Commercial Agency
and
Distribution Agreements:
Law and Practice in the
Member States of the European Community

Commercial Agency
and
Distribution Agreements:
Law and Practice in the
Member States of the European Community

General Editor
Guy- Martial Weijer
Chairman of AIJA EEC Law Commission

Graham & Trotman
A member of the Kluwer Academic Publishers Group
LONDON/DORDRECHT/BOSTON

Graham & Trotman Limited
Sterling House
66 Wilton Road
London SW1V 1DE
UK

Graham & Trotman
Kluwer Academic Publishers Group
101 Philip Drive
Assinippi Park
Norwell, MA 02061
USA

© AIJA, 1989
First published in 1989

British Library Cataloguing in Publication Data
Commercial agency and distribution agreements: law and
  practice in the member states of the European
  Community.
  1. European Community countries. Agency &
  distribution agreements. Law
  I. Weijer, Guy-Martial
  342.6'29

  ISBN 1-85333-358-1

Library of Congress Cataloging-in-Publication Data
Commercial agency and distribution agreements: law and practice in
  the member states of the European community/general editor, Guy
  -Martial Weijer.
    p. cm.
  Includes bibliographical references.
  ISBN 1-85333-358-1
  1. Commercial agents —European Economic Community countries.
2. Franchises (Retail trade)—European Economic Community countries.
3. Sales—European Economic Community countries. I. Weijer, Guy
  -Martial.
  KJE2079.C66   1989
  343.4'0887—dc20
  [344.03887]

Typeset in Times by BookEns, Saffron Walden, Essex
Printed and bound in Great Britain by Billing & Sons Ltd, Worcester

CONTENTS

PART II
NATIONAL RULES AND APPLICATION OF EEC LAW

CHAPTER 2—BELGIUM   81

CHAPTER 4—FEDERAL REPUBLIC OF GERMANY

PREFACE

It may well be that Agency and Distribution agreements are the backbone of cross-border commercial activity. In any event lawyers, such as the young lawyers who have participated in preparing this book, are constantly confronted with the drafting of such agreements.

Bearing in mind the approach of 1992, the conclusion of which will see the economic unity of EEC as a reality, and the coming into effect of EEC Council Directive 86/653 relating to self-employed Commercial Agents, it seemed logical that the Commission on EEC law of the Young Lawyer's International Association begin work on the subject.

The fruit of those endeavours is the present book, which does not pretend to be a scientific work. Rather, the aim shared by the 40 or more contributors, has been to set out, as systematically and schematically as possible, the law and practice in the 12 member states of the European Economic Community.

The credit for each contribution goes to the individual authors, who will be glad to give you further advice if you might need it.

My task, as President of the AIJA Commission on EEC law, following the original initiative made by our former President, François de Bourgerel, has been limited to putting the writing of this book into motion and to coordinating and harmonizing the various elements of its development as much as I could.

Paris, 1989

G.-M.A.X. Weijer
President, EEC Commission, AIJA
Dutilh, van der Hoeven & Slager
Attorneys at Law
Rotterdam, Breda, Amsterdam, Paris, Madrid, Brussels

ABOUT AIJA

THE ASSOCIATION INTERNATIONALE DES JEUNES AVOCATS is a non political organisation founded in 1962 to encourage meetings and to promote cooperation and mutual respect between young lawyers from all countries around the world. It contributes to the provision of full and effective protection in all circumstances and places of the right of every lawyer to practice his profession freely and of every person to be aided, counselled or represented by a lawyer freely chosen and to be entitled to a fair trial by an impartial and independent Judge within a reasonable period of time.

To this end, AIJA examines throughout the year general or specific subjects within Permanent Commissions, promotes Regional and Intercontinental Meetings of young lawyers, organises Courses and Seminars as well as an annual Congress and issues professional publications.

Any qualified lawyer under the age of 45 may join the association.

For more information contact:
AIJA
Me. Marie-Anne Bastin
Avenue Louis Lepoutre 59-Bte-20
B-1060 Brussels
Belgium
TEL: 32-2-347 28 08
TELEX. 65079 aija b
FAX: 32-2 347 55 22

LIST OF CONTRIBUTORS

Chapter 1 - EEC

Mr. JAAP FEENSTRA
Dutilh, van der Hoeven & Slager
Postbus 1110
3000 BC Rotterdam
The Netherlands
Tel. 31-10-402-06-00
Fax. 31-10-413-35-74

Chapter 2 - BELGIUM

GENERAL COORDINATOR

MR. OLIVIER VAES
Donnet, Vaes & Wouters
Mechelsesteenweg 195
2018 Antwerpen
Belgium
Tel. 32-3-239-78-40
Fax. 32-3-239-34-20

COMMERCIAL AGENCY

MRS. CHRISTINE DE KEERSMAEKER
Advokatenkantoor de Keersmaeker Bureau d'Avocats
Vrijheidsplein 4 Place de la Liberté
1000 Brussels
Belgium
Tel. 32-2-217-74-74
Fax. 32-2-218-80-53

DISTRIBUTORSHIP AGREEMENTS

MR. GEERT BOGAERT
De Caluwe, Putzeys, T'kint, van Fraeyenhoven
Rue St. Bernard 98
1060 Brussels
Belgium
Tel. 32-2-735-45-11
Fax. 32-2-536-59-11

FRANCHISING

MRS. NICOLE VAN RANST
Lafili & van Crombrugghe
Voss<ndreef 6 (B1) Drève des Renards
1180 brussels
Belgium

Tel. 32-2-374-92-00
Fax. 32-2-375-45-25

Chapter 3 – DENMARK

MR. JOHN KAHLKE
T. Ingemann, Hanssen
Meurs-Gerken & Co.,
Amaliegade 22
DK-1265 Copenhagen K
Denmark
Tel. 45-1-11-34-00
Fax. 45-1-32-46-25

MR. CARSTEN IVERSEN
Thyregod & Partners
Vimmelskaflet 42
1161 Copenhagen K
Denmark
Tel. 45-1-15-25-61
Fax. 45-1-15-47-15

Chapter 4 – FEDERAL REPUBLIC OF GERMANY

COMMERCIAL AGENCY

DR. ROLF BEEKER
Beeker, Berkenbusch
Kaiserswerther Str. 45
4000 Dusseldorf 30
West Germany
Tel. 49-211-49-20-91
Fax. 49-211-498-03-85

DISTRIBUTORSHIP AGREEMENTS

DR. ULRICH LOHMANN
Boetticher, Bernet & Partner
Widenmayerstr. 4
8000 München 22
West Germany
Tel. 49-89-22-33-11
Fax. 49-89-22-47-28

FRANCHISING

DR. RENATE BRAEUNINGER-WEIMER
Wangler, Braeuninger-Weimer
Kriegsstr. 135
7500 Karlsruhe 1
West Germany
Tel. 49-721-84-30-94
Fax. 49-721-85-33-40

Chapter 5 – GREECE

MRS. HELEN PAPACONSTANTINOU

Law Offices
Michael G. Papaconstantinou
10 Lycabettus Str.
106 71 Athens
Greece
Tel. 30-1-363-15-35
Fax. 30-1-361-91-68

Chapter 6 – SPAIN

COMMERCIAL AGENCY

MRS. INMACULADA UMBERT MILLET
Estudio Legal
Avda. Diagonal 442
08037 Barcelona
Spain
Tel. 34-3-237-95-82
Fax. 34-3-218-88-12

MR. ENRIC ENRICH MULS
KPMG Estudio Juridico y Tributario
Edificio Masters
Pedro i Pons 9–11
08034 Barcelona
Spain
Tel. 34-3-205-32-12
Fax. 34-3-205-30-04

MR. RAMON GIRBAU PEDRAGOSA
Arthur Andersen & CIA
Avda. Diagonal 654
08034 Barcelona
Spain
Tel. 34-3-205-10-12
Fax. 34-3-205-12-50

DISTRIBUTORSHIP AGREEMENTS

MR. RAFAEL ALONSO DREGI
Bufete Catrecasas
Balmes 76
08007 Barcelona
Spain
Tel. 34-3-215-44-78
Fax. 34-3-216-08-47

FRANCHISING

MR. SANTIAGO MONTANER GOMIS
Montaner, Defoin, Suils & Lafora
Avda. Diagonal 405
08008 Barcelona
Spain
Tel. 34-3-237-17-22

Chapter 7 – FRANCE

COMMERCIAL AGENCY

MRS. LILYANE ANSTETT-GARDEA
Merckel-Schmidt & Associés
22 rue du Général de Castelnau
6700 Strasbourg
France
Tel. 33-88-35-55-82
Fax. 33-88-35-54-71

DISTRIBUTORSHIP AGREEMENTS

MR. JEROME DEPONDT
19 Avenue Rapp
75007 Paris
France
Tel. 33-1-45-55-72-00
Fax. 33-1-47-53-76-14

SELECTIVE DISTRIBUTION

MR. PIERRE SERVAN-SCHREIBER
SCP Dubarry, Gaston-Dreyfus, Leveque, Le Douarin, Servan-Schreiber,
Veil & Associés
9 rue le Tasse
75116 Paris
France
Tel. 33-1-45-27-39-00
Fax. 33-1-45-27-31-20

FRANCHISING

MRS. CHANTAL COUTURIER-LEONI
52 Boulevard Malesherbes
75008 Paris
France
Tel. 33-1-42-94-18-05
Fax. 33-1-42-94-01-74

Chapter 8 – IRELAND

MR. R. JOHN McBRATNEY
40 Percy Place
Dublin 4
Ireland
Tel. 0001-68-70-13
Fax. 0001-68-78-77

Chapter 9 – ITALY

MRS. ANNA MARIA FULGONI
Studio Ughi & Nunziante
Via S. Andrea 19
20121 Milano XI
Italy
Tel. 39-2-79-39-51
Fax. 39-2-78-41-40

MRS. NICOLLETA CONTARDI
Studio Legale Contardi
Via Aurispa 2
20122 Milano XI
Italy
Tel. 39-2-58-10-06-37
Fax. 39-2-55-18-56-83

MRS. ALESSANDRA PANDARESE
Studio Legale Rampino e Giordano
Via Freguglia 4
20122 Milano XI
Italy
Tel. 39-2-551-27-15
Fax. 39-2-55-18-14-37

Chapter 10 – LUXEMBURG

MR. GUY HARLES and MR. PATRICK KINSCH
Arendt & Medernach
4 Avenue Marie-Thérèse
2010 Luxemburg
Luxemburg
Tel. 352-46-22-22
Fax. 352-47-18-80

Chapter 11 – THE NETHERLANDS

GENERAL COORDINATOR

MR. ROBERT BOSMAN
Derks, de Gier, Pentinga
Avenue Louise 391 B 11
1050 Brussels
Belgium
Tel. 32-2-640-35-25
Fax. 32-2-648-50-86

COMMERCIAL AGENCY

MR. RICHARD NORBRUIS
Dutilh, van der Hoeven & Slager
Postbus 7061
1007 JB Amsterdam
The Netherlands
Tel. 31-20-66-21-214
Fax. 31-20-66-20-194

DISTRIBUTORSHIP AGREEMENTS

MR. GERARD VAN DER WAL
MR. J.M.C. MONTIJN-SWINKELS
Barents, Gasille & Mout
223 rue de la Loi B1
1040 Brussels
Belgium
Tel. 32-2-230-44-45
Fax. 32-2-230-26-13

FRANCHISING

MR. ERIC KEYZER
MRS. CORINNA WISSELS
Loeff & van der Ploeg
Postbus 5088
Peter van Anrooystraat 7
1007 AB Amsterdam
The Netherlands
Tel. 31-20-574-12-00
Fax. 31-20-571-87-75

Chapter 12 – PORTUGAL

EEC ASPECTS

MR. NUNO RUIZ
Botelho Moniz, Magalhaes Cardoso, Marques Mendes & Ruiz
Sociedade de Advogados
Rua Castilho 63, 6°
1200 Lisbon
Portugal
Tel. 351-1-54-33-21
Fax. 351-1-52-23-75

COMMERCIAL AGENCY

MR. CARLOS DE OLIVEIRA COELHO
Av. Fontes Pereira de Melo 7/13
1000 Lisbon
Portugal
Tel. 351-1-57-70-00

DISTRIBUTORSHIP AGREEMENTS

MRS CLEMENTINA PAIVA
Av. de Republica
1000 Lisbon
Portugal
Tel. 351-1-53-03-21
Fax. 351-1-52-40-02

FRANCHISING

MR. ANA REIS SANTOS
Av. Conselheiro Fernando de Sousa 25-14° A
1000 Lisbon

Portugal
Tel. 351-1-65-12-10

Chapter 13 - UNITED KINGDOM

MR. LEONARD HAWKES
Stanbrook & Hooper
42 rue du Taciturne
1040 Brussels
Belgium
Tel. 32-2-230-50-59
Fax. 32-2-230-57-13

MR. FERGUS RANDOLPH
European Law Chambers
45 Boulevard Charlemagne
1040 Brussels
Belgium
Tel. 32-2-230-11-74

PART I
EEC Law and Jurisprudence

CHAPTER 1

Distribution and Commercial Agency and EEC Law

Jaap Feenstra

Holland

SECTION A

Introduction to European Competition Law

1. EEC Competition Law

This book contains a description of the national legal rules of the Member States of the European Community regarding distribution and commercial agency agreements. This description is mainly based on the rules of civil law.

The impact of European Community law on distribution and commercial agency agreements is different from that of the various national laws. European Community law restricts the content of the various distribution and commercial agency agreements in many aspects. These restrictions are dictated by the competition rules of the Community. It is mainly from a point of view of competition policy that European Community law affects distribution and commercial agency agreements.

National civil law may prescribe positively the inclusion of specific clauses in an agreement or may force parties to an agreement to insert clauses of a certain content in the agreement. European competition law only prevents the inclusion of specific clauses while not compelling parties positively to insert such and such provisions. Of course, this also applies to national competition laws. This difference between (national) civil law and (European) competition law is illustrated by the fact that Articles 85 and 86 of the EEC Treaty are based on a system of prohibitions.

It is only in the field of agency agreements that the Council of the European Communities adopted a Directive which contains certain clauses which must be included in commercial agency agreements.[1] The Directive obliges the Member States to adapt their legislation on agency agreements. In most Member States this legislation is included in the Civil Code or is part of civil law.

In this introduction some general aspects of European competition law will be highlighted (Section A). Subsequently, the principles of the decisions rendered by the Commission of the European Communities (the 'Commission') in Brussels and the judgments of the European Court of Justice in Luxemburg with regard to distribution and commercial agency agreements will be discussed (Section B).

2. Article 85 of the EEC Treaty

2.1. Elaborating the basic principle of Article 3(f) of the EEC Treaty, Articles 85 and 86 contain the substantive Treaty provisions on European competition law. Legal practice of the European Community demonstrates that Article 85 of the EEC Treaty is more important for distribution and commercial agency agreements. The description of the consequences of European competition law on distribution and commercial agency agreements will, therefore, be based on Article 85.

According to Article 85, paragraph 1 of the EEC Treaty agreements between undertakings, decisions by associations of undertakings and concerted practices are prohibited as incompatible with the Common Market if they may restrict competition within the Common Market and may affect trade between the Member States. Article 85 (2) provides that agreements or decisions prohibited pursuant to Article 85 (1) shall be automatically void. An exemption of the prohibition of Article 85 (1) is included in paragraph 3 of Article 85.

In the following, four elements of Article 85 (1) will be discussed briefly, i.e. the notions 'undertaking', 'agreement', 'restriction of competition' and 'influence on trade' (2.2–2.6). In paragraph 3 of this introduction I will deal with some general aspects of application of Article 85 (3). In addition to this, I will touch briefly on the mechanism of enforcement of Article 85 (paragraph 4).

2.2. The Notion 'Undertaking'

The word 'undertaking' is a wide term which extends to almost any legal or natural person carrying on activities of an economic or commercial nature,[2] in different stages of industry (production, distribution) and in different industrial sectors.

An agreement between a parent company and a subsidiary or between two subsidiaries of the same parent company, in principle does not fall within Article 85 (1) if the undertakings form an economic unit within which the subsidiaries have no real freedom to determine their economic

---

[1] Official Journal (OJ) L 382/17 of 31 December 1986.
[2] Bellamy and Child, *Common Market Law of Competition*, London, 1987, p. 45.

activities on the market. The Commission and the Court interpret the word 'undertaking' as an economically independent unit. In its *Béguelin* judgment[3] the Court held that Article 85 (1) does not apply to an agreement between a parent company and a subsidiary which, although having separate legal personality, enjoys no economic independence. In its judgment in the *Centrafarm/Sterling Drug* case[4] the Court said that Article 85 (1) does not apply to agreements between undertakings belonging to the same group and having the status of parent company and subsidiary, if the undertakings form an economic unit within which the subsidiary has no real freedom to determine its course of action on the market, and if the agreements or practices are concerned merely with the internal allocation of tasks as between the undertakings. In the *Hydrotherm/Compact* case[5] the Court held that in competition law the term undertaking must be understood as designating an economic unit even if in law that economic unit consists of several legal or natural persons.

In recent years the examination of the Commission in applying this principle has become more strict. The Commission investigates very precisely all the circumstances to see whether there are in fact autonomous activities of the subsidiary with regard to the parent company. Furthermore, even if subsidiaries are strictly governed by parent companies' instructions, the Commission is looking into agreements of the subsidiaries with third parties in which the instructions are laid down.

In the recent *Konica* case[6] the Commission objected to restraints of exports and imports effected by Konica Europe GmbH and Konica UK intended to protect each other's territories. These restraints were imposed upon distributors. The Commission considered such restraints to be part of the agreements of the subsidiary with its distributors. Unlike the instructions or the common policy of the Konica group, the distributorship agreements could fall within Articles 85 (1). The Commission imposed fines of 75,000 ECU both on Konica UK and Konica Europe GmbH.[7]

2.3. Agreements within the meaning of Article 85 (1)

The notion 'agreement' has also been given an extensive interpretation. Legally binding arrangements are considered as agreements within the meaning of Article 85 (1).[8] Such an agreement may be written or oral, and may even be inferred from the circumstances.[9] An exchange of letters may constitute an agreement within the meaning of Article 85 (1). Furthermore,

---

3   [1971] ECR 949.
4   [1974] ECR 1147. This was confirmed in the recent *Bodson* judgment of 4 May 1988, case 30/87, not yet recorded.
5   [1984] ECR 2999.
6   OJ L 78/34 of 23 March 1988.
7   See also previous decisions in the *Kawasaki* case (OJ 16/9 of 23 January 1979) and the *Johnson and Johnson* case (OJ L 377/16 of 31 December 1988).
8   Which degree of legal force is required for the notion 'agreement' is not clear. Gentlemen's agreements can be considered to be agreements. The difference with concerted practices within the meaning of Article 85 (1) can be rather vague.
9   Bellamy and Child, p. 49.

standard conditions of sale are agreements, within the meaning of this provision. Provisions which, at first glance, look like being unilaterally imposed, can be seen as an agreement within the meaning of Article 85 (1) if, for example, a supplier operates a restricted system of distribution and if it results from an understanding, tacit or express, between the supplier and his existing dealers, that the unilaterally imposed conditions are to be included in the distribution system. Similarly, the sales policy of a manufacturer who maintains a restricted system of distribution may be regarded as impliedly accepted by that manufacturer's dealers and may give rise to an agreement within the meaning of Article 85 (1).[10]

2.4.1. Restriction of competition within the meaning of Article 85 (1)

Article 85 (1) does not apply unless the agreement in question has as its object or effect the prevention, restriction or distortion of competition within the Common Market.[11] A restriction of competition occurs if the agreement limits the freedom of action for the parties to the agreement or for competitors of these parties.

Distribution and commercial agency agreements are so-called vertical agreements. These are agreements between undertakings which do not perform their activities at the same level of industry. Parties to a vertical agreement do not compete with each other because their activities are confined to different markets. An important kind of a vertical agreement is an agreement between a supplier and a customer to whom he supplies. Vertical agreements often contain (a) a restriction accepted by the supplier not to supply goods to anyone except the acquirer, for example a distributor or a dealer in a particular area; (b) a restriction accepted by the acquirer not to acquire goods from anyone except the supplier; and (c) restrictions on the acquirer's freedom to determine his own course of economic transactions.[12]

In the *Grundig–Consten*[13] case the Court established that not only horizontal arrangements or cartels but also vertical agreements may fall within Article 85 (1). According to the Court, Article 85 refers in a general way to all agreements which distort competition within the Common Market and does not lay down any distinction between those agreements based on whether they are concluded between competitors operating at the same level in the economic process or between non-competing persons operating at different levels. Vertical agreements fall within Article 85 (1) if they restrict the freedom of action of one of the parties towards a third competitor. For instance, an exclusive sales agreement prevents the producer selling his products to a different distributor within a certain area. Subsequently, distributors in that area have no possibilities of purchasing products from that manufacturer.

2.4.2. In European Community competition policy the Commission and the Court apply a slightly moderated interpretation of the word 'competition' for

---

[10] Cf. the *Konica* decision mentioned in note 6.
[11] Bellamy and Child, p. 62.
[12] Bellamy and Child, p. 64.
[13] [1966] ECR 449 and OJ 161/2545 of 20 October 1964.

certain groups of agreements. In the famous *Metro/SABA I* judgment[14] of 25 October 1977 on selective distribution systems the Court held that the requirements set out in Articles 3 and 85 of the EEC Treaty that competition shall not be distorted, implies the existence on the market of a workable competition, that is to say the degree of competition necessary to ensure the observance of the basic requirements and the attainment of the objectives of the Treaty, in particular the creation of a single market achieving conditions similar to those of a domestic market. In accordance with this requirement, the nature and intensiveness of competition may vary to an extent dictated by the products or services in question and the economic structure of the relevant market sectors. As the *Metro/SABA* case dealt with the distribution of consumer electronics, the Court continued by saying that in the sector covering the production of high quality and technically advanced consumer durables, where a relatively small number of large and medium-scale producers offer a varied range of items which, or so consumers may consider, are readily interchangeable, the structure of the market does not preclude the existence of a variety of channels of distribution adapted to the peculiar characteristics of the various producers and the requirements of the various categories of consumers. The Court adhered to the view of the Commission that selective distribution systems constitute an aspect of competition which accords with Article 85 (1) provided that resellers are chosen on the basis of objective criteria of a qualitative nature relating to the technical qualifications of the reseller and his staff and the suitability of his trading premises and that such conditions are laid down uniformly for all potential resellers and are not applied in a discriminatory fashion.

The recognition by the Court of the requirements of workable competition may have as a consequence that not all restrictions of the freedom of the parties and their competitors to determine their own course of economic transactions are prohibited by Article 85 (1). Some restrictions can be maintained provided that they are necessary for acheiving the objectives of the distribution system. These restrictions may even increase competition. Moreover, such approach will reduce the role of Article 85 (3) for balancing the positive and negative effects of the agreements.

This mitigated approach was followed in the *Nutricia* judgment[15] (non-competition clause in a takeover agreement), the *Nungesser* judgment[16] (licence agreement), the *Pronuptia* judgment[17] (franchise) and the *Philip Morris* judgment[18] (acquisition agreement).

It is not clear which legal or economic theory constitutes a basis for this approach. It is presumed that the Commission and the Court are inspired by US antitrust practice. The approach of the *Metro/SABA* judgment could be seen as an application of the US rule of reason doctrine or of the (also American) theory of ancillary restraints. This second doctrine appears to have been applied in the *Nutricia, Pronuptia* and *Philip Morris* judgments.

---

14 [1977] ECR 1875.
15 [1985] ECR 2545.
16 [1982] ECR 2015.
17 [1986] ECR 353.
18 Judgment of 17 November 1987, joined cases 142 and 156/84, not yet recorded.

It should be borne in mind that it depends on the Commission, and in the last resort the Court of Justice, whether such a mitigated interpretation of the notion 'restriction of competition' for a specific type of agreement will be accepted. With regard to the distribution and commercial agency agreements discussed in this book, the Court, until now, in addition to selective distribution systems, has been prepared to adopt such an interpretation only for agreements on franchising (the *Pronuptia* judgment).

2.5. Influence on Trade between the Member States

The effect on trade between the Member States is a second condition of a substantive character for applying Article 85 (1) to agreements between undertakings. Agreements which do not have an influence on trade between the Member States do not fall within Article 85 (1) and may only be examined in the light of national competition law.

The notion 'effect on trade' is interpreted as meaning an alteration of trade flows.[19] This condition of applying Article 85 (1) is closely connected with the basic concept of the Common Market and the objective of the EEC Treaty to withdraw all impediments to the free movement of goods, persons, services and capital. Separation of the Common Market by restoring national markets must be avoided.

Many agreements between undertakings can clearly be regarded as having an effect on trade between the Member States. Agreements between undertakings which are established in different Member States undoubtedly influence trade patterns between the Member States. Agreements which contain clauses with regard to imports or exports into or from Member States can easily have effects on trade between the Member States as well.

Agreements covering one Member State may also influence the trade between the Member States within the meaning of Article 85 (1). These are agreements between parties situated in one Member State or agreements which regulate economic transactions which take place in one Member State. In its judgment in the *Cementhandelaren* case[20] the Court of Justice held that an agreement extending over the whole territory of a Member State by its very nature has the effect of reinforcing the partitioning of markets on a national basis and therefore impedes the aims of the EEC Treaty.

Even agreements between parties which are situated in one Member State and which have a very small market share may fall within Article 85 (1) if that agreement is one of a network of agreements between, for example, a manufacturer and its distributors. If the agreement is part of a network, interstate trade may well be affected within the meaning of Article 85 (1) even if the effect of the agreement, standing alone, would be insignificant. Agreements between undertakings which are established outside the Community also fall within Article 85 if such agreements are related to production or distribution of goods within the Community.[21]

---

[19] Bellamy and Child, p. 108.

[20] [1972] ECR 977.

[21] The extraterritorial application of EEC competition law raises a very intricate question. The Commission seems to adhere to the doctrine of effect. The Court of Justice accepted the point of view of the Commission in its *Wood Pulp* judgment of 27 September 1988.

The Commission and especially the Court conclude very easily that intra community trade is being affected.

2.6. Appreciability

According to the competition policy of the Commission and the case law of the Court, agreements only fall within Article 85 (1) if they restrict competition and affect trade between the Member States to an appreciable extent. This is called the *de minimis* rule (*de minimis non curat praetor*). This means that agreements which do not restrict competition and influence trade to a sufficient degree do not fall within Article 85 (1). For determining the appreciability of the restriction on competition and the effect on trade it is necessary to consider the whole economic and legal context of the agreement involved, including the existence of other agreements to the same effect. The existence of similar contracts may be taken into consideration for this purpose to the extent to which the general body of contracts of this type is capable of restricting the freedom of trade.[22]

The Commission has sought to materialize the notion 'appreciability' by determining quantitive criteria. In its Notice concerning agreements of minor importance,[23] the Commission takes the view that agreements do not have an appreciable effect on trade and do not appreciably restrict competition if the parties involved together have a turnover of less than 200 million ECU and if the product which is the subject of the agreement together with the parties' similar goods does not represent more than 5 per cent of the relevant product market. A Notice of the Commission, however, does not have a binding effect. National courts and the Court of Justice are in no way compelled to apply this Notice.

3. Application of Article 85 (3)

3.1. Agreements which are prohibited pursuant to Article 85 (1) can be exempted from this provision if the conditions of Article 85 (3) can be fulfilled. Article 85 (3) provides:

'The provisions of paragraph 1 may, however, be declared inapplicable in case of:

— any agreement or category of agreements between undertakings;
— any decision or category of decisions by associations of undertakings;
— any concerted practice or category of concerted practices;

which contributes to improving the production or distribution of goods or to promoting technical or economic progress, while allowing consumers a fair share of the resulting benefit and which does not:

(a) impose on the undertakings concerned restrictions which are not indispensable to the attainment of these objectives;
(b) afford such undertakings the possibility of eliminating competition in respect of a substantial part of the products in question'.

---

[22] *Brasserie de Haecht (I)* judgment, [1967] ECR 407.
[23] OJ C 213/2 of 12 September 1986.

3.2. Notification of the agreement to the Commission is a condition for a favourable decision on Article 85 (3). Under Regulation 17 the Commission has the exclusive competence to grant exemptions pursuant to Article 85 (3), notwithstanding judicial review by the Court of Justice under Article 173 of the EEC Treaty. National courts are not allowed to apply Article 85 (3).

EEC competition policy demonstrates that the Commission is prepared to recognize certain advantages of distribution and commercial agency agreements within the meaning of the first condition for application of Article 85 (3). Distribution and commercial agency agreements as such can be exempted. However, unnecessary clauses have to be deleted.

3.3. Article 85 (3) is applied by the Commission to individual agreements. However, for several categories of agreements the Commission adopted Regulations containing block exemptions. These Regulations list which clauses may be inserted in agreements and which may not. Important Regulations adopted by the Commission in this respect concern exclusive distribution agreements and exclusive purchasing agreements. The Regulation on franchise agreements was adopted on 30 November 1988.

Unlike individual exemptions under Article 85 (3), national courts are allowed and even obliged to apply the block exemption Regulations of the Commission. Under Community law, Regulations shall have general application and shall be directly applicable in all Member States (Article 189, EEC Treaty). This is very important for the effectiveness of European competition law. Applicants may invoke provisions of Regulations of the Commission before national courts in order to argue that a specific agreement does not fulfil the conditions of the block exemption involved or, conversely, that a specific agreement complies with the provision of such block exemption and therefore is legal.

Agreements justified under a block exemption do not need to be notified to the Commission. Agreements which do not fall within the block exemption may be exempted by the Commission on the basis of a separate decision. Such agreements must be notified.

4. Enforcement of European Competition Law

4.1. In the foregoing, the implementation of European competition law has already been mentioned. Two ways of enforcing Article 85 can be distinguished: enforcement via the national courts and via the Commission.

Article 85 (1) has been given direct effect.[24] This means that Article 85 (1) can be invoked by undertakings in proceedings before national courts. National courts are bound to examine whether or not an agreement falls within Article 85 (1). If a national court has doubts on the interpretation of Article 85 (1) it may ask for a preliminary ruling of the Court of Justice under Article 177 of the EEC Treaty. According to Article 85 (2), clauses of an agreement which are regarded as infringing European competition law are void. The remainder of an agreement which is not infringing Article 85

---

[24] *Sacchi* judgment, [1974] ECR 409.

(1) may preserve its legal effect. This point has to be decided within the framework of national civil law. Article 85 (2) underlines that the provision of paragraph 1 of Article 85 is based on a system of prohibition. An agreement which falls within Article 85 (1) is prohibited and void unless an exemption is granted under Article 85 (3).

Block exemption Regulations of the Commission must be applied by national courts as well. According to Article 189 of the EEC Treaty, Regulations do not have to be implemented by national legislation. As Community law takes precedence over the domestic law of Member States, national courts are prevented from applying national provisions which do not comply with Community law.

4.2. Until now, the problem of enforcement of European competition law has been discussed from the angle of proceedings before national courts. Another important role for monitoring compliance with Articles 85 and 86 is entrusted to the European Commission. Under Regulation 17[25] the Commission is entitled to examine agreements which may fall within Article 85 (1). According to Article 4 of Regulation 17, agreements which might come within the ambit of Article 85 have to be notified to the Commission.

Within the framework of Regulation 17, the Commission may take three categories of decisions:

(a) the Commission may give a negative clearance, i.e. the Commission certifies that an agreement does not fall within Article 85 (1);
(b) the Commission may decide that an agreement falls within Article 85 (1) but can be exempted under Article 85 (3);
(c) the Commission may decide that an agreement falls within Article 85 (1) and cannot be granted an exemption under Article 85 (3).

Exemptions under Article 85 (3) can be granted only if the agreement concerned is notified to the Commission.

4.3. In some recent block exemption Regulations, the Commission included a so-called opposition procedure. According to this procedure, agreements which do not fulfil the terms of the block exemption are permitted if the agreement is notified and if the Commission does not oppose such exemption within a period of six months. The information furnished with the notification must be complete and must be in accordance with the facts. The opposition procedure is inserted in Regulation 4078/88 on franchise agreements. Unfortunately, the block exemptions on exclusive dealing and on motor car servicing do not contain such an opposition procedure.

4.4. Investigations of the Commission can be prompted by a notification or a complaint made by third parties. The Commission may also start proceedings on its own initiative. Regulation 17 authorizes the Commission to investigate undertakings. Officials of the Commission are authorized to investigate on the spot, to examine books and other business records of undertakings, to take copies of extracts from the books and business records and to enter any premises, land and means of transport of undertakings.

[25] OJ 1959–1962, p. 87.

4.5. Regulation 17 enables the Commission to impose fines upon undertakings which violate Articles 85 or 86. These fines may vary from 1000 to 1,000,000 ECU or a sum in excess thereof but not exceeding 10 per cent of the turnover in the preceding business year. In fixing the amount of the fines, the Commission must have regard both to the gravity and to the duration of the infringement. Vertical agreements that contained severe infringements of Article 85, for instance obligations on resale prices or restrictions on imports or exports, have resulted in the imposition of fines. Commission decisions to impose fines can be brought before the Court of Justice under Article 173 of the EEC Treaty.

4.6. Finally, it should be mentioned that the Court of Justice held in its *Camera Care* judgment[26] that Regulation 17 affords the Commission the power to take interim measures that are indispensable for the effective exercise of its function and, in particular, for ensuring the effectiveness of any decisions requiring undertakings to bring to an end infringements which it has found to exist. An interim measure may extend to ordering positive measures to be taken as well as to the issue of prohibitory orders.

4.7. In conclusion it can be noted that provisions of European competition law impose directly enforceable obligations on undertakings. It offers protection to those who comply with the rules and it may constitute a threat to those who infringe these rules. Undertakings that feel injured by infringements of European competition law by other companies may use two courses of action, by either starting proceedings before a national court or by lodging a complaint with the Commission, or it may even follow both avenues simultaneously.

SECTION B

European Competition Law

1. Commercial Agency Agreements

Introduction

This section on commercial agency agreements will, first of all, deal with aspects of European competition law with regard to agency agreements (a). It is necessary to examine whether and to what extent competition law restricts the contents of an agency agreement. Subsequently, Council Directive 86/353 on the harmonization of legislation of the Member States concerning independent agents will be discussed (b). Unlike European competition law, this Directive obliges the Member States to provide that certain clauses must be inserted in agency contracts.

---

[26] [1980] ECR 119.

(a) Competition Law: Application of Article 85 to Agency Agreements

1.1. In its Notice of 24 December 1962 on exclusive agency contracts made with commercial agents[27] the Commission considers that agency contracts in which the agents undertake, for a specified part of the territory of the Common Market, to negotiate transactions on behalf of an enterprise, or to conclude transactions in their own name and on behalf of this enterprise, do not fall under the prohibition of Article 85 (1).

It is essential that there is a genuine agency agreement. If the agent appears to be an independent trader the agreement will fall within Article 85 (1). The true commercial agent should neither undertake nor engage in activities proper to an independent trader in the course of commercial operations. The Commission regards as the decisive criterion, which distinguishes the commercial agent from the independent trader, the way in which the agreement, express or implied, deals with the responsibility for the financial risks bound up with the sale or the performance of the contract. Except for the usual *del credere* guarantee, a commercial agent must not by the nature of his functions assume any risk resulting from the transaction. If he does assume such risks, his function becomes economically akin to that of an independent trader and he must therefore be treated as such for the purposes of the rules of competition. the Commission regards the agent as an independent trader if he is required to keep or does in fact keep, as his own property, a considerable stock of the products covered by the contract, or is required to organize, maintain or ensure at his own expense a substantial service to customers free of charge, or does in fact organize, maintain or ensure such a service or if he can determine or does in fact determine prices or terms of business.

1.2. According to the Notice, the Commission takes the view that genuine agency contracts have neither the objective nor the effect of preventing, restricting or distorting competition within the Common Market. The commercial agent performs only an auxiliary function in the market for goods. In that market he acts on the instructions and in the interest of the enterprise on whose behalf he is operating. Unlike the independent trader, he himself is neither a purchaser nor a vendor but seeks purchasers or vendors in the interest of the other party to the contract who is the person doing the buying or selling. In this type of exclusive dealing contracts, the selling or buying enterprise does not cease to be a competitor; it merely uses an auxiliary. The selling or buying enterprise is free to decide the product and the territory in respect of which he is willing to give these powers to his agent. The obligation assumed by the agent, i.e. to work exclusively for one principal for a certain period of time, entails a limitation of supply on the market. The obligation assumed by the other party to the contract, i.e. to appoint him sole agent for a given territory, involves a limitation of demand of the market. Nevertheless, the Commission regards these restrictions as a result of the special obligation between the commercial agent and his principal to pro-

[27] OJ 1962/2921.

tect each other's interests and therefore considers that they involve no restriction of competition.

1.3. In the final paragraph of the Notice, the Commission remarks that it is without prejudice to any interpretation that may be given by other competent authorities and in particular by the courts.

1.4. The view of the Commission on agency agreements was confirmed by the Court of Justice in the *Sugar* case.[28] In this judgment the Court held that Article 85 does not apply to a clause in an agreement prohibiting an agent from trading products competing with those of his principal where the agent has undertaken to sell goods in the name and for the account of his principal, to promote the principal's interests and to carry out the principal's instructions. If such an agent works for his principal he can in principle be regarded as an auxiliary organ forming an integral part of the latter's undertaking bound to carry out the principal's instructions and thus, like a commercial employee, forms an economic unit with this undertaking.

1.5. Article 85 (1) may also apply where the agent, although acting as agent vis-à-vis his principal, also carries on a business of his own.[29] In the *Pittsburgh Corning* decision[30] the Commission held that an agency agreement has to be tested within the light of Article 85 (1) if the agent is an independent manufacturer or distributor of products unconnected with the agency. In the *Sugar* case the Court had decided that the creation of such an ambivalent relationship cannot escape the prohibitions of Article 85.

1.6. In the literature it is argued that an agent has to be considered as an independent trader if he acts for more than one principal, where those principals are in competition with one other and agree to appoint the same agent to transact business on their behalf.[31]

1.7. This view is not contradicted by the judgment of 1 October 1987 of the Court in case 311/85 (*Vlaamse Reisbureaus*).[32] In this judgment the Court held that a travel agent has to be considered as a independent intermediary who provides services autonomously in as far as he sells organized trips of a large number of tour operators. Equally, a tour operator sells his trips through a large number of travel agents, according to the Court. Thus, a travel agent cannot be characterized as an auxiliary organ that is integrated into the undertaking of some tour operator. Agreements between tour operators and travel agents therefore have to be assessed in the light of Article 85 (1).

In the literature[33] it has been argued that the *Vlaamse Reisbureaus* judgment of the Court of Justice results in a rather odd solution. Agency agreements which are based on mutual exclusivity escape the applicability of Article 85 (1) while agency agreements between parties that act for or with several competing undertakings fall within Article 85 (1). However, it is fair

[28] [1975] ECR 1663.
[29] Bellamy and Child, p. 245.
[30] OJ L 272/35 of 5 December 1972.
[31] Bellamy and Child, p. 245.
[32] This judgment has not yet been included in the European Court Reports.
[33] Koch and Marenco, "L'article 85 du Traité CEE et les contracts d'agents", CDE 1987, p. 603.

to argue that this interpretation already results from the Commission Notice of 1962.

1.8. The Commission is considering adjusting the Notice to new developments in the field of agency contracts.

1.9. If it has been established that the agent has to be regarded as an independent trader, the agreement has to be assessed along the lines of the European competition policy on vertical agreements like distribution and franchise agreements. These agreements are discussed in the following paragraphs of this chapter.

(b) Directive 86/653 Relating to Self-Employed Commercial Agents

1.1. Definition

Council Directive 86/653 of 18 December 1986[34] contains provisions on self-employed commercial agents to which the legislation of the Member States must be adapted. Article 189 of the EEC Treaty provides that a Directive shall be binding, as to the result to be achieved, on each Member State to which it is addressed but shall leave to the national authorities the choice of form and methods. Member States must adapt their legislation to Directives. Unlike regulations, Directives require complementation. However, provisions of Directives can have direct effect.[35] Article 22 obliges the Member States to implement the provisions of this Directive before 1 January 1990. Adapted national legislation shall apply at least to contracts that come into force on or after that date. Such provisions shall apply to contracts in operation by 1 January 1994 at the latest. The Directive enables Ireland, the United Kingdom and Italy to implement this Directive or some provisions of it at a later stage.

Article 1, paragraph 2 of the Directive defines the notion 'commercial agent' as a self-employed intermediary who has continuing authority to negotiate the sale or the purchase of goods on behalf of another person, the principal, or to negotiate and conclude such transactions on behalf of and in the name of that principal. A commercial agent shall be understood within the meaning of this Directive as not including, in particular:

- a person who, in his capacity as an officer, is empowered to enter into commitments binding on a company or association;

[34] OJ L 382/17 of 31 December 1986.
[35] *Van Duyn* judgment, [1974] ECR 1337. However, in the *Marshall* judgment ([1986] ECR 7237) the Court held that with respect to the so-called horizontal direct effect a Directive may not of itself impose obligations upon an individual and that a provision of a Directive may not be relied upon as such against such a person. Such provision can be invoked in principle only in proceedings against a Member State. However, this restriction of the direct effect does not necessarily prevent that provisions of Directives can be relied upon *otherwise* in proceedings against private parties (see Timmermans, "Directives: their Effect within the National Legal Systems", CML Rev. 1979, p. 533). In the *Kolpinghuis* judgment (8 October 1987, case 80/86, not yet reported), the Court of Justice held that national courts are bound to interpret national provisions in accordance with underlying Community Directives.

- a partner who is lawfully authorized to enter into commitments binding on his partners;
- a receiver and manager, a liquidator or a trustee in bankruptcy.

According to Article 2, Directive 86/653 shall not apply to commercial agents whose activities are unpaid. Article 2 (2) provides that the Member States have the right to provide that the Directive shall not apply to those persons whose activities as commercial agents are considered secondary by the law of that Member State.

1.2. Conclusion of the Contract

Article 13 of Directive 86/653 provides that each party shall be entitled to receive from the other on request a signed written document setting out the terms of the agency contract, including any terms subsequently agreed. Waiver of this right shall not be permitted. Member States are allowed to provide that an agency contract shall not be valid unless evidenced in writing.

1.3. The Principal's Duties and Rights

1.3.1. The principal's duties

1.3.1.1. Commission

Articles 6–12 of the Directive are related to the payment of commission by the principal to the agent.

According to Article 6, in the absence of any agreement on this matter between the parties and without prejudice to the application of the compulsory provisions of the Member States concerning the level of remuneration, a commercial agent shall be entitled to the remuneration that commercial agents appointed for the goods forming the subject of this agency contract are customarily allowed in the place where he carries on his activities. If there is no such customary practice, a commercial agent shall be entitled to reasonable remuneration taking into account all the aspects of the transaction. Any part of the remuneration which varies with the number or value of business transactions shall be deemed to be commission within the meaning of this Directive.

Article 7 states that a commercial agent shall be entitled to commission on commercial transactions concluded during the period covered by the agency contract where the transaction has been concluded as a result of his action or where the transaction is concluded with a third party whom he has previously acquired as a customer for transactions of the same kind. A commercial agent shall also be entitled to commission on transactions concluded during the period covered by the agency contract, either where he is assigned a specific geographical area or group of customers or where he has an exclusive right to a specific geographical area or group of customers and where the transaction has been entered into with a customer belonging to that area or group.

Article 8 is related to paying commission on transactions concluded after the agency contract has terminated. A commercial agent is entitled to such commission if the transaction is mainly attributable to the commercial agent's efforts during the period covered by the agency contract and if the transaction was entered into within a reasonable period after that contract terminated or if the order of the third party reached the principal or the commercial agent before the agency contract terminated.

According to Article 9, a commercial agent shall not be entitled to the commission if that commission is payable, pursuant to Article 8, to the previous commercial agent unless it is equitable for the commission to be shared between the commercial agents.

Article 10 of the Directive provides that the commission shall become due as soon as and to the extent that one of the following pre-requisites is fulfilled:

(a) the principal has executed the transactions; or
(b) the principal should, according to his agreement with the third party, have executed the transaction; or
(c) the third party has executed the transaction.

The commission shall become due at the latest when the third party has executed his part of the transaction or should have done so if the principal had executed his part of the transaction as he should have. The commission shall be paid not later than on the last day of the month following the quarter in which it became due. Agreements to derogate from these provisions to the detriment of the commercial agent shall not be permitted.

Article 11 of the Directive refers to the expiry of the right to commission. This right can be extinguished only if and to the extent that it is established that the contract between the third party and the principal will not be executed and that fact is due to a reason for which the principal is not to blame. Any commission which the commercial agent has already received shall be refunded if the right to it is extinguished. Agreements to derogate from this provision to the detriment of the commercial agent shall not be permitted.

Article 12 obliges the Member States to provide that the principal shall supply his commercial agent with a statement of the commission due, not later than the last day of the month following the quarter in which the commission has become due. This statement shall set out the main components used in calculating the amount of commission. A commercial agent shall be entitled to demand that he be provided with all the information, and in particular an extract from the books, which is available to his principal and which he needs in order to check the amount of the commission due to him. Derogations to the detriment of the commercial agents shall not be permitted. According to Article 12 (4), this Directive shall not conflict with the internal provisions of Member States which recognize the right of a commercial agent to inspect a principal's books.

1.3.1.2. Information

First of all, reference is made to Article 12 of the Directive, discussed in the previous paragraph. Furthermore, Article 4 of the Directive obliges a principal to act dutifully and in good faith in relations with his commercial agent. A principal must in particular provide his commercial agent with the necessary documentation relating to the goods concerned and obtain for his commercial agent the information necessary for the performance of the agency contract, and in particular notify the commercial agent within a reasonable period once he anticipates that the volume of commercial transactions will be significantly lower than that which the commercial agent could normally have expected. In addition to this, a principal must inform the commercial agent within a reasonable period of his acceptance, refusal and/or any non-execution of a commercial transaction which the commercial agent has procured for the principal. Parties may not derogate from these provisions.

1.4. The Commercial Agent's Duties and Rights

1.4.1. The commercial agent's duties

Article 3 of Directive 86/653 is related to the obligations of the commercial agent. According to this provision, the commercial agent must look after his principal's interests and act dutifully and in good faith in performing his activities. In particular, a commercial agent must make proper efforts to negotiate and, where appropriate, conclude the transactions he is instructed to take care of, communicate with the principal all the necessary information available to him and comply with reasonable instructions given by his principal. The parties may not derogate from these provisions.

Article 20 is related to non-competition clauses according to which the business activities of a commercial agent are restricted following termination of the agency contract. Such non-competition clause shall be valid only if and to the extent that it is concluded in writing and it relates to the geographical area or the group of customers and the geographical area entrusted to the commercial agent and to the kind of goods covered by his agency contract. A restraint of trade clause shall be valid for not more than two years after termination of the agency contract. Article 20 (4) provides that this shall not affect provisions of national law which impose other restrictions on the validity or enforceability of restraint of trade clauses or which enable the courts to reduce the obligations on the parties resulting from such an agreement.

The Directive does not mention other obligations for the commercial agent to be inserted in the agency contract.

1.4.2. The commercial agent's rights

Several rights of the commercial agent can be inferred from the corresponding obligations of the principal. Such obligations have been discussed under 1.3.1.

1.5. Liabilities of Principal and Agent during the Term of the Agency

The Directive does not contain separate provisions concerning the liabilities of the principal and the commercial agent.

1.6. Term and Termination

1.6.1. Term

The Directive states neither a minimum nor a maximum term for the agency agreement. Article 14 of the Directive provides that an agency contract for a fixed period which continues to be performed by both parties after that period has expired shall be deemed to be converted into an agency contract for an indefinite period.

1.6.2. Termination

Articles 15 and 16 of the Directive refer to the termination of the agency agreement. Article 15 provides that where an agency contract is concluded for an indefinite period, either party may terminate it by notice. The period of notice shall be one month for the first year of the contract, two months for the second year commenced and three months for the third year commenced and subsequent years. The parties may not agree on shorter periods of notice. Paragraph 3 of Article 15 enables the Member States to fix the period of notice at four months for the fourth year of the contract, five months for the fifth year and six months for the sixth and subsequent years. They may decide that the parties may not agree to shorter periods. If the parties agree on longer periods than those laid down in this Directive, the period of notice to be observed by the principal must not be shorter than that to be observed by the commercial agent. Unless otherwise agreed by the parties, the end of the period of notice must coincide with the end of a calendar month. According to Article 15 (6), the provisions of this Article shall apply to an agency contract for a fixed period where it is converted under Article 14 into an agency contract for an indefinite period subject to the proviso that the earlier fixed period must be taken into account in the calculation of the period of notice.

Article 16 of the Directive provides that nothing in this Directive shall affect the application of the law of the Member States where the latter provides for the immediate termination of the agency contract because of the failure of one party to carry out all or part of his obligations or where exceptional circumstances arise.

1.7. Indemnity and Compensation for Damages

Article 17 (1) of the Directive obliges the Member States to take the measures necessary to ensure that the commercial agent is, after termination of the agency contract, indemnified in accordance with paragraph 2 of Article 17 or compensated for damage in accordance with paragraph 3 of Article 17.

Entitlement to the indemnity as provided for in paragraph 2 of Article 17 or to compensation for damage as provided for under paragraph 3 of Article 17 shall also arise where the agency contract is terminated as a result of the commercial agent's death. The commercial agent shall lose his entitlement to the indemnity or to the compensation for damage if within one year following termination of the contract he has not notified the principal that he intends pursuing his entitlement.

Article 18 is devoted to circumstances in which the indemnity or compensation shall not be payable. This occurs:

(a) where the principal has terminated the agency contract because of default attributable to the commercial agent which would justify immediate termination of the agency contract under national law.

(b) where the commercial agent has terminated the agency contract, unless such termination is justified by circumstances attributable to the principal or on grounds of age, infirmity or illness of the commercial agent in consequence of which he cannot reasonably be required to continue his activities;

(c) where, with the agreement of the principal, the commercial agent assigns his rights and duties under the agency contract to another person.

The parties may not derogate from Articles 17 and 18 on indemnity and compensation for damage to the detriment of the commercial agent before the agency contract expires.

1.7.1. Indemnity

Paragraph 2 of Article 17 provides that the commercial agent shall be entitled to an indemnity if and to the extent that:

- he has brought the principal new customers or has significantly increased the volume of business with existing customers and the principal continues to derive substantial benefits from the business with such customers; and
- the payment of this indemnity is equitable having regard to all the circumstances and, in particular, the commission lost by the commercial agent on the business transaction with such customers. Member States may provide for such circumstances also to include the application or otherwise of a restraint of trade clause within the meaning of Article 20.

Furthermore, Article 17 (2) mentions that the amount of the indemnity may not exceed a figure equivalent to an indemnity for one year calculated from the commercial agent's average annual remuneration over the preceding five years and if the contract goes back less than five years the indemnity shall be calculated on the average for the period in question. The grant of such an indemnity shall not prevent the commercial agent from seeking damages.

1.7.2. Compensation for damages

Article 17 (3) stipulates that the commercial agent shall be entitled to compensation for the damage he suffers as a result of the termination of his relations with the principal. Such damage shall be deemed to occur particularly when the termination takes place in circumstances:

- depriving the commercial agent of the commission which proper performance of the agency contract would have procured him while providing the principal with substantial benefits linked to the commercial agent's activities; and/or

- which have not enabled the commercial agent to amortize the costs and expenses that he had incurred for the performance of the agency contract on the principal's advice.

2. Distributorship Agreements

Introduction

The notion 'distribution contracts' covers a whole range of vertical agreements between a vendor and a seller or distributor who are situated at different levels of economic transactions. Several categories of distribution agreements may be distinguished:

- exclusive distribution agreement, i.e. an agreement by which the supplier agrees to deliver certain products only to the distributor for resale within a certain area;
- exclusive purchasing agreement, i.e. an agreement by which the reseller agrees with the supplier to purchase certain goods for resale only from the supplier;
- selective distribution agreement, i.e. the establishment of a system in which the supplier sells his products only through outlets that fulfil certain minimum requirements concerning staff training, technical expertise, etc.[36]

Additional subdivisions will be made in the rest of this paragraph.

Not every vertical agreement on the supply of goods falls within Article 85 (1). In general, purchase agreements which lack exclusivity for either or both parties do not infringe Article 85 (1) unless other clauses in the agreements involved may result in a restriction of competition. This may occur, for instance, if parties agree on a vertical price restraint for the distributor.

Apart from that, a purchasing obligation of a longer duration and concerning a large quantity of goods may fall within Article 85 (1) and could result in the distributor being tied to the contract for a long period and unable to go to another supplier.[37]

Agreements which contain exclusivity for one or for both parties have to be assessed within the light of Article 85 (1). Such agreements may be combined with additional clauses which also restrict competition, for instance, again, clauses on vertical price restraints or provisions on preventing parallel imports.

This second part of this chapter deals with exclusive dealing and selective distribution agreements. Exclusive dealing occurs if the producer or the distributor obtains exclusivity in reselling the products within a specific area. Selective distribution takes place if distributors are limited according to their compliance with certain requirements. Limitation of the number of distributors and/or granting them protection within a certain territory is not permitted under Article 85 (1) within a system of selective distribution.

[36] Bellamy and Child, pp. 246-7.
[37] *BP Kemi/DDSF* decision (OJ L 286/32 of 14 November 1979).

In section 2.1 ('Exclusive Dealing') exclusive distribution agreements (A), exclusive purchasing agreements (B), two specific categories of exclusive purchasing agreements, i.e. beer supply agreements (C) and service station agreements (D), and, finally, motor vehicle distribution and servicing agreements (E) are discussed. Section 2.2 is devoted to selective distribution agreements.

2.1. Exclusive Dealing

A. Exclusive Distribution (Regulation 1983/83)

2.1.1. Definition and preliminary remarks

Exclusive distribution contracts are agreements by which the supplier agrees with the distributor to supply certain goods for resale within a defined area only to that distributor. Thus, it is the distributor who obtains the exclusive right to sell the products. Regulation 1983/83 of the Commission contains the block exemption for this category of agreements. Regulation 1984/83 provides the block exemption for categories of exclusive purchasing agreements. Such agreements constitute the opposite of exclusive distribution contracts and provide the supplier with an exclusive right. Together, these categories of agreements are called exclusive dealing contracts.

The predecessor of Regulations 1983/83 and 1984/83 was Regulation 67/67. This Regulation dealt with exclusive dealing contracts in general. The Regulations of 1983 make a distinction between exclusive distribution and exclusive purchasing. However, exclusive distribution agreements which are combined with clauses on exclusive purchasing fall within Regulation 1983/83 only. Agreements which are limited to exclusive purchasing have to be examined in the light of Regulation 1984/83.

Exclusive dealing agreements give rise to certain problems of competition policy. Such agreements normally prevent the supplier from appointing another distributor in the territory, or selling in the territory himself, while the distributor undertakes not to sell competing products. Such restrictions not only limit the freedom of the parties, but may additionally affect third parties. For those reasons, the Commission has constantly regarded exclusive distribution provisions of this kind as falling within Articles 85 (1), subject to an exemption under Article 85 (3).

Exclusive dealing agreements may have a number of benefits. In the preamble to Regulation 1983/83 the Commission considers that exclusive distribution agreements facilitate the promotion of sales of a product and lead to intensive marketing and to continuity of supplies while at the same time rationalizing distribution. These agreements stimulate competition between the products of different manufacturers. The appointment of an exclusive distributor who will take over sales promotion, customer services and carrying of stocks is often the most effective way and sometimes indeed the only way for the manufacturer to enter a market and to compete with other manufacturers already present. In general, exclusive distribution agreements lead to an improvement in distribution because the manufacturer is able to concentrate its sales activities, does not need to maintain numerous business relations with a larger number of dealers and is able, by dealing with only one dealer, to overcome more easily distribution difficulties in international trade resulting from linguistic, legal and other differences. As a rule such exclusive distribution agreements also allow customers a fair share of the resulting benefit as they gain directly from the improvement in distribution. Their economic and supply position is improved as they can obtain products manufactured in other countries more quickly and more easily.

However, issues with regard to the territorial protection of the distributor raise complications in the Community context. Distribution agreements often intend to ensure that the distributor will be the only person to market the contract goods in the territory assigned to him. The simplest means of achieving this aim is to impose export restrictions on other distributors of the same supplier. In order to protect distributors in other areas similar restrictions are imposed upon the distributor himself. Further devices for achieving the same end are the exercise of trade marks, pricing policies designed to make imports and exports between territories uneconomic and other measures such as refusing to honour a guarantee for parallel imports.[38] A distributor who is entirely protected against competition from imports of the contract products by third parties is said to enjoy absolute territorial protection.

As indicated above, European competition law, in general, and Regulation 1983/83, specifically, do not prescribe inserting special clauses in exclusive distribution agreements. Articles 85 and 86 are based on a system of prohibitions which means that Regulation 1983/83 is only useful for assessing whether a certain clause is permitted.

Regulation 1983/83 is designed to establish a fair balance between the interests of the manufacturer and the distributor and advantages of an exclusive distribution system on the one hand and the requirements of the Common Market on the other. Some protection for the distributor is allowed. Absolute territorial protection is forbidden under Regulation 1983/83. Furthermore, the distributor must be free to set resale prices.

2.1.2. Conclusion of the contract

Regulation 1983/83 does not contain provisions which prohibit methods of concluding the contract.

2.1.3. The supplier's duties and rights

2.1.3.1. The supplier's duties

It results from the definition of exclusive distribution agreements included in Article 1 of Regulation 1983/83 that the supplier may be obliged not to supply goods for resale to anyone other than the distributor within the defined area.

---

[38] Bellamy and Child, p. 248.

According to Article 2 (1) of Regulation 1983/83, the supplier may also accept the obligation not to supply himself the goods involved to end users in the contract's territory. End users can be defined as the consumers who buy the products in the final stage of marketing. According to Article 3(d) of Regulation 1983/83, the supplier must refrain from hindering intermediaries or users in obtaining the contract goods from other dealers inside the Common Market or, in so far as no alternative source of supply is available there, from outside the Common Market, in particular where the supplier exercises industrial property rights or other rights or takes other measures so as to prevent dealers or users from obtaining the contract goods outside, or from selling them in the contract territory.[39]

It follows from the competition policy of the Commission that the supplier must refrain from resale price restraints.[40]

2.1.3.2. The supplier's rights

First of all, there are rights of the supplier which reflect the counterpart of obligations of the distributor. These duties will be discussed in paragraph 2.1.4.1.

Article 2 (1) of Regulation 1983/83 provides that the supplier may be restricted in supplying the contract goods to users in the contract territory. However, in the Notice concerning Regulations 1983/83 and 1984/83[41] the Commission considers that the exclusive supply obligation does not prevent the supplier from providing the contract goods to other resellers who afterwards sell them in the exclusive distributor's territory. The supplier is not in breach of his obligation to the exclusive distributor provided that he supplies the distributors who resell the contract goods in the territory only at their request and that the goods are handed over outside the territory. However, supplies of this nature are permissible only if the reseller and not the supplier bears the costs for transporting the goods into the contract territory.

In addition to this, the Commission notes that the restriction on the supplier himself supplying the contract goods to end users in the exclusive distributor's contract territory need not be absolute. Clauses permitting certain customers in the territory to be supplied—with or without payment of compensation to the exclusive distributor—are compatible with the block exemption provided the customers in question are not resellers.

2.1.4. The distributor's duties and rights

2.1.4.1. The distributor's duties

Article 2 (2) and (3) of Regulation 1983/83 contains the exhaustive list of

---

[39] The principles that absolute territorial protection, export and import bans and prevention of parallel imports violate Article 85 were established in the *Grundig-Consten* decision of the Commission and were upheld by the Court of Justice (OJ 161/2545 of 20 October 1964 and [1966] ECR 449). They have been repeated in many decisions and judgments (*Tepea*, [1979] ECR 39, *Pioneer*, [1983] ECR 1825 and *Konica*, OJ L 78/34 of 23 March 1988).

[40] See the *Gero* decision (OJ L 16/8 of 19 January 1977), the *Hasselblad* decision (OJ L 161/18 of 12 June 1982) and the *Binon* judgment ([1985] ECR 2015).

[41] OJ C 101/2 of 13 April 1984.

obligations which the exclusive distribution agreement may impose upon the distributor.

According to Article 2 (2), no restriction on competition shall be imposed other than:

(a) the obligation not to manufacture or distribute goods which compete with the contract goods;
(b) the obligation to obtain the contract goods for resale only from the other party;
(c) the obligation to refrain, outside the contract territory and in relation to the contract goods, from seeking customers, from establishing any branch and from maintaining any distribution depot.

As indicated before, Regulation 1983/83 does not prescribe inserting all these clauses in exclusive distribution agreements.

With respect to Article 2 (2) (b) of Regulation 1983/83, it is worth noting that including this provision in an exclusive distribution agreement results in reciprocal exclusivity. The supplier is prevented from supplying the contract goods to anyone other than the distributor while the distributor is prevented from purchasing these goods or competing products from anyone other than the supplier. Agreements which contain only an exlcusive purchasing clause for the distributor and do not allot a specific territory to one distributor have to be examined in the light of Regulation 1984/83 and do not fall within Regulation 1983/83.

Article 2 (2) (c) of Regulation 1983/83 provides that the distribution agreement may restrict the distributor in actively marketing the products outside his territory. This section of Article 2 defines very precisely which restrictions may be imposed on the distributor. It results from this provision that the distributor may never be prevented from accepting orders from outside his territory. If a supplier were to neglect this provision (or other provisions of Article 2), Regulation 1983/83 would not apply because such policy might lead to absolute territorial protection. A partial prohibition on exporting the products, i.e. a prohibition on exportation in cases of an actively marketing policy, is acceptable to the Commission.

Paragraph 3 of Article 2 of Regulation 1983/83 enables parties to agree on obligations for the exclusive distributor related to:

(a) purchasing complete ranges of goods or minimum quantities;
(b) selling the contract goods under a trade mark, or packed and presented as specified by the other party;
(c) taking measures for promotion of sales, in particular to advertise, maintain a sales network or stock of goods, provide customer and guarantee services and employ staff with specialized or technical training.

The imposition of such obligations upon the distributor is justified under Regulation 1983/83.

2.1.4.2. The distributor's rights

To some extent the rights of the distributor which are guaranteed by the Regulation 1983/83 have already been mentioned above.

The distributor should be given the right to respond to requests to deliver from outside his territory. It is irrelevant whether these demands are made by distributors in that other territory or by end users in so far the distributor has the right to export.

Regulation 1983/83 does not as such prevent vesting the distributor with industrial property rights related to the contract goods. An important industrial property right in this respect is the right to use a trade mark. However, Article 3 (d) of Regulation 1983/83 applies also to the distributor and obliges him not to exercise industrial property rights so as to prevent dealers or users from obtaining outside, or from selling in, the contract territory properly marked or otherwise properly marketed contract goods. This rule was established in the famous *Grundig-Consten* case.[42]

Furthermore, the distributor must be free to set resale prices. Free movement of goods is considered a correction mechanism for price differences in the various territories. Substantial price differences constitute an indication that parallel imports are restricted.

According to the *Pronuptia* judgment, suppliers appear to have the right to establish a system of advisory prices provided that such a system will not result in a concerted practice to maintain uniform prices within a certain territory.

B. Exclusive Purchasing (Regulation 1984/83)

2.1.1. Definition and preliminary remarks

Article 1 of Regulation 1984/83 defines an exclusive purchasing agreement as an arrangement by which the reseller agrees with the supplier to purchase certain goods specified in the agreement for resale only from the supplier or from a connected undertaking. In principle, Article 85 (1) may apply to such agreements since the reseller deprives himself of the freedom to obtain those goods elsewhere, while at the same time other suppliers are denied an outlet for their products.

The basic approach of the Commission to exclusive purchasing agreements is rather favourable. Such agreements lead in general to an improvement in distribution. They stimulate competition between the products of different manufacturers. Resale price maintenance, restrictions on parallel imports and absolute protection of a territory are not permitted. This approach is reflected by the decisions of the Commission and judgments of the Court of Justice.[43]

2.1.2. Conclusion of the contract

Regulation 1984/83 does not contain prohibitions on methods of establishing an exclusive purchasing agreement.

---

[42] See note 39.
[43] *Brasserie de Haecht I* ([1967] ECR 407), *De Norre* ([1977] ECR 65), *Bilger* ([1970] ECR 127) and *Stremsel* ([1981] ECR 851).

2.1.3. The supplier's duties and rights

2.1.3.1. The supplier's duties

According to Article 2 (1) of Regulation 1984/83, the supplier is allowed to accept the obligation not to distribute himself the contract goods or goods which compete with the contract goods in the reseller's sales area and at the reseller's level of distribution. This provision allows the reseller to protect himself against direct competition from the supplier in his principal sales area. The reseller's sales area is determined by his normal business activity. It may be more closely defined in the agreement. However, the supplier cannot be forbidden to supply dealers who obtain the contract goods outside this area and afterwards resell them to customers inside it or to appoint other resellers in that area.

2.1.3.2. The supplier's rights

Regulation 1984/83 does not contain rights for the supplier other than those which reflect duties of the distributor.

2.1.4. The distributor's duties and rights

2.1.4.1. The distributor's duties

The main obligation which may be imposed upon the distributor is contained in Article 1 of Regulation 1984/83. According to this provision, the distributor may be impeded from purchasing certain goods specified in the agreement for resale from suppliers other than his contracting party. In addition to this, following Article 2 (2) and (3) of Regulation 1984/83, the distributor may be obliged not to manufacture or distribute goods which compete with the contract goods. Other obligations may involve the duty to purchase complete ranges of goods, to purchase minimum quantities of goods which are subject to the exclusive purchasing obligation, to sell the contract goods under trademarks, or packed and presented as specified by the supplier, and to take measures for the promotion of sales (in particular to advertise, maintain a sales network or stock of goods, provide customer and guarantee services and employ staff with specialized or technical training). Paragraph 3 of Article 2 of Regulation 1984/83 is similar to Article 2 (3) of Regulation 1983/83.

Further obligations imposed upon the distributor are not permitted under Regulation 1984/83. Additional duties require an individual exemption under Article 85 (3).

2.1.4.2. The distributor's rights

Regulation 1984/83 does not mention distributor's rights other than those which reflect duties of the supplier.

2.1.5. Liabilities

Regulation 1984/83 is not concerned with liabilities of the supplier or the distributor.

2.1.6. Term and termination

Article 3 (d) of Regulation 1984/83 provides that the block exemption does not apply if the agreement is concluded for an indefinite duration or for a period of more than five years. Agreements which do not comply with this term are prohibited under Article 85 (1) and require a specific exemption of the Commission under Article 85 (3). Agreements which specify a fixed term but are automatically renewable unless one of the parties gives notice to terminate are considered to have been concluded for an indefinite period.

C. Beer Supply Agreements (Regulation 1984/83)

2.1.1. Definition

Articles 6–9 of Regulation 1984/83 contain specific provisions for beer supply agreements. According to Article 6, such agreements oblige the reseller to purchase only from the supplier certain beers or certain beers and other drinks for resale in premises.

According to the Commission, it is necessary to lay down specific rules for beer supply agreements which take account of the particularities of the market in question. Like service station agreements, beer supply agreements are generally distinguished by the fact that, on the one hand, the supplier confers on the reseller special commercial or financial advantages by contributing to his financing, granting him or obtaining for him a loan on favourable terms, equipping him with a site or premises for conducting his business, providing him with equipment or fittings, or undertaking other investments for his benefit, and on the other hand, the reseller enters into a long-term exclusive purchasing obligation which in most cases is accompanied by a ban on dealing in competing products.

Since the mid-1960s the Community institutions have been compelled to examine beer supply agreements in the light of Article 85. In the *Brasserie de Haecht (I)* case[44] the Court of Justice held that such an individual agreement will not of its nature fall within Article 85 (1), but that this provision will apply if the agreement forms part of a network of agreements which, taken together, appreciably restrict competition and affect trade. Competition policy has been established through different decisions and judgments.[45]

2.1.2. Conclusion of the contract

The Regulation doe not contain obligations to be complied with when concluding a beer supply agreement.

2.1.3. The supplier's duties and rights

Article 9 of Regulation 1984/83 provides that Article 2 (1) of this Regulation on the obligation not to distribute the contract goods himself in the reseller's sales area applies to beer supply agreements as well.

---

[44] [1967] ECR 407.
[45] See the *De Norre* and *Bilger* judgments mentioned in note 43.

2.1.4. The distributor's duties and rights

2.1.4.1. The distributor's duties

The definition of beer supply agreements of Article 6 contains the main obligation for the distributor. In consideration for according special commercial or financial advantages the reseller undertakes to purchase only from the supplier certain beers, or certain beers and other drinks, specified in the agreement for resale and premises used for the sale and consumption of drinks and designated in the agreement.

According to the Notice of the Commission[46], the beers and other drinks covered by the exclusive purchasing obligation must be specified by brand or denomination in the agreement.

The exclusive purchasing obligation can be agreed in respect of one or more premises used for the sale and consumption of drinks which the reseller runs at the time the contract takes effect. The name and location of the premises must be stated in the agreement.

The reseller may enter into exclusive purchasing obligations both with a brewery in respect of beers of a certain type and with a drinks wholesaler in aspect of beers of another type and/or other drinks. The two agreements can be combined into one document. Article 6 also covers cases where the drinks wholesaler performs serveral functions at once, signing the first agreement on the breweries' and the second on his own behalf and also undertaking delivery of all the drinks. The provision of Article 6–9 do not apply to the contractual relations between the brewery and the drinks wholesaler.

Article 7 of Regulation 1984/83 contains an exhaustive list of additional obligations which may be imposed upon the reseller. The reseller may be obliged not to sell beers and other drinks which are supplied by other undertakings and which are of the same type as the beers or other drinks supplied under the agreement. Furthermore, the reseller may be held, in the event that the reseller sells beers which are supplied by other undertakings and which are of a different type from the beers supplied under the agreement, to sell such beers only in bottles, cans or other small packages, unless the sale of such beers in draught form is customary or is necessary to satisfy a sufficient demand from consumers. Finally, the reseller may be obliged to advertise goods supplied by other undertakings only in proportion to the share of these goods in the total turnover realized in the premises.

2.1.4.2. The distributor's rights

The reseller's right to purchase drinks from third parties may be restricted only to the extent allowed by Articles 6 and 7 of Regulation 1984/83. In his purchases of goods other than drinks and in his procurement of services which are not directly connected with the supply of drinks by the other party, the reseller must remain free to choose his supplier. Under Article 8 (1) (a) and (b), any action of the other party to prevent the reseller exercising his right in this regard will entail the loss of the benefit the block exemption.

[46] OJ C 101/2 of 13 April 1984.

According to Article 8 (2), specific provisions must be inserted if the agreement relates to premises which the supplier lets to the reseller or allows the reseller to occupy on some other basis. The agreement must provide for the reseller to have the right to obtain:

- drinks, except beer, supplied under the agreement from other undertakings where these undertakings offer them on more favourable conditions which the supplier does not meet;
- drinks, except beer, which are of the same type as those supplied under the agreement but which bear different trademarks, from other undertakings where the supplier does not offer them.

With respect to this last paragraph it should be noted that a threshold is crossed. Notwithstanding the primarily negative impact of European competition law on agreements concluded between private parties, Article 8 (2) of Regulation 1984/83 positively prescribes the inserting of several clauses in beer supply agreements in order to qualify for an exemption. This can only be explained by the intention of the Commission to protect the interests of the distributor in such agreements.

2.1.5. Liabilities

Regulation 1984/83 does not mention clauses on liabilities of the supplier or the distributor of beer.

2.1.6. Term and termination

The block exemption of Regulation 1984/83 is not applicable if the agreement is concluded for an indefinite duration or for a period of more than five years and the exclusive purchasing obligation relates to specific beers and other drinks or if the agreement is concluded for an indefinite duration or for a period of more than ten years and the exclusive purchasing obligation relates only to specified beers. The block exemption does not apply either if the supplier obliges the reseller to impose the exclusive purchasing obligation on a successor for a longer period than the reseller would himself remain tied to the supplier.

D. Service Station Agreements (Regulation 1984/83)

2.1.1. Definition

Finally, Regulation 1984/83 contains additional provisions for service station agreements. Such agreements are also a specific category of exclusive purchasing agreements and are defined as agreements by which the reseller agrees with the supplier, in consideration for the according of special commercial or financial advantages, to purchase only from the supplier certain petroleum-based motor vehicle fuels or certain petroleum-based motor vehicle and other fuels specified in the agreement for resale in a service station.

Parallel to beer supply agreements, special provisions for service station agreements are included in Regulation 1984/83 in order to protect the distributor from unjustified restrictions.

The exclusive purchasing obligation may cover, either motor vehicle fuels (for instance petrol, diesel fuel, LPG, kerosene) alone or motor vehicle fuels and other fuels (for instance heating oil, bottled gas, paraffin). All the goods concerned must be petroleum-based products. The motor vehicle fuels covered by the exclusive purchasing obligations must be for use in motor-powered land or water vehicles or aircraft. The term 'service station' is to be interpreted in a correspondingly wide sense. The Regulation applies to petrol stations adjoining public roads as well as to fuelling installations on private property not open to public traffic.

2.1.2. Conclusion of the contract

The Regulation does not contain specific provisions on the conclusion of a service station agreement.

2.1.3. The supplier's duties and rights

These duties and rights have been clarified in the foregoing. Because of the objectives of these special provisions on service station agreements, i.e. the protection of the distributor, the discussion of the relevant provisions of Regulation 1984/83 will focus on the rights and duties of the distributor.

2.1.4. The distributor's duties and rights

2.1.4.1. The distributor's duties

In addition to the general exclusive purchasing obligation, Article 11 provides that certain other restrictions can be imposed related to supply by other undertakings, advertising and equipment.

2.1.4.2. The distributor's rights

Article 11 of Regulation 1984/83 contains an exhaustive list of obligations which may be imposed upon the distributors. Other restrictions violate Article 85. Consequently, the distributor has the right to obtain goods other than fuels and services from an undertaking of his choice.

2.1.5. Liability

The section of Regulation 1984/83 relating to service station agreements does not provide for special clauses on liability.

2.1.6. Term and termination

Article 12 of Regulation 1984/83 provides that the block exemption does not apply where the agreement is concluded for an indefinite duration or for a period of more than ten years or if the supplier obliges the reseller to impose the exclusive purchasing obligation on his successor for a longer period than the reseller would himself remain tied to the supplier.

E. MOTOR VEHICLE DISTRIBUTION AND SERVICING AGREEMENTS (REGULATION 123/85)

2.1.1. Definition

Motor vehicle distribution and servicing agreements have features common to exclusive dealing agreements. The Commission adopted a specific Regulation concerning the distribution and servicing of automobiles (Regulation 123/85).

Article 1 of Regulation 123/85 defines such agreements as contracts to which only two undertakings are party and in which one contracting party agrees to supply within a defined territory only to the other party, or only to the other party and to a specified number of other undertakings within the distribution system, for the purpose of resale, certain motor vehicles intended for use on public roads and having three or more roadwheels, together with spare parts for them. Other definitions can be found in Article 13 of the Regulation. Such agreements fall within the block exemption of Regulation 123/85 if the conditions mentioned in the Regulation are met.

In Regulation 123/85 the Commission tried to find a compromise between the need to protect small distributors on the one hand and the justified demands of producers of motor cars for an efficient distribution network on the other.

The Commission based the Regulation on its previous decisions related to distribution systems in the motor car industry.[47] One of the main concerns of the Commission is that parallel exports are not restricted. Prohibitions of exporting by dealers are only permitted in so far as the dealer must refrain from selling motor cars and spare parts to dealers who do not belong to the distribution network set up by the manufacturer.[48]

This regulation is part of the more general policy of the Commission to establish a true Common Market in the field of motor cars. Until now, national borders have remained as a result of diverging national legislation (registration, certifications, fiscal distortions) and as a result of the restrictive practices of manufacturers.

2.1.2. Conclusion of the contract

Regulation 123/85 does not contain specific requirements for the conclusion of a motor vehicle and servicing agreement.

2.1.3. The supplier's duties and rights

Article 1 of Regulation 123/85 mentions the most important obligation for the supplier, i.e. to supply certain motor vehicles together with spare parts within a defined territory of the Common Market only to the other party, or

---

[47] See the *BMW I* decision (OJ L 29/1 of 3 February 1975, the *BMW II* decision (OJ L 46/13 of 17 February 1978) and the *Ford* decision (OJ L 327/31 of 24 November 1983). The Court dealt with such agreements in the *BMW* case ([1979] ECR 2435) and the *Ford* case ([1984] ECR 1129 and 1985, 2735).

[48] See the second *BMW* case mentioned in note 47.

only to the other party and to a specified number of other undertakings within the distribution system for the purpose of resale. Parties may agree that the supplier reserves the right to conclude distribution and servicing agreements for contract goods with specified further undertakings operating within the contract area or to alter the contract territory only where the supplier shows that there are objectively valid reasons for doing so (Article 5 (2), under (1) (b). Furthermore, Article 2 enables parties to agree that the supplier is bound neither to sell contract goods to final consumers nor to provide them with servicing for contract goods in the contract territory.

According to Article 5 (1) (2) (d), the supplier shall also supply to the dealer, for the purpose of performance of a contract of sale concluded between the dealer and a consumer in the Common Market, any passenger car which corresponds to a model within the contract programme and which is marketed by the manufacturer or with the manufacturer's consent in the Member State in which the vehicle is to be registered.[49]

In addition to this, Regulation 123/85 mentions rights for the supplier to be included in the agreement, which are connected with specific obligations for the dealer. Such duties for the distributor will be described in the next paragraph.

2.1.4. The distributor's duties and rights

Regulation 123/85 contains an exhaustive list of obligations which may be imposed on the dealer and conditions to be complied with in that respect. These obligations are mentioned in Articles 3 and 4 of the Regulation. The main obligations will be discussed.

The Regulation accepts that the dealer may be bound not to manufacture products which compete with contract goods (Article 3 (2)).

The distributor may be prohibited from selling new motor vehicles which compete with contract goods or from selling, at the premises used for the distribution of contract goods, new motor vehicles other than those offered for supply by the manufacturer (Article 3 (3)).

Furthermore, the dealer may be prohibited from selling spare parts which compete with contract goods and do not match the quality of contracts goods or to use them for repair or maintenance of contract goods or corresponding goods (Article 3 (4)).

The dealer may be bound not to conclude distribution or servicing agreements with third parties for goods which compete with contract goods (Article 3 (5)). Article 5 (2) (1) provides that the parties must agree that the supplier shall release the dealer from the obligations referred to in Article 3 (3) and (5) where the dealer shows that there are objectively valid reasons for doing so.

Article 3 (6) enables parties to agree that the dealer is prohibited, without the supplier's consent, from concluding distribution or servicing agreements with undertakings operating in the contract area for contract goods or corresponding goods. For the applicability of the block exemption, the dealer has to undertake to impose on the sub-dealers on obligation to honour guaran-

---

[49] See the *Ford II* case mentioned in note 47.

tees and to perform free servicing and vehicle recall work, at least to the extent to which the dealer himself is obliged (Article 5 (1) (1) (b)). The supplier shall not without objectively valid reasons withhold consent to conclude, alter or terminate sub-dealer agreements.

Article 3 (7) refers to the duty of the dealer to impose on undertakings with which he has concluded sub-dealer agreements obligations corresponding to those which he (the dealer) has accepted in relation to the supplier and which are covered by Article 3 of Regulation 123/85.

Article 3 (8) provides that the dealer may be obliged not to maintain branches or depots for the distribution of contract goods or corresponding goods outside the contract territory and not to seek customers for contract goods or corresponding goods outside the contract territory. In relation to this, the dealer may be obliged not to entrust third parties with the distribution or servicing of contrast goods or corresponding goods outside the contract territory.

According to Article 3 (10), the dealer may be obliged to supply to a reseller contract goods or corresponding goods only where the reseller is an undertaking within the distribution system or to supply to a reseller spare parts within the contract programme only where they are for the purposes of repair or maintenance of a motorvehicle by the reseller. The first part of this provision is a very substantial element of distribution systems.

Article 4 of Regulation 123/85 contains additional obligations which do not prevent application of the block exemption of the Regulation. The main obligations are:

- to observe, for distribution and servicing, minimum standards which relate in particular to the equipment of the business premises and of the technical facilities for servicing, the specialized and technical training of staff, advertising, etc.;
- to endeavour to sell, within the contract territory and within a specified period, a certain minimum quantity of contract goods;
- to keep in stock a certain quantity of contract goods;
- to keep such demonstration vehicles within the contract programme;
- to perform guarantee work, free servicing and vehicle recall work for contract goods and corresponding goods;
- to use only spare parts within the contract programme or corresponding goods for guarantee work, free servicing and vehicle recall work in respect of contract goods or corresponding goods.

With respect to the obligation to perform guarantee work, free servicing and recall work, Article 5 (1) (1) (a) requires the dealer to undertake to honour guarantees in respect of motor vehicles which have been supplied within the Common Market by another undertaking within the distribution network and to perform free servicing and vehicle recall work to an extent which corresponds to the dealer's obligations.

2.1.5. Liability

This subject has already been dealt with in the previous paragraph.

2.1.6. Term and termination

Article 5 (2) (2) of Regulation 123/85 contains some minimum provisions to be inserted in certain types of motor vehicle distribution and servicing agreements. In this respect the Regulation refers to agreements according to which the dealer has assumed obligations for the improvement of distribution and servicing structures and the obligations of Article 3 of the Regulation with respect to the distribution and servicing of motor vehicles of other manufacturers. Such agreements shall be concluded for a period of at least four years. If the agreement is concluded for an indefinite period such agreements shall contain the provision that the period of notice for regular termination of the agreement is at least one year for both parties, unless

- the supplier is obliged by law or by special agreement to pay appropriate compensation on termination of the agreement; or
- the dealer is a new entrant to the distribution system and the period of the agreement, or the period of notice for regular termination of the agreement, is the first agreed by the dealer.

For such agreements each party must undertake to give the other at least six months' prior notice of intention not to renew an agreement concluded for a definite period. These requirements do not apply if the agreement is terminated with mutual consent. These provisions do not affect the right of a party to terminate the agreement for cause.

Article 3 (12) of Regulation 123/85 enables parties to agree that the dealer is obliged to comply with certain non-competition clauses for a maximum period of one year after termination or expiry of the agreement.

2.2. Selective Distribution

2.2.1. Definition and preliminary remarks

Selective distribution systems can be defined as networks of resellers chosen on criteria relating to the sale of the product and which may include a minimum of technical expertise.[50] The manufacturers supply their products only to the selected resellers while those resellers are prohibited from selling to non-members of the network. The products involved may constitute goods for which some information is required for the sale to consumers. Systems of selective distribution occur, among others, in the field of motor cars,[51] consumer electronics and luxury products. Selective distribution systems usually consist of selected resellers at several levels of distribution. The manufacturer may choose an exclusive distributor for one country, who, in return, deals with some selected wholesalers, who supply only the chosen dealers. At each level obligations apply to ensure that the marketing of the products involved follows the channels set up by the manufacturer.[52]

[50] Bellamy and Child, p. 292.
[51] Selective distribution systems of BMW and Ford were assessed by the Commission. The motor vehicle and servicing agreements covered by Regulation 123/85 have characteristics common to selective distribution systems.
[52] See, for instance, the *Saba* distribution system described in the decisions' of the Commission (OJ L 28/19 of 3 February 1976 and L 376./41 of 31 December 1983).

In the following description, the rights and duties of the manufacturer and the dealer will be emphasized. This description is based on decisions of the Commission and case law of the Court. The Commission did not establish a block exemption for selective distribution contracts.

Systems of selective distributions may have features common to other systems of distribution. Selective distribution may be combined with some degrees of territorial protection. In that respect selective distribution has characteristics which are similar to exclusive distribution. The borderline between those categories of distribution systems may be difficult to draw because suppliers may require also a minimum of technical expertise and advertising for exclusive distributors. On the other hand, selective distribution systems are often very similar to franchise agreements.[53]

The Community's approach to selective distribution systems is based on a rule of reason. Article 85 (1) does not apply to such systems if the resellers are selected exclusively on the basis of non-discriminatory qualitative criteria relating to their technical ability to handle the goods and the suitability of their premises.

This approach was established by the Court in the *Metro-Saba (I)* case.[54] In the judgment the Court held that the provisions of Articles 3 and 85 imply the existence on the market of workable competition, that is to say the degree of competition necessary to ensure the observance of the basic requirements and the attainment of the objectives of the Treaty. In the sector covering the production of high quality and technically advanced consumer durables, the structure of the market does not preclude the existence of a variety of channels of distribution adapted to the peculiar characteristics of the various producers and the requirements of the various categories of consumers. In such systems of distribution price competition is not generally emphasized either as an exclusive or indeed as a principal factor. Although price competition is so important that it can never be eliminated, it does not constitute the only effective form of competition or that to which absolute priority must be accorded in all circumstances. Therefore selective distribution systems accord with Article 85 (1) provided that resellers are chosen on the basis of objective criteria of a qualitative nature relating to the technical qualitifications of the reseller and his staff and the suitability of his trading premises and that such conditions are laid down uniformally for all pretential resellers and not applied in a discriminatory fashion.

In the *AEG* judgment,[55] the Court summarized its approach of selective distribution. There are legitimate requirements, such as the maintenance of the specialist trade capable of providing specific services as regards high quality and high technology products which may justify a reduction of price competition in favour of competition relating to factors other than price. Systems of selective distribution constitute an element of competition which is in conformity with Article 85 (1) in as far as they aim at the attainment of a legitimate goal capable of improving competition in relation to factors other than price. The operation of a selective distribution system which is

---

[53] Bellamy and Child, p. 292.
[54] [1977] ECR 1875.
[55] [1983] ECR 3151.

not based on objective criteria of a qualitative nature constitutes an infringement of Article 85 (1).

It is appropriate to examine in more detail the circumstances under which the rule of reason approach of selective distribution systems of the Commission and the Court can be applied.

Article 85 (1) is violated where resellers are selected on the basis of requirements other than objective criteria of a qualitative nature, or where such objective conditions are not being laid down uniformly for all potential resellers or are applied in a discriminatory fashion. The position is the same where a system which is in principle in conformity with Community law is applied in practice in a manner incompatible with it. According to the *AEG* judgment, a selective distribution system is unlawful where the manufacturer, with a view to maintaining a high level of prices or to excluding certain modern channels of distribution, refuses to approve distributors who satisfy the qualitative criteria of the system.

Where a producer restricts the number of resellers and organizes the selective distribution system on the basis of quantitative criteria, Article 85 (1) is violated because such a practice results in a degree of territorial protection. Under those circumstances the Commission must examine the selective distribution system within the framework of the exemption of Article 85 (3).

Another requirement of applying the rule of reason approach to selective distribution systems was mentioned in the *Metro-Saba (I)* judgment. The Court held that the Commission must ensure that the structural rigidity resulting from a selective distribution system is not reinforced, as might happen if there were an increase in the number of selective distribution networks for marketing the same product. This point was discussed in the *Metro-Saba (II)* judgment[56] as well. The Court held that the existence of a large number of selective distribution systems for a particular product does not in itself permit the conclusion that competition is restricted or distorted.

A final condition for applying the rule of reason approach is the requirement that the product involved constitutes a rather sophisticated good. The objective criteria of a qualitative nature used for the selection of resellers should be related to the products concerned. This point is seldom used by the Commission to deny application of the rule of reason approach. In the *L'Oréal* judgment,[57] the Court held that in order to determine the exact of qualitative criteria for the selection of resellers it is also necessary to consider whether the characteristics of the product in question necessitate a selective distribution system in order to preserve its quality and to ensure its proper use and whether those objectives are not already satisfied by national rules governing admission to the resale trade or the conditions of sale of the product in question. In the *Grohe* case,[58] the Commission refused application of the rule of reason approach by stating that it is doubtful whether plumbing fittings can be considered as technically advanced products. Furthermore, wholesalers generally do not sell plumbing fittings directly to final consumers but to retailers. Therefore it is questionable

---

[56] [1986] ECR 3021.
[57] [1980] ECR 3775.
[58] OJ L 19/7 of 23 January 1985.

whether the characteristics of the product necessitate a selective distribution system in order to preserve their quality and ensure their proper use. It is thus doubtful whether the purely qualitative criteria which Grohe imposed in its dealership agreement with wholesalers are compatible with Article 85 (1).

In general, the Commission rather easily decides to apply the rule of reason approach to selective distribution systems.

2.2.2. Conclusion of the contract

Community law does not provide specific requirements for the conclusion of selective distribution contracts.

2.2.3. The supplier's duties and rights

In most selective distribution systems the manufacturer undertakes not to supply dealers outside the distribution network. This obligation does not violate Article 85 (1) if the access to the distribution network is based solely on objective grounds of a qualitative nature.

Limitation of the number of dealers in a specific area violates Article 85 (1) and will only under exceptional circumstances qualify for an exemption under Article 85 (3). For that purpose it is necessary that such territorial protection is the only means to encourage dealers to undertake the investment.

Another obligation usually imposed upon the manufacturer is the duty to enforce strictly its distribution arrangements and to proceed immediately against dealers by all means at its disposal.[59] This obligation is permitted as long as it is not used for objectives other than to protect a selective distribution network based on qualitative criteria.

2.2.4. The distributor's duties and rights

2.2.4.1. The distributor's duties

The basic obligation for dealers in selective distribution systems is the prohibition to supply dealers who have not been appointed by the manufacturer. In so far as admission to a selective distribution network is given only to those dealers who fulfil general qualitative requirements, this obligation does not violate Article 85 (1).

The general objective criteria are similarly obligations for the dealer. The imposition of such obligations is allowed by the Commission. Important objective criteria are, among others:

- technical qualifications of the dealers;
- specialist knowledge of their staff;
- suitability of trading premises;
- adequacy of customer services;
- participation in a guarantee arrangement;
- submission of advertisements for approval of the manufacturer;

---

[59] See the *Saba I* case mentioned in note 52.

- maintaining a record of customers' names and addresses, serial numbers of purchases and dates of delivery and making the record available to the manufacturer.[60]

The objective criteria of a qualitative nature may not be used in a discriminatory way.[61] In accordance with the *Saba II* decision,[62] Saba undertook to fulfil specific requirements for the admission procedure. A system giving the manufacturer the sole and unrestricted right of admission opens the door to discriminatory application of the admission criteria. Admission may not be dependent on the dealer's willingness to comply with severe price maintenance system.

Saba undertook to take a decision within four weeks on each application. If it fails to do so, the dealer in question is deemed admitted to the network and Saba is obliged to conclude a dealership agreement with him immediately.

2.2.4.2. The distributor's rights

Cross-supplies by the dealer to other appointed resellers may not be prohibited. Consequently, the dealer has a right to supply contract goods from other distributors, including distributors established in other Member States. To that extent imports and exports by the dealer may not be prohibited by the selective distribution system.[63]

A system of resale price maintenance is not permitted. The dealer must be free to determine his prices. According to the *AEG* judgment, the existence of a price undertaking constitutes a condition which is manifestly foreign to the requirements of a selective distribution system.[64]

2.2.5. Liability

EEC competition does not provide specific requirements for liabilities of suppliers and distributors in selective distribution systems.

2.2.6. Term and termination

Community law does not contain provisions related to the term and termination of selective distribution agreements. However, selection of dealers is related to the expulsion of dealers from the network. Termination of an agreement because of failure to comply with criteria other than the general objective criteria infringes Article 85. In the *Saba II* case the Commission sought guarantees from Saba in this respect. Under the new agreement such termination is only possible in the event of a complete change of the distribution system involving the termination of all dealership agreements. The new Saba agreements provide that termination is possible without notice but reasons must always be given. If a dealer disputes an allegation, final

[60] See the *Saba I* case mentioned in note 52 and the *IBM* case (OJ L 118/24 of 4 May 1984).
[61] *AEG* decision, OJ L 117/15 of 30 April 1982.
[62] OJ L 376/41 of 31 December 1983.
[63] See for instance the *BMW II* decision mentioned in note 47.
[64] [1983] ECR 3151.

expulsion is only possible after a decision by a Court. Finally, the agreements now contain a reference to the applicability of the appropriate national competition law. This ensures that a dealer can only be penalized on account of actions which are considered unfair under national regulations.[65]

3. Franchise Agreements (Regulation 4087/88)

3.1. Definition and Preliminary Remarks

Franchise agreements have only recently been examined within the framework of European competition law. The *Pronuptia* judgment of the Court of 28 January 1986[66] was the first decision of one of the institutions of the European Communities on franchise networks. After that judgment the Commission adopted some decisions concerning specific franchise networks.[67] Based on these developments, the Commission adopted Regulation 4087/88 containing a block exemption for catagories of franchise agreements on 30 November 1988.[68] This Regulation entered into force on 1 February 1989.

Apart from distribution agreements, franchise agreements demonstrate similarities with patent licence agreements and know-how licence agreements. It would be interesting to examine more closely the differences between these agreements and the block exemptions of the Commission.

In general, the following types of franchise can be distinguished: industrial franchise which concerns the manufacturing of goods, distribution franchise on the retailing of goods and service franchise which concerns the supply of services. The *Pronuptia* judgment and the Regulation of the Commission are mainly concerned with distribution franchises. The Regulation applies to service franchise as well. In the *Pronuptia* decision, the Court defines distribution franchise agreements as contracts under which the franchise simply sells certain products in a shop which bears the franchisor's business name or symbol. The definition of franchise agreements applied in the Regulation has a more extended ambit. According to Article 1 (3) (b), a franchising agreement means an agreement whereby one undertaking, the franchisor, grants the other, the franchise, in exchange for financial consideration, the right to exploit a franchise for the purpose of marketing determined goods and/or services. A franchise means a package of industrial or intellectual property rights relating to trade marks, trade names, shop signs, utility models, designs, copyrights, know-how or patents, to be exploited for the resale of goods or the provision of services to end users.

According to Article 1 (2) of the Regulation, the exemption also applies to

---

[65] *Saba II* decision, paragraph 25, mentioned in note 52.

[66] [1986] ECR 353.

[67] *Pronuptia* decision (OJ L 13/39 of 15 January 1987), *Yves Rocher* decision (OJ L 8/49 of 10 January 1987), *Computerland* decision (OJ L 222/12 of 10 August 1987), *Service Master* decision (OJ L 332/38 of 3 December 1988) and *Charles Jourdain* decision (OJ L 35/31 of 7 February 1989).

[68] OJ L 359/46 of 28 December 1988.

master franchise agreements, i.e. agreements between two undertakings whereby the franchisor grants the other, the master franchisee, in exchange for financial consideration, the right to exploit a franchise in a specified territory for the purposes of concluding with third parties, the franchisees, franchise agreements as defined in this Regulation.

In the *Pronuptia* judgment, the Court adopted a rule of reason approach for the application of Article 85 (1) to franchise agreements. The Court defined a system of distribution franchises as a network of agreements whereby an undertaking which has established itself as a distributor on a given market and thus developed certain business methods, grants independent traders, for a fee, the right to establish themselves in other markets using its business name and the business methods which have made it successful. Rather than a method of distribution, it is a way for an undertaking to derive financial benefit from its expertise without investing its own capital. Moreover, the system gives traders who do not have the necessary experience access to methods which they could not have learnt without considerable effort and allows them to benefit from the reputation of the franchisor's business name. Such a system, which allows the franchisor to profit from his success, does not in itself interfere with competition. In order for the system to work two conditions must be met. The Court held that, first, the franchisor must be able to communicate his know-how to the franchisees and provide them with the necessary assistance in order to enable them to apply his methods, without running the risk that the know-how and assistance might benefit competitors. It follows that provisions which are essential in order to avoid that risk do not constitute restrictions on competition for the purposes of Article 85 (1). Secondly, the franchisor must be able to take the measures necessary for maintaining the identity and reputation of the network bearing his business name or symbol. It follows that provisions which establish the means of control necessary for that purpose do not constitute restrictions on competition for the purposes of Article 85 (1), either.

The Court of Justice and the Commission have established the borderlines to be complied with under Article 85. From the *Pronuptia* judgment, the individual decisions and the Regulation of the Commission, it has become clear that European competition law is regarding franchise agreements rather favourably.

According to the Court, provisions in franchise agreements which are strictly necessary, in order to ensure that the know-how and assistance provided by the franchisor do not benefit competitors, do not constitute restrictions of competition for the purposes of Article 85 (1). Provisions which establish the control strictly necessary for maintaining the identity and reputation of the network identified by the common name or symbol do not constitute restrictions of competition for the purpose of Article 85 (1), either. However, provisions which share markets between the franchisor and the franchisees or between franchisees do constitute restriction of competition for the purposes of Article 85 (1). Finally, the fact that the franchisor makes price recommendations to the franchisee does not constitute a restriction of competition, as long as there is no concerted practice between the franchisor and the franchisees or among the franchisees for the actual application of such prices. Obligatory price restraints will not be permitted by the Commission, not even under Article 85 (3) or under the block exemption.

An exemption will not be granted, as well, if parallel imports are restricted. Therefore, cross-deliveries between franchisees should always be possible. Furthermore, where a franchise network is combined with a selective distribution system, franchisees should be free to obtain supplies from approved distributors. Even if franchisees can be prohibited from competing with the franchisor, they should never be prevented from investing in competing companies, in particular, where they do not have control, or are not a member of the board of a competing company. The franchisee must be able to obtain supplies of goods of equivalent quality to those offered by the franchisor from other manufacturers, unless such a restriction is justified for reasons related to the protection of the franchisor's know-how or maintaining the common identity and reputation of the franchised network.

3.2. Conclusion of the Contract

Community law does not contain specific provisions for the conclusion of franchise contracts.

3.3. The Supplier's Duties and Rights

Article 2 of the Regulation on franchise agreements provides that the main obligations to be imposed upon the supplier are the obligation not to give the right to exploit all or part of the franchise to third parties in a defined area of the Common Market and the obligation not to exploit itself the franchise or supply of the goods or services which are subject of the franchise under a similar formula in the contract territory.

3.4. The Distributor's Duties and Rights

3.4.1. The distributor's duties

The *Pronuptia* judgment of the Court and the Regulation of the Commission are to a large extent devoted to the obligations which may be imposed upon the distributor.

Article 2 of the Regulation contains several obligations to be imposed upon the franchisee which are essential to franchise agreements. These obligations fall under the block exemption. First, most franchise agreements will contain an obligation for the franchisee to exploit the franchise only from the contract premises. In addition to this, the Regulation permits an obligation to be included in the agreement for the franchisee to refrain from seeking customers outside the contract territory. Finally, Article 2 enables parties to oblige the franchisee not to manufacture or distribute goods competing with the goods which are the subject of the franchise in the contract territory or in a territory allotted to another member of the franchised work.

These restrictions belong to the most sensitive clauses in franchise agreements. In the *Yves Rocher* decision the Commission noticed that the selection of only one franchisee for a given territory combined with the prohibition on the opening by franchisees of a second shop results in a degree of sharing of markets between the franchisor and the franchisees or between franchisees. The prohibition on cross-supplies between franchisees was deleted by the contracting parties. The remaining restrictions caught by Article 85 (1) were indispensable to the establishment of the network: none of the franchisees would, in all probability, have agreed to undertake the investment had he not been certain of receiving a degree of protection in his territory.[69]

Article 3 provides a list of additional obligations which may be imposed on the franchisee:

(a) in so far as it is necessary to protect the franchisor's know-how or to maintain the common identity and reputation of the franchised network, to sell exclusively goods matching minimum objective quality specifications laid down by the franchisor;

(b) to sell goods which are manufactured only by the franchisor or by third parties designated by it, where it is impracticable, owing to the nature of the goods which are the subject of the franchise, to apply objective quality specifications;

(c) not to engage, directly or indirectly, in any similar business in a territory where it would compete with a member of the franchised network. The franchisee may be held to this obligation after termination of the agreement for a reasonable period which may not exceed one year, within the territory where it has exploited the franchise;

(d) to sell the goods which are the subject matter of the franchise only to end users, to other franchisees and to resellers within other channels of distribution supplied by the manufacturer or with its consent;

(e) not to use the know-how licensed by the franchisor for purposes other than the exploitation of the franchise. The franchise may be held to this obligation after termination of the agreement;

(f) not to disclose to third parties the know-how provided by the franchisor. The franchisee may be held to this obligation after termination of the agreement;

(g) to inform the franchisor of infringements of the licensed industrial or intellectual property rights, to take legal action against infringers or to assist the franchisor in any legal actions against infringers;

(h) to communicate to the franchisor any experience gained in exploiting the franchise and to grant it, and other franchisees, a non-exclusive licence for the know-how resulting from that experience;

(i) to attend or to have its staff attend training courses arranged by the franchisor;

(j) to use its best endeavours to sell the goods or provide the services that are the subject of the franchise, to offer for sale a minimum range of goods, achieve a minimum turnover, plan his orders in advance, keep minimum stocks and provide customer and warranty services;

---

[69] *Yves Rocher* decision, pts 54 and 63; see also the *Pronuptia* decision, pts 28 and 36, and the *Computer land* decision, pts 25 and 33.

(k) to pay to the franchisor a specified proportion of its revenue for advertising and obtain the franchisor's approval for the nature of the advertising it carries out itself;

(l) to apply the commercial methods devised by the franchisor and use the licensed industrial or intellectual property rights;

(m) to comply with the franchisor's standards for the equipment and presentation of the contract premises and/or means of transport;

(n) to allow the franchisor to carry out checks;

(o) not to change the location of the contract premises without the franchisor's consent.

Under Article 4 (b) the franchisee must honour guarantees. This also applies to goods applied by other members of the franchised network. According to Article 4 (c), the franchisee must indicate its status as an independent undertaking.

3.4.2. The distributor's rights

Articles 4 and 5 of Regulation 4087/88 provide for certain rights of the franchisee which constitute conditions for applying the block exemption.

According to Article 4 (a), the franchisee must be free to obtain the goods that are the subject matter of the franchise from other franchisees.

Article 5 (b) enables the franchisee to obtain supplies of goods of a quality equivalent to those offered by the franchisor from other manufacturers unless it is impracticable, owning to the nature of the goods which are the subject matter of the franchise, to apply objective quality specifications. The franchisor may not refuse to designate third parties proposed by the franchisee as authorized manufacturers for reasons other than protection of the franchisor's industrial and intellectual property rights or maintaining the common identity and reputation of the franchised network. Furthermore, the franchisee must have the opportunity to use the licensed know-know after termination of the agreement where the know-how has become generally known or easily accessible. The franchisee may not be restricted by the franchisor to determine resale prices.

The provisions included in Article 5 of the Regulation constitute essential rights of the franchise. If these rights are not mentioned in the agreement, the block exemption will not apply. In addition to this, individual exemptions will not be granted by the Commission if such rights are not provided for in the agreement.

3.5. Liability

The Regulation of the Commission does not contain provisions dealing with liability of the franchisor or the franchisee.

3.6. Term and Termination

Regulation 4087/88 does not regulate the term and termination of the franchise agreements. The fact that franchise agreements which were exempted prior to the entry into force of Regulation 4087/88 were concluded for periods of five or ten years did not provoke special comments of the Commission.

Annex 1

COUNCIL DIRECTIVE

of 18 December 1986

on the coordination of the laws of the Member States relating to self-employed commercial agents

(86/653/EEC)

THE COUNCIL OF THE EUROPEAN COMMUNITIES,

Having regard to the Treaty establishing the European Economic Community, and in particular Articles 57 (2) and 100 thereof,

Having regard to the proposal from the Commission (¹),

Having regard to the opinion of the European Parliament (²),

Having regard to the opinion of the Economic and Social Committee (³),

Whereas the restrictions on the freedom of establishment and the freedom to provide services in respect of activities of intermediaries in commerce, industry and small craft industries were abolished by Directive 64/224/EEC (⁴);

Whereas the differences in national laws concerning commercial representation substantially affect the conditions of competition and the carrying-on of that activity within the Community and are detrimental both to the protection available to commercial agents *vis-à-vis* their principals and to the security of commercial transactions; whereas moreover those differences are such as to inhibit substantially the conclusion and operation of commercial representation contracts where principal and commercial agent are established in different Member States;

Whereas trade in goods between Member States should be carried on under conditions which are similar to those of a single market, and this necessitates approximation of the legal systems of the Member States to the extent required for the proper functioning of the common market; whereas in this regard the rules concerning conflict of laws do not, in the matter of commercial representation, remove the inconsistencies referred to above, nor would they even if they were made uniform, and accordingly the proposed harmonization is necessary notwithstanding the existence of those rules;

Whereas in this regard the legal relationship between commercial agent and principal must be given priority;

Whereas it is appropriate to be guided by the principles of Article 117 of the Treaty and to maintain improvements

already made, when harmonizing the laws of the Member States relating to commercial agents;

Whereas additional transitional periods should be allowed for certain Member States which have to make a particular effort to adapt their regulations, especially those concerning indemnity for termination of contract between the principal and the commercial agent, to the requirements of this Directive,

HAS ADOPTED THIS DIRECTIVE:

CHAPTER I

Scope

Article 1

1. The harmonization measures prescribed by this Directive shall apply to the laws, regulations and administrative provisions of the Member States governing the relations between commercial agents and their principals.

2. For the purposes of this Directive, 'commercial agent' shall mean a self-employed intermediary who has continuing authority to negotiate the sale or the purchase of goods on behalf of another person, hereinafter called the 'principal', or to negotiate and conclude such transactions on behalf of and in the name of that principal.

3. A commercial agent shall be understood within the meaning of this Directive as not including in particular:

— a person who, in his capacity as an officer, is empowered to enter into commitments binding on a company or association,

— a partner who is lawfully authorized to enter into commitments binding on his partners,

— a receiver, a receiver and manager, a liquidator or a trustee in bankruptcy.

Article 2

1. This Directive shall not apply to:

— commercial agents whose activities are unpaid,

(¹) OJ No C 13, 18. 1. 1977, p. 2; OJ No C 56, 2. 3. 1979, p. 5.
(²) OJ No C 239, 9. 10. 1978, p. 17.
(³) OJ No C 59, 8. 3. 1978, p. 31.
(⁴) OJ No 56, 4. 4. 1964, p. 869/64.

— commercial agents when they operate on commodity exchanges or in the commodity market, or

— the body known as the Crown Agents for Overseas Governments and Administrations, as set up under the Crown Agents Act 1979 in the United Kingdom, or its subsidiaries.

2.   Each of the Member States shall have the right to provide that the Directive shall not apply to those persons whose activities as commercial agents are considered secondary by the law of that Member State.

CHAPTER II

Rights and obligations

Article 3

1.   In performing has activities a commercial agent must look after his principal's interests and act dutifully and in good faith.

2.   In particular, a commercial agent must:

(a)   make proper efforts to negotiate and, where appropriate, conclude the transactions he is instructed to take care of;

(b)   communicate to his principal all the necessary information available to him;

(c)   comply with reasonable instructions given by his principal.

Article 4

1.   In his relations with his commercial agent a principal must act dutifully and in good faith.

2.   A principal must in particular:

(a)   provide his commercial agent with the necessary documentation relating to the goods concerned;

(b)   obtain for his commercial agent the information necessary for the performance of the agency contract, and in particular notify the commercial agent within a reasonable period once he anticipates that the volume of commercial transactions will be significantly lower than that which the commercial agent could normally have expected.

3.   A principal must, in addition, inform the commercial agent within a reasonable period of his acceptance, refusal, and of any non-execution of a commercial transaction which the commercial agent has procured for the principal.

Article 5

The parties may not derogate from the provisions of Articles 3 and 4.

CHAPTER III

Remuneration

Article 6

1.   In the absence of any agreement on this matter between the parties, and without prejudice to the application of the compulsory provisions of the Member States concerning the level of remuneration, a commercial agent shall be entitled to the remuneration that commercial agents appointed for the goods forming the subject of his agency contract are customarily allowed in the place where he carries on his activities. If there is no such customary practice a commercial agent shall be entitled to reasonable remuneration taking into account all the aspects of the transaction.

2.   Any part of the remuneration which varies with the number or value of business transactions shall be deemed to be commission within the meaning of this Directive.

3.   Articles 7 to 12 shall not apply if the commercial agent is not remunerated wholly or in part by commission.

Article 7

1.   A commercial agent shall be entitled to commission on commercial transactions concluded during the period covered by the agency contract:

(a)   where the transaction has been concluded as a result of his action; or

(b)   where the transaction is concluded with a third party whom he has previously acquired as a customer for transactions of the same kind.

2.   A commercial agent shall also be entitled to commission on transactions concluded during the period covered by the agency contract:

— either where he is entrusted with a specific geographical area or group of customers,

— or where he has an exclusive right to a specific geographical area or group of customers,

and where the transaction has been entered into with a customer belonging to that area or group.

Member States shall include in their legislation one of the possibilities referred to in the above two indents.

Article 8

A commercial agent shall be entitled to commission on commercial transactions concluded after the agency contract has terminated:

(a)   if the transaction is mainly attributable to the commercial agent's efforts during the period covered by the agency contract and if the transaction was entered into within a reasonable period after that contract terminated; or

b) if, in accordance with the conditions mentioned in Article 7, the order of the third party reached the principal or the commercial agent before the agency contract terminated.

Article 9

A commercial agent shall not be entitled to the commission referred to in Article 7, if that commission is payable, pursuant to Article 8, to the previous commercial agent, unless it is equitable because of the circumstances for the commission to be shared between the commercial agents.

Article 10

1. The commission shall become due as soon as and to the extent that one of the following circumstances obtains:

a the principal has executed the transaction; or

b the principal should, according to his agreement with the third party, have executed the transaction; or

c the third party has executed the transaction.

2. The commission shall become due at the latest when the third party has executed his part of the transaction or should have done so if the principal had executed his part of the transaction, as he should have.

3. The commission shall be paid not later than on the last day of the month following the quarter in which it became due.

4. Agreements to derogate from paragraphs 2 and 3 to the detriment of the commercial agent shall not be permitted.

Article 11

1. The right to commission can be extinguished only if and to the extent that:

— it is established that the contract between the third party and the principal will not be executed, and

— that face is due to a reason for which the principal is not to blame.

2. Any commission which the commercial agent has already received shall be refunded if the right to it is extinguished.

3. Agreements to derogate from paragraph 1 to the detriment of the commercial agent shall not be permitted.

Article 12

1. The principal shall supply his commercial agent with a statement of the commission due, not later than the last day of the month following the quarter in which the commission has become due. This statement shall set out the main components used in calculating the amount of commission.

2. A commercial agent shall be entitled to demand that he be provided with all the information, and in particular an extract from the books, which is available to his principal and which he needs in order to check the amount of the commission due to him.

3. Agreements to derogate from paragraphs 1 and 2 to the detriment of the commercial agent shall not be permitted.

4. This Directive shall not conflict with the internal provisions of Member States which recognize the right of a commercial agent to inspect a principal's books.

CHAPTER IV

Conclusion and termination of the agency contract

Article 13

1. Each party shall be entitled to receive from the other on request a signed written document setting out the terms of the agency contract including any terms subsequently agreed. Waiver of this right shall not be permitted.

2. Notwithstanding paragraph 1 a Member State may provide that an agency contract shall not be valid unless evidenced in writing.

Article 14

An agency contract for a fixed period which continues to be performed by both parties after that period has expired shall be deemed to be converted into an agency contract for an indefinite period.

Article 15

1. Where an agency contract is concluded for an indefinite period either party may terminate it by notice.

2. The period of notice shall be one month for the first year of the contract, two months for the second year commenced, and three months for the third year commenced and subsequent years. The parties may not agree on shorter periods of notice.

3. Member States may fix the period of notice at four months for the fourth year of the contract, five months for the fifth year and six months for the sixth and subsequent

years. They may decide that the parties may not agree to shorter periods.

4. If the parties agree on longer periods than those laid down in paragraphs 2 and 3, the period of notice to be observed by the principal must not be shorter than that to be observed by the commercial agent.

5. Unless otherwise agreed by the parties, the end of the period of notice must coincide with the end of a calendar month.

6. The provisions of this Article shall apply to an agency contract for a fixed period where it is converted under Article 14 into an agency contract for an indefinite period, subject to the proviso that the earlier fixed period must be taken into account in the calculation of the period of notice.

Article 16

Nothing in this Directive shall affect the application of the law of the Member States where the latter provides for the immediate termination of the agency contract:

(a) because of the failure of one party to carry out all or part of his obligations;

(b) where exceptional circumstances arise.

Article 17

1. Member States shall take the measures necessary to ensure that the commercial agent is, after termination of the agency contract, indemnified in accordance with paragraph 2 or compensated for damage in accordance with paragraph 3.

2. (a) The commercial agent shall be entitled to an indemnity if and to the extent that:

— he has brought the principal new customers or has significantly increased the volume of business with existing customers and the principal continues to derive substantial benefits from the business with such customers, and

— the payment of this indemnity is equitable having regard to all the circumstances and, in particular, the commission lost by the commercial agent on the business transacted with such customers. Member States may provide for such circumstances also to include the application or otherwise of a restraint of trade clause, within the meaning of Article 20;

(b) The amount of the indemnity may not exceed a figure equivalent to an indemnity for one year calculated from the commercial agent's average annual remuneration over the preceding five years and if the contract goes back less than five years the indemnity shall be calculated on the average for the period in question;

(c) The grant of such an indemnity shall not prevent the commercial agent from seeking damages.

3. The commercial agent shall be entitled to compensation for the damage he suffers as a result of the termination of his relations with the principal.

Such damage shall be deemed to occur particularly when the termination takes place in circumstances:

— depriving the commercial agent of the commission which proper performance of the agency contract would have procured him whilst providing the principal with substantial benefits linked to the commercial agent's activities,

— and/or which have not enabled the commercial agent to amortize the costs and expenses that he had incurred for the performance of the agency contract on the principal's advice.

4. Entitlement to the indemnity as provided for in paragraph 2 or to compensation for damage as provided for under paragraph 3, shall also arise where the agency contract is terminated as a result of the commercial agent's death.

5. The commercial agent shall lose his entitlement to the indemnity in the instances provided for in paragraph 2 or to compensation for damage in the instances provided for in paragraph 3, if within one year following termination of the contract he has not notified the principal that he intends pursuing his entitlement.

6. The Commission shall submit to the Council, within eight years following the date of notification of this Directive, a report on the implementation of this Article, and shall if necessary submit to it proposals for amendments.

Article 18

The indemnity or compensation referred to in Article 17 shall not be payable:

(a) where the principal has terminated the agency contract because of default attributable to the commercial agent which would justify immediate termination of the agency contract under national law;

(b) where the commercial agent has terminated the agency contract, unless such termination is justified by circumstances attributable to the principal or on grounds of age, infirmity or illness of the commercial agent in consequence of which he cannot reasonably be required to continue his activities;

(c) where, with the agreement of the principal, the commercial agent assigns his rights and duties under the agency contract to another person.

Article 19

The parties may not derogate from Articles 17 and 18 to the detriment of the commercial agent before the agency contract expires.

Article 20

1. For the purposes of this Directive, an agreement restricting the business activities of a commercial agent following termination of the agency contract is hereinafter referred to as a restraint of trade clause.

2. A restraint of trade clause shall be valid only if and to the extent that:

a it is concluded in writing; and

b it relates to the geographical area or the group of customers and the geographical area entrusted to the commercial agent and to the kind of goods covered by his agency under the contract.

3. A restraint of trade clause shall be valid for not more than two years after termination of the agency contract.

4. This Article shall not affect provisions of national law which impose other restrictions on the validity or enforceability of restraint of trade clauses or which enable the courts to reduce the obligations on the parties resulting from such an agreement.

CHAPTER V

General and final provisions

Article 21

Nothing in this Directive shall require a Member State to provide for the disclosure of information where such disclosure would be contrary to public policy.

Article 22

1. Member States shall bring into force the provisions necessary to comply with this Directive before 1 January 1990. They shall forthwith inform the Commission thereof. Such provisions shall apply at least to contracts concluded after their entry into force. They shall apply to contracts in operation by 1 January 1994 at the latest.

2. As from the notification of this Directive, Member States shall communicate to the Commission the main laws, regulations and administrative provisions which they adopt in the field governed by this Directive.

3. However, with regard to Ireland and the United Kingdom, 1 January 1990 referred to in paragraph 1 shall be replaced by 1 January 1994.

With regard to Italy, 1 January 1990 shall be replaced by 1 January 1993 in the case of the obligations deriving from Article 17.

Article 23

This Directive is addressed to the Member States.

Done at Brussels, 18 December 1986.

For the Council
The President
M. JOPLING

Annex 2

I

(Acts whose publication is obligatory)

COMMISSION REGULATION (EEC) No 1983/83

of 22 June 1983

on the application of Article 85 (3) of the Treaty to categories of exclusive distribution
agreements

THE COMMISSION OF THE EUROPEAN
COMMUNITIES,

Having regard to the Treaty establishing the
European Economic Community, and in particular
Article 87 thereof,

Having regard to Council Regulation No 19/65/EEC
of 2 March 1965 on the application of Article 85 (3)
of the Treaty to certain categories of agreements and
concerted practices (¹), as last amended by the Act of
Accession of Greece, and in particular Article 1
thereof,

Having published a draft of this Regulation (²),

Having consulted the Advisory Committee on
Restrictive Practices and Dominant Positions,

(1) Whereas Regulation No 19/65/EEC empowers
the Commission to apply Article 85 (3) of the
Treaty by regulation to certain categories of
bilateral exclusive distribution agreements and
analogous concerted practices falling within
Article 85 (1);

(2) Whereas experience to date makes it possible to
define a category of agreements and concerted
practices which can be regarded as normally
satisfying the conditions laid down in Article 85
(3);

(3) Whereas exclusive distribution agreements of the
category defined in Article 1 of this Regulation
may fall within the prohibition contained in
Article 85 (1) of the Treaty; whereas this will
apply only in exceptional cases to exclusive
agreements of this kind to which only undertakings from one Member State are party and
which concern the resale of goods within that

Member State; whereas, however, to the extent
that such agreements may affect trade between
Member States and also satisfy all the
requirements set out in this Regulation there is
no reason to withhold from them the benefit of
the exemption by category;

(4) Whereas it is not necessary expressly to exclude
from the defined category those agreements
which do not fulfil the conditions of Article 85
(1) of the Treaty;

(5) Whereas exclusive distribution agreements lead
in general to an improvement in distribution
because the undertaking is able to concentrate
its sales activities, does not need to maintain
numerous business relations with a larger
number of dealers and is able, by dealing with
only one dealer, to overcome more easily distribution difficulties in international trade resulting
from linguistic, legal and other differences;

(6) Whereas exclusive distribution agreements facilitate the promotion of sales of a product and
lead to intensive marketing and to continuity of
supplies while at the same time rationalizing
distribution; whereas they stimulate competition
between the products of different manufacturers; whereas the appointment of an exclusive
distributor who will take over sales promotion,
customer services and carrying of stocks is often
the most effective way, and sometimes indeed
the only way, for the manufacturer to enter a
market and compete with other manufacturers
already present; whereas this is particularly so in
the case of small and medium-sized undertakings; whereas it must be left to the
contracting parties to decide whether and to
what extent they consider it desirable to
incorporate in the agreements terms providing
for the promotion of sales;

(7) Whereas, as a rule, such exclusive distribution
agreements also allow consumers a fair share of

(¹) OJ No 36, 6. 3. 1965, p. 533/65.
(²) OJ No C 172, 10. 7. 1982, p. 3.

the resulting benefit as they gain directly from the improvement in distribution, and their economic and supply position is improved as they can obtain products manufactured in particular in other countries more quickly and more easily;

(8) Whereas this Regulation must define the obligations restricting competition which may be included in exclusive distribution agreements; whereas the other restrictions on competition allowed under this Regulation in addition to the exclusive supply obligation produce a clear division of functions between the parties and compel the exclusive distributor to concentrate his sales efforts on the contract goods and the contract territory; whereas they are, where they are agreed only for the duration of the agreement, generally necessary in order to attain the improvement in the distribution of goods sought through exclusive distribution; whereas it may be left to the contracting parties to decide which of these obligations they include in their agreements; whereas further restrictive obligations and in particular those which limit the exclusive distributor's choice of customers or his freedom to determine his prices and conditions of sale cannot be exempted under this Regulation;

(9) Whereas the exemption by category should be reserved for agreements for which it can be assumed with sufficient certainty that they satisfy the conditions of Article 85 (3) of the Treaty;

(10) Whereas it is not possible, in the absence of a case-by-case examination, to consider that adequate improvements in distribution occur where a manufacturer entrusts the distribution of his goods to another manufacturer with whom he is in competition; whereas such agreements should, therefore, be excluded from the exemption by category; whereas certain derogations from this rule in favour of small and medium-sized undertakings can be allowed;

(11) Whereas consumers will be assured of a fair share of the benefits resulting from exclusive distribution only if parallel imports remain possible; whereas agreements relating to goods which the user can obtain only from the exclusive distributor should therefore be excluded from the exemption by category; whereas the parties cannot be allowed to abuse industrial property rights or other rights in order to create absolute territorial protection; whereas

this does not prejudice the relationship between competition law and industrial property rights, since the sole object here is to determine the conditions for exemption by category;

(12) Whereas, since competition at the distribution stage is ensured by the possibility of parallel imports, the exclusive distribution agreements covered by this Regulation will not normally afford any possibility of eliminating competition in respect of a substantial part of the products in question; whereas this is also true of agreements that allot to the exclusive distributor a contract territory covering the whole of the common market;

(13) Whereas, in particular cases in which agreements or concerted practices satisfying the requirements of this Regulation nevertheless have effects incompatible with Article 85 (3) of the Treaty, the Commission may withdraw the benefit of the exemption by category from the undertakings party to them;

(14) Whereas agreements and concerted practices which satisfy the conditions set out in this Regulation need not be notified; whereas an undertaking may nonetheless in a particular case where real doubt exists, request the Commission to declare whether its agreements comply with this Regulation;

(15) Whereas this Regulation does not affect the applicability of Commission Regulation (EEC) No 3604/82 of 23 December 1982 on the application of Article 85 (3) of the Treaty to categories of specialization agreements (¹); whereas it does not exclude the application of Article 86 of the Treaty,

HAS ADOPTED THIS REGULATION:

Article 1

Pursuant to Article 85 (3) of the Treaty and subject to the provisions of this Regulation, it is hereby declared that Article 85 (1) of the Treaty shall not apply to agreements to which only two undertakings are party and whereby one party agrees with the other to supply certain goods for resale within the whole or a defined area of the common market only to that other.

Article 2

1.   Apart from the obligation referred to in Article 1 no restriction on competition shall be imposed on

---

(¹) OJ No L 376, 31. 12. 1982, p. 33.

the supplier other than the obligation not to supply the contract goods to users in the contract territory.

2. No restriction on competition shall be imposed on the exclusive distributor other than:

(a) the obligation not to manufacture or distribute goods which compete with the contract goods;

(b) the obligation to obtain the contract goods for resale only from the other party;

(c) the obligation to refrain, outside the contract territory and in relation to the contract goods, from seeking customers, from establishing any branch, and from maintaining any distribution depot.

3. Article 1 shall apply notwithstanding that the exclusive distributor undertakes all or any of the following obligations:

(a) to purchase complete ranges of goods or minimum quantities;

(b) to sell the contract goods under trademarks, or packed and presented as specified by the other party;

(c) to take measures for promotion of sales, in particular:
   — to advertise,
   — to maintain a sales network or stock of goods,
   — to provide customer and guarantee services,
   — to employ staff having specialized or technical training.

Article 3

Article 1 shall not apply where:

(a) manufacturers of identical goods or of goods which are considered by users as equivalent in view of their characteristics, price and intended use enter into reciprocal exclusive distribution agreements between themselves in respect of such goods;

(b) manufacturers of identical goods or of goods which are considered by users as equivalent in view of their characteristics, price and intended use enter into a non-reciprocal exclusive distribution agreement between themselves in respect of such goods unless at least one of them has a total annual turnover of no more than 100 million ECU;

(c) users can obtain the contract goods in the contract territory only from the exclusive distributor and have no alternative source of supply outside the contract territory;

(d) one or both of the parties makes it difficult for intermediaries or users to obtain the contract goods from other dealers inside the common market or, in so far as no alternative source of supply is available there, from outside the common market, in particular where one or both of them:

   1. exercises industrial property rights so as to prevent dealers or users from obtaining outside, or from selling in, the contract territory properly marked or otherwise properly marketed contract goods;

   2. exercises other rights or take other measures so as to prevent dealers or users from obtaining outside, or from selling in, the contract territory contract goods.

Article 4

1. Article 3 (a) and (b) shall also apply where the goods there referred to are manufactured by an undertaking connected with a party to the agreement.

2. Connected undertakings are:

(a) undertakings in which a party to the agreement, directly or indirectly:
   — owns more than half the capital or business assets, or
   — has the power to exercise more than half the voting rights, or
   — has the power to appoint more than half the members of the supervisory board, board of directors or bodies legally representing the undertaking, or
   — has the right to manage the affairs;

(b) undertakings which directly or indirectly have in or over a party to the agreement the rights or powers listed in (a);

(c) undertakings in which an undertaking referred to in (b) directly or indirectly has the rights or powers listed in (a).

3. Undertakings in which the parties to the agreement or undertakings connected with them jointly have the rights or powers set out in paragraph 2 (a) shall be considered to be connected with each of the parties to the agreement.

Article 5

1. For the purpose of Article 3 (b), the ECU is the unit of account used for drawing up the budget of the Community pursuant to Articles 207 and 209 of the Treaty.

2. Article 1 shall remain applicable where during any period of two consecutive financial years the total turnover referred to in Article 3 (b) is exceeded by no more than 10 %.

3. For the purpose of calculating total turnover within the meaning of Article 3 (b), the turnovers achieved during the last financial year by the party to the agreement and connected undertakings in respect of all goods and services, excluding all taxes and other duties, shall be added together. For this purpose, no account shall be taken of dealings between the parties to the agreement or between these undertakings and undertakings connected with them or between the connected undertakings.

Article 6

The Commission may withdraw the benefit of this Regulation, pursuant to Article 7 of Regulation No 19/65/EEC, when it finds in a particular case that an agreement which is exempted by this Regulation nevertheless has certain effects which are incompatible with the conditions set out in Article 85 (3) of the Treaty, and in particular where:

(a) the contract goods are not subject, in the contract territory, to effective competition from identical goods or goods considered by users as equivalent in view of their characteristics, price and intended use;

(b) access by other suppliers to the different stages of distribution within the contract territory is made difficult to a significant extent;

(c) for reasons other than those referred to in Article 3 (c) and (d) it is not possible for intermediaries or users to obtain supplies of the contract goods from dealers outside the contract territory on the terms there customary;

(d) the exclusive distributor:

1. without any objectively justified reason refuses to supply in the contract territory categories of purchasers who cannot obtain contract goods elsewhere on suitable terms or applies to them differing prices or conditions of sale;

2. sells the contract goods at excessively high prices.

Article 7

In the period 1 July 1983 to 31 December 1986, the prohibition in Article 85 (1) of the Treaty shall not apply to agreements which were in force on 1 July 1983 or entered into force between 1 July and 31 December 1983 and which satisfy the exemption conditions of Regulation No 67/67/EEC (¹).

Article 8

This Regulation shall not apply to agreements entered into for the resale of drinks in premises used for the sale and consumption of beer or for the resale of petroleum products in service stations.

Article 9

This Regulation shall apply *mutatis mutandis* to concerted practices of the type defined in Article 1.

Article 10

This Regulation shall enter into force on 1 July 1983.

It shall expire on 31 December 1997.

This Regulation shall be binding in its entirety and directly applicable in all Member States.

Done at Brussels, 22 June 1983.

For the Commission
Frans ANDRIESSEN
Member of the Commission

(¹) OJ No 57, 25. 3. 1967, p. 849/67.

Annex 3

COMMISSION REGULATION (EEC) No 1984/83

of 22 June 1983

on the application of Article 85 (3) of the Treaty to categories of exclusive purchasing
agreements

THE COMMISSION OF THE EUROPEAN
COMMUNITIES,

Having regard to the Treaty establishing the
European Economic Community,

Having regard to Council Regulation No 19/65/EEC
of 2 March 1965 on the application of Article 85 (3)
of the Treaty to certain categories of agreements and
concerted practices (¹), as last amended by the Act of
Accession of Greece, and in particular Article 1
thereof,

Having published a draft of this Regulation (²),

Having consulted the Advisory Committee on
Restrictive Practices and Dominant Positions,

(1) Whereas Regulation No 19/65/EEC empowers
the Commission to apply Article 85 (3) of the
Treaty by regulation to certain categories of
bilateral exclusive purchasing agreements
entered into for the purpose of the resale of
goods and corresponding concerted practices
falling within Article 85 (¹);

(2) Whereas experience to date makes it possible to
define three categories of agreements and
concerted practices which can be regarded as
normally satisfying the conditions laid down in
Article 85 (3); whereas the first category
comprises exclusive purchasing agreements of
short and medium duration in all sectors of the
economy; whereas the other two categories
comprise long-term exclusive purchasing
agreements entered into for the resale of beer in
premises used for the sale and consumption
(beer supply agreements) and of petroleum
products in filling stations (service-station
agreements);

(3) Whereas exclusive purchasing agreements of the
categories defined in this Regulation may fall
within the prohibition contained in Article 85 (1)
of the Treaty; whereas this will often be the case

with agreements concluded between undertakings from different Member States; whereas
an exclusive purchasing agreement to which
undertakings from only one Member State are
party and which concerns the resale of goods
within that Member State may also be caught by
the prohibition; whereas this is in particular the
case where it is one of a number of similar
agreements which together may affect trade
between Member States;

(4) Whereas it is not necessary expressly to exclude
from the defined categories those agreements
which do not fulfil the conditions of Article 85
(1) of the Treaty;

(5) Whereas the exclusive purchasing agreements
defined in this Regulation lead in general to an
improvement in distribution; whereas they
enable the supplier to plan the sales of his goods
with greater precision and for a longer period
and ensure that the reseller's requirements will
be met on a regular basis for the duration of the
agreement; whereas this allows the parties to
limit the risk to them of variations in market
conditions and to lower distribution costs;

(6) Whereas such agreements also facilitate the
promotion of the sales of a product and lead to
intensive marketing because the supplier, in
consideration for the exclusive purchasing
obligation, is as a rule under an obligation to
contribute to the improvement of the structure
of the distribution network, the quality of the
promotional effort or the sales success; whereas,
at the same time, they stimulate competition
between the products of different manufacturers; whereas the appointment of several
resellers, who are bound to purchase exclusively
from the manufacturer and who take over sales
promotion, customer services and carrying of
stock, is often the most effective way, and
sometimes the only way, for the manufacturer to
penetrate a market and compete with other
manufacturers already present; whereas this is
particularly so in the case of small and medium-
sized undertakings; whereas it must be left to
the contracting parties to decide whether and to
what extent they consider it desirable to
incorporate in their agreements terms
concerning the promotion of sales;

(¹) OJ No 36, 6. 3. 1965, p. 533/65.
(²) OJ No C 172, 10. 7. 1982, p. 7

(7) Whereas, as a rule, exclusive purchasing agreements between suppliers and resellers also allow consumers a fair share of the resulting benefit as they gain the advantages of regular supply and are able to obtain the contract goods more quickly and more easily;

(8) Whereas this Regulation must define the obligations restricting competition which may be included in an exclusive purchasing agreement; whereas the other restrictions of competition allowed under this Regulation in addition to the exclusive purchasing obligation lead to a clear division of functions between the parties and compel the reseller to concentrate his sales efforts on the contract goods; whereas they are, where they are agreed only for the duration of the agreement, generally necessary in order to attain the improvement in the distribution of goods sought through exclusive purchasing; whereas further restrictive obligations and in particular those which limit the reseller's choice of customers or his freedom to determine his prices and conditions of sale cannot be exempted under this Regulation;

(9) Whereas the exemption by categories should be reserved for agreements for which it can be assumed with sufficient certainty that they satisfy the conditions of Article 85 (3) of the Treaty;

(10) Whereas it is not possible, in the absence of a case-by-case examination, to consider that adequate improvements in distribution occur where a manufacturer imposes an exclusive purchasing obligation with respect to his goods on a manufacturer with whom he is in competition; whereas such agreements should, therefore, be excluded from the exemption by categories; whereas certain derogations from this rule in favour of small and medium-sized undertakings can be allowed;

(11) Whereas certain conditions must be attached to the exemption by categories so that access by other undertakings to the different stages of distribution can be ensured; whereas, to this end, limits must be set to the scope and to the duration of the exclusive purchasing obligation; whereas it appears appropriate as a general rule to grant the benefit of a general exemption from the prohibition on restrictive agreements only to exclusive purchasing agreements which are concluded for a specified product or range of products and for not more than five years;

(12) Whereas, in the case of beer supply agreements and service-station agreements, different rules should be laid down which take account of the particularities of the markets in question;

(13) Whereas these agreements are generally distinguished by the fact that, on the one hand, the supplier confers on the reseller special commercial or financial advantages by contributing to his financing, granting him or obtaining for him a loan on favourable terms, equipping him with a site or premises for conducting his business, providing him with equipment or fittings, or undertaking other investments for his benefit and that, on the other hand, the reseller enters into a long-term exclusive purchasing obligation which in most cases is accompanied by a ban on dealing in competing products;

(14) Whereas beer supply and service-station agreements, like the other exclusive purchasing agreements dealt with in this Regulation, normally produce an appreciable improvement in distribution in which consumers are allowed a fair share of the resulting benefit;

(15) Whereas the commercial and financial advantages conferred by the supplier on the reseller make it significantly easier to establish, modernize, maintain and operate premises used for the sale and consumption of drinks and service stations; whereas the exclusive purchasing obligation and the ban on dealing in competing products imposed on the reseller incite the reseller to devote all the resources at his disposal to the sale of the contract goods; whereas such agreements lead to durable cooperation between the parties allowing them to improve or maintain the quality of the contract goods and of the services to the customer and sales efforts of the reseller; whereas they allow long-term planning of sales and consequently a cost effective organization of production and distribution; whereas the pressure of competition between products of different makes obliges the undertakings involved to determine the number and character of premises used for the sale and consumption of drinks and service stations, in accordance with the wishes of customers;

(16) Whereas consumers benefit from the improvements described, in particular because they are ensured supplies of goods of satisfactory quality at fair prices and conditions while being able to choose between the products of different manufacturers;

(17) Whereas the advantages produced by beer supply agreements and service-station agreements cannot otherwise be secured to the

same extent and with the same degree of certainty; whereas the exclusive purchasing obligation on the reseller and the non-competition clause imposed on him are essential components of such agreements and thus usually indispensable for the attainment of these advantages; whereas, however, this is true only as long as the reseller's obligation to purchase from the supplier is confined in the case of premises used for the sale and consumption of drinks to beers and other drinks of the types offered by the supplier, and in the case of service stations to petroleum-based fuel for motor vehicles and other petroleum-based fuels; whereas the exclusive purchasing obligation for lubricants and related petroleum-based products can be accepted only on condition that the supplier provides for the reseller or finances the procurement of specific equipment for the carrying out of lubrication work; whereas this obligation should only relate to products intended for use within the service station;

(18) Whereas, in order to maintain the reseller's commercial freedom and to ensure access to the retail level of distribution on the part of other suppliers, not only the scope but also the duration of the exclusive purchasing obligation must be limited; whereas it appears appropriate to allow drinks suppliers a choice between a medium-term exclusive purchasing agreement covering a range of drinks and a long-term exclusive purchasing agreement for beer; whereas it is necessary to provide special rules for those premises used for the sale and consumption of drinks which the supplier lets to the reseller; whereas, in this case, the reseller must have the right to obtain, under the conditions specified in this Regulation, other drinks, except beer, supplied under the agreement or of the same type but bearing a different trademark; whereas a uniform maximum duration should be provided for service-station agreements, with the exception of tenancy agreements between the supplier and the reseller, which takes account of the long-term character of the relationship between the parties;

(19) Whereas to the extent that Member States provide, by law or administrative measures, for the same upper limit of duration for the exclusive purchasing obligation upon the reseller as in service-station agreements laid down in this Regulation but provide for a permissible duration which varies in proportion to the consideration provided by the supplier or generally provide for a shorter duration than that permitted by this Regulation, such laws or measures are not contrary to the objectives of this Regulation which, in this respect, merely sets an upper limit to the duration of service-station agreements; whereas the application and enforcement of such national laws or measures must therefore be regarded as compatible with the provisions of this Regulation;

(20) Whereas the limitations and conditions provided for in this Regulation are such as to guarantee effective competition on the markets in question; whereas, therefore, the agreements to which the exemption by category applies do not normally enable the participating undertakings to eliminate competition for a substantial part of the products in question;

(21) Whereas, in particular cases in which agreements or concerted practices satisfying the conditions of this Regulation nevertheless have effects incompatible with Article 85 (3) of the Treaty, the Commission may withdraw the benefit of the exemption by category from the undertakings party thereto;

(22) Whereas agreements and concerted practices which satisfy the conditions set out in this Regulation need not be notified; whereas an undertaking may nonetheless, in a particular case where real doubt exists, request the Commission to declare whether its agreements comply with this Regulation;

(23) Whereas this Regulation does not affect the applicability of Commission Regulation (EEC) No 3604/82 of 23 December 1982 on the application of Article 85 (3) of the Treaty to categories of specialization agreements (¹); whereas it does not exclude the application of Article 86 of the Treaty,

HAS ADOPTED THIS REGULATION:

TITLE I

General provisions

Article 1

Pursuant to Article 85 (3) of the Treaty, and subject to the conditions set out in Articles 2 to 5 of this Regulation, it is hereby declared that Article 85 (1) of the Treaty shall not apply to agreements to which only two undertakings are party and whereby one party, the reseller, agrees with the other, the supplier, to purchase certain goods specified in the agreement for resale only from the supplier or from a connected undertaking or from another undertaking which the supplier has entrusted with the sale of his goods.

(¹) OJ No L 376, 31. 12. 1982, p. 33.

Article 2

1.   No other restriction of competition shall be imposed on the supplier than the obligation not to distribute the contract goods or goods which compete with the contract goods in the reseller's principal sales area and at the reseller's level of distribution.

2.   Apart from the obligation described in Article 1, no other restriction of competition shall be imposed on the reseller than the obligation not to manufacture or distribute goods which compete with the contract goods.

3.   Article 1 shall apply notwithstanding that the reseller undertakes any or all of the following obligations;

(a) to purchase complete ranges of goods;

(b) to purchase minimum quantities of goods which are subject to the exclusive purchasing obligation;

(c) to sell the contract goods under trademarks, or packed and presented as specified by the supplier;

(d) to take measures for the promotion of sales, in particular:
— to advertise,
— to maintain a sales network or stock of goods,
— to provide customer and guarantee services,
— to employ staff having specialized or technical training.

Article 3

Article 1 shall not apply where:

(a) manufacturers of identical goods or of goods which are considered by users as equivalent in view of their characteristics, price and intended use enter into reciprocal exclusive purchasing agreements between themselves in respect of such goods;

(b) manufacturers of identical goods or of goods which are considered by users as equivalent in view of their characteristics, price and intended use enter into a non-reciprocal exclusive purchasing agreement between themselves in respect of such goods, unless at least one of them has a total annual turnover of no more than 100 million ECU;

(c) the exclusive purchasing obligation is agreed for more than one type of goods where these are neither by their nature nor according to commercial usage connected to each other;

(d) the agreement is concluded for an indefinite duration or for a period of more than five years.

Article 4

1.   Article 3 (a) and (b) shall also apply where the goods there referred to are manufactured by an undertaking connected with a party to the agreement.

2.   Connected undertakings are:

(a) undertakings in which a party to the agreement, directly or indirectly:
— owns more than half the capital or business assets, or
— has the power to exercise more than half the voting rights, or
— has the power to appoint more than half the members of the supervisory board, board of directors or bodies legally representing the undertaking, or
— has the right to manage the affairs;

(b) undertakings which directly or indirectly have in or over a party to the agreement the rights or powers listed in (a);

(c) undertakings in which an undertaking referred to in (b) directly or indirectly has the rights or powers listed in (a).

3.   Undertakings in which the parties to the agreement or undertakings connected with them jointly have the rights or powers set out in paragraph 2 (a) shall be considered to be connected with each of the parties to the agreement.

Article 5

1.   For the purpose of Article 3 (b), the ECU is the unit of account used for drawing up the budget of the Community pursuant to Articles 207 and 209 of the Treaty.

2.   Article 1 shall remain applicable where during any period of two consecutive financial years the total turnover referred to in Article 3 (b) is exceeded by no more than 10 %.

3.   For the purpose of calculating total turnover within the meaning of Article 3 (b), the turnovers achieved during the last financial year by the party to

the agreement and connected undertakings in respect of all goods and services, excluding all taxes and other duties, shall be added together. For this purpose, no account shall be taken of dealings between the parties to the agreement or between these undertakings and undertakings connected with them or between the connected undertakings.

TITLE II

Special provisions for beer supply agreements

Article 6

1. Pursuant to Article 85 (3) of the Treaty, and subject to Articles 7 to 9 of this Regulation, it is hereby declared that Article 85 (1) of the Treaty shall not apply to agreements to which only two undertakings are party and whereby one party, the reseller, agrees with the other, the supplier, in consideration for according special commercial or financial advantages, to purchase only from the supplier, an undertaking connected with the supplier or another undertaking entrusted by the supplier with the distribution of his goods, certain beers, or certain beers and certain other drinks, specified in the agreement for resale in premises used for the sale and consumption of drinks and designated in the agreement.

2. The declaration in paragraph 1 shall also apply where exclusive purchasing obligations of the kind described in paragraph 1 are imposed on the reseller in favour of the supplier by another undertaking which is itself not a supplier.

Article 7

1. Apart from the obligation referred to in Article 6, no restriction on competition shall be imposed on the reseller other than:

(a) the obligation not to sell beers and other drinks which are supplied by other undertakings and which are of the same type as the beers or other drinks supplied under the agreement in the premises designated in the agreement;

(b) the obligation, in the event that the reseller sells in the premises designated in the agreement beers which are supplied by other undertakings and which are of a different type from the beers supplied under the agreement, to sell such beers only in bottles, cans or other small packages, unless the sale of such beers in draught form is customary or is necessary to satisfy a sufficient demand from consumers;

(c) the obligation to advertise goods supplied by other undertakings within or outside the premises

designated in the agreement only in proportion to the share of these goods in the total turnover realized in the premises.

2. Beers or other drinks of the same type are those which are not clearly distinguishable in view of their composition, appearance and taste.

Article 8

1. Article 6 shall not apply where:

(a) the supplier or a connected undertaking imposes on the reseller exclusive purchasing obligations for goods other than drinks or for services;

(b) the supplier restricts the freedom of the reseller to obtain from an undertaking of his choice either services or goods for which neither an exclusive purchasing obligation nor a ban on dealing in competing products may be imposed;

(c) the agreement is concluded for an indefinite duration or for a period of more than five years and the exclusive purchasing obligation relates to specified beers and other drinks;

(d) the agreement is concluded for an indefinite duration or for a period of more than 10 years and the exclusive purchasing obligation relates only to specified beers;

(e) the supplier obliges the reseller to impose the exclusive purchasing obligation on his successor for a longer period than the reseller would himself remain tied to the supplier.

2. Where the agreement relates to premises which the supplier lets to the reseller or allows the reseller to occupy on some other basis in law or in fact, the following provisions shall also apply:

(a) notwithstanding paragraphs (1) (c) and (d), the exclusive purchasing obligations and bans on dealing in competing products specified in this Title may be imposed on the reseller for the whole period for which the reseller in fact operates the premises;

(b) the agreement must provide for the reseller to have the right to obtain:

— drinks, except beer, supplied under the agreement from other undertakings where these undertakings offer them on more favourable conditions which the supplier does not meet,

— drinks, except beer, which are of the same type as those supplied under the agreement but which bear different trade marks, from other undertakings where the supplier does not offer them.

Article 9

Articles 2 (1) and (3), 3 (a) and (b), 4 and 5 shall apply *mutatis mutandis*.

TITLE III

Special provisions for service-station agreements

Article 10

Pursuant to Article 85 (3) of the Treaty and subject to Articles 11 to 13 of this Regulation, it is hereby declared that Article 85 (1) of the Treaty shall not apply to agreements to which only two undertakings are party and whereby one party, the reseller, agrees with the other, the supplier, in consideration for the according of special commercial or financial advantages, to purchase only from the supplier, an undertaking connected with the supplier or another undertaking entrusted by the supplier with the distribution of his goods, certain petroleum-based motor-vehicle fuels or certain petroleum-based motor-vehicle and other fuels specified in the agreement for resale in a service station designated in the agreement.

Article 11

Apart from the obligation referred to in Article 10, no restriction on competition shall be imposed on the reseller other than:

(a) the obligation not to sell motor-vehicle fuel and other fuels which are supplied by other undertakings in the service station designated in the agreement;

(b) the obligation not to use lubricants or related petroleum-based products which are supplied by other undertakings within the service station designated in the agreement where the supplier or a connected undertaking has made available to the reseller, or financed, a lubrication bay or other motor-vehicle lubrication equipment;

(c) the obligation to advertise goods supplied by other undertakings within or outside the service station designated in the agreement only in proportion to the share of these goods in the total turnover realized in the service station;

(d) the obligation to have equipment owned by the supplier or a connected undertaking or financed by the supplier or a connected undertaking serviced by the supplier or an undertaking designated by him.

Article 12

1. Article 10 shall not apply where:

(a) the supplier or a connected undertaking imposes on the reseller exclusive purchasing obligations for goods other than motor-vehicle and other fuels or for services, except in the case of the obligations referred to in Article 11 (b) and (d);

(b) the supplier restricts the freedom of the reseller to obtain, from an undertaking of his choice, goods or services, for which under the provisions of this Title neither an exclusive purchasing obligation nor a ban on dealing in competing products may be imposed;

(c) the agreement is concluded for an indefinite duration or for a period of more than 10 years;

(d) the supplier obliges the reseller to impose the exclusive purchasing obligation on his successor for a longer period than the reseller would himself remain tied to the supplier.

2. Where the agreement relates to a service station which the supplier lets to the reseller, or allows the reseller to occupy on some other basis, in law or in facts, exclusive purchasing obligations or prohibitions of competition indicated in this Title may, notwithstanding paragraph 1 (c), be imposed on the reseller for the whole period for which the reseller in fact operates the premises.

Article 13

Articles 2 (1) and (3), 3 (a) and (b), 4 and 5 of this Regulation shall apply *mutatis mutandis*.

TITLE IV

Miscellaneous provisions

Article 14

The Commission may withdraw the benefit of this Regulation, pursuant to Article 7 of Regulation No 19/65/EEC, when it finds in a particular case that an agreement which is exempted by this Regulation nevertheless has certain effects which are incompatible with the conditions set out in Article 85 (3) of the Treaty, and in particular where:

(a) the contract goods are not subject, in a substantial part of the common market, to effective competition from identical goods or goods considered by users as equivalent in view of their characteristics, price and intended use;

(b) access by of other suppliers to the different stages of distribution in a substantial part of the common market is made difficult to a significant extent;

(c) the supplier without any objectively justified reason:

1. refuses to supply categories of resellers who cannot obtain the contract goods elsewhere on suitable terms or applies to them differing prices or conditions of sale;

2. applies less favourable prices or conditions of sale to resellers bound by an exclusive purchasing obligation as compared with other resellers at the same level of distribution.

Article 15

1. In the period 1 July 1983 to 31 December 1986, the prohibition in Article 85 (1) of the Treaty shall not apply to agreements of the kind described in Article 1 which either were in force on 1 July 1983 or entered into force between 1 July and 31 December 1983 and which satisfy the exemption conditions under Regulation No 67/67/EEC (¹).

2. In the period 1 July 1983 to 31 December 1988, the prohibition in Article 85 (1) of the Treaty shall not apply to agreements of the kinds described in Articles 6 and 10 which either were in force on 1 July 1983 or entered into force between 1 July and 31 December 1983 and which satisfy the exemption conditions of Regulation No 67/67/EEC.

3. In the case of agreements of the kinds described in Articles 6 and 10, which were in force on 1 July 1983 and which expire after 31 December 1988, the prohibition in Article 85 (1) of the Treaty shall not apply in the period from 1 January 1989 to the expiry of the agreement but at the latest to the expiry of this Regulation to the extent that the supplier releases the reseller, before 1 January 1989, from all obligations which would prevent the application of the exemption under Titles II and III.

Article 16

This Regulation shall not apply to agreements by which the supplier undertakes with the reseller to supply only to the reseller certain goods for resale, in the whole or in a defined part of the Community, and the reseller undertakes with the supplier to purchase these goods only from the supplier.

Article 17

This Regulation shall not apply where the parties or connected undertakings, for the purpose of resale in one and the same premises used for the sale and consumption of drinks or service station, enter into agreements both of the kind referred to in Title I and of a kind referred to in Title II or III.

Article 18

This Regulation shall apply *mutatis mutandis* to the categories of concerted practices defined in Articles 1, 6 and 10.

Article 19

This Regulation shall enter into force on 1 July 1983.

It shall expire on 31 December 1997.

This Regulation shall be binding in its entirety and directly applicable in all Member States.

Done at Brussels, 22 June 1983.

For the Commission

Frans ANDRIESSEN

Member of the Commission

(¹) OJ No 57, 25. 3. 1967, p. 849/67.

Annex 4

COMMISSION REGULATION (EEC) No 123/85

of 12 December 1984

on the application of Article 85 (3) of the Treaty to certain categories of motor
vehicle distribution and servicing agreements

THE COMMISSION OF THE EUROPEAN
COMMUNITIES,

Having regard to the Treaty establishing the European
Economic Community,

Having regard to Council Regulation No 19/65/EEC
of 2 March 1965 on the application of Article 85 (3) of
the Treaty to certain categories of agreements and
concerted practices (¹), as last amended by the Act of
Accession of Greece,

Having published a draft of this Regulation (²),

Having consulted the Advisory Committee on Restrictive Practices and Dominant Positions,

Whereas :

(1) Under Article 1 (1) (a) of Regulation No
19/65/EEC the Commission is empowered to
declare by means of a Regulation that Article 85
(3) of the Treaty applies to certain categories of
agreements falling within Article 85 (1) to which
only two undertakings are party and by which
one party agrees with the other to supply only
to that undertaking other certain goods for
resale within a defined territory of the common
market. In the light of experience since
Commission Decision 75/73/EEC (³) and of the
many motor vehicle distribution and servicing
agreements which have been notified to the
Commission pursuant to Articles 4 and 5 of
Council Regulation No 17 (⁴), as last amended
by Regulation (EEC) No 2821/71 (⁵), a category
of agreements can be defined as satisfying the
conditions laid down in Regulation No
19/65/EEC. They are agreements, for a definite
or an indefinite period, by which the supplying
party entrusts to the reselling party the task of
promoting the distribution and servicing of
certain products of the motor vehicle industry
in a defined area and by which the supplier

(¹) OJ No 36, 6. 3. 1965, p. 533/65.
(²) OJ No C 165, 24. 6. 1983, p. 2.
(³) OJ No L 29, 3. 2. 1975, p. 1.
(⁴) OJ No 13, 21. 2. 1962, p. 204/62.
(⁵) OJ L 285, 29. 12. 1971, p. 49.

undertakes to supply contract goods for resale
only to the dealer, or only to a limited number
of undertakings within the distribution network
besides the dealer, within the contract territory.

A list of definitions for the purpose of this
Regulation is set out in Article 13.

(2) Notwithstanding that the obligations imposed
by distribution and servicing agreements which
are listed in Articles 1, 2 and 3 of this Regulation normally have as their object or effect the
prevention, restriction or distortion of competition within the common market and are
normally apt to affect trade between Member
States, the prohibition in Article 85 (1) of the
Treaty may nevertheless be declared inapplicable to these agreements by virtue of Article 85
(3), albeit only under certain restrictive conditions.

(3) The applicability of Article 85 (1) of the Treaty
to distribution and servicing agreements in the
motor vehicle industry stems in particular from
the fact that restrictions on competition and the
obligations connected with the distribution
system listed in Articles 1 to 4 of this Regulation are regularly imposed in the same or
similar form throughout the common market
for the products supplied within the distribution
system of a particular manufacturer. The motor
vehicle manufacturers cover the whole common
market or substantial parts of it by means of a
cluster of agreements involving similar restrictions on competition and affect in this way not
only distribution and servicing within Member
States but also trade between them.

(4) The exclusive and selective distribution clauses
can be regarded as indispensable measures of
rationalization in the motor vehicle industry
because motor vehicles are consumer durables
which at both regular and irregular intervals
require expert maintenance and repair, not
always in the same place. Motor vehicle manufacturers cooperate with the selected dealers and
repairers in order to provide specialized
servicing for the product. On grounds of
capacity and efficiency alone, such a form of

cooperation cannot be extended to an unlimited number of dealers and repairers. The linking of servicing and distribution must be regarded as more efficient than a separation between a distribution organization for new vehicles on the one hand and a servicing organization which would also distribute spare parts on the other, particularly as, before a new vehicle is delivered to the final consumer, the undertaking within the distribution system must give it a technical inspection according to the manufacturer's specification.

(5)   However, obligatory recourse to the authorized network is not in all respects indispensable for efficient distribution. The exceptions to the block exemption provide that the supply of contract goods to resellers may not be prohibited where they :

— belong to the same distribution system (Article 3, point 10 (a)),

or

— purchase spare parts for their own use in effecting repairs or maintenance (Article 3, point 10 (b)).

Measures taken by a manufacturer or by undertakings within the distribution system with the object of protecting the selective distribution system are compatible with the exemption under this Regulation. This applies in particular to a dealer's obligation to sell vehicles to a final consumer using the services of an intermediary only where that consumer has authorized that intermediary to act as his agent (Article 3, point 11).

(6)   It should be possible to bar wholesalers not belonging to the distribution system from reselling parts originating from motor vehicle manufacturers. It may be supposed that the system of rapid availability of spare parts across the whole contract programme, including those with a low turnover, which is beneficial to the consumer, could not be maintained without obligatory recourse to the authorized network.

(7)   The ban on dealing in competing products and that on dealing in other vehicles at stated premises may in principle be exempted, because

they contribute to concentration by the undertakings in the distribution network of their efforts on the products supplied by the manufacturer or with his consent, and thus ensure distribution and servicing appropriate for the vehicles (Article 3, point 3). Such obligations provide an incentive for the dealer to develop sales and servicing of contract goods and thus promotes competition in the supply of those products as well as between those products and competing products.

(8)   However, bans on dealing in competing products cannot be regarded as indispensable in all circumstances to efficient distribution. Dealers must be free to obtain from third parties supplies of parts which match the quality of those offered by the manufacturer, for example where the parts are produced by a sub-contract manufacturer who also supplies the motor vehicle manufacturer, and to use and sell them. They must also keep their freedom to choose parts which are usable in motor vehicles within the contract programme and which not only match but exceed the quality standard. Such a limit on the ban on dealing in competing products takes account of the importance of vehicle safety and of the maintenance of effective competition (Article 3, point 4 and Article 4 (1), points 6 and 7).

(9)   The restrictions imposed on the dealer's activities outside the allotted area lead to more intensive distribution and servicing efforts in an easily supervised contract territory, to knowledge of the market based on closer contact with consumers, and to more demand-orientated supply (Article 3, points 8 and 9). However, demand for contract goods must remain flexible and should not be limited on a regional basis. Dealers must not be confined to satisfying the demand for contract goods within their contract territories, but must also be able to meet demand from persons and undertakings in other areas of the common market. Dealers' advertising in a medium which is directed to customers in the contract territory but also covers a wider area should not be prevented, because it does not run counter to the obligation to promote sales within the contract territory.

(10) The obligations listed in Article 4 (1) are directly related to the obligations in Articles 1, 2 and 3, and influence their restrictive effect. These obligations, which might in individual cases be caught by the prohibition in Article 85 (1) of the Treaty, may also be exempted because of their direct relationship with one or more of the obligations exempted by Articles 1, 2 and 3 (Article 4 (2)).

(11) According to Article 1 (2) (b) of Regulation No 19/65/EEC, conditions which must be satisfied if the declaration of inapplicability is to take effect must be specified.

(12) Under Article 5 (1), points 1 (a) and (b) it is a condition of exemption that the undertaking should honour the minimum guarantee and provide the minimum free servicing and vehicle recall work laid down by the manufacturer, irrespective of where in the common market the vehicle was purchased. These provisions are intended to prevent the consumer's freedom to buy anywhere in the common market from being limited.

(13) Article 5 (1), point 2 (a) is intended to allow the manufacturer to build up a coordinated distribution system, but without hindering the relationship of confidence between dealers and sub-dealers. Accordingly, if the supplier reserves the right to approve appointments of sub-dealers by the dealer, he must not be allowed to withhold approval arbitrarily.

(14) Article 5 (1), point 2 (b) obliges the supplier not to impose on a dealer within the distribution system requirements, as defined in Article 4 (1), which are discriminatory or inequitable.

(15) Article 5 (1), point 2 (c) is intended to counter the concentration of the dealer's demand on the supplier which might follow from cumulation of discounts. The purpose of this provision is to allow spare-parts suppliers which do not offer as wide a range of goods as the manufacturer to compete on equal terms.

(16) Article 5 (1), point 2 (d) makes exemption subject to the conditions that the dealer must be able to purchase for customers in the common market volume-produced passenger cars with the specifications appropriate for their place of residence or where the vehicle is to be registered, in so far as the corresponding model is also supplied by the manufacturer through undertakings within the distribution system in that place (Article 13, point 10). This provision obviates the danger that the manufacturer and undertakings within the distribution network might make use of product differentiation as between parts of the common market to partition the market.

(17) Article 5 (2) makes the exemption of the no-competition clause and of the ban on dealing in other makes of vehicle subject to further threshold conditions. This is to prevent the dealer from becoming economically over-dependent on the supplier because of such obligations, and abandoning the competitive activity which is nominally open to him, because to pursue it would be against the interests of the manufacturer or other undertakings within the distribution network.

(18) Under Article 5 (2), point 1 (a), the dealer may, where there are exceptional reasons, oppose aplication of excessive obligations covered by Article 3, point 3 or 5.

(19) The supplier may reserve the right to appoint further distribution and servicing undertakings in the contract territory or to alter the territory, but only if he can show that there are exceptional reasons for doing so (Article 5 (2), point 1 (b) and Article 5 (3)). This is, for example, the case where there would otherwise be reason to apprehend a serious deterioration in the distribution or servicing of contract goods.

(20) Article 5 (2), points 2 and 3 lay down minimum requirements for exemption which concern the duration and termination of the distribution and servicing agreement; the combined effect of a no-competition clause or a ban on dealing in other makes of vehicle, the investments the dealer makes in order to improve the distribution and servicing of contract goods and a short-term agreement or one terminable at short notice is greatly to increase the dealer's dependence on the supplier.

(21) In accordance with Article 1 (2) (a) of Regulation No 19/65/EEC, restrictions or provisions which must not be contained in the agreements, if the declaration of inapplicability of Article 85 (1) by this Regulation is to take effect, are to be specified.

(22) Agreements under which one motor vehicle manufacturer entrusts the distribution of its products to another must be excluded from the block exemption under this Regulation because of their far-reaching impact on competition (Article 6, point 1).

(23) An obligation to apply minimum resale prices or maximum trade discounts precludes exemption under this Regulation (Article 6, point 2).

(24) The exemption does not apply where the parties agree between themselves obligations concerning goods covered by this Regulation which would be acceptable in the combination of obligations which is exempted by Commission Regulations (EEC) No 1983/83 (¹) or (EEC) No 1984/83 (²) on the application of Article 85 (3) of the Treaty to categories of exclusive distribution agreements and exclusive purchasing agreements respectively, but which go beyond the scope of the obligations exempted by this Regulation (Article 6, point 3).

(25) Distribution and servicing agreements can be exempted, subject to the conditions laid down in Articles 5 and 6, so long as the application of obligations covered by Articles 1 to 4 of this Regulation brings about an improvement in distribution and servicing to the benefit of the consumer and effective competition exists, not only between manufacturers' distribution systems but also to a certain extent within each system within the common market. As regards the categories of products set out in Article 1 of this Regulation, the conditions necessary for effective competition, including competition in trade between Member States, may be taken to exist at present, so that European consumers may be considered in general to take an equitable share in the benefit from the operation of such competition.

(26) Articles 7, 8 and 9, concerning the retroactive effect of the exemption, are based on Articles 3 and 4 of Regulation No 19/65/EEC and Articles

---

(¹) OJ No L 173, 30. 6. 1983, p. 1.
(²) OJ No L 173, 30. 6. 1983, p. 5.

4 to 7 of Regulation No 17. Article 10 embodies the Commission's powers under Article 7 of Regulation No 19/65/EEC to withdraw the benefit of its exemption or to alter its scope in individual cases, and lists several important examples of such cases.

(27) In view of the extensive effect of this Regulation on the persons it concerns, it is appropriate that it should not enter into force until 1 July 1985. In accordance with Article 2 (1) of Regulation No 19/65/EEC, the exemption may be made applicable for a definite period. A period extending until 30 June 1995 is appropriate, because overall distribution schemes in the motor vehicle sector must be planned several years in advance.

(28) Agreements which fulfil the conditions set out in this Regulation need not be notified.

(29) This Regulation does not affect the application of Regulations (EEC) No 1983/83 or (EEC) No 1984/83 or of Commission Regulation (EEC) No 3604/82 of 23 December 1982 on the application of Article 85 (3) of the Treaty to categories of specialization agreements (³), or the right to request a Commission decision in an individual case pursuant to Council Regulation No 17. It is without prejudice to laws and administrative measures of the Member States by which the latter, having regard to particular circumstances, prohibit or declare unenforceable particular restrictive obligations contained in an agreement exempted under this Regulation ; the foregoing cannot, however, affect the primacy of Community law,

HAS ADOPTED THIS REGULATION :

Article 1

Pursuant to Article 85 (3) of the Treaty it is hereby declared that subject to the conditions laid down in this Regulation Article 85 (1) shall not apply to agreements to which only two undertakings are party and in which one contracting party agrees to supply within a defined territory of the common market

— only to the other party, or

— only to the other party and to a specified number of other undertakings within the distribution system,

---

(³) OJ No L 376, 31. 12. 1982, p. 33.

for the purpose of resale certain motor vehicles intended for use on public roads and having three or more road wheels, together with spare parts therefor.

Article 2

The exemption under Article 85 (3) of the Treaty shall also apply where the obligation referred to in Article 1 is combined with an obligation on the supplier neither to sell contract goods to final consumers nor to provide them with servicing for contract goods in the contract territory.

Article 3

The exemption under Article 85 (3) of the Treaty shall also apply where the obligation referred to in Article 1 is combined with an obligation on the dealer :

1. not, without the supplier's consent, to modify contract goods or corresponding goods, unless such modification is the subject of a contract with a final consumer and concerns a particular motor vehicle within the contract programme purchased by that final consumer ;

2. not to manufacture products which compete with contract goods ;

3. neither to sell new motor vehicles which compete with contract goods nor to sell, at the premises used for the distribution of contract goods, new motor vehicles other than those offered for supply by the manufacturer ;

4. neither to sell spare parts which compete with contract goods and do not match the quality of contract goods nor to use them for repair or maintenance of contract goods or corresponding goods ;

5. not to conclude with third parties distribution or servicing agreements for goods which compete with contract goods ;

6. without the supplier's consent, neither to conclude distribution or servicing agreements with undertakings operating in the contract territory for contract goods or corresponding goods nor to alter or terminate such agreements ;

7. to impose upon undertakings with which the dealer has concluded agreements in accordance with point 6 obligations corresponding to those which the dealer has accepted in relation to the supplier and which are covered by Articles 1 to 4 and are in conformity with Articles 5 and 6 ;

8. outside the contract territory

   (a) not to maintain branches or depots for the distribution of contract goods or corresponding goods,

   (b) not to seek customers for contract goods or corresponding goods ;

9. not to entrust third parties with the distribution or servicing of contract goods or corresponding goods outside the contract territory ;

10. to supply to a reseller :

    (a) contract goods or corresponding goods only where the reseller is an undertaking within the distribution system, or

    (b) spare parts within the contract programme only where they are for the purposes of repair of maintenance of a motor vehicle by the reseller ;

11. to sell motor vehicles within the contract programme or corresponding goods to final consumers using the services of an intermediary only if that intermediary has prior wirtten authority to purchase a specified motor vehicle and, as the case may be, to accept delivery thereof on their behalf ;

12. to observe the obligations referred to in points 1 and 6 to 11 for a maximum period of one year after termination or expiry of the agreement.

Article 4

1.   Articles 1, 2 and 3 shall apply notwithstanding any obligation imposed on the dealer to :

(1) observe, for distribution and servicing, minimum standards which relate in particular to :

   (a) the equipment of the business premises and of the technical facilities for servicing ;

   (b) the specialized and technical training of staff ;

   (c) advertising ;

   (d) the collection, storage and delivery to customers of contract goods or corresponding goods and servicing relating to them ;

   (e) the repair and maintenance of contract goods and corresponding goods, particularly as concerns the safe and reliable functioning of motor vehicles ;

(2) order contract goods from the supplier only at certain times or within certain periods, provided that the interval between ordering dates does not exceed three months ;

(3) endeavour to sell, within the contract territory and within a specified period, such minimum quantity of contract goods as may be determined by agreement between the parties or, in the absence of such agreement, by the supplier on the basis of estimates of the dealer's potential sales ;

(4) keep in stock such quantity of contract goods as may be determined by agreement between the parties or, in the absence of such agreement, by the supplier on the basis of estimates of the dealer's potential sales of contract goods within the contract territory and within a specified period ;

(5) keep such demonstration vehicles within the contract programme, or such number thereof, as may be determined by agreement between the parties or, in the absence of such agreement, by the supplier on the basis of estimates of the dealer's potential sales of motor vehicles within the contract programme ;

(6) perform guarantee work, free servicing and vehicle recall work for contract goods and corresponding goods ,

(7) use only spare parts within the contract programme or corresponding goods for guarantee work, free servicing and vehicle recall work in respect of contract goods or corresponding goods ;

(8) inform customers, in a general manner, of the extent to which spare parts from other sources might be used for the repair or maintenance of contract goods or corresponding goods ;

(9) inform customers whenever spare parts from other sources have been used for the repair or maintainance of contract goods or corresponding goods for which spare parts within the contract programme or corresponding goods, bearing a mark of the manufacturer, were also available.

2.   The exemption under Article 85 (3) of the Treaty shall also apply where the obligation referred to in Article 1 is combined with obligations referred to in paragraph 1 above and such obligations fall in individual cases under the prohibition contained in Article 85 (1).

Article 5

1.   Articles 1, 2 and 3 and Article 4 (2) shall apply provided that :

(1) the dealer undertakes

(a) in respect of motor vehicles within the contract programme or corresponding thereto which have been supplied in the common market by another undertaking within the distribution network, to honour guarantees and to perform free servicing and vehicle recall work to an extent which corresponds to the dealer's obligation covered by point 6 of Article 4 (1) but which need not exceed that imposed upon the undertaking within the distribution system or accepted by the manufacturer when supplying such motor vehicles ;

(b) to impose upon the undertakings operating within the contract territory with which the dealer has concluded distribution and servicing agreements as provided for in point 6 of Article 3 an obligation to honour guarantees and to perform free servicing and vehicle recall work at least to the extent to which the dealer himself is so obliged ;

(2) the supplier

(a) shall not without objectively valid reasons withhold consent to conclude, alter or terminate sub-agreements referred to in Article 3, point 6 ;

(b) shall not apply, in relation to the dealer's obligations referred to in Article 4 (1), minimum requirements or criteria for estimates such that the dealer is subject to discrimination without objectively valid reasons or is treated inequitably ;

(c) shall, in any scheme for aggregating quantities or values of goods obtained by the dealer from the supplier and from connected undertakings within a specified period for the purpose of calculating discounts, at least distinguish between supplies of

— motor vehicles within the contract programme,

— spare parts within the contract programme, for supplies of which the dealer is dependent on undertakings within the distribution network, and

— other goods ;

(d) shall also supply to the dealer, for the purpose of performance of a contract of sale concluded between the dealer and a final customer in the common market, any passenger car which corresponds to a model within the contract programme and which is marketed by the manufacturer or with the manufacturer's consent in the Member State in which the vehicle is to be registered.

2.   In so far as the dealer has, in accordance with Article 5 (1), assumed obligations for the improvement of distribution and servicing structures, the exemption referred to in Article 3, points 3 and 5 shall apply to

the obligation not to sell new motor vehicles other than those within the contract programme or not to make such vehicles the subject of a distribution and servicing agreement, provided that

(1) the parties

  (a) agree that the supplier shall release the dealer from the obligations referred to in Article 3, points 3 and 5 where the dealer shows that there are objectively valid reasons for doing so ;

  (b) agree that the supplier reserves the right to conclude distribution and servicing agreements for contract goods with specified further undertakings operating within the contract territory or to alter the contract territory only where the supplier shows that there are objectively valid reasons for doing so ;

(2) the agreement is for a period of at least four years or, if for an indefinite period, the period of notice for regular termination of the agreement is at least one year for both parties, unless

  — the supplier is obliged by law or by special agreement to pay appropriate compensation on termination of the agreement, or

  — the dealer is a new entrant to the distribution system and the period of the agreement, or the period of notice for regular termination of the agreement, is the first agreed by that dealer.

(3) each party undertakes to give the other at least six months' prior notice of intention not to renew an agreement concluded for a definite period.

3.   A party may only invoke particular objectively valid grounds within the meaning of this Article which have been exemplified in the agreement if such grounds are applied without discrimination to undertakings within the distribution system in comparable cases.

4.   The conditions for exemption laid down in this Article shall not affect the right of a party to terminate the agreement for cause.

Article 6

Articles 1, 2 and 3 and Article 4 (2) shall not apply where :

1. both parties to the agreement or their connected undertakings are motor vehicle manufacturers ; or

2. the manufacturer, the supplier or another undertaking within the distribution system obliges the

dealer not to resell contract goods or corresponding goods below stated prices or not to exceed stated rates of trade discount ; or

3. the parties make agreements or engage in concerted practices concerning motor vehicles having three or more road wheels or spare parts therefor which are exempted from the prohibition in Article 85 (1) of the Treaty under Regulations (EEC) No 1983/83, or (EEC) No 1984/83 to an extent exceeding the scope of this Regulation.

Article 7

1.   As regards agreements existing on 13 March 1962 and notified before 1 February 1963 and agreements, whether notified or not, falling under Article 4 (2), point 1 of Regulation No 17, the declaration of inapplicability of Article 85 (1) of the Treaty contained in this Regulation shall apply with retroactive effect from the time at which the conditions of this Regulation were fulfilled.

2.   As regards all other agreements notified before this Regulation entered into force, the declaration of inapplicability of Article 85 (1) of the Treaty contained in this Regulation shall apply from the time at which the conditions of this Regulation were fulfilled, or from the date of notification, whichever is the later.

Article 8

If agreements existing on 13 March 1962 and notified before 1 February 1963 or agreements to which Article 4 (2), point 1 of Regulation No 17 applies and which were notified before 1 January 1967 are amended before 1 October 1985 so as to fulfil the conditions for application of this Regulation, and if the amendment is communicated to the Commission before 31 December 1985, the prohibition in Article 85 (1) of the Treaty shall not apply in respect of the period prior to the amendment. The communication shall take effect from the time of its receipt by the Commission. Where the communication is sent by registered post, it shall take effect from the date shown on the postmark of the place of posting.

Article 9

1.   As regards agreements to which Article 85 of the Treaty applies as a result of the accession of the United Kingdom, Ireland and Denmark, Articles 7 and 8 shall apply except that the relevant dates shall be 1 January 1973 instead of 13 March 1962 and 1 July 1973 instead of 1 February 1963 and 1 January 1967.

2. As regards agreements to which Article 85 of the Treaty applies as a result of the accession of Greece, Articles 7 and 8 shall apply except that the relevant dates shall be 1 January 1981 instead of 13 March 1962 and 1 July 1981 instead of 1 February 1963 and 1 January 1967.

Article 10

The Commission may withdraw the benefit of the application of this Regulation, pursuant to Article 7 of Regulation No 19/65/EEC, where it finds that in an individual case an agreement which falls within the scope of this Regulation nevertheless has effects which are incompatible with the provisions of Article 85 (3) of the Treaty, and in particular :

1. where, in the common market or a substantial part thereof, contract goods or corresponding goods are not subject to competition from products considered by consumers as similar by reason of their characteristics, price and intended use ;

2. where the manufacturer or an undertaking within the distribution system continuously or systematically, and by means not exempted by this Regulation, makes it difficult for final consumers or other undertakings within the distribution system to obtain contract goods or corresponding goods, or to obtain servicing for such goods, within the common market ;

3. where, over a considerable period, prices or conditions of supply for contract goods or for corresponding goods are applied which differ substantially as between Member States, and such substantial differences are chiefly due to obligations exempted by this Regulation ;

4. where, in agreements concerning the supply to the dealer of passenger cars which correspond to a model within the contract programme, prices or conditions which are not objectively justifiable are applied, with the object or the effect of partitioning the common market.

Article 11

The provisions of this Regulation shall also apply in so far as the obligations referred to in Articles 1 to 4 apply to undertakings which are connected with a party to an agreement.

Article 12

This Regulation shall apply *mutatis mutandis* to concerted practices of the types defined in Articles 1 to 4.

Article 13

For the purposes of this Regulation the following terms shall have the following meanings.

1. 'Distribution and servicing agreements' are framework agreements between two undertakings, for a definite or indefinite period, whereby the party supplying goods entrusts to the other the distribution and servicing of those goods.

2. 'Parties' are the undertakings which are party to an agreement within the meaning of Article 1 : 'the supplier' being the undertaking which supplies the contract goods, and 'the dealer', the undertaking entrusted by the supplier with the distribution and servicing of contract goods.

3. The 'contract territory' is the defined territory of the common market to which the obligation of exclusive supply in the meaning of Article 1 applies.

4. 'Contract goods' are motor vehicles intended for use on public roads and having three or more road wheels, and spare parts therefor, which are the subject of an agreement within the meaning of Article 1.

5. The 'contract programme' refers to the totality of the contract goods.

6. 'Spare parts' are parts which are to be installed in or upon a motor vehicle so as to replace components of that vehicle. They are to be distinguished from other parts and accessories according to customary usage in the trade.

7. The 'manufacturer' is the undertaking

   (a) which manufactures or procures the manufacture of the motor vehicles in the contract programme, or

   (b) which is connected with an undertaking described at (a).

8. 'Connected undertakings' are :

   (a) undertakings one of which directly or indirectly

      — holds more than half of the capital or business assets of the other, or

      — has the power to exercise more than half the voting rights in the other, or

— has the power to appoint more than half the members of the supervisory board, board of directors or bodies legally representing the other, or

— has the right to manage the affairs of the other;

(b) undertakings in relation to which a third undertaking is able directly or indirectly to exercise such rights or powers as are mentioned in (a) above.

9. 'Undertakings within the distribution system' are, besides the parties to the agreement, the manufacturer and undertakings which are entrusted by the manufacturer or with the manufacturer's consent with the distribution or servicing of contract goods or corresponding goods.

10. A 'passenger car which corresponds to a model within the contract programme' is a passenger car

— manufactured or assembled in volume by the manufacturer, and

— identical as to body style, drive-line, chassis, and type of motor with a passenger car within the contract programme.

11. 'Corresponding goods', 'corresponding motor vehicles' and 'corresponding parts' are those which are similar in kind to those in the contract programme, are distributed by the manufacturer or with the manufacturer's consent, and are the subject of a distribution or servicing agreement with an undertaking within the distribution system.

12. 'Distribute' and 'sell' include other forms of supply such as leasing.

Article 11

This Regulation shall enter into force on 1 July 1985.

It shall remain in force until 30 June 1995.

This Regulation shall be binding in its entirety and directly applicable in all Member States.

Done at Brussels, 12 December 1984.

For the Commission
Frans ANDRIESSEN
Member of the Commission

Annex 5

COMMISSION REGULATION (EEC) No 4087/88

of 30 November 1988

on the application of Article 85 (3) of the Treaty to categories of franchise
agreements

THE COMMISSION OF THE EUROPEAN COMMUNITIES,

Having regard to the Treaty establishing the European Economic Community,

Having regard to Council Regulation No 19/65/EEC of 2 March 1965 on the application of Article 85 (3) of the Treaty to certain categories of agreements and concerted practices ('), as last amended by the Act of Accession of Spain and Portugal, and in particular Article 1 thereof,

Having published a draft of this Regulation (²),

Having consulted the Advisory Committee on Restrictive Practices and Dominant Positions,

Whereas :

(1) Regulation No 19/65/EEC empowers the Commission to apply Article 85 (3) of the Treaty by Regulation to certain categories of bilateral exclusive agreements falling within the scope of Article 85 (1) which either have as their object the exclusive distribution or exclusive purchase of goods, or include restrictions imposed in relation to the assignment or use of industrial property rights.

(2) Franchise agreements consist essentialy of licences of industrial or intellectual property rights relating to trade marks or signs and know-how, which can be combined with restrictions relating to supply or purchase of goods.

(3) Several types of franchise can be distinguished according to their object : industrial franchise concerns the manufacturing of goods, distribution franchise concerns the sale of goods, and service franchise concerns the supply of services.

(4) It is possible on the basis of the experience of the Commission to define categories of franchise agreements which fall under Article 85 (1) but can normally by regarded as satisfying the conditions laid down in Article 85 (3). This is the case for franchise agreements whereby one of the parties supplies goods or provides services to end users. On the other hand, industrial franchise agreements should not be covered by this Regulation. Such agreements, which usually govern relationships between producers, present different characteristics than the other types of franchise. They consist of manufacturing licences based on patents and/or technical know-how, combined with trade-mark licences. Some of them may benefit from other block exemptions if they fulfil the necessary conditions.

(5) This Regulation covers franchise agreements between two undertakings, the franchisor and the franchisee, for the retailing of goods or the provision of services to end users, or a combination of these activities, such as the processing or adaptation of goods to fit specific needs of their customers. It also covers cases where the relationship between franchisor and franchisees is made through a third undertaking, the master franchisee. It does not cover wholesale franchise agreements because of the lack of experience of the Commission in that field.

(6) Franchise agreements as defined in this Regulation can fall under Article 85 (1). They may in particular affect intra-Community trade where they are concluded between undertakings from different Member States or where they form the basis of a network which extends beyond the boundaries of a single Member State.

(7) Franchise agreements as defined in this Regulation normally improve the distribution of goods and/or the provision of services as they give franchisors the possibility of establishing a uniform network with limited investments, which may assist the entry of new competitors on the market, particularly in the case of small and medium-sized undertakings, thus increasing interbrand competition. They also allow independent traders to set up outlets more rapidly and with higher chance of success than if they had to do so without the franchisor's experience and assistance. They have therefore the possibility of competing more efficiently with large distribution undertakings.

(') OJ No 36, 6. 3. 1965, p. 533/65.
(²) OJ No C 229, 27. 8. 1987, p. 3.

(8) As a rule, franchise agreements also allow consumers and other end users a fair share of the resulting benefit, as they combine the advantage of a uniform network with the existence of traders personally interested in the efficient operation of their business. The homogeneity of the network and the constant cooperation between the franchisor and the franchisees ensures a constant quality of the products and services. The favourable effect of franchising on interbrand competition and the fact that consumers are free to deal with any franchisee in the network guarantees that a reasonable part of the resulting benefits will be passed on to the consumers.

(9) This Regulation must define the obligations restrictive of competition which may be included in franchise agreements. This is the case in particular for the granting of an exclusive territory to the franchisees combined with the prohibition on actively seeking customers outside that territory, which allows them to concentrate their efforts on their allotted territory. The same applies to the granting of an exclusive territory to a master franchisee combined with the obligation not to conclude franchise agreements with third parties outside that territory. Where the franchisees sell or use in the process of providing services, goods manufactured by the franchisor or according to its instructions and or bearing its trade mark, an obligation on the franchisees not to sell, or use in the process of the provision of services, competing goods, makes it possible to establish a coherent network which is identified with the franchised goods. However, this obligation should only be accepted with respect to the goods which form the essential subject-matter of the franchise. It should notably not relate to accessories or spare parts for these goods.

(10) The obligations referred to above thus do not impose restrictions which are not necessary for the attainment of the abovementioned objectives. In particular, the limited territorial protection granted to the franchisees is indispensable to protect their investment.

(11) It is desirable to list in the Regulation a number of obligations that are commonly found in franchise agreements and are normally not restrictive of competition and to provide that if, because of the particular economic or legal circumstances, they fall under Article 85 (1), they are also covered by the exemption. This list, which is not exhaustive, includes in particular clauses which are essential either to preserve the common identity and reputation of the network or to prevent the know-how made available and the assistance given by the franchisor from benefiting competitors.

(12) The Regulation must specify the conditions which must be satisfied for the exemption to apply. To guarantee that competition is not eliminated for a substantial part of the goods which are the subject of the franchise, it is necessary that parallel imports remain possible. Therefore, cross deliveries between franchisees should always be possible. Furthermore, where a franchise network is combined with another distribution system, franchisees should be free to obtain supplies from authorized distributors. To better inform consumers, thereby helping to ensure that they receive a fair share of the resulting benefits, it must be provided that the franchisee shall be obliged to indicate its status as an independent undertaking, by any appropriate means which does not jeopardize the common identity of the franchised network. Furthermore, where the franchisees have to honour guarantees for the franchisor's goods, this obligation should also apply to goods supplied by the franchisor, other franchisees or other agreed dealers.

(13) The Regulation must also specify restrictions which may not be included in franchise agreements if these are to benefit from the exemption granted by the Regulation, by virtue of the fact that such provisions are restrictions falling under Article 85 (1) for which there is no general presumption that they will lead to the positive effects required by Article 85 (3). This applies in particular to market sharing between competing manufacturers, to clauses unduly limiting the franchisee's choice of suppliers or customers, and to cases where the franchisee is restricted in determining its prices. However, the franchisor should be free to recommend prices to the franchisees, where it is not prohibited by national laws and to the extent that it does not lead to concerted practices for the effective application of these prices.

(14) Agreements which are not automatically covered by the exemption because they contain provisions that are not expressly exempted by the Regulation and not expressly excluded from exemption may nonetheless generally be presumed to be eligible for application of Article 85 (3). It will be possible for the Commission rapidly to establish whether

this is the case for a particular agreement. Such agreements should therefore be deemed to be covered by the exemption provided for in this Regulation where they are notified to the Commission and the Commission does not oppose the application of the exemption within a specified period of time.

(15) If individual agreements exempted by this Regulation nevertheless have effects which are incompatible with Article 85 (3), in particular as interpreted by the administrative practice of the Commission and the case law of the Court of Justice, the Commission may withdraw the benefit of the block exemption. This applies in particular where competition is significantly restricted because of the structure of the relevant market.

(16) Agreements which are automatically exempted pursuant to this Regulation need not be notified. Undertakings may nevertheless in a particular case request a decision pursuant to Council Regulation No 17 (¹) as last amended by the Act of Accession of Spain and Portugal.

(17) Agreements may benefit from the provisions either of this Regulation or of another Regulation, according to their particular nature and provided that they fulfil the necessary conditions of application. Theys may not benefit from a combination of the provisions of this Regulation with those of another block exemption Regulation,

HAS ADOPTED THIS REGULATION :

Article 1

1.   Pursuant to Article 85 (3) of the Treaty and subject to the provisions of this Regulation, it is hereby declared that Article 85 (1) of the Treaty shall not apply to franchise agreements to which two untertakings are party, which include one or more of the restrictions listed in Article 2.

2.   The exemption provided for in paragraph 1 shall also apply to master franchise agreements to which two undertakings are party. Where applicable, the provisions of this Regulation concerning the relationship between franchisor and franchisee shall apply *mutatis mutandis*

(¹) OJ No 13, 21. 2. 1962, p. 204/62.

to the relationship between franchisor and master franchisee and between master franchisee and franchisee.

3.   For the purposes of this Regulation :

(a) 'franchise' means a package of industrial or intellectual property rights relating to trade marks, trade names, shop signs, utility models, designs, copyrights, know-how or patents, to be exploited for the resale of goods or the provision of services to end users ;

(b) 'franchise agreement' means an agreement whereby one undertaking, the franchisor, grants the other, the franchisee, in exchange for direct or indirect financial consideration, the right to exploit a franchise for the purposes of marketing specified types of goods and/or services ; it includes at least obligations relating to :

— the use of a common name or shop sign and a uniform presentation of contract premises and/or means of transport,

— the communication by the franchisor to the franchisee of know-how,

— the continuing provision by the franchisor to the franchisee of commercial or technical assistance during the life of the agreement ;

(c) 'master franchise agreement' means an agreement whereby one undertaking, the franchisor, grants the other, the master franchisee, in exchange of direct or indirect financial consideration, the right to exploit a franchise for the purposes of concluding franchise agreements with third parties, the franchisees ;

(d) 'franchisor's goods' means goods produced by the franchisor or according to its instructions, and/or bearing the franchisor's name or trade mark ;

(e) 'contract premises' means the premises used for the exploitation of the franchise or, when the franchise is exploited outside those premises, the base from which the franchisee operates the means of transport used for the exploitation of the franchise (contract means of transport) ;

(f) 'know-how' means a package of non-patented practical information, resulting from experience and testing by the franchisor, which is secret, substantial and identified ;

(g) 'secret' means that the know-how, as a body or in the precise configuration and assembly of its components, is not generally known or easily accessible ; it is not limited in the narrow sense that each individual component of the know-how should be totally unknown or unobtainable outside the franchisor's business ;

(h) 'substantial' means that the know-how includes information which is of importance for the sale of goods or the provision of services to end users, and in particular for the presentation of goods for sale, the processing of goods in connection which the provision of services, methods of dealing with customers, and administration and financial management; the know-how must be useful for the franchisee by being capable, at the date of conclusion of the agreement, of improving the competitive position of the franchisee, in particular by improving the franchisee's performance or helping it to enter a new market;

(i) 'identified' means that the know-how must be described in a sufficiently comprenhensive manner so as to make it possible to verify that it fulfils the criteria of secrecy and substantiality; the description of the know-how can either be set out in the franchise agreement or in a separate document or recorded in any other appropriate form.

Article 2

The exemption provided for in Article 1 shall apply to the following restrictions of competition:

(a) an obligation on the franchisor, in a defined area of the common market, the contract territory, not to:

— grant the right to exploit all or part of the franchise to third parties,

— itself exploit the franchise, or itself market the goods or services which are the subject-matter of the franchise under a similar formula,

— itself supply the franchisor's goods to third parties;

(b) an obligation on the master franchisee not to conclude franchise agreement with third parties outside its contract territory;

(c) an obligation on the franchisee to exploit the franchise only from the contract premises;

(d) an obligation on the franchisee to refrain, outside the contract territory, from seeking customers for the goods or the services which are the subject-matter of the franchise;

(e) an obligation on the franchisee not to manufacture, sell or use in the course of the provision of services, goods competing with the franchisor's goods which are the subject-matter of the franchise; where the subject-matter of the franchise is the sale or use in the course of the provision of services both certain types of goods and spare parts or accessories therefor, that obligation may not be imposed in respect of these spare parts or accessories.

Article 3

1. Article 1 shall apply notwithstanding the presence of any of the following obligations on the franchisee, in so far as they are necessary to protect the franchisor's industrial or intellectual property rights or to maintain the common identity and reputation of the franchised network:

(a) to sell, or use in the course of the provision of services, exclusively goods matching minimum objective quality specifications laid down by the franchisor;

(b) to sell, or use in the course of the provision of services, goods which are manufactured only by the franchisor or by third parties designed by it, where it is impracticable, owing to the nature of the goods which are the subject-matter of the franchise, to apply objective quality specifications;

(c) not to engage, directly or indirectly, in any similar business in a territory where it would compete with a member of the franchised network, including the franchisor; the franchisee may be held to this obligation after termination of the agreement, for a reasonable period which may not exceed one year, in the territory where it has exploited the franchise;

(d) not to acquire financial interests in the capital of a competing undertaking, which would give the franchisee the power to influence the economic conduct of such undertaking;

(e) to sell the goods which are the subject-matter of the franchise only to end users, to other franchisees and to resellers within other channels of distribution supplied by the manufcturer of these goods or with its consent;

(f) to use its best endeavours to sell the goods or provide the services that are the subject-matter of the franchise; to offer for sale a minimum range of goods, achieve a minimum turnover, plan its orders in advance, keep minimum stocks and provide customer and warranty services;

(g) to pay to the franchisor a specified proportion of its revenue for advertising and itself carry out advertising for the nature of which it shall obtain the franchisor's approval.

2. Article 1 shall apply notwithstanding the presence of any of the following obligations on the franchisee:

(a) not to disclose to third parties the know-how provided by the franchisor; the franchisee may be held to this obligation after termination of the agreement;

(b) to communicate to the franchisor any experience gained in exploiting the franchise and to grant it, and other franchisees, a non-exclusive licence for the know-how resulting from that experience;

(c) to inform the franchisor of infringements of licensed industrial or intellectual property rights, to take legal action against infringers or to assist the franchisor in any legal actions against infringers :

(d) not to use know-how licensed by the franchisor for purposes other than the exploitation of the franchise ; the franchisee may be held to this obligation after termination of the agreement ;

(e) to attend or have its staff attend training courses arranged by the franchisor ;

(f) to apply the commercial methods devised by the franchisor, including any subsequent modification thereof, and use the licensed industrial or intellectual property rights ;

(g) to comply with the franchisor's standards for the equipment and presentation of the contract premises and/or means of transport ;

(h) to allow the franchisor to carry out checks of the contract premises and/or means of transport, including the goods sold and the services provided, and the inventory and accounts of the franchisee ;

(i) not without the franchisor's consent to change the location of the contract premises ;

(j) not without the franchisor's consent to assign the rights and obligations under the franchise agreement.

3. In the event that, because of particular circumstances, obligations referred to in paragraph 2 fall within the scope of Article 85 (1), they shall also be exempted even if they are not accompanied by any of the obligations exempted by Article 1.

Article 4

The exemption provided for in Article 1 shall apply on condition that :

(a) the franchisee is free to obtain the goods that are the subject-matter of the franchise from other franchisees ; where such goods are also distributed through another network of authroized distributors, the franchisee must be free to obtain the goods from the latter ;

(b) where the franchisor obliges the franchisee to honour guarantees for the franchisor's goods, that obligation shall apply in respect of such goods supplied by any member of the franchised network or other distributors which give a similar guarantee, in the common market ;

(c) the franchisee is obliged to indicate its status as an independent undertaking ; this indication shall however not interfere with the common identity of the franchised network resulting in particular from the common name or shop sign and uniform appearance of the contract premises and/or means of transport.

Article 5

The exemption granted by Article 1 shall not apply where :

(a) undertakings producing goods or providing services which are identical or are considered by users as equivalent in view of their characteristics, price and intended use, enter into franchise agreements in respect of such goods or services ;

(b) without prejudice to Article 2 (e) and Article 3 (1) (b), the franchisee is prevented from obtaining supplies of goods of a quality equivalent to those offered by the franchisor ;

(c) without prejudice to Article 2 (e), the franchisee is obliged to sell, or use in the process of providing services, goods manufactured by the franchisor or third parties designated by the franchisor and the franchisor refuses, for reasons other than protecting the franchisor's industrial or intellectual property rights, or maintaining the common identity and reputation of the franchised network, to designate as authorized manufacturers third parties proposed by the franchisee ;

(d) the franchisee is prevented from continuing to use the licensed know-how after termination of the agreement where the know-how has become generally known or easily accessible, other than by breach of an obligation by the franchisee ;

(e) the franchisee is restricted by the franchisor, directly or indirectly, in the determination of sale prices for the goods or services which are the subject-matter of the franchise, without prejudice to the possibility for the franchisor of recommending sale prices ;

(f) the franchisor prohibits the franchisee from challenging the validity of the industrial or intellectual property rights which form part of the franchise, without prejudice to the possibility for the franchisor of terminating the agreement in such a case ;

(g) franchisees are obliged not to supply within the common market the goods or services which are the subject-matter of the franchise to end users because of their place of residence.

Article 6

1 The exemption provided for in Article 1 shall also apply to franchise agreements which fulfil the conditions laid down in Article 4 and include obligations restrictive of competition which are not covered by Articles 2 and 3 (3) and do not not fall within the scope of Article 5, on condition that the agreements in question are notified to the Commission in accordance with the provisions of Commission Regulation No 27 (¹) and that the Commission does not oppose such exemption within a period of six months.

(¹) OJ No 35, 10. 5. 1962, p. 1118/62.

2. The period of six months shall run from the date on which the notification is received by the Commission. Where, however, the notification is made by registered post, the period shall run from the date shown on the postmark of the place of posting.

3. Paragraph 1 shall apply only if :

(a) express reference is made to this Article in the notification or in a communication accompanying it ; and

(b) the information furnished with the notification is complete and in accordance with the facts.

4. The benefit of paragraph 1 can be claimed for agreements notified before the entry into force of this Regulation by submitting a communication to the Commission referring expressly to this Article and to the notification. Paragraphs 2 and 3 (b) shall apply *mutatis mutandis.*

5. The Commission may oppose exemption. It shall oppose exemption if it recives a request to do so from a Member State within three months of the forwarding to the Member State of the notification referred to in paragraph 1 or the communication referred to in paragraph 4. This request must be justified on the basis of considerations relating to the competition rules of the Treaty.

6. The Commission may withdraw its opposition to the exemption at any time. However, where that opposition was raised at the request of a Member State, it may be withdrawn only after consultation of the advisory Committee on Restrictive Practices and Dominant Positions.

7. If the opposition is withdrawn because the undertakings concerned have shown that the conditions of Article 85 (3) are fulfilled, the exemption shall apply from the date of the notification.

8. If the opposition is withdrawn because the undertakings concerned have amended the agreement so that the conditions of Article 85 (3) are fulfilled, the exemption shall apply from the date on which the amendments take effect.

9. If the Commission opposes exemption and its opposition is not withdrawn, the effects of the notification shall be governed by the provisions of Regulation No 17.

Article 7

1. Information acquired pursuant to Article 6 shall be used only for the purposes of this Regulation.

2. The Commission and the authorities of the Member States, their officials and other servants shall not disclose information acquired by them pursuant to this Regulation

of a kind that is covered by the obligation of professional secrecy.

3. Paragraphs 1 and 2 shall not prevent publication of general information or surveys which do not contain information relating to particular undertakings or associations of undertakings.

Article 8

The Commission may withdraw the benefit of this Regulation, pursuant to Article 7 of Regulation No 19/65/EEC, where it finds in a particular case that an agreement exempted by this Regulation nevertheless has certain effects which are incompatible with the conditions laid down in Article 85 (3) of the EEC Treaty, and in particular where territorial protection is awarded to the franchisee and :

(a) access to the relevant market or competition therein is significantly restricted by the cumulative effect of parallel networks of similar agreements established by competing manufacturers or distributors ;

(b) the goods or services which are the subject-matter of the franchise do not face, in a substantial part of the common market, effective competition from goods or services which are identical or considered by users as equivalent in view of their characteristics, price and intended use ;

(c) the parties, or one of them, prevent end users, because of their place of residence, from obtaining, directly or through intermediaries, the goods or services which are the subject-matter of the franchise within the common market, or use differences in specifications concerning those goods or services in different Member States, to isolate markets ;

(d) franchisees engage in concerted practices relating to the sale prices of the goods or services which are the subject-matter of the franchise ;

(e) the franchisor uses its right to check the contract premises and means of transport, or refuses its agreement to requests by the franchisee to move the contract premises or assign its rights and obligations under the franchise agreement, for reasons other than protecting the franchisor's industrial or intellectual property rights, maintaining the common identity and reputation of the franchised network or verifying that the franchisee abides by its obligations under the agreement.

Article 9

This Regulation shall enter into force on 1 February 1989.

It shall remain in force until 31 December 1999.

This Regulation shall be binding in its entirety and directly applicable in all Member States.

Done at Brussels, 30 November 1988.

For the Commission

Peter SUTHERLAND

Member of the Commission

———————

PART II

National rules and application of EEC law

CHAPTER 2
BELGIUM

Geert Bogaert
Christine De Keersmaeker
Nicole Van Ranst
Olivier Vaes

1. Commercial Agency

1.1. Definition of Various Types of Agencies and Intermediaries

1.1.1. Independent

1.1.1.1. Introduction

According to Belgian law there is only one kind of "commercial agent", as against English law where the term "agent" can mean "commission agent", "mandatory", etc.[1] All of these are intermediaries, according to Belgian law, but there can only be one "commercial agent". We will nevertheless analyse both "commercial agency" (agence commerciale or handelsagentuur) and "commercial representation" (représentation de commerce or hendelsvertegenwoordiging) because a commercial agent, in Belgian law, is an "independent" commercial representative.[2]

The commercial representative has a legal status in Belgian law often referred to in the literature and in jurisdiction in connection with commercial agency.

The commercial agent and the commercial representative are intermediaries who contact and visit clients with a view to negotiating transacting business for the account of and in the name of one or more principals. The commercial representative does so under the authority of his principal, while the commercial agent acts independently.

---

[1] Brussels, 18.3.69, Pas. 1969, II, 141.
[2] F. Bortolotti and A. Previsiani, *Guide pour la conclusion des contrats d'agence et de concession a l'étranger*, Ed. du Montieur, (Paris, 1981), 136. P. Crahay, "La directive européenne relative aux agents commerciaux indépendants", B.R.H. 1987, 564 ff. see also: D. Struyven, A. Van Cauwelaert and C. Wouters-de Cuyper. Tussenpersonen in Rechtstaktoren in de onderneming, (Kluwer Anterp, 1982). VII B, 2-17 (aanvullingen Sept. 1987).

1.1.1.2. The legal presumption

Article 4, paragraph 2 of the law of 3 July 1978[3] concerning labour agreements embodies a legal presumption, namely that:

> "the agreement concluded between the principal and an intermediary, however it is described, shall be considered to be a labour agreement for a commercial representative".

Every intermediary is thus, until proof of the contrary, a commercial representative.

However, article 4 (3) enumerates certain intermediaries who are not commercial representatives, such as the commission agent, the broker, the concessionaire for sole sale, the intermediary who can pass his orders to whom he wants and in general the commercial agent who does not act under the authority of his principal. But this list must be read subject to article 4 (2) and every intermediary remains, therefore, until proof to the contrary, a commercial representative.

Article 87 of the Law Concerning Labour Agreements, stipulates moreover that the regulations applicable to labour agreements for employees are also applicable to commercial representatives. Every commercial representative is thus an employee.

The legal presumption is therefore that every agreement between a principal and intermediary, except where there is proof to the contrary is an agreement for a commercial representative who is an employee. The legal provisions concerning the labour agreement for employees will be applicable to intermediaries and an intermediary will enjoy the social security rights of wage-earning employees (such as annual vacation, Sunday as a non-working day, working hours and guaranteed monthly wages).

Proof to the contrary should be given by the principal who has to prove that the activities of the intermediary do not correspond to the legal definition of commercial representative. He will be able to restrict himself largely to proving the absence of a tie of subordination. Elements which presume such a tie will be discussed later.

Because of the legal presumption mentioned above we suggest that you first read 1.1.2. and then 1.1.1.3.

1.1.1.3. The commercial agent (l'agent commercial or de Handelsagent)

Until recently, the commercial agent had no legal status in Belgian law. On 26 November 1973 the three Benelux countries adopted the Benelux Agreement concerning agency agreement, but this agreement has not yet been incorporated in the Belgian legislation.

A bill approving the Benelux Agreement on agency agreements[4] was passed in both the Chamber and the Senate on 3 June 1976 and 5 July 1979 respectively but was never published. Another bill was deposited concerning

---

[3] Relevant sections of the Law on Labour Agreements are given in translation on pp. 139–146 and unless otherwise indicated all references are to this Law.

[4] Parl. St., Kamer, 1975-76, nr. 831.

commercial agency agreements[5] but it was not approved by either house and lapsed on 8 November 1987 with the fall of the Belgian Government. The bill number 486/1 is pending in the Commission of Justice.

Belgium must now bring into force the provisions necessary to comply with the EEC Commercial Agents Directive before 1 January 1990. As some of the provisions of the bills discussed above are contrary to the provisions of the EEC Directive, work on them is likely to be discontinued. The text which follows is based on the assumption that the Directive will be properly implemented in Belgian law.

In the absence of a legal status, there is no definition in Belgian law of commercial agency. Jurisdiction[6] and the literature,[7] however, both defined commercial agency. The commercial agent does exactly the same as the commercial representative, namely he contacts and visits clients with a view to negotiating or transacting business for the account of and in the name of one or more principal(s) but he does it independently. Thus the Commercial Agent is not under the authority of his principal, and is an independent intermediary. The relation of the commercial agent with his principal is like the relation of the commercial representative, a durable relation (if it were an occasional relationship, he would be a broker). The commercial agent is in principle a trader.

According to article 2 of the Commercial Code every enterprise of an agency is an act of trade. The commercial agent should be registered on the Register of Commerce. Registration on the Register of Commerce establishes his quality as that of trader, according to article 3 of the law of 3 July 1951.

It is evident, however, that someone can only be a trader when acting on his own account and in his own name and the Commercial Agent is someone who acts in the name of one or more principals. The Court of Cassation took the view in a judgment of 26 November 1970[8] that a Commercial Agent is not necessarily a trader in the absence of proof that he acts in his own name. No definite position on this matter has been reached.

The Council Directive defines the Commercial Agent in article 1, paragraph 2 as:

> "a self-employed intermediary who has continuing authority to negotiate the sale or the purchase of goods on behalf of another person, called the 'principal', or to negotiate and conclude such transactions on behalf of and in the name of that principal".

The Directive adds in article 1, paragraph 3:

> "A comercial agent shall be understood within the meaning of this Directive as not including in particular:
> –a person who, in his capacity as an officer, is empowered to enter into commitments binding on a company or association.

[5] Parl. St., Senaat, 1975-76, nr. 871/1.
[6] Antwerp 4.2.80, B.R.II. 1980, 456; Brussels, 21.1.81, B.R.II. 1981, 493.
[7] W. Van Gerven, *Overzicht van het recht betreffende tussenpersonen in het handelsverkeer*, R.W. 1969-79, 1271.
[8] Cass. 26.11.70, J.T. 1971, 149; R.W. 1970-71, 1419; Brussels, 26.6.78, B.R.H. 1978, 451.

–a partner who is lawfully authorized to enter into commitments binding on his partners.

–a receiver and manager, a liquidator or a trustee in bankruptcy".

Article 2 of the Directive states:

"1. This Directive shall not apply to:
 –commercial agents whose activities are unpaid.
 –commercial agents when they operate on commodity exchanges or in the commodity market, or
 –the body known as the Crown Agents for Overseas Governments and Administrations, as set up under the Crown Agents 1979 in the United Kingdom, or its subsidiaries.

2. Each of the Member States shall have the right to provide that the Directive shall not apply to those persons whose activities as commercial agents are considered secondary by the law of that Member State".

1.1.2. Employed (Le représentant de commerce or de handelsvetegenwoordiger)

The commercial representative unlike the commercial agent, has a legal status. It is defined by the law of 13 July 1963 establishing the status of the commercial representative (Mon. Belge 7 August 1963) as modified by the law of 3 July 1978 on labour agreements (Mon. Belge 22 August 1968).

As previously stated, article 4, paragraph 2 of this law embodies the legal presumption that each intermediary is a commercial representative until proof to the contrary, and according to article 87 the commercial representative is subject to the legal regulations concerning labour agreements for employees.

Article 4, paragraph 1 gives a definition of commercial representation:

"The commercial representative is an intermediary who contacts and visits clients with a view to negotiating or transacting business, insurances excepted, under the authority, for the account and in the name of one or more principals".

1.1.2.1. A "physical person"

The commercial representative, as an employee, is necessarily a "physical person".

1.1.2.2. Contacting and visiting clients

This means both finding new clients (contacting and visiting) and keeping up existing clients (visiting). These activities must be exercised outside the offices of the enterprise. Clients should be visited at home. Receiving clients, for example, at trade fairs is not sufficient. This does not mean that a commercial representative could not be appointed to receive clients at a fair or in a shop on an *ad hoc* basis. Visiting clients door to door falls under the definition of commercial representation. A touring booth does not.[9] Contacting and visiting clients must be done personally, i.e. there must be direct contact with the client.[10]

[9] Coor. Brussels, 9.1.70, J.T. 1970, 396; Arbrb. Dinant, 6.1.81, J.T.T. 1981, 110.
[10] Arbrb. Brussels, 7.2.78, J.T.T. 1978, 145.

1.1.2.3. With a view to negotiating or transacting business

While contacting and visiting clients, the commercial representative must negotiate and eventually transact for business. However, the transaction need not be concluded by the commercial representative himself and will often, in fact, be concluded by the principal.

Visiting a client to take an order or to acquaint the client with a new product or service is not sufficient. A medical representative who visits doctors to acquaint them with new pharmaceutical products will therefore often not be considered as a commercial representative because he does not negotiate or transact business.[11]

"Business" can be the sale, rent, etc. of goods or the granting of a service, anything except insurance.[12] [13]

1.1.2.4. Under the authority

Whereas article 3 of the Law Concerning Labour Agreements states that employees work under the authority, the guidance and the surveillance of the employer, article 4 states that the Commercial Representative merely acts under the "authority" of his principal. Authority, however, includes guidance (giving orders) and surveillance (looking after the execution of the orders).

In this sense, one could say that by merely restricting the element of authority little or nothing has been modified by comparison with the classic notion of subordination characterized by the criteria of article 3 of "authority, guidance and surveillance".[14] [15] [16]

Whether or not a subordinate relationship exists, and hence the authority of the principal, is a question of fact which a judge might have to decide, taking into account all the circumstances. The terms of the agreement do not bind the judge.[17] [18]

Elements of subordination are:

- receiving instructions from the principal;[19]

[11] Cass. 8.1.70, Arr. Cass. 1970, 415; Arbrb. Luik, 25.274, J.L. 1974-75, 30; Arbrb. Brussels, 7.2.86, Rechtspr. Arb. Br. 1986, 152. Arbrb. Nijvel, 21.9.84, Soc. Kron. 1986, 17, A. de Theux, noot.
[12] Arbh. Luik, 18.10.79, J.T.T. 1980, 47; Arbh. Brussels, 3.9.1975, J.T.T. 1976, 166.
[13] Cass. 14.6.82, Pas. 1982, 1182.
[14] H. Tielemans and R. Nockels, "Le Statut Social du représentant de commerce", 1981, dans Promouvoir, CNE, I, 1-2, 8 ff. G. Delagrange, R. de Paepe, J. Herman, and D. Parisis-Dresse, Handelsvertegenwoordigers en Handelsagenten, CED-Samson, Brussels 1982, 1.1/10 ff.
[15] Taquet and Denis, "La représentation commerciale, le lien de subordination et la notion d'autorité", J.T. 1969, 361 ff.
[16] Taquet and Wautiez, "Les indices de l'autorité en matière de représentation commerciale", J.T.T. 1971, 193, ff.
[17] Cass. 11.5.77, Arr. Cass. 1977, 932; J.T.T. 1978, 144; Cass. 24.11.77, Arr. Cass. 1978, 341; Pas. 1978, I, 326; Arbh. Luik, 22.11.84, Soc. Kron. 1985, 208, A. de Theux; Arbrb. Ieper, 8.2.85, J.T.T. 1985, 261; Arbrb. Brussels, 26.10.82, J.T.T. 1983, 298; Cass. 16.3.81, Pas. 1981, I, 761; Arbrb. Brussels, 29.1.82, J.T.T. 1982, 229.
[18] Struyven et al., op. cit. VII B, 2-3. See also: A. de Theux, "Handelsvertegenwoordiger – Vermoeden van ondergeschiktheid", Soc. Kron. 1985, 210.
[19] Arbh. Bergen, 10.4.78, J.T.T. 1978, 348; Arbrb. Bergen, 14.1.85, J.T.T. 1985, 151; Arbh. Luik, 22.9.83, J.T.T. 1984, 460; Arrond. Rb. Charleroi, 19.2.85, T.S.R. 1985, 627.

- obligation to report on the fulfilment of a task;[20]
- attending meetings organized by the principal at which instructions are received;[21]
- regulation of time, vacation and absence;[22]
- total restriction on competition;
- use of a company car;
- reimbursement of costs except for travel expenses;[23]
- price determination;[24]
- guarantee of a minimum wage;[25]
- mandatory period of probation;
- payment of a fixed wage.[26] [27] [28]

Elements which could indicate the absence of subordination:

- no repayment of costs;[29]
- affiliation to a security fund for independence;
- registration on the Register of Commerce and liability for VAT;[25] [30]
- use of letters with a personal letterhead;[25]
- payment of commission only;
- no guarantee of a minimum wage;[31]
- freedom of organization and free use of time;[32]
- no obligation to report, however the absence of reporting does not automatically mean the absence of authority;[33]
- no obligation to attend meetings;[19]
- nomination as commercial agent in the agreement.[34]

The question of subordination is usually raised if several of the above-mentioned elements are present.

1.1.2.5. For the account of and in the name of one or more principals

The commercial representative negotiates or transacts busines on behalf

[20] Arbh. Brussels, 3.9.75, J.T.T. 1976, 54; Arbh. Brussels, 7.11.77, J.T.T. 1978, 41; Arbh. Bergen, 10.4.78, J.T.T. 1978, 348; vgl. Arbh. Luik, 9.11.77, J.T.T. 1978, 147.
[21] Arbh. Luik, 18.5.77, T.S.R. 1978, 83; Arbh. Brussel, 7.11.78, J.T.T. 1978, 145.
[22] Arbh. Luik, 2.5.77, J.L. 1977-78, 174; Arbh. Luik, 18.5.77, T.S.R. 1978, 83.
[23] Cass. 11.5.77, J.T.T. 1978, 144, Arbrb. Luik, 11.1.80, J.T.T. 1980, 153.
[24] Arbrb. Verviers, 31.1.79, J.T.T. 1979, 352.
[25] Arbh. Bergen, 10.4.78, J.T.T. 1978, 348.
[26] R. Blanpain, "Arbeidsovereenkomsten voor handelsvertegenwoordigers. Begrip en bewijs", in *Juridisch statuut van de handelsvertegenwoordiger*, Kluwer, Antwerp, 1980, II 2.
[27] Delagrange et al; *op. cit.*, 2.1/7, 10 e.v.
[28] Y. Merchiers, "Overzicht van Rechtspraak, Bijzonder Afwijkend handelsrecht, 1979-81, TPR 1982, 748.
[29] Arbh. Luik, 11.1.80, J.T.T. 1980, 153.
[30] Arbh. Ghent, 19.11.87, T.S.R. 1973, 82.
[31] Arbh. Luik, 9.11.77, J.T.T. 1978, 147; Arbh. Luik, 18.11.80, J.L. 1981, 150; Arbrb. Brussels, 11.3.83, J.T.T. 1983, 301.
[32] Arbh. Luik, 11.1.80, J.T.T. 1980, 153; Arbh. Luik, 18.11.79, J.T.T. 1980, 196; Arbh. Luik, 18.12.80, J.L. 1981, 150.
[33] Arbrb. Verviers, 29.9.77, J.T.T. 1978, 42; Contra: Arbh. Luik, 18.5.77, T.S.R. 1978, 85; Arbh. Luik, 17.9.80, J.L. 1980, 317.
[34] Delagrange et al. *op. cit.*, 3.1/11 e.v.

of his principal. Hence the principal's name is known and clearly communicated.

The commercial representative may act for more than one principal. One visit to a client may be for the benefit of different principals at the same time.

The commercial representative usually, but not necessarily, represents principals who are not in competition with one other.

The only legal relationship resulting from the commercial representative's contact with a client is the relationship between client and principal.

The commercial representative is not a party to the business transacted and does not have any responsibility for the consequences of the transaction provided that his activities remain those of representation.

1.1.3. Others

1.1.3.1. The commision agency (La commission or de commissie)

The commission agent, just as the commercial agent (who is independent), acts within a continuing relationship with his principal(s), for the account of his principal(s) but, unlike the commercial agent, in his own name. Commission agency is governed by articles 12-17, Title VII of the Code of Commerce.

1.1.3.2. The "mandatory" (Le mandat or de lastgeving)

The mandatory is an independent commercial agent who is also legally allowed to undertake transactions. The mandate is governed by the article 1984, Title XIII of the Civil Code.

1.1.3.3. Work by contract (Le louage d'ouvrage or de Aanneming)

Legal writers often refer to the legal regulations concerning work by contract in dealing with commercial agency. Work by contract and commercial agency are similar, although work by contract specifically provides for the execution of a piece of work. Work by contract is governed by article 1787 ff. of the Civil Code.

1.1.3.4. The broker (Le courtier or de makelaar)

A broker is an independent commercial agent who does not have a continuing relationship with his principal. He puts the parties (principal and client) together, this is where his relation with the principal and the client ends. Many professional organizations have specific regulations for their broker-members.

Travel agents and stock exchange brokers are subject to particular legal regulations.

1.1.3.5. Distribution (La distribution or de distributie)

The distributor, unlike the commercial agent, both independent and employed, acts in his own name and for his own account.

1.2. Conclusion of the Contract (Special Conditions)

Whether the intermediary, including the commercial representative, and the principal have a written agreement is not conclusive, nor are the contents or the name of the agreement. The existence or absence and the contents of an agreement of commercial representation are determined according to the facts of a particular case.

The legal presumption remains that the agreement between an intermediary and principal should be considered as a labour agreement for a commercial representative, and thus, according to article 87 of the Law Concerning Labour Agreements as a contract of employment. Proof to the contrary must be established.

Broadly speaking, the agreement for commercial representation need not be written, but there are some exceptions.

Where the agreement is in writing, article 6 must be considered. It states that:

> "any stipulations contrary to the regulations of this law and its enforcement are null and void in so as far as they have the intention of diminishing the rights of the employee or increasing his obligations".

The commercial representative is advised to make a written agreement with his principal, notably on the territory in which to operate, clients to visit and products to sell. These are essential elements of the representation and once set out in a written agreement, they cannot be modified except by agreement of both parties. The principal cannot modify the agreement unilateraly.

If the commercial representative does not agree with a proposed modification, the principal has to resign or decide to end the representation with all its consequences such as having to give a notice of termination to the commercial representative or pay him or her a termination indemnity, together with an indemnity for the number of clients.

The principal is, however, allowed to redivide the territories, to decide to reach other clients and to sell other products if these modifications are necessary for the prosperity and the preservation of his company. The modification, however, may not be disadvantageous to the commercial representative, which would be the case if his salary were diminished.[35][36]

A written agreement is obligatory for:

- the period of probation;
- an agreement for a fixed term;
- an agreement for specified work;
- the competition clause;

[35] Arbh. Luik, 17.3.80, J.L. 1980, 317. Arbh. Brussels, 7.11.77, J.T.T. 1978, 41. Cass., 19.12.79, T.S.R. 1980, 93; Arbrb. Brussels, 25.5.73, J.T.T. 1974, 15; Arbrb. Brussels, 15.2.79, J.T.T. 1979, 222; Arbrb. Brussels, 25.11.74, V.B.O. 1976, 364.
[36] Delagrange et al., *op cit.*, 3.1/17 e.v.

- the *del credere* clause;
- replacement;
- a part-time job.

The agreement must be drawn up, at the latest, at the moment when employment starts, on penalty of nullity.

The clause on the period of probation is governed by the articles 67, 79 and 81 of the Law Concerning Labour Agreements, which are also applicable to the commercial representative.

A general clause referring to all commercial representatives in service is not valid.

The period of probation should not last less than one month but not more than 6 or 12 months, according to whether the annual salary is lower or higher than 812,000 Belgian Francs. This wage level is linked every year on 1 January to the fluctuations of the wage index figures according to article 131.

If the clause on the period of probation does not specify the length of time, the period will be one month.

The period of probation can be suspended (arts. 70–72 of the Law Concerning Labour Agreements); when reinstated, a period equal to the suspension will be added.

The labour agreement for a commercial representative can be ended unilaterally during the period of probation and without specific cause, but the probation must have lasted at least one month. A specific cause is a serious shortcoming which makes professional co-operation between principal and commercial representative immediately and permanently impossible.

A period of notice of at least seven days should be given (art. 81, para. 1) in default of which the party who has ended the agreement will be held liable to pay the other party compensation equal to the wages and advantages specified in the agreement, in accordance with the remaining period of the month plus the period of notice (art. 81, para. 2).

If the commercial representative is unable to work for more than seven days during the period of probation, the agreement may be ended without compensation.

The notice of termination has, on penalty of nullity, to be given in writing by registered post or by writ which will take effect on the third day after the date of sending. The letter must state when the period of notice starts and ends (art. 37).

A fixed-term labour agreement must be written and prepared separately for each employee. If there is no written contract, the agreement will come under the conditions for labour agreements of indeterminate duration (art. 9). This is also the case if the parties extend the agreement beyond its fixed term (art. 11). When the parties have signed successive agreements for fixed terms without interruption, they will be supposed to have signed an agreement for an indefinite period unless the employee proves that these agreements were justified by the nature of the work, or for another legal reason (art. 10).

According to article 11 an agreement for *part-time work* should also be written and signed individually by each employee. The contract should also mention the conditions and hours of work. If it does not, the employee may apply the rules of working conditions which are most favourable to him.

Article 11 (c) states that in an agreement for *temporary replacement* of an employee, the reason for replacement should be given, the identity of the replaced employee, and the condition of entering upon one's duties. The duration of the replacement agreement (also when there are several successive agreements considered as one) should never exceed two years, but also should not, contrary to the normal legal regulations, be fixed precisely.

If the period of two years is exceeded or if there is no written contract, the agreement is considered as an agreement for an indeterminate duration. It is useful to mention that parties may deviate in these agreements from the normal legal regulations concerning the period of notice.

The no competition clause will also, on penalty of nullity, be in writing (art. 107, see para. 1.4.). The obligation does however only exist where the annual usage is more than 677.000 Belgian Francs, as the competition clause, is null where the annual wage is lower.

The same applies for the *del credere* clause (see 1.4.).

Finally, the following regulations cover the obligatory use, of language:

- articles 52 and 59 of the Law Concerning Labour Agreements;
- the decree of 19 July 1973 of the Dutch Community (Mon. Belge, 6 September 1973);
- the decrees of 12 July 1978 and 30 June 1982 of the French Community (Mon. Belge, 9 September 1978. erratum 16 September 1978);
- the judgment of the Arbitration Court of 30 January 1986 and 18 November 1986.

The Council Directive provides that a commercial agency agreement can be signed for a fixed period or for an indefinite period and further, under article 13:

> "1. Each party shall be entitled to receive from the other on request a signed written document setting out the terms of the agency contract including any terms subsequently agreed. Waiver of this right shall not be permitted.
> 2. Notwithstanding paragraph I a Member State may provide that an agency contract shall not be valid unless evidenced in writing".

The commercial agency agreement does not have to take a specified form. This follows from the absence of any legal statute. But precisely because of this absence clear written agreements are strongly advised. Without any written agreements there are no legal provisions.

The usefulness of a written agreement is evident when one considers the legal presumption in article 4 of the Law Concerning Labour Agreements: the agreement will be considered an agreement for commercial representation in the absence of a written agreement.

A written agreement showing that the commercial agent does not have a subordinate relationship will, provided it is based on fact, preclude further discussion.

Every element of the agreement should be interpreted to show the absence of subordination. A written agreement is therefore useful but it is the facts that are decisive.

In specifying a particular territory, clients, and products, this exclusivity indicates merely the economic needs, not subordination, which could lead to the agreement being interpreted as one for commercial representation.[37]

One should bear in mind that an exclusivity clause is subject to the EEC competition rules, particularly article 85 (1) of the EEC Treaty. The exclusivity clause restricts competition and is therefore contrary to article 85 (1) of the EEC Treaty if the commercial agent is an independent economic entity and if the agreement perceptibly influences trade between member states. After notice such a clause could, however, be subject to the exemption provided for by article 85 (3) of the EEC Treaty.

1.3. The Principal's Duties and Rights

1.3.1. The principal's duties

The duties and rights of the principal in relation to a commercial representative are legally regulated, contrary to his duties and rights in his relation to a commercial agent. The principal owes the commercial representative respect and esteem and has to observe decency and good morals (art. 16) while the agreement is in force (art. 16 of the Law Concerning Labour Agreements).

According to article 20, the principal is obliged:

"1. To make the employee labour in the manner, at the time and in the place agreed upon particularly, if the circumstances require it and except contrary stipulation by giving him the necessary help, aid and materials in order to execute this work.
2. To administer with due diligence the work to be done in fitting circumstances with respect to the security and the health of the employee and to assure that the employee gets, if an accident occurs, first aid. A first-aid kit should therefore permanently be accessible to the personnel.
3. To pay the wages in the manner, at the time and in the place agreed upon.
4. If such has been agreed, to properly house the employee and to give him adequate, healthy food.
5. To give the employee the necessary time to fulfil his religious duties and his legal civil obligations.
6. To give the necessary care and attention to the welcome of the employees, especially young employees.
7. To administer with due diligence the worktools that belong to the employee, his personal belongings given in custody; in no circumstances the principal may refuse to give them back".

The principal must respect the agreement made with the commercial representative, which means that he cannot unilaterally change the nature of the agreement by modifying or reducing the territory or taking away the best paying product, even if a wage is guaranteed.[38] The commercial representative undergoes a real moral damage, a modification is to be assimilated with a unilateral breach of contract. Any clause whereby the principal

---

[37] Arbrb. Brussels, 9.5.73, J.T.T. 1974, 59; Arbrb. Luik, 13.12.73, J.L. 1974-75, 142; Arb. Luik, 18.9.79, J.T.T. 1980, 204.
[38] Arbrb. Brussel, 26.9.77, J.T.T. 1978, 148.

reserves the right of unilateral breach is therefore also null (art. 25). If the commercial representative is unable to prove he registered a protest against the unilaterial breach, he will be considered to have accepted it.[39]

A protest by the commercial representative against a unilateral breach of contract by the principal will not be a breach of contract.

If the unilateral modifications do not affect the essential elements of the agreement or if they are justified by the interest of the company and the commercial representative, in such a case, suffers no loss of wages, and his work is not essentially modified, the unilateral modifications will be considered admissible.[40]

The principal must pay the commercial representative for work done (art. 20.3). Article 89 specifies that the commercial representative's wages should include a fixed wage or commission or both. "Wages" include the premium, bonus payments and all other advantages obtained by virtue of the agreement.[41] [42] [43]

1.3.1.1. Commission

Commission is due for every order accepted by the principal, even if no execution follows the order, except if the non-execution is the commercial representative's fault, which has to be proved by the employer.

The order is considered, except stipulation in the agreement of another duration, to be accepted within a period of one month after passing the order, except where the principal (article 90), within this period and in writing, refuses to fulfil the order. This gives the principal the freedom to refuse what he does not wish to accept but guarantees the commercial representative that it will be done within a certain time. The principal cannot refuse without due cause. The commercial representative has a right to work (art. 20).

The commercial representative also has, apart from direct commissions, and in so far as he has an exclusive right over his territory, the right to indirect comissions on the business transacted by the principal without his assistance but with clients from his territory (art. 93).

The basis for the calculation is stipulated in the agreement, if it is not, the price that is shown on the order or on the accepted order will be the basis for calculation. Failing this the price list, the current price or price tariff, will be used (art. 96).

The principal must provide the commercial representative with a monthly statement of the commissions due to him, together with all exhibits relating to these commissions.

---

[39] Arbh. Luik, 8.3.50, R.D.S. 1951, 52.

[40] Arbh. Brussels, 25.5.73, J.T.T. 1974, 15; Arbh. Brussels, 15.2.79, J.T.T. 1979, 222, Arbh. Ghent, 24.1.73, T.S.R. 1974, 50,; J.T.T. 1974, 24; Arbrb. Brussels 13.2.76, J.T.T. 1976, 167.

[41] Tielemans and Nockels, op. cit., II 3-4, 41 e.v. Delegrange et al., op. cit., 3.2/3 e.v.

[42] V. Vannes, "Quelques aspects du droit à la commission du représentant de commerce", J.T.T. 1984, 453.

[43] Arbrb. Antwerp, 27.1.76, J.T.T. 1976, 282; Arbh. Brussels, 31.7.79, J.T.T. 1980, 218; Arbrb. Bergen, 22.9.80, T.S.R. 1984, 78; Arbh. Luik, 27.4.83, J.T.T. 1983, 296; Arbh. Luik, 19.1.82, J.T.T. 1982, 227.

If wages are based both on commissions and a fixed wage, they will be payable monthly. Commissions alone may be claimed 15 days after the delivery of the monthly statement.

The principal is obliged to provide a monthly statement, but if the commercial representative has accepted an omission, this omission will not be an acceptable ground for claiming a breach of contract without a period of notice.[44]

Non-payment, partial payment, or late payment of wages due will be considered a unilateral breach of contract by the principal. The payment of the agreed wages at the agreed time is one of the essential elements of the agreement between the principal and his commercial representative.

When an agreement is terminated *without* due cause by the principal or by the commercial representative *with* due cause, the principal will have to pay the commercial representative *an indemnity for goodwill and/or clients* (see chapter 1.7.).

In absence of a specific legal status for the commercial representative, the duties and rights of the principal are subject only to general legal principles and can thus be agreed upon between parties without restriction, but the parties will benefit from a detailed arrangement.

The most important duty of the *principal towards the commercial agent* is to pay him for work done. A fixed wage paid to the commercial agent will often be interpreted as a sign of subordination and the agreement between principal and intermediary as an agreement for commercial representation.

This is not always correct. It is more usual to pay commission and only commission to the commercial agent, but nothing prevents the parties from agreeing to a fixed wage during a starting period.[45]

The commission can be directly or indirectly. The parties usually agree on the percentage according to what is customary.[46]

It may be useful to explain what is meant by indirect sales. The commission will be calculated, as agreed on the basis of a percentage on the amount of the invoices. The parties should also agree on the time the payment should become due, for example, after acceptance of the order by the principal, after execution of the order, at delivery or at the time of payment by the client. Article 1134 of the Civil Code states:

> "All agreements which have been legally concluded, engage, those who concluded, as law.
> They cannot be revoked except by mutual agreement or on legal grounds.
> They have to be executed in good faith".

Except with good reason, which does not necessarily have to be communicated but which does have to exist, the principal has to execute the orders passed on to him by the commercial agent. A systematic or arbitrary refusal cannot be accepted, because the commercial agent is not remunerated with a fixed wage but from the orders submitted. The principal should inform his commercial agent if he is not able to execute an order. He should

---

[44] Cass. 29.9.76, T.S.R. 1977, 278.
[45] Arbh. Brussels, 14.11.79, T.S.R. 1980, 104.
[46] Brussels, 21.11.79, R.W. 1980-81, 194.

also give his commercial agent all necessary information and documentation in order to perform the best he can (general conditions, price lists, etc.). If granted, the principal must respect the commercial agent's exclusivity.

As with the commercial representation, it is the rule that any unilateral modification by the principal of an essential element of the agreement should be considered unacceptable and a unilateral breach of contract, unless the modification does not bring any damage, financial or other, to the commercial agent.

The rights and duties of the principal in relation to his commercial agent are laid down in the Directive of the Council, article 4:

> "1. In his relations with his commercial agent a principal must act dutifully and in good faith.
>   (a) provide his commercial agent with the necessary documentation relating to the goods concerned;
>   (b) obtain for his commercial agent the information necessary for the performance of the agency contract, and in particular notify the commercial agent within a reasonable period once he anticipates that the volume of commercial transactions will be significantly lower than that which the commercial agent could normally have expected.
> 3. A principal must, in addition, inform the commercial agent within a reasonable period of his acceptance, refusal, and of any non-execution of a commercial transaction which the commercial agent has procured for the principal".

Article 5 states that the parties may not derogate from these provisions.

1.4. The Commercial Agent's (and Representative's) Duties and Rights

From the definition of commercial representation it follows that the commercial representative has to contact and visit clients, with a view to negotiating or transacting business, except insurance, on behalf of, and in the name of one or more principals. (Article 4 of the Law Concerning Labour Agreements). In addition to the general regulations of this law, he is subject to certain *general obligations*, i.e., he owes his principal respect and esteem and during the agreement he has to consider decency and good character (art. 16).

According to article 17, he is obliged:

(1) to carry out his work with carefulness, honesty and exactness, in the time, place and manner agreed;
(2) to act according to the orders and instructions given to him by the principal with a view to carrying out the agreement;
(3) after the termination of the agreement not
    (a) to divulge any trade secrets, business or other secrets concerning personal or confidential matters acquired during the execution of his work;
    (b) to execute or help others execute acts of unfair competition;

(4) to avoid endangering his own safety, or that of his fellow-employees, his principal or third parties;
(5) to return to his principal in good condition, the materials used by him.

The commercial representative also has a number of rights (the law cited in this list is the Law Concerning Labour Agreements, unless otherwise stated):

- the right to respect from his principal (art. 16);
- the right to work (art. 20(1));
- the right to safety and healthy work conditions (art. 20(2));
- the right to fulful his religious and civil duties (art. 20(5));
- the right to a kind welcome when visiting the principal (art. 20(6));
- the right to care from his principal over worktools and personal belongings (art. 20(7));
- the right to remuneration (arts. 20(3) and 89) (see 1.3.);
- the right to an indemnity for goodwill and for clientèle (art. 101) (see 1.7.);
- the right to observe legal feast-days (see the Law on Feast-Days of 4 January 1974 and the decree of 18 April 1974);
- the right not to work on Sunday (art. 66 of the Labour Law of 15 March 1971);
- the right to regulated working hours for young employees in respect of night work and maternity (arts. 30, 35, and 39 of the labour law of 19 March 1971.[47]

Apart from this, the parties are free to agree any other conditions.

1.4.1.2. Del credere

The *del credere* clause holds the commercial representative responsible for the insolvency of the client (see also 1.5.3.).

Stipulations concerning products sector, clients and organization, mentioned in the agreement, either commit the commercial representative to certain obligations or confer rights on him.

Finally, the commercial representative can be obliged to deliver a bond, which guarantees the execution of his obligations (arts. 23, 23 bis and 24).

The duties and rights of the commercial agent are not specified by law, but from the definition of the commercial agency, it follows that the commercial agent contacts and visits clients, with a view to negotiating or transacting business on behalf of, and in the name of one or more principal(s).

The commercial agent can be *obliged by agreement*:

- to remain within a certain territory;
- to visit specific clients;
- to suggest only certain products;
- to place a certain infrastructure at the disposal of the commercial agency and bear all the costs of it (this obligation, however, should never give evidence of subordination of the commercial agent to the principal or

---

[47] Delagrange et al., *op. cit.*, 3.2/26 e.v.

the agreement would be interpreted as one of commercial representation);

- to achieve a minimum turnover under penalty of losing his exclusivity or having his territory reduced (recent jurisprudence has decided that imposing a minimum turnover is not evidence of subordination.[48]
- to remain *del credere* for the insolvency of his clients:
- not to compete with his principal after termination of the contract:[49] The non-competition clause is subject to the EEC competition rules, particularly article 85(1) of the EEC Treaty if of course the agreement has a perceptible influence on trade between Member States. It would be called a competition restrictive clause if the agent was an independent economic entity and therefore contrary to article 85(1) of the EEC Treaty. An exemption could be obtained according to article 85(3) of the EEC Treaty;
- not to transfer the agreement or not to transfer without consent of the principal.

The agreement can also specify the rights of the commercial agent. In absence of an agreement, the commercial agent will in any case have the right to negotiate (or contract) in a totally independent way. Unless it is stipulated to the contrary in the contract, it is accepted that the commercial agent collaborates with others, with sub-agents, etc.[50] Working with helpers may not result in a total substitution, otherwise a transfer of agreement would have occurred which could, depending on the stipulation in the agreement, be rendered null by default of the consent of the principal.[51]

The commercial agent also has the right to remuneration.

The commercial agent, like the commercial representative, must act according to general legal principals, of which the most important is to execute the agreement in good faith (art. 1134 of the Civil Code). This means he must:

- further the negotiations;
- keep clients informed;
- report on his activities to the principal;
- safeguard the interests of the principal by executing his work carefully and precisely,[52] [53] by keeping the principal's trade secrets confidential, and so on.

The Council Directive regulates the commercial agent's rights and duties in articles 3, 5, 6–12 and 20. Article 3 states:

> "1. In performing his activities a commercial agent must look after his principal's interests and act dutifully in good faith.
> 2. In particular, a commercial agent must:

---

[48] Arbrb. Verviers 28.9.77, J.T.T. 1978, 42; Arbrb. Luik, 18.9.79, J.T.T. 1980, 204.
[49] Cass. 11.5.77, J.T.T. 1978, 144.
[50] Kh. Brussels, 3.12.63, J.C.B. 1064, 118.
[51] Delagrange et al., *op. cit.*, 2/2/8 e.v.
[52] Brussels, 8.11.79, Pas. 1980, II, 1; Kh. Brussels, 15.3.79, B.R.H. 1980, 8.
[53] Kh. Kortrijk, 4.9.81, R.W. 1982-83, 1399; Kh. Brussels, 31.1.80, B.R.H. 1980, 2120.

(a) make proper efforts to negotiate and, where appropriate, conclude the transactions he is instructed to take care of;
(b) communicate to his principal all the necessary information available to him;
(c) comply with reasonable instructions given by his principal".

According to article 5 parties cannot derogate from these provisions. Articles 6–12 provide for regulations concerning remuneration. Article 17 regulates the indemnification and compensation due to the commercial agent after termination of the agency contract. These articles cannot be analysed in detail for reasons of space.

Finally, articles 20(2) and 3 provide in the validity requirements for a competition clause called "restraint of trade clause":

"2. A restraint of trade clause shall be valid only if and to the extent that:
(a) it is concluded in writing; and
(b) it relates to the geographical area or the group of customers and the geographical area entrusted to the commercial agent and to the kind of goods by his agency under the contract.
3. A restraint of trade clause shall be valid for not more than two years after termination of the agency contract".

Two clauses deserve particular attention, namely the non-competition clause and the *del credere* clause.

1.4.1.3. Non-competition

The non-competition clause forbids the commercial representative, when leaving his principal's company, to compete with his principal. He is prevented from exercising similar activities, either on his own behalf or by entering a contract with a competitive employer. (Unfair competition is legally, forbidden by articles 17(3) and 4 of the Law Concerning Labour Agreements, notwithstanding any agreement to the contrary).

An employee who does not earn more than 677,000 Belgian Francs cannot be subject to a non-competition clause. This clause will, if included in the agreement, be null (art. 104). If the employee's wage is higher than 677,000 Belgian Francs, the non-competition clause will be acceptable. By "wage", is meant a fixed wage, commissions and all other advantages due according to the agreement is meant. The wage level is adjusted every year on 1 January to the fluctuations of the wage index figure.

To be valid, the competition clause must satisfy four requirements. It must:

(a) concern only similar activities;[54]
(b) be limited to one year;
(c) be limited to the sector in which the commercial representative executes his work;
(d) be written, under penalty of nullity (art.104).

---

[54] Brussels, 23.1.81, J.T. 1981, 289. Cass. 25.6.70, Pas. 1970, I, 947; Arbrb. Doornik, 9.5.80, J.T.T. 1980, 251; Arbrb. Brussels, 12.2.79, T.S.R. 1979, 349. Arbrb. Kortrijk, 28.5.74, J.T.T. 1974, 280.

If one of the three first requirements is not fulfilled, the clause is null.

The no-competition clause, will have no effect if the agreement is terminated:

(a) during the period of probation;
(b) after the period of probation by the employer without proper cause;
(c) by the representative with proper cause.

The fact that the commercial representative's agreement mentions a competition clause (whether valid or not), presumes a contribution of clients by the commercial representative and thus a right to an indemnity for goodwill and/or clients (art. 105). The principal can refute this presumption by proving that the commercial representative has not contributed clients (see 1.7.)

When enforcing a valid non-competition clause which has been violated, article 106 of the Law Concerning Labour Agreements says, the principal may claim compensation, if the agreement so provides to a maximum of three months' wages. He can claim a higher compensation if he proves the existence and extent of the damage caused by the violation. If the principal can prove that he has suffered disadvantage and also its seriousness, he will be allowed to claim a compensation of more than three months' wages. But the agreement cannot fix compensation for violation in excess of three months' wages or the compensation clause will be null.

1.5. Liabilities of the Principal and Agent during the Term of the Agency

1.5.1. The principal as against the agent

Every employer, hence also the principal, is according to article 1384 of the Civil Code, responsible for his employees, hence also commercial representatives. He is responsible for damages caused to his employees, for example through an accident.

Article 19 of the Law Concerning Labour Agreements stipulates that the employer is responsible for damage or wear and tear caused by the normal use of worktools and for accidental loss by the employee. Despite the absence of legal regulation, the same principles in our view, apply to the principal in his relations with the commercial agent.

1.5.2. The principal as against third parties

The commercial agent, like the commercial representative, acts on behalf of and in the name of one or more principal(s). Third parties may therefore rightly presume they will be legally bound only to the principal.

According to article 18 of the Law Concerning Labour Agreements, the employee, including the commercial representative, is responsible to third parties for deception and serious offences as well as less serious but recurring offences. It follows that the employer–principal is responsible against third parties for the faults of his commercial representative with the exception of deception, serious offence and any less important but recurring offences of his commercial representative. This principle, in our view, applies in commercial agency.

It may normally be presumed that the commercial representative or agent has the competence to negotiate or transact business. However, if the commercial representative or agent was not competent to represent his principal for a particular transaction but failed to inform the client, the client may rely on the presumption of the responsibility of the principal for the acts of his representative or agent and the principal will be held responsible for the consequences of the business concluded.

The principal, on grounds of accountability, remains responsible as against third parties for acts of this commercial representative or agent, even if he and his commercial representative or agent decided in common to restrict the scope of representation.

The employer–principal will also, according to article 19 of the Law Concerning Labour Agreements, be responsible for the work delivered, if defective.

The Council Directive of 25 July 1985 on products liability should also be borne in mind.[55] The provisions of this Directive should have been incorporated in Belgian law by 1 August 1988, but have not as yet been incorporated. This Directive provides that the producer shall be liable for damage caused by a defect in his product. The injured person is required to prove the damage, the defect and the causal relationship between defect and damage.

Article 3 gives an extensive definition of producer, i.e. anyone who puts his name, trade mark or other distinguishing feature on a product or who gives himself out as its producer as well as any person who imports into the community a product for sale, hire, leasing or any form of distribution in the course of his business.

In Belgium a third party may also invoke article 1381 of the Civil Code to claim indemnification for damage as a result of the principal's fault.

1.5.3. The agent as against the principal

The responsibility of the *commercial representative* is governed by articles 18, 19 and 107 of the Law Concerning Labour Agreements. From article 18 it follows that the employee, (and hence the commercial representative) who, in the execution of the agreement, causes damage to his principal (or third parties, see 1.5.4.) is responsible for any deception he has caused and any serious offence. The commercial representative cannot avoid this responsibility, except through a collective labour agreement which has been declared obligatory by the King.

From article 19 it follows that the commercial representative will be held responsible during the whole execution of the agreement for his defective work until acceptance of his work by the principal.

Finally, according to article 107 the commercial representative will be

---

[55] O.J.L. 382/17 (86/653/EEC).

held responsible for the insolvency of the clients. An obligatory *del credere* clause regulates this responsibility.

In the absence of deception or serious offences the representative's liability will be limited to repaying the commission received in respect of the irrecoverable claim on the client; in cases of deception or serious offence, his responsibility will not be restricted to his commission.

The *commercial agent*, according to general legal principles concerning responsibility, may be held responsible for deception he has caused and serious offences.

In such an agreement, a *del credere* clause, may be used. There is of course no legal restriction on the responsibility of the commercial representative, but such restriction can be agreed between the agent and his principal. It is advisable to put such a clause in writing.

1.5.4. The agent as against third parties

The *commercial representative* is responsible as against third parties for deception or serious offences or less important but recurring faults (article 18 of the Law Concerning Labour Agreements). He cannot avoid this responsibility. The general theory on responsibility is also applicable to the *commercial agent*, i.e. that he will also be responsible for deception and serious offences or less serious but recurring faults.

1.6. Term and Termination

1.6.1. Term

The labour agreement and therefore the agreement of *commercial representation* can be concluded for an indefinite or fixed duration, for part-time work, for fixed work or for replacement of a commercial representative who cannot execute his work for a certain period of time.

As agreements for a fixed term, for part-time work, fixed work and replacement have to be in writing, it will be easy to take cognisance of the term of the agreement. Only an agreement for commercial representation of an indeterminate duration need not be in writing and will therefore cause more difficulty in determining the term thereof.

An agreement for a *commercial agency* may also be concluded for a fixed or indefinite period. Such agreements may be concluded in writing or orally. In addition, a written agreement which does not specify duration will be considered to be concluded for an indefinite period.

1.6.1.1. Suspension

The execution of an agreement of commercial representation may sometimes be legally suspended, in cases such as:

- disablement;
- maternity (art. 76 of the Law Concerning Labour Agreements);
- technical disorder (art. 49 of the same law);
- bad weather (art. 50);
- lack of work for economic reasons (art. 51).

The Council Directive provides that the agreement of Commercial Agency may be concluded either for an indefinite duration (article 14) or for a fixed period (art. 15).

1.6.2. Termination

An agreement of commercial representation can be terminated according to article 32 which stipulates that, subject to the general rules of termination of obligations, they terminate:

" • in course of time;
  • on completion of the work;
  • by the will of both parties if the agreement was concluded for an indeter-minate duration or in case of a proper reason to terminate;
  • through the death of the employee, i.e. the commercial representative;
  • by force majeur".

The agreement is not terminated by the death of the principal (art. 33).

Article 32(3) stipulates that the labour agreement for employees and hence for commercial representatives, can be terminated by the will or desire of both parties.

Article 37(1) re-affirms and states that each party has the right to terminate an agreement for an indefinite duration provided notice is given to the other party. This notice can be a period of time or compensation (art. 39) or if neither if there is a proper reason for termination.

Article 37 regulates notice on penalty of nullity; it should be given in writing, and by registered post or by writ, and should specify the starting and ending dates of the period of notice.

Notice by registered letter takes effect only on the third working day (all days, except for Sundays and public holidays) after the date of forwarding.

Article 82 stipulates that the period of notice begins on the first day of the month following the month in which notice is given.

Periods of notice differ according to whether the annual remuneration is lower or higher than 677,000 Belgian Francs or higher than 1,354,000 Belgian Francs. the wage level is adjusted every year to the wage index figure (art. 131).

If annual remuneration is lower than 677,000 Belgian Francs, the period of notice should be at least three months for employees with less than five years' service. This period will be augmented by three months at the beginning of every new period of five years' service. If the agreement is terminated by the employee, those periods will be halved.

If annual remuneration is higher than 677,000 Belgian Francs, either the parties can agree upon a notice period at the earliest at the time of termination or a judge will fix the period. If notice is given by the employer, the period of notice should not be shorter than the periods mentioned above. If the notice is given by the employee, the period of notice should not be longer than four and a half months for remuneration between 677,000 Belgian Francs and 1,354,000 Belgian Francs, and not longer than six months in cases of remuneration higher than 1,354,000 Belgian Francs.

Length of service is calculated from the time when the employee took up the principal's duties, in whatever capacity. Suspensions do not affect length of service, unless they were differently agreed. If, however, the agreement had already been terminated once and had really been interrupted, only the period after the interruption is considered.

If one party receives notice and is not satisfied with the period of notice,this party may ask the court to fix a reasonable period according to one of the formulae available, such as Claeys, Van Geel, Major, and Chavez; these formulae determine notice according to length of service, age, remuneration and the nature of the job.[56]

If the party who terminates the contract does not give a notice period that party must give the other compensation in lieu of notice, according to article 39 of the Law Concerning Labour Agreements (see 1.7.).

An agreement with a commercial representative can also be terminated without a period of notice or compensation if dismissal is justified by a serious shortcoming which makes it impossible, immediately and permanently, to continue employing the representative (art. 35).[57] [58]

A principal can only terminate an agreement with due cause:

(1) if he dismisses the other party within three working days of cognisance of the cause (no formality has to be observed in dismissal; it can be done in writing or orally, though dismissal in writing and by registered letter is advised); and

(2) if he gives to the party dismissed, within three working days of dismissal, by registered post or through a writ, a detailed account of the cause.

If the dismissed party does not accept the reasons for dismissal and therefore the termination without notice or compensation in lieu, he may claim through the courts, payment of compensation and an indemnity for goodwill and/or clientèle (see 1.7.).

An agreement for a *commercial agency* can be terminated in the course of time, on completion of the work, or through death of the agent.

An agreement for a commercial agency for an indefinite duration can be terminated at any time by either party with or without notice or compensation in lieu, according to the terms of the agreement.

An agreement for a fixed duration which continues *de facto* after the date of termination should be considered as an agreement for an indefinite duration. So too should an agreement for a fixed duration which provides for an extension but not its duration.

The general rule is that the commercial agent, when his agreement for an

---

[56] W. Van Eeckhoutte, *Sociaal zakboekje*, Kluwer, Antwerp, 1987, 1, 56 e.v.

[57] E. Leboucq, "De beeindiging van de arbeidsovereenkomst wegens dringende reden in de wet van 3 juli 1978, betreffende de arbeid overeenkomsten", J.T.T. 1979, 53.

[58] Cass., 2.2.81, T.S.R. 1980, nr. 3., 246; Arbh. Luik, 17.4.84, T.S.R. 1984, nr. 7, 487; Arbrb. Brussels, 2.6.82, J.T.T. 10.12.84, 488; Arbrb. Antwerp, 15.5.84, T.S.R. 1984, nr. 8, 589; Arbh. Brussels, 22.5.84, T.S.R. 1984, 299; Arbh. Luik, 11.6.79, J.L. 1980, 316; Arbh. Brussels, 2.11.83, J.T.T. 1984, 483; Arbh. Antwerp, 14.1.85, R.W., 1984-85, 2218; Arbh. Brussels, 22.12.82, J.T.T. 1984, 486; Arbh. Luik, 29.1.80, J.T.T. 1981, 18.

indefinite period is terminated, is entitled to receive compensation if the notice of termination is given contrary to the requirements of good faith and equity.[59]

In absence of any written agreement article 1134 Civil Code which gives an obligation to execute the agreement in good faith, should be referred to. Article 1134 Civil Code contains a stipulation, that an agreement should not be terminated in an abusive, untimely and unreasonable way.[60] In such a case, the agreement should be terminated after a period of notice or with compensation in lieu if it seems impossible for the principal and agent to continue to work together.[61]

The source rule applies to the early termination of an agreement of fixed duration.

In case of termination with due cause, no notice or compensation in lieu will be due. On the contrary, compensation for damages could be claimed.

The Council Directive provides that an indemnity and compensation should be paid to the agent after termination of the agency agreement (but see 1.7.).

1.7. Indemnity

1.7.1. Indemnity for goodwill and/or clientèle

If the principal terminates the agreement without due cause or if the *commercial representative* terminates the agreement for valid reasons, the principal must pay the commercial representative an indemnity for goodwill and/or clientèle for the clientèle he has brought and which he loses because of the termination of the agreement, unless the principal proves that the commercial representative suffers no loss at all through the termination (art. 101 of the Law Concerning Labour Agreements) for example if the commercial representative starts to work for a competitor selling identical products within the same territory.[62] [63] [64] [65]

It is important to identify the introduction of clientèle (through client lists, etc.), with the onus of proof being on the employee.[66]

Indemnity is payable only after service of at least one year and will be equal to the three months' wages for a commercial representative who has been acting for the same principal for a period of one to five years. This period will be increased by one month for each period of five years' service.[67] [68]

[59] Cass. 19.9.83, T.B.H. 1984, 276; Kh. Ghent, 1.6.84, RKW 84-85, 1721.
[60] Brussel, 13.10.80, J.L.B. 1981, I, 149; Liège, 20.4.61, Pas. 1961, II, 244; Rb.Kh. Ghent, 9.4.75, J.T. 1975, 511; Rb.Kh. Brussel, 15.1.79, J.L.B. 1979, 602.
[61] Brussels, 13.10.80, J.L. 1981, I, 149; Antwerp, 4.2.80, J.L.B. 1980, I, 456; Rb.Kh. Brussels, 10.5.82, T.B.H. 1983, 244.
[62] Thielemans and Nockels, *op. cit.*, 98 e.v.
[63] W. Reynders, "Indemnité d'éviction", Aperçu de la Jurisprudence".
[64] Delagrange et al., *op. cit.*, 3.4/63.
[65] Arbh. Brussels, 22.4.75, R.D.S. 1976, 357.
[66] Arbh. Ghent, 24.3.75, R.D.S. 1975, 171; Arbh. Brussels, 8.5.74, V.B.O. 1975, 387; Arbrb. Antwerp, 20.10.80, R.W. 1980-81, 1731.
[67] P. Crahay and J. Jadot, *L'indemnité d'éviction du représentant de commerce*, Larcier, Brussels, 1980, 15 e.v.
[68] B. Graulich, "L'indemnité d'éviction du représentant de commerce", Soc. Kron; 1982, 434.

If wages consist partly of commission, this part will be taken as the average commission over the last 12 months. "Wages" also cover the advantages acquired by the agreement (art. 101 of the Law Concerning Labour Agreements).[69] [70]

If the commercial representative wants to claim an indemnity for goodwill and/or clientèle, he must:

(a) have been acting on behalf of the same principal for at least one year as a commercial representative, including periods of suspension;[71]

(b) have brought clients to his principal either on entering upon his principal's duty by bringing clients with him or during the term of the agreement by increasing the existing clientèle or, if there is none, finding new clients. The introduction of clientèle need not be substantial but neither may it be insignificant.[72] The clients need not to stay loyal to the principal.[73] The commercial representative has to prove the introduction by him of clientèle except if his agreement provides for a non-competition clause. He then is presumed to have brought clientèle to his principal and his principal should, if he wishes to do so, prove the contrary;[74]

(c) have terminated the agreement with due cause or been dismissed without due cause;[75]

(d) have suffered a disadvantage by the loss of clientèle, but he does not have to proof this loss. The principal, if he wants to avoid payment, will have to prove the contrary. There is no disadvantage for the commercial representative if the clientèle has followed him to his new job or if he stops his activities.[76]

The supplementary indemnity to the indemnity for goodwill and/or clientèle will be due to the commecial representative:

(a) if the agreement is terminated by the principal;

(b) if there is due cause for which the principal is responsible;

(c) if the commercial representation is subject to an indemnity for goodwill and/or clientèle; and

(d) if the disadvantages suffered through the termination of the agreement

[69] Arbh. Luik, 25.2.82, J.T.T. 1982, 226; Arbh. Brussels, 5.10.82, R.W. 1983-84, 449; Arbh. Brussels, 16.12.81, T.S.R. 1984, 162, H. Demeester; Arbrb. Antwerp, 15.11.83, Soc. Kron. 1984, 353, D. Rijck; Otherwise: Arbh. Brussels, 29.6.82, T.S.R. 1982, 627; Arbh. Antwerp 4.10.82, J.T.T. 1983, 95.

[70] D. Rickx. "De berekeningsbasis van de uitwinningsvergoeding voor handelsvertegenwoordigers", Soc. Kron., 1984, 358-360.

[71] Cass. 12.9.83, T.S.R. 1983, 484; Soc. Kron. 1983, 439; Cass. 30.1.84, T.S.R. 1984, 153.

[72] Cass. 24.3.86, R.W. 1985-86, 2796.

[73] Arbh. Brussel, 12.1.82, J.T.T. 1983, 301; Arbh. Brussel, 2.12.83, T.S.R. 1984, 277.

[74] Cass. 22.6.81, R.W. 1981-82, 2118.

[75] Arbh. Brussels, 9.1.80, Med. UBO, 1981, 237.

[76] Arbrb. Namen, 7.12.81, J.T.T. 1982, 169; Cass. 21.12.81, J.T.T. 1982, 200; Arbh. Brussels, 11.1.83, J.T.T. 1983, 297; Cass. 14.9.81, Soc. Kron. 1982, 44.

are greater than those compensated by the indemnity for goodwill and/or clientèle (art. 103).[77]

The *commercial agent* has, in principle, no right to an indemnity for goodwill and/or clientèle,[78] as there is no legal statute covering this point. The parties can, however, provide for such indemnity in the agreement and the court may also decide whether a commercial agency is entitled to an indemnity.[79] Jurisprudence is divided on this question.

The Council Directive, in Article 17(2) provides for the entitlement of the commercial agent to an indemnity for goodwill and/or clientèle and states:

"(a) The commercial agent shall be entitled to an indemnity if and to the extent that:
–he has brought the principal new customers or has significantly increased the volume of business with existing customers and the principal continues to derive substantial benefits from the business with such customers, and
–the payment of this indemnity is equitable having regard to all the circumstances and, in particular, the commission lost by the commercial agent on the business transacted with such customers. Member States may provide for such circumstances also to include the application or otherwise of a restraint of trade clause, within the meaning of article 20;
(b) The amount of the indemnity may not exceed a figure equivalent to an indemnity for one year calculated from the commercial agent's average annual remuneration over the preceding five years and if the contract goes back less than five years the indemnity shall be calculated on the average for the period in question;
(c) The grant of such an indemnity shall not prevent the commercial agent from seeking damages".

Article 18 specifies that:

"The indemnity or compensation referred to in Article 17 shall not be payable:
(a) where the principal has terminated the agency contract because of default attributable to the commercial agent which would justify immediate termination of the agency contract under national law;
(b) where the commercial agent has terminated the agency contract, unless such termination is justified by circumstances attributable to the principal or on grounds of age, infirmity or illness of the commercial agent in consequence of which he cannot reasonably be required to continue his activities;
(c) where, with the agreement of the principal, the commercial agent assigns his rights and duties under the agency contracts to another person".

Finally, according to article 19, parties may not derogate from articles 17 and 18 to the detriment of the commercial agent before the agency contract expires.

---

[77] Arbh. Antwerp, 21.11.81, J.T.T. 1982, 166.
[78] H. Willemart, "La résiliation du contrat d'agence autonome", J.T. 1981, 617.
[79] Antwerp, 4.2.80, B.R.H. 1980, 456; Brussel, 13.10.80, B.R.H. 1981, 148; Contra: Antwerp 13.2.80, R.B.H. 1983, 351; Rb.Kh. Brussels, 21.1.81, B.R.H. 1981, 493.

1.7.2. Compensation for damages

The unilateral notice of termination of an agreement of a *commercial representative* for an indefinite period or the early termination of an agreement for a fixed term shall, except where there is proper cause or notice is given, entitle the other party to compensation in lieu of notice (art. 39 of the Law Concerning Labour Agreements).

This compensation should be equal to the actual remuneration over the period of notice or the remaining period of notice. If the period of notice does not seem satisfactory, supplementary compensation in lieu of notice should be due.

When calculating compensation in lieu of notice, the basis is the wages set out in the agreement and covers other benefits, including those elements which are not defined as wages according to the law of 12 April 1965 concerning the calculation of the remuneration by the employees. This is multiplied by the number of months constituting that period of notice.

If the wages are based partly on commission then the average commission over the last 12 months, is taken into account.

For the exact period of notice, see 1.6.

Finally, certain employees are subject to special protection, so that unreasonable dismissal will have financial implications for the principal. No details are given here, but categories of protected employees are:

- employees with military responsibilities (art. 38, para. 3 - article 39, para. 2 of the Law Concerning Labour Agreements);
- pregnant women (art. 40 of the labour law of 16 March 1971);
- political representatives (art. 5 of the law of 19 July 1976);
- delegates (collective labour agreement no. 5 of 24 May 1971);
- members of the Enterprise Council and Committee for Security, Health and Safety in the Workplace (Royal Decree no. 4 of 11 October 1978).

No period of notice or compensation in lieu of notice is prescribed in the case of termination for due cause; but the party terminating the agreement could seek damages caused by serious offences, deception recurring less serious faults of the other party (art. 18 of the Law Concerning Labour Agreements).

The *commercial agent* has, in specific circumstances, the right to compensation in lieu of notice. there is no legal rule on this point but it follows from the application of article 1134 of the Civil Code.

If the commercial agency agreement, whether it be for an indefinite or fixed period, is terminated by the principal in an abusive, untimely or unreasonable way, the principal would then have to pay the agent a compensation notice (see 1.6).

The Council Directive also foresees the payment of compensation to the commercial agent for the damage suffered as a result of the termination of his relations with the principal. Article 17(3) determines the circumstances of termination which will certainly lead to compensation, stating that:

"The Commercial Agent shall be entitled to compensation for the damage he suffers as a result of the termination of his relations with the principal.

Such damage shall be deemed to occur particularly when the termination takes place in circumstances:
–depriving the commercial agent of the commissions which proper performance of the agency contract would have procured him whilst providing the principal with substantial benefits linked to the commercial agent's activities.
–and/or which have not enabled the commercial agent to amortize the costs and expenses that he had incurred for the performance of the agency contract on the principal's advice".

The intention of pursuing his entitlement to compensation should be notified to the principal within one year following termination.

Finally, article 18 provides that:

"The indemnity or compensation referred to in article 17 shall not be payable:
  (a) where the principal has terminated the agency contract because of default attributable to the commercial agent which would justify immediate termination of the agency contract under national law.
  (b) where the commercial agent has terminated the agency contract, unless such termination is justified by circumstances attributable to the princpal or on grounds of age, infirmity or illness of the commercial agent in consequences of which he cannot reasonably be required to continue his activities;
  (c) where, with the agreement of the principal, the commercial agent assigns his rights and duties under the agency contract to another person.

Article 19 re-affirms that the parties should not derogate from articles 17 and 18 to the detriment of the commercial agent before the agency contract expires.

1.8. Specific Application of EEC Law

1.8.1. Applicable law and jurisdiction

No problems should rise between two Belgian contractual parties as they will most probably provide for the application of the national Belgian law and for the competence of the national Belgian judge. Parties are free to provide for the application of the law of another country[80] but such provision should, at least as far as commercial representation is concerned, never cause the commercial representative a disadvantage, which would be contrary to article 6 of the Law Concerning Labour Agreements.

When agreements have a foreign element, for example, parties of different nationalities, they can choose which law will be applicable. The agreement usually comes under the application of the legal system with which it has the most points of contact, for example the country of execution.

If no specific choice has been made in the agreement, the applicable legal system will be the one closest to the agreement.[81] This is also provided for in

---

[80] Cass. 25.6.75, T.S.R. 1975, 439.
[81] Kh. Brussels, 12.11.79, B.R.H. 1980, 299; Kh. Brussels, 3.9.81, B.R.H. 1982, 630; Kh. Brussels, 10.5.82, T.B.H. 1983, 24; Hof van Justitie EG 18.3.81, zaak 139/80, Publiekatieblad EG 10.4.81.

the European Convention on the law applicable to the undertakings of agreements.[82]

Belgian law will thus usually be applicable if the intermediary has his activity in Belgium. This application of the International private law results from both jurisprudence and doctrine. (See also Crahay and Jadot).[83]

As regards the competent judge, the labour courts will be competent for the commercial representative who has his activity in Belgium. This principle should also be applied by any foreign judge, but for the countries who have joined the Brussels Convention of 27 September 1968 on the recog-nition of foreign judgments, application is made of article 17 of the Convention which accepts the clauses of derogation of competence.

Parties could also opt for arbitration and insert an arbitration clause in their agreement. Arbitration in commercial representation is limited to the commercial representative who has an annual remuneration higher than 1,300,000 Belgian Francs and who is involved in daily management or who has management responsibility (art. 69). Note that the Brussels Convention excludes arbitration.

The commercial courts are competent for the commercial agent. A dero-gation of competence in favour of a foreign judge seems acceptable. Articles 4 and 5 (except 5(5); see the European Court of Justice, 18 March 1981, case 139–80, O.J., EC 10 April 1981 of the Brussels Convention have priority over national competence rules and should always be applied granted the national authorities have approved this convention (arts. 67, 79, 81).

2. Distributorship Agreements

2.1. Distribution

2.1.1. Definition

The Belgian law of 27 July 1961, modified by the law of 13 April 1971, gives a definition of a "contract of concession", "contrat de concession" or "verkoopsconcessieovereenkomst".

Article 1, paragraph 2 states that a distributorship agreement is:

"every agreement by which the manufacturer who grants the distributorship to one or more distributors offers them the right to sell the products manufac-tured or distributed by the manufacturer, in their own name and for their account".

This definition contains several elements.

(a) An agreement

There must be a mutual willingness to behave on the market as distri-

---

[82] European Convention of July first 1964 on the international sale of tangible movable prop-erty.

[83] P. Crahay and J. Jadot, *L'indemmité d'eviction du représentant de commerce*, Lancier, Brussels, 1980, 15 e.v.

butor and supplier. There is no need for a written agreement, but the existence of a written agreement will be helpful in proving the agreement and its contents.

The agreement can furthermore be proved by referring to the circumstances of the commercial relationship.

(b) By which the manufacturer or distributor grants the right to sell the products he manufactured or distributed by himself

A distributorship agreement is not a succession of various sales agreements and consequently is not regulated by the Civil Code rules on sales agreements.

The manufacturer grants special rights to the distributor, by which the distributor is distinguished from other distributors. He can call on special rights from the supplier and has specific obligations. He therefore can claim the protection foreseen in the 1961 law.

A distributorship agreement means a permanent relationship between parties which continues to exist, even if for some time there are no sales.

Several sales with the intention of resale do not constitute a distributorship agreement: the distributor must have granted special rights. The law is not applicable to the sale of "services".

(c) To one or several distributors

The supplier can grant the same rights to several distributors in the same territory. The supplier can also reserve the right to sell himself his product within his territory, unless the contract explicitly forbids it (see exclusive/non-exclusive distributorship).

(d) In his own name and for his own account

This element is essential and distinguishes the distributor from other categories of intermediaries.

The agreement obliges the supplier in the first place to sell the products to the distributor for the duration of the contract, while the distributor must promote the sale of these products in his territory.

The distributorship agreement differs from the sales agreement and is consequently not subject to the Code Civil regulations on the sales agreement. Likewise, a distributorship agreement will not be regulated by general sales conditions specified on the supplier's or distributor's invoice.

The agreement is specifically regulated by the law of 27 July 1961 on the unilateral termination of the exclusive distributorship agreements of indefinite duration – (*Belgian Office Journal* – 5 October 1961, modified 13 April 1971) which contains the definition mentioned above.

Jurisprudence has played an important part in determining whether the agreement is a distributorship agreement or not.

As well as specific rules as to the rights and duties of suppliers and distributors in case of unilateral termination, the agreement is regulated by the Civil Code rules and, more specifically, by the chapter on the obligations. This means that the parties have great freedom in determining their rights and duties.

The name given by the parties to the agreement (agency agreement, representation, franchising) is not significant; what matters is the economic reality, which has to be examined in order to determine whether the distributor sells in his own name and for his own account.

This last element " own name – own account" is essential in the definition. It distinguishes the distributor from:

(a) An agent

An agent contacts potential clients in order to conclude agreements in the name of and for the account of one or more principals.

An agent carries out his activities either for a fixed or for indefinite period as an independent trader.

The agent does not carry the financial risk of the transaction. The insolvency of the buyer will be at the expense of the principal.

(b) A commission agent (commissionaire or commissionaris)

A commission agent undertakes to carry out, in consideration of remuneration, one or several commercial operations in his own name but for the account of somebody else (the principal).

(c) A broker (courtier or makelaar)

A broker is an independent commercial intermediary whose professional activity consists in bringing two or more persons together in order to conclude a legal transaction to which the broker is not a party.

(d) A commercial representative (représentant de commerce or handelsvertegenwoordiger)

A commercial representative has the same function as an agent but is linked to the principal by an employment contract: the commercial representative is, in fact, subordinated to his principal–employer.

On the question of the existence of a distributorship agreement, several cases are relevant.

There is no distributorship agreement when the supplier did not mean to link himself to the distributor and to grant him special rights, which would distinguish him from other resellers.[84]

The existence of a distributorship agreement is not proved by the immediate delivery by the supplier of certain products, the mailing of administrative and publicity material or the supplier's contribution to publicity costs.[85]

A regular flow of sales agreements during a period of 13 years and of publicity material representing the distributor as being the "sales distributor of the products", the interference of the supplier in fixing prices, must lead to the conclusion of the existence of a "priviliged position", "granting special rights" to the distributor.[86]

[84] Verviers, 30 June 1986, R.G. 1085/84, not published.
[85] Comm. Brussels, 30 June 1983, R.D.C. 1984, 451.
[86] Cass., 12 June 1986, R.W. 1986-87, 1146.

2.1.1.1. Exclusive/non-exclusive/exclusive purchasing

The distinction between exclusive and non-exclusive distributorship agreements is important since the protection granted by the law of 27 July 1961 applies only to:

- *fully exclusive distributorships* in which no other distributor is appointed in the territory;
- *nearly exclusive distributorships* in which the distributor sells more or less all contractual products;
- *distributorships implying important obligations*, which would put a heavy burden on the distributor after having terminated the distributorship.

Exclusive distributorship: The Law does not provide any definition of "exclusive" distributorship but we can rely on the statements of the Belgian Conseil d'Etat and the Supreme Court.

According to the Conseil d'Etat, an exclusive distributorship is any agreement by which the supplier is obliged to sell to the distributor, and only to the distributor, products intended for resale in the distributor's territory, with the exclusion of all other distributors.

The Belgian Supreme Court at first followed the above definition (Decision of 11 March 1971, but later gave an enlarged definition:

> "An agreement is exclusive even when the supplier appoints several distributors, to sell all or some of the products in a given territory, or when he reserves the right to sell these products to himself".[87]

According to this definition an exclusive distributorship can be shared by several distributors.

In connection with the nature of the distributorship agreement, this raises the question of third parties. In what way could a distributor oppose the selling by a third party of products while he has an exclusive distributorship with a supplier? The distributor has legal claims against the supplier for not respecting his exclusive rights. The third party is aware, or should be, of the existence of the exclusive rights of the distributor, but he cannot be responsible for acts of unfair competition.

This discussion on the nature of the distributorship agreement (exclusive/non-exclusive) must be seen from the point of view of EEC law and jurisprudence (article 85).

2.1.1.2. Nearly exclusive distributorships in which the distributor sells more or less all contractual products

In Belgium, a disposition protects the open or incomplete distributorship, in which the distributor sells almost all products which are the subject of a distributorship agreement, whereas the supplier, or a third party acting in collaboration with this supplier, sells only a small part of the products of a distributorship agreement. The law used the word "almost" without specifying further, and is up to the court to interpret each case separately.

---

[87] Cass., 22 January 1981, Pas. I, 541.

Recently, the Brussels Court stated that the distributor who sells 30–35 per cent of all products on the market is not engaged in a quasi-exclusive distributorship.

2.1.1.3. Distributorships implying onerous obligations from the distributor would suffer damages in the event of the termination of the distributorship

This disposition protects the "weaker" party with a large investment in the concession, who had considerable expenses.

For this clause to be valid four conditions must be fulfilled.

(1) The obligations imposed by the supplier must be large. The question of "large" relates to the nature and extent of the distributorship, and interpretation is left to the court.

Some examples can be found in court decisions:

- restrictions on selling outside a given area;
- the prohibition to sell to a certain type of purchaser;
- the obligation to organize work according to the supplier's instructions;
- the obligation to organize after sales service;
- the obligation to sell/purchase a minimum quota during a certain period;
- the obligation to have a stock of goods/equipment according to the supplier's wishes;
- the obligation to advertise or to spend money on publicity;
- restrictions on selling competitive products.

(2) These obligations must be imposed by the supplier on the distributor and do not include agreements by which a distributor accepts obligations, not set out in the contract, but on his own initiative.

(3) These obligations must be closely linked to the distributorship, and must not simply be the outcome of a normal commercial activity. As a result of these obligations the distributor has received his distributorship.

(4) The extent of these obligations must be so great that the distributor would suffer considerable damages in the event of the termination of the agreement.

This condition excludes distributorship agreements which contain onerous obligations already contracted during the execution of the contract.

In conclusion, most of the distributorship agreements fall into one of the three categories mentioned above. The 1961 Law is applicable to distributorships of these three types as long as they are concluded for an indefinite period.

As we will see further on, an agreement is considered to be for an indefinite period if it is impossible to know at the time when the agreement was made when it will come to an end.

2.1.2. Conclusion of the contract (special conditions)

The Belgian Law does not impose any special conditions for the conclusion of a distributorship agreement. There is no need for a written agreement. Nevertheless, a written agreement is helpful in avoiding discussion between suppliers and distributors as to the existence of an agreement and their reciprocal rights and duties.

A fortiori, there are no formal regulations as to the draft of written agreement.

In the absence of a written agreement, the existence of a distributorship agreement may be proved by all means, including testimonies, depositions, and the contents of all exchanged correspondence.

2.1.3. The supplier's duties and rights

As discussed earlier, a distributorship agreement, according to Belgian law, is regulated:

(a) at the end of an agreement, in accordance with the Law of 27 July 1961 (see 2.1.6. and 2.1.7.);
(b) during the term of the distributorship agreement, by common law principles and in particular by the Civil Code rules on agreements.

Consequently, parties are free to agree on their reciprocal rights and duties within the limits imposed by public order, morality and the compulsory legal provisions of the Law of 27 July 1961 with regard to the termination of a contract for indefinite period.

The agreement between the parties has the force of law, ie the parties are bound to their agreement and that agreements must be executed in good faith (article 1134 of the Civil Code). The following clauses are most the frequently used in distributorship agreements.

2.1.3.1. The supplier's duties

The supplier must first guarantee the right to sell his products on the agreed territory. This right may be exclusive or not. In an exclusive distributorship, the supplier will refrain from selling his products directly or indirectly to persons other than the distributor. He can eventually also compel other dealers not to sell his products in the territory specified in the contract.

The supplier can also agree not to sell directly in the specified territory himself.

Exclusive distribution clauses are forbidden by article 85 of the EEC Treaty. But the obligation to guarantee the right to sell does not mean that the supplier has to accept all orders the distributor may give to him. In accordance with the general principles of article 1134 of the Civil Code (all agreements must be executed in good faith), the supplier must not, systematically or arbitrarily, refuse to fulfil the orders the distributor gives him.

The parties may freely agree the terms of their agreement, except for matters subject to the compulsory rules of the 1961 Law.

2.1.3.2. The supplier's rights

The supplier's rights are the counterpart of the distributor's duties. They may also be freely established in the agreement. The supplier will seek a clause in the contract which allows him to end the contract immediately without any term of notice whenever a certain event (e.g. a contractual short-coming) occurs. This clause is known as "la clause résolutoire expresse", and most frequently used where certain sales quota are not fulfilled. In this case, resolution occurs automatically. The court, when faced with this clause, can only examine whether the event actually occurred or the short-coming really existed. It is not competent to examine the seriousness of the shortcoming.

Distributors should clearly try to avoid the insertion of this type of clause, which, from a legal point of view, is valid (see also 2.1.6.2.2.).[88]

2.1.4. The distributor's duties and rights

2.1.4.1. The distributor's duties

The chief obligation for the distributor is the promotion of products as specified. The parties also have the right to agree other clauses on matters such as a minimum quota, exclusivity, and non-competition clause.

2.1.4.2. The distributor's rights

The distributor's rights broadly correspond to the supplier's duties (see 2.1.3.1.), but the distributor is almost completely free to organize his market-ing policy, and the supplier should never intervene in the fixing of prices by the distributor.

2.1.5. Liabilities of supplier and distributor during the term of the distributorship agreement

There is a contractual relationship between suppliers and distributors in a distributorship agreement, and the distributor sells the supplier's products in his own name and for his own account. The supplier and distributor may, in their agreement, freely agree their reciprocal liabilities, while suppiler and distributor will have an extra-contractual liability towards third parties. This can only be a product of liability.

2.1.5.1. The supplier as against the distributor

The liability can only be invoked in so far as it has been provided for in the contract (see 2.1.3.).

2.1.5.2. The supplier as against third parties

For the supplier, third parties are consumers. The general principles of the Civil Code as regards liability and the rules of product liability are appli-cable.

2.1.5.3. The distributor as against the supplier

See 2.1.5.1.

2.1.5.4. The distributor as against third parties

See 2.1.5.2.

[88] Cass., 29 April 1979, J.C.B. 1980, 440.

2.1.6. Term and termination

The Belgian distributor, or the distributor whose territory is in Belgium, benefits from strong protection under the Law of 27 July 1961, (as modified on 13 April 1971) on the unilateral termination of distributorship agreements. Legal protection varies according to whether the agreement is concluded for an indefinite or fixed period.

2.1.6.1. Term distributorship agreements of determinate duration

An agreement is concluded for a fixed period when it ends through a definite future event which will occur independently of the will of the parties and which is known by them or which can be known at the moment of the moment of the conclusion of the contract.[89]

Since the Law of 13 April 1971 who passed, a distributorship for a fixed duration must be terminated by notice given by registered mail, at least three months and at most six months before the end of the term.

By not doing so, the parties are considered to have tacitly renewed the agreement, either for an indefinite duration or for the duration provided in clause of renewal.

If there is no specific clause in the contract on duration, the renewed agreement will be considered to be for an indefinite period.[90]

Furthermore, a distributorship agreement for a fixed period is considered to be concluded for an indefinite period as soon as it is renewed for the third time between the same parties, whether the clauses of the agreement have been modified or not.

This also applies where the distributorship has been tacitly renewed as a result of a clause in the agreement (article 3 bis, para. 2).

Parties may not agree to modify the nature of their agreement before it ends; the Belgian Supreme Court has held that parties are not entitled to change an agreement for an indefinite period into one for a fixed period. They must end the first agreement and then conclude a new agreement for a fixed period.

Distributorship agreements for an indefinite period

It is generally accepted that the distributorship agreement is an agreement for an indefinite period of time when it is impossible at the moment of conclusion of the contract to know when it will end.[91]

The concept of "at the moment of the conclusion" is important and means that parties cannot decide during the agreement term to fix a date to end the contract: in this case the agreement will be considered to be for an indefinite period.

2.1.6.2. Termination

Termination of an agreement for a fixed period

Neither parties could make any claims if the agreement is terminated as

---

[89] Brussels, 11 June 1977, J.T. 1974, 641; Comm. Louvain, 3 April 1966, J.C.B. 1969, 286.
[90] Comm. Brussels, 8 March 1977, J.C.B., 409.
[91] Brussels, 11 June 1977, J.T. 1974, 641.

originally planned at the end of the term. The parties are free to stipulate what will happen in the event of a termination of the relationship before the end of the term. They can provide for an indemnification of the party who is not responsible for the unexpected ending, or they can provide for an enforced execution of the agreement until the final date, but Belgian case law most emphatically does not admit claims for the enforced execution of the contract.

The distributor can only claim before the courts for damages resulting from the ending of the agreement before the fixed date.

Termination of an agreement for an indefinite period

According to article 2 of the 1961 Law, any exclusive distributorship agreement for an indefinite period of time and regulated by this Law cannot be terminated by either party, except with a reasonable period of notice or a fair indemnification to be agreed between parties at the conclusion of the agreement, unless there has been a serious breach of duty.

This rule is applicable in the event of a unilateral termination of the contract by one of the parties, unless a serious breach of the agreement can be proved.

The Law will not intervene when an annulment automatically occurs as a consequence of the so-called "clause résolutoire expresse", i.e. a clause providing for the automatic cancellation of the agreement, when a contractual obligation is not fulfilled.

The distributor's obligations to sell a certain quantity of the supplier's products or to achieve a certain annual turnover are frequently used clauses which, if they are not observed, cause the immediate termination of the agreement. The judge in this type of case, determines only the existence of the clause, but cannot evaluate the seriousness of it.

Distributors should try to avoid the insertion of such clause.

Serious breach of the agreement

In most cases, it is up to the court to examine whether the alleged breach by the distributor or the supplier is serious. The parties may agree as to what will be considered a serious breach. They may agree on the immediate termination of the agreement whenever a serious breach occurs. A "serious breach" is one which makes any further collaboration immediately and totally impossible; even during a given term of notice.

The party who has alleged a serious breach must immediately stop any further collaboration.

The supplier who has given the distributor notice cannot allege serious fault from the distributor to justify an insufficient period of notice.

The sudden termination of the existing relationship can harm both parties as well as the consumer. Recently, the Brussels Court of Appeal ordered the provisional continuation of the relationship, which was terminated because of an alleged serious fault, in order to avoid the distributor's imminent bankruptcy.

The legislation gives both parties the possibility of terminating the agreement, as long as they agree on a period of notice. The court may not undo a decision to terminate: it can only determine an annulment or regulate the consequences of a sudden annulment.

Even, in the event of a serious breach, parties may agree on measures to be taken during a transitional period, e.g. the liquidation of existing stock, or the discovery of a list of clients.

The law has not given a definition of "serious fault" in the sense of article 2.

According to some jurisprudence,[92] a "serious fault" must necessarily be a contractual shortcoming. This view has been criticized by Bricmont who gives examples of agreements ended because of the use of violence by one of the parties, and because the distributor was in prison for a period of six months.

The following have been considered "serious faults":

- unilateral modification of his territory by the distributor;
- non-fulfilment at regular times of payment due;
- serious financial problems which endanger the distributorship agreement;
- unilateral modification of the selling quota agreed;
- sale by the distributor of competitive products despite an exclusive purchasing clause;
- sale by the supplier of his products to another distributor, despite an exclusivity clause;
- unilateral modification of the prices by the supplier, althuogh these prices have been fixed by the parties together.

When a distributorship agreement for an indefinite period is terminated, and no serious fault is invoked or accepted by the court, the party who has caused the annulment has the choice between:

- giving a reasonable period of notice;
- a compensation instead of notice.

The distributor – and the distributor only – can also claim a just supplementary indemnity in cases where the supplier terminated the distributorship for reasons other than a "serious fault" on the part of the distributor, or when the distributor terminated the agreement due to a "serious fault" on the part of the supplier (see 2.1.7.1.).

Determination of a reasonable period of notice

According to case law and jurisprudence, compensation for the lack of notice cannot be calculated in a general, predetermined way, as happens when a representative's agreement is terminated.

The principle is that a reasonable period of notice corresponds with the period which is in theory necessary to enable the distributor (or the supplier) to find a similar distributorship agreement, i.e. a situation offering the same commercial advantages as the previous one.

Determination of the length of notice is always theoretical, since the parties must agree at the moment when the notice of termination is given. If parties cannot agree, the court will settle the matter in equity, taking into consideration the particular circumstances.

---

[92] Brussels Court, 10 December 1973, quoted by Bricmont.

The court will be guided by commercial custom and by case law which offers valuable criteria, such as:

- duration of the distributorship agreement (the most important element);
- effect of the termination of the distributorship agreement on the total activity of the distributor. In other words, the greater the impact of the termination on the distributor's overall activities, the longer the notice will have to be;
- development of turnover during the distributorship agreement;
- complexity of the organization and the obligations assumed by the distributor in order to perform the contract;
- extent of the territory and the number of the clients and the other advantages linked to the distributorship agreement;
- renown of the supplier's products and the possibility of selling similar products;
- recoupment of efforts and expenses, e.g. publicity costs, rental, costs for material; if these costs are of no further use to the distributor, the court will award compensation for this loss.

It is quite hard to estimate what the unilateral termination of a distributorship agreement for an indefinite period will "cost" in terms of length of notice (see, G. Bogaert in the *De Rechtsgids*, which gives a list of all published decisions with regard to the Law of 27 July 1961).

As guidance, examples of lengths of notice granted by Case law are given:

- The longest period of notice to date is the one granted by the Brussels Court of Appeal, which gave 42 months' notice for a distributorship agreement which lasted for 32 years;[93]
- a period of notice of three years was given to a distributor selling a product (whisky) for 22 years, with an annual profit of 870,000 Belgian francs;[94]
- a period of notice of 30 months was determined for a distributorship agreement of 5 years selling cars in the Liège region which was the only activity of the distributor;[95]
- a period of notice of 20 months was determined for the distributorship agreement of cars which lasted over 10 years and which was the only activity of the distributor;[96]
- a period of notice of 24 months for the distributorship agreement of motorcycles which lasted over 11 years and which was the main activity of the distributor.[97]

2.1.7. Indemnity

2.1.7.1. Compensatory indemnities

Article 2 of the 1961 Law states that a distributorship agreement for an

[93] Brussels, 9 May 1985, R.W. 1985-86, 1210.
[94] Comm. Court Brussels, 4 June 1971, J.T. 1971, 595.
[95] Liège, 1979 November R.G., 698.
[96] Gand, 27 June 1985 Rev. Dr. Comm. 1986, 135.
[97] Gand, Comm. Court, 1900, not published.

indeterminate period of time and subject to this Law cannot be terminated otherwise than with a reasonable period of notice or a fair indemnification, to be agreed by the parties at the moment of the termination of the agreement unless there is a serious breach of duty by one of the parties.

If the parties fail to reach an agreement, as often happens, the judge will decide in equity, if necessary taking into account the practices of the trade.

Both parties are free to end the agreement without giving any justification, but have to observe the Law which obliges them to give reasonable notice, unless a serious breach by the other party can be proved.

The party who breaches the agreement will have the choice between giving notice or paying an indemnity. This decision cannot be disputed and even the court must respect the decision to terminate the contract. The court can only state the termination and regulate its consequences.

The Brussels President of the Commercial Court broke new ground when he granted an injunction to suspend termporarily a sudden termination, because an immediate rupture would inevitably lead to the bankruptcy of the distributor.[98]

The decision to terminate a contract is irreversible, which means that once a decision to terminate an agreement without notice or with insufficient notice has been taken neither the supplier nor the distributor can claim or propose a (longer) period of notice.

If no period of notice is granted or if the period granted is insufficient, the distributor is entitled to compensation for any damage suffered as a result of the lack of notice period. The law does not give any indication as to the method to be used for calculating that compensation. The indemnity should only correspond to the profits the other party would have enjoyed during the term of notice, if it had given.

Since 1961 Law was passed authors have drafted two formulae to calculate compensation:

- The compensatory indemnity is equal to the net profit which the distributor would have enjoyed if a reasonable period of notice had been given, increased by the irreducible overheads up to the percentage represented by the distributorship in the total turnover of the distributor. The figures are based on the figures of the two or three years prior to the termination unless these years were exceptional. Basically, the years of reference are those which most resemble the year in which notice has been given.
- Another method has been proposed by which the compensatory indemnity is equal to the gross profit realized on the sale of the products subject to the concession during the period corresponding to the reasonable period of notice after deduction of the reducible overheads directly related to the distributorship.

Net profit

The salary of the business manager of a small family company who possesses all the shares (which is in fact an advanced deduction of the profit of the company) is added to the profit of the company itself. If there is no

[98] Brussels, réf., 6 October 1983, J.T. 1984, 134.

profit at all with regard to the distributorship, the distributor will not be entitled to any indemnity.

The compensatory indemnity calculation

The compensatory indemnity is equal to the gross profit realized on the sale of the products subject of the concession during the period corresponding to the reasonable period of notice and after deduction of the reducible overheads directly related to the concession.

Irreducible/reducible overheads

Irreducible overheads are rent, real estate withholding tax, insurance, heating, water, lighting and cleaning costs.

Reducible overheads are all costs which can directly be linked to the products of the distributorship agreement and which disappear at the termination of it, such as cleaning costs of the products.

Stock

The 1961 Law does not cover stock at the end of a contract. Most Belgian court decisions require the supplier to take over the stock or to pay for its value. The parties may freely agree on how to dispose of the stock at the end of an agreement.

Questions about the responsibility for the termination of the termination of the agreement stock and discussions about the stock are not linked to one another.

The Belgian court rarely determines immediately the amount of the compensatory indemnity, and generally seeks expert advice, as the information given by the distributor is in most cases insufficient.

When seeking expert advice, the court usually grants provisional indemnity, as the outcome of the advice may take time.

2.1.7.2. Supplementary indemnity

While article 2 of the 1961 Law provides for a period of notice when the agreement is terminated by the supplier or the distributor, article 3 grants an indemnification only to a distributor suffering from a sudden termination.

Article 3

If the distributorship agreement, as referred to in article 2, is terminated by the supplier for reasons other than serious breach by the distributor, or if the distributor terminates the agreement because of a serious breach by the manufacturer, the distributor will be entitled to an equitable supplementary indemnity.

This supplementary indemnity consists of three elements, and each case is evaluated on its merits.

The enumeration as stipulated in the Law is restrictive and excludes all other indemnifications for whatever reason, such as moral damages.

1. Any substantial increase of the clientèle which has been created by the distributor and which remains attached to the manufacturer after the termination of the contract.

The Law imposes four conditions:

- there must be an increase in the number of clients at the end of the distributorship;
- this increase must be substantial;
- the clientèle must remain attached to the supplier after the termination of the contract;
- the clientèle must have been brought in by the distributor.

If the distributor stops doing business after the termination of the agreement, he will not be entitled to any indemnity.

In some cases, the court orders an expert's report as to the value of the clientèle; in other cases, the court will make an evaluation *ex aequo et bono*. Crahay and Jadot, in their study *L'Indemnite de clientèle du concessionnaire de vente*, (J.T., 1982, p. 609), stated that the courts generally allow an indemnity equal to half or twice the average net profit over the last two years.

2. All expenses incurred by the distributor in furtherance of the distributorship which will benefit the manufacturer after the termination of the contract.

These expenses should not be confused with the irreducible overheads which are taken into consideration in the determination of the compensatory indemnity.

In most of the cases, it is difficult to determine which expenses will be profitable for the supplier.

The following expenses will without any further discussion be accepted:

- costs for the development of the distribution;
- costs for the training of employees.

Expenses made for tests, laboratory controls and technical files have been rejected because of their non-profitable character.[99] Similarly newspaper advertising expenses, which have temporary effect on the consumer, will also be rejected.[100]

It often is hard to evaluate the costs of running the distributorship and even more difficult to evaluate in what way these expenses were profitable to the supplier; this is why the courts often make an evaluation *ex aequo et bono*.

3. Amounts to be paid by the distributor to employees he is obliged to make redundant as a result of the termination of the distributorship.

When the supplier decides to terminate the distributorship agreement without notice, and if this obliges the distributor to dismiss his employees, the supplier must compensate for the redundancy payments which the distributor has to make. The supplier must also indemnify the distributor for the wages and redundancy payments made by the distributor during the period of notice which exceeds the term of notice.

---

[99] Brussels, 25 June 1982, J.C.B. 1983, 66.
[100] Comm. Brussels, 9 March 1963, J.T., 1963, 513.

2.1.8. Specific application of EEC-law

2.1.8.1. Applicable law and competency

Applicable law

The presumption is made here that the agreement is subject to the Belgian Law 1961 and to the Civil Code. Parties are free to agree on the Law which will be applicable to their agreement. However, the Belgian distributor who has a distributorship agreement having its effect on Belgian territory will be better off with the application of Belgian law, especially the 1961 Law. The Belgian distributor benefits from strict protection under the law of 27 July 1961. In order to ensure distributors benefit from the protection set out in articles 2 and 3, two rules have been written:

(a) a distributor can always sue the supplier in Belgium before a Belgian court (Article 4, paragraph 1);
(b) in cases where the Belgian court has to decide on such a matter, Belgian law has to be applied imperatively (Article 4, paragraph 2).

This means that the Belgian court must always apply Belgian law, if nothing is agreed in the contract and even when the application of foreign law is provided for.

This is because Article 4, paragraph 2 must be taken together with Article 6, paragraph 1 of the law:

"notwithstanding any contrary agreements, the articles of this Law are applicable to all agreements that are concluded before the end of the distributorship agreement, whereby the distributorship is granted. They govern all exclusive distributorship agreements before the entering into force of this Law".

Article 4, paragraph 1 refers only to ". . . the articles of this Law . . ." We must assume that other provisions of the Civil Code are not compulsory. Consequently, other clauses in this agreement, which are not governed by the 1961 Law, can be regulated by foreign law.

We can deduce from article 6, paragraph 1, on agreements concluded before the end, that parties can agree to submit any litigation to foreign law or to arbitration, at the moment of termination of the agreement or afterwards.

This shows that agreements enforcing the imperative rules of the 1961 Law will be valid when concluded after the termination of the contract.

Belgian law is not, of course, binding on foreign courts; foreign courts can refuse to apply Belgian law.[101] It is also possible, and even probable, that a foreign court will refuse to give an exequatur for a Belgian sentence, if the court takes the view that Article 4, paragraph 2 of the 1961 Law conflicts with national law as regards applicable law or competence.

In some cases, distributors and suppliers prefer to insert an arbitration clause, agreeing to submit the case to one or more arbiters who will, if the need arises, apply the legislation chosen by both parties.

The Brussels Convention of 27 September 1968 includes the rules set out

---

[101] Paris, 20 May 1965, 578.

by article 4, paragraph 1 of the 1961 Law (priority of international rule over national principles, but excludes arbitration from its field of application.

The Belgian Supreme Court, asked to determine the validity of an arbitration clause, decided:

> "A litigation relating to the termination by the supplier of an exclusive distributorship agreement having effect in part or in the whole of the Belgian territory, cannot be ruled by an arbitration, agreed prior to the end of the agreement, and which has as an aim and effect the application of a foreign law".[102]

Consequently, an arbitration clause is in itself valid, but only in so far as it provides for the application of Belgian law. An arbitration sentence in Belgium, in which Belgian law has not been applied, cannot be executed. But an arbitration clause dealing with problems which are not regulated by the Belgian 1961 Law can be applied without any problem.

Competency

The questions of competency must be answered according to the nationality of the parties or the location of their registered office.

According to article 4, the distributor who suffers damage can always on the termination of a distributorship which covers part or the whole of the Belgian territory, sue the manufacturer in Belgium, either before the court of the place of residence or of business of the manufacturer.

If an action is brought before a Belgian court, the court will apply Belgian law exclusively. The imperative character of this rule prevents any derogation, e.g. by inserting a clause of competence.

This rule applies only for claims made by Belgian *distributors* when the claim is made when the agreement is terminated by the supplier.

The "competency" rule of article 4, paragraph 1 arguably applies not only to claims for damages resulting from the unilateral termination of a distributorship agreement, but also for claims for damages resulting from a failure in the execution of an agreement, in so far as the claim is introduced at the termination of the agreement.

This view is not accepted by certain authors who believe that the 1961 Law has a restrictive interpretation.

Other items likely to be disputed by the parties and which have nothing to do with the termination of the agreement will, if necessary, be heard by the competent court, according to Belgian Processual Law.

Disputes between a foreign supplier and a Belgian distributor will be subject to the EEC Treaty, Brussels 27 September 1969, if the national authorities of the supplier signed this Treaty. The Treaty takes priority over national competency rules. The application of article 5(1) and article 17 of the Brussels Treaty are frequent in jurisprudence and case law.

On a question of prejudice, the European Court of Justice stated that national judges should decide whether the compensatory indemnity is an independent contractual obligation or an obligation replacing the non-executed obligation to give a period of notice.[103]

---

[102] Cass., 20 June 1979, J.T. 1979, 625.
[103] Court of Justice, 16 October 1976, J.T. 1976, 739.

The Belgian national judge, i.e. the Supreme Court, decided that this obligation is not an independent contractual obligation; consequently, the obligation to pay an indemnity must, according to Belgian law, be executed in Belgium, if the distributorship is executed on Belgian territory.

Applying article 5(1) EEC Treaty, Belgian courts are competent to decide on the claim for payment of a compensatory indemnity.

Recently, the Supreme Court argued that the supplementary indemnity which article 3 of the 1961 Law provides for, is an independent obligation: this means that the court of the place of residence of the supplier is competent.

However, Belgian courts can decide on the claim in accordance with article 3 when the claim is made together with a claim for a compensatory indemnity based on article 3 of the Law. This is possible thanks to the procedural rules of article 22 EEC Treaty.

2.1.9. Bibliography

Beniot-Moury, A. et Matray, D., "Les Concessions exclusives de Vente", Ann. Fac. Dr. Liège, 1980, 127;

Bogaert, G., "Concessieovereenkomsten", *Rechtsgids, Handels- en Economisch Recht*, (Story);

Bricmont, G. et Philips, J.M., "Commentaire des Dispositions de Droit Belge et Communautaire applicables aux Concessions de Vente en Belgique", Bruxelles, Jeune Barreau, 1979;

Crahay, P. and Jadot, F., "L'indemnité de clientèle du concessionnaire de vente", J.T. 1982, 609;

Fierens, J.P. et Kileste, P., "Chronique de Jurisprudence: Les Concessions de Vente", J.T., 1988, 34;

Mallerbe, J., "Les Concessions de Vente en droit Belge et Communautaire", J.C.B., 1973, 53;

Sunt, C., "Overzicht van de Belangrijkste Rechtspraak" in J.C.B., 1981, 431; Vereniging van Belgische Ondernemingen, Alleenverkoopsovereenkomsten, Brussel 1978.

2.1.10. Legislation

Law of 27 July 1961, modified by the Law of 13 April 1971.

2.2. Selective Distribution

2.2.1. Definition

Selective distribution is a system by which the distribution of a certain product is restricted to a limited number of qualified traders at different levels of production.

It consists of a network of recognized exclusive distributors, importers and wholesalers to whom the manufactuer will exclusively supply; in turn, these distributors will supply only to other recognized retailers or dealers.

The discussion on the validity of a selective distributorship system must be seen from the point of view of EEC law. The Court of Justice and the Commission have both accepted the fundamental validity of selective distribution.[104]

The Court admits certain systems of selective distribution, provided the choice of the distributors is an objective one and only quantified criteria are used, uniformly imposed without discrimination.

Belgian courts have integrated this jurisprudence in their discussions. A recent decision of the Brussels President defines what is to be understood by "quantitative criteria".[105] A quantitative criterion is any criterion based on quantifiable elements which are not justified by considerations related to the improvement of the product or service.

The Court gave some examples:

- limitation of the number of points of sale based on the number of inhabitants;[106]
- criterion of distance between two point of sale;[107]
- the obligation to achieve a minimum turnover;[108]
- the obligation to maintain a permanently minimum selection.[109]

In Belgian law, no specific regulations are provided concerning selective distribution. The courts deal only indirectly with the problem when a potential purchaser is confronted with a manufacturer refusing to sell a product or to integrate himself in the selective distribution network.

According to Belgian civil law, everybody is free to choose the person he wants to contract a sales agreement with and everybody has a subjective right not to sell. However, if this refusal to sell is based on illegal grounds, the court can order this practice to be stopped. Moreover, the refusal to sell may also be illegal in so far as it is forbidden by a specific regulation, such as the law of the 22 January 1945 on economic regulations and prices, sanctioning sales under conditions contrary to the rules.[110]

A selective distribution system can also be sanctioned in an indirect way in so far as it leads to a refusal to sell as a result of the abuse of an economic position of strength by the manufacturer or a group of manufacturers (arts. 1 and 2 of the law of 27 May 1960 protecting the abuse of the economic position of power).

2.2.2. Conclusion of the contract (special conditions)

See 2.1.2.

[104] M.P. Piriou, "La Distribution sélective et les règles communautaires de concurrence", R.T.D.E., 1978, 602; I.S. Chard, "The Economics of the Application of Article 85 to Selective Distribution Systems", E.L. Rev., 1982, 83.

[105] Président du Tribunal de Commerce de Bruxelles, 23 October 1985, J.C.B., 1987, 293.

[106] W. Van Gerven, M. Maresceau, and J. Stuyck, *Handel en Economisch Recht, II Mededingingsrecht*, B. Kartelrecht.

[107] J. Stuyck and Van de Walle de Ghelcke, *Weigering van Verkoop en van Levering*, JCB 1984, 324.

[108] Law of 22 January 1945 concerning economic regulations and prices

[109] Law of 27 May 1960 concerning the protection of abuse of economic position of strength.

[110] J. Stuyck and Van de Walle de Ghelcke, "Weigering van Verkoop en van Levering", J.C.B., 1984, 324.

2.2.3. The supplier's duties and rights

2.2.3.1. The supplier's duties

2.2.3.2. The supplier's rights

See 2.1.3.

2.2.4. The distributor's duties and rights

2.2.4.1. The distributor's duties

2.2.4.2. The distributor's rights

See 2.1.4.

2.2.5. Liabilities of supplier and distributor during the term of the distributorship agreement

See 2.1.5.

2.2.6. Term and termination

2.2.6.1. Term

2.2.6.2. Termination

See 2.1.6.

2.2.7. Indemnity

See 2.1.7.

2.2.8. Specific application of EEC law

See 2.1.8.

3. Franchise Agreements

3.1. Definition

Under Belgian law, there are no specific rules governing franchising. If the Bill on franchise agreements, which has been before the Belgian Parliament since 4 February 1982[111] becomes law, the parties' liberty to draft franchise agreements would be severely restricted. From Parliamentary Question no. 16 and the corresponding answer, it appears that the government is not considering intervening in this field, since it is becoming increasingly European and any new national law might seriously complicate European and transnational co-operation.[112]

It is also argued that the national Code of Ethics drafted by the Belgian

---

[111] Wetsvoorstel tot regeling van de franchise overeenkomst, zitting 1981-1982, 4 February 1982, Parl. Doc. 90, no. 1.

[112] A Lombart and P. Van Hooghten, "Parliamentary question no. 16 of Mr. Lagneau 11 April 1986", *Journal of International Franchising and Distribution Law*, September, 1986, 51.

Franchsing Association, supplemented by the European Code of Ethics, is sufficient to deal with the present situation. The European Code has been submitted to the European Commission, who considered that it contains no clause which is contradictory to notices 85 or 86 of the Treaty of Rome.[113]

The Belgian Franchising Association defines a franchise agreement as follows:[114]

> "A franchise agreement is an agreement between independent parties, in which one (the franchisor) grants to another (the franchisee) in exchange for payment, the use of his know how, trademark and/or brand name and any other symbols, developed by the franchisor, tested and found to work. Additionally, support and regular services may be provided for. As a result of such an agreement, the franchisee becomes part of a co-ordinated system".

3.1.1. Characteristics

The essential elements of a franchise agreement under Belgian law are:

- *Independence*: The parties to the franchise agreement must remain independent and when drafting a franchise agreement, it is advisable to stress this.[115] There should be no suggestion of subordination of the franchisee; in such an event the Labour Law and its disadvantages could well apply.[116] The independence of the parties supposes that each must comply with social and fiscal regulations for independent traders as well as with the rules of bookkeeping and annual accounts.[117]
- *Collaboration*: The franchisor and the franchisee collaborate in the commercial exploitation of a product.[118]
- *Reputation*: What distinguishes a franchise agreement from a distributorship agreement and other agreements is the element of recognition, reputation and originality (of the product, services or commercial formula), which are the determinant reasons for the franchisee to enter into the agreement.[119]
- *Intuita personae*: A franchise agreement is usually an *intuita personae* agreement because the importance to each party of the identity and personality of the other party. This *intuita personae* character may have consequences for the continuity of the franchise agreement in the event of death or bankruptcy. Unless otherwise agreed, a franchisee may not grant subfranchises.[120]
- *Licence*: There is no franchise without the licence of commercial know how, intellectual property (the trade mark, name, sign and other sym-

---

[113] J. Billiet, "Franchising", B.R.H., 1982, 124.

[114] Belgian Code of Loyal Practice Concerning Franchising.

[115] C. Sunt, "Franchising", *Bedrijf en recht*, suppl. 1 (November 1982), VII.A., 2.1.1.1. Th. Bourgoignie, "Le contrat de franchise", J.T., 1974, 21.

[116] Law on Labour Contracts of 3 July 1978.

[117] Law on Bookkeeping and Annual Accounts of 17 July 1975.

[118] J. de Lat and B. Maes, "franchising. Een juridische schets van een succesformule", 1985, Brussels, Swinnen, 26. W. Van Gerven, "Handels - en economisch recht, deel 1 mededingingsrecht", *Standaard*, 343.

[119] Belgisch Comité voor de distributie, "Juridische aspecten van de franchising", I, 4.

[120] Van Gerven, *op. cit.*, 334. De Lat and Maes, *op. cit.*, 27.

bols) and/or of a technical specialization. These elements serve to advertise the originality, quality and image of a product or service.[121]

3.2. Conclusion of a Contract (Special Conditions)

Since a franchise agreement is one of the "unnamed" contracts which are not explicitly regulated by Belgian law, the general rules of contract apply.[122] These general rules contain two fundamental principles:

- *freedom to contract*: The parties are free to fix their rights and obligations within the limits imposed by public order, morality and any compulsory legal provisions. The agreement of the parties has force of law.[123]
- *consent*: Basically parties are free to conclude contracts, in whatever form, even orally.

Notwithstanding the principles contained in the Civil Code, in particular as regards the form of contract, the Code of Loyal Practices of the Belgian Franchising Association stipulates in article 2 that the basic agreement between franchisor and franchisee should be in writing.[124]

In Belgium there is a tendency towards the use of "take it or leave it" agreements ("contracts of accession") in which the franchisee has very little say, which implies that the franchisor has a standard contract and the franchisee has the choice only of whether to sign or not.

3.3. The Supplier's Duties and Rights

3.3.1. The supplier's duties

The franchisor grants the use of a complete system, which has been tried and found to work. This system may include the trade mark, brand name and other symbols which are the property of the franchisor and which are part of the collective image of the system. On this subject, in one of the few examples of case law, it was held that a franchisee's sign board bearing the name of the franchisor does not amount to publicity. The sign board is the property of the franchisor, who grants a licence to use it for the duration of the agreement.[125] [126]

The franchisor must grant free use of the trade mark, brand name and other symbols, which implies that in the event of imitation by third parties, he must start both civil and criminal proceedings against the infringer.[127]

The franchisor should provide a range of services and assistance consistent with the image of the network so that the outlet can be identified as

---

[121] Sunt, *op. cit.*, VII A 2222.
[122] Article 1107 of the Civil Code.
[123] Article 1134 of the Civil Code.
[124] Belgian Code of Loyal Practice concerning Franchising, article 2.
[125] Corr. Antwerp, 21 December, 1978, J.C.B., 1981, 256 C. Sunt.
[126] Article 6, Royal Decree of 14 December 1959.
[127] Article 13, Benelux Trade Mark Law of 19 March 1962; Article 1382 of the Civil Code; Article 54 of the Law of 14 July 1971 on Commercial Practices; Article 8 of the law of 1 April, 1879.

being a part of it. The assistance and services rendered by the franchisor include advertising by or under the supervision of the franchisor, the management of the business and training of the franchisee and his staff.[128]

It is accepted that the franchisor must make full disclosure to the franchisee of every matter which is relevant to his decision to enter into the agreement.[129]

In addition to the franchisee's obligations to purchase from the franchisor, the latter has to guarantee a decent, regular and sufficient supply to the franchisee. Through a failure to guarantee such a supply, the network might suffer, which would be contrary to the aim of a franchise agreement. In such cases, the franchisee would have a claim for damages against the franchisor.[130] An exclusive supply clause has the disadvantage that it may compromise the independence of the parties and that the agreement might be considered a kind of a labour agreement in which the franchisee takes little or no risk and only shares in the profits.[131]

3.3.2. The supplier's rights

The supplier has the right of control, i.e. the franchisor is entitled to receive all information relating to the quality and progress of the franchising business and which will enable the franchisor to evaluate the extent of his own obligations and how far the identity and reputation of the network are being observed.[132]

All the rights pertaining to any name or trademark are the exclusive property of the franchisor.

Non-competition and secrecy clauses may be used to prevent competitors from using the know how of the franchisor or from benefiting indirectly from the franchisor's know how.[133] One has to distinguish between the non-competition clause during the franchise agreement and any analogous obligation after termination of the agreement. In addition to the franchisee's obligation to purchase particular products from the franchisor, the parties can incorporate in their agreement a non-competition clause during the performance of the agreement, based on article 1134 of the Civil Code, which states that parties must perform the contract in good faith. Protection of the integrity of the franchised system would be inconsistent with the distribution of products of the competitors.[134]

In order to maintain a consistent commercial policy, a franchisor may wish to impose prices on the franchisee, but *contractual clauses which directly or indirectly fix purchase or sale prices infringe article 85(1) of the Treaty of Rome. The franchisor, however, can communicate price guidelines which are not binding on the franchisee.*

---

128 Billiet, *op. cit.,* 116-117.
129 Billiet, *op.cit.,* 113.
130 Bourgoignie, *op. cit.,* 19, paragraph 2 1-b.
131 De Lat and Maes, *op. cit.,* 109-110.
132 Billiet, *op. cit.,* 117.
133 Van Bael and Bellis, *Competition Law of the EEC,* paragraph 354.
134 Van Bael and Bellis, *op. cit.,* paragraph 354.

3.4. The Distributor's Duties and Rights

3.4.1. The distributor's duties

The franchisee has first of all the obligation to pay a form of remuneration, which is usually in two parts:

- an entrance fee which may be fixed or variable and which is in effect a payment for the advantages of the use of the system;
- royalties, which are often a percentage calculated on the annual turnover and are paid on a recurring basis.

The franchisee must comply with the franchisor's plans and designs for the business premises and with instructions and standards for operating the business.

Unless otherwise agreed, the franchisee may not grant sublicences and must respect the *intuita personae* character of the agreement.

The franchisee may be required to sell only products supplied by the franchisor or by suppliers selected by him. *There is no infringement of article 85(1) as far as the obligation of exclusive purchasing is necessary to allow the franchisor to control the quality of the products sold by the franchisee and, as a result, protect the network. Such exclusive purchase obligation may not, however, prevent the franchisee from buying from other franchises, belonging to the same network.*[135]

3.4.2. The distributor's rights

The distributor, i.e. the franchisee, has the right to operate under the franchisor's trade name or mark and avail himself of the continuing services provided by the franchisor.

He is entitled to commercial assistance and services rendered by the franchisor. Based on his experience, the franchisor has to inform the franchisee as to the best way of running the system.

3.5. Liabilities of Supplier and Distributor during the Term of the Franchise Agreement

The general rules of contract apply. Under Belgian law, a distinction is made between contractual liability and non-contractual liability (i.e. Tortious liability).

Contractual liability can only be relied upon by one of the contracting parties while tortious liability may be invoked by anyone even if not privy to the contract.

Tortious liability is dealt with in article 1382 *et seq.* of the Belgian Civil Code. Unlike some other legal systems, contractual and tortious liability can be invoked simultaneously. The Belgian Supreme Court (Hof van Cassatie) has held that the rules of tortious liability can also be applied to contracts where the behaviour or acts, including breach of contract are of such nature

---

[135] Van Bael and Bellis, *op. cit.*, paragraph 356.

that it would be covered by article 1382 Civil Code had there not been a contract.

Another basic rule of liability is applied to the franchisor and franchisee by article 1384, paragraph 1 of the Civil Code, which states that the one who has custody of goods can be held liable for damage caused by those goods provided they are in his possession.[136]

3.5.1. The supplier as against the distributor

3.5.1.1. Pre-contractual

If the franchisor misleads the franchisee into believing that the system is tried and proven to work, and the franchisee discovers that he has not received what he contracted for and that the franchisor did not make full disclosure, he can proceed on the basis of imperfect consent or absence of all relevant facts.[137]

Imperfect consent can give rise to proceedings for nullity (which is relative) of the franchise agreement based on the principles of error, fraud or misrepresentation. In the case of error, the franchisee must show that the error was not an inexcusable error which a reasonable person would not have made. As for proceedings on the ground of fraud, the franchisee would have to prove bad faith on the part of the franchisor.

If the franchisor was silent, it must be determined whether that silence amounted to fraud and whether or not the franchisee did all that was necessary to obtain information.[138] [139] Either in subsidiary or separate proceedings, the franchisee can sue on the principle of *culpa in contrahendo*. According to this principle, the franchisor can be held liable for damages caused by false or erronerous information on matters that he should have been aware of. The importance of the information in relation to the franchisee's consent must be assessed when it appears that the information was insufficient. The advantages of this principle are its less stringent criteria and when it is used in subsidiary pleadings, the franchisee can claim not only nullity but also damages.[138]

3.5.1.2. Contractual

If the franchise contains the grant of a licence of commercial know how, intellectual property (trade mark, brand name, sign) or of a technical speciality, its protection must be assured if the franchisee is to have full use of it. If the franchisor does not safeguard what has been licensed or allows the franchise network to run down, this could result in a claim by the franchisee. In the case of imitation or trade mark infringement, it is the franchisor who has the capacity to act. If he fails to perform his funda-

---

[136] R. Kruithof, "Aansprakelijkheid voor schde veroozaakt door produkten", *Economisch en financieel recht vandaag*, Gakko, 1972, 423-450.

[137] M. Fallon, "La cour de cassation et la responsabilité liée aux biens de consommation", R.C.B.J., 1979, 164-182.

[138] Articles 1131, 1110, 1116 of the Civil Code.

[139] W. Wilms, "Het recht op informatie in het verbintenissenrecht een grondslagonderzoek", R.W., 1980-81, 489-520.

mental obligations, it could give grounds for the termination of the franchise agreement.[140]

If any condition for the validity of a trade mark is absent, the franchisee can claim nullity of the licence. The effect of the nullity of the licence on the whole of the franchise agreement depends on the importance of the licence in the context of the legal operation of the franchise. Since the licence of a trade mark is often one of the essential elements, some authors hold that the nullity of the licence would automatically make the whole agreement null.[140]

Where a franchisor sells a product to the franchisee, it is important to stress that the franchisor warrants that the product is free from hidden defects.

Belgian law has specific regulations as to the liability of vendors towards purchasers, in respect of hidden defects where the purchaser would not have bought the goods, at least not at the same price.[141] To repair the damage, the franchisor would be liable to take back the goods and reimburse the price.

However if the damage has been caused by the goods, article 1645 stipulates that the vendor is not only liable to reimburse the price but also to indemnify the purchaser for damages incurred.

Jurisprudence now tends towards the principle that the manufacturer, the professional vendor and the distributor are deemed to be aware of the defects of the products they sell and are thus liable for all damages caused by the defects of the product; the only defence is to prove that it was not possible to have known of the defect.[142]

Where a franchisee is sued for damages caused by the product supplied by the franchisor, he would be able to turn to the franchisor for indemnification.

3.5.2. The supplier as against third parties

Where a third party has suffered damage caused by defective franchise goods sold to that third party, he has a direct course of action, which in a franchise system enables him to claim indemnification from the franchisor.[143]

Alternatively, the third party could also claim indemnification on the basis of article 1382 of the Civil Code if he can prove that the franchisor was at fault and that such fault has a causal link with the damage suffered.

3.5.3. The distributor as against the supplier

3.5.3.1. Pre-contractual

A franchisee can be prosecuted if it appears that his motives for entering into the franchise agreement were fraudulent and with the intent of obtaining secrets of commercial know how, industrial processes, etc.[144]

Proceedings can be based on article 1382 et seq. of Civil Code or on article

---

[140] Bourgoignie, op. cit., section 2, paragraph 1.
[141] Article 1641 of the Civil Code.
[142] Cass., 6 October 1961, Pas., 1962, I, 152.
[143] H. Cousy, "Productaansprakelijkheid", Bedrijf en Recht, IX.B 2-6.
[144] Article 1116 of the Civil Code.

54 of the Law on Loyal Commercial Practices. The franchisor can in such a case claim damages, but he can also obtain a cessation order.[145]

Criminal proceedings could be based on theft, fraud and abuse of confidence.[146]

If the franchisor wants to start criminal and civil proceedings, based on article 1382 of the Civil Code, the criminal proceedings will first have to be terminated, based on the adage that "le criminel tient le civil en état". But if the franchisor would proceed for a cessation order and start at the same time as criminal proceedings, this principle does not apply.[147] [148]

3.5.3.2. Contractual

Although it is the franchisor who in his capacity as owner of the intellectual property can act against infringement, the franchisee can institute a criminal prosecution. The franchisee can issue a writ as a civil party without the support of the franchisor in order to have one of the crimes set out in the law of 1 April 1879, modified by Royal Decree on 29 January 1935, penalised.

The franchisee can also start proceedings to stop infringement and unfair trading by unauthorised use of a trade mark or brand name.[149] In these last two cases, the franchisee could claim damages he personally suffered.

3.5.4. The distributor as against third parties

The franchisee's liability can be both contractual and tortious.

There is contractual liability where the third party has bought a product or a service from the franchisee. Where a third party suffers damage because of a product he has not purchased directly from the franchisee there is no contractual relationship and the franchisee can only be liable under article 1382 *et seq.* of the Civil Code, if the fault, the damage and the causal link can be proved.

The EEC Council Directive of 25 July 1985 on product liability must be incorporated in Belgian law before 1 August 1988. According to this Directive, the producer shall be liable for damage caused by a defect in his product and the injured person shall be required to prove the damage, the defect and the causal relationship between defect and damage.[150]

Article 3 states that anyone putting his name, trade mark or other distinguishing feature on a product gives himself out as its producer. Moreover, without prejudice to the liability of the producer, any person who imports into the community a product for sale, hire, leasing or any form of distri-

---

[145] Article 54 of the Law on Commercial Practices of 14 July 1971.
[146] Article 491, 309, 461 of the Criminal Code; Article 61 of the Law on Commercial Practices of 14 July 1971;
[147] Article 59 of the Law on Commercial Practices of 14 July 1971.
[148] Commercial Court, Brussels, 21 March 1979, B.R.H., 1981, 242.
[149] Article 54 of the Law on Commercial Practices of 14 July 1971; Note: article 56 of the Law on Commercial practices of 14 July 1971.
[150] Council Directive of 25 July, 1985 on product liability, no. L 210/29, notified to the Member States on 30 July 1985.

bution in the course of his business shall be deemed to be a producer within the meaning of this Directive and shall be responsible as a producer.[151]

The provisions of the Directive may make it necessary for an injured party to commence proceedings against the franchisee and franchisor, either alternatively or for joint and several liability based on article 5 of the Directive. It rather depends on the rules of procedure which the Belgian legislator will apply to this question.[151]

Franchising may be a two-tier business but from the point of view of the public, there is only one business, namely that whose name, brand mark and sign can be seen everywhere.

Third parties have a direct course of action against the franchisor who may be liable in his capacity as the professional vendor for the defects caused by the products supplied to the franchisee.

Alternatively, third parties may proceed against the franchisee from who they have bought the final product, in which case the franchisee may have recourse against the franchisor.

To date, there is no case law to the effect that a franchisor is liable for defective products which bear his trade mark.

3.5.5. Disclaimer clause

Belgian law recognizes the freedom of contract, and disclaimer clauses are generally allowed. There are however three provisos:

- such clauses may not contravene Belgian public order, be against the public interest, or involve certain protected contracting parties;
- no disclaimer may constitute a fraud, i.e. may not benefit a contracting party who does not intend to perform;
- a disclaimer will not be upheld if it is so widely phrased as to give the party claiming its benefit, relief from obligations which form the substance of the contract.[152]

3.6. Term and Termination

3.6.1. Term

Although franchise agreements may be for a fixed or indefinite duration, they are usually made for a fixed term. It is quite common to provide an explicit or tacit renewal clause. If, however, a franchise agreement has been renewed several times, it may be considered as being for indefinite term.[153]

3.6.2. Termination

The view is expressed by some authors that the law of 27 July 1961, as modified by the law of 13 April 1971 on the termination of distributorship

---

[151] M. Faure and W. Vanbuggenhout, "Productaansprakelijkheid. De Europese richtlijn: Harmonisatie en consumentenbeschreming?", R.W., 1987-1988, 8. Editions du Jeune Barreau, 1987, "la vente", 283.

[152] P. Van Ommselaghe, *droit des obligations*, vol. 3, 705-709.

[153] Billiet, *op. cit.*, 117.

agreements, would apply also to franchise agreements which are exclusive or quasi-exclusive distributorship of goods and not of services.

For that law to apply it would be necessary to show that the franchisee purchases the goods directly from the franchisor in order to sell them in his own name and for his own account. To date, however, there is no case law to support this theory.[154] [155]

A clause stipulating that the contract is a franchise agreement, and that as a consequence the law on the termination of distributorship agreements does not apply, will not suffice for the parties to escape from the application of that law. A judge is not bound by the qualification given by the parties to their contract.[156]

Franchise agreements can be terminated as follows:

(a) At the *expiry of the term* where the agreement was for a fixed term and has not been renewed.

(b) By giving reasonable *notice* in the case of franchise agreements of indefinite duration or in the case of franchise agreements for a fixed term which have been renewed several times and are considered as being indefinite.

  Franchise agreements usually contain provisions for terms of notice which must be given or an equivalent indemnity which should correspond with the profit the franchisee would have been able to earn had he been given a proper notice period.[157] [158]

  Contrary to the provisions of the law on the termination of distributorship agreements, no compensation for the clientèle or any other supplementary compensation need be paid to the franchisee.[159]

(c) *Early dissolution* based on article 1184 of the Belgian Civil Code: if one of the parties does not carry out his obligations, the other party may be entitled to ask the judge to terminate the contract and award damages.

  The parties to a franchise agreement, can explicitly provide for automatic termination when certain conditions or events occur. A court is bound to apply such a clause subject to verifying whether or not the conditions for its application have effectively occurred.[160]

(d) If one of the parties is guilty of a *serious breach of contract*, the other party can immediately terminate the franchise agreement, without having to give a reasonable term of notice, although there may be some liable to pay compensation.

  It is advisable, therefore, to stipulate in a franchise agreement what is considered to be a serious breach. Examples of such conditions are:

---

[154] P. Crahay, "Le contrat de franchise de distribution et la loi relative à la résiliation unilaterale des concessions de vente.", T.B.H., 1985, 660.

[155] Law on the termination of Distributorship agreements of 27 July 1961, modified by the law of 13 July 1971.

[156] Article 1156 of the Civil Code.

[157] De Lat and Maes, *op. cit.*, 162.

[158] Cass., 19 September, 1983, R.W., 1983-84, 1480.

[159] Belgisch Comité voor de distributie, "Juridische aspecten van de franchising", II, 12.

[160] Cass, 19 April, 1979, B.R.H., 1980, 440 with note of F. Maussion; Commercial Court, Brussels, 22 November, 1985, T.B.H., 1987, 120; Commercial Court of Neufchâteau, 10 December 1985, T.B.H., 1987, 123.

- failure by the franchisee to pay commissions, a radical change in style of appearance of the business, obstructing the franchisor's right of control in view of the protection of the identity of the network;
- failure by the franchisor to supply, absence of substantive know how, failure to promote the national image.[161]

(e) The *death or bankruptcy of one of the parties* results in the termination of a franchise agreement, since a franchise agreement is a contract *intuitu personae*,[162] unless there is a clause granting successors a right to continue the franchise agreement.

The majority of franchise agreements provide for a termination *de jure* when one of the parties goes into bankruptcy.

If the franchisor's trustee in bankruptcy does not continue the franchise agreement, the franchisee's obligations of non-competition and confidentiality are no longer binding, he may not continue to use the trade mark, or the emblem, since they are a part of the assets of the bankrupt estate.[162]

(f) *Transfer of the franchise agreement*: Because of the *intuita personae* character of the franchise agreement, a transfer of the agreement is only possible with the consent of the other party, unless the principle of transfer has been accepted in the agreement together with the conditions under which such a transfer would operate.

A difference should be made with the transfer of the business which does not include the transfer of the franchise agreement.[163] Since the trade marks, signs and name have to be returned to the franchisor and, as a consequence, the worth of the business would decrease enormously.

The agreement may contain a right of pre-emption whereby the franchisor has the right of first option to buy the business for a price which is equal to the offered price of the proposed transferee or at the price estimated by an expert.

3.7. Indemnity

Compensation payable on termination of a franchise agreement, can take various forms.

- damages for early termination of the agreement in the absence of serious breach of contract and compensation for loss of profit which the franchisee would otherwise have earned up to the end of the term;
- return of the franchise equipment and materials;
- discontinued use of the name and the insignia. After the termination of the agreement, the franchisee may not use that name or give the impression that he is still part of the franchise system.[164] He must also take all necessary measures to avoid any confusion with the franchise system;

---

[161] De Lat and Maes, *op. cit.*, 152; Bourgoignie, *op. cit.*, 24.
[162] Commercial Court, Brussels, 9 December 1982, J.T., 1983, 399-400.
[163] I. Moreau-Margreve, "Heurs et malheurs du gage sur fonds de commerce", R.C.J.B., 1980, 139.
[164] Court of Appeal, Brussels, 6 May 1980, B.R.H., 1981, 51.

- further use of know how: it would be impossible to make the franchisee forget everything he has learnt from the franchisor. It is therefore usual to insert a confidentiality clause in order to prevent dissemination of know how during the post-contractual period. In the case of a bankruptcy and when the trustee does not continue the franchise, the confidentiality clause no longer applies);
- since the clients are not an element of the franchise agreement, but only a result of it, it is difficult to make out a case for compensation for loss of clientèle;
- the contract can provide for buy-back of goods by the franchisor or the continued sale by the franchisee but without reference to the trademark.[165]

3.8. Specific Application of EEC Law

Although to date there has not been any case law in Belgium where specific application has been made of EEC law to franchise agreements, Reg. 4087/88 granting block exemption to certain categories of franchising agreements has direct effect. It is therefore an integral part of the legal framework within which an ever growing number of contracting parties will have to work and which the courts of Belgium must now interpret and apply.

3.8.1. Applicable law and jurisdiction

3.8.1.1. Applicable law

International contracts, which have a point of contact with different legal systems, are traditionally governed in Belgium by the law chosen by the parties. Based on the general principle of the contractual freedom of the parties as stated in article 1134 Civil Code, parties are free to choose the applicable law.

Problems arise, however, when the will of the parties as to their choice is unclear.

Components such as the element of connection with a specific country, the individual features of the contract can be withheld to be decisive for the applicable law.

3.8.1.2. Jurisdiction

Parties may choose the competence of the Belgian courts in their contract.

If the contract does not contain a clause of jurisdiction, a foreign defendant can be assigned before a Belgian court according to article 635 of the Judicial Code. The competence of the Belgian court can for instance be based on the defendant's residence, the place where the contractual obligations have been performed.[166]

Except for the competence rules provided for in article 635 Judicial Code, the foreign defendant can challenge the competence of the Belgian court, if he raises this challenge before any other defence.

---

[165] De Lat and Maes, *op. cit.,* 161.
[166] Article 635 Judicial Code.

If the defendant does not appear before the Belgian court, he is presumed to decline the competence of the Belgian court. The judge has to examine *de officio* whether or not he is competent.[167]

In daily practice, the problem of jurisdiction is governed by the provisions of bilateral and multilateral treaties, which have priority over national rules.

In that respect, the Treaty of Brussels, of 27 September 1968, which states as a main principle that the jurisdiction of the domicile of the defendant is competent, is of special importance. This Treaty applies, notwithstanding contrary regulations of older bilateral treaties or Belgian law.

Arbitration does not fall within the scope of the Treaty but the validity of arbitration clauses is fully recognized by Belgian law.[168]

As to validity of an arbitration clause, the problem is raised under 3.6.2. If indeed the law of 27 July 1961, as modified by the law of 13 April 1971 on the termination of distributorship agreements would apply on the termination of franchise agreements, the arbitration clause providing for the application of a foreign law could give problems for the exequatur of the award.[168]

The Belgian Supreme Court was asked whether an arbitration clause in an exclusive distributorship agreement was valid and gave the following answer:[169]

"A litigation relating to the termination by the supplier of an exclusive distributorship agreement having effects in part or in the whole of the Belgian territory, cannot be ruled by an arbitration, agreed prior to the end of the agreement and which has as its aim and effect the application of foreign law".

---

[167] Article 636 Judicial Code.
[168] Article 1676 ff. of the Judicial Code.
[169] Cass. 20 June 1979, J.T., 1979, 625.

LAW OF 3RD JULY 1978 CONCERNING
LABOUR AGREEMENTS
(=Arbeidsovereenkomstenwet)
(=AOW)

Article 4. A labour agreement for a trade representative shall be a contract in which a worker, the trade representative, undertakes to prospect and visit clients with a view to negotiating or concluding business, excluding insurance, for the account of and in the name of one or more principals.

Notwithstanding any express stipulation or absence thereof in the contract, any contract concluded between a principal and an intermediary, whatever the description thereof, shall be deemed to be a contract of employment for a trade representative until provided otherwise.

The following are not deemed to be trade representatives for the purposes of this law: commission agents, brokers, holders of exclusive sales concessions, intermediaries who are free to pass on orders received to any party they see fit, and in general any commercial agent linked to his principal by a business contract, a salary mandate or any other contract by virtue of which a commercial agent is not acting under his principal's authority.

Article 7. A labour contract shall be concluded either for a fixed period, or for a clearly defined piece of work, or for an indeterminate period.

It may never be concluded for life.

Article 9. Any labour contract entered into for a fixed period of time or for a clearly defined piece of work shall be produced in writing for each employee individually by the date upon which he begins employment.

If there is no written confirmation that it is entered into for a fixed period of time or for a clearly defined piece of work, the contract shall be subject to the same conditions as a contract entered into for an indeterminate period of time.

Production of a written contract entered into for a fixed period of time or for a clearly defined piece of work shall not be required in those industries and for those categories of worker where this form of work contract is covered by a collective labour agreement made compulsory by Royal Decree.

Article 10. Where the parties have entered into more than one successive contract of work for a fixed period of time without there having been any interval between them which is attributable to the worker, they shall be deemed to have entered into a contract for an indeterminate period of time, unless the employer proves that these contracts were justified by the nature of the work or other legitimate reasons.

Article 11 (a). (Any labour contract entered into for part-time work must be produced individually in writing for each employee, by the date upon which the worker begins fulfilment of his contract.

This written contract shall specify the agreed conditions and hours of part-time work.

The hours of part-time work may be variable.

In the absence of any written contract in conformity with the provisions of the first and second paragraphs above, the worker may choose the conditions and hours of part-time work which are most convenient to him from those which are either:

- Specified in the conditions of work, or
- Failing this, are given in any document produced compulsorily under Royal Decree no. 5 dated 23rd October 1978 relating to the keeping of company documents).

Article 11 (b). (Any person replacing a worker who is termporarily unable to fulfil his contract for a reason other than economic reasons, bad weather, strike or lock-out, may be taken on under conditions which depart from the regulations laid down by this law as far as the duration of the contract and the amount of notice required are concerned.

The reason, the identity of the worker(s) replaced and the conditions under which they are taken on shall be specified in writing for each worker individually, by the date upon which they commence employment.

The duration of any contract of replacement entered into under the provisions of this Article may not exceed two years.

Where the parties have entered into more than one successive contract of work for a fixed period of time without there having been any interval between them which is attributable to the worker, the total duration of these successive contracts may not exceed two years.

Unless written agreement is made to the contrary or the period of two years specified in paragraphs 3 and 4 is exceeded, the contract shall be subject to the same conditions as contracts entered into for an indeterminate period of time.

Article 16. The employer and the worker owe each other a duty of mutual respect and regard.

They are obliged to ensure and observe that propriety and correctness are respected during the fulfilment of the contract.

Article 17. The worker shall be obliged:

1. To carry out his work with due care, integrity and conscientiousness, at the time and place agreed;
2. To act according to the orders and instructions given to him by the employer, his agents and officials, for the purpose of fulfilling the contract;
3. To refrain from doing any of the following during the contract or after it has ceased:

(a) Divulging any trade or business secret, or any secret of a personal or confidential nature which he may come to know during the course of his professional activity;

(b) Taking part in or co-operating with any act of disloyal competition;

4. To refrain from anything which might harm either his own safety or that of his colleagues, his employer or any third party;

5. To return to the employer in good condition any tools or unused materials given to him.

Article 18. In the event of damage caused by the worker to the employer or to any third party whilst fulfillilng his contract, the worker shall be liable only for wilful misrepresentation or gross negligence.

He shall not be liable for trivial negligence unless this constitutes a habitual rather than accidental feature of his behaviour.

He may not be absolved from the liability laid down in paragraphs 1 and 2 except by a collective work agreement which is compulsory under a Royal Decree, and this shall relate only to his liability to his employer.

The employer may, subject to the conditions laid down in Article 23 of the law dated 12th April 1965 on the protection of employees' remuneration, deduct from his remuneration any compensation or damages due to him under this Article, which have been agreed on the facts with the employee or fixed by a judge.

Article 19. A worker shall not be held liable for deterioration or wear and tear caused by normal use of an item, nor for its accidental loss.

Article 20. The employer shall be obliged:

1. To ensure that the worker works in the agreed conditions, and at the agreed time and place, notably by making available, if required and in the absence of any stipulation to the contrary, the assistance, instruments and materials required to carry out the work;

2. To take due pains to ensure that the work is carried out in conditions which favour both the safety and the health of the employee, and that first aid is available to him in the event of accident. A first aid box must therefore be available to staff at all times;

3. To pay the employee's remuneration under the conditions and at the time and place agreed;

4. To provide the worker with suitable accommodation and healthy and adequate food where he is obliged to accommodate and feed the worker;

5. To give the employee the time required to carry out the duties of his religion, and any civic duties imposed by law;

6. To give due care and attention to the comfort of workers, especially young workers;

7. To give due care to the preservation of tools belonging to the worker and personal effects held in trust for the worker; under no circumstances shall the employer be entitled to refuse to return these tools or personal effects.

Article 23. (A worker shall not be obliged to provide a deposit unless specified by a collective work agreement or, in the absence of such an agreement, by a collective work agreement with the *Conseil national du travail* which is compulsory under a Royal Decree).

Any deposit paid to ensure that the worker fulfils his obligations shall be deposited with the *Banque National de Belgique*, the *Caisse des Dépôts et Consignations*, the *Caisse Générale d'Epargne et de Retraite*, the *Crédit Communal de Belgique*, or with a private bank or building society covered by the provisions of the Royal Decree dated 23rd June 1967.

The deposit shall be made in the worker's name and its purpose shall be described.

The employer shall deposit the money within fourteen days of the date it is paid by the worker or deducted from his pay.

Solely by the fact of the deposit having been made, the employer shall acquire a preferential claim to the deposit for any debt arising from the worker's total or partial failure to fulfil his obligations.

The amount of the deposit may only be returned to the employee or paid to the employer by agreement of both parties or by production of an extract from a judicial decision on the issue.

The amount of the deposit may not exceed the equivalent of six months' remuneration.

Article 23 (a). (Deposits made before this law comes into force shall be adapted to the provisions of the collective employment agreements referred to in Article 23, paragraph 1, of the law dated 3rd July 1978 on contracts of work, within a period of six months from the day when the employer became bound by the collective work agreement.)

Article 24. The following shall be punished by imprisonment of seven days to six months and a fine of 26 to 500 francs or only one of these penalties:

(1. Any employer who contravenes the provisions of Article 23, paras. 2, 3, 4 and 7).

2. Any person making it a condition of granting employment or of paying allowances or commissions that the worker subscribe to, pay for or purchase shares, shares of interests or obligations of any kind or who are made to return funds in a title other than that of the worker's deposit.

Article 25. Any clause in which the employer reserves the right to unilaterally amend the conditions of the contract shall be null and void.

Article 32. Without prejudice to general laws on the expiry of obligations, undertakings resulting from contracts covered by this law shall cease:

1. When the contract expires;
2. When the work for which the contract was entered into has been competed;
3. By the wish of one of the parties when the contract has been entered into for an indeterminate period of time or there is a serious cause for breaching it;
4. By the death of the employee;
5. By Act of God.

Article 33. The death of the employer shall not terminate the contract. If it leads to a situation where the work which the employee was taken onto carry out no longer exists, or if the contract was for direct work with the deceased person, the judge shall decide in equity whether any compensation is due and, if so, how much.

Article 37. Where the contract has been entered into for an indeterminate period of time, either of the parties may revoke it having first given notice.

The notice shall only be valid if the party sends the other party written notice of the beginning and the duration of the period of notice.

If this party then signs a copy of this communication, this shall be deemed only to constitute acknowledgement that the notice has been received.

This may also be done either by recorded delivery, taking effect from the third working day after posting, or by a writ served by a process-server.

Article 39. § 1 If the contract has been entered into for an indeterminate period of time, any party revoking the contract without serious cause or without giving the period of notice specified in Articles 59, 82, 83, 84 and 115, shall pay the other party compensation equal to the current remuneration corresponding either to the length of the period of notice or to the part of the period of notice still to run. However the compensation shall always be equal to the amount of current remuneration corresponding to the period of notice where the employer terminates the contract in ignorance of the provisions of Article 38 § 3 of this law or article 40 of the law on employment dated 6th March 1971.

Compensation for the dismissal shall include not only current remuneration, but also the benefits acquired under the contract.

§ 2. Without prejudice to the provisions of § 1, any employer who, during one of the periods specified in Article 29, points 1, 6 and 7, and Article 38, § 3, paragraphs 1, 3 and 4, does not comply with the provisions of Article 38, § 3 shall pay compensation equal to the normal remuneration due for the periods or parts of periods referred to in Article 38, § 3, paragraphs 1, 3 and 4, during which the employee has not been occupied.

However this compensation may not exceed an amount corresponding to three months of this remuneration if a manual worker or domestic is involved, or six months if a non-manual worker or trade representative is involved.

§ 3. Without prejudice to the provisions of § 1, any employer not complying with the provisions of Article 40 of the law on work dated 16th March 1971 shall pay compensation under paragraph 3 of the said Article 40.

Article 67. § 1. The contract may include a probation clause. This clause shall, if it is to be valid, be stated in writing for each employee individually, no later than the date upon which he begins employment.

§ 2. The probationary period may not be less than one month. It may not be more than (six months or twelve months) respectively depending on whether the annual remuneration is less or greater than (780,000 francs).

In the absence of any specification as to its duration, either in the individual or collective labour contract, or in the work regulations, the probationary period shall be one month.

§ 3. In the event that fulfilment of the contract is suspended during the probationary period, this period shall be extended by a period equal to that of the suspension.

Article 69. Notwithstanding Art. 13, the arbitration clause shall apply to any employee whose annual remuneration exceeds (1,300,000) francs and who is responsible for the day-to-day administration of the organisation or assumes within one division of the organisation or one production unit management responsibilities which are comparable to those exercised at overall company level.

Article 70. Any employee taken on for an indeterminate period of time, or for a fixed period of at least three months, or for a clearly defined piece of work which would normally take at least three months to complete, shall retain a right to remuneration for the first thirty days of being unable to work through illness or accident.

Article 72. An employee as specified in Article 71 shall, in the event of being unable to work because of occupational illness, an accident at work or an accident occurring on the way to or from work, to (. . .) payment for a period of seven days beginning from the first day of inability to work.

Any day of work which is interrupted by reason of occupational illness, an accident at work or an accident occurring on the way to or from work, for which the employee is paid by virtue of the provisions of Article 27, shall be considered as the first day of this period.

The provisions of Article 54, § 2, paras. 1 and 2 shall apply to this remuneration.

Article 79. Where the contract provides for a probationary period, and the worker is unable to work because of illness or accident, the employer may revoke the contract without compensation, if it has a duration of more than seven days.

The same shall apply to contracts entered into for a fixed period of less than three months or for a clearly defined piece of work which would normally take less than three months to carry out.

Article 81. § 1 Without prejudice to article 79, the contract may not be revoked unilaterally during the probationary period without serious cause without giving seven days' notice in the form specified in Article 37, paras. 2 to 4. If this notice is given during the course of the first month, it shall take effect by the last day of the month.

§ 2 If either party revokes the contract without serious cause or without observing the period of notice specified in § 1, it shall pay the other party compensation equal to the current remuneration (including benefits acquired by virtue of the contract) corresponding either to the period of notice or to that part of the period of notice which is still left to run.

If the contract is revoked during the first month of probation, the compensation shall be equal to the current remuneration (including benefits acquired by virtue of the contract) corresponding to that part of the month which is still to run, increased by the length of the period of notice.

Article 82. § 1 The period of notice speicified in Article 37 shall begin on the first day of the month following that during which the notice was given.

§ 2. Where the annual remuneration is less than (650,000) francs, the period of notice to be observed by the employer shall be at least three months for employees who have been employed for at least five years.

This period of notice shall be increased by three months at the beginning of each new period of five years with the same employer.

If notice is given by the employee, the period of notice specified in paras. 1 and 2 shall be reduced by one half, not exceeding three months.

§ 3. Where the annual remuneration exceeds (650,000) francs, the amount of notice to be observed by the employer and the employee shall be specified by agreement made on or before the date upon which the notice is given, or by a judge.

If notice is given by the employer, the period of notice may not be less than that specified in § 2, paras. 1 and 2.

If notice is given by the employee, the period of notice may not be more than four and a half months if the annual remuneration is over (650,000) francs and under (1,300,000) francs, and may not exceed six months if the annual remuneration exceeds (1,300,000) francs.

§ 4. The period of notice shall be calculated based on the seniority acquired at the moment when the notice takes effect.

Article 87. The provisions of section III, with the exception of Article 86, and this section shall apply to labour contracts for trade representatives.

Article 93. Any trade representative whose contract specifies that he is responsible for visiting only a fixed number of clients or a fixed area shall be entitled during the period of the contract to commission on business concluded by the employer with these clients or in this area without his assistance.

He shall also be entitled to commission on business concluded while the contract is suspended or after it is terminated where the order was passed on during the period of the contract.

Article 96. The contract shall lay down the basis upon which commission is calculated. In the absence of any contractual provisions, commission shall be calculated on the price appearing on the order form or on the order accepted by the employer; in the absence of either of these, it shall be calculated on current prices, rates or price lists, and, in the absence of these, on the price paid.

Article 101. Where a contract is terminated, either by the employer with no serious cause, or by the trade representative with serious cause, compensation shall be payable for dismissal to a trade representative who has created a clientèle, unless the employer is able to prove that no prejudice arises to the trade representative from the breach of contract.

This compensation shall only become payable after the employee has been employed for one year.

It shall be equal to three months' remuneration where a trade representative has been employed by the same employer for a period of one to five years. It shall be increased by one month's remuneration at the beginning of each additional period of five years of employment with the same employer.

Where the trade representative's remuneration consists wholly or partly of commission, this shall be calculated based on the average monthly commission earned during the twelve months prior to the date upon which the contract is terminated.

(Indemnity for dismissal shall include not only current remuneration, but also the benefits acquired under the contract).

Article 103. Where a contract is terminated for a serious reason imputable to the employer and the amount of compensation for dismissal specified in Article 101 does not cover the whole of the damage actually suffered, the trade representative may, provided he is able to prove the extent of the alleged damage, also obtain the compensation specified in Article 101, of damages and interest equal to the difference between the amount of damage actually suffered and that of this compensation.

Article 104. In contracts where the annual remuneration does not exceed (650,000) francs, the non-competition clause shall be deemed not to exist.

In contracts where the annual remuneration is above this amount, any non-competition clause shall only be valid provided that it relates to similar activities, that it does not exceed twelve months and it is limited to the territory in which the trade representatives carries out his activities.

The non-competition clause shall not have effect after the contract has been terminated, either during or after the probation period, by the employer wihtout serious cause or by the trade representative with serious cause.

A non-competition clause shall only be valid if it is in writing.

Article 105. A non-competition clause creates a presumption in favour of the representative of having created a body of customers; the employer may prove the contrary if necessary.

Article 107. Unless there is gross negligence or wilful misrepresentation, any clause making a trade representative liable for a client's insolvency shall only be valid up to an amount equal to the commission payable on the debts irrecoverable from the client.

Any guaranteed commission clause must be in writing.

Article 131. For the purposes of Articles 65, 67, 69, 82, 84, 85, 86 and 104, the commissions and benefits payable shall be calculated on the amount of remuneration paid in the past twelve months.

(The amounts of remuneration specified in Articles 65, 67, 69, 82, 84, 85, 86 and 104 shall be adjusted each year by the third-quarter index of salaries for employees using the following formula: the new amount is equal to the basic amount multiplied by the new index and divided by the opening index. The result obtained shall be rounded up to the nearest thousand.

The new amounts are published in the *Moniteur belge*. They come into force on 1st January following that of their adjustment.

For the purposes of paragraph 2, the following definitions shall apply:

1. Index of conventional salaries for employees: the index calculated by the Ministry of Employment and Labour based on the calculation of the average benefits received by adult employees in the private sector as specified in the collective labour agreement;
2. Base amount: the amount applying on 1st January 1985;
3. New index: the index for the third quarter of 1985 and subsequent years;
4. Opening index: the index for the third quarter of 1984).

CONVENTION 1 JULY 1964

Article IV. "1. Any state which has already ratified one or more conventions on the conflicts of law concerning the international sale of tangible moveable property or has confirmed it, may declare, in a notification addressed to the Government of the Netherlands when it desposits its instrument of ratification or confirmation, that it will only apply the uniform law in the cases specified by one of these conventions if this leads to the uniform law being applied.

2. Any state making the above declaration shall indicate to the Government of the Netherlands the conventions intended in its declaration."

Article V. "Any state may, in a notification addressed to the government of the Netherlands, when it deposits its instrument of ratification or confirmation, declare that it will only apply the uniform law to contracts where the parties have chosen this law as governing the contract under Article 4 of the uniform law."

CHAPTER 3

Denmark

John Kahlke, Carsten Iversen

INTRODUCTION

Danish law on agents will be substantially altered by the application in national law of the EC directive no. 653 of 8 December 1986.

Consequently, it is fair to deal rather briefly with the present national aspects of distribution and agency in Danish law.

The EEC-law provisions on distribution and agency has had little impact in Denmark till now. A new Danish legislation on agency is presently being prepared by a working group composed of Ministry of Justice officials and trade association representatives. The working group is expected to present its suggestions in December 1988. However, the actual legislation will be drafted by a parliamentary commission and may be subject to many digressions from the path drawn by the specialists. The new legislation will take effect from 1 January 1990. Agency agreements concluded before that date will be governed by the rules previously in force until 1 January 1992 or, if terminated, to expire on or before 30 June 1992 until such date.

This text relies to a certain extent on AIJA Reports on Distribution and Agency by John Kahlke and Patrice Caron, presented in Vancouver in 1986, and on Business Format Franchising, by Christian T. Kjølbye, presented in Copenhagen in 1987.

Copenhagen
October 1988

1. Commercial Agency

1.1 Definition of Various Types of Agencies and Intermediaries

A commercial agent is defined as a person who brings about contracts of purchase in the name of another person (the principal). He does not—except when legally provided—have the power to bind the principal. He is entitled to a remuneration for his efforts based on the results obtained. The legislation concerning commercial agents is contained in the Act on Commission, Commercial Agency and Itinerant Salesmen, *Kommissionsloven*.

The legislation was enacted in 1917 and—as with other commercial codifications from that time—*Kommissionsloven* may be deviated from by agreement.

1.1.1. Independent

According to *Kommissionsloven*, three categories of independent commercial agents exist under Danish law: the *kommissionær* (the commission-aire—chapter II), the *agent* (commercial agent—chapter III) and the *selvstændinge handelsrejsende* (independent salesman—chapter IV).

The *kommissionær* sells or buys at the request of a principal but in his own name. In modern terms: he is a broker. In Denmark, a *kommissionær* is known within the trades of commodities, bonds and shares and real estate. Specific legislation is enacted for stock brokers, real estate agents, etc. largely in order to secure the position of their principal. For the purpose of this text it is thought to be appropriate not to deal with these special categories.

An agreement for sale in commission (*kommissionssalg*) is further used as a device to secure manufacturer's or wholesaler's claim against a distributor for unpaid deliveries of stock. Such agreements for sale in commission are directed by security interests only and are rarely brought to the attention of the distributor's customers as title of the goods is held to pass from distributor to customer directly. However, the manufacturer/wholesaler gains security in the purchase sum provided certain formalities are complied with.

An *agent* procures promises for deliveries from customers or solicits orders from customers while acting in the name of an identified principal. The *agent* has no power to enter into contracts binding on the principal.

An *selvstændig handelsrejsende* is an independent tradesman who travels from place to place procuring orders for delivery from his principals for goods that he does not carry with him.

As the legal rules applying are almost identical to the three categories, the term of *agent* will cover them all unless specifically excepted.

The revised Danish legislation will cover agents and *selvstændige handelsrejsende* who will be fused into one category in law whereas the *kommissionær* will not see his position altered.

1.1.2. Employed

According to *Komissionsloven*, only one category of employed agents exists, that of the *handelsrejsende* (the itinerant salesman). He is defined as a person who travels from place to place soliciting orders from customers for goods that he does not bring along with him.

The status of *handelsrejsende* is normally but not necessarily that of a salaried employee, i.e. he is employed by one principal, he receives instructions from this principal and has to report to him. Furthermore, he is subject to the principal's control. Much case-law has dealt with this distinction, e.g. 60.880,

Ø, where much importance was attached to the formal (but not exercised) power of instruction of the principal. It is fair to assume that the courts when in doubt will conclude that the position of the *handelsrejsende* has been that of a salaried employee.

As an employee the *handelsrejsende* now enjoys the protection of a legislation set up for salaried employees long after the enactment of *Kommissionsloven*, such as minimum notice period, protection against unfair dismissal, sickness pay, leave for maternity and military service, reimbursement of travel expenses, etc. according to Lov om Retsforholdet mellem Arbejdsgivere og Funktionærer—*Funktionærloven*. It is a precondition to obtain this protection that the employee works for a minimum of time per week (at present 15 hours) and that his appointment is not a temporary one.

The general development in commercial distribution has led to the establishment of further categories of employed agents. The distinction between them is of no great significance in this context and the term of *sælger* (salesman) will be used in the following to identify all employed agents who— under the supervision and control of a principal—solicit orders or obtain promises for delivery from customers, and whose remuneration partially or fully is dependent on the results of their efforts.

1.1.3. Others

1.2. Conclusion of the Contract (Special Conditions)

A contract in Danish law is concluded through the acceptance by one party of the offer of another party. Offer and acceptance are binding upon the offeror/acceptor until withdrawn or rejected. An offer must be accepted without delay unless it specifically states a delay of acceptance—*Aftaleloven*, sections 1–9. An offer may be binding even though it is not directed towards the offeree. There are no requirements for agreements to be in writing. This is true as well for agreements between commercial agents and principals.

However, within specific areas of business, a written and well-specified agreement between principal and agent has now become a pre-condition for the agent's right to obtain a remuneration for sales concluded through his efforts, e.g. in real estate sales where the *kommissionær* (broker) acting for a consumer may find himself deprived of a remuneration, unless he has had his consumer principal enter into an agreement of commission following administrative order requirements specifying size of remuneration, expenses to be covered, notice periods for termination, etc.

In practice, agreements for sale in commission—*kommissionssalg*—must be in writing to secure the manufacturer/creditor in dispute with the distributor/debtor's other creditors or bankrupt estate.

Notwithstanding the absence of formal requirements new agency agreements will normally be concluded in writing. They will either adapt the models proposed by the Danish Chamber of Commerce—out of which one standard form already provides for the application of Directive No. 653—or they will follow the standard form agreed upon between the associations of agents in the Nordic countries. In some relationships the standard form published by the ICC (publication no 410), the ORGALIME model form of Exclusive Agency Contract, will be used.

The contract is interpreted and may eventually be modified if too onerous on one party. This is carried through by virtue of section 36 of *Aftaleloven*, a general clause on limitation of contracts. Such modifications are administered by the courts and they have shown themselves extremely reluctant to modify terms of contracts concluded by parties that could be qualified as 'businessmen' as opposed to 'consumers'.

1.3. The Principal's Duties and Rights

1.3.1. The principal's duties

1.3.1.1. Commission

The principal is under a duty to pay the agent a commission on sales concluded through the agent's intervention or sales concluded with customers located in a territory where the agent enjoys a position of exclusivity (*Kommissionsloven*, sections 68 and 70).

There are no legal requirements for the quantification of commission to an agent. In case no agreement has been made about how to calculate the commission the agent is entitled to whatever commission he claims provided it is not openly excessive (*Kommissionsloven*, section 68 and parallel *Købeloven* Sales of Goods Act, section 5).

However, jurisprudence has in recent years developed so that an intermediary may not obtain remuneration above the normal commission when no specific agreement has been made as to the calculation of commission.

The principal is not liable to pay the commission until he has received payment in full from the customer. If the customer terminates the agreement in virtue of a breach of contract by the principal or in virtue of an agreement with the principal the agent remains entitled to his commission. If the purchase sum is paid only partially the agent loses his right to the commission. He will, however, be entitled to a part of the commission if the outstanding purchase sum is smaller than the commission to the agent (viz. *Kommissionsloven* section 69).

In many trades it has become customary to pay a proportion of the commission in respect to the proportion of the purchase sum that has been paid.

1.3.1.2. Protection of agent, information

When the agent has been granted the exclusivity either to sell certain objects or to sell within a certain territory, the principal is restricted from placing his products for sale himself or through other agents.

However, this restriction is of a purely economical nature, i.e. the principal will remain liable to pay the commission on the transactions even though he does not use the services of his exclusive agent.

When the agent enjoys exclusivity he is entitled to receive information of all customers' inquiries concerning the objects he is selling or his territory.

The principal is under a duty to treat as confidential all secret commercial information about the agent obtained as a result of their collaboration.

This inhibition is specified in Act on Fair Marketing Practices—*Markedsføringsloven*—section 9. Violations of the duty is sanctioned by damages and even fines when public interest is concerned. Nor must any third party use information passed on in contravention of *Markedsføringsloven*, section 9. Such third party, e.g. the new employer or collaborator, may be held liable to pay damages provided bad faith can be established. Jurisprudence relating to *Markedsføringsloven*, section 9, hardly deals with agent-principal business relations. The losses for which a claimant could expect to be compensated through damages would be calculated on the basis of a fair estimate made by the court of the consequences of loss of business or disruption of the market. Danish courts have accepted that it is difficult if not impossible to evidence directly a loss caused through a breach of confidence.

1.3.1.3. Supply of written statement

The agent who acts on a permanent basis for a principal is entitled to a *provisionsnota* (a written statement) at the beginning of each half-year (2 January and 1 July). The written statement shall specify all sales effected through the efforts of the agent or concluded with persons within the agents exclusive territory.

The written statement must further specify what amount of commission the agent is entitled to for each transaction and the reason for which the commission has not yet been paid out.

The agent who is not representing the principal on a permanent basis is entitled to a written statement for each sale concluded through his efforts. This written statement shall indicate the amount of commission outstanding or—when the principal finds that no commission is due—include the reason given by the principal to this effect.

1.3.2. The principal's rights

In addition to his contractual obligations the agent is under a general duty according to *Kommissionsloven*, section 66, to act in the best interests of his principal. He shall keep the principal informed of any matter of importance to his and the product's performance on the market. Especially, he is under the duty to forward purchase orders without delay. The *kommissionær* is further under the duty to make prompt accounts for transactions closed by him for the principal and promptly to hand over money belonging to the principal. The *kommissionær* but not the agent is under the duty to obtain the best possible price for the principal and shall keep the stock of the principal separate from any other stock. The *kommissionær* is not obliged to inform the principal of the name of the purchaser of goods. However, he must inform the principal if he himself is a party to the transaction.

The principal is entitled to damages from the agent if the latter fails to comply with his statutory duties and thereby causes a foreseeable loss to the principal (*Kommissionsloven*, section 67). Failure to comply with contractual obligations may, depending on the contract, give rise to further claims for damages.

The principal has proprietary rights to stock belonging to him in the possession of the *kommissionær* and to money received by the *kommissionær* for sales of that stock. Such stock must be kept separate from any other stock of the *kommissionær* and efficient control must be exercised by the principal. The principal of an agent does not enjoy the same privilege. However, an agent unlike the *kommissionær* is not held legitimated to recover money for transactions effected between his principal and the customers.

The principal may impose upon the agent secrecy concerning secret commercial information divulged from the principal in accordance with *Markedsføringsloven*, section 9. cf. section 1.3.1.2. above.

The agent is free to represent other principals, even competing principals, unless he has specifically undertaken not to do so.

Certain restrictions on the agent's freedom of action in this respect may be deducted from his general obligation to act in the principal's best interests (*Kommissionsloven*, section 66). Further requirements for loyal behaviour may ensue from the general clause of *Markedsføringsloven*, section 1, according to which enterprises may not act in contravention of good marketing practice. This 'general clause' has in jurisprudence been applied to prevent business methods that—though violating no contractual obligations—were regarded by the courts as being abusive, e.g. U.82.1095.H.

1.4. The Commercial Agent's Duties and Rights

1.4.1. The commercial agent's duties

1.4.1.1. Trustworthiness, duty to inform

As mentioned above in 1.3.2. the agent is under a duty to take care of principal's best interests and to inform him of any circumstance of importance to the thrift of his business. You may say that the agent is bound by a general duty to act loyally to his contractual partner, i.e. to take any adequate steps to sell the products, not to misinform him, to pass on any relevant information, not to dis-recommend the products, etc.

The *kommissionær* has a duty to examine products received for the purpose of sale and to inform the principal of any defects found. This duty is incumbent on the agent as well as he holding products in stock at the wish of the principal (*Kommissionsloven*, sections 21 and 75).

1.4.1.2. Del credere

The agent is under no duty to guarantee the payment by the customers of the purchase sum—to act *"del credere"*.

To act or stand *"del credere"* in Danish law signifies acting as a bail. It is disputed whether the *"del credere"* agent's duty to pay the sum in guarantee arises immediately when the purchaser has failed to pay or only when the purchaser's inability to pay has been evidenced, e.g. through bankruptcy, vain recovery procedures, etc. Of course you may say that the agent always stands *"del credere"* for his commission (viz. section 1.3.1.1. above.).

Danish legislation does not contain any restrictions as to the extent to which the agent may stand *"del credere"*. In principle, the agent may stand *"del credere"* for the entire purchase price without any compensation through the quantum of his commission. Principal's abuse of his power to dictate such contract conditions could be reduced in virtue of *Aftaleloven*, section 36 (viz. section 1.2. above).

When the *kommissionær* does not disclose to his principal the identity of the purchaser he stands "*del credere*" for the payment of the purchase sum. A similar situation arises when the *kommissionær* has allowed purchaser credit on the payment contrary to the instructions of the principal.

1.4.1.3. Non-competition

The agent may represent competitors or even himself compete with the principal. The general duty of loyalty may compel him not to represent competitors, not to take over competing firms, etc. even if he has not specifically undertaken to refrain from doing so. It should be noted that even if the agent has undertaken a competition clause the principal may see it reduced by the courts in virtue of *Aftaleloven*, section 38. The court may limit such clauses if they are considered excessive as to the geographical scope, time or other circumstances when compared with the principal's need of protection against competitors.

Normally, it is part of the competition clause that a breach is sanctioned by liquidated damages, i.e. it is agreed that one party will pay a fixed amount regardless of what losses the other party may evidence. Such sanctions are normally considered fair on the agent. Danish law contains very strict requirements to evidence of loss, so strict that it is difficult to obtain adequate compensation for disruption of the market position of a product caused by the serious breach of a competition clause. In excessive cases, however, the courts may reduce the amount of liquidated damages.

A *sælger* may be subjected to competition clauses only if he is in a particular position of trust and only for a time period of one year (*Funktionærloven*, section 18). This period of time may be extended when a specific remuneration is paid as a fair compensation.

1.4.1.4. Secrecy

The agent is under a duty to treat the principal's trade secrets as confidential in accordance with *Markedsføringsloven*, section 9.

The principal's trade secrets comprise both commercial and technical secrets. Not all information about the principal's business is trade secrets. Only information known by a restricted number of persons within the enterprise concerning essential operations and not being accessible through other sources may be qualified as trade secrets.

Confidence may not be extended to any information concerning the principal's business or to information ordinarily acquired during the normal operation of a business in that field.

Confidence as prescribed by *Markedsføringsloven*, section 9, must be observed only as to a commercial exploitation of the trade secrets. The agent may without violating *Markedsføringloven*, section 9, devolve information to journalists, scientists, public controlling officials, etc.

Given the rather limited scope of the duty to keep information confident in the *Markedsføringsloven* the agent will normally be asked contractually to undertake a specific clause of secrecy.

Employees are under a general duty to act loyally to their principal and thus to keep confident the trade secrets of the enterprise. The extent of an employee's duty to keep information confident is certainly larger than the duty of the independent agent. However, it remains unclear in jurisprudence where to draw the line. In recent jurisprudence much importance has been attached to the position of trust of the employee. If the employee is in a particular position of trust or, generally, if he holds a position with a principal that is very dependent on the trust of his customers (an accountant, a solicitor), the breach of confidence is likely to lead to a termination of the appointment without notice. In other positions, such as that of the *sælger*, such steps would only occur following a warning by the employer against abuse of confidence.

1.4.2. The commercial agent's rights

1.4.2.1. Commission

The agent is entitled to a commission on all orders obtained through his efforts or—in case he enjoys exclusivity, for a certain period of time or over a certain geographical area—on all transactions concluded within that time-limit or within that area.

The commission falls due for orders obtained during the term of agent's appointment (*Kommissionsloven*, section 68). The issue of "after commission" is referred to at 1.7.2. The commission falls due when the purchaser has paid the full purchase sum and will eventually be reduced if the principal receives only such proportions of the purchase sum as do not cover the commission in full. In many fields of business commission is paid out proportionate to the fraction of the purchase sum actually paid. In addition to the commission the agent is entitled to reimbursement of all expenses that are extraordinary and which he may evidence that the commission is not meant to cover.

The agent may exercise a lien over samples of products, etc. in his possession to exert payment of commission for the principal. The employee agent may further claim reimbursement of travel and accommodation expense for displacement outside the area he is appointed to cover.

The principal of an employee agent who has paid to him a commission on account and who at the termination of the employment has a balance in his favour on such payments is barred from recovering such amount from the employee, i.e. the employee is entitled to regard the commission paid on account as a minimal remuneration or wage.

1.5. Liabilities of Principal and Agent during the Term of the Agency

1.5.1. The principal as against the agent

The principal is liable in tort against the agent according to the general rules of Danish law, i.e. if he has intentionally or negligently committed an act whereby a foreseeable loss has occurred to the agent.

The principal may be held liable to the agent for payment of commissions though he has not obtained payment from the purchaser or not even delivered goods according to the purchase orders, when the non-fulfilment of the contract was not solely the fault of the purchaser, e.g. if the purchase sum cannot be recovered because of prescription the principal would still have to pay the commission to the agent (*Kommissionsloven*, section 68 (2)).

The agent may be liable directly towards the customer by virtue of his passing on information about the products (*Købeloven*, sections 84 and 85). In such cases he may direct a claim of relief against the principal.

The principal is liable for the negligence of the *sælger* as though it was committed by himself. The principal is not liable for the independent agent's errors or omissions, notably he is not immediately liable to comply with terms of delivery, prices or performance criteria established between the agent and the customer, and which exceed the agent's authority as agreed between the principal and himself. See 1.5.2. below.

The principal has in older case-law been held liable for the agent's loss of expected profit in cases where he has concealed essential information to him or failed to prevent the marketing of his products through other sources when in a legal position to do so (viz. U.60.422 S.).

1.5.2. The principal as against third parties

Generally the agent has no power to bind the principal towards third parties. However, the *sælger* may be held to have a limited proxy for his principal in virtue of the position he holds with the enterprise – if it falls within the scope of his position to conclude certain agreements. In such cases the principal is bound to a third party, in good faith the agreement entered into by the employee (*Aftaleloven*, section 10 (2)).

An independent agent is not able to bind the principal to third parties, but the principal will be contractually obliged if he does not immediately object to the third party when he finds that the agent has exceeded his mandate, *Kommissionsloven*, section 78. This rule is enacted in order to protect the third party. Any objections by the principal should be made without delay, as should be made in Danish any objection regarding quantity, quality or delay in purchase transactions between businessmen.

It should be noted that it is fairly normal for a Danish agent to issue an order confirmation to the customer with a copy to the principal in order to avoid misunderstandings and in order to bind the potential customer until such time as the principal may accept his offer, and to establish a time-limit for any objections to be made.

A *handelsrejsende* (itinerant salesman)—who normally cannot bind his principal to third parties—is regarded as holding a special proxy for the principal if he has been supplied by the principal with standard forms for agreements, bearing the principal's name, and worded such that they are apt to evidence final agreements (*Kommissionsloven*, section 88 (2)).

When the principal has accepted the offer or is deemed to have accepted it the relationship between him and the purchaser will be judged according to *Købeloven* as to price-fixing, delay, defects, etc.

1.5.3. The agent as against the principal

The agent is liable to principal for any foreseeable loss occurring through a breach of duty on his part, viz. *Kommissionsloven*, sections 17 and 66, such as lack of diligence in passing on orders to the principal, lack of information about claims made by customers concerning delays or defects, lack of support to marketing efforts within this area, etc. Contracts often provide for summary or liquidated damages as factual loss may be difficult to evidence.

Danish tort law is quite strict as to requirements for the evidence of loss to be compensated. The principal may find himself with little or no compensation for the disruption of the market of his products caused by a negligent agent. Liquidated damages, however, may be reduced when considered excessive, *Aftaleloven*, section 36 (2).

Principal must immediately make a reservation of his claim against the agent once the alleged negligence has come to his knowledge (*Kommissionsloven*, sections 20 and 67 (2)).

1.5.4. The agent as against third parties

The agent will incur liability towards third parties if he negligently or intentionally fails to pass on relevant information.

The agent is not liable against third parties for the fulfilment of contracts as long as he acts in the principal's name and does not exceed his authority. However, he is a party to the agreement and may be adjoined in an ensuing dispute by virtue of a jurisdiction clause contained therein, viz. II 1969.125H.

When the agent erroneously pretends that he holds a proxy for his principal he remains liable to the third party as if the contract was concluded by himself, *Aftaleloven*, section 25. One may say that the agent has a strict liability for the existence of the proxy. Of course, the *komissionær* who trades in his own name and on behalf of the principal remains liable directly to the third party even if he exceeds the instructions of his principal relating to price or other terms. The third party will gain title to the goods and the principal must content himself with a claim for damages against the *kommissionær*.

1.6. Term and Termination

1.6.1. Term

There are no legal requirements for the duration of an agency agreement. Any agreement may be terminated with reasonable notice even if the terms of it do not provide for termination. Agreements which expire at a given date without notice are rarely seen.

1.6.2. Termination

Kommissionsloven contains no facultative delays of termination. In principle the contract may be terminated at any time without delay, *Kommissionsloven*, sections 46 and 76. In case substantial investments in marketing or material have been required by agent in order to establish and maintain a product on the market, recent case-law has required the principal to give a fair notice period. This period will depend on the specific business, the length of agent's appointment, the possibilities of agent or principal of minimizing their expenditure in relation to the termination, the prospect of a work-force to be dismissed, etc. A fair termination period normally would be between 1 and 6 months.

1.7. Indemnity

1.7.1. Indemnity for goodwill and/or clientèle

It is debatable whether an agent in Danish law could be entitled to claim for damage for loss of goodwill or clientèle. Case-law has so far refused to award compensation to agents under this headline. The reasons for such positions have been individualistic and factual and it may not be altogether excluded that such compensation would be awarded upon the individual merits of an agent terminated without cause.

1.7.2. Compensation for damages

Apart from loss of expected profit the agent may suffer loss from having incurred expenses in the expectation of maintaining the agency. Furthermore, he may have devoted substantial time to obtain orders that may be placed with principal or with successor without any effort on their behalf. In such cases the agent may be entitled to partial or full commission on the orders.

Compensation for expenses of marketing material have been awarded only at a rather specific basis by the Danish Court, e.g. the principal has been judged to buy off useless brochures and publishing material, to buy back samples, etc.

The *kommissionær* who has an exclusive agreement for a certain period may claim a fair remuneration—usually full commission—for the work performed if the appointment is terminated before envisaged (*Kommissions-loven*, section 50). It is not possible for the principal to reduce or limit his duty to pay commission on orders obtained within the fixed period by terminating the appointment.

A *sælger* during the notice period is entitled to his ordinary commission on account even though no transactions are obtained through his efforts (*Funktionærloven*, section 9). He is further entitled to 'after commission' on orders obtained after the period of employment through his preparatory efforts.

1.8. Specific Application of EEC Law

Provisions of the EEC law have until now been rarely applied on agents in Denmark. No judgments have been published concerning such disputes.

1.8.1. Disputes

Agreements may be entered into for the application of foreign law to contracts of agency between Danish agents and foreign principals. If no agreements exist the applicable law will be determined by applying the rules of Danish International Private law.

In virtue of these rules a test is carried through whereby all the points of attachment to the two different legal systems are examined. Such points may be place of contract, place of delivery, place of payment, language of contract, currency, choice of venue, place of performance, etc. The place of performance in agency agreement may be considered preponderant.

Denmark has ratified the 1955 Hague Convention on international sales of goods and enacted *International Løsørekøbslov* (Act on International Sales of Goods). The principles of the Convention apply, i.e. the choice of the parties is respected but if no choice has expressly been made the law of the seller's country is applicable or the law of the country in which the seller is permanently established and did receive the order.

The Rome Convention of 1980 on Choice of Applicable Law on Contractual Obligations has been ratified by Denmark and has been in force since 1 July 1984.

It is possible as well to agree to the application of a foreign legal system in a contract with a *sælger*. However, he may not thereby be deprived of the statutory minimal protection that any employee enjoys under *Funktionærloven* or other protective legislation concerning employees.

1.8.2. Jurisdiction

The ordinary Danish courts are competent to hear cases between principals and agents. Most cases are heard before the *Byret* (District Court) (abbrev.: "B") in first instance. From the *Byret* appeal lies to the *Landsret* (High Court) (abbrev.: "L"). The *Landsret* historically was the court of first instance for larger cases. Now it only deals with cases involving issues of principle or cases above DKK 500.000. when the parties so request. An appeal against its decisions lies to *Højesteret* (Supreme Court) (abbrev.: "H"). Cases involving maritime law issues or commercial issues may be brought before *Sø- og Handelsretten* (Maritime and Commercial Court) (abbrev.: "S"). The last-mentioned are collegiate courts where the presiding judge only is legally educated. He sits with two or four law assessors appointed because of their skill in the specific field. *Sø og Handelsretten in Copenhagen* covers the greater Copenhagen area, ranking along with *Landsretten*, i.e. appeals lie to *Højesteret*. In the rest of the country there is no permanent *Sø- und Handelsret* but it may be established as an "*ad hoc*" tribunal by the district judge and two (local) lay assessors. Appeal then lies to the *Landsret*.

The Brussels Convention of 1968 on Enforcement of Foreign Judgments has been ratified by Denmark and has been in force since 1 November 1986.

A lot of cases are referred to arbitration. There are no inhibitions against arbitration clauses in agency agreements provided the clause is clear, specific and the composition of the Arbitration Court fair to both parties.

The New York Convention of 1958 on the Recognition and Enforcement of Foreign Arbitral Awards is ratified by Denmark and has been in force since 7 March 1973.

1.9. Bibliography

Peter Arndorff, *Erhvervslivets Kontrakthåndbog* (Copenhagen, 1980).

Mogens Bjerre and Claus Fog, *Franchising—Et Forretningssystem for Fremtiden* (Copenhagen, 1985).

Foighel & Gammeltoft-Hansen, *Automobilforhandlerkontrakter* (Copenhagen).

Bent Iversen, *Handelsagenter og Eneforhandlere* (Copenhagen, 1987).

Ole Lando, *Agenter og Eneforhandlere i Vesteuropæisk Ret* (Copenhagen, 1965).

——*Kontraktsstatuttet*, 3rd edn. (Copenhagen, 1981).

——*Udenrigshandelens Kontrakter*, 3rd edn. (Copenhagen, 1980).

——*Udenrigshandelsretten IV, International Procesret m.v.* (Copenhagen, 1986).

Johan Lansdorff, Didier Rigault, Elisabeth Thuesen, Börge Villard and J.C. Warnich-Hansen, *Agentregler i Europa* (Copenhagen, 1985).

Lennart Lynge Andersen, Palle Bo Madsen and Jørgen Nørgaard, *Aftaler og Mellemmænd* (Copenhagen, 1987).

Jakob Nørager-Nielsen and Søren Theilgaard, *Købeloven med Kommentarer* (Copenhagen, 1979).

Allan Philip, *EF/IPI Lovvalget i Kontraktforhold* (Copenhagen, 1982).

Niels Erik Segerfos and Josef Fischler, *Agentavtalet* (Stockholm, 1968).

Torben Svenné Schmidt, *International Formueret* (Copenhagen, 1987).

Betaenking nr. 1151 om handelsagenter og handelsrejsende (Copenhagen, 1988).

1.10. Legislation

Aftaleloven, Act on Formation of Contracts. Lovbekendtgørelse no. 600, 8 September 1986, om aftaler og andre retshandler på formuerettens område.

Benzinforhandlerkonktraktloven, Act on Petrol Distributor Contracts. Lovbekendtgørelse no. 234, 6 June 1985.

Funktionærloven, Act on Legal Relationship between Employers and Salaried Employees. Lovbekendtgørelse no. 413, 30 August 1986, om retsforholdet mellem arbejdsgivere og funktionærer som ændret ved lov no. 313, 10 August 1976 og lov 162, 12 April 1978.

International Løsørekøbslov, Act Applying the Convention on International Sales of Goods (CISG). Lovbekendtgørelse no. 722, 24 October 1986, som indeholder hvilke retsregler, som skal anvendes på løsørekøb af international karakter.

Kommissionsloven, Act on Commission, Commercial Agents and Itinerant Salesmen, Lovbekendtgørelse no. 363, 15 September 1986 on Kommission, Handelagentur og Handelsregsende.

Købeloven, Sales of Goods Act. Lovbekendtgørelse no. 28, 21 January 1980, af Købelov.

Lejeloven, The Lease Act. Lovbekendtgørelse no. 524, 11 August 1986, om leje en.

Markedsføringsloven, Act on Good Marketing Practices. Lovbekendtgørelse no. 55 af 28 January 1987, om markedsføring.

Monopolloven, Act on supervision of monopolies and restriction of competition no. 108 of 11 March 1986.

Forslag til Lov om Produktansvar, Project for Act on Product Liability, L 19, submitted to the "Folketing", 7 October 1987 by the Minister of Justice.

1.11 Case Law

Case-law is published in the legal gazette *Ugeskrift for Retsvæsen* (abbrev. "U"). Cases are referred to by the year of publication, page and an indication of the court that has pronounced the judgments. All Supreme Court cases are published whereas only a part of High Court and Maritime and Commercial Court cases are published. The courts in fact decide themselves what cases they would find relevant for publication. The Board of Editors is composed of a Supreme Court judge, two High Court judges—one for the Eastern and one for the Western division—a practising lawyer and a City Court judge. Cases from the *Byret* are published only when found exceptionally relevant. Below are listed cases published 1960–July 1988.

1.11.1. Employed/independent agents

U.1960.97.Ø, U.1960.880.H, U.1981.159.Ø

1.11.2. Entitlement to commission

U.1960.594.H, U.1962.503.H, U.1966.533.H, U.1967.79.H, U.1973.642.H, U.1974.709.H, U.1983.20.H, U.1983.122.H, U.1984.809.B, U.1986.263.S, U.1987.433.H.

1.11.3. Indemnity

U.1962.820.H, U.1965.307.S, U.1969.29.H, U.1973.267.H, U.1976.947.S, U.1976.655.H, U.1980.195.H, U.1981.301.H, U.1982.227.H, U.1987.326.H.

1.11.4. Relationship to third parties

U.1969.125.H, U.1973.901.H, U.1973.976.S, U.1972,502.H, U.1980.4.H, U.1985.933.H.

1.11.5. Competition

U.1968.576.H, U.1980.7171.H, U.1982.1149.S, U.1983.157.H, U.1983.164.H, U.1983.559.S, U.1986.268.S, U.1987.543.S.

2. Distributorship Agreements

2.1. Distribution

2.1.1. Definition

No general legislation exists in Denmark concerning distributors or sole distributors. A specific legislation is enacted concerning distributors of petrol by the Act on Petrol Distributors Contracts, *Benzinforhandler-kontraktloven*.

A distributor is an independent trader who undertakes to purchase products for the purpose of resale and to maintain additional customer facilities necessary for the needs of the product. Normally a distributor will work within a specific area. The term of distribution applies both to the perfume sales at the local drugstore and the sales of Mercedes lorries and spare parts, so the general definition is not very elaborate.

2.1.1.1. Exclusive/non-exclusive/exclusive purchasing

A distributor will normally expect to enjoy a monopoly over a certain geographical area, a certain set of customers, etc. He will expect to enjoy exclusivity to such an extent that it will justify his work and expense in setting up and maintaining the specific facilities required to commercialize the products.

The supplier on his part will expect the distributor to represent solely his products or at least to represent no competing products. The notion of sole distributor is fairly common. A sole distributor is the sole trader who within a given geographic area may purchase from a supplier a given product for the purpose of resale. Normally the notion implies belonging to supplier's business organization, using trade marks, receiving current information, sharing marketing expenses, etc.

The notion of sole purchasing distributor is more rare. It is well known, e.g. within the automobile trade. A sole purchasing distributor is a trader who undertakes to take all deliveries from one supplier and who within a given geographic area is the only one who may purchase from that supplier for the purpose of resale.

It should be noted that by application of *Aftaleloven*, § 36 and eventually the EEC-law provisions, the duty to purchase solely from one supplier may be held not enforceable by the supplier when the distributor is in a position to take deliveries of equal quality from other suppliers and legally distribute it within the EEC.

2.1.2. Conclusion of the contract (special conditions)

For the general rules on formation of contracts refer to section 1.2. above. There are no requirements for writing of distributorship contracts. It is common that fairly elaborate distributorship contracts are set up. They will either follow the standard forms of the Danish Chamber of Commerce or of the Council of Danish Industries or be drafted by counsel for the supplier or the distributor.

The distributors of some trades, e.g. the automobile trade, are organized in relatively powerful associations. Sometimes these associations will act as a negotiating body on behalf of their members.

Distributor contracts may eventually have to be submitted to the Monopolies' Supervisory Board. Generally this will be the case if they are concerned with suppliers having a national market share exceeding 15–20%.

2.1.3. The supplier's duties and rights

2.1.3.1. The supplier's duties

The supplier's sole legal duties to the distributor are under *Købeloven*. In addition, he will normally be under a contractual duty to grant an exclusivity to the distributor within a certain geographical area. He will be bound to supply goods or services within specific delays and to supply them at prices agreed for a certain period, subject to change only at the change of given external circumstances.

In common the supplier will be under a contractual duty to provide the distributor's personnel with specific formation and the maintenance thereof. He will be under a duty to pass on information concerning the products or services to the distributor and even to contribute to the distributor's marketing or to undertake certain overall marketing activities. Like the principal the supplier is bound to observe confidence concerning commercial secrets (*Markedsføringsloven*, section 9, viz. section 1.3.1.2. above).

2.1.3.2. The supplier's rights

Often the supplier will require certain minimum quantities to be sold by the distributor in given periods. He will reserve his right to discontinue without notice or with a shorter notice his appointment of the distributor in case of failure to meet such sales targets. He will require the distributor to keep him informed of the development of his market, to maintain stock at a certain level, to pass on immediately any complaints from the customers concerning the products, and even impose upon the distributor and his personnel a requirement to continue providing information concerning the products.

Købeloven applies only in so far as the parties have not contracted otherwise. Normally the distributor contract will provide for specific terms that supersede the rules of *Købeloven*. The supplier in principle remains liable to the distributor for any delay in delivery, for defects in the goods delivered and for product liability (which is not dealt with in *Købeloven*). The supplier may be liable for damages paid by the distributor to his customers because of the delay but only if he has contractually undertaken a guarantee of delivery time. Damages for delay calculated in accordance with *Købeloven* may not include compensation for delay claimed by a second or third purchaser.

Denmark is expected to enact legislation for the implementation of the 25/374 EEC-Directive on product liability as from 1 January 1990. This legislation concerns product liability relating to personal injury and damages in consumer products.

2.1.4. The distributor's duties and rights

2.1.4.1. The distributor's duties

(See above 2.1.3.2.)

2.1.4.2. The distributor's rights

(See above 2.1.3.1.)

2.1.5. Liabilities of supplier and distributor during the term of the distributorship agreement

2.1.5.1. The supplier as against the distributor

(See above 2.1.3.2.)

2.1.5.2. The supplier as against third parties

The supplier will become liable directly towards third parties in matters of product liability and even in "consumer purchases", i.e. purchases made by a consumer from a man of business when the goods purchased are destined mainly for the non-commercial use of the purchaser and the seller knew or ought to know this. In relation to such purchases the supplier remains liable towards the consumer if he has given information on the label through publicity or by other sources concerning the products, and such information is revealed to be inexact.

Product liability is expected to be altered as from 1 January 1990 (see section 2.1.3.2. above).

2.1.5.3. The distributor as against the supplier

The distributor may claim damages from the supplier if the supplier negligently has failed to pass on information concerning the product or inquiries coming from the area of his exclusivity.

Likewise the distributor is liable to the supplier for failing to pass on relevant information, i.e. concerning marketing conditions, development of competitors, immaterial rights infringements, etc. to the supplier.

The distributor finally has all the rights of *Købeloven* in case of delay, defects in quality or quantity, etc.

2.1.5.4. The distributor as against third parties

By "third parties" are understood the purchaser of products offered for sale by the distributor, though of course a contractual link exists directly between distributor and purchaser.

The legal relationship of distributor to his customers is still governed by *Købeloven*. The distributor will remain directly liable towards his customers for delay, defects and damages caused to the product even though he may claim relief from the supplier. He cannot claim to be excused from the product liability by virtue of the argument that the product defect has not been caused by him. When the products sold are consumer goods and the supplier is domiciled outside the EEC the distributor will incur product liability for economic loss. He will further incur product liability for personal injury caused by the products. In both cases the legislation is expected to be enacted as from 1 January 1990.

2.1.6. Term and termination

2.1.6.1. Term

There are no requirements for the term of a distributorship contract. As such contracts normally will require considerable expenditure in building up the distributor's name, the initial term for a distributorship contract will rarely be shorter than 12 months. Normally distributorship contracts are entered into for indefinite periods.

2.1.6.2. Termination

There are no legal requirements for the termination or notice period. However, jurisprudence has developed according to which termination period cannot be shorter than 3 to 6 months (viz. U.1980.42.H.).

Furthermore, jurisprudence has found that during a termination period the supplier is not entitled to appoint a parallel distributor, nor may he modify the distributor's area or possibilities of economic results during that period (viz. U.1985.192.S.).

2.1.7. Indemnity

Till now Danish case-law has not awarded damages for loss of good will or loss of investments at the termination of a distributorship contract (viz. U.80.42.H.). In case of termination without notice of a distributor, he has been awarded a compensation for "good will" corresponding to the profit he would have made during the termination period, i.e. damages for loss of expected profit (U.88.101.H.). The Danish courts have awarded compensation for marketing material turned useless through the termination. The courts have imposed on the supplier a duty to buy back at market price the distributor's stock of products and spare parts (U.80.42.H.).

2.1.8. Specific applications of EEC law

Jurisprudence concerning EEC-law in relation to distributorship contract is rare. However, Danish courts have rejected to make injunctions against the sale of products based on the submission that the marketing of such products was a contravention of an exclusive distributorship contract (U.85.632.V.).

2.1.8.1. Disputes

(See above 1.8.1.).

2.1.9. Bibliography

(See above 1.9.).

2.1.10. Legislation

(See above 1.10.)

2.1.11. Case law

2.1.11.1. Case law concerning indemnity

U.1960.422.S, U.1980.42.H, U.1986.747.H, U.88.101.H.

2.1.11.2. Unfair contract terms

H.8.5.632.V, U.1987.576.H, U.1987.531.H.

2.1.11.3. Parallel import

2.2 Selective Distribution

2.2.1. Definition

Selective distribution is defined as a system of distribution whereby a supplier seeks to ensure a specific level of quality and quantity with the businesses distributing his products through contracts with the distributors and through refusal to sell his products to anybody who does not comply with his concept of distribution to the consumer. As far as the law of contract is concerned there is no reason to distinguish between distributors in general and distributors belonging to a selective distributor system. Their rights and duties are identical. The admissibility of selective distribution has been tried several times under the Act on Supervision of Monopolies and Restrictions on Competition—*Monopolloven*. Selective distributor systems may have to be registered with the Monopolies Supervisory Board if the products enjoy a substantial market share (15–20%) so that restrictions on distribution may be said to create an unreasonable inequity in competition. The Monopolies' Supervisory Board may compel a supplier to change his criteria for selecting distributors or—eventually—to sell against cash payment to anybody who wants to buy his products. The Monopolies' Supervisory Board have till now admitted selective-distributor systems in the case of technically refined high-quality products, e.g. U.78.361.H., concerning radios and television sets from Bang & Olufsen. The selective-distributors system may be accepted and no order to sell on request issued if the products require a specifically trained sales personnel, special sales or test facilities or if the value of the product would substantially deteriorate by its being marketed under circumstances different from those offered by the selective-distribution system. E.g. well-known perfumes may not be sold in low-price warehouses, etc.

2.2.2. Conclusion of the contract (special conditions)

(See above 2.1.2.).

2.2.3. The supplier's duties and rights

2.2.3.1. The supplier's duties

(See above 2.1.3.1.)

2.2.3.2. The supplier's rights

(See above 2.1.3.2.)

2.2.4. The distributor's duties and rights

2.2.4.1. The distributor's duties

(See above 2.1.3.2.)

2.2.4.2. The distributor's rights

(See above 2.1.3.1.)

2.2.5. Liabilities of supplier and distributor during the term of the distributorship agreement

2.2.5.1. The supplier as against the distributor

(See above 2.2.5.2.)

2.2.5.2. The supplier as against third parties

(See above 2.2.5.2.)

2.2.5.3. The distributor as against the supplier

(See above 2.1.5.3.)

2.2.5.4. The distributor as against third parties

(See above 2.1.5.4.)

2.2.6. Term and termination

2.2.6.1. Term

(See above 2.1.6.1.)

2.2.6.2. Termination

(See above 2.1.6.2.)

2.2.7. Indemnity

(See above 2.1.7.)

2.2.8. Specific application of EEC-Law

(See above 2.1.8.)

2.2.8.1. Disputes

(See above 1.8.1.)

2.2.9. Bibliography

(See above 1.9.)

2.2.10. Legislation

(See above 1.10.)

2.2.11. Case law

(See above 2.1.11.)

3. Franchise Agreements

3.1. Definition

Franchising in Danish law is defined as a contract whereby the owner of a product system for a fee normally based on the turnover puts his business characteristics at the disposal of a moral or physical person with a view to retail exploitation.

The franchising concept includes a well-defined product system comprising products, accessories, trademarks, appearance in general and possibly specifically developed machinery or patented items.

3.2. Conclusion of the Contract (Special Conditions)

Denmark has no specific legislation about franchising. There is no doubt, however, that the franchising contract or rather the contract complex is legally recognized under Danish law. The agreement between the franchisor and the franchisee does not have to be in writing but given the comprehensive nature of the agreement it will in practice always be written down and signed by both parties.

The contract may in fact be several agreements comprising:

- a licence agreement concerning trademarks;
- a purchase or lease agreement concerning specific machinery and equipment;
- a licence agreement concerning the know-how necessary to exploit the product system;
- a distributorship agreement concerning the actual products to be resold—eventually in territorial exclusivity—by the franchisee;
- a lease agreement concerning the premises from which the exploitation will take place;
- an agreement on joint advertising along with the franchisor and other franchisees for the marketing of the product system.

3.3. The Supplier's Duties and Rights

3.3.1. The supplier's duties

In addition to the duties already mentioned under section 2.1.3.1. the supplier will normally be under a duty to inform the distributor or franchisee loyally of a realistic budget for the exploitation. He will further be under a duty to bring to the disposal of the distributor the trademarks, consultancy services, marketing services and the equipment needed for an efficient exploitation.

Since all the agreements listed above form parts of the co-operation the supplier may be faced with the risk of the entire contract complex being terminated by the franchisee when serious breach of one contract has occurred.

One of the few application of the *Aftaleloven*, section 36, possibility of reducing contract clauses between businessmen, has in fact been to a distributorship agreement with certain franchising elements (petrol distribution), e.g. U.1987.326.H and 531.H. Since the supplier generally will be much more powerful than the distributor in the franchising relationship it is realistic to expect further application of *Aftaleloven*, section 36, in this field.

3.3.2. The supplier's rights

The supplier's remuneration for the exploitation will normally be a percentage of the turnover. Further, the supplier will normally reserve the rights to trade marks, trade features and trade methods following the termination of the collaboration. Hereby he may secure himself of additional rights of protection further to the position he may already claim under *Markedsføringsloven*, section 9.

3.4. The Distributor's Duties and Rights

3.4.1. The distributor's duties

In addition to what has been specified under 2.1.3.2. the distributor may be under a duty to comply with purchase targets and turnover targets. Further duties may be conferred on the distributor or franchisee by virtue of the agreements. No legal requirements exist under Danish law to such agreements other than the lease agreement. The Lease Act, *Lejeloven*, contains very specific rules as to the formation and administration of lease agreements. These rules in general are given to protect the tenant, i.e. the distributor or franchisee. Protection is individual and the tenant is under a duty not to assign his lease without the consent of the landlord, i.e. the franchisor or supplier. If the tenant complies with the terms of his lease it is in principle not terminable.

3.4.2. The distributor's rights

Apart from the rights mentioned under 2.1.3.1. the distributor or franchisee may enjoy a certain protection in virtue of his being overwhelmingly dependent upon supplies of goods and services from the supplier.

This observation is not based on any actual jurisprudence. It is a transcript of the general principles underlying Danish contract law when it comes to interpretation of contract between parties whose position of strength is radically different. It may be expected of *Aftaleloven* section 36 and *Markedsføringsloven* section 1 may be applied by the courts to prevent any abuse by the franchisor of his position of strength over the franchisee.

It seems clear that by virtue of the EEC-law provisions the distributor may not be prevented from taking delivery of the products from sources other than the franchisor provided that these other sources have access to goods legally distributed within the EEC. However, the franchisee can be held to sell exclusively goods which are manufactured by the franchisor or by third parties designed by it where it is impracticable, owing to the nature of the goods which are the subject-matter of the franchise, to apply objective quality specifications.

Territorial exclusivity with the EEC are no more enforceable by virtue of franchising contracts than by virtue of distributorship contracts.

3.5. Liabilities of Supplier and Distributor During the Term of the Distributorship Agreement

3.5.1. The supplier as against the distributor

(See above 2.1.3.2.)

3.5.2. The supplier as against third parties

(See above 2.1.5.2.)

3.5.3. The distributor as against the supplier

(See above 2.1.3.2.)

3.5.4. The distributor as against third parties

(See above 2.1.5.4.)

3.6. Term and Termination

3.6.1. Term

(See above 2.1.6.1.)

3.6.2. Termination

(See above 2.1.6.2.)

3.7. Indemnity

As for distributors in general it is doubtful if franchisees may under the present legislation expect indemnity at a lawful termination. It should be noted that a lease agreement may be terminated without cause only for very specific reasons such as demolition, landlord's proper use of premises, etc. and only if the landlord pays damages corresponding to the tenant's costs of moving his business to other premises, loss of goodwill, loss of investment in inventory, etc.

3.8. Specific Application of EEC Law

No specific application of EEC-law has yet been seen in jurisprudence. The principles upon which the Pronuptia case was decided already forms part of Danish contract law.

3.8.1. Disputes

(See above. 1.8.2.)

3.9 Bibliography

(See above 1.9.)

3.10 Legislation

(See above 1.10.)

3.11 Case Law

(See above 2.1.11.)

3.12 Terminology

Kommissionær	Commissionary, a person who sells or buys in the name of a principal whose identity is undisclosed.
Handelsrejsende	Itinerant salesman, i.e. a person who travels from place to place to solicit orders from customers for goods that he does not bring along with him.
Funktionær	Salaried employee who complies with the requirements of *Funktionærloven* (min. 20 hours work per week, administrative sales or executive work, etc.).
Sælger	Salesman employed by one employer and subject to his control (salaried employee).

CHAPTER 4
FEDERAL REPULIC OF GERMANY

Rolf Beeker,
Ulrich Lohmann,
Renate Braeuninger-Weimer

INTRODUCTION

1. Commercial Agency

In Germany the legal position of commercial agents (or commercial representatives) was first made statutory in 1900. It soon became clear that the law would have to be amended. The Amending Law of 6 August 1953 brought about a clearer differentiation between the legal standing of a commercial agent (a "Handelsvertreter") and that of a commercial assistant (a "Handlungsgehilfe"). It clarified the legal standing of commercial agents with regard to their generally accepted status as semi-employees and included provisions on the degree of competence which the "Labour Courts" have for dealing with cases concerning disputes between commercial agents and principals and on preferential claims in bankruptcy proceedings.

It should be noted that the term "Handelsvertreter" is not a professional title protected by law and that it may be used by or applied to individuals whose situation does not match all the characteristics of that of a commercial agent.

Within the EEC the law on commercial agents is to be harmonized. On 18 December 1986 the Council adopted a Directive on this subject. Member States must adapt their legislation before 1 January 1990.

1.1. Definition of Various Types of Agencies and Intermediaries

1.1.1. Independent

An independent commercial agent is an individual or a legal entity who or which

- acts as intermediary in the conclusion of transactions or concludes transactions;
- works for a principal or group of principals;
- acts independently;

- and is appointed to do so on a permanent basis.

The terms and conditions of the contractual relationship and their actual implementation will be decisive for judging whether these characteristics are present in a given case and not what the agreement in question may be called, e.g. possibly a Co-operation, Service or Distribution Agreement.

Any individual, legal entity, general or limited partnership or other corporate body may be a commercial agent.

1.1.2. Employed

A distinction has to be made between commercial agents with employee status and independent agents. The distinction is made according to individual freedom of action and not according to economic independence. An independent agent is defined by law, as a person who is essentially free to organize his activities and his working time.

Characteristics which tend to indicate independent status are:

> Being responsible for one's expenses; occupying one's own business premises; having one's own office, equipment, etc.; keeping a record of accounts; working under one's own name; representing more than one principal.

Characteristics of employee status are:

> Working according to instructions; fixed working hours; a fixed salary; the deduction of tax and national insurance contributions from one's wage; travel expenses being fully refunded; the right to annual leave; the agent being perhaps prohibited from representing other firms.[1]

An agent with employee status is a commercial assistant ("Handlungsgehilfe"). He enjoys the same social protection as do other salaried employees.

1.1.3. Others

Commercial agents have to be distinguished from:

(a) Traders and contractual dealers who buy goods—for resale—in their own name and on their own account;

(b) Factors whose business is to conclude transactions in their own name for third parties as well as for commission agents who are appointed by contract on a permanent basis to conclude transactions—in their name—with third parties;

(c) Brokers whose business is to conclude transactions or who are professionally engaged in concluding transactions in the name of third parties—without being appointed by contract to do so and without being under any obligation to act.

1.2. Conclusion of the Contract (Special Conditions)

1.2.1. Informal

Commercial Agency Agreements may be concluded informally. A com-

[1] BGH NJW 82, 1758.

mercial agency agreement may be established by actions which imply that such a relationship exists, e.g. by the agent having repeatedly acted as an intermediary in concluding transactions and by the the principal having accepted the transactions so concluded.[2]

1.2.2. In writing

Both parties in such a Commercial Agency Agreement will, however, be entitled to demand that such an agreement and any amendment thereof or agreement supplementary thereto be put in writing and delivered, signed by the other party. A claim for an instrument or instruments to be delivered will have to be implemented and any understanding purporting to debar a party from raising such a claim shall be null and void. Refusal to carry this out and deliver such an instrument or instruments will be considered as constituting cogent reason for terminating the contractual relationship with immediate effect and for claiming compensation.[3]

1.3. The Principal's Duties and Rights

1.3.1. The principal's duties

1.3.1.1. Commission

The principal is obliged to pay the agreed commission to the commercial agent.[4] The rate of commission will be as agreed; in the absence of such an agreement the normal rate will apply. Claims for payment of commission will arise in so far and as soon as either the principal or the third party has carried out a deal. In this regard there may be various, different arrangements agreed between the parties.

Claims for commission arise whilst the Agency Agreement is in force in respect of all concluded transactions which were brought about by the agent's activities and in respect of all transactions concluded with customers who were canvassed for similar orders by the agent.

A commercial agent responsible for a defined area can claim for commission in respect of transactions concluded with customers in his area and/or with parties within his group of customers whilst the Agency Agreement was in force— even though he may not have acted as intermediary in connection with the particular order.[5]

In addition, a commercial agent can claim for commission in respect of transactions which were concluded after the contractual relationship ended, where he acted as an intermediary in bringing about such transactions or where he initiated them—or prepared the ground for them—in such a manner that the conclusion of the deal was predominantly due to his actions and where the transactions were concluded within a reasonable period after the termination of the contractual relationship.[6] Moreover, a commercial

---

[2] BGH NJW 83, 1727.
[3] § 85 HGB: German Law of Commerce.
[4] § 87 HGB: German Law of Commerce.
[5] § 87 Abs. 2 HGB: German Law of Commerce.
[6] § 87 Abs. 3 HGB: German Law of Commerce.

agent can claim for "commission collection" in respect of amounts collected by him in accordance with instructions he was given.

If a commercial agent undertakes to assume personal liability for the indebtedness arising from a transaction he will be entitled to claim a special "*del credere* commission".[7] Such liability can, at any time, be assumed only in respect of a particular third party, and only if the agent concludes, or acts as an intermediary in concluding such transactions. The undertaking of such a risk will be binding only if established in writing.

A claim for commission will become null and void if the third party in the transaction, for which the agent acted as intermediary, completely fails to fulfil its obligations in terms of the transactions.[8]

In addition, a claim for commission will become void if the prinicpal does not carry out the transaction because it is impossible to do so due to circumstances outside his control. The same will apply where it cannot reasonably be expected that the principal will carry out the deal.[9]

1.3.1.2. Protection of the agent, information

The principal is bound by loyalty and good faith to the commercial agent; the principal must therefore refrain from doing anything which would be to the agent's disadvantage. This applies in particular—depending on the Commercial Agency Agreement—to competitive activities and/or arrangements.

The principal must support the commercial agent by making available such documentation as may be necessary for his activities (specimen drawings, pricelists, printed advertising material, terms and conditions for transactions).[10]

The principal has to advise the agent whether to accept and/or reject orders in connection with which the agent has acted as intermediary.

The principal has to advise the agent of any proposed limited acceptance of an order.[11]

1.3.1.3. Supply of written statements

The principal has to submit regular commission statements in writing—at least every three months.[12]

1.3.2. The principal's rights

The principal has the right to insist that the commercial agent observes his contractual and statutory obligations as set out below.

1.4. The Commercial Agent's Duties and Rights

---

[7] § 86b HGB: German Law of Commerce.
[8] § 87a Abs. 2 HGB: German Law of Commerce.
[9] § 87a Abs. 3 5.2 HGB: German Law of Commerce.
[10] § 86a Abs. 1 HGB: German Law of Commerce.
[11] § 86a Abs. 2 HGB: German Law of Commerce.
[12] § 86a Abs. 2 HGB: German Law of Commerce.

1.4.1. The commercial agent's duties

1.4.1.1. Trustworthiness, duty to inform

A commercial agent must make an earnest attempt to conclude transactions or to act as intermediary in concluding transactions.[13]

A commercial agent is appointed, on a permanent basis, to act as intermediary for such purposes. A commercial agency relationship will not be established towards these goals where there is only infrequent activity. Failure on the part of the commercial agent to carry out his duties may give rise to claims for compensation being made by the principal.

In carrying out his duties the commercial agent must promote the principal's interests.

The obligation to promote the principal's interests is a basic one. Acting in the principal's interests, the commercial agent cannot be an impartial broker working even-handedly with the parties involved in a transaction which is to be concluded. A commercial agent cannot act as the buyer's broker.

A commercial agent is not allowed to accept bribes, other payments of commission or similar benefits from third parties.

A commercial agent will generally be bound by particular directives given by the principal in so far as such directives do not conflict with the independent character of the agent's activities.

A commercial agent has to keep the principal notified about the necessary matters; in particular he must notify the principal without delay about every transaction concluded, or to be concluded, in connection with which he has acted as intermediary.[14]

The obligation to keep the principal notified arises from the agent's obligation in terms of § 666 L3 to give an account of the situation and supply information; this relates to the business matters in connection with which the agent acts as intermediary, to the transactions concluded, as well as to all other particulars arising from the agent's activities which are of importance to the principal—e.g. advertising methods, agreements reached at in connection with anticipated transactions, reports on calls on customers, etc.

In carrying out his work for the principal, the commercial agent has to conduct himself in the appropriate manner for a prudent businessman.

The appropriate manner for a prudent businessman includes, e.g. such matters as checking the credit rating of customers and rendering reports on their worthiness with regard to credit, reporting wishes expressed by customers, carefully observing the principal's directives relating to advertising, keeping a range of samples on hand, etc.

In general the location of a commercial agent's activities will, in as far as his obligations are concerned, be the legal location of activity.

1.4.1.2. Del credere

The commercial agent may undertake responsibility for the obligations arising from a transaction being discharged.

An agreement to this effect has to be set out in writing and it is valid only

---

[13] § 86 HGB: German Law of Commerce.
[14] § 86 Abs. 2 HGB: German Law of Commerce.

if it applies to a particular transaction or to such transactions with certain third parties.

In such a case the commercial representative is entitled to claim a special "del credere".[15]

The aforementioned restrictions for such agreements do not apply in cases in which the commercial agent acts for a foreign firm.[16]

1.4.1.3. Non-competition

Specific obligations, particularly with regard to the prohibition of competitive activities, arise from the duty to promote the principal's interests. It is prohibited to engage in competitive activities for the period of the Agency Agreement relationship.[17] Thereafter such prohibition will continue to be in force only if this is expressly agreed.

In the event of infringement of the prohibition to engage in competitive activities the commercial agent will be liable to pay compensation for loss or damage sustained but will not be liable to hand over earnings received as a result of such infringement to the principal.

1.4.1.4. Secrecy

The commercial agent is obliged to maintain secrecy regarding all business and operational secrets.

In addition he is under an obligation to refrain from utilizing such secrets or divulging them to third parties after the contractual relationship has ended—in so far as this would, all circumstances taken into consideration, run counter to the professional standards of a responsible businessman.[18] (§ 90).

In principle, infringement of a commercial agent's obligation to maintain secrecy is not a criminal offence.

In the absence of contractual provisions on competition, due weight has to be given to the consideration that a commercial agent is a free and independent party and is not restricted in his activities.[19]

1.5. Liabilities of Principal and Agent During the Term of the Agency

Culpable violation of any of the obligations listed under sections 1.3 and 1.4 above may lead to claims for damages by the other contracting party. Depending on the circumstances, claims to act and/or claims to desist may also be raised.

The principal is liable for the reimbursement of a commercial agent's expenditure only if this has been agreed or if such reimbursement is usual in the trade.[20]

---

[15] § 86 HGB: German Law of Commerce.
[16] § 86 Abs. 2 HGB: German Law of Commerce.
[17] § 86 Abs. 1 HGB: German Law of Commerce.
[18] § 90 HGB: German Law of Commerce.
[19] BGH NJW 82, 1758.
[20] § 87d HGB: German Law of Commerce.

Undertaking relating to exclusive agency agreements will be construed in terms of the standards of loyalty and good faith. Following on from court decisions, § 18[21] does not apply to exclusivity arrangements with commercial agents; in any case, it does not apply in so far as such arrangements are in accordance with the provisions of the second part of the clause of para. 1 of § 86[22] (cf. Note 2 to § 86).

The prohibition of controlled prices laid down in § 15[23] does not apply to commercial agents.

It is permissible to agree upon a minimum turnover to be guaranteed by the commercial agent.

In this regard it may be stipulated that in the event of failure to achieve such a turnover the agent shall be liable for damages, shall forgo claims for commission previously earned and/or become subject to a special notice of termination of service.

1.5.2. The principal as against third parties

The principal is liable for ensuring that the goods sold are freed of legal and material defects and that they possess the warranted characteristics.

If, before a contract is concluded, the commercial agent makes false statements as regards the features of the object under contract then the principal shall be liable for the damages suffered by the other contracting party.

In such an event the commercial agent shall be liable for damages to the principal.

1.6. Term and Termination

1.6.1. Term

The contracting parties will be at liberty to fix the contractual period; if no such period is laid down in the agreement then the agreement will be considered to have been concluded for an indefinite term.

1.6.2. Termination

The statutory period for giving notice of termination during the first three years of the contractual period will be six weeks for such notice to take effect at the end of any quarter of the calendar year.

Where the contractual period is longer, not less than three months' notice will have to be given.

Where a period for giving notice of termination is laid down in the agreement it must be less than one month, to take effect at the end of any calendar month and the period must be the same for both contracting parties.

---

[21] GWB: Antitrust Law.
[22] HGB: German Law of Commerce.
[23] GWB: Antitrust Law.

1.6.2.1. Cogent reasons

In addition there is the right to terminate the relationship with immediate effect for congent reaon.[24]

Cogent reason is considered in effect if the party giving such notice cannot reasonably be expected to continue the relationship until the end of the contractual term or the end of the period of ordinary notice of termination.

A grave breach of the agreement must therefore occur. A "once only" breach will not be considered to be sufficient but a breach of the agreement which has been committed after a specific warning has been given will usually be considered to give rise to such cogent reason.

Any purported exclusion of the right to terminate the relationship with immediate effect for cogent reason will be ineffective.[25]

1.6.2.2. Compensation

The party giving notice of termination with immediate effect for good and cogent reason can claim for compensation from the other contracting party.[26]

1.7. Indemnity

1.7.1. Indemnity for goodwill and/or clientèle

After the contractual relationship has ended, the commercial agent can claim for indemnification.[27]

1.7.1.1. Amount

Such indemnification will not excede one year's commission calculated as the average of the amount of commission earned by the agent during the preceding five years.[28]

1.7.1.2. Exceptions

There will be no such claim for indemnification where the commercial agent gave notice of termination of the contractual relationship—except if

- the principal's conduct gave well-founded reason for giving notice; or
- the commercial agent cannot reasonably be expected to continue his activities due to old-age or ill health.[29]

1.7.1.3. Misconduct

Moreover, there shall be no such claim where the principal gave notice terminating the relationship because there was good reason to do so, due to culpable misconduct on the part of the commercial agent.[30]

---

[24] § 89a HGB: German Law of Commerce.
[25] § 89a 1.2 HGB: German Law of Commerce.
[26] § 89a 2 HGB: German Law of Commerce.
[27] § 89a HGB: German Law of Commerce.
[28] § 87 Abs. 0 HGB: German Law of Commerce.
[29] § 89b 3 HGB: German Law of Commerce.
[30] § 89 3 HGB: German Law of Commerce.

1.7.1.4. Purported exclusion

Any purported exclusion of the right to claim such indemnification will be ineffective.[31]

Such claims for indemnification have to be raised within the three months following the end of the contractual relationship.

1.7.1.5. Criteria

The amount of indemnity payable will depend on the circumstances, in particular on

- what advantages the principal is expected to derive from customers who may have been enlisted recently by the commercial agent;
- what disadvantages the commercial agent can expect will follow from the ending of the contractual relationship;
- considerations of equity and fairness.[32]

1.7.2. Compensation for damages

Separate from and in addition to the commercial agent's claim to be indemnified, the commercial agent can claim for compensation if the contractual relationship was terminated by the principal in contravention of the legal provisions. This is the case if the statutory and/or contractual periods of notice are not observed by the principal.

The amount of compensation will depend on the turnover which the commercial agent could have produced during the period by which the contractual relationship was illegally shortened.

Such earnings are considered to be lost earnings which is what would in the ordinary course of events have been expected to have been earned.[33] This provision facilitates the procedure of producing evidence of loss/damage. Furthermore, the court is authorized by § 287, para. 1, ZPO,[34] to assess the damage at its own discretion, taking all circumstances into account.

1.8. Specific Application of EEC-Law

As yet there is no specific EC law on commercial agents.

The Directive on Co-ordinating the Legal Provisions on Commercial Agents of the Member Countries of 18 December 1986 (Ref. EC 1986 No. L 382/17) made provision for the Member Countries to implement the guideline by 1 January 1990 (Italy by 1 January 1993, Great Britain and Ireland by 1 January 1994).

The Hague Convention of 14 March 1978 on Principal-and-Agent Law was not enforced because it was not ratified by a sufficient number of countries.

---

[31] § 89b 4 HGB: German Law of Commerce.
[32] § 89b 1 HGB: German Law of Commerce.
[33] § 252, Cl. 2, BGB: German Civil Law.
[34] German Law of Civic Procedure.

1.8.1. Applicable law and place of jurisdiction

1.8.1.1. Applicable law

The contracting parties have free choice in deciding what code of law is to be made applicable.

In addition to the law of the country in which the commercial agent has his place of business or the law of the country in which the principal's headquarters are located, the law of a third country may also be selected.

In order to establish a uniform legal basis for all their commercial agents, multinational companies in particular often avail themselves of this possibility in their own interests.

German law allows agents abroad to operate subject to less favourable legal provisions than agents inland.

1.8.2. Tasks

If the applicable law is not expressly indicated then the Commercial Agency Agreement will be determined by what the characteristic tasks of the agent are to be. It is officially laid down in Art. 28 para. 2 Cl. 2[35] that the law of the country in which he has his place of business is applicable.[36]

The *lex fori* determines whether a person is a commercial agent in the sense of the German standards for distinguishing between commercial agency and other occupations.

Up to the present day, jurisdiction in Germany has predominantly relied upon the law applicable to the commercial agent.[37]

In cases in which the commercial agent's activities are in a country other than the one in which he has his place of business, German jurisdiction recommends that the law of the country where his activities take place should prevail.

In cases where the applicable law is implied any relevant indications which are available have to be relied upon. Guidance may be derived from the agreed place of jurisdiction or the agreed place of performance. In such cases, all circumstances have to be taken into account—even earlier contractual arrangements, nationality, the code of law applicable and actually referred to in sale contracts, etc.

1.8.3. Place of jurisdiction

The place of jurisdiction may be selected at will. Usually it is agreed that either the principal's or the commercial agent's place of business is to be the place of jurisdiction.

Alternatively it is of course permissible to agree upon an Arbitration Clause. An agreed appointment of a place of jurisdiction is valid only if expressly stated and set out in writing. The European Convention on Competence and Applicable Law in Civil and Commercial Cases of 27 Septem-

---

[35] EGBGB: German Introduction Law for German Civil Law.
[36] BGH 53, 337.
[37] BGH 16 Mar. 1970 = Bd 53, 332; 28 Nov. 1980 = NJW 1981/1899.

ber 1968[38] states that in the absence of such an agreement, a case may be instituted at the place of performance. Quite apart from this, the court of law competent for the defendant is competent in such cases.

1.9. Bibliography

Küstner, *Handbuch des gesamten Aussendienstrechts*, vols. 1–3, (1983–6) (*Complete Manual of the Laws Relating to Field Service for Sales*).
Baumbach, Duden and Hopt, *Handelsgesetzbuch (The Commercial Code)*, 27th edn. (1987), as well as other commentaries on the Commercial Code.
Stumpf, *Internationales Handelsvertreterrecht*, vol. 1 (1977) and vol. 2 (1986).
Schröder, *Recht der Handelsvertreter*, 4th edn. (1969).
Reithmann and Martin, *Internationales Vertragsrecht*, 4th edn. (1988), pp. 748 ‡ ff. (Martiny).
G. Kegel, *Internationales Privatrecht*, 6th edn. (1987), pp. 396 ‡ ff.
H. H. Eberstein, *Handelsvertretervertrag*, 6th edn. (1986).

1.10. Legislation

The legal position of commercial agents is codified in § § 84 to 94 c of the "Handelsgesetzbuch" (Commercial Code).

Jurisdiction relating to commercial agents is collated in "Rechtsprechungssammlung HVR" (almost 600 decisions made between 1982 and 1983)—and in many other sources.

2. Distributorship Agreements

German law concerning distributorship agreements is based on case law and, to some extent, on the above-described provisions of the German Commercial Code dealing with commercial agents. There is no statute dealing specifically with distributorship agreements.

In German, a distributor is referred to as "Vertragshändler", as "Eigenhändler" or as "Vertriebshändler". Consequently, a distributorship agreement is referred to as "Vertragshändlervertrag", "Eigenhändlervertrag" or "Vertriebshändlervertrag".

2.1. Distribution

2.1.1. Definition

2.1.1.1. Exclusive / non-exclusive / exclusive purchasing

The prevailing definition of a distributorship agreement under German case-law is as follows:

> A distributorship agreement is deemed to be a skeleton agreement ("Rahmenvertrag"), entered into for a certain period of time, under which one

---

[38] EuGVü: European Convention of 29 Sept. 1968.

party (the distributor or dealer) agrees to distribute goods supplied by the other party (the manufacturer or supplier) in his own name and on his own account, which agreement incorporates the distributor into the manufacturer's sales organisation.[39]

The detailed statutory provisions of the German Commercial Code (Handelsgesetzbuch—"HGB") relating to commercial agency, which are described in the preceding part, may be applied to a distributorship agreement only where the legislative intent behind these provisions applies also in the case of a distributor.[40] In addition, the provisions of the German Civil Code (Bürgerliches Gesetzbuch—"BGB") concerning the sale of goods (Secs. 433 *et seq*.), service agreements (Secs. 611 *et seq*.) and mandate (Sec. 675) may apply to a distributorship agreement.[41]

Exclusivity

Exclusive dealing ("Alleinvertrieb")

A distributorship agreement is referred to as an exclusive-distributorship agreement if the supplier undertakes not to appoint another distributor or agent in the contract territory. Such an agreement would also oblige the supplier to refrain from making direct sales in the territory, unless otherwise stated in the agreement.[42]

Exclusive purchasing ("Bezugsbindung")

Where the distributor undertakes to purchase the contract goods only from the supplier, the agreement may be referred to as exclusive-purchasing agreement. Exclusive-distributorship agreements often contain an exclusive-purchasing provision.

2.1.2. Conclusion of the contract (special conditions)

There is no general form requirement for the conclusion of distributorship agreements. Such agreements may be concluded in writing, orally or even impliedly.

An exception applies to those distributorship agreements which contain restraints of competition (including, in particular, exclusive dealing, exclusive purchasing, selective distribution, restrictive covenants and similar clauses, for which see below): According to Sec. 34 of the Act against Restraints of Competition ("Gesetz gegen Wettbewerbsbeschränkungen"—"GWB"),[43] such agreements are valid only if they are entirely in writing. Reference may be made to certain other written materials, most importantly existing or future price lists and general business conditions.[44] The purpose of this form requirement is to permit the cartel offices (see below) to verify

---

[39] BGH 21 Oct. 1970, BGHZ 54, 338. See also BGH 11 Dec. 1958, BGHZ 29, 84; BGH 16 Feb. 1961, BGHZ 34, 282; BGH 4 Apr. 1979, BGHZ 74, 136.

[40] Stumpf, *Der Vertragshändlervertrag*, 2nd edn. (Heidelberg, 1979), Sec. 4.

[41] Ibid.

[42] BGH 12 Nov. 1969, DB 1970, 44.

[43] Relevant sections of the Act Against Restraints of Competition (GWB) are given in translation on pp. 214–218.

[44] Gloy (ed.), *Handbuch des Wettbewerbsrechts* (Munich, 1986), Sec. 29 n. 31.

the complete contents of agreements containing possibly anticompetitive clauses. In practice, the requirement caters rather more to parties who wish to get out of an agreement which they no longer deem to be advantageous. It is therefore important to observe the form requirement. Failure to do so makes the entire agreement void. It is currently (in May of 1989) expected that Sec. 34 of the GWB will be repealed with effect as of January 1, 1990.

2.1.3. The supplier's duties and rights

In the absence of statutory provisions governing the contents of distributorship agreements, the duties and rights of the parties are primarily defined by the terms of the agreement. The parties' freedom to contract is limited to a certain extent by the GWB and by the Act concerning Standardized Business Conditions (AGBG).[45] The purpose of the AGBG is, generally speaking, consumer protection against unfair business conditions. Certain provisions of the AGBG, most importantly Sec. 9,[46] apply even where both parties to a given agreement are businesses ("Kaufmann"). Clauses failing to comply with the requirements of Sec. 9 AGBG are void, which may affect the validity of the whole agreement, at least if the clause at issue is of decisive importance to the parties (Sec. 139 BGB) and there is no severability clause. Agreements between businesses which are not governed by German law do not fall under the AGBG, according to its Sec. 24.

2.1.3.1. The supplier's duties

Supply of contract goods

Unless otherwise agreed the existence of a distributorship agreement does not generally oblige the supplier to accept all orders the distributor may place with him. This applies in particular where the supplier is prevented from making or purchasing the goods concerned for reasons beyond his control, e.g. failure of a subcontractor to deliver certain components.[47] However, pursuant to his general duty of good faith, the distributor may not refuse to honour the supplier's orders arbitrarily without any business-related reason.[48]

Where the agreement provides for a minimum purchase obligation on the part of the dealer, the supplier is generally under obligation to supply the minimum quantity agreed on, except if he is prevented from doing so by valid business reasons.[49] The presence of a no-compete clause does not per se trigger a supply obligation on the part of the supplier.[50]

If the supplier desires to subject the individual contracts of sale with the distributor to certain general business conditions, these conditions should be expressly incorporated into the distributorship agreement. A copy of the general conditions should be attached to the agreement.

---

[45] For translation of Section 9 see below, p. 219.
[46] Ibid.
[47] BGH 29 Apr. 1958, NJW 58, 1138.
[48] Ibid.
[49] BGH 19 Jan. 1972, BB 72, 193; OGL Bremen 10 June 1966, BB 66, 756.
[50] Stumpf, Sec. 62.

In this context, the distributor sometimes insists on a clause in the distributorship agreement requiring the supplier to give him advance notice if the supplier has reason to believe that he may not be able to fulfil all orders of the dealer in the ordinary course of business. Such a clause is lawful. Conversely, it may be advisable for the supplier to insist on a clause authorizing him, in case of a shortage of the contract goods, to fill orders made by his distributors only in part, in proportion to the amount of contract goods available to him; in this way, each distributor receives a fair share of his requirements.

Supply of documentation, promotion material and information

There are no specific rules governing the supply of documentation, promotion material and information by the supplier. Such obligations may arise, however, under the general duty of good faith, according to the circumstances of the specific case.[51]

Exclusivity

No other distributor

General

The supplier may agree to refrain from appointing another distirbutor or agent for a certain territory (the contract territory). Even where no such obligation is expressly agreed on, there is a certain risk that it will be deemed to be implied by the distribution agreement.[52] It is therefore advisable to address this point in the agreement and to state clearly whether the supplier may appoint another distributor or not.

Competition law

Under the terms of the GWB, an exclusivity agreement is valid and enforceable, but subject to scrutiny by the national German cartel (antitrust) offices pursuant to Sec. 18 (1)2 GWB. An injunction may only be issued if the prerequisites listed under Sec. 18 (1) (a)-(c) GWB are fulfilled. In practice, an injunction under Sec. 18 is rare and need generally not be anticipated, because exclusive distribution agreements almost never have either of the effects on the market set out in Sec. 18 (1) (a)-(c).[53]

There are cartel offices at national level, the Federal Cartel Office (Bundeskartellamt), and at state level (Landeskartellämter). The procedure to be observed by these offices is set out in the GWB. The provisions of the GWB apply—irrespective of the law of the distributorship agreement—to any and all restrictions of competition having an effect within Germany (Sec. 98 (2) GWB). Thus, the GWB would apply to any distributorship agreement where Germany is part of the contract territory.

Exclusive distribution clauses are in principle permitted under the GWB, which is contrary to EEC law, where such agreements covered by Art. 85 (1) of the EEC Treaty would in principle be prohibited. A prohibition similar to Art. 85 (1) of EEC Treaty exists under the GWB only with respect to hori-

---

[51] Ibid. Secs. 57–59.
[52] BGH 11 Dec. 1958, BGHZ 29, 84; BGH 16 Feb. 1961, BGHZ 34, 282.
[53] Niederleithinger and Ritter, *Die kartellrechtliche Entscheidungspraxis zu Liefer-, Vertriebs- und Franchiseverträgen* (Cologne, 1986), pp. 98, 99.

zontal agreements and practices (Secs. 1, 25 GWB) and with respect to resale price maintenance and agreements providing for restrictions with respect to the business conditions which one party may use vis-à-vis third parties (Sec. 15 GWB). Consequently, there is no need for an exemption procedure with respect to vertical restrictions falling under Sec. 18 GWB, such as the one at issue here, and there is no equivalent under German law to the EEC Regulations 1983/83 and 1984/83 described in the introduction to this book. There is also no risk of fines being imposed with respect to such restrictions, except where a specific injunction issued by a cartel office is disregarded (Sec. 38 (1)2 GWB).

The relationship between EEC and German competition law has not yet been fully clarified.[54] Generally, the GWB applies irrespective of EEC competition law, which means in practice that both laws have to be observed and the stricter law prevails. A conflict may arise where the Commission has granted an exemption pursuant to Art. 85 (3) of the EEC Treaty, although the agreement concerned would violate a provision of the GWB; in such a case, the German courts and authorities may not use the GWB to enjoin the enterprise concerned from making use of the exemption granted by the Commission.[55]

It should be note that the distributor, if he enjoys a dominant market position, is under a statutory obligation not to abuse that position (Sec. 22 GWB, L 1). Pursuant to Sec. 22 (3) GWB, a company is deemed to hold a dominant market position if its share of the relevant market exceeds one third or if it is part of an oligopoly. An exclusivity provision may be regarded as an abuse of such a dominant market position, if it forecloses a significant part of the market to other suppliers.[56] In such a case, the cartel offices could, irrespective of Sec. 18 GWB, enjoin the respective provision under Sec. 22(5) GWB. Similarly, an exclusivity provision benefitting a distributor who enjoys a dominant market position or on whom the supplier is dependent, because there is no other competitive distribution channel available to the supplier, might, under certain circumstances, be regarded as unfair or discriminatory vis-à-vis the supplier under Sec. 26(2) GWB, in which case the provision would be void (Sec. 134 BGB) and subject to fines (Sec. 38 (1)8 GWB).[57] In practice, however, the number of such cases appears to be small.

Public policy

Finally, an exclusivity provision may be held to contravene public policy, in particular, if it is of extraordinarily long duration. there are no hard and fast rules in this respect. However, there is case-law to the effect that an exclusitivity agreement of 20 years is just about the maximum which would be acceptable.[58] If the period for which the exclusivity agreement shall be

[54] EC 13 Feb. 1969, ECR 69, 1 "Walt Wilhelm v Bundeskartellamt", Kammergericht. WuW/E OLG 1745 "Sachs".
[55] BGH Immenga and Mestmäcker. in eid., GWB-Kommentar zum Kartellgesetz (Munich, 1981), Introd. nn. 44 ff.
[56] Möschel, in Immenga and Mestmäcker. Sec. 22 n. 131.
[57] Markert, in Immenga and Mestmäcker. Sec. 26 n. 130.
[58] BGH 17 Jan. 1979, WuW/E BGH 1641.

valid is found to be too long, the court or the parties may shorten this period, if the distributorship agreement contains a severability clause, in accordance with the terms of such clause.[59]

Direct sales

In addition to undertaking not to appoint another dealer for the contract territory, the supplier may agree to refrain from selling the contract goods in the territory himself, so that he would not be permitted to make any direct sales. It has been held that such an undertaking is implied where the supplier has agreed not to appoint another dealer in the territory.[60] It is therefore advisable to state clearly in the agreement whether or not the supplier may make such direct sales.

The undertaking to refrain from making direct sales is also covered by Sec. 18 (1)2 GWB; see the section on Competition Law under 2.1.3.1. above.

Restrictions on other dealers

An undertaking on the part of the supplier to impose on other dealers the obligation not to sell in the contract territory would, strictly speaking, be void and subject to fines pursuant to Sec. 15 GWB. Nevertheless, courts and legal writers are of the opinion that such a clause is permissible,[61] because it is closely related to the undertaking not to appoint another distributor in the contract territory, which in turn is permitted under Sec. 18 (1)2 GWB, as described above.

No discrimination

Irrespective of the terms of the distributorship agreement, the supplier may be under a particular duty to refrain from discriminating certain of his distributors in accordance with the terms Sec. 26 (2) GWB. (See below). If this provision applies, the supplier may be unable, e.g. to refuse to supply a certain distributor with contract goods which he supplies freely to other, comparable distributors, or to use different bonus systems for different groups of distributors without justification.[62]

Sec. 26 (2) GWB applies if either the supplier has a dominant market position (see below) or if the distributor concerned is dependent on the supplier for the supply of the contract goods, there being no other source of supply for the contract goods of which the distributor could make reasonable use. Such dependence may exist where a distributor establishes his business solely with a view to distributing his supplier's products, which may be the case, in particular, in a selective distribution system. Under such circumstances, Sec. 26 (2) GWB would make it unlawful for the supplier to obstruct the distributor's business unfairly (which would be hard to show in practice) or to treat one distributor or a group of distributors differently from other, similar distributors. Based on this provision, it has been held unlawful for a supplier of brandy to grant a special 5% bonus only to those distributors who undertook to resell the brandy only to restaurants and bars, if the

---

[59] BGH 23 Nov. 1983, GRUR 1984, 298, 300.
[60] BGH 12 November 1969, C 2; BGH 9 February 1984, BB 84, 1313.
[61] Ibid.; Emmerich, Immenga and Mestmäcker, Sec. 18 n. 93.
[62] BGH 24 Feb. 1976, BB 76, 1334; "Asbach-Fachroßhändlervertrag".

supplier could not show any valid business reasons for such differentiation.[63]

A supplier holding a dominant market position would have to observe the requirements of Sec. 26 (2) GWB even vis-à-vis those distributors who are not dependent on him in the sense described. In addition, such a supplier would be under a statutory obligation not to abuse his dominant market position (Sec. 22 (1) GWB, see below). A dominant market position would be presumed to exist where the supplier holds a market share of more than one third of the relevant market or where he is part of an oligopoly, pursuant to Sec. 22 (3) GWB (see below). In practice, however, the number of claims brought against a supplier by his distributor and based on a dominant market position appears to be small.

An infringement of Sec. 26 GWB would be subject to fines (Sec. 38 (1)8 GWB, see below), while the abuse of a dominant market position would give rise to fines only when a specific injunction by a cartel office is disregarded (Sec. 38 (1)4 GWB). In either case, the distributor concerned could request a court injunction or damages pursuant to Sec. 35 GWB (see below).

The scope of Sec. 26 (2) GWB is different from Art. 85 (1) d of the EEC Treaty, because it requires no agreement or concerted practice and is directed primarily against unilateral discrimination. The GWB rules concerning dominant market positions are roughly comparable to Art. 86 to the EEC Treaty.

2.1.3.2. The supplier's rights

The supplier's rights under the distribution agreement correspond largely to the distributor's duties set out below. In addition, the following rights are of importance:

Product policy

The supplier has a right to establish his own product policy. This right is not restricted by the existence of a distribution agreement. The supplier may therefore decide, e.g. to modify certain products or to cease making certain products without giving rise to claims on the part of the distributor. Unless otherwise agreed, the supplier may refuse to accept orders from the distributor on the ground that he has ceased to manufacture the product in question, and is not under an obligation to observe a certain notice period before putting such a change into effect.[64]

Unilateral modifications to the agreement

The supplier may generally reserve the right to make unilateral modifications and amendments to the distribution agreement. Where the supplier uses a standardized agreement, however, such clauses may be invalid and unenforceable pursuant to Sec. 9 AGBG if they fail to take fairly into account the distributor's interests.

Under this provision, for instance, a clause contained in a standardized agreement used by a car manufacturer which gave the manufacturer the

---

[63] Ibid.
[64] BGH 26 Nov. 1984, BGHZ 93, 29 "Opel".

right to reduce the contract territory unilaterally was held to be invalid because, *inter alia*, it gave the manufacturer discretion to make use of the clause even where no valid business reasons were present and failed to provide for an indemnification for the distributor concerned to compensate him for the loss of income caused by the reduction of the territory.[65] Likewise, the supplier may generally reserve the right to change the prices applicable to the individual orders placed by the distributor.[66] On the other hand, the supplier may not retroactively change the prices applicable to orders which he has already accepted, if the distributor cannot legally reserve the right to change the corresponding resale price vis-à-vis his customers.[67]

2.1.4. The distributor's duties and rights

2.1.4.1. The distributor's duties

Promotion

A duty to promote the contract goods is normally implied by the existence of a distributorship agreement, particularly if the distributor has been appointed as exclusive distributor.[68] The details of such promotion, which may also include exhibiting the contract goods at trade fairs and exhibitions, should be regulated in the distributorship agreement.

No agency

A distributor is generally not authorized to act as agent for the supplier.[69] However, it is advisable to state clearly in the distributorship agreement that the distributor may not do so.

Minimum purchases

The distributor may agree to make minimum purchases of the contract goods. These minimum purchases would have to be specified in the agreement. It is of particular importance to state also the sanction that is to apply if the distributor fails to make the minimum purchases agreed. A sanction which is frequently agreed on is the right to withdraw the distributor's exclusivity,[70] irrespective of the supplier's right to request specific performance or damages (see section 2.1.5.4. below).

Exclusive purchasing

The distributor may agree to purchase the contract goods exclusively from the supplier. Such an obligation would be covered by Sec. 18 (2) GWB. Consequently, it would generally be permitted, subject, however, to scrutiny by the cartel offices, as explained above with respect to exclusive-dealing clauses. In practice, the most important consequence of an exclusive-purchasing clause is that—if concluded before January 1, 1990—the entire agreement must be made in writing according to Sec. 34 GWB, whether or

---

[65] BGH 21 December 1983, BGHZ 89, 206 "Ford".
[66] BGH 16 Jan. 1985, BGHZ 93, 252.
[67] Ulmer, in Ulmer, Brandner and Hensen, *AGB-Gesetz*, 5th edn. (Cologne, 1987), Secs. 9–11 n. 884.
[68] Stumpf, Sec. 30.
[69] Ibid. Secs. 16, 17.
[70] Ibid. Secs. 28, 29.

not it contains other exclusivity clauses (see section 2.1.2. above). Sec. 34 GWB would also apply if the agreement does not contain an explicit exclusive-purchasing clause, but requires the distributor to purchase a certain percentage of his requirements of the supplier, or provides for economic incentives (such as rebates) if the distributor purchases exclusively from the supplier.[71]

The scope of German competition law concerning exclusive-purchasing obligations is thus similar to EEC law,[72] but the approach is different in that there is no blanket prohibition comparable to Art. 85 (1) of the EEC Treaty and thus no exemption procedure. What has been said in the section on competition law at 2.1.3.1. above applies here again.

Territorial restrictions

The distributor may agree to refrain from selling the contract goods outside the contract territory. Such an obligation is normally provided for in exclusive distributorship agreements, but the appointment as exclusive distributor does not imply per se that the distributor may not sell outside the territory concerned.

The obligation at issue here would fall under Sec. 18 (1)3 GWB. This statutory provision would also cover an extended territorial restriction, i.e. a clause obliging the distributor to impose a corresponding territorial restriction on his customers other than end users.[73] Here again, the comments under the section on Competition Law under 2.1.3.1. above apply accordingly.

The territorial restrictions permitted under German competition law would be broader than the territorial restrictions permitted under Art. 2 (2) (c) of Regulation 1983/84, in that Sec. 18 (1)3 GWB would also permit a prohibition of "passive" sales outside the territory. Consequently, where the agreement is covered by Article 85 of the EEC Treaty, the more limited provisions of EEC-law would have to be observed irrespective of the foregoing.

No-compete clause

A clause whereby the distributor agrees not to sell other products which are competitive with the contract goods is generally permissible, subject again to Sec. 18 (1)2 GWB; reference is made to the section on Competition Law under 2.1.3.1. above.

Sec. 18 (1)2 GWB would not per se prohibit a no-compete clause covering the time after termination of the agreement. Here again, German law is less stringent than EEC-law which would not permit any post-contractual no-compete clause.[74]

Customer service

The distributor's responsibility for after-sales customer service is generally implied by the fact that the distributor sells the contract goods in his own name and on his own account. Nevertheless, it is advisable to provide

---

[71] Niederleithinger and Ritter, p. 16.
[72] Ibid.
[73] Langen, Niederleithinger, Ritter and Schmidt, *Kommentar zum Kartellgesetz*, 6th edn. (Neuwied and Darmstadt, 1982), Sec. 18.
[74] Commission Notice of 22 June 1983, n. 10.

for an express obligation vis-à-vis the supplier to carry out customer service in the distributorship agreement. Such a provision could also include an obligation on the part of the distributor to maintain a certain stock of contract goods and spare parts therefor as well as certain facilities for customer service.[75]

Secrecy

Even where it is not explicitly stated in the distributorship agreement, the distributor would be under a secrecy obligation vis-à-vis the supplier. In addition, the passing on of the supplier's business secrets to third parties would constitute unfair competition prohibited by Sec. 1 of the German Act Against Unfair Competition.[76] Nevertheless, German case law as to what constitutes a business secret is not entirely clear.[77] It is therefore generally advisable to include an express secrecy obligation in the distributorship agreement and to clarify what business secrets shall be covered by that provision. Observance of such a secrecy obligation is often secured by agreeing on a contractual penalty to be paid in case of an infringement (Secs. 339–345 of the German Civil Code). The duration of a secrecy obligation may legally extend beyond the termination of the agreement, which is often agreed in practice.

2.1.4.2. The distributor's rights

The distributor's rights under the distribution agreement correspond largely to the supplier's duties set out above. In addition, the following rights are of importance.

Prices

As an independent business entity, the distributor has a right to determine the prices which he charges for the contract goods, independently from the supplier. Any agreement purporting to give the supplier a right to determine the distributor's prices would be void under Sec. 15 GWB and subject to fines under Sec. 38 (1) 1 GWB. A concerted practice to the same effect would also be prohibited under Sec. 25 (1) GWB, and be subject to fines under Sec. 38 (1)8 GWB. Furthermore, the supplier may not exercise any pressure whatsoever or promise certain rewards to the distributor in order to control the distributor's pricing (Sec. 25 (2) GWB); such conduct would also be subject to fines (Sec. 38 (1)8 GWB).

A limited exception is available for manufacturers of branded products under Sec. 38 a GWB. This provision permits resale price recommendations, provided that such recommendations are expressly marked as non-binding and that no pressure is exerted in order to enforce them.

Use of third parties

Although the distributor is generally under an obligation to provide his services in person[78] he may use employees, agents and other distributors in

---

[75] Stumpf, Secs. 52–55.
[76] Gesetz gegen den unlauteren Wettbewerb—"UWG"; translation of Section 1 given on p. 219.
[77] Stumpf, Sec. 36.
[78] Ibid. Sec. 38.

order to distribute the contract goods.[79] Therefore, if the supplier has reason to impose certain restrictions on the distributor in this regard, such restrictions should be set out in the distributorship agreement.

2.1.5. Liabilities of supplier and distributor during the term of the distributorship agreement

If one party fails to comply with his obligations under the distributorship agreement, the other party may in principle claim specific performance. In addition, a serious breach may give the other party the right to terminate the distributorship agreement without notice (see section 2.1.6. below). In those cases where the breach was committed negligently or intentionally, the other party may claim damages (Secs. 325, 326 BGB).

2.1.5.1. The supplier as against the distributor

In addition to the foregoing, the supplier warrants that the contract goods delivered pursuant to the individual contracts of sale entered into under the distributorship agreement are free of defects (Secs. 459, 463 BGB). This liability may be modified or restricted by the distributorship agreement or by the general business terms used by either party, provided that the latter has been incorporated into the distributorship agreement (see section 2.1.3.1. above).

Where a restriction of the supplier's liability for defects of the contract goods is contained either in a standardized distributorship agreement or in the supplier's general business terms, it is valid only if it takes into account the distributor's liability vis-à-vis his customers.

To the extent that the distributor resells the contract goods to private customers (rather than business entities), the distributor would be able to restrict his liability for defects of the goods concerned only within certain limits set out in Secs. 10, 11 AGBG. For instance, the distributor serving private customers may not shorten the statutory warranty period of generally 6 months (Sec. 477 BGB). Consequently, the supplier must observe the same limitations when devising his standardized distributorship agreements or business terms, because otherwise the distributor alone would bear the liability for defects of the contract goods.[80]

2.1.5.2. The supplier as against third parties

The distributorship agreement in and of itself would normally not generate rights of any third party vis-à-vis the supplier.

The supplier may, and often does, undertake to warrant the quality of the contract goods directly vis-à-vis the end user. This is frequently done by issuing certain warranty cards which the distributor or retailer gives to the final customer when he buys the product. Unlike his liability for defects of the contract goods vis-à-vis the distributor, the supplier is here free to formulate the warranty at his discretion.[81] Where the supplier undertakes to give

---

[79] Ibid.
[80] Ulmer, Brandner and Hensen, n. 890.
[81] Ibid.

such a direct warranty, the procedure following a claim by a customer under the warranty should be set out in the distributorship agreement.

Apart from the contractual warranty for defects of the contract goods, the supplier would bear the product liability for defects of the contract goods vis-à-vis any purchaser or user of these products. Product liability under German law is based on tort principles (Sec. 823 BGB); a new act regulating product liability is expected to be adopted in 1989 or in 1990. Where the distributorship agreement is individually negotiated (rather than standardized), it may require the distributor to hold the supplier harmless from any product liability claims; the same clause in a standardized agreement might be held invalid, if, as normally, the distributor himself would not be subject to any product liability under statutory law (but see section 2.1.5.4. below).

Finally the supplier's duty to refrain from discrimination and from abusing a dominant market position (see section 2.1.3.4. above) would apply also with respect to third parties. This may require the supplier, e.g., to supply an outsider with the contract goods. Since this is of particular importance only in case of selective distribution systems, this point will be addressed in that context (see the section on claims for supply by outsiders under 2.2.3.1. below).

2.1.5.3. The distributor as against the supplier

As indicated above, the supplier would be entitled to request specific performance if the distributor failed to comply with his obligations under the distributorship agreement. If the distributor commits a material breach of the agreement, the supplier may normally terminate the agreement without notice (see section 2.1.6. below) and, if the breach was caused by negligence or intent, claim damages.

The distributor's liability for the payment of the purchase price for the contract goods would arise under the individual contracts of sale entered into on the basis of the distributorship agreement. The distributorship agreement may contain a provision obliging the distributor to pay default interest at a specified rate, typically a certain percentage above the prevailing discount rate of the German bundesbank. The distributorship agreement should contain a reservation of title clause, according to which title to the contract goods remains with the supplier until full payment of his invoice. Typically, such a retention of title clause permits the distributor to resell the contract goods in the ordinary course of business, providing at the same time for an assignment of his claims for payment under the resale agreements to the supplier. No registration is required for a retention of title clause to be valid.

2.1.5.4. The distributor as against third parties

The distributorship agreement does not normally give rise to any liability on the part of the distributor vis-à-vis third parties, except as follows:

Where the distributor is the exclusive distributor for a foreign supplier with respect to Germany, the distributor, beside the supplier, also bears product liability vis-à-vis any purchasers or users of the contract goods, on the theory that a domestic distributor has a duty to observe the domestic market and to warn the supplier if defects of the contract goods which may lead to product liability become apparent on the German market. The distributor's product liability would arise whenever he failed to comply with this duty.[82]

In addition, the distributor is—as any independent business—liable vis-à-vis other market participants to observe the requirements of the Unfair Competition Act.[83] Where it can be shown that the supplier instructed the distributor to commit acts of unfair competition, the supplier may also be held liable.[84] If the supplier wishes to dismiss any appearance that he gave such instructions, it may be helpful to state in the distributorship agreement that it is the distributor's duty to observe all pertinent legal requirements.

2.1.6. Term and termination

2.1.6.1. Term

The parties are free to determine the term of the distributorship agreement as they see fit. Distributorship agreements which have been preformulated by the supplier and which require major investments on the part of the distributor should provide for a term which is long enough to allow the distributor to recoup his investment, in order to conform to Sec. 9(1) AGBG.[85]

2.1.6.2. Termination

Either party may terminate the distributorship agreement, either observing reasonable notice or, if there is cause, without notice, irrespective of whether this is expressly provided for in the agreement. Nevertheless, it is advisable to state clearly in the distributorship agreement the duration of the notice period in case of a termination without cause, as well as those causes for termination without notice which both parties deem to be important.

The notice period applicable in case of termination without cause may be determined by the parties as they see fit. In a standardized distributorship agreement devised by the supplier, however, the notice period must take into account the distributor's interest in recouping the investments which he was required to make under the agreement.[86] The actual length of the notice period must be determined in accordance with the circumstances of the case. It has been suggested that the period should not be less than one year, as provided by Art. 5 (2)2 of EEC-Regulation 123/85, which, however, appears to be too long, at least where the distributor has a claim for indemnity upon termination of the agreement (see below). On the other hand, a period of three months may be too short, as suggested by the decision in the *Ford* case.[87]

[82] BGH 9 December 1986, NJW 87, 1009.
[83] See below, pp. 219.
[84] Baumbach and Hefermehl, *Wettbewerbsrecht*, 15th edn. (Munich, 1988), Sec. 13 UWG n. 66.
[85] Ulmer, Brandner and Hensen, n. 891.
[86] BGH 26 Nov. 1984, BGHZ 93, 29 "Opel".
[87] BGH 21 Dec. 1983, BGHZ 89, 206 "Ford".

A termination without notice is generally permitted only in cases which make it unreasonable to expect the party concerned to continue the co-operation envisaged under the agreement. It is advisable to state explicitly in the agreement all those reasons which are, in the opinion of these parties under the specific circumstances of the case, so important that they would warrant a termination without notice. The following reasons for a termination without notice are frequently contained in distributorship agreements:

- Breach of material provisions of the distributorship agreement, e.g. appointment of another distributor in contravention of an exclusivity agreement;[88]
- Material or repeated breaches of individual contracts of sale entered into under the distributorship agreement;[89]
- Failure of the distributor to achieve reasonable sales;
- Change of ownership or control of the distributor;[90]
- Insolvency or bankruptcy of the distributor.

A termination without notice must be declared within a reasonable period from the date on which the terminating party learns of the reason justifying such a termination; it has been suggested that a period of two months may be adequate.[91] Negligence or intent on the part of the other party is not required. Reasons for a termination without notice contained in a standardized agreement may be invalid if they do not in fact make it unreasonable for the other party to continue complying with its obligations under the agreement.[92]

Repurchase of distributor's stock

The supplier may agree to buy back the distributor's stock of contract goods and spare parts upon termination of the agreement. Such an obligation may be implied if, under the terms of the distribution agreement, the distributor has agreed to maintain a certain stock and if the distributor cannot reasonably sell that stock to third parties.[93]

In any event, it is advisable to state clearly in the distributorship agreement whether or not the supplier shall be obliged to repurchase the distributor's stock. If the distributorship agreement is a standardized agreement prepared by the supplier, it may not totally exclude such an obligation on the part of the supplier if the distributor has no other reasonable opportunity to sell that stock.[94]

Note that if the agreement is terminated due to a breach thereof committed by the supplier, the distributor's claims for damages may include a claim that the supplier repurchase the stock irrespective of what has been said in the agreement.[95]

---

[88] BGH 23 Feb. 1966, DB 66, 577.
[89] BGH 27 Jan. 1982, BB 82, 515.
[90] Stumpf, Secs. 111, 115.
[91] BGH 27 Jan. 1982, BB 82, 515.
[92] Ulmer, Brandner and Hensen, n. 891.
[93] BGH 21 Oct. 1970, BGHZ 54, 338; OLG Frankfurt 1 Dec. 1981, BB 82, 209; OLG Köln 28 Nov. 1985, BB 87, 148.
[94] Ulmer, Brandner and Hensen, n. 892.
[95] BGH 21 Oct. 1970, BGHZ 54, 338.

2.1.7. Indemnity

2.1.7.1. Basis

Although there is no statutory provision which would require the supplier to pay an indemnity to the distributor upon termination of the agreement, numerous court decisions have held that Sec. 89 b HGB which entitles a commercial agent to claim such an indemnity (see section 1 above) is to be applied as well to the benefit of those distributors who

- are incorporated into the supplier's sales organization to such an extent that, from an economic point of view, their position is comparable to that of a commercial agent; and
- are obliged to disclose to the supplier the customers acquired by them,

without regard to the question whether the distributor merits particular protection in the specific case.[96] In more detail:

Incorporation into the supplier's sales organization

Under case-law, certain factors have been deemed to show that a distributor is incorporated into the supplier's sales organization in a fashion comparable to commercial agency. These include, in particular,[97]

- appointment for a certain contract territory, even in the absence of an exclusivity provision or a no-compete clause;
- an obligation on the part of the distributor to do business under the supplier's trade mark or logo;
- an obligation to promote the sale of the contract products by maintaining specified business premises, a specified repair shop or a certain minimum stock;
- an obligation to purchase certain minimum quantities of the contract goods;
- an obligation to carry out warranty and other customer service repairs;
- an obligation on the part of the distributor to train certain employees according to suggestions or recommendations made by the supplier; and/or
- a right on the part of the supplier to investigate the distributor's business and financial standing and to be consulted beforehand with respect to any major investment or modification of the distributor's business structure.

There are no hard and fast rules as to how many of these factors must be present and in which combination in order to come to the conclusion that a distributor is incorporated into the supplier's sales organization. However, where one or more of these factors are present, the supplier should be advised to take into account an eventual indemnity.

Disclosure of customers

This requirement is fulfilled where the distributor is under obligation to

---

[96] Baumbach, Duden and Hopt, *Handelsgesetzbuch*, 27th edn. (Munich, 1987) Sec. 84 n. 2 A.
[97] BGH 3 Mar. 1983, NJW 83, 1789; BGH 14 Apr. 1983, NJW 83, 2877; BGH 20 Oct. 1983, NJW 83, 2102; BGH 21 Oct. 1987, WM 87, 542.

identify his customers to the supplier during the life of the distributorship agreement or after its termination, even if the supplier has no intention of using these data to make sales to the customers concerned. Even where the distributorship agreement does not mention, or expressly excludes, such an obligation, the requirement may be held to be fulfilled if the distributor has implicitly agreed to make such a disclosure, for instance by submitting to the supplier sales reports on forms prepared by the supplier which identify the customer concerned.[98] The requirement is deemed to be fulfilled even where the contract goods are branded products and there is reason to believe that the customers would buy these products irrespective of the distributor's efforts.[99]

Exclusion

The distributor's claim to indemnity cannot be contractually excluded, irrespective of whether or not the distributorship agreement has been preformulated by the supplier,[100] except if the distributor does not have his seat in the Federal Rupublic of Germany (Sec. 92 c (1) HGB). A decision dating back to 1961, holding that where the supplier has his seat outside the Federal Republic of Germany he may avoid an agent's claim for indemnity by subjecting the agreement to the law of his country,[101] could also be applied to distributorship agreements.

No claim for indemnity exists further if the distributor has terminated the distributorship agreement, unless the supplier has given cause for such a termination, or if the supplier has terminated the distributorship agreement for cause given by the distributor.[102]

To avoid being exposed to a claim for indemnity, the supplier should always consider not obliging the distributor to disclose his customers, and avoiding any implied understanding to that effect. Where this is not possible, he should consider requesting an indemnification (or 'entrance fee') from the distributor for good will taken over from the supplier or his predecessor in the contract territory, as the case may be.[103]

2.1.7.2. Amount

Where the prerequisities set out herein are fulfilled, the distributor may claim a "fair indemnity" for the customers identified to the supplier upon termination of the distributorship agreement. Pursuant to Sec. 89 b (2) HGB, the maximum indemnity is the agent's average annual commission during the last five years or the entire life of the agreement, whichever is shorter, which limit would apply equally in case of a distributor.

---

[98] BGH 3 Mar. 1983, NJW 83, 1789; BGH 14 Apr. 1983, NJW 83, 2877; BGH 20 Oct. 1983, NJW 83, 2102; BGH 16 Jan. 1985, BGHZ 93, 252.
[99] BGH 14 Apr. 1983, NJW 83, 2877; BGH 16 Jan. 1985, BGHZ 93, 252.
[100] BGH 26 Feb. 1985, BB 85, 1085.
[101] BGH 30 Jan. 1961, NJW 61, 1061.
[102] Sec. 89d (3) HGB; BGH 7 July 1983, BB 84, 166.
[103] Stumpf and Hesse, *Der Ausgleichsanspruch des Vertragshändlers - Probleme und Gestaltungsmöglichkeiten,* BB (1987), 1474.

2.1.8. Specific applications of EEC-law

There are very few decisions rendered by German courts dealing with EEC-law concerning distribution agreements (except selective distribution agreements, see section 2.2. below). It appears that there is only one BGH decision which is perhaps of some interest,[104] where the BGH referred the following questions concerning the applicability of EEC-Regulation 67/67 to the European Court of Justice, to wit whether the Regulation could be applied if:

- there are several parties to the agreement on one side, which parties form an economic unit;
- the contract territory includes countries outside the EEC; and
- the distributor is authorized to register a certain trade mark in various member states of the EEC, without anything in the contract giving rise to the suspicion that the distributor might use these trade marks to block intra-EEC parallel imports.

The European Court[105] answered all three questions in the affirmative. The BGH[106] duly adopted the European Court's reasoning in its final decision.

2.1.8.1. Applicable law and jurisdiction

German law generally recognizes the validity of choice of law clauses (Art. 27 EGBGB), including those contained in distributorship agreements. In the absence of such a clause, the agreement will generally be deemed to be governed by the law of the distributor's country,[107] on the theory that his activities are characteristic for the agreement (Art. 28 (2) EGBGB).

Likewise, German law recognizes choice of forum clauses under Art. 17 of the Brussels Convention. Otherwise, such clauses concerning German courts (prorogation as well as derogation) contained in distributorship agreements are generally valid pursuant to Sec. 38 (1) of the German Code of Civil Procedure (ZPO) which permits choice of forum clauses if both parties thereto are businesses, which is normally the case in distributorship agreements. German law does not provide for exclusive jurisdiction in respect of distributorship agreements.

2.2. Selective Distribution

Since 1973, when the German Act Against Restraints of Competition was amended to prohibit resale price maintenance, which before had been permitted at least for branded goods, selective-distribution agreements have become increasingly popular in Germany.

2.2.1. Definition

The definition of selective-distribution systems prevailing in Germany is not different from the one prevailing at EEC level: A selective-distribution

---

[104] BGH 28 June 1983, GRUR 84, 183 "Ghibli".
[105] EC 12 July 1984, GRUR 1984, 629 "Hydrotherm".
[106] BGH 2 Dec. 1984, GRUR 85, 472 "Ghibli II".
[107] Kindler, *Handelsvertreter- und Vertragshändlerverträge im IPR*, RIW (1987), 660.

system is generally understood to be a system of distributorship agreements designed to restrict the distribution of the products concerned to qualified, "selected" distributors and retailers.[108] The German term for selective distribution is "Selektive Vertriebsbindung".

2.2.2. Conclusion of the contract (special conditions)

While Sec. 34 GWB is in force, selective distributorship agreements are valid only if they are in writing (see 2.1.2. above).

2.2.3. The supplier's duties and rights

What has been said under section 2.1.3. above applies also with respect to selective-distribution agreements. In addition, the following rules apply.

2.2.3.1. The supplier's duties

The existence of a selective-distribution system implies a paramount duty on the part of the supplier to maintain the selective distribution system, i.e. to refrain from supplying outsiders and, if necessary, to take action against outsiders who attempt to sell contract goods outside the selective-distribution system.[109] Consequently, the distributor's duty to observe specified quality standards and to resell the contract goods only to qualified retailers is only enforceable if the supplier can show that (i) all other distributors are under a corresponding, valid legal obligation to observe specified quality standards and to resell the contract goods only to qualified retailers ("theoretical comprehensiveness'—"gedankliche Lückenlosigkeit") and (ii) the said obligations of all other distributors are enforced in practice ("practical comprehensiveness"—"praktische Lückenlosigkeit").[110]

If the supplier has established a comprehensive selective- distribution system, he can successfully defend himself against claims for supply by outsiders based on Sec. 26 (2) GWB (see below) and he can enjoin outsiders from selling the contract goods (see the sections on Claims for Supply by Outsiders and Action Against Outsiders under 2.2.3.1. below). If the supplier fails to make use of these rights, the selective-distribution system would lose its comprehensiveness and would thus be destroyed.

Theoretical comprehensiveness

In order to establish theoretical comprehensiveness, the supplier must show that all of his distributors are legally bound to observe the same quality standards and to refrain from selling to outsiders. This means that the supplier may have to furnish legal opinions confirming the legality of the selective-distribution agreement in all countries concerned, except with respect to those countries from where, under the circumstances of the case,

---

[108] Stumpf, Sec. 172.

[109] Bundesgerichtshof ("BGH") 14 June 1963, Entscheidungen des Bundesgerichtshofes in Zivilsachen ("BGHZ") 40, 135 "Trockenrasierer II"; BGH 9 Nov. 1967, GRUR 68, 272 "Trockenrasierer III"; Baumbach and Hefermehl, *Wettbewerbsrecht*, Sec. 1 UWG n. 744; Hootz, *Die Durchsetzung zulässiger selektiver Vertriebs-systeme nach deutschem Wettbewerbsrecht*, Betriebsberater ("BB") 84, 1649.

[110] Ibid.

no imports or re-imports into Germany are made or are to be expected.[111] In one case, a selective-distribution system was held not to be theoretically comprehensive because the supplier, a manufacturer of cosmetics, had failed to show that his distributors in Denmark and Burma(!) were bound under the terms of their respective contracts to respect the selective-distribution system, and there was reason to believe that parallel imports into Germany had been made from both countries.[112]

In this context, a particular problem arises under EEC-law with respect, to those selective distribution agreements which are not solely based on objective technical requirements and thus fall under Article 85 (1) of the EEC Treaty. Frequently, a notification has been made of selective-distribution systems requiring exemption under Art. 85 (3) of the EEC Treaty in accordance with EEC-Regulation 17/62, but an exemption has not (yet) been granted by the Commission. Strictly speaking, such distribution agreements are void pursuant to Art. 85 (2) of the EEC Treaty, because they are not covered by the European Court's decision in the "Brasserie De Haecht" case;[113] this would mean that the selective-distribution system concerned would not be theoretically comprehensive. Nevertheless, German courts have consistently treated such selective-distribution systems as lawful, provided that the systems concerned had been, if necessary under EEC-law, notified to the Commission and respected the criteria set out in the European Court's "Metro/Saba" decision.[114] A comfort letter from the Commission may be helpful in this respect,[115] but where the Commission has issued a statement of objections it is up to the supplier to show that the Commission's objections are unfounded under EEC law.[116] Consequently, even a distribution system which violates Art. 85 (1) of the EEC Treaty and has not been exempted by the Commission may be regarded as valid and comprehensive.

Practical comprehensiveness

Regarding the practical comprehensiveness of the system, the supplier must show not only that he has acted against infringements of the system, but also that he has done everything that could reasonably be expected in order to maintain the system and, in particular, to prevent infringements beforehand. Thus, a system was found not to be comprehensive because the supplier could show only that he had given certain instructions to his French and Italian distributors, but not that he had verified compliance with these instructions.[117]

To conclude, only where the supplier undertakes to maintain his selective-distribution system legally and practically comprehensive may he claim adherence to the system by his distributors. It should be noted that the strict-

---

[111] BGH 21 Feb. 1968, GRUR 69, 222 "Le Galion"; OLG Frankfurt 30 Aug. 1979, GRUR 80, 49 "5-Sterne-Programm".
[112] OLG Düsseldorf 7 Nov. 1985, WRP 86, 150 "Dior".
[113] EC 6 Feb. 1972, ECR 1973, 77.
[114] EC 25 Oct. 1977, ECR 1977 II 1875.
[115] OLG Frankfurt 30 Aug. 1979, GRUR 80, 49 "5-Sterne-Programm".
[116] BGH 9 May 1985, GRUR 85, 1059 "Vertriebsbindung".
[117] Ibid.

ness of these requirements has been severely criticized,[118] but no relaxation of the standards established under case-law is presently in sight.

Claims for supply by outsiders

In practice, the major threat against the comprehensiveness of a selective-distribution system consists of claims by outsiders based on Sec. 26 (2) GWB. Such a claim would require, firstly, that either the supplier holds the dominant market position (see section 2.1.3.1.4. above) or the outsider is dependent on the supplier, most importantly if the outsider needs the contract products to complete his product range in order to remain competitive vis-à-vis his own customers, there being no other source of supply for the products concerned of which he could make reasonable use. This may be the case where the supplier's products are absolutely leading in the market, so that virtually no distributor or retailer can do without offering those products.[119] An outsider would also be considered dependent on a supplier whose products are part of a group of several branded products which together are leading in the market, so that the claimant needs to offer at least a certain number of these products in order to remain competitive.[120]

Secondly, the outsider would have to show that the supplier's refusal to supply him constitutes unfair obstruction or unjustified discrimination in the meaning of Sec. 26 (2) GWB. Neither of these requirements is met, however, if the supplier can show that the products concerned are distributed in a comprehensive selective-distribution system, which provides for fair and objective standards justified by valid business reasons, unless the outsider can show that he meets the standards set by the distribution agreements.

The requirement that the standards set out in the selective-distribution agreements be justified by valid business reasons has been the subject of many court decisions[121] which may be summarized as follows: Qualitative standards, such as those relating to staff qualification, showroom facilities and customer service are generally permitted; the standards may be stricter the more sophisticated the product at issue is.[122] The supplier may define these standards at his discretion, but must then apply the so-defined standards without discrimination. Thus, a supplier requiring certain showroom facilities may not restrict his deliveries to specialized retailers only and refuse to supply department stores, provided that the latter have equally well-equipped specialized departments.[123] A quantitative limitation may be lawful, if the supplier can show that there is no economically feasible alter-

[118] Beier, *Der Schutz selektiver Vertriebsbindungen gegenüber Außenseitern—Die Lückenlosigkeit in Theorie und Praxis, Gewerblicher Rechtsschutz und Urheberrecht* ("GRUR") 87, 131.
[119] "Spitzenstellungsabhängigkeit", BGH 20 Nov. 1975, GRUR 76, 206 "Rossignol".
[120] "Spitzengruppenabhängigkeit", BGH 30 June 1981, Neue juristische Wochenschrift ("NJW") 81, 2357 "Belieferungsunwürdige Verkaufsstätten I"; BGH 16 Dec. 1986, GRUR 87, 459 "Belieferungsunwürdige Verkaufsstätten II".
[121] Markert, in Immenga and Mestmäcker, Sec. 26 nn. 222 ff.: Niederleithinger and Ritter, p. 112 ff.; Langen, Niederleithinger, Ritter and Schmidt, Sec. 26 n. 199 ff.
[122] BGH 8 Mai. 1983, GRUR 83, 396 "Modellbauartikel III"; BGH 16 Dec 1986 C 10.
[123] BGH 30 June 1981, Neue juristische Wochenschrift ("NJW") 81, 2357 "Belieferungsunwürdige Verkaufsstätten I"; BGH 16 Dec. 1986, GRUR 87, 459 "Belieferungsunwürdige Verkaufsstätten II". Markert, in Immenga and Mestmäcker, n. 225.

native to such limitation.[124] It may be unlawful for the supplier to refuse to supply an outsider who does meet the standards set by the supplier solely because other distritbutors have threatened to stop the distribution of the contract goods if the outsider is supplied.[125]

The foregoing requirements are roughly similar to those used by the EEC Commission in connection with the negative clearance or exemption of a selective-distribution system.[126] In all those cases, however, where the selective-distribution system at issue is covered by stricter standards under Art. 85 (1) of the EEC Treaty, failure to comply with the (stricter) EEC standards would permit outsiders to request supplies pursuant to Sec. 26 (2) GWB. This would make it impossible for the supplier to maintain a comprehensive system and would thus destroy the system.

Action against outsiders

The supplier's duty to maintain a comprehensive selective-distribution system also requires him to take action against outsiders who are selling the contract goods. Under German law, the supplier may enjoin outsiders from selling the contract goods if he can show that (i) either the outsider has incited an inside distributor to breach the distribution agreement, or has at least knowingly made use of such a breach, thereby gaining an undeserved competitive advantage with respect to insiders or other outsiders, or (ii) has bought the contract goods from an inside distributor through third parties or otherwise in a fashion concealing his intention to resell the goods outside the selective-distribution system.[127] While the latter can rarely be proven, a breach of the selective-distribution agreement can be established, at least *prima facie*, by showing that the selective-distribution system is—as explained above—theoretically and practically comprehensive.[128] Under these circumstances, the outsider's selling the contract goods would be regarded as unfair pursuant to Sec. 1 UWG[129] and could thus be enjoined by the supplier.[130]

If the supplier cannot establish the comprehensiveness of his selective-distribution system, he has no claim against an outsider for disclosure of the outsider's source of supply.[131]

The fact that the outsider is selling contract goods where the code numbers have been removed which the supplier has affixed in order to verify adherence to the selective-distribution system is not in and of itself a violation of unfair competition law.[132]

---

[124] Ibid. n. 228.
[125] BGH 16 Dec. 1986, GRUR 87, 459 "Belieferungsunwürdige Verkaufsstätten II".
[126] EC Commission, OJ C 140 of 28 May 1983, p. 3 "Saba".
[127] BGH 14 June 1963, Entscheidungen des Bundesgericht-shofes in Zivilsachen ("BGHZ") 40, 135 "Trockenrasierer II"; Baumbach and Hefermehl, n. 745 ff.
[128] BGH 14 June 1963, Entscheidungen des Bundesgericht-shofes in Zivilsachen ("BGHZ") 40, 135 "Trockenrasierer II".
[129] *Act Against Unfair Competition*, for translation of relevant provisions see p. 219.
[130] BGH 14 June 1963, Entscheidungen des Bundesgericht-shofes in Zivilsachen ("BGHZ") 40, 135 "Trockenrasierer II".
[131] OLG Düsseldorf 7 Nov. 1985, WRP 86, 150 "Dior".
[132] BGH 21 April 1988, NJW 88, 3152 "Entfernung von Kontrollnummern I" BHG 15 May 1988, NJW 88, 3154 "Entfernung von Kontrollnummern II".

2.2.3.2. *The supplier's rights*

As already indicated above, the supplier may request the distributor to observe the quality standards set out in the distribution agreement and to refrain from selling the contract goods to outsiders, provided that the system is comprehensive as explained in the preceding paragraphs.

2.2.4. The distributor's duties and rights

As described under Claims for Supply by Outsiders under 2.2.3.1. above, the supplier may generally determine the particular duties and rights of the distributor under a selective-distribution agreement, provided always that the particular duties imposed on the distributors are justified by valid business reasons. Ohterwise, there is a risk that outsiders could claim to be supplied with the contract goods, which in turn would entitle the distributor to disregard his particular duties under the selective-distribution agreement.

2.2.5. Liabilities of supplier and distributor during the term of the distributorship agreement

The liabilities of the parties to a selective-distribution agreement are not different from those of the parties to an ordinary distributorship agreement (see section 2.1.5. above).

2.2.6. Term and termination

There are no particular rules regarding the term and termination of a selective-distribution agreement.

2.2.7. Indemnity

The fact that a distributor is party to a selective-distribution agreement may be a factor showing that he is incorporated into the supplier's sales organization. Consequently, it is generally more likely that a distributor in a selective-distribution agreement has a claim to indemnification than an ordinary distributor, provided always that he is obliged to disclose the customers acquired by him to the supplier (see section 2.1.7. above).

2.2.8. Specific applications of EEC-law

Except for those already mentioned under section 2.2.3.1. above, there are no specific applications of EEC-law regarding selective-distribution systems in Germany.

3. Franchise Agreements

3.1. Definition

The franchise contract, not yet subject to legal regulation and definition in Germany, is a contract *sui generis*. The official definition of the German Franchise Association e.V. runs as follows:

Franchising is a distribution system used by legally independent entreprises with a vertical co-operative organization, based on a permanent contractual relationship. The system is standardized on the market and is characterized by an operating programme which divides the tasks among the different partners, as well as by a system of instructions and controls to secure compliance with the system.

The franchisor's operating programme is the franchise package, consisting of a concept of supply, distribution and organization, use of industrial property rights, and training of the franchisee, as well as the franchisor's obligations of active and continuous support to the franchisee and of constant development of the concept.

The franchisee, acting on his own name and at his own risk, has the right and the duty to use the franchise-package subject to payment. He, on his part, has to contribute work, capital and information.

3.1.1. Characteristics

Franchise contracts can be viewed as mixed or combined contracts because they contain elements of various types of contracts, legally regulated. Thus, the franchise contract contains elements of a licensing agreement for the utilization of industrial property rights of various types (patents, trade marks, designs), a know-how agreement on the interchange of technical, operational and other data and practical provisions such as an organization and marketing structure. Components of a franchise contract are frequently a supply agreement, an agency agreement for special services of the franchisor such as guidance and additional information; further it contains delivery and payment conditions, tenancies, non-competition clauses, arbitration agreements, etc.

As franchising is mainly considered to be a new form of distribution, the legal rules concerning dealerships are largely applied. Like franchise agreements, distributorship systems are not subject to statutory provisions. The courts have extensively developed legal standards for distributor agreements, applying by analogy the provisions concerning commercial agents in the German Commercial Code. Thus, if no rulings exist for franchise or distributor agreements, a court is likely to refer to the provisions ruling commercial agents. Thus, the legal regulations appropriate to the nature of a particular part of a contract are applied.

3.2. Conclusion of the Contract (Special Conditions)

3.2.1. Act against restraints on competition (GWB)

3.2.1.1. Distinction between German and European competition law

The Act against Restraints on Competition (GBW) distinguishes between horizontal and vertical restraints of trade, whereas Art. 85 of the EEC Treaty makes no distinction. European Competition Law therefore covers franchise contracts as mere vertical co-operation agreements, in contrast to German Competition Law, which takes a narrower standpoint.

According to German Competition Law only horizontal restrictions functioning as cartels are basically prohibited (§ 1 GWB) unless one of the specifically standardized exceptions exists (§ §2 ff., GWB). Such co-operation agreements have to be registered with the Cartel (Antitrust) Office and become effective only if the latter does not oppose them.

Compared with Art. 85 of the EEC Treaty, German Competition Law lacks a blanket prohibitive clause on vertical restraints of trade. According to § 15 GWB only contracts which restrain one partner with regard to the content (e.g. prices, terms of trade, etc.) of deals to be made with a third party are generally prohibited. Otherwise vertical restraints of trade are subject only to a control of abuse, and registration or authorization are not required. (cf., § § 15 ff., GWB).

3.2.1.2. Franchise contracts as contracts of vertical co-operation

Normally a franchise contract is to be considered as a contract of vertical co-operation and is consequently subject only to control of abuse by the Cartel Office (see § 18 GWB). If franchisees are partners of their franchisors, or if all franchisees are members of a board of trustees, founded by the franchisor whose duty it is to support them in their business policy, it is disputed whether the franchise contract in such a case becomes a horizontal association and consequently a trust which has to be licensed.[133] As a rule, these cases will not be the subject of a horizontal co-operation, but this question finally depends on the individual situation. The situation changes as soon as the franchise system is integrated into other vertical combines like co-operative associations, buyers' associations, commercial chains, or joint ventures. If there is a horizontal connection this complex can consequently be regarded as a horizontal association and will be prohibited under § 1 GWB.[134]

Summing up, it may be said that the typical franchise contract is to be considered as mere vertical co-operation and is only subject to control of abuse by the Cartel Office. Exclusive agreements, supply and distribution agreements as well as restrictions on use (cf. § 18 GWB), or restraints of trade concerning patent licences, registered trade marks, designs, etc. (cf. § § 20.21 GWB) are particularly subject to control of abuse. The franchisor must always ensure that the commitments provided in his franchise contract are not inconsistent with German Antitrust Law (see sections on Direct Sales and Restrictions on Other Dealers under 2.1.3.1. above).

3.2.1.3. Requirement for writing § § 18, 34 GWB

Under § 34 GWB, a franchise contract must be drawn up in writing if it contains restraints of trade. A non-written franchise contract can be totally or partly void. (§ § 125, 126 BGB = German Civil Code) § 34 para. 3 GWB furthermore demands that documents like resolutions, statutes and price-lists to which the franchise contract refers have to be drawn up in writing

---

[133] Blaurock, Uwe, Kartellrechtliche Grenzen von Franchise-Systemen, in *Festschrift für Winfried Werner* (Berlin and New York, 1984), pp. 23 ff.

[134] Steindorff, BB 1961, 377 ff.

and be accessible at any time and the reference has to be unequivocal and therefore explicit. The reason for this provision is to enable the Cartel Office to examine, within the scope of its control of abuse, such documents at any time. Care has to be taken that such documents, above all price-lists for the supply of goods, exist in writing, are accessible to the Cartel Office, and are referred to unequivocally in the franchise contract.[135]

3.2.1.4. Commitment to take delivery § 18 GWB

Exclusive or far-reaching commitments of the franchisee can cause problems as far as antitrust law is concerned. An obligation to accept the supply of goods exclusively from the franchisor is only admissible under competition law, if the goods are produced by the franchisor, and the restriction aims to guarantee quality. It is inadmissible to oblige the franchisee to purchase from the franchisor products which are not typical for the system. If the franchisor himself obtains the goods from a third party, an exclusive commitment to take delivery is not necessary to make the franchise system function, and is therefore invalid under Competition Law. In this case the franchisee must be allowed partly to make his own supply arrangements irrespective of the commitment. The Cartel Office has not approved a universal percentage but everything above 50% is doubtful. Whether the purchase obligation is accepted depends on the individual case. If the obligation is necessary for establishing and maintaining small independent businesses, approval may be easier to achieve.

3.2.1.5. Price maintenance § 15 GWB

Under § 15 GWB it is not permissible to restrict the franchisee's freedom to determine prices or terms of trade for the ultimate buyer.

Commitment to general terms of trade

General terms of trade can only be arranged for the direct relationship between franchisor and franchisee. According to § 15 GWB the franchisor is not allowed to instruct the franchisee as to his terms of trade with the customer. Of course, the franchisee is at liberty to agree with his customers on the same conditions and above all on the same liability arrangements as between him and the franchisor but he cannot be bound by contract.

Price maintenance

Under no circumstances can the franchisee be restricted in his freedom to determine prices. The prohibition of price maintenance under § 15 GWB has been found to be applicable to franchise contracts.[136]

Price recommendation

According to § 38 a GWB, price recommendations for branded goods (i.e. products having a label to show their origin) are allowed on the following conditions:

---

[135] BGH 14 Nov. 1978, BB 1979, 592; BGH of 6 Mar. 1978, WuW 1979, 1592; BGH of 9 July 1985, DB 1985, 2609.
[136] OLG Köln of 14 June 1975, WuW/E OLG 1715, 1716 ff. "Wimpy" KG Berlin of 16 July 1980, WuW/E OLG 2452, 2454, "Meierei-Zentrale".

- The price has to be significant marked and recommended as "non-compulsory". All records have to show distinctly that the price recommendation is subject to change.
- No economic or other pressure may be applied in order to enforce the price.
- The price recommendation has to be in conformity with the market and may be made only for products which are in price competition with similar products of competitors.
- Only one single consumer price may be recommended, no approximate, maximum, minimum or skeleton prices.
- No price recommendations can be made for services.

Small business recommendation

The small business recommendation, according to § 38 para. 2 GWB, offers another possibility for smaller and medium-sized franchise systems which are in competition with large-scale enterprises. A price recommendation in accordance with this regulation is valid on condition that:

- the recommendation contributes to an increase in efficiency for smaller franchise systems compared with large-scale enterprises and thereby improves general competition in the market-place, and
- the price is explicitly designated as "non-compulsory" and no economic, social or other pressure is used to enforce it.

3.2.1.6. Discrimination

See section on No Discrimination under 2.1.3.1. above.

3.2.2. Law on general terms of trade (AGBG)

The law on General Terms of Trade (AGBG) is designed to protect the weaker partner from being forced to accept unreasonable contractual conditions. This law applies to all contractual clauses standardized for a large number of contracts, and which one party presents to the other as the terms of a contract. It does not apply to individually negotiated contracts.

Because as a rule standardized contracts are produced by the franchisor, franchise systems are basically subject to the controls in the Law on General Terms of Trade.[137] If the franchisee is not a merchant, the Law on General Terms of Trade, which contains detailed regulations concerning the validity of special clauses, will be applicable. If, however, the franchisee is a merchant, which normally is the case, the Law on General Terms of Trade is only applicable in a qualified sense. § 24 para. 2 9 AGBG provides that a so-called examination of the franchise contract or control of subject-matter is to be carried out. Accordingly, terms become void if they place the franchisee at a disadvantage which is contrary to the principle of good faith in business policy. This is a discretionary decision exercised by the courts, which in recent years have more and more used the AGBG to remove "unfair" contractual clauses.

---

[137] BGH of 3 October 1984, NJW 1985, 1894 ff., "McDonalds".

3.2.3. Instalment business act (AbzG)

In order to protect the consumer, there is in Germany a Law concerning Instalment Purchases (AbzG), containing contractual safeguard clauses for purchase contracts in which the parties have agreed on a payment by at least two instalments. The law is not applicable to registered merchants (§ 8 AbzG).

In connection with a franchise contract a judgment completely unexpected by all persons concerned has been given by the Federal Supreme Court.[138] The Court decided that the obligation of the franchisee, contained in the franchise contract which was the subject-matter of the proceedings, to obtain goods repeatedly from the franchisor, was covered by the provision of § 1 c no. 3 AbzG. The effect of this is that under § 1 b AbzG the instalment buyer, i.e. the franchisee, is entitled to withdraw from the contract by notice in writing within one week. This one week period, however, does not start running until the franchisor has notified the franchisee in writing about his right to withdraw. In the case decided by the Federal Supreme Court, the franchisor's failure could withdraw from the franchise contract although it had been in operation for years.

Although this judgment of the Federal Supreme Court has received much general criticism from experts, the franchise business has had to adapt to it. As far as current franchise contracts, not concluded with a registered merchant, are concerned, there is now the danger, if no notification of the possibility of withdrawal was given, that the franchisees could avoid these contracts. In that case, it has to be considered if it is advisable and meaningful to insert a supplementary clause in existing contracts. As far as future franchise contracts to be concluded with non-traders are concerned, the franchisor must inform the franchisee in a clear written statement, also to be signed by the franchisee, about his right to withdraw in accordance with the Instalment Business Act. In view of the fact that the right to withdraw has to be exercised within one week, no considerable disadvantages are caused to the franchisor.

3.3. The Supplier's Duties and Rights

The main duty of the franchisor is to integrate the franchisee in the franchise (distribution) system and to give him permanent assistance. The detailed duties of assistance depend on the specific franchise system and are contained in the franchise agreement. The Federal Labour Court has stated that between the parties to a franchise contract there is no employment but a kind of distributorship, yet at the same time it imposed a number of onerous duties on the franchisor. If the franchisor has considerable expert knowledge and a well-proven system, he must advise the franchisee competently and protect him from investment failures.[139] A logical development of this jurisdiction, but up to now not yet decided, would be liability for damages in the event of inadequate information or advice.

---

[138] BGH of 16 Apr. 1986. BB 1986, 1115 "Yves Rocher".
[139] BAG of 24 Apr. 1980. BB 1980. 1471.

3.4. The Distributor's Duties and Rights

3.4.1. The distributor's duties

The main duty of the franchisee is to promote sales in accordance with the marketing strategy of the franchisor and to pay the franchise fees.

3.4.2. The distriubor's rights

Franchise agreements often impose non-competition clauses on the franchisee. In order to judge the validity of non-competition clauses, it is essential to distinguish between prohibitions imposed for the period of the contract and those which continue to be applicable after termination.

3.4.2.1. Non-competition during the term of the contract

Non-competition for the duration of a contract is, according to German understanding, an inherent element of the franchisee's loyalty to his system and a covenant to this effect in the contract is therefore valid. This may change as soon as the Group Exemption Regulation of the EC-Commission comes into force, where participation in a competing enterprise is allowed under certain conditions.

3.4.2.2. Non-competition after termination of contract

Non-competition clauses for the time after termination of a contract are valid only to a limited extent. The right of a commercial agent to earn a living can only be overridden by such a non-competition clause for a period of two years and only in cases where the commercial agent is paid adequate compensation for the period of restraint of trade (§ 90 a HGB).[140] Accordingly jurisprudence treats non-competition clauses in franchise contracts in the same way. A post-termination non-competition clause in a franchise contract was considered illegal and therefore void, for no compensation was paid for it. A post-termination non-competition clause for three years was also declared void in analogous application of the right of the commercial agent.[141] A different judgment did not declare a non-competition clause without compensation void but it awarded an adequate indemnity payment to the franchisee.[142]

In view of this jurisprudence a post-termination non-competition clause should only be imposed for a period of two years after termination of the contract. In addition, it is advisable to settle the amount and the nature of the compensation. There is no difficulty if the non-competition clause is armed with a proportionate penalty clause. The application of the non-competition clause can only be extended to the contractual activity and related ones in the contractual and neighbouring territories, and is not effective to the extent that it attempts to encompass other activities or areas.

Moreover it is advisable to record the non-competition clause in a sep-

---

[140] See below, pp. 000 (L 5).
[141] KG Berlin of 10 July 1973, MDR 1974, 144 ff.; LG Berlin of 25 Apr. 1973, BB 1975, 61 ff.
[142] OLG Düsseldorf of 24 May 1975, WuW/E; OLG 1683 "Wimpy".

arate document and to insert the possibility for the franchisor to waive the clause, this reducing the compensation to be paid. A waiver will only be regarded as valid if it was stated in writing prior to the termination of the contract (§ 90 a HGB).[143]

3.5. Liabilities of Supplier and Distributor During the Term of the Distributorship Agreement

3.5.1. The supplier as against the distributor

The contractual liability between franchisor and franchisee on the one hand and franchisee and consumer (third party) on the other hand is governed by the German Civil Code.

According to the Civil Code the franchisor can be held liable for defective goods, in which case he must reduce the price or take the goods back. The franchisor may under certain conditions also be liable for damages. In addition to the warranty of proper quality, a contractual party is responsible for breach of contract (e.g. non-delivery, or delayed delivery).

Restrictions of liability are possible if the contract is separately negotiated. If, however, liability is restricted by general terms of trade, the Law on General Terms of Trade allows only few restrictions. Liability for damages based on a grossly negligent or wilful act of a contracting party or its employees cannot be limited or excluded.

3.5.2. The supplier as against third parties

Product liability is based on tort law. The manufacturer whose product injures a person or damages property has to prove that he is not responsible for the fault and that he has taken all possible measures to prevent the fault. If he cannot provide such proof he is fully liable for all damages. A limitation of liability is only possible where there is a contractual relationship (franchisor = manufacturer—franchisee = consumer). The provisions in the Law on General Terms of Trade (referred to above) must be taken into account. A restriction of liability of the manufacturer vis-à-vis the customers of the franchisee is not possible.

Product liability rules will change with the application of the EC-Directive on Product Liability, as this directive will introduce strict liability not only of the manufacturer but also of all enterprises affixing their name to the product.

3.6. Term and Termination

3.6.1. Term

The term of a franchise contract normally differs, according to the importance of the investment, between three and ten years, or even longer. It is possible to agree on any duration. As to the franchise contract of Holiday

---

[143] For translation of § 90 a see below p. 220–221.

Inns, however, the Federal Court of Justice decreed that a contractual obligation of 50 years is inappropriate, conflicts with national policy and public morals (*contra bonos mores*) and is therefore void under § 138 BGB (German Civil Code). As far as a contractual term of 20 years is concerned, no legal objections were raised.[144]

3.6.2. Termination

The contract usually provides for an appropriate notice of termination to be served. A clause making provision for the automatic extension of a contract with fixed duration if no notice is given within a certain time, is usual and to be recommended.

The maximum fixed duration of a contract can be up to 20 years. The right to give notice of summary termination for an important reason, however, cannot be excluded. An important reason would be the breach by one party of its contractual duties in a way that endangered the main concept of the system. In a franchise contract it is advisable to specify the major contract violations which may give rise to summary termination. In a case relating to a summary termination clause in a McDonalds franchise contract, the Federal Court of Justice stated that notice given pursuant to such a clause is effective only in so far as a lasting breach of duty which makes further successful co-operation doubtful has taken place. Summary termination is justified only where the franchisee's breach of duty is sufficiently severe that the franchisor's realization of his entrepreneurial aims seems to be jeopardized. Clauses which give the franchisor a right of summary termination in cases of slight breaches of duty are void.[145]

In addition, it was stated that even if an important reason for giving notice exists, the termination notice can only be given within a reasonable time after the constituent facts have come to the franchisor's knowledge. A termination notice given months after having received information on the facts of the case is not issued within a reasonable time and is therefore void.[146]

In analogous application to the regulations of § 89 a para. 2 HGB (German Commercial Code),[147] applicable to commercial agents, the one whose behaviour or activities caused the summary termination will be obliged to indemnify the damage incurred by the other party due to the premature termination of the contract.

3.7. Indemnity

3.7.1. Indemnity for goodwill and/or clientèle

According to § 89 b HGB,[148] a commercial agent is entitled to receive compensation after termination of a contract. The basic idea of the legal regulation is, that during the term of the contract the commercial agent has formed business relations with new customers which will also be of further advantage to the principal. A contractual exclusion of the compensation

[144] BGH of 5 Oct. 1981, ZIP 1982, 578 ff.
[145] BGH of 3 Oct. 1984, NJW 1985, 1895.
[146] Ibid.
[147] For translation of § 89 see below p. 220.
[148] Ibid.

claim is invalid and ineffective. By analogy, jurisprudence has applied this principle of the German Commercial Code to distributors on condition that:

- The distributor is fully integrated into the marketing organization of the manufacturer (see section on Incorporation into the Supplier's Sales Organization under 2.1.7.1. above).
- The distributor is bound by contract to make the names and addresses of his customers available to the manufacturer if he leaves the marketing organization, or the manufacturer is in the position to take advantage of the distributor's customers in a different way.[149] Continuous information during the period of contract is also a method of naming the customers. It is decisive that the manufacturer is actually put into the position of being able to continue to take advantage of the customers after termination of the contract. A conclusive activity like the transmission of accounting data, copies of invoices, sales analyses, summary and sales reports, etc. is sufficient if it supplies the particulars of the cusomters[150] (see section on Disclosure of Documents under 2.1.7.1. above).

A court decision concerning a claim for compensation on termination of a franchise contract has yet to be made. It can be presumed that the jurisprudence will be the same as for distributorship contracts, if similar conditions exist. Thus, there should be no compensation if the client data are not made available to the franchisor. It is therfore advisable not to include an obligation to transmit the client data in the franchise contract. It may also be important if the franchisor, through the actual implementation of the franchise contract, is enabled to take advantage of the franchisee's customers. These facts do not apply to franchise systems in which there are either no regular customers or the customers are not registered, a typical feature of over-the-counter transactions. An analogous application of § 89b HGB giving rise to a compensation claim would fail because of the analogous precondition that the customer-data must be ceded.

3.7.2. Compensation for damages

In analogous application to the rule of § 89 a para. 2 HGB (see below), which applies to commercial agents, the one who caused the termination of the franchise contract for an important reason, i.e. by his behaviour or activities, will be obliged to reimburse the losses of the other party arising out of the premature termination of the contract.

3.8. Specific Application of EEC Law

There are no specific aspects to mention.

3.8.1. Applicable Law, Choice of Law

See section 2.1.8.1. above.

---

[149] BGH of 20 Feb. 1981, NJW 1981, 1961; BGH of 25 Mar. 1982, NJW 1982, 2819; BGH of 3 Mar. 1983, NJW 1983, 1789; BGH of 14 Apr. 1983, NJW 1983, 2877; BGH of 20 Oct. 1983, NJW 1984, 2102.
[150] Ibid.

List of Abbreviations

AGBG	Gesetz zur Regelung des Rechts der Allgemeinen Geschäftsbedingungen
BB	Betriebsberater
BGB	Bürgerliches Gesetzbuch
BGH	Bundesgerichtshof
BGHZ	Entscheidungen des Bundesgerichtshofs in Zivilsachen
DB	Der Betrieb
EGBGB	Einführungsgesetz zum BGB
GRUR	Gewerblicher Rechtsschutz und Urheberrecht
GWB	Gesetz gegen Wettbewerbsbeschränkungen
HGB	Handelsgesetzbuch
NJW	Neue Juristische Wochenschrift
OLG	Oberlandesgericht
RIW	Recht der Internationalen Wirtschaft
WM	Wertpapiermitteilungen
WuW/E	Wirtschaft und Wettbewerb/Entscheidungssammlung
ZPO	Zivilprozeßordnung

ACT AGAINST RESTRAINTS OF COMPETITION

Clauses printed in bold type are expected to enter into force on January 1, 1990, according to the Executive Draft (Regierungsentwurf) of February 1, 1989 -

Section 1

(1) Agreements made for a common purpose by enterprises or associations of enterprises and decisions of associations of enterprises shall be of no effect, in so far as they are likely to influence, by restraining competition, production or market conditions with respect to trade in goods or commercial services. This shall not apply in so far as this Act provides otherwise.

(2) The term "decision of an association of enterprises" shall include decisions of meetings of the members of a legal entity, in so far as its members are enterprises.

Section 15

Agreements between enterprises concerning goods or commercial services relating to markets located within (Germany) shall be null and void, in so far as they restrict a party to them in its freedom to determine prices or terms of business in such contracts which it concludes with third parties in regard to the goods supplied, other goods, or commercial services.

Section 18

(1) The cartel authority may declare agreements between enterprises concerning goods or commercial services to be of no effect either immediately or as from some future date to be determined by it, and prohibit the implementation of new, similar agreements, in so far as they

1. restrict one of the parties in its freedom to use the supplied goods, other goods or commercial services; or
2. restrict one of the parties in the purchase of other goods or commercial services from, or their sale to, third parties; or
3. restrict one of the parties in the sale of the supplied goods to third parties; or
4. oblige one of the parties to accept goods or commercial services not related to the subject-matter of the agreements by their nature or the custom of the trade.

and in so far as

(a) by virtue of such agreements a number of enterprises significant in relation to competition in the market are similarly bound and unfairly restricted in their freedom of competition, or
(b) by virtue of such agreements other enterprises are unfairly foreclosed from market entry, or
(c) by the extent of such restrictions competition in the market for these or other goods or commercial services is substantially impaired.

(2) A restriction which is insignificant in relation to the sources of supply and demand that remain available to other enterprises shall not be deemed unfair in the sense of subsection (1) (b).

Section 22

(1) An enterprise is market dominating in the meaning of this Act in so far as, in its capacity as a supplier or buyer of a certain type of goods or commercial services,
   1. it has no competitior or is not exposed to any substantial competition, or
   2. it has a supreme market position in relation to its competitors; in this context, its financial strength, its access to the supply or sales markets, its links with other enterprises and legal or factual barriers to the market entry of other enterprises, **its ability to switch its offer or demand to other goods or commercial services as well as the ability if the opposing parties on the market to switch to other enterprises,** shall in particular be taken into account in addition to its market share.
(2) Two or more enterprises shall also be deemed market dominating to the extent that, with respect to a certain type of goods or commercial services, no substantial competition exists between them for factual reasons, either in general or in specific markets, and taken together they meet the requirements of subsection 1.
(3) It shall be presumed that
   1. an enterprise is market dominating in the meaning of subsection 1, if it has a market share of at least one third for a certain type of goods or commercial services; this presumption shall not apply when the enterprise concerned achieved sales of less than DM 250 mio. during the last full business year;
   2. the requirements specified in subsection 2 are met if, with respect to a certain type of goods or commercial services,

      (a) three or more enterprises hold a combined market share of 50% or more, or
      (b) five or more enterprises hold a combined market share of two thirds or more; . . .
(4) The cartel authority shall have the powers set forth in subsection 5 vis-à-vis market dominating enterprises, to the extent that these enterprises abuse their dominant position on the market for the goods concerned or other goods or commercial services. . . .
(5) If the requirements of subsection 4 are met, the cartel authority may enjoin market dominating enterprises from abusive practices and may invalidate agreements; . . .

Section 25

(1) Concerted actions of enterprises or associations of enterprises which under this Act may not be made the subject of a contractual commitment are prohibited.
(2) Enterprises and associations of enterprises shall not threaten or inflict disadvantages, or promise or grant advantages, to other enterprises in order to induce them to adopt conduct which may not be made the subject of a contractual commitment under this Act or a decision issued thereunder by the cartel authority.

Section 26

(1) Enterprises and associations of enterprises shall not instigate another enterprise or association of enterprises to refuse to sell or purchase with intent to restrict certain other enterprises unfairly.
(2) Market dominating enterprises, associations of enterprises within the meaning of Section 2 to 8, 99 **(1) 1 and 2,** Section 100 (1) and (7), Sections 102 to 103, and enterprises fixing prices under Section 16, 100 (3), or Section 103 (1) no. 3, shall

not unfairly obstruct, directly or indirectly, another enterprise in business activities which are usually open to similar enterprises, nor in the absence of facts justifying such differentiation treat such enterprise directly or indirectly in a manner different from the treatment accorded to similar enterprises. Sentence 1 shall also apply to enterprises and associations of enterprises, in so far as suppliers or purchasers of a certain type of goods or commercial services depend on them to such an extent that sufficient and reasonable possibilities of dealing with other enterprises do not exist. For the prohibition procedure pursuant to Section 37a (2), a supplier of a certain type of goods or commercial services shall be presumed to depend on a purchaser within the meaning of sentence 2, if, in addition to the price reductions or other considerations customary in the trade, that purchaser regularly obtains special benefits not granted to similar purchasers.

(3) Market dominating enterprises and associations of enterprises within the meaning of subsection 2, sentence 1, shall not use their market position to cause other enterprises to grant preferential business terms to them in the absence of facts justifying such terms. Sentence 1 shall also apply to enterprises and associations of enterprises within the meaning of subsection 2, sentence 2, in relation to the enterprises depending on them.

(4) **Enterprises holding superior market power vis-à-vis small and medium sized competitors may not make use of their market power to obstruct such competitors unfairly, whether directly or indirectly.**

Section 34 (to be repealed)

Cartel agreements and cartel decisions (Sections 2 to 8), as well as agreements containing restrictions of the nature described in Sections 16, 18, 20 and 21, must be in writing. Sections 126 (1) of the Civil Code shall apply. It shall be sufficient for the parties to sign documents which refer to a written decision, to a written charter, or to a price list. Section 126 (2) of the Civil Code shall not apply.

Section 35

(1) Whoever breaches negligently or intentionally one of the provisions of this Act or a decision issued under this Act by the cartel office or the court of appeals shall, if such provision or decision is intended to protect another person, be liable vis-à-vis such other person for damages caused by such breach.

Section 37a

(1) The cartel authority may prohibit the implementations of an agreement or decision which is of no effect or null and void under Sections 1, 15, 20 (1), 21, 100 (1) sentence 3, or 103 (2).

(2) The cartel authority may prohibit enterprises and associations of enterprises from adopting conduct prohibited under Sections 25, 26, and 38 (1) no. 11 or 12.

(3) **(to be repealed)** The cartel authority may also prohibit an enterprise which, as a result of its superior market power vis-à-vis its small and medium-sized competitors is in a position to influence the market conditions substantially from adopting conduct that, directly or indirectly, unfairly hinders such competitors and is likely to lastingly impair competition with lasting effect.

Section 38

(1) An offence is committed by any person who:
   1. disregards the non-effectiveness or nullity of an agreement or decision which is of no effect or null and void under Sections 1, 15, . . .
   2. wilfully or negligently diregards the non-effectiveness of an agreement or a decision which the cartel authority under . . . Sections 18, 22 (5) . . . has declared to be of no effect by a decision that has become final; . . .
   4. wilfully or negligently contravenes a final decision of the cartel authority taken under . . . Sections 18, 22 (5), . . . 37a, 38a (3) or (6) . . . in so far as it refers explicitly to this provision governing administrative fines; . . .
   8. contravenes any of the prohibitions laid down in Sections 25 or 26; . . .
  10. by means of recommendations contributes to the commission of one of the offences specified in Nos. 1 to 9;
  11. issues recommendations which, through uniform conduct, result in the circumvention of prohibitions laid down in this Act or of decisions taken by the cartel authority pursuant to this Act;
  12. recommends purchasers of his goods to charge or quote specified prices when reselling them to third parties or to use specific price-fixing methods or to observe certain maximum or minimum limits in pricing.
(4) The offence may be punished by a fine of up to DM 1,000,000 or, beyond this, of up to three times any additional profits made as a result of the infringement. The amount of the additional profits may be estimated.

Section 38a

(1) Section 38 (1) nos. 11 and 12 shall not apply to non-binding price recommendations issued by an enterprises for the resale of its branded goods which are in price competition with similar goods of other manufacturers, if the recommendations
   1. are expressly declared to be non-binding, exclusively contain a specific price mark and no economic, social or other pressure is exerted to enforce them, and
   2. are issued with the expectation that the recommended price will correspond to the price likely to be charged by the majority of those to whom the recommendation is addressed.
(2) Branded goods within the meaning of subsection (1) are products which the price recommending enterprises guarantee to be delivered in consistent or improved quality and:
   1. which themselves, or
   2. whose packaging or presentation for delivery to the consumer, or
   3. whose containers in which they are sold are provided with a mark indicating their origin (a firm's symbol, a word or other sign).
    Sentence 1 shall apply to agricultural products on the understanding that minor quality fluctuations which are due to the nature of the product and which cannot be remedied by the producer by measures that can be reasonably required of him shall be left out of account.
(3) The cartel authority may declare recommendations of the nature specified in subsection 1 unlawful and prohibit new, similar recommendations, if it determines that the recommendations constitute an abuse of the exemption from Section 38 (1) nos. 11 or 12. An abuse is present in particular, if
   1. the recommendation alone or in combination with other restraints of competition is likely, in a manner not justified by the overall economic situ-

ation, to increase the price of the goods or prevent their price from decreasing or restrict the production or the sale of such goods, or

2. the recommendation is likely to deceive the consumer as to the price charged by the majority of those to whom the recommendation is addressed, or

3. the recommended price in the majority of cases considerably exceeds the price actually charged in (Germany) or a substantial part thereof, or

4. by distribution arrangements or other measures of the recommending enterprise, certain enterprises or certain groups of buyers are excluded from the distribution of the goods without any reason justifying such action.

ACT AGAINST UNFAIR COMPETITION

Section 1

Any person who, in the course of business activity for purposes of competition, commits acts contrary to fair practices, may be enjoined from these acts and held liable for damages.

ACT CONCERNING GENERAL BUSINESS CONDITIONS

Section 9

(1) Provisions in general business terms are invalid, if they put the other party against public policy at an unfair disadvantage.
(2) If in doubt, an unfair disadvantage shall be presumed to exist if a provision
   1. does not correspond to the characteristic basic intent of the statutory provision from which it derogates, or
   2. limits characteristic rights and duties which arise from the nature of the contract, to such an extent that there is a risk that the object of the contract may not be achieved.

COMMERCIAL CODE (HGB)

Para 89b

(1) The commercial agent can, after termination of the contractual relationship, demand from the principal reasonable compensation if and in so far as
  1. the principal obtained substantial advantages, after expiration of the contractual period, from business relations with new customers solicited by the commercial agent,
  2. the commercial agent lost, by reason of termination of the contractual relationship, rights to commission relating to concluded business or business to be concluded in the future with those customers he had solicited, to which he would have been entitled had the contractual relationship continued, and
  3. the payment of compensation is equitable, considering all the circumstances.

  The expansion of business by the commercial agent with an existing customer so significantly that this corresponds commercially to the introduction of a new customer, shall be considered to be the introduction of a new customer.

(2) Compensation may be awarded of more than the average of the annual commission or other annual compensation over the last five years of the activity of the commercial agent; in the event that the contractual relationship continued for less than five years, the average for the actual period will be awarded.

(3) There is no right to compensation if the commercial agent terminated the contractual relationship, unless conduct of the principal provided reasonable grounds therefor or the commercial agent cannot reasonably be expected to continue because of age or ill health. In addition, there is no right to compensation if the principal terminated the contractual relationship for good reason based on the fault of the commercial agent.

(4) The right to compensation cannot be excluded in advance. It must be asserted within three months following termination of the contractual relationship.

(5) Subsections (1) to (4) apply to insurance agents, provided, however, that instead of the introduction of business relations with new customers, the introduction of new insurance agreements by the insurance agent shall apply and the claim is limited to no more than three years' commission or remuneration.

Para 90a

(1) An agreement by which a commercial agent is restricted in his commercial activity following termination of the contractual relationship (agreement prohibiting competition) must be in writing and the document containing the conditions agreed on, signed by the principal, must be given to the commercial agent. The agreement can extend for no longer than two years following the termination of the contractual relationship. The principal must pay reasonable compensation to the commercial agent for the duration of the prohibition on competition.

(2) The principal can waive the prohibition on competition in writing at any time up to the end of the contractual relationship with the effect that he will be freed

from the obligation to pay compensation upon the expiration of six months from the date of such waiver. Where the principal terminates the contractual relationship for good reason based on the default of the commercial agent, the commercial agent has no right to compensation.

(3) Where the commercial agent terminates the contractual relationship for good reason based on the default of the principal, he can, in writing, within one month following the termination, declare himself unrestricted by the prohibition on competition.

(4) Agreements differing from these provisions to the prejudice of the commercial agent are invalid.

CHAPTER 5

GREECE

Helen Papaconstantinou

Commercial Agency

1.1. Definition of the Various Types of Agencies and Intermediaries

1.1.1. Independent
1.1.2. Employed

Greek law does not contain any legislative or other provisions regarding commercial agencies or commercial agents in general with the exception of L. 307/76 "on commercial agents for imports and exports" which is strictly limited to the setting out of the requirements for the practice of the profession and the penalties imposed for non-compliance therewith. In view of Greece's entry into the EEC, P.D. 407/87 duly amended the above-mentioned law by including the citizens of EEC Members States among those entitled to exercise the profession of commercial agents for imports or exports.

According to Greek academics and case-law a commercial agency agreement is an agreement whereby the commercial agent undertakes, in consideration of a certain remuneration, to negotiate or enter into agreements in a consistent and continuous way on account and in the name of a certain principal.[1] In the absence of specific provisions in the law, commercial agency has been considered equivalent to commission agency and held to be governed by the relevant articles of the Commercial Code (Art. 90–94) in conjunction with the articles on mandate (Art. 713–729) and agency (Art. 211–215) of the Civil Code.[2] Certain academics,[3] considering that the parties

---

[1] T. Mitroulis, "The Commercial Agency Agreement", *JCL* (1963), 12; D. Androutsopoulos, *The Commercial Agency Agreement* (1968), p. 8; E. Anapliotis, "Comments on Commercial Agency and Respondeat Superior", *JCL* (1969), 305.

[2] F.I.C. of Trikala 496/68, *JCL* (1968), 375; A.C. of Athens 485/69, *JCL* (1969), 368; A.C. of Athens 1793/69, *JCL* (1970), 46; F.I.C. of Athens 401/71, *JCL* (1971), 200; A.P. 1072/72, *JCL* (1973), 338; A.C. of Salonica 567/73 *JCL* (1973), 503; A.P. 887/74, *JCL* (1974), 393; A.P. 70/77, *JCL* (1977), 553; F.I.C. of Athens 12785/77, *JCL* (1978), 396; A.C. of Athens 7964/82, *JCL* (1983), 44; F.I.C. of Heraklion 158/86, *JCL* (1987), 38.

[3] Perdikas, *Handbook on Commercial Law*, vol. "A", 3 edn. (1960), p. 225.

of an agency agreement are mainly interested in the results to be achieved by the agent, have also put forward the view that an agency agreement is in fact an agreement for the performance of a certain project and should therefore be regarded in the context of the relevant provisions of the Civil Code (Art. 681–702). Alternatively, other academics[4] have suggested that as the commercial agent is actually providing independent services his agreement with the principal should also be regarded within the context of the employment provisions of the Civil Code (Art. 648–680) to the extent that these are consistent with the nature of a commercial agency agreement. In conclusion, it could be said that commercial agency agreements must be interpreted in good faith by giving regard primarily to the real intention of the parties (Art. 173 of the Civil Code) and the relevant commercial practice (Art. 200 of the Civil Code),[5] these being supplemented by the provisions of the Civil Code which are consistent with the nature of commercial agency.

In addition to the fact that a commercial agent always acts on account and in the name of his principal, among the main characteristics of a commercial agency agreement are

(a) its duration and consistency;
(b) the undertaking of obligations by both parties thereto; and
(c) the independence of the commercial agent's activity.[6]

Although, in the absence of specific provisions on the matter, there is a certain disagreement among academics as to whether the independence of the commercial agent is an essential characteristic of a commercial agency agreement, such independence is more akin to the nature of commercial agency without, however, being an absolutely necessary prerequisite thereof. Whether the commercial agent is actually exercising an independent activity of his own is a question of fact the essence of which is the control which the principal is capable of exercising upon his agent. Among the criteria which will be taken into consideration by the court in deciding whether the commercial agent is independent of his principal without, however, any of those being conclusive, are, indicatively, the following:[7]

• the type of the agent's remuneration (commission as opposed to salary);
• the maintenance of a separate establishment the expenses of which are borne by the agent;
• the form and name under which the agent exercises his activity and the employment of personnel by the agent;
• the conduct of the agent's activity and the control of the principal thereon.

1.1.3. Others

1.1.3.1. The commission agency

Contrary to a commercial agent who acts both on account and in the

---

[4] Kapodistrias, *Interpretation of the Civil Code*, Arts. 648–80; Androutsopoulos, p. 125.
[5] A.P. 70/77, *JCL* (1977), 553.
[6] Androutsopoulos, p. 10 *et seq.*; Anapliotis, p. 305.
[7] A.P. 546/69, *JCL* (1970), 247.

name of another a commission agent is a person who acts in his own name but on account of another. An additional characteristic of a commission agent is that, again contrary to a commercial agent who normally acts on account of a principal with whom he has a contractual relationship of a certain duration, the commission agent is free to provide his services to anybody who may request them.

The commission agency is governed by Art. 90 *et seq.* of the Commercial Code.

1.1.3.2. The broker

Contrary to a commercial agency agreement whereby both parties undertake obligations towards each other a broker does not undertake an obligation to execute the work assigned to him, in the sense that he does not become liable for the non-execution thereof. If, however, as a result of the broker's intervention an agreement is concluded, the broker is entitled to the agreed remuneration. In addition to the above, while the commercial agent has a relation of trust and confidence with his principal (as will be explained below), the broker plays a neutral role towards the parties to the contract.

Brokerage agreements are governed by Art. 703 *et seq.* of the Civil Code.

1.1.3.3. The mandatory

The mandate is an agreement whereby the mandatory is under the obligation to accomplish the task assigned to him by the principal without any remuneration.

The mandate is governed by Art. 713 *et seq.* of the Civil Code and its essential difference from the commercial agency is that the mandatory provides his services without remuneration.

As mentioned above, the provisions on mandate of the Civil Code are also applicable to commercial agency.

1.1.3.4. The distributor

Contrary to the commercial agent who acts on account and in the name of a principal, the distributor acts in his own name and account by virtue of a right granted to him by a prinicpal. Greek law does not contain any provisions regarding these agreements, which shall be dealt with under part 2 of this report.

1.2. Conclusion of the Contract (Special Conditions)

In view of the fact that commercial agency is not explicitly governed by Greek law, the general rules of contract apply.

1.2.1. Absence of particular requirements

In the absence of any particular requirements as to form the parties are free to conclude the agency agreement in whatever form they wish and even orally.

1.2.2. Rights and obligations

The parties are free to decide on their rights and obligations within the limits of good morals and compulsory legal provisions (Arts. 174 and 178 of the Civil Code). In addition, the conclusion of the contract must be the result of the parties' free will, i.e. it must not be the result of a mistake, threat or fraud as these are defined in the Civil Code. If this is so the party which has been mistaken, threatened or defrauded may ask for the annulment of the contract as well as for compensation under the conditions provided in the Civil Code (Arts. 140, 147 and 150).

1.2.3. The negotiations

The Civil Code also provides that the negotiations for a commercial agency agreement must take place in good faith and that if during the negotiations one party intentionally or negligently causes damage to the other the former shall be liable to compensation even in the case in which no agreement has been concluded between the parties (*culpa in contrahendo*) (Arts. 197 and 198 of the Civil Code).

1.3. The Principal's Duties and Rights

1.3.1. The principal's duties

1.3.1.1. Commission

Prima facie the parties are free to decide on the type of remuneration to be given to the commercial agent unless the agreement is contrary to good morals. The obligation of the principal to pay the agent a certain remuneration derives from the agreement itself. To the extent that the commercial agent is considered as providing independent services the obligation of the principal to compensate the agent also derives from Art. 648 of the Civil Code regarding employment contracts. Under Art. 649 of the Civil Code even in the absence of an express agreement a remuneration is considered as having been implicitly agreed if under the circumstances the specific services would have only been provided for remuneration. Normally the remuneration paid to the agent is a commission on the value of the transactions effected through him. In the absence of an agreement to the contrary the agent is entitled to his remuneration upon the execution of his mandate. Thus, it has been held that the mere delivery of a certain purchase order by the agent to his principal was not sufficient. The agent was only entitled to remuneration upon the acceptance of the order by the principal.[8]

1.3.1.2. Protection of agent, information

The obligation of the principal to assist the agent in the exercise of his activity derives from the nature of commercial agency combined with the principles of good faith and commercial practice.[9] This obligation also

---

[8] A.C. of Athens 485/69 *JCL* (1969), 368.
[9] Androutsopoulos, p. 193; F.I.C. of Salonica 1671/71, *JCL* (1972), 52.

derives from Arts. 380 and 381 of the Civil Code which, in general terms, provide that if one of the parties cannot perform its task as a result of the fault of the other the former is released from its respective obligations. In addition the failure of the principal to assist the agent may make him liable towards the latter for all the expenses incurred by him in the performance of his duties (Art. 358 of the Civil Code).[10]

The content of this obligation depends on the circumstances. Thus, while the principal may be allowed by the contract to appoint additional agents in the same area he should avoid exercising this right to the point that the original agent may no longer exercise his activity. The principal must not compete illegally with the agent.

Furthermore, the principal should supply the agent with samples, documents, brochures, and other necessary information in order to assist the agent in promoting the principal's products.[11]

1.3.1.3. Supply of written statement

This obligation of the principal is consistent with the above and also derives from the nature of the commercial agency and the principles of good faith and commercial practice. The principal must give the agent both general and specific instructions and also promptly inform the agent with respect to any matter which may be material in the performance of his task.[12]

1.3.1.4. Obligation to cover exceptional expenses

Articles 721 and 722 of the Civil Code on mandate, which provide that the principal is under the obligation to cover all the expenses incurred by the mandatory in the performance of his mandate, do not apply to commercial agents who provide their services for a remuneration. However, the above articles do apply, by analogy, with respect to exceptional expenses which the commercial agent makes further to the instructions of the principal.[13]

1.4. The Commercial Agent's Duties and Rights

1.4.1. The commercial agent's duties

The basic duties of the agent, which derive from the nature of the commercial agency agreement as one of trust and confidence, are the following.

1.4.1.1. Trustworthiness, duty to inform

The obligation of the agent to inform the principal on any matter relevant to his task derives from the nature of the agency agreement and the principles of good faith and commercial practice (Arts. 200 and 288 Civil Code) as well as from Art. 718 of the Civil Code which imposes such obligation on the mandatory. The particular content of this obligation will depend on the terms of the agreement and the relevant circumstances.

[10] F.I.C. of Salonica 1671/71, JCL (1972), 52;
[11] Ibid.
[12] Androutsopoulos, p. 199.
[13] A.C. of Salonica 567/73, JCL (1973), 503.

Duty to follow the principal's instructions

This duty also derives from the nature of the commercial agency agreement as well as from Art. 717 of the Civil Code regarding mandate. According to Art. 717 the mandatory (and for our purposes also the commercial agent) is allowed to divert from the limits of his mandate only when it is impossible for him to notify the principal and provided it is clear that had the principal been aware of the particular circumstances he would have allowed the diversion.

Duty to protect the principal's interests

This duty also derives from the nature of the commercial agency and the general principles of good faith and commercial practice. It implies that the agent must make sure that in negotiating or making agreements with third parties the principal's interests are adequately protected.

1.4.1.2. Del credere

Greek law does not contain any specific provisions on "*del credere*" clauses. Therefore, the inclusion of a "*del credere*" clause in a commercial agency contract as well as the specific obligations of the "*del credere*" agent are up to the agreement of the parties.[14]

1.4.1.3. Non-competition

In the absence of specific provision in the agency agreement permitting the agent to compete during the duration thereof the commercial agent is under the obligation not to compete with his principal. This obligation derives from the nature of the commercial agency and the principles of good faith as well as from Art. 919 of the Civil Code which provides that whoever wilfully causes damage to another in a way contrary to good morals is liable to compensation.[15]

After the termination of the agreement the obligations of the agent not to compete *prima facie* ceases to apply. However, the agent's freedom to compete is then subject to the above-mentioned Art. 919 of the Civil Code as well as to L. 146/1914 "on unfair competition".[16]

Non-competition clauses contained in the commercial agency agreements are *prima facie* valid unless they are contrary to good morals (Art. 178 of the Civil Code). According to Art. 179 a clause is contrary to good morals if it unduly restricts the freedom of the other to exercise his activity. In view of the above a non-competition clause is valid provided it is of limited duration and applies to a specific restricted territory.[17]

1.4.1.4. Secrecy

The agent has the duty not to disclose, either during the duration of the agreement or after the termination thereof, any information of a confidential nature which may have come to his knowledge during the term thereof.

---

[14] F I T C. of Athens 6834/69 (1970) 248.

[15] F.I.C. of Athens 11486/80 *JCL* (1981), 50, 131.

[16] F.I.C. of Athens 11486/80 *JCL* (1981), 50, 131; F.I.C. of Athens 14284/81, *JCL* (1982), 144; F.I.C. of Heraklion 158/86, *JCL* (1987), 38.

[17] Ibid.

This obligation of the agent derives from the nature of the commercial agency and the principles of good faith and commercial practice (Arts. 200 and 288), as well as from L. 146/14 "on unfair competition"[18] and Art. 57 of the Civil Code regarding the protection of someone's personality.[19]

Duty to inform—duty to account

The commercial agent is under the obligation to inform the principal on the progress of his mandate as well as to account to him at the end thereof. Art. 718 of the Civil Code, which imposes such obligation on the mandatory, applies by analogy. The parties may provide, either in writing or by implication, that the agent shall be under obligation to account to the principal even before the end of the mandate.[20]

In addition, the commercial agent is under obligation to return to the principal whatever he has acquired from third parties during the performance of his taks. Art. 719 of the Civil Code, which imposes such an obligation on the mandatory, applies by analogy. Within the context of the performance of this duty the agent must return to the principal, among other things, any advertising or other material given to him by the principal, any merchandise not disposed off, the proceeds of any sales, etc. as well as any monies received from the principal and not spent.[21]

1.5. Liabilities of Principal and Agent During the Term of the Agency

1.5.1. The principal as against the agent

1.5.1.1. Contractual liability

As mentioned under section 1.2. above, between the principal and the agent there is a contractual relationship and therefore the general rules of contract apply. The rights and liabilities of the parties as between themselves primarily depend on the terms of the contract, regard being given to the general rights and duties derived from the nature of the commercial agency agreement (see sections 1.3. and 1.4. above), as well as to the relevant articles on contracts of the Civil Code.

Thus, under Art. 330 of the Civil Code one party (the debtor) is liable towards the other (the creditor) if he or his legal representatives intentionally or negligently contravene any of his obligations under the contract. A person is negligent if he fails to exercise the necessary duty of care. Any agreement excluding or restricting liability for fraud or gross negligence is void (Art. 332 of the Civil Code).

1.5.1.2. Pre-contractual liability

See under sections 1.2.2. and 1.2.3. above

---

[18] Mitroulis, p. 24.
[19] Androutsopoulos, p. 169.
[20] F.I.C. of Patras 1042/76, *JCL* (1976), 409.
[21] Justice of Peace of Athens 1060/69, *JCL* (1969), 369.

1.5.2. The principal as against third parties

1.5.2.1. Contractual liability

There is a distinction between the commercial agents who are authorized to enter into contracts in the name and on account of their principal and those who are only authorized to act as intermediaries and only undertake negotiations in the name and on account of the principal without, however, having authority to bind them.

With respect to the former category of commercial agents (i.e. those authorized to bind their principals) there is a distinction between actual authority (the content of which is determined by the terms of the power of attorney) and apparent authority towards third parties.

Actual authority is determined by the power of attorney granted by the principal to the commercial agent (Art. 216 et seq. of the Civil Code). The power of attorney is not subject to any form and may be either written or oral, explicit or implied, unless the contract to which it refers is subject to a certain form in which case the power of attorney must also be subjected to the same form (Art. 217 para. 2 of the Civil Code). For example, in view of the fact that a contract for the sale of immovables must take the form of a notarial deed, a power of attorney granted for such purpose must also be signed before a notary public.

In determining the content and extent of the actual authority of the agent regard must be given to the real intention of the parties without abiding by the words (Art. 173 of the new Civil Code).

Apparent authority is the authority which third parties are led to believe that the commercial agent has. Whether the commercial agent has apparent authority with respect to a certain issue or transaction is a question of fact and is deduced from the general behaviour of the principal.

Regarding apparent authority the generally accepted view in Greece is that third parties are entitled to believe that the commercial agent has authority to bind his principal with respect to all matters pertaining to the task assigned to him.[22] Any particular restrictions are valid only if the third party is aware thereof.

As a result of the above-mentioned presumption of full authority of the commercial agent the principal is bound towards third parties for all the contracts entered into by the commercial agent within the scope of his general authority unless the principal can prove that the third party was aware of the lack of authority of the agent. Thus, an agent having authority to sell has been held by the court as also having apparent authority to receive the proceeds of the sale.[23]

For the commercial agent to bind his principal it is not sufficient to act within the scope of his apparent authority. He must also act in the name and on account of his principal.

The general rule expressed in Art. 211 of the Civil Code is that a statement of will made by one person (agent) in the name of another (principal) within

---

[22] Androutsopoulos, p. 244 et seq.; F.I.C. of Patras 1042/76, JCL (1976), 409.
[23] Justice of Peace of Athens 1060/69, JCL (1969), 369.

the scope of his authority produces direct effects in favour and against the principal. The statement of will need not be made explicitly in the name of the principal. It is sufficient if it may be derived from the circumstances that the agent is in fact acting in the name of a principal. The name of the principal need not be disclosed at the time of the transaction.[24]

However, Art. 212 provides that if it may not be determined that a person acts in the name of another he is considered as acting in his own name.

Therefore, in the light of the above, as long as the commercial agent acts in the name and on account of his principal within the scope of his apparent authority the principal acquires direct rights and liabilities towards the third party and the agent is not privy thereto.

The authority of the commercial agent to act on account and in the name of the principal ends automatically upon the termination of the agency agreement or upon the death or incapacity of either the principal or the agent (Arts. 222 and 223 of the Civil Code).

The power of attorney is also freely revocable and the principal's resignation from his right to revoke a power of attorney is void unless such resignation concerns exclusively the benefit of the agent (Art. 218 of the Civil Code—see also under 1.6. of this report).

If after the termination of his authority and without being aware thereof the agent enters into a contract with the third party in the name and on account of the principal this is binding upon the principal unless the third party was or should have been aware of the expiration of the agent's authority (Art. 224 of the Civil Code). If the agent was aware of the termination of his authority while the third party was not aware thereof and the principal invokes such termination against the third party the principal may be liable for compensation if it would have been possible for him to notify the third party of the termination of the agent's authority but failed to do so (Art. 225 of the Civil Code).

1.5.3. The agent as against the principal
(Liability of the principal for the fault of the agent)

With respect to the liability of the principal for the fault of the agent there are two articles of the Civil Code which are relevant and the application of which has caused considerable debate.

On the one hand Art. 334 provides that a party to a contract is liable for the fault of the persons which he used for the performance of his obligations as for his own faults. Such liability may, however, be excluded or restricted at the time of the conclusion of the contract.

The generally accepted view is that Art. 334 applies to faults occurring both during the negotiations of the contract and after its conclusion and that the person used for the performance of the obligations referred therein need not have a relation of dependence with the contracting party.[25] In fact the agent, not-withstanding his independence from the principal, often

---

[24] F.I.C. of Patras 1042/76, *JCL*, 409.
[25] Anapliotis, p. 307 *et seq.*; A.C. of Athens 7863/74, *JCL* (1975), 401.

plays an active role in the performance of the principal's obligations under the contract and the principal should not be able to escape liability for the faults of his agent on the ground that the latter is not his employee.

Therefore, in the light of the above we may conclude that article 334 of the Civil Code is applicable on commercial agents and that the principal is liable for the fault of his agent to the extent that the latter is used by the principal for the performance of his obligations and his activity is directed to that end.

On the other hand Art. 922 of the Civil Code establishes the strict liability of the employer for the acts of his employee during the course of his employment. In view of the fact that the commercial agent does not have a relation of dependence with his principal as the employee has with his employer the generally accepted view is that Art. 922 does not apply to commercial agents.[26] However, whether the so-called commercial agent is in fact independent or not is a question of fact which shall be determined by the court by taking account of all surrounding circumstances.

1.5.4. The agent as against third parties

1.5.4.1. Contractual liability

There is a distinction between the acts of an agent within the scope of his authority and those outside or beyond the scope thereof. A commercial agent acting in the name and on account of his principal within the scope of his actual authority does not become personally liable towards the third party, all the rights and obligations deriving from his acts having effect directly on his principal (Art. 211 of the Civil Code). As a result thereof the principal is alone responsible towards the third party (see 1.5.2.1. above).

On the other hand a commercial agent who does not have authority to enter into contracts on behalf of the principal or who acts beyond his authority, is under the obligation, assuming that the principal does not subsequently ratify the contract, at the option of the third party either to execute the contract or to pay compensation. The commercial agent who acts without authority is absolved from all liability if the third party was aware or should have been aware of the lack of authority (Art. 231 of the Civil Code).[27]

1.5.4.2. Tortious liability

While the general rule is that the principal is liable, under Art. 334 of the Civil Code, for the faults of his agent (see also 1.5.3. above), the commercial agent may be personally responsible towards third parties under the tort provisions. Thus under Art. 914 of the Civil Code the commercial agent shall be liable for compensation to the third party for any damage caused to the latter as a result of his illegal intentional or negligent act. In addition, under Art. 922 of the Civil Code the commercial agent shall be liable towards the third party for any damage caused to the latter by the illegal acts of his employees.

[26] Anapliotis, p. 311 et seq.
[27] Androutsopoulos, p. 260.

1.6. Term and Termination

A commercial agency agreement may be either of definite or of indefinite duration.

An agreement of definite duration automatically expires at the end of the term thereof. However, if the activities of the agent continue after the relevant term has expired without the principal objecting thereto the agreement becomes of indefinite duration.

The general view adopted by case-law is that a commercial agency agreement of indefinite duration may be terminated by the principal at any time.[28] In this respect analogy is drawn from Art. 724 of the Civil Code which provides that a mandate may be revoked at any time, the reason being the relation of trust and confidence between the principal and the agent.[29] Consistent with this view, the termination by the principal of a commercial agency agreement of indefinite duration has been held not to be contrary to good morals even if the agent had made much effort and spent a lot of money for many years in promoting the principal's products.[30]

Notwithstanding the above there are certain academics[31] who, drawing analogies from the provisions of the Civil Code regarding employment contracts and, in particular, from Art. 669 thereof, according to which an employment contract of indefinite duration may be determined at any time by giving fifteen days' notice, believe that appropriate notice of termination must be given also with respect to agency agreement. This view, which finds support in case-law,[32] is also consistent with the general principle of commercial and labour law that agreements of indefinite duration may be terminated at any time by giving reasonable notice.[33] In view of the above we would consider it advisable to avoid terminating an agency agreement without giving some reasonable notice. What is reasonable notice will, of course, depend on the circumstances, but in view of the fact that in principle an agreement of indefinite duration may be terminated at any time the notice of termination need not be long.

The above-mentioned Art. 724 of the Civil Code also provides that an agreement preventing the agent from revoking the mandate is void unless the mandate also concerns the benefit of the agent or a third party, this being, for example, the case when the agency has been agreed to be of definite duration or terminable upon certain notice. In such case the principal can terminate the agency agreement only for serious reasons.[34] The burden of proving the occurrence of a serious reason is upon the party invoking it.[35] The final decision lies with the judge who must each time take into account

---

[28] A.C. of Athens 485/69, *JCL* (1969), 368; F.I.C. of Athens 401/71, *JCL* (1971), 200; A.P. 1072/72, *JCL* (1973), 338; A.C. of Salonica 567/73, *JCL* (1973), 503; A.P. 887/74, *JCL* (1975), 393; F.I.C. of Athens 12785/77, *JCL* (1978), 396; A.C. of Athens 7964/82 (1983), 44.
[29] A.C. of Salonica 567/73, *JCL* (1973), 503.
[30] A.C. of Athens 7964/82, *JCL* (1983), 44.
[31] Androutsopoulos, pp. 276–7; Mitroulis, p. 35.
[32] A.C. of Salonica 567/73 (1973), 503.
[33] A. Argryriadis, "Legal Opinion", *JCL* (1987), 153.
[34] A.C. of Athens 485/69, *JCL* (1969), 368; A.P. 1072/72, *JCL* (1973), 338.
[35] A.P. 887/74, *JCL* (1975), 393.

the particular circumstances of the case.[36] Thus, the termination of an agency agreement before the lapse of its duration was held to be justified in a case where the agent instead of passing to his principal the orders which he was supposed to get on his behalf, bought and supplied machinery of his principal's competitors.[37] On the same line the termination of an agency agreement was held justified in a case where the agent collected money on behalf of the principal without the latter's authority.[38]

1.7. Indemnity

In the case in which the principal terminates a commercial agency agreement of definite duration without serious reason he is liable towards the agent for any damage which the latter incurred as a result thereof. The damage may consist of the loss of commission as well as of any future damage, in the sense that the agent's image and prestige in commercial circles is harmed as a result of the fault of the principal.[39] The loss of clientèle may also be taken into account in the calculation of the damages.[40] The general expenses of the agent are borne by the latter and cannot be recovered.[41]

1.8. Specific Application of EEC-Law

The draft bill implementing into Greek law the EEC Directive on Commercial Agents was given by the Minister of Trade to the interested parties for comment in August 1989. This bill is therefore expected to be submitted to Parliament before the end of 1989 or the beginning of 1990. Greece is under the obligation to adapt its legislation to the above-mentioned Directive until January 1990 at the latest.

1.8.1. Applicable law

With respect to the contractual relationship between principal and agent, Art. 25 of the Civil Code applies according to which the law governing the contract may be freely chosen by the parties. The same article provides that in the absence of such express provision by the parties the applicable law will be determined by taking account of all the surrounding circumstances. In such cases the place of conclusion of the contract, the place of residence of the parties, the place where the agent will exercise his activities, etc. will be relevant in determining the applicable law.

Art. 25 of the Civil Code is also relevant in deciding the law governing the relationship between the principal and the third party with which the agent entered into a contract on behalf of his principal.

However, according to academics, Art. 25 of the Civil Code is not applicable in determining the content of the power of attorney of the agent as this

---

[36] A.C. of Salonica 567/73 (1973), 503.
[37] A.C. of Athens 485/69, *JCL* (1969), 368.
[38] A.C. of Salonika 567/73 (1973), 503.
[39] F.I.C. of Athens 401/71, *JCL* (1971), 200.
[40] Androutsopoulos, p. 293 *et seq.*
[41] A.C. of Salonica 567/73, *JCL* (1973), 503.

is not based on an agreement but is granted by virtue of a unilateral deed. In view thereof the prevailing opinion in Greece is that the existence and content of the power of attorney of an agent will be governed by the law of the place where the agent carries out his activities.[42]

1.8.2. Jurisdiction

Greek law does not provide for specific jurisdiction (exclusive or non-exclusive) with respect to agency agreements. Therefore agency agreements fall under the general rule according to which a court assumes territorial jurisdiction over a certain case on the basis of the residence of the defendant unless the law provides otherwise (Art. 22 of the Code of Civil Procedure). With respect to disputes concerning the existence or validity of a contract or the rights and obligations derived therefrom, Art. 33 of the Greek Code of Civil Procedure also provides for the concurrent jurisdiction of the place where the contract was concluded or should be performed. Both Greeks and foreigners may fall within the jurisdiction of the Greek courts.

Greek law also recognizes choice of forum clauses in the sense that the above-mentioned provisions regarding territorial jurisdiction may be set aside by private agreement between the parties, provided the dispute has a value object. Thus, by express or implied agreement of the parties a Greek Court may assume jurisdiction over a certain matter for which it would not otherwise be competent and the other way around (Art. 42 of the Code of Civil Procedure).

Regarding future disputes, a choice of forum clause shall be valid only if it is in writing and makes specific reference to the legal relationship from which a dispute might derive. Similarly, Greek law also recognizes arbitration clauses.

Notwithstanding the above, the submission of a purely domestic matter to the territorial jurisdiction of a foreign court may be considered an abuse or right.

The jurisdiction of the Greek courts over applications for provisional measures may never be set aside by private agreement.

2. Distributorship Agreement

2.1. Distribution

2.1.1. Definition

2.1.1.1. Exclusive / non-exclusive / exclusive purchasing

As with respect to commercial agency agreements Greek law does not contain any legislative or other provisions regarding distributorship agreements. Agreements whereby a supplier agrees to sell to a distributor certain products in consideration of the latter undertaking to market and sell these products in his own name and account within a certain territory are gen-

---

[42] Androutsopoulos, pp. 91–92.

erally considered as a type of commercial agency agreements also governed by the provisions on commission agents of the Commercial Code in conjunction with the mandate provisions of the Civil Code.[43] It has been held that in view of the fact that the legal provisions which are applicable to commercial agency (see section 1.1.2. above) are not of compulsory character, the parties are free to adapt them to their own needs and thus also provide that the distributor will act in his own name and account by following only certain guidelines and instructions of the supplier.[44] Consequently, what was mentioned under section 1.1. regarding the characteristics of commercial agency also applies with respect to distributorship agreements to the extent that this is consistent with the nature of the latter.

In addition to the above regarding the particular sale transactions which take place between the supplier and the distriubtor the provisions of the Civil Code concerning the sale of goods are applicable.

Exclusive distribution

A distributorship agreement is referred to as an exclusive distributorship agreement if the supplier undertakes to sell his products exclusively to the distributor and not to supply anybody else within the contract territory.[45] Exclusive distributorship agreements are *prima facie* valid under Greek law unless they contravene national or EEC competition law or the market policing law (see section 2.1.8. below).

Selective distribution

Selective distribution systems have been considered by case-law within the context of competition law. A selective-distribution system is generally understood to be a system of distribution agreements designed to restrict the distribution of the products concerned only to selected distributors and retailers. The validity of such agreements within the context of national and community competition law and the market-policing law shall be considered under section 2.1.8. below.

2.1.2.–2.1.3.

No special comment is called for.

2.1.4. The distributor's duties and rights

In view of the above, what was mentioned under sections 1.2., 1.3. and 1.4. above regarding the conclusion of the contract and the rights and duties of the principal and the agent also applies in the case of distributorship agreements. In order to avoid any problems of interpretation and clearly to distinguish a distributorship agreement from any agency agreement it is advisable to set out in detail in the contract the respective rights and liabilities of the parties as well as to stress the fact that the distributor does not act as an agent of the supplier.

In addition to the above the rights and liabilities of the parties in the case of the exclusive or selective distribution agreements must also be consistent

---

[43] F.I.C. of Salonica 1271/82, *JCL* (1983), 401; A.C. of Athens 3857/83, *JCL* (1984), 584.
[44] A.C. of Athens 3857/83, *JCL* (1984), 584.
[45] F.I.C. of Salonica 1271/82, *JCL* (1983), 401.

with national and community competition law as well as with the market policing law. As is the case on the EEC level, national competition law does not prescribe inserting special clauses in distribution agreements. Instead it prohibits the inclusion of certain clauses which are considered to be restrictive of competition. The prohibition imposed by national and EEC competition law will be discussed in detail under section 2.1.8. below.

2.1.5. Liabilities of supplier and distributor during the term of the distributorship agreement

2.1.5.1. The supplier as against the distributor

As with respect to the relationship between principal and agent the relationship between supplier and distributor is a contractual relationship and, therefore, what was mentioned under section 1.5. above is also relevant in the case of distribution agreements.

2.1.5.2. The supplier as against third parties

The supplier has no contractual liability against third parties. For the supplier third parties are normally consumers, in which case the general rules on tort and product liability apply. In order to avoid any misunderstanding as to the liability of the supplier towards third parties distribution agreements normally contain a clause making clear that the distributor is not an agent of the supplier.

2.1.5.4. The distributor as against third parties

The liability of the distributor towards third parties will depend on the terms of their contract and in this respect what was mentioned under 2.1.5.1. is also applicable in this case.

2.1.6. Term and termination

2.1.7. Indemnity

What was mentioned under sections 1.6. and 1.7. regarding commercial agency also applies in the case of distributorship agreements.

2.1.8. Specific application of EEC-law

2.1.8.1. Free competition

As is the case on the EEC level, distributorship agreements must also be examined within the context of the national competition rules. The relevant Law 703/77 "on the control of monopolies and oligopolies and the protection of free competition", which was first introduced in 1977 in an attempt to adapt Greek legislation to the community rules in view of Greece's prospective entry into the EEC (1 January 81), virtually adopted word for word the relevant provisions of the EEC Treaty and has to a large extent been applied in consistence therewith.

In particular, Art. 1 of the above-mentioned L. 703/77 reads as follows:

Article 1.1. All agreements between undertakings, decisions by associations of undertakings and any kind of concerted practices of undertakings, which have as their object or effect the prevention, restriction, or distortion of competition are prohibited. In particular those consisting of:

(a) directly or indirectly fixing purchase. or selling price or any other trading conditions;
(b) limiting or controlling production, supply, technical development or investment;
(c) sharing markets or sources of supply;
(d) applying dissimilar conditions to equivalent transactions in trade thus making difficult the operation of competition and, in particular, unjustifiably refusing to sell, purchase or conclude any other transaction;
(e) making the conclusion of contracts subject to acceptance by the other parties of supplementary obligations which, by their nature or according to commercial usage, have no connection with the subject of such contracts.

2. The agreements and decisions which are prohibited pursuant to the above-mentioned paragraph shall be absolutely void, unless the present law provides otherwise.

3. Agreements, decisions and concerted practices or categories thereof falling under paragraph 1 of the present article may by decision of the Minister of Trade be declared valid in toto or in part, provided that they fulfil all of the following:

(a) contribute to improving the production or distribution of goods or to promoting technical or economic progress, while allowing consumers a fair share of the resulting benefit;
(b) do not impose on the undertakings concerned restrictions beyond those which are indispensable for the attainment of these objectives;
(c) do not afford such undertakings the possibility of eliminating competition in a substantial part of the relevant market.

Article 11 also provides for the granting of a negative clearance at the request of an interested undertaking in the case in which it is found that there has been no distortion of competition.

The body responsible for the application and enforcement of the provisions of the above law is the Department for the Protection of Competition set up within the Ministry of Trade. The power to issue all relevant decisions was originally vested to a Competition Committee set up for this purpose but pursuant to L. 1232/82 and Joint Ministerial Decision of the Ministers of Presidency and Trade B 3/395 (O.J. B 217/26.4.82) all the decisive powers of the Committee were transferred to the Ministry of Trade whereas the Committee acquired a consultative character. The decisions of the Minister are subject to judicial review by the Administrative Courts.

Since the promulgation of L. 703/77, several distributorship agreements have been subject to review by the Competition Committee and the Minister of Trade as well as by the Administrative Courts. The decisions issued by the above have consistently followed the interpretation of the respective Community provisions as this has been developed by the

European Court of Justice and the EEC Commission. In several national decisions community case-law and the competition reports of the EEC Commission have been specifically invoked and there have even been two decisions of the Minister of Trade (adopted pursuant to a respective recommendation of the Committee) where the relevant exclusive distributorship agreements were examined solely within the context of the EEC block exemption provided under Regulation 1983/83. Whereas in the first of these cases (PLAYTEX)[46] a negative clearance was eventually granted because the agreement affected only a very small share of the market (below 5%), in the second case (BLYTHE COLOURS)[47] the Committee and the Minister after considering that the agreement fell within the ambit of the Regulation decided to exempt it also under national law.

In the light of the above we shall proceed to an examination of the relevant opinions and decisions of the competent Greek authorities by considering separately: exclusive distribution agreements, selective distribution agreements, and selective distribution of motor vehicles (EEC REG. 123/85).

A. Exclusive distribution agreements

As has been held by the Administrative Court of First Instance and upheld on appeal, an agreement providing for the exclusive importation and distribution of certain products in Greece is not *per se* contrary to Art. 1 of L. 703/77 provided that the agreement does not contain any terms which are restrictive of competition such as terms which prohibit parallel imports or exports or which enable the distributor to determine retail prices in an arbitrary way. The obligation imposed on the distributor to obtain his supplies of raw materials exclusively from the supplier was upheld as it was considered necessary in order to maintain the high quality and reputation of the products.[48]

Consistent with the above the Minister of Trade granted negative clearance to an exclusive distribution agreement in which the supplier agreed not to appoint another distributor or importer in Greece while the distributor undertook to concentrate his activities in Greece, attain a certain high level of sales, provide sufficient spare parts and service as well as inform the supplier about the selling prices whenever the latter requested so.[49]

Similarly, the Competition Committee in the case of BIOLIGNIT[50] held that an exclusive distributorship agreement does not contravene the competition provisions as long as it does not contain restrictive terms providing, for example, for absolute territorial protection. In that case a

---

[46] PLAYTEX, Competition Committee Opinion 34/85 adopted by Ministerial Decision K6-104/86.
[47] BLYTHE COLOURS, Competition Committee Opinion 53/87 adopted by Ministerial Decision K6-346/87.
[48] F.I.Adm.C. 1040/84 and Adm.C.A. 2267/84.
[49] VIANE, Competition Committee Opinion 7/84 adopted by Ministerial Decision K6-937/84.
[50] BOILIGNIT, Competition Committee Opinion 2/83 adopted by Ministerial Decision K6-956/83.

negative clearance was granted because the agreement affected only a very small percentage of the local market.

In the cases of **REVLON** and **WRANGLER** exclusive distributorship agreements containing restrictive terms such as an obligation upon the distributor not to sell the supplier's products outside his territory, were held by Ministerial Decisions[51] not to be contrary to L. 703/77 because the products in question represented only a very small share of the market and could not therefore have any effect on competition.

In the case of **LAVIPHARM**[52] distributorship agreements permitting sales exclusively through pharmacists were held not to distort competition in view of the large number of existing substitutes, the small market share of the product and the large number of pharmacists.

B. Selective distribution agreements
Following the example set on the EEC level a large number of agreements which were examined within the context of L. 703/77 concerned the selective distribution of various brands of perfumes and beauty products. In this field the relevant practice of the Commission and the case-law of the European Court provided considerable guidance to the Greek Competition Committee which examined the various agreements by making consistent and specific reference to the relevant community precedents. Thus, several selective distribution systems of perfumes and beauty goods have been held consistent with L. 703/77 as long as the selection of resellers was based on objective and qualitative criteria and there was no discrimination between the retailers. Furthermore, it has been held that although the prohibition to sell to retailers outside the network, which is normally contained is such agreements, *prima facie* appears to contravene article 1 of L. 703/77, nevertheless, in view of the existence of a fairly large number of competing firms, none of which held a really prominent position, there was no distortion of competition.[53]

In a recent decision adopted pursuant to an investigation of the actual

---

[51] REVLON, Ministerial Decision K6-448/84; WRANGLER, Ministerial Decision K6-729/84.
[52] LAVIPHARM Competition Committee Opinion 27/85 adopted by Ministerial Decision K6-393/85.
[53] GUY LAROCHE I, Competition Committee Decision 1/79; GUY LAROCHE II, Competition Committee Decision 6/80; GUY LAROCHE III, Competition Committee Decision 19/82; ZETA I, Competition Committee Decision 20/82; ZETA II, Competition Committee Decision 21/82; PARFUMS CHRISTIAN DIOR, Competition Committee Opinion 3/83 adopted by Ministerial Decision K6-1019/83; LANCASTER I, Competition Committee Opinion 35/86 adopted by Ministerial Decision K6-138/86; LANCASTER II, Competition Committee Opinion 43/86 adopted by Ministerial Decision K6-713/86; PACO RABANNE and CLARINS I, Competition Committee Opinion 36/86 adopted by Ministerial Decision K6-137/87; PACO RABANNE and CLARINS II, Competition Committee Opinion 44/86 adopted by Ministerial Decision K6-714/86; VIOTHERM, Competition Committee Opinion 37/86 adopted by Ministerial Decision K6-136/86; CHARLES OF THE RITZ, Competition Committee Opinion 42/86 adopted by Ministerial Decision K6-564/86; YVES ST LAURENT, Competition Committee Opinion 46/86 adopted by Ministerial Decision K6-716/86; CACHAREL II, Competition Committee Opinion 48/86 adopted by Ministerial Decision K6-715/86; CHRISTIAN DIOR, Competition Committee Opinion 49/86 adopted by Ministerial Decision K6-712/86.

implementation of a selective distribution system with respect to which a negative clearance had previously been granted, it was held that the application of subjective criteria for the selection of resellers (e.g. solely on the basis of the location of their shops), the granting of discounts on an arbitrary basis and the indirect fixing of prices, was contrary to Art. 1 of L. 703/77 (ZETA III).[54]

C. Selective distribution of motor vehicles (EEC REG. 123/85)

The attempt by an importer of motor vehicles to apply the above-mentioned Regulation in Greece has met obstacles both on an administrative and on a judicial level. The problem has mainly arisen because of the existence of Market Policing Provisions regarding the sale of motor vehicles and spare parts, compliance with which is ensured by the imposition of administrative as well as penal sanctions.

Art. 31 para 2 of the Greek Trade Law provides that:

> "Whoever withholds objects referred to in the above-mentioned paragraph (i.e. consumer goods and in general goods of any kind satisfying one's necessities), which were produced or acquired by him for the purpose of resale, is punishable with imprisonment and fine."

Furthermore, Trade Law 62/87 of 20 October 87 setting maximum retail prices for spare parts of motor vehicles as well as compulsory minimum discounts to retailers, provides that all importers of vehicles and spare parts must grant a compulsory minimum discount to all retailers wishing to buy spare parts from them.

Importers who have attempted to establish a selective distribution system of motor vehicles in accordance with Regulation 123/85 by supplying the market only through approved dealers, have been consistently prosecuted on the basis of the above-mentioned provisions. Notwithstanding the invocation of Regulation 123/85, the Penal Court of First Instance convicted an importer for refusing to sell. Although the importer was acquitted on appeal other criminal prosecutions may ensue. The matter has also been brought before the Administrative Court of the EEC Commission. The results remain to be seen.

2.1.8.2. Unfair competition

Since 1970 a series of court decisions, overruling the previously prevailing view,[55] held that the sale by a third party of the products sold by the exclusive distributor in the latter's territory does not amount to unfair competition and is not therefore contrary to L. 146/14 "On Unfair Competition". The action of the third party may, however, be considered to be contrary to L. 146/14 "On Unfair Competition" in the case in which the third party obtained the products by using unlawful means. Mere knowledge by the

---

[54] ZETA III, Competition Committee Opinion 57/87 adopted by Ministerial Decision K6-346/87.

[55] President of the F.I.C. of Athens, 929/67, *JCL* (1967), 136; President of the F.I.C. of Athens, 9/68, *JCL* (1968), 134; President of the F.I.C. of Salonica 1572/67, *JCL* (1968), 137; President of the F.I.C. of Athens 13310/67, *JCL* (1968), 453.

third party of the existence of an exclusive distributor does not make the sale of the distributor's products by the third party unlawful.[56]

2.1.8.3. Applicable law and jurisdiction

What was mentioned under section 2.1.8. regarding commercial agency also applies in the case of distributorship agreements.

3. Franchise Agreements

3.1. Definition

As with respect to commercial agency and distribution agreements Greek law does not contain any legislative or other provisions regarding franchise agreements. Furthermore, franchise agreements, although widely used in practice, have not been considered under this term or any Greek translation thereof either by the Greek courts or by the Competition Committee. Nevertheless, in view of the wide use thereof the Ministry of Trade has announced that it is in the process of examining this new notion and intends to produce a relevant bill shortly.

In the absence of any guidance either by the courts or by academics we believe that producing a report on franchising would involve a lot of guesswork which should be avoided. To the extent that franchise agreements are a type of distribution agreement which, in their turn, have been held to be a type of commercial agency agreement, reference is made to the previous sections of this report.

3.2. Franchise Agreements and Competition Law

Agreements which could qualify as franchise agreements have been examined by the antitrust authorities twice so far.

INTERNATIONAL ENTERPRISES OF FASHION involved an agreement between a supplier and a distributor whereby the distributor undertook to establish a special boutique from which he would sell exclusively the products supplied to it by the supplier. The location of the boutique as well as the decoration thereof was subject to the approval of the supplier who also provided the distributor with know-how, advice on promotion and advertising and the right to use the supplier's title. Furthermore the supplier had the right to fix minimum prices in order to protect the high quality of the products. In view of the fact that the market share of the supplier was below 1% the Competition Committee granted negative clearance.[57] In reaching this decision the Competition Committee also invoked the decision of the Court of Justice in the case *Volk v Vervaecke* (Case 5/69).

PIGI Ltd., a distributor of single-use baby slips, established a chain of

---

[56] F.I.C. of Athens 13321/72, *JCL* (1973), 122; F.I.C. of Corinth 59/77, *JCL* (1977), 477; A.C. of Athens 5808/76, *JCL* (1977) 484.
[57] INTERNATIONAL ENTERPRISES OF FASHION, Competition Committee Decision 22/ 82.

retail shops under the name of PIGI, on which it imposed the obligation (a) to sell only those products supplied by PIGI Ltd. or by suppliers nominated by PIGI Ltd., (b) to buy only from PIGI Ltd. even if the same goods were offered from other sources at lower prices, (c) to sell at prices fixed by PIGI Ltd. The retail shops were operated by independent distributors who rented their shops from PIGI Ltd. PIGI Ltd. further undertook to abstain from appointing new distributors at a distance less than 1,000 metres from existing distributors. Those agreements were held to contravene Art. 1 of L. 703/77 and were therefore declared void.[58]

The development of franchising under Greek law remains to be seen. However, the above indicate that in so far as the law of competition is concerned the trend is to follow EEC-law.

---

[58] PIGI/AVLON, Competition Committee Opinion 50/87 adopted by Ministerial Decision K6-756/87.

List of Abbreviations

F.I.C.	First Instance Court
F.I.T.C.	First Instance Tax Court
F.I.Adm.C.	First Instance Administrative Court
A.C.	Appeals Court
Adm.C.A.	Administrative Court of Appeals
A.P.	Arios Pagos (Supreme Court on Civil and Criminal Matters)
JCL	Journal of Commercial Law (Epitheorisi Emporikou Dikaiou)
L.	Law
P.D.	Presidential Decree

CHAPTER 6
SPAIN

Rafael Alonso Dregi,
Santiago Montaner Gomis,
Inmaculada Umbert Millet,
Enric Enrich Muls,
Ramon Girbau Pedragosa

1. Commercial Agency

1.1. Definition of Various Types of Agencies and Intermediaries

According to the Spanish Commercial Code (article 244), in relation to the Spanish Civil Code (article 1709), the contract of commercial agency (comisión mercantil) is the contract whereby one person (the agent) performs a special commercial service on behalf of another person (the principal). It is commercial (and therefore ruled by the Spanish Commercial Code) provided that the service or the action to be perfromed falls into the category of commercial services, and either the agent or the principal are businessmen.

In Spain there are two main kinds of commercial agents, independent and employed.

1.1.1. Independent

Independent agents are those individuals who work in commercial operations on behalf of one or more principals carrying out their work effectively and assuming the risk of the operation in which they participate (*del credere* agents). They are subject to the Commercial Code (articles 244–280).[1]

1.1.2. Employed

Employed agents are those individuals who work in commercial operations on behalf of one or more principals, without assuming the risk of the

---

[1] Independent agents and their contractual relations with the principal and third parties are subject to the general provisions of the *Commercial Code (Articles 244–280)*, and to the general rules of the *Civil Code* concerning the contracts and their resolution.

operation in which they participate. They are known in commercial practice as representatives (representantes).

In this respect, a presumption of labour relationship between the agent and the employer is established when the former follows the instructions of the latter concerning labour time, distribution, prices, or acts of soliciting orders and contracts. They are categorized as employees, in need of certain protection and subject to mandatory rules (Royal Decree 1438/1985 of 1 August, and labour law generally.[2]

1.1.3. Others

There are no other categories of commercial agents in Spanish law.

1.2. Conclusion of the Contract (Special Conditions)

The Royal Decree 1438/1985 of 1 August, which establishes the position of the commercial representative, provides that the contract should be in writing and in triplicate: one for each party and the third to be registered at the Employment Office corresponding to the domicile of the agent. The contracts must establish the following fundamental points:

(a) identification of the parties;
(b) type of commercial operations to be promoted by the agent, indicating the products concerned by the contract;
(c) powers and faculties of the agent-employee, indicating if he can or cannot enter into operations on behalf of the principal–employer;
(d) whether the agent has to work exclusively for the principal–employer, or not;
(e) territory and category of clients in relation to which the agent has to provide his services, indicating whether or not the principal grants him an exclusive right to them;
(f) type of remuneration to be received by the agent;
(g) duration of the contract.

The contract of commercial agency does not have to be formalized in writing, nor has it to be registered. Article 249 of the Commercial Code confirms the possibility of tacit acceptance by agent. There are, however, two special points:

(a) If an Agent, who is tied to a principal, receives instructions from the latter and does not want to be committed in contract, he is under an obligation to notify his rejection to the principal (article 248 of the Commercial Code).

This is a derogation of the general principle of Spanish law where silence is

---

[2] Employed agents, as defined in 1.1.2. above, are ruled by *Royal Decree 1438/1985* of 1 August, concerning the specific labour relations of agents who undertake the risks of the operations in which they participate and for the *Labour Statute* (Estatuto de los Trabajadores, Article 8/ 1980 of 10 March) to which the Royal Decree refers on many points concerning the general rules governing the relation between an employee and his employer. Finally, the special Social Security rules to which commercial representatives are subject are determined by the *Royal Decree 2621/1986* of 24 December.

never deemed to be acceptance (the Civil Code establishes that consent has to be given explicitly).

(b) Once an agent has accepted, in any manner, the contract, he can suspend work until he receives from the principal the monies, if any, stipulated therin, unless it has been agreed that the agent has to advance them.

1.3. The Principal's Duties and Rights

1.3.1. The principal's duties

The principal is obliged:
- To pay commission and justified expenses, plus any interests;
- to provide his agent with the documents and material necessary to carry out his work;
- to notify promptly all the circumstances of every operation, its acceptance, or reasons for refusal;
- to inform the agent of any circumstance which might affect the relation with the clients (change of products or services, prices and conditions, volume of operations, list of other representatives or agents and so on);
- to inform the agent of any order placed directly by any client assigned to the agent by virtue of the contract;
- to comply with any other obligation established in the contract.
- to perform, under the agreed conditions, the specific operations agreed within the contractual limits.

1.4. The Commercial Agent's Duties and Rights

1.4.1. The commercial agent's duties

1.4.1.1. Trustworthiness, duty to inform

- A general obligation established in the Commercial Code is to carry out business and to give account of it.

A non-competition clause should be specifically provided in the contract. Secrecy arises from the general principle of good faith.
Specific obligations of the Royal Decree 1438/1985 of 1 of August are:

- to carry out the promotion of the business on behalf of the principal, protecting his interests and following his instructions;
- to act prudently, without adversely affecting the interests of the principal and without incurring unfair competition;
- to communicate frequently with the principal on the operations within the contract and particularly on any contracts entered into with third parties, and to inform him generally of any circumstance that could affect the clientele and the position of the principal in the market;
- to collect any amount due to the principal and to pay the balance due to him;

- not to perform any duties for competing companies;
- to disclose to the principal any other company for whom he is working;
- to comply with any other obligation established in the contract;
- the agent of said Royal Decree is never a *del credere* agent.

1.4.1.2. Del credere

When the agent is an undisclosed agent he is liable vis-à-vis third parties as if he were the principal. In the case of the *del credere* agent, in consideration of a higher percentage of commission, the agent guarantees the payment of the price of the goods sold by him. When the agent acts not only on his behalf but also in the name of the principal, the results of the contracts he enters into belong to the principal.

1.5. Liabilities of Principal and Agent during the Term of the Agency

1.6. Term and Termination

Concerning the commercial representatives, the most important mandatory rules of the Royal Decree 1438/1985 relate to duration and termination.

1.6.1. Term

In Spanish labour law, there is a strong tendency to treat labour contracts as agreed for an indefinite period of time. The Royal Decree establishes the following in article 3:

(a) The duration of the contract shall be that expressed in the contract itself. Should the contract not stipulate the duration, it shall be deemed indefinite.
(b) Fixed-period contracts may not be for a period longer than three years.
(c) Where contracts are drawn up for a period of less than three months, these contracts may be extended before termination for periods of at least six months, while not exceeding in total the maximum period allowed.
(d) Where contracts have been drawn up for a period of less than three years and have reached termination, and are neither renounced nor extended, it is to be deemed that they have been automatically extended up to the completion of the three-year period but not for an indefinite period.

With regard to probationary periods, the new Royal Decree refers to article 14 of the Labour Act (Estatuto de los Trabajadores): six months for qualified technical staff; three months for other qualified workers; and fifteen days for unqualified workers.

When the relation is not subject to labour law (*del credere* agent) the term of the contract can be freely agreed between the parties.

1.7. Indemnity

The agent shall be entitled to compensation when the contract is terminated without sufficient motive.

Possible compensation shall be determined in accordance with the regulations of the Estatuto de los Trabajadores, (Labour Act ET) (45 days of salary per year of service). For this purpose, the monthly salary shall be calculated on the basis of the average income obtained over the two years preceding the dismissal or termination of the contract.

Compensation provided for in the ET varies from an amount equal to 42 months' salary when termination is not based on any reason recognized by the law ("despido improcedente"), to no compensation at all, if some fault has been committed by the employee.

With the enactment of the new Royal Decree compensation for clientele is now regulated differently. This type of compensation shall only be provided when the termination of the contract is not due to non-fulfilment on the part of the agent and if, on termination the agent is obliged not to compete with the principal. The new Royal Decree requires compensation to be calculated by comparing the lists of clients at the beginning and at the end of the agency, but this compensation may not exceed the total amount of commission received in one year.

In respect of *del credere* agents if a fixed duration has been agreed, the principal may in any event terminate the relationship but, according to the general rule of service contracts (article 1594 of the Civil Code), he must compensate the agent for the lost profits.

In a one-off contract, or where the contract is for an indefinite duration, the principal may terminate at any moment (article 279 of the Commercial Code). However, in an established relationship, the courts will require a *bona fide* termination, and reasonable notice; otherwise, the agent will be entitled to damages.

Death and insolvency are grounds of termination when applicable to the agent, but not to the principal, unless their representatives or successors so decide so (article 280 of the Commercial Code).

The Labour law agency contracts can be terminated only where there is sufficient reason; otherwise the agent is entitled to compensation.

1.8. Specific Application of EEC Law

1.8.1. EEC law

There is no specific application of the EEC rules in this matter. The Royal Decree 1438/1985[2] follows the criteria established in the 1962 Notice by the Commission on exclusive dealing contracts with commercial agents in that it considers the lack of responsibility of the agent for the financial risks bound up with the sale as the essential definition of the relation between him and his employer.

As for the Directive of 18 December 1986 concerning the co-ordination of the law of the Member States in relation to independent commercial agents, no great changes, if any at all, in Spanish Law should be necessary for its implementation in Spain on 1 January 1990.

1.8.2. Applicable Law and Jurisdiction

1.8.2.1. Applicable law

Rules as to jurisdiction are laid down in the Organic Judicial Powers Act on the Organisation of the Judiciary (LOPJ), No. 6/1985, 1 July 1985 and in the Civil Procedure Act, 3 February 1881 which has been modified many times. When the contract is submitted to labour law, the applicable rules are those of the Labour Procedure Act, (Royal Decree No. 1568/1980) of 13 June 1980).

1.8.2.2. Jurisdiction

Conflicts between a principal and his employed agents, (as defined in 1.1.2., when the relation is subject to the Royal Decree no. 1438/1985)[2], are submitted to the labour courts (Magistraturas de Trabajo). Disputes arising from contracts between an independent agent and his principal, come within the competence of the civil courts, who will decide according to the Commercial and Civil Codes.[1]

A common contractual clause usually specifies where any disputes between the parties will be heard, normally in a court in the principal's area of residence. These kinds of clauses are effective only in agreements with independent agents. In the case of employees, the Labour Procedure Act does not accept such clauses as valid and lays down in article 2 that the competent court must be determined by the plaintiff, who can choose between the courts of the place where the services were rendered and those of the domicile of the other party. When services are rendered in different places, the plaintiff may choose between the place of the domicile of the agent, or the place where the contract was signed when the other party can be found in it.

1.9. Bibliography

E. Ortega Prieto, *Representantes de comercio y agentes comerciales*, Ediciones Deusto, Bilbao, 1987.

L.F. Ragel Sanchez, "La denuncia unilateral sin justa causa en el contrato de agencia por tiempo indeterminado", *Anuario de Derecho Civil*, XXXVIII (1985), pp. 61-87.

1.11. Case Law

Principles established or clarified by jurisprudence are given here, but the judgments referred to are only a few among many others. The judgments of the Spanish Supreme Court (Tribunal Supremo) are referred to as TS and those of the Spanish Central Labour Court (Tribunal Central de Trabajo) as TCT.

The legal nature of the contract does not depend on the name or qualification given to it by the parties, but on the obligations of the parties established in the contract (TS 11.3.1962; 29.1.1975; TCT 26.3.1980).

There is a presumption that the relation between the principal and the agent is of the nature of labour law, and an obligation to prove the contrary by the party who denies such a character to the relation (TS 23.6.1977; TCT 9.1.1980).

Responsibility of the agent means that he is subrogated in the responsibility of the principal in the case that the principal does not fulfil his obligations 9TS 4.10.1984, 5.10. 1984; TCT 25.1.1980, 6.3.1980).

The loss of commissions due to the failure of an operation does not imply the assumption by the representative of the risk of such operation (TS 16.6.1980, 14.10.1980).

The activity of collection does not imply either the assumption by the representative of the risk of the operations concerned (TS 1.3.1980; TCT 12.11.1980).

2. Distributorship Agreements

2.1. Distribution

2.1.1. Definition

The distribution contract is not expressly regulated by Spanish legislation. Nevertheless Spanish jurisprudence characterizes it as atypical, based on the principle of free will as set out in article 1255 of the Spanish Civil Code[3] which states, "The contracting parties may enter into any agreement, clauses and conditions that they think suitable, which are not contrary to the laws, public morals or public order".

In this respect, the judgment of 30 November, 1964[4] states:

"Article 1255 of the Civil Code stands for the free will principle, with the limitations as set forth therein; and such principle is not contradicted, but is accepted by the Commercial Code in article 50[5] and in the first paragraph of article 51.[6] Under Spanish law there exist, in addition to 'typical' and 'mixed' contracts, both of which are regulated under the two Codes, those contracted which are called 'atypical'. Even so, a contract classified as 'typical' in form, but which contains special provisions which exceed the bounds of this form, or which contain agreements or conditions aimed at accomplishing definite goals, must be deemed and interpreted in accordance with the intentions of the

---

[3] Spanish Civil Code of 1889, article 1255.
[4] Supreme Court judgment of 30 November 1964.
[5] Spanish Commercial Code of 1885, article 50: "The regulation of commercial contracts, in everything relating to their prerequisites, modifications, exceptions, interpretations, extinction and capacity of the contracting parties, will be provided, where not expressly found in this code or in special laws, by general common law rules".
[6] Spanish Commercial Code of 1885, article 51, paragraph 1: "Commercial contracts, of whatever from, language, class, or monetary value, will be valid and will give rise to legally enforceable duties and claims, if their existence may be made certain by any of the means provided under the Civil Law. Nevertheless, the declaration of a witness will not, in and of itself, be sufficient to prove the existence of a contract whose amound exceeds 1.500 pesetas . . . .".

parties, except if they are contrary to any legal dispositions, public morals or public order".

In agreement on this subject are the judgments of 27 February 1950,[7] 5 November 1957,[8] and 18 November 1980.[9]

Jurisprudence and legal doctrine classify the distribution contract as a "commercial grant" ("concesión mercantil"). It is important to note, however, that it is often not clear if a certain case fits within this legal form (judgment of 14 February 1973[10] or of 19 February 1979)[11]. An imprecise terminology is associated with this lack of clarity, with the use of such terms as "concession" (grant), "representative", "distributor", "agent", and the like, which make identification under the law more difficult.

For this reason, attention must be focused on the essential characteristics and the economic function underlying the distribution contract as factors which determine its classification as an independent and "atypical" contract or a "mixed" contract with its own character.

Spanish jurisprudence, scarce on this question, tends to classify it as an atypical contract of a mixed nature which shares some elements with the agency contract, the commission contract, the services contract, the purchase and sale contract, etc. (see the judgments of 14 November 1970[12] and of 29 October 1955[13] and the opinions of such authors as Garrigues,[14] Uria,[15] and Cano and Rico[16]).

Iglesias Prada[17] classifies it, and in our opinion rightly, as:

"Every agreement by which the entrepeneur (distributor) places his network at the service of another entrepreneur, industrialist, or merchant (supplier), to distribute, for an indefinite or definite period, in a specific geographical area, and under the supervision of the supplier, even though acting in his own name and on his own account, the products whose exclusive resale is granted under predetermined conditions".

The same author defines the distribution contract as a contract of collaboration and technical integration into the business network through

---

[7] Supreme Court judgment of 27 February 1950.
[8] Supreme Court judgment of 5 November 1957.
[9] Supreme Court judgment of 18 November 1980.
[10] Supreme Court judgment of 14 February 1973.
[11] Supreme Court judgment of 19 February 1979.
[12] Supreme Court judgment of 14 November 1970.
[13] Supreme Court judgment of 29 October 1955.
[14] Garrigues, *Curso de derecho mercantil*, Edt. Aguiree, Madrid, 1962.
[15] Uria, *Derecho mercantil*, Edt. Aguirre, Madrid, 1985.
[16] Cano and Rico, *Manuel práctico de contratación mercantil*, Vol I, Edt. Tecnos, 2nd edition 1987.
[17] Iglesias Prada, Estudios de derecho mercantil (en homenaies a Rodrigo Uria), Edt. Civitas, Madrid, 1978.
Other Works
Puente Muñoz, *"El pacto de exclusiva en la compraventa y el suministro*. RDM, 1966, pp. 75 ff. and *El contrato de concesión mercantil.*
Sanchez Calero, *"Las costumbres de probidad en la competencia y los secretos industriales, Anales de Moral Social y Económica*, XII, Madrid, 1966 e *Instituciones de Derecho Mercantil*, Valladolid, 1976.
Diez Velasco, *Notas para el estudio de la competencia ilicita*. RDM, 1946.
Hernandez and Rodriguez, *Diccionario de Formularios Generales*, Colección Nereo, 1979.

which co-operation between both producers and distributors is accomplished, permitting the new activity to be extended through the marketing phase.

As a result, exclusive sale constitutes the essential element of the contract which is closely related to the other elements which characterize it, permitting the final integration into the supplier's activity. Iglesias therefore, characterizes this contract as "atypical" and "independent".

2.1.1.1. Exclusive / non exclusive / exclusive purchasing

An essential element of the exclusive distribution contract is the exclusivity of resale conferred on the distributor by the supplier within a specific geographic area.

Keeping in mind the economic function of this contract, we agree with Iglesias Prada that the commercial concession should be thought of as a contract of business collaboration and integration in which an exclusive resale agreement forms the bases for its achievement.

The exclusive distribution agreement must therefore, be distinguished from such other contractual forms as the authorized distribution contract (in which the distributor maintains legal autonomy) because its purpose is distinct from that of the commercial concession, in as much as the distributor does not enjoy an exclusivity, or a geographic monopoly, in the sale of the supplier's products, and in as much as exclusivity is not pursued by a contract of this form, which represents a lower level of business collaboration.

The fact that under a distribution contract the distributor normally acquires the supplier's products is supplementary to the purpose of this contract, in which the business relations existing between the parties is the most important goal, resulting in a greater interdependence between them.

2.1.2. Conclusion of the contract (special conditions)

The final agreement on the distribution contract, in the absence of a specific regulation in Spain, is subject to the general provision on contracts that are contained in Title II of Book IV of the Spanish Civil Code (Obligations and Contracts) and specific ones, in that the parties are normally businessmen or carry out acts of trade and so remain subject to the Spanish Commercial Code, where it is specifically relevant.

The contract is completed by simple agreement between the parties. The contract itself may be either written or oral, and often an oral contract is subsequently confirmed by occasional written correspondence. On this point, article 54 of the Spanish Commercial Code[18] states that commercial contracts concluded by means of correspondence will be deemed finalized from the time of the answer accepting the proposals or modifications. The place of the contract is deemed under article 1252 of the Civil Code[19] to be the place where the offer was made.

[18] Spanish Commercial Code of 1855, article 54: "Contracts made by correspondence will be deemed finalized from the time of the acceptance of the proposals or the modifications".

[19] Spanish Civil Code of 1889, article 1252: "Consent is manifested by concurrence of the offer and the acceptance regarding the object and the purpose which constitute the contract. Acceptance by letter does not oblige the offerer until he learns of it. The place of contracting, in this case, is presumed to have been the place in which the offer was made".

The object of the distribution contract is often the distribution itself, and terms are often agreed through a "contract of adhesion" in cases where the creation of a distribution network is intended to achieve the same conditions. In these cases, the terms offered to each of the distributors are substantially the same.

2.1.3. The supplier's duties and rights

Spanish jurisprudence and legal opinion on distribution contracts indicate several rights and duties created by the contents of the contract which determine its special legal nature. The relations between the supplier and the distributor, owing to the special elements of the distribution contract, come dangerously close to the boundaries of public policy, as set forth in Spanish anti-trust law.[20]

2.1.3.1. The supplier's duties

As Iglesias Prada (*op. cit.*) has indicated, the supplier's duties are divided into two types: positive duties and negative duties, each imposed according to the contract's particular contents, which must be compatible with the free will of the parties, as article 1255 (previously cited) of the Spanish Civil Code provides. Typical duties imposed include the following:

(a) regarding the resale exclusivity conferred, negative duties (obligations not to do something) implied by the terms of this type of contract are imposed on the supplier, and originate in the very nature of the concession contract itself as well as in its purpose. Any breach will give the distributor the right to pursue legal action, as provided in article 1099 of the Spanish Civil Code[21] and in article 925 of the Civil Procedure Act (Ley de Enjuiciamento Civil);[22]

(b) an obligation to advertise actively the products which are the subject of the concession contract;

(c) compulsory supply of a minimum quantity of the agreed products, subject to a predetermined date and time period;

(d) provision of some products at no cost for purposes of demonstration.

2.1.3.2. The supplier's rights

The supplier's rights are the exact reverse of the distributor's duties as established generally by the law and specifically by the terms of the contract, subject to the limits to contractual freedom previously mentioned. See also 2.1.4. and 2.1.4.1.

---

[20] Spanish Restricted Trade Practice Act, 1963.

[21] Spanish Civil Code of 1889, article 1099: "That regulated in paragraph one of the previous article will also apply to negative obligations where the obligor has carried out the prohibited act". Article 1098 states that the obligor who violates the spirit of the obligation will be compelled to rectify the situation.

[22] Spanish Civil Procedure Act of 1881, article 925: "If a person subject to a judgment not to do something violates the judgment, it will be understood that he chooses to amend the damages, and those having obtained the judgment will be indemnified by the violator in a form expressed by the preceding article".

2.1.4. The distributor's duties and rights

Discussion is limited here to those rights and duties of the distributor which originate in the contractual relation of the commercial concession, bearing in mind its special economic function. Spanish jurisprudence is aware of the weak position of the distributor in this type of contract, and tends to strengthen his position, thus balancing the same with respect to the supplier (this is examined under contractual responsibility).

2.1.4.1. The distributor's duties

The distributor's fundamental obligation is, as pointed out by Iglesias Prada, the marketing of the products which are the subject of the distribution contract. Marketing implies positive, active conduct, qualitatively and quantitatively spelt out in the concession contract, in order to comply with the contract. From this primary duty, several secondary duties are derived:

(1) to follow the supplier's instructions on the promotion and sale of the products in question;
(2) to accept the administrative, accounting and financial systems established by the supplier;
(3) to permit the supplier to verify the books;
(4) to acquire a specified minimum quantity of the contract products;
(5) to fulfil a minimum resale volume;
(6) to refrain from acquiring products of identical or similar characteristics to the contract products;
(7) to refrain from maintaining stocks outside the territory defined in the contract;
(8) to refrain from advertising ouside of the contract area.

2.1.4.2. The distributor's rights

We refer to the supplier's dutes (see 2.1.3.1.) as the distributor's rights flow directly from them. In addition, a distribution contract of this type may provide for quantity discounts; that is, the price may be reduced according to the volume of the purchases by the distributor. A term providing for resale commissions may also be included in the contract.

2.1.5. Liabilities of supplier and distributor during the term of the distributorship agreement

We can first, distinguish the liabilities associated with the distribution contract, i.e. the liabilities of the supplier and of the distributor, bearing in mind the specific conditions expressed in the contract. Secondly, we shall make reference to the liabilities of both the supplier and the distributor, vis-à-vis third parties, as an extracontractual consequence of the distribution contract.

2.1.5.1. The supplier as against the distributor

The liabilities of the supplier depend on his duties as expressly set out in the distribution contract. Any non-performance of the contract gives rise to a right of action by the distributor to enforce it, as well as to damages or indemnity where appropriate. For this reason, the liabilities of the supplier are determined according to specific circumstances.

In general the supplier's primary duty under the contract is to respect the resale exclusivity of the distributor, who has the right to enforce it (see 2.1.3.1.). Upon such enforcement action, the supplier may have incurred liability under the terms of the contract itself, which may contain a non-competition clause.

In the normal distribution contract the supplier sells to the distributor the products to be resold, and for this reason, under a supplementary duty, the supplier is liable to the distributor in accordance with the provisions relating to commercial purchasing found in the Commercial Code.

2.1.5.2. The supplier as against third parties

An exclusivity clause in a distribution contract does not imply that the supplier's other distributors will be entitled to the same exclusivity. This is because the object of an exclusivity clause is the benefit of the parties to it, not the benefit of third parties, although they may be in similar positions. An exclusivity clause between a supplier and a particular distributor gives third parties no rights to demand the same treatment.

In addition, an exclusivity clause gives to no right of action by the distributor as against the supplier where third parties selling the same products obtained the products either from the supplier (but purchased outside the contract territory), or from other sources, whether inside or outside of the contract territory.

2.1.5.3. The distributor as against the supplier

The liability of the distributor as against the supplier also depends on specific circumstances, as reflected in the distribution contract. The distributor will also be liable where the contractual duties give rise to an action by the supplier to enforce the contract by arbitration or through the courts (see 2.1.4.1.).

The normal distribution contract contains a non-competition clause, which the distributor must also respect.

The distributor may also be subject by special provisions concerning commercial purchasing if so provided in the distribution contract.

2.1.5.4. The distributor as against third parties

Where one distributor deliberately invades the exclusive distribution contract territory of another, his acts may constitute unfair trading as defined by article 10 of the Treaty of Paris,[23] the treaty is directly applicable under Spanish law where the act of competition goes against notions of the integrity of trade practices. However, this article cannot be invoked before

---

[23] Treaty of Paris (1883), article 10. Spanish authorities signed, in Stockholm, on 14 July 1970 an Act modifying the Treaty of Paris, and ratified the Act, by signing it into law on 14 April 1972.

Spanish national courts; the distributor must base his action on article 1902 of the Spanish Civil Code.[24]

2.1.6. Term and termination

2.1.6.1. Term

In so far as the period of validity is concerned, the parties to an exclusive distribution contract may freely agree upon its term. In the case of an exclusive distribution (or commercial concession) which does not specify a period of duration, the Spanish Supreme Court has given to understand that any one of the parties may rescind the contract by means of a request made over a reasonable period of time and in a suitable form (see the judgments of the Supreme Court of 2 February 1973).[13] Moreover, contracting parties cannot provide in the distribution contract for a perpetuity clause, which is illegal under Spanish jurisprudence and under the Civil Code, as stated by the Supreme Court in its judgment of 14 February 1973.[25] However, the parties may provide for an unlimited duration in the contract if either or both are expressly given the power to terminate the contract, within a predetermined period of time, the occurence of a specified event. Where the contract gives no such powers, normal commercial practice will be applied, if it exists. If it does not, Iglesias Prada has suggested that the problem could be resolved by the application of article 302 of the Commercial Code (concerning the contract of commercial representation) which states that a period of one month is necessary to permit both parties to terminate the contract or to leave the judge to decide if the unilateral termination of the contract has been carried out in accordance with the parties' general duty of good faith.

Spanish case law has not fully addressed the question of the extension or renewal of a distribution contract of limited duration which does not provide for an extension. However, an interesting judgment of the Supreme Court has been delivered on the subject of unilateral termination without just cause of a distribution contract before its term has expired. This decision, of 21 December 1963,[26] held that the cancelling party must pay an indemnity to the other party for the premature and unjustified termination of the contract if any damages have resulted.

2.1.6.2. Termination

Several causes for termination under Spanish law have been identified. These are:

(1) expiration of the term, if the contract has so provided;
(2) where the parties have not so agreed, on the occurrence of a specified event, as stated in the contract (for contracts of unlimited duration, see 2.1.6.1.);

---

[24] Spanish Civil Code of 1899, article 1902: "Any person, who by action or inaction causes damage to another, due to negligent or intentional behaviour, will be obliged to make reparations for the damages incurred".
[25] Supreme Court judgment of 2 February 1973.
[26] Supreme Court judgment of 21 December 1963.

(3) upon unilateral termination by one of the parties before the period of the contract has expired, (for contracts of limited duration, see 2.1.6.1.);

(4) upon the death or incapacity of the distributor, in so far as the choice of distributor was an essential element of the contract. Iglesias Prada has suggested that the distribution contract would not terminate upon the death of the distributor, on the grounds that modern suppliers do not contract for the person, but for the enterprise.

2.1.7. Indemnity

Spanish law does not expressly provide for indemnity in distribution contracts. Reference must therefore, be made to the general rules of the Civil and Commercial Codes. Article 1255 of the Civil Code provides that:

> "Contracts are finalized by simple agreement, and from that point on oblige the parties, not only to the performance of the express clauses under the contract, but also to the consequences flowing therefrom, according to their nature, to custom, to good faith, and to law".

Article 1101 of the Spanish Civil Code states that:

> "Those who in the performance of their duties cause damage through fraud, negligence, or delay , as well as those who in any way violate the spirit of their duties, remain subject to indemnification".

Article 1106 of the Spanish Civil Code states that:

> "Indemnification for damages incurred comprises not only the value of the loss suffered, but also the value of the gains that the claimant would have had, but for the act giving rise to indemnity, except as noted in the following articles".

Article 1107 of the Spanish Civil Code states that:

> "The damages for which the good faith obligor is responsible are those foreseen or which could have been foreseen at the time the duties were incurred and which were the necessary consequence of such non-performance. In case of fraud the obligor will be responsible for all damages which he knows flow from such non-performance of the obligations".

2.1.8. Specific application of EEC law

There is no specific application of EEC law. However, the Spanish Act on Competition was highly influenced by the EEC competition rules. The Spanish Restrictive Practices Court has followed, to some extent, the case law of the EEC court on competition, while disagreeing in other cases, with the Spanish court taking a more restrictive and nationalistic view.

2.1.8.1. Applicable law and jurisdiction

Two main problems may arise when one of the parties to the distribution contract (the supplier or the distributor) seeks enforcement by the court of the contract breached by the other party. The first is to establish which law will be applied to the contract, and the second, which court will have jurisdiction.

2.1.8.2. Applicable law

The supplier and the distributor may provide expressly in the distribution contract which law will be applicable, in that case, if any problem of interpretation or execution of the contract should arise, it will be resolved under the law chosen by the parties, provided it has some connection with the purpose of the contract, and it has been expressly designated.

In absence of a specific submission of the parties in the distribution contract, the Spanish Civil Code provides in article 10(5)[27] that:

"The law applicable to contractual duties will be the law to which the parties have expressly submitted in as much as it has some connection with the business which is the subject of the contract; by default, the common national law of the parties; failing this, that of their regular common residence, and, in the last instance, the law of the place of contracting. Notwithstanding the provisions of the previous paragraph where such express submission is lacking, in the case of land is located will be applied, and in relation to the sale of tangible goods carried out between business establishments the applicable law will be that of the place where the places of business are located."

2.1.8.3. Jurisdiction

As for the competent jurisdiction for resolving claims arising regarding performance under, or interpretation of the distribution contract, we may distinguish three situations:

(a) *The parties have not agreed upon this matter.* In this case, Spanish courts will have jurisdiction if the defendant is resident in Spain. A submission to Spanish jurisdiction may be implied under article 22(2) of the Jurisdiction Act of 1985 (Ley Orgánica del Poder Judicial)[28] if the defendant appears in court and does not challenge its jurisdiction. If such submission cannot be implied, article 22(3) of the same law provides that the Spanish civil courts will have jurisdiction over contractual obligations when they arise in or must be performed in Spain.

(b) *A clause in the contract chooses the Spanish jurisdictional forum.* In conformity with article 22(2) of the above-mentioned law, the Spanish civil courts will be competent to hear the case.

(c) *A clause in the contract chooses a foreign jurisdictional forum.* In a distribution contract where, according to article 22(3) of the Jurisdiction Act, Spanish courts have jurisdiction, and, at the same time, no grounds for exclusive jurisdiction exist, it is not clear whether such clause is effective. Before the Jurisdiction Act, such clauses were not recognized as valid. However, since the enactment of this law, no jurisprudence has directly covered the problem.

Lastly, the parties may agree that any difference arising from the performance or interpretation of the distribution contract may be resolved by means of arbitration, whether in Spain or in a foreign country (see the Law on Arbitration of 1953[29]. In this regard, Spain has ratified the New York Convention of 1958 without the reservations for reciprocity or the limited application to commercial questions.

---

[27] Spanish Civil Code of 1889, article 10(5).
[28] Spanish Jurisdiction Act, 1985.
[29] Spanish Arbitration Law, 1953.

2.2. Selective Distribution

2.2.1. Definition

The selective distribution contract is not expressly regulated by Spanish legislation. Nevertheless Spanish jurisprudence characterizes it as atypical, based on the principle of free will as set out in article 1255 of the Spanish Civil Code. On the elements of the selective distribution contract which are common to distribution contracts in general, see 2.1.1. A discussion on the unique and more complex elements of the selective distribution contract follows.

Incorporating the definition proposed by Iglesias Prada for the distribution contract in general (see 2.1.1.) into a definition containing the more specific elements of the selective distribution contract, the selective distribution contract may be defined as any agreement by which the entrepreneur (distributor) places his network at the disposal of another entrepreneur, industrialist or merchant (supplier), in order to market, for a definite or indefinite period, within a specific geographical area, and under the supervision of the supplier, even though acting in his own name and on his own account, those products whose exclusive resale is granted under predetermined conditions. These conditions make it mandatory for the supplier to take extraordinary precautions in selecting the distributors of his products in order to maintain the level of their quality, preserve the carefully nurtured public opinion of these products and the supplier, assure the best presence in the market and the most advantageous channels of distribution for resale, and maintain a strict level of control over their presentation and resale.

The selective distribution contract has been described by Spanish jurisprudence in several decisions, one of the most important and interesting of which was delivered by the Competition Court on 30 March 1974.[30] In defining the essence of this type of contract, the Court stated, in reference to a contract between a French supplier of perfumes and a Spanish distributor, that:

> "the large makers of important brands of perfumes and cosmetics take great care to protect the image of the product offered to the public, concerning themselves not only with the intrinsic quality of the product, but also with its marketing and advertising, with the channels of its distribution and the establishment of points of resale by which the products are placed before the public; with the organization of territorial distribution, especially as regards the selection of retailers, as the distributor is obligated under the contract agreed with the French company to follow its terms, reserving to the supplier the right of its inspectors to visit such retailers".

2.2.2. Conclusion of the contract (special conditions)

See 2.1.2.

2.2.3. The supplier's duties and rights

---

[30] Judgment of the Competition Court, 30 March 1974. Información Comercial Española, no. 1414, p. 1322 ff. See 2.1.11.

See 2.1.3.

2.2.3.1. The supplier's duties

See 2.1.3.1.

2.2.3.2. The supplier's rights

See 2.1.3.2. and 2.2.4.1.

2.2.4. The distributor's duties and rights

Because the selective distribution contract constitutes a more complex form of the simple distribution contract, it normally provides for increased duties which specifically concern the distributor and special rights which are accorded the supplier. Each of these is regulated by Spanish law, but the adjudication of such contracts depends more on the contents of the specific selective distribution contract as well as on Spanish case law. Also 2.1.4.

2.2.4.1. The distributor's duties

On the basic duties of distributors, see 2.1.4.1. The selective distributor is normally subject to duties which go beyond the scope of those listed in point 2.1.4.1.; he has, for example:

(1) to follow the supplier's specific instructions regarding the promotion and sale of the supplier's products through appropriate channels of distribution and through the establishment of points of resale by which the products are placed before the public;

(2) to maintain the level of product quality to the satisfaction of the supplier;

(3) to preserve, and if possible enhance, public opinion of these products and the image of the supplier;

(4) to permit the maintainance by the supplier of a strict level of control over the presentation and resale of the products;

(5) to maintain the integrity of the products and the supplier through appropriate marketing and advertising;

(6) to follow the supplier's instructions regarding the organization of territorial distribution, especially as regards the selection of retailers;

(7) to follow the contract provisions regarding the supplier's right to have inspectors visit such retailers.

2.2.4.2. The distributor's rights

See 2.1.4.2.

2.2.5. Liabilities of supplier and distributor during the term of the distributorship agreement

2.2.5.1. The supplier as against the distributor

Because of the extraordinary care with which the supplier selects the distributor most appropriate to its special needs, the supplier must retain significant control over the distributor. The selective distribution contract may provide for a right of termination for the supplier should the resale situation change or should the supplier feel that its products are not being presented under the conditions called for in the contract. Where the contract has made provision for such exigencies, the supplier incurs no liability.

2.2.5.2. The supplier as against third parties

See 2.1.5.2.

2.2.5.3. The distributor as against the supplier

Regarding basic distributor liability under distribution contracts, see 2.1.5.3. Additionally, where the selective distribution contract specifies particular conditions as to the marketing, promotion, etc. of the products, it may be in breach of the contract when deviating from such conditions.

2.2.5.4. The distributor as against third parties

See 2.1.5.4.

2.2.6. Term and termination

See 2.1.6.

2.2.6.1. Term

See 2.1.6.1.

2.2.6.2. Termination

See 2.1.6.2.

2.2.7. Indemnity

See 2.1.7.

2.2.8. Specific application of EEC law

There exists no specific application of EEC law.

2.2.8.1. Applicable law and jurisdiction

See 2.1.9.

2.2.8.2. Applicable law

See 2.1.8.1.

3. Franchise Agreements

3.1. Definition

The franchising contract is one in which one party (the franchisor, or the grantor) gives to the order party (the franchisee or grantee) the authorization to utilize his trademark (generally an international trademark), while at the same time he integrates him into his commercial network.

3.1.1. Characteristics

In this second characteristic, a franchise differs from a trademark licence, in as much as it is the business style to which the franchisee binds himself, as well as the control and assistance of the franchisor which make the trademark licence not the material component of the franchising contract.

This definition is much clearer if we look at the situation in which – at least in contracts which have been known as franchise distributions – the franchisor buys the products with the trademark already incorporated.

One final element which serves to differentiate the franchise from the trademark licence is that in a franchising contract, the franchisee is not paying only for the right to use the trademark, but also for the right to form part of the system.

Nevertheless, the definition of franchising is not complete unless we also make reference to certain of its inherent characteristics which caused it to appear in the business world in the first place. The law now seeks to fit these circumstances into a proper framework.

These circumstances are that the franchising formula should be original, that it should demonstrate a record of success and that such success should be capable of repetition. Because of the force of these characteristics, we can speak of franchising contracts today.

3.2. Conclusion of the Contract (Special Conditions)

Before we examine the form of the contract, which for lack of specific regulations in Spanish law, is governed by the provisions contained in the Civil Code, it is necessary to realize, that even if one form doesn't deal with an in-depth study of the variations in franchising, each contract will operate according to the specific formula that the sale deals with.

There are four principal kinds of franchising:

(a) the integrated franchise, between the manufacturer and the retailer;
(b) the semi-integrated franchise between the manufacturer and the wholesalers;
(c) horizontal franchising between manufacturers or between retailers;
(d) vertical franchising, which breaks the initial pattern of this type of agreement and which is produced when the franchisor is the retailer who franchises to manufacturers.

Based on these four ways of franchising, we also find a number of cases in which there are special covenants, arising from the original formula which, is an essential, though non-legal, component of franchising.

We can distinguish the following components:

(a) the franchisor contributes his know-how and corresponding technical and trade assistance, (this must be considered confidential by the franchisee and is normally transmitted by an operating manual);
(b) the franchisor indicates to the franchisee the sources of supply of the products that he markets;

(c) the franchisor contributes those industrial property rights which are directly related to the subject of the contract;

(d) the franchisee pays the franchisor an initial sum or down payment for rights of entry, as well as periodic payments according to the volume of the sales;

(e) the franchisor will not normally grant the contract for a determined geographic zone.

(f) the franchisee is usually also obliged not to sell products other than those which are subject of the contract.

(g) the franchise contract therefore supposes a partial loss to the franchisee of independent management control, as a result of the control exercised by the franchisor in the management, sale and accounting of the products.

3.3. The Supplier's Duties and Rights

3.3.1. The supplier's duties

The supplier's duties are as follows:

- to add and incorporate new products;
- to grant to the franchisee those of his industrial and intellectual property rights that have a direct relation to the subject of the franchise;
- to place at the franchisee's disposal that merchandise comprising his stock or to guarantee its provision even though not manufactured by the franchisor;
- to promote with advertisements those articles or products; however, on occasions when the franchisor promotes these products through point of sale advertisements, these expenses may be on the franchisor's account;
- to provide instruction, technical training, and technical assistance to the franchisee;
- to ensure that the pricing policy maintains the compatibility of his own interests with those of franchisee's profitability and security under the contract;
- to keep control of royalties and stocks of the franchisee, as well as the quality of products and services offered to the public;
- to respect the exclusivity clauses granted to the franchisee.

3.3.2. The supplier's rights

The supplier's rights are the exact reverse of the distributor's duties (see 3.4.1.).

3.4. The Distributor's Duties and Rights

3.4.1. The distributor's duties

The distributor's duties are as follows:

- to maintain adequate stock to meet demand and according to the plan;

- to follow the advice on prices suggested by the franchisor;
- to respect the franchise's public image;
- to pay the initial sum or down-payment for right of entry as well as the periodic payments set out in the contract;
- to respect the rules of exploitation and management covenanted, adequately carrying out accounting and permitting the agreed controls by the franchisor;
- to inform the franchisor of the market's development and growth;
- to respect the exclusivity set forth in the contract.

3.4.2. The distributor's rights

The distributor's rights are the exact reverse of the supplier's duties (see 3.3.1.).

3.5. Liabilities of Supplier and Distributor during the Term of the Distributorship Agreement

We can distinguish the liabilities associated with the contract by considering those of the supplier and those of the distributor, bearing in mind the specific conditions expressed in the contract. We also make reference to the liabilities of both the supplier and the distributor, vis-à-vis third parties, as an extracontractual consequence of the contract.

3.5.1. The supplier as against the distributor

The liabilities of the supplier depend on his duties as expressly set forth in the contract. Any non-performance of the contract gives rise to a right of action by the distributor to enforce it, as well as to damages or indemnity in the appropriate circumstances. For this reason, the liabilities of the supplier are determined by specific circumstances.

In general the supplier's primary duty under the contract is to respect the resale exclusivity of the distributor, who has the right to enforce in. Upon such enforcement action, the supplier may have incurred liability under the terms of the contract itself, which may contain a non-competition clause.

In the normal franchising contract the supplier sells to the distributor the products to be resold, and for this reason, under a supplementary duty the supplier is liable to the distributor in accordance with the provisions relating to commercial purchasing found in the Commercial Code.

3.5.2. The supplier as against third parties

An exclusivity clause in a franchising contract does not imply that the supplier's other distributors will be entitled to the same exclusivity. This is because the object of an exclusivity clause is the benefit of the parties to it, not the benefit of third parties, although they may be in a similar situation. An exclusivity clause between a supplier and a particular distributor gives no rights of action to third parties to demand the same treatment.

In addition, an exclusivity clause gives no right of action to the distributor as against the supplier where third parties selling the same products, obtained the products either from the supplier (but purchased outside of the contract territory), or from other sources, whether inside or outside the contract territory.

3.5.3. The distributor as against the supplier

The liability of the distributor as against the supplier also depends on the specific circumstances, as reflected in the contract. The distributor will also be liable where the contractual duties give rise to an action by the supplier to enforce the contract by arbitration or through the courts.

The normal franchising contract contains a non-competition clause, which the distributor must also respect.

The distributor is also subject to special provisions concerning commercial purchasing if so provided in the contract.

3.5.4. The distributor as against third parties

Where one distributor deliberately invades the exclusive franchising contract territory of another, its acts may constitute unfair trade as defined under Article 10 of the Treaty of Paris,[31] the treaty is directly applicable under Spanish law where the act of competition goes against notions of the integrity of trade practices. However, this article cannot be invoked before Spanish national courts; the distributor must base his action on Article 1902 of the Spanish Civil Code.[32]

3.6. Term and Termination

3.6.1. Term

In so far as the period of validity is concerned, the parties to an exclusive franchising contract may freely agree upon its term. In the case of an exclusive distribution which is concluded without specifying duration, the Spanish Supreme Court has given to understand that any one of the parties may rescind the contract by means of a request made over a reasonable period of time and in a suitable form. Moreover, contracting parties cannot provide in a franchising contract for a perpetuity clause, which is illegal under Spanish case law and under the Civil Code. However, the parties may provide for an unlimited duration in the contract if either one or both of the parties are expressly given the power to terminate the contract, within a predetermined period of time, upon the occurrence of a specified event. Where the contract gives no such powers, commercial practice will be applied, if it exists.

3.6.2. Termination

Several causes for termination have been identified under Spanish law:

---

[31] Treaty of Paris (1883), Art. 10. Spanish authorities signed, in Stockholm, on 14 July 1970 an Act modifying the Treaty of Paris, and ratified the Act, by signing it into law on 14 April 1972.
[32] Spanish Civil Code of 1899, Art. 1902 states that "Any person who by action or inaction causes damage to another, due to negligent or intentional behaviour, will be obliged to make reparations for the damages incurred".

- expiration of the term, if the contract has so provided;
- where the parties have not so agreed, upon the occurrence of a specified event, as stated in the contract;
- upon unilateral termination by one of the parties before the period of the contract has expired.

3.7. Indemnity

3.7.1. Indemnity for goodwill and/or clientèle

This term may also be set out in the franchising contract, but where such a term is absent or in the absence of agreement or in the case of diverging interpretation, the damaged party must demonstrate the extent of damages sustained either through arbitration or by an ordinary judicial proceeding.

3.7.2. Compensation for damages

Article 1101 of the Spanish Civil Code states that:

"Those who in the performance of their duties cause damages through fraud, negligence, or delay, as well as those who in any way violate the spirit of their duties, remain subject to indemnification".

Article 1106 of the Spanish Civil Code states that:

"Indemnification for damages incurred comprises not only the value of the loss suffered, but also the value of the gains that the claimant would have had, but for the act giving rise to indemnity, except as noted in the following articles".

Article 1107 of the Spanish Civil Code states that:

"The damages for which the good faith obligor is responsible are those foreseen or which could have been foreseen at the time the duties were incurred and which were the necessary consequence of such non-performance.
   In case of fraud the obligor will be responsible for all damages which he knows flow from such non-performance of the obligation".

3.8. Specific Application of EEC Law

There is no specific application of EEC law.

3.9. Bibliography

Nothing has yet been published in Spanish devoted specifically to the subject of franchising contracts.

3.10. Legislation

Apart from general references to the contracts previously mentioned, there are no specific references in Spanish legislation to these types of contract.

3.11. Case Law

There is no jurisprudence directly covering franchising, although there is one judicial reference in the judgment of the First Division (the Civil Division) of the Supreme Court, promulgated on the 15 May 1985 which includes franchising contracts as well as the concession or sole right of distribution contracts and which defines franchising as:

> "the authorization that the grantor gives to the grantee in order to utilize his trademark, generally international in nature, thus integrating him into his trade network".

CHAPTER 7
FRANCE

Jérôme Depondt,
Lilyane Anstett-Gardea,
Chantal Couturier-Leoni
Pierre Servan-Schreiber

1. Commercial Agency

1.1. Definition of Various Types of Agencies and Intermediaries.

French law offers several statutes for intermediaries in commercial sales. These statutes depend on the nature of the activity concerned or on the level of dependence or subordination requested.

1.1.1. Independent

A commercial agent is defined by Article 1D of 23 December 1958[1], as amended.[2] He acts for and on behalf of one or several principals, usually and independently[3]. Under these conditions, if he is both registered and if he is bound by a contract according to the stipulations of the decree, he will profit by the special statute of the commercial agents.[4]

Not being a merchant by nature, because his mandate is purely civil, the commercial agent is subject to stipulations related to improving commercial and industrial professions.[5]

---

[1] Decree of 23.12.1958 No. 58-1345. *Article*: "est agent commercial le mandataire qui, à titre de profession habituelle et indépendante, sans être lié par un contrat de louage de services, négocie et, éventuellement, conclut des achats, des ventes, des locations ou des prestations de services, au nom et pour le compte de producteurs, d'industriels ou de commerçants. Le contrat qui lie l'agent à ses mandants est écrit et indique la qualité des deux parties contractantes. Il peut être à durée déterminée ou indéterminée. Il peut contenir une convention d'exclusivité, une convention ducroire, une convention de consignation de marchandises en vue de livraison à la clientèle".

[2] Arrêté of 22.8..1968.

[3] Alfred Jauffret, *Manuel de droit commercial*, 18th edn. by J. Mestre ed. (LGDJ No. 564 et seq.)

[4] Didier Ferrier "Distribution—agents commerciaux" in *Jurisclasseur commercial—contracts—distribution*, Vol. 3, Pt. 1230-1253. Cf. references cited.

[5] *Ordonnance no. 59-26 of 3.1.1959*, "portant application aux activités de représentation de loi du 30 août 1947, relative à l'assainissement des professions commerciales et industrielles" O.J. 6.1.1959).

It is important to notice that the courts change the commercial agent contract into a labour contract as soon as a bond of subordination between the principal and the agent exists.[6]

The present examination is confined to the statute of commercial agency.

1.1.2. Employed

Among dependent intermediaries, can be distinguished the wage earner representative and the commercial traveller ("V.R.P."). The first is bound to the employer by a current labour contract of common law, and placed in a complete state of dependence but the second works in legally defined conditions and benefits[7] from certain advantages, such as the indemnity of clientele.[8] Only physical persons can be bound by a labour contract.

The statutory "V.R.P." is distinguished from other wage-earners primarily by his independence.

The "V.R.P." statute is defined by Article L.751.1–L.751.15 of the "Labour Code".

Because of its specific character, it is one of the few professions which benefits from the statute governed by the "Labour Code" (such as pressmann, caretakers of flats).

In pursuance of Article L.751.1 of the Labour Code, the following must be considered as a sole "V.R.P." or multicards and benefits from this statute: every agent who:

- works for one or more employer;
- performs his work in a selective or steadfast way;
- does not carry out any commercial operation for himself;
- is bound to his employer by an agreement when settles the nature of the services or products offered for sale, the territory or kind of clients which he visits and the rate of remuneration.

The question of the activity is determining, notwithstanding any express stipulation of the contract or in the case silence (Article L.751.1 AL.1).

The essential force of the statute consists in the right which is acquired by the "V.R.P." over the clients he acquires, develops or creates for his profit or that of his principal.

Indeed, in case of dismissed without serious fault, the "V.R.P." can claim an indemnity for his clientele.

1.1.3. Others

Among other intermediaries, business agents should be mentioned. Their activity generates commercial acts within the meaning of Article 632 of the

---

[6] Cass. Soc. 9.5.1979 no. 983. Pourvoi no. 77–41–406 of 16.9.1977 and 3.5.1978. Pourvoi no. 78–40–794 of 16.9.1977 and 3.5.1978 *in lexis*. Cass. Soc. 18.11.1976 no. 1–449. Pourvoi no. 75–12–135 of 9.5.1975 *in lexis*. Cass. Soc. 27.1.1971 Arrêt no. 98. Pourvoi no. 69–13–367 of 20.8.1969.

[7] Labour Code, Article L751.

[8] Mireille Bouteloup, "Distribution VRP" in *Jurisclasseur commercial—contrats—distribution*, Vol. 3, Pt. 1200-1224.

Commercial Code.[9] Jurisprudence defines this profession as formed by private intermediaries, devoid of official character, who usually manage other business for a consideration.

The following are generally included in this definition: Advertising and artistic agents, matrimonial agencies, patent of inventions agencies, engineering consultants for patent rights, insurance agents.

Many of these professions have been brought under regulation: for example, travel agencies (Law no. 75–627 11 July 1975), intermediaries in sales of real estates or businesses (Law no. 70–9 2 January 1970).

The broker 'courtier' is an intermediary whose only function is to introduce two parties to one another, without acting for and on behalf of his principal. He is a merchant but he only interposes in punctual businesses.

The commissioner "commissionnaire" is a merchant who acts on his own behalf and also for his principal's interest.[10]

Finally, an important category of intermediaries consists of trustee representatives, physical or moral persons. Their situation is ruled by the stipulations of Articles 1984 et seq. of the "Civil Code"[11]

The representatives governed by these clauses are those who cannot meet the broad requirements of the Commercial Agent Statute. Thus, their profession does not consist in representation of a principal, and this is not a producer, merchant or industrial. The judicial position would be the same if the agent did not take the precaution of being registered or having a written contract which sets out the position of each party.

Their duties are defined in the contract and can be the same as the obligations in a commercial agency contract.

As far as the contract is concerned, two kinds of intermediaries must be distinguished: the simple representative and the authorized agent in common interest of the parties. The first acts only in the interest of the principal. The second acts in his own interest in proportion to the interest of the principal in the procuration of agency carrying out. It is thus when the agent's remuneration corresponds to a percentage of the profits of the principal. The simple procuration can be cancelled ad nutum without indemnity. This kind of agent acts generally for punctual operations.

A procuration in common interest cannot be terminated except with indemnity due to the party on whom the terminated is imposed. In the care of a termination for a legitimate reason such as an industrial reorganization, no indemnity is payable.

Consequently, therefore, the position of agents in common interest is the same as that of commercial agents one, because their contract is qualified by law: procuration in common interest (Article 3 Decree 23 December 1958).

---

[9] Commercial code, Article 632. Law no. 67–563 of 13.7.1967: "toutes opérations d'intermédiaires pour l'achat, la souscription ou la vente d'immeubles, de fonds de commerces, d'actions ou parts de sociétés immobilières . . .".

[10] Cass. Com. 6.7.1960, Bulletin Civil III no. 279, Rev. Trim. Dr. Com. 1961, 664.

[11] Civil Code, Article 1984: "Le mandat ou procuration est un acte par lequel une personne donne à une autre le pouvoir de faire quelque chose pour le mandant et en son nom. Le contrat ne se forme que par l'acceptation du mandataire".

1.2. Conclusion of the Contract (Special Conditions)

According to Article 1 of the Decree of 23 December 1958[12] the contract which binds the principal and the agent is written and states the position of both parties.

Article 3 Arr of 19 June 1959,[13] subordinates to the presentation of a written contract, the possibility for the agent to be registered on the special register.

The doctrine considers whether the written contract is required *ad probationem*[14] or *ad validitatem*[15]. Jurisprudence and the High Court consider that without a written contract, the agent can not benefit from the special statute of commercial agency.[16] Written contract is so required *ad validitatem*.

In the absence of a written contract, the courts consider whether the working conditions of the agent oblige him to comply with the principal rules of conduct, to write frequent reports, etc. When those conditions show a binding obligation, the contract will be a qualified labour contract.[17] Without a binding obligation, it will be a procuration in common interest.[18]

In a word, commercial agency needs a written contract.

The EEC Directive of 18 December 1986 does not prescribe a written contract as a condition of validity[19]. No Jurisprudence has not yet used this directive, which has not yet come into force, in French law.

A contract signed but not witnessed is sufficient for a commercial agency. A simple exchange of letters is not sufficient, but very subsidiary if the subject matter is wholly included in them.

In fact, the contract must indicate the position of the parties:[20] this means that the agent exercises his rights within the limits of the Decree of 23 December 1958. These specifications and the written ones are particularly important as risks of recalling can not be excluded. Article L.291, Book One, of the Labour Code explains "in the absence of a written contract, persons whose activity consists of intermediary work are presumed to be "V.R.P.".

In addition, the great care must be taken in the written contract to state

---

[12] Decree of 23.12.1968, Article 3: "Les contrats intervenus entre les agents commerciaux et leurs mandants sont conclus dans l'intérêt commun des parties.

Leur résiliation par le mandant, si elle n'est pas justifiée par une faute du mandataire ouvre droit au profit de ce dernier, nonobstant toute clause contraire, à une indemnité compensatrice du préjudice subi".

[13] Arrêté of 19.6.1959.

[14] Georges Edeline, "La representation commerciale" in *La vie moderne et le droit* (Etudes et Editions Juride'ques et Sociales: "EJUS").

See also, *op. cit.* n.4, Pts 1230 No. 49 et seq and No. 1240 and G. Cas, D. Ferrier, R. Bout, *Droit Economique Concurrence Distribution Consommation*, No. 3111 et seq (Editions Lamy SA).

[15] B. Mercadal, Ph. Jarin, *Les accords de coopérations inter entreprises* (Editions juridiques Lefevre).

[16] Cass. Com. 17.2.1987 JCP (E) 1987 no. 16297. Cass. Com. 11.12.1973 Bull. Civ. IV 319.

[17] Cass. Com. 16.7.1982—JCP no. 1984 II 20286. Cass. Soc. 9.5.1979 Bul. Civ. V 286.

[18] CA Nancy 6.4.1987 Doc. Jurisdata Doc. 041416. CA Poitiers 16.7.1987 Doc. Jurisdata no. 044965.

[19] Directive Communautaire of 18.12.1986 no. 86/653/CEE. Art. 13.

[20] Decree of 1958. Art. 1 alinéa 2 and Arreté of 22.8.1968, Art. 3A 3.

the rate of commission due to the agent. This specification is essential for the validity of the contract.

Article 4–7 of the Decree of 23 December 1958[21] forecasts that the agent has to register himself on the special agent register, kept at the Record Office by the commercial court or county court, in the judicial areas of the district in which the agent is resident. This registration is done by furnishing the written commercial contract, in French. Foreign agents need a foreign trading licence[22], even if the agent is not a merchant.

This register declaration must be accompanied by a copy of identification papers, an official report or request of affiliation to an old-age no wage insurance among others. . . Societies must also give up a certificate from the commercial register and a copy of identification papers concerning for example, the responsibilities.[23]

When all the formalities have been completed, the clerk of the court delivers to the agent a receipt of declaration including the register number. This number and the register must be listed[24] on all professional documents and letters belonging to the agent. This duty is sanctioned from a penal point of view.[25]

The registering formalities must be done before the agent begins his activity. Registering is valid for 5 years[26] and must be renewed after that time. Any changes in the new registration must be declared to the clerk of the court.[27]

Finally, the agent will be taken off the register in the two months following the end of his contract. In the case fault or of the agent's death he will be taken off the register automatically according to normal legal conditions.[28]

All these agents duties are sanctioned from a penal point of view, consisting of fine or imprisonment.[29] It should be noticed that the civil sanction of failing to register deprives the agent of the benefit of the status of a commercial agent. But the mere fact of registering will not confer this status if the basic conditions concerning his activity are not complied with.[30]

1.3. The Principal's Duties and Rights

1.3.1. The principal's duties

1.3.1.1. Commission

The principal has to pay the agreed remuneration to the agent for his work.

The remuneration consists generally of a percentage amount computed on the accepted orders and not a fixed lump sum. If the remuneration is not

---

[21] Decree of 1958, Arts. 4 *or* 7.
[22] Arrêté of 22.8.1968, Art. 3A 2.
[23] Cf. Cas *et al op. cit.* n. 14, No. 3114 et seq.
[24] Decree of 1958, Art. 10.
[25] *Ibid.* Art. 13.
[26] *Ibid.* Art. 5.
[27] *Ibid.* Art. 4 alinéa 4.
[28] *Ibid.* Arts. 7, 8.
[29] *Ibid.* Arts. 11, 12.
[30] Cass. Com. 19.11.1973. Arrêt 702—Pourvoi No. 72–13.282 of 4.8.1972 *in lexis.*

fixed in the contract, it is invalid.[31] The agreed rate can be changed only by a common agreement between the parties, in due form and must be in writing. But the agent's agreement of a lower rate can be considered as an approved modification.[32]

The commission rate fixed by contract cannot be changed by a judge even if the rate seems to be exorbitant, or paltry, or when, in fact, the situation has been changed.

The rate is higher if the agent is engaged either in a *del credere* duty, in an exclusivity or in an activity of deposit or addition to his mandate.

The conditions for payment of the commission are usually provided for in the contract.

Article 1999 al.2 of the French Common Law[33] makes provision for the situation where the mission has failed, despite the fact that the agent has commited no fault: the remuneration is owed to him.

If the contract does not clearly otherwise stipulate, the courts consider that the commission is owed when the principal is irrevocably bound[32] and when the delivery is made in the territory where the agent works, especially in case of exclusivity.

In practice, the contacts often stipulate that the remuneration is owed only if the order has been accepted, delivered, and paid for. It is a question of bringing the business to a successful conclusion.

The contract may provide that the remuneration be paid to the agent even if the order is cancelled for a reason beyond his control or if fulfilling the order becomes impossible through some absolute necessity.

The basis of commission can be either the net or gross amount of the principal's invoice, with some expenses like packing, transport or refund either deducted or not.

Usually, exceptional discounts consented by the principal are excluded from the basis.

Commissions are paid periodically, either monthly or quarterly, in contrast to the simple agent's commissions, which are paid after each operation.

Jurisprudence admits that the principal has to make the agent able to check commissions basis by supplying him with details of the orders.[34]

After the contract has expired, the agent can indisputably claim as a right the commissions issued from previous operations. It can be provided in the contract that commissions issued from operations signed after the end of the contract could be owed to the agent if these operations are the result of his activity or the direct consequence of the making up of samples he made.

The EEC Directive of 18 December 1986[35] provides that in default of written conditions, the remuneration must conform with uses. It points out exhaus-

---

[31] CA Paris 8.2.1984—Gaz. Pal. 84—1 Somm. 1974.

[32] Cass. Soc. 11.2.1944 D.soc. 44-156.

[33] Civil Code, Art. 1999 al 2: "s'il n'y a aucune faute imputable au mandataire, le mandant ne peut se dispenser de faire ces remboursements et paiements, lors même que l'affaire n'aurait pas réussi, ni fait réduire le montant des frais et avances sous le prétexte qu'ils pouvaient être moindres".

[34] Cass. Com. 4.11.1980 JCP CI—1984—no. 9409.

[35] Directive Communautaire of 18.12.1986 No. 86/653 CEE, Arts. 6-12.

tively cases in which the agent can claim commissions during the contract and afterwards as well. It also provides the conditions of commission sharing. It fixes beyond their date of payment as well as the documents the principal has to furnish in support.

The commissions which the agent may claim usually constitute his whole remuneration[36], for acting as an independant professional, he has with expenses in the execution of his duties: for example transport, insurance, social contributions, taxes, staff and so on.

Exceptionally, the contract may define the cost sharing between the principal and the agent.

1.3.1.2. Protection of agent, information

To protect the agent, three main duties devolve to the principal:

First, he has to act upon the orders of the agent.

Article 1998 of the Common Law[37] fixes the conditions in which the principal has to execute the duties undertaken by the agent. Obviously, the principal is only responsible within the limits of the power he gave the agent.

The principal has a general obligation to execute the duties undertaken by the agent. This obligation is particularly difficult to determine when the agent only has an obligation to negotiate and not to conclude operations. The principal can only dismiss orders sent by the agent for objective reasons like insolvency of the client.

The principal must also respect his duty to confer exclusivity. This protection means that, unless otherwise stipulated, neither the principal nor a third party may canvas the clientele in the agent's area, and must agree to pay him a remuneration based on every operation concluded in this area, directly or not.

So, the exclusivity clause protects both the activity and the remuneration of the agent. The courts can infer the existence of an exclusivity clause from circumstances of the case or from the interpretation of the contract.

When the principal transgresses the exclusive rights of the agent, he is responsible for the cancelling of the contract, and will be paid a compensation for abusive breaking.

The principal must give the agent all necessary information for order taking or negotiation. He must also make the agent's activity easier by supplying him with all necessary information for concluding a contract: such as the salient points about quality, quantity, services, available stocks, delay of delivery, after-sales services, etc.

The principal must also supply the agent with samples, up-to-date techniques and advertising documents.

This last obligation is mentioned in Artical 4.2. of the Directive of 18 December 1986.

In addition, the principal may be obliged to fulfil other obligations according to particular conditions of agency contract. Thus he will have to furnish the necessary stock, in case of agreement or consignment.

[36] Cass. Soc. 19.1.1961—D61 page 238.
[37] Civil Code. Art. 1998.

1.3.1.3. Supply of written statement
Cf.1.2.

1.3.2. The principal's rights

The principal may demand periodic accounts on the agent's activity without threatening his independence, nor imposing directives about his use of time nor his method of canvasing.

In this regard, the principal's rights are generally less than those which a principal holds over a simple agent, who has to give an account of his stewardship[38]. They are also less than the rights allowed to an employer over a wage-earning agent who has generally to make a precise report about his activity.

The principal can meanwhile ask the commercial agent to give information about the situation of the market, the response of the clientele, the difficulties faced during the execution of his activity, about the state or the evolution of competition.

The principal can also ask the commercial agent to interpose amicably in order to recover unpaid sums or to send him the information about a client's financial situation.

Finally, the principal is allowed to insist on the genuine execution of the contract by the agent, in pursuance of the fundamental principle according to which contracts must be executed in good faith.[39]

1.4. The Commercial Agent's Duties and Rights

1.4.1. The commercial agent's duties

1.4.1.1. Trustworthiness, duty to inform

The agent commits himself to use his best efforts in order to conclude or negotiate operations on behalf and in the name of the principal.

In this aim, the agent faces four duties:

(1) He has to find clients for the operations required by the principal. Unless he has special instructions, he settles freely the clientele but cannot buy himself the goods sold. He must make the buyer know his qualification. As he is the intermediary between the customers and the principal, he both has to render an account to the principal and to transmit orders received from the clients.

(2) The agent negotiates with clients, advising them of the clauses governing sales which have been given to him by the principal. Exceptionally, he will be allowed to deal under other conditions, especially in the matter of prices, discounts, terms of payment into limits previously fixed by the principal.

(3) Sometimes, the agent can conclude contracts and in this case he has to supply the accounts of his mission to the principal. Exceptionally, the agents may be able to draft invoices and pay cheques in on behalf and for the principal's account.

[38] *Ibid.* Art. 1993.
[39] *Ibid.* Art. 1134 al 3.

(4) After the sale, the agent may be entrusted with a technical and commercial aid obligation.

Directive Article 3 provides that the commercial agent acts fairly and sincerely, and defines the agent's duties.

1.4.1.2. Del credere

Article 1 al.4 of the 1958 Decree[40]: the commercial agency contract shall not involve a *del credere* convention.

This particular agent's engagement must result from a explicit written clause of the contract or of an endorsement, subsidiarily in unambiguous letters passed between the two parties. As a matter of fact, the rules of evidence concerning the commercial agent are French common law ones, which require the production of a written document by the principal who avails himself of a *del credere* engagement, as soon as the value is higher than FRF 5000.

It is different when the commercial agent is a tradesman or a commercial society:[41] these rules, by contast, being free.

The *del credere* engagement makes the commercial agent answerable to the principal for the execution of contracts concluded on his behalf. Thus, he is obliged to pay for the goods or services on behalf of a debtor. He will bear the cost of the procedure against the client and the interest resulting from the payment at maturity of the amounts due to the principal.[42]

He bears the risk of non-execution of contract owing to circumstances outside his control[43], but not non-execution owing to any fault of the principal. He also bears the risk if contract is cancelled because of a latent defect, or because of a case of clearing agreement of debts between the principal and the client.

Without being *del credere*, the commercial agent's responsibility towards the principal shall be binding if he concluded a contract without due consideration, even though a client's insolvency was obvious or could be easily detected.

Exceptionally, the agent may be *del credere* of the duties of delivery or service execution due by the principal towards his clients.

The *del credere* engagement can be limited or not in his quantum. When it is limited, it is generally equal to the agent's commissions or to the businesses or the clients.

Consequently the rate of commissions in a *del credere* engagement, are higher than commissions paid to an ordinary agent. Indeed, the rate can be doubled.

Furthermore, the remuneration is due at the conclusion of the contract between the principal and the client and not when the engagement has been successfully completed.

If the *del credere* obligation is limited to an amount equal to the commission,

---

[40] See n. 1 above.
[41] Civil Code, Art. 109.
[42] Cass. Com. 6.1.1981 Bul. Civ. IV no. 4.
[43] Cass. Req. 6.3.1935 S. 1935—1—210.

the date of payment is delayed until payment has been received from the client.

The Directive of 18 December 86 does not govern any *del credere* obligation.

1.4.1.3. Non-competition

Article 2 al.1 of the Decree of December 58 stipulates that the agent is allowed to accept other mandates without referring to his principal. But he is not authorized to be a representative of a competitive company of his principal without his agreement.

The notion of "competitive company" is explained with restriction by the courts. Similar products with similar uses and characteristics as the principal's products are considered to be competitive.[44]

Article 2 a1.2 stipulates that the agent is authorized to perform commercial operations on his own. So, is he allowed to engage in any activity which could compete with his principal? The answer must be negative, unless there is a written agreement to the contrary from the principal or unless the principal knew of the competitive activity before the conclusion of the contract. In this last case proof of the tacit consent would be required.

The obligation of no competition is an obligation of good faith towards the principal[45]. It's violation is sanctioned by cancellation of the contract through fault of the agent, without indemnity. The agent may not be blamed if the principal changes his range of products and this interferes with the products already represented by the agent.

The commercial agent's contract stipulates that the agent is authorized to represent a competitive company after agreement with the principal or obliges the agent to submit all new contracts to him before signature. This clause makes the principal judge the kind of company which would be a competitive one.

At the termination of the contract, a special and clear stipulation may oblige the agent to respect no competition clause. This clause must be limited to the nature of the prohibited activity and the term and territory.

The directive of 18 December 86 regulates only the validity of conditions of a clause of no competition at the termination of the contract. Article 20 stipulates that this clause must be written and relate a geographic area and/or agent's clientele and the kind of products which he represented. The term of this clause cannot go beyond two years after the end of the contract.

1.4.1.4. Secrecy

Authors don't consider this matter which is not specific to commercial agent's settlement. But the agent is certainly obliged to respect a duty of secrecy because, since acting on behalf and in name of the principal, he owes him a loyal collaboration.[46] The secrecy duty figures in all obligations of the agent stipulated in the official model of contract written by the professionals.

Generally these clauses stipulate that during and after the contract the

---

[44] Cass. Com. 20.3.1966—Bul. Civ. III no. 180.
[45] Ripert, Roblot, *Traité de droit commercial*, Vol. 2, No. 2625 (Editions LGDJ 1986).
[46] J. P. Casinur, A. Couret, *Droit des affaires*, No. 853 (Editions Sirey, 1987).

agent must keep confidential all technical and commercial information which he knew about the principal, his products or services during the execution of the contract.

This obligation is not limited in time and devolves also on the wage earner or under agents of the agent.

The case of no explicit clause of secrecy, the courts sanctioned the disclosures on the base of common law of civil responsibility[47] and specially upon unloyal competition towards the principal[48]. Courts also consider that the only real risk involving the agent releasing information would be where a bond with a third competitor proves the loss of trust in the agent and so permits cancellation of the contract, without indemnity, in the face of the wrong-doing of the agent.

The directive of 18 December 86 does not clearly stipulate an obligation of secrecy. Nevertheless it results from Article 3rd al.1 which states that the agent has, during the contract execution, to watch over principal's interests and to act loyally and sincerely. The validity of this legal engagement is limited during contracts period.

After the end of the contract, only the swindling and unloyal working may be sanctioned by the common law of responsibility.

1.4.2. The commercial agent's rights

1.4.2.1. Commission

The agent has the right to receive the agreed remuneration as explained in section 1.3.1.1. above. In fact, the commercial agent exercises his activity as a professional and so must be paid.

This situation is very different from an ordinary agent[49] whose intervention is generally ponctual and free.

Fixing the rate of commissions in relation to the turnover by the principal is an important element of the commercial agent's contract. If the rate or a part of it is fixed by only one of both parties, the contract should be annulled.[50]

The commission must also apply to operations which are not originally foreseen in the contract, for example, in a new geographic area, or with a new kind of clientele. In this event, a written statement enables the agreement of both parties to extend the initial mandate.

If the principal does not pay the commission due to the agent, the contract would be cancelled because of the wrong of the principal.[51]

1.5. Liabilities of Principal and Agent during the Term of the Agency

---

[47] Civil Code, Arts. 1382, 1383.
[48] CA Poitiers 16.7.1987 Jurisdata no. 044965. CA Versailles 12ème Chambre 1.7.1987 Jurisdata no. 044873.
[49] Civil Code, Art. 1986.
[50] CA Paris 4ème Chambre 8.2.1984—Gaz. Pal. 1 Somm. p. 174.
[51] Cass. Com. 1.12.1981 Bull. Com. 1981 IV 333.

1.5.1. The principal as against the agent

The principal involves his liability if he does not execute his engagements towards the agent.

The directive of 18 December 86 includes several obligations which fall on the principal (Article 12 and 4 al.3).

1.5.2. The principal as against third parties

The engagements signed by the agent in the scope of his mission bind the principal with regard to third parties, because the agent acts on his behalf and in his name.

In the same way, the principal is engaged by the consequences of the signed act. He is supposed to have received payment if the agent has received payment. He must take over all objections and claims received by the agent.

The principal's liability is not engaged if the agent has exceeded given orders or if he perpetrates misdemeanours. However, the client could assert the benefit of the apparent mandate if the agent gets the disputed powers after a long time or if those powers belong usually to a commercial agent.

A third party does not know the real powers described in the contract because of the theory of the relativity of contracts.[52]

So the principal can be engaged by contracts signed by the agent after the end of the contract if the third party does not know this development.

1.5.3. The agent as against the principal

The agent's contractual liability arises from non fulfilment or an insufficient execution of his engagements. The commercial agent is liable for willful lacks and negligence.[53] For example, in case of lessening of profitability due to shirking his obligations.

The agent can see his penalty liability engaged for breach of trust[54] or false pretences[55] because of misappropriation of goods, or money which he was supposed to transmit. The burden of proof rests with the principal.

In the case of a reduction in profitability, the principal must prove that the turnover of operations handled by the agent was also reduced.

The agent should prove there is no link between his attitude and the reduction of turnover.[56] The agent's liability can be increased if he is *del credere*: in this case he will be guilty of theft.[57]

His liability can have two consequences:

- it can justify termination of the contract and deprive the agent of the profit of any indemnity provided by Law (Article 3rd-1-from Decree L.7.);

[52] Civil Code, Art. 1165.
[53] CA Dijon 9.9.1987 Jurisdata no. 044571.
[54] Penal Code, Art. 408.
[55] *Ibid.* Art. 405.
[56] Cass. Com. 9.2.1982 Gaz. Pal. 1982 2 panor, p. 278.
[57] CA Versailles 13ème Chambre 30.9.1987 Doc Jurisdata no. 043748.

- the principal can claim damages.

The agent's faults are considered with harshness because he is a professional from whom the principal can expect professional competency and consciousness.

1.5.4. The agent as against third parties

The agent is not part of the operation signed between the principal and the client.

In consequence, he is not liable for the execution of the orders of the principal's insolvency or failure or for his non respect of regulations concerning the products or for fraud. Some exceptions have to be opposed to this principle when the agent's liabilily could be invoked:

- In a case of complicity with the principal or as main author of any misdemeanour,
- When the agent is *del credere* of the principal's engagements towards the clients or the suppliers,
- In a case of negligence or voluntary fault of the agent during his canvassing activity; for example, if he engages in unfair competition, or if he commits a fraud[58], or if he instigates a mistake which causes the annulment of the sale contract[59],
- In case of precontractual faults, such as if concluding the contract becomes impossible and this causes damage to the client.

1.6. Term and Termination

1.6.1. Term

The contract term may be fixed or unfixed (Article 1 al.3) [60]. The difference between the two solutions primarily concerns the allowance of damages which will be studied in section 1.7. A term may not be too short because commercial agency is a regular profession. The term must be about one year minimal.

The contract may provide that the first term would be renewed by tacit agreement for the same or a different period, which must be stated, but each party may cancel before every new term. This party must inform the other one of his decision within the notice stipulated in the contract, or within reasonable notice.

Parties can also be bound by a contract with a fixed term without tacit renewal, so that they can sign a new contract at the end of the first one.

The EEC Directive provides in Article 14 that a contract with fixed term which is continued after it's termination is considered as changed to a contract with an unfixed term.

This solution, in favour of the agent, will be the same as the one a wage

---

[58] Cass Com. 4.6.1971 Arrêt no. 369. Pourvoi 70–12.322 of 22.6.1970 *in lexis*.
[59] Civil Code, Art. 1109.
[60] See n. 1 above.

earner will profit by[61], in French law. The French solution will change when the Directive comes into force. Until then, a contract will be renewed for successive terms without changing the determined nature of the contract[62]. When the contract is concluded for an unfixed term, it generally stipulates the conditions and notice with respect for cancelling at any time.

Failing this, the notice to respect may be about 3 or 6 months to prevent cancellation being considered too fast which might justify an allowance of damages.

The EEC Directive regulates expressly the commercial agency with fixed term and the notice, which depends on the term of the contract.

1.6.2. Termination

The end of the contract may result from many causes coming from either one or both parties, or from the *intuitu personae* nature of the contract.

The contract is signed in consideration of the person of the principal or of the agent, i.e. the physical person or the managers of the firm;[63] this circumstance is presumed by courts, even if the contract does not specify anything[64] about the agent who is a physical person. It will be the same when the agent is a moral person only in the case where the manager by reference to whom the contract has been concluded is specified by name in the contract. Concurrently, the same situation can be found concerning the principal.

So, the contract ends by the agent's death if he is a physical person, without the possibility for his rightful owners to claim any compensation.[65] When the manager of the commercial agency dies, without being specified by name in the contract, the agency contract goes on with the successors.[66] The parties may forecast that with the occurrence of death the contract will be transmitted either to the heirs, or to a successor introduced by them.

In these last assumptions, if the principal still refuses to go through with the contract, he will have to pay the heirs compensation in cash. The transmission of the contract to the heirs can be deducted from the fact that the contract goes through with them, even in absence of a precise clause.

- The same rules must be observed in case of permanent disability of the agent.
- Cancelling the contract may result from the incapacity of one of the parties by application of the law about the stabilization of commercial professions.[67]

So is it when the agent or the principal is guilty of, for example, a crime, theft, swindling, breach of trust, receiving and concealing stolen goods for example according to the conditions defined by law.

---

[61] Cass. Soc. 23.10.1974 JCP 75 II 18082.
[62] Cass. Civ. 24.4.1974 DS 75-764.
[63] Civil Code, Art. 2003.
[64] Cass. Com. 20.4.1967 JCP 68 II 15389.
[65] CA Paris 5ème Chambre 13.6.1984 Jurisdata no. 022938.
[66] CA Amiens 15.12.1960 Gaz. Pal. 61-1.98.
[67] See n. 5, above.

Article 2003 al.4 "Code Civil"; the legal incapacity of one of the parties could also terminate the agency contract.

According to the same article, failure of one party would also cause breach of contract.

Nevertheless, Article 37 of the law of 25 January 85, in order to safeguard the interests of both debtor and his creditors, forbids automatic breach of contract.

The contract terminates at the term or with the agreement of both parties.

- This is so in the case of a non renewal of a fixed-term contract. The lower jurisdictions[68] according to some authors,[69] consider that a sequence of short periods confer to the contract an undetermined term, because its aim is to divert the provisions of the Article 3rd al.2 of the Decree of 1958.[70] The agent has to prove the fraud to obtain his indemnity.
- A breach can occur by common agreement between both parties, without indemnity.
- The agent can give up the contract with the principal's agreement, because of the *intuitu personae* nature of the contract. When the right to give the contract up is provided in its clauses, the price and conditions must be determined or determinable objectively in the contract; they must not depend on the will of one party or go back to an ulterior agreement.[71]
- Breach can result from cancelling a contract of unfixed period by one of the parties. Those in breach must respect the notice and the payment of indemnity to the agent to offsetting his loss of rights, when breach is due to the principal.

The same conditions could apply to the agent who must respect the contractual period or reasonable notice. The principal could only claim for indemnity if he proves the agent's faults and his damage.

A Contract could end for circumstances outside one's control.

The reorganization of the principal's firm can lead to a break of contract if it does not reveal the will to divert the law in the aim to avoid the payment of any indemnity. Each reorganization of the principal's firm gives the agent a right to an indemnity if his clientele is continued to be exploited by the principal.

On the other hand, the termination of the concerned activity, branch or the stoppage of commercialization of the products of the contract, will justify a lawful cause of breaking, without indemnity.

Finally, the contract could be cancelled by one party because of the failings of the other.

The EEC Directive reserves the right of each Member State about causes for termination of contract. It only provides two special cases of termination with notice:

---

[68] Trib. Com. Paris 1ère Chambre 17.5.1976 in "L'agent commercial" Mardi, April 1977, p. 11.
[69] Cantoni, "Les contrats d'agence à durée déterminée" in *L'agent commercial*, May, June 1975, p. 67 and 135.
[70] See n. 12, above.
[71] CA Paris 5ème Chambre 28.1.1982 Gaz. Pal. 1982 1 Somm. p. 107.

non-fulfilment by one party of his engagements
unexpected occurrence of "exceptional circumstances".

1.7. Indemnity

1.7.1. Indemnity for goodwill and for clientèle

Contrary to the wage earner intermediary, as the V.R.P., it is generally acknowledged that the commercial agent cannot claim an indemnity for clientele – *sticto sensu*.

In fact, the clientele he canvasses in respect of his contract, belong to the principal. Several authors attribute the statutory commercial agent with a patrimonial right for the clientele.[72]

In these conditions the agent does not make a profit from an indemnity in any case of breach of contract. The grounds for breach without indemnity are essentially the following:

- the non-renewal of a contract of fixed duration.[73]
- the death of the agent or of the principal, if he is a physical person, or the winding up of a company if the contract does not provide the transferable nature of the contract.[74]
- deed of assignment of the contract or of the goodwill of the agent with the principals agreement.[75]
- deprivation of rights, incapacity or failure of one of the parties (cf § 1.6.2.).
  Nevertheless, it must be noted that an indemnity could be due to the agent, if the failure trustee of the principal has continued the contract before terminating it.
- reorganization of the principal's company with suppression of the agent's activity.
- termination by the agent.
- termination following mistakes by the agent. Jurisprudence seems only to retain those faults of a certain importance or of repeated negligence. However, as already indicated, the agent being a professional, his short-comings will be severely assessed.

So it is in the case of infringement of an exclusive clause, lack of honesty, in case of misdemeanour, negligence in canvass of clientele, non-respect of sale conditions.

The decline of business, or the non respect of quotas do not by themselves prove the fault of the agent. The principal must prove agent's failings.[76] Likewise judges check that the agents fault is not the consequence of a fault by the principal himself.

Article 3rd al.2 of the Decree of 1958 stipulates that the termination of the

---

[72] Yves Reinhard, *Droit commercial*, No. 238 et seq (Editions Litec, 1987).
[73] Cass. Com. 17.11.1980 Bul. Civ. IV 303.
[74] See n. 64, above.
[75] Cass. Com. 4.11.1980 Bull. Civ. IV 292.
[76] See n. 56 above.

contract gives the agent a right to an indemnity to compensate prejudice against him, when the termination is not due to his fault.

The termination must be a matter for the principal during a contract of fixed or unfixed duration before the end of such contract.

An unilateral alteration of the contract made by the principal may be assimilated to a breach of the contract. For example, in case of modification of the commissions,[77] or of the activity area. When a clause forecasts the possibility of a transfer of the contract, the principal can refuse the proposed successor with an objective reason or he has to pay an indemnity. In the same way, the principal cannot refuse each successor proposed by the agent without good reasons. The amount of indemnity can be fixed in the contract or by the courts.

Any clause by which the agent would renounce to claim an indemnity is null and void. The same solution would be given to a clause which fixed contractually the amount. The only admissible clause is the one which provides the method of calculation of the indemnity, for example double the average value of commissions remit during the last three years.[78]

This clause is a penalty clause.[79] In consequence, courts can reduce it, if it seems to be manifestly too high, or can increase it if it seems to be too low.

In the asbence of the contractual clause, lower jurisdictions have to supremely assess the indemnity amount,[80] by taking into account these indications:

- the duration of the contract,
- the loss of commissions, especially until the end of the determined contract,
- the loss or decrease of the profits that the agent could hope to gain from his investments,
- the expenses caused by breach of contract,
- the disbanding indemnity of wage earners,
- the costs of adaptation and reconversion of the commercial agency,
- the costs of a depot which is no longer in use,
- etc.

Courts generally work out this amount from two years of commission,[81] but this is not an absolute rule.

The EEC Directive of 18 December 1986 provides in its article 17.2 the conditions for granting indemnity:

- in case the agent has brought new clients
- if the indemnity appears just with regard to circumstances.

These two alternative criterions regulate the whole French law concerning commercial agent and labour law and especially the V.R.P., whether the term of the contract is determined or not.

---

[77] Cass. Com. 16.7.1982 Gaz. Pal. 1982—2—panor 361.
[78] CA Bordeaux 12.2.1969 Gaz. Pal. 1969—2—288.
[79] CA Aix en Provence: 2.5.1975 et CA Paris 6.11.1975—D S 1976, p. 344.
[80] Cass. Com. 10 mai 1977 JCP 1979 II 19048.
[81] See n. 79, above.

Article 17.2.b establishes the amount of indemnity on the yearly average of the agents remuneration during the last five years or on the average of the period if the contract has been executed for less than five years.

1.7.2. Compensation for damages

The circumstances of termination can lead to a conviction to pay damages to the agent. So it is, in case of sudden breach, with or without insufficient notice, insulting notice or in case of breach because of swindling or unfair proceedings such as disparagement.

It often happens that courts allow a single indemnity including compensation for damages and indemnity.

The European Directive completes the indemnity due to the agent with damages (Article 17 al.3) in order to compensate the damage suffered because of termination of the contract.

These damages cover the prejudice redressed by the indemnity under French law (cf § 1.7.1.) than the compensation of a prejudice as understood by French courts (cf § 1.7.2.).

Article 17.3 enacts the following cause of damages:

- the fact for the agent to be deprived of commissions even when the principal gets substantial monetary gain from agent's activity.

The directive provides (Article 17.al 4) that the agent's right about indemnity and damages is acquired in case of death. This solution is new in French law. The official regulations of Article 17.5 of the European Directive obliges the agent to notify his right to indemnity within one year after the end of the contract.

The prescription conditions of the law suit is not governed by the Directive. Nevertheless, the conditions stipulated in Article 17.5 are more restrictive that the French law prescription which is about 10[82] or 30 years.[83]

1.8. Specific Application of EEC-law

- The European Directive has not yet been introduced into French law because its provisions will be included in French law up to January 1990 at least.
- Commercial agency is not liable to the provisions of Article 85 and 86 of the EEC treaty.

It has been asserted that the registering obligation of commercial agents would have the effect of preventing the agent resident out of France to benefit from the statute.

Such circumstances would constitute a restriction of freedom of establishment (Article 59 and 60 EEC Treaty).

In consequence, a break without wants of such a contract should allow the agent to claim the legal indemnity. This solution has not been adopted by the High Court.[84]

[82] Cass. Com. 24.6.1986—Inédit—Pourvoi no. 84—16.993.
[83] Civil Code. Art. 2262.
[84] Cass. Com. 21.3.1983. Pourvoi no. 81–10-869—Rejet *in lexis*.

1.8.1. Jurisdiction and Law

1.8.2.1. Applicable law

As for any contract, the applicable law is the one choosen by the parties.[85]

In the absence of choice, the court will check the will of the parties by usual criterions of attachment: execution place of the contract, settlement place, language, currency etc.

In the absence of lack of elements, the applicable law will be the one of the residence of the agent or of his main firm in the country in which he exercizes his activity. If the agent acts especially in the country in which the principal has his main firm, the law of this country will be applicable.[86]

1.8.2.2. Competent jurisdiction

The *ratione materiae* jurisdiction competency depends on the nature of the contract.

The commercial agent is not a merchant[87] and jurisdictions and the High Court consider that the contract is civil and not commercial.[88]

So, only the "Tribunaux de Grande Instance" (T.G.I.) will be competent, but not the commercial or labour courts, concerning trials between the principal and the commercial agent.

When the commercial agent is a commercial company, the commercial court will by exception be competent.

If the agent brings an action against the principal, he can choose the court: the civil (T.G.I.) or the commercial one.

The predicative competence clause—*ratione loci*, is only valid between two merchants. In consequence, it cannot be opposed to the commercial agent who is not a commercial person.

Artical 46 of the New Civil Process Code (N.C.P.C.) determines the competent court, and it is in contractual matter: the place where the defendant is domicilied or the place where the contract has been executed.

2. Distributorship Agreements

2.1. Distribution

While distribution has taken on various legal guises over the last few years, like franchising (see 3.1) it is no less true that the accepted conception of distribution in France is a commercial distributorship.

The distributor's agreement in fact originated at the beginning of the 20th

---

[85] Law 85-8 of 2.1.1985, OJ 3.1.1985, "approuvant la Convention de LA Haye du 14.3.1978 sur la loi applicable aux contrats d'intermédiaire et à la représentation." DPCI 1981, Vol. 7 no. 3-387.
[86] Brussels Convention of 27.9.1968, Art. 5, 1 and see n. 82, above.
[87] Ripert, Roblot, *Traité étémentaire de droit commerical*, Vol. 2, 10th edn. no. 2620 (LGDJ, 1986). Yves Guyon, *Droit des affaires*, Vol. 1, *Droit commercial général et des sociétés*, 4th edn. no. 811 et seq (Economica, 1986).
[88] Civil Code, Art. 1984. Cass. Civ. 19.10.1979 JCP 81 Ed. G II 19591. Cass. Civ. 28.10.1980 DS 1981 IR 196).

Century in monopoly selling, the commercial concept appeared in its present form on the eve of the second world war at a time when trade structures were beginning to undergo substantial changes, they made way for the setting up of a new type of relationship between manufacturer and trader.

A distributorship is of little interest in distributing high volume consumer products, which do not require a professional attitude nor special technical skills of the distributor, and the marketing of which requires neither a technical installation, after sales service nor guarantee.

It is on the other hand particularly well suited to the sale of durable consumer goods and in particular branded products, which have to be marketed by salesmen with professional aptitude suited to the nature and character of the product and the requirements of the customers who buy them.

The exclusive distributorship first appeared in the car industry.

It was then extended to agricultural machinery, household electricals, televisions, furniture, clocks, photographic equipment, beauty products and computer equipment.

Acting in his own name and on his own behalf, buying his products from the supplier to sell on to his own customers, the distributor must be distinguished from other trade and industry intermediaries.

He is different from the commercial agent (1.1 and following) who is an agent selling products for and on behalf of a principal who remains the owner of the products the agent sells.

The distributor is also different from a commission agent who also sells under his own name but does so on behalf of a principal from whom he does not buy the goods.

The Court of Cassation however decided that a distributor could be in a similar situation to that of a commission agent whenever he undertakes to centralise orders and forward delivery orders or goods to the supplier who then delivers direct to the customer.

An exclusive distributor is also different from an approved distributor, in fact, approved distribution, called "agreation" or "habilitation" or even selective distribution, constitutes a kind of acknowledgement of technical skills which the manufacturer gives to certain selling agents who become preferred distributors, in preference to others.

However, such acknowledgement of skills does not under any circumstances confer a sales monopoly on the approved distributor, nor the allocation of a specific territory, as does an exclusive distributorship.

An exclusive distributorship is also different from a brand licence, in fact, the distributor has no rights to the brand name, the supplier remains the owner and does not transfer his patent rights to his distributor. A distinction should also be made, particularly with regard to competition law, between a commercial distributorship, which covers exclusive selling rights, and a manufacturing concession which is based on exploiting technical processes, licences, patents or trademarks.

2.1.1. Definition

An exclusive distributor's agreement is an agreement by which the supplier sells products exclusively to a distributor in his network. The distributor—a legally independent trader—sells to his own customers in a given territory, products which he undertakes to buy exclusively from his supplier.

It is interesting to note at this stage that the choice of the word distributorship ["un concession"] comes from an analogy with public law describing a trading monopoly in a public service by which the State, the holder of the monopoly, handed over the provision of services or rights to a private individual in exchange for a royalty and obligations set down in what was called a specification. There is therefore a similarity of objectives between a private law commercial distributorship and a public service distributorship.

In both cases, a privilege, or even a monopoly, is granted to a Company.

French internal law does not specifically regulate an exclusive distributor's agreement.

However, ministerial answers to two written questions put by members of parliament show that this legislative gap will perhaps soon be filled (legislation regulating this type of agreement can therefore be expected).

2.1.1.1. Exclusive/Non-exclusive/exclusive purchasing

An exclusive distributor's agreement of necessity contains a territory clause by which the supplier grants the distributor a monopoly to sell his products in a specific geographic area.

The effect of this clause is to protect the territory of the distributor who is the sole trader to be supplied by the supplier in that area.

The supplier undertakes in fact not to sell his products to another trader in the distributor's area.

This network may be large or small, a "department", a commune, a district, sometimes even a single shopping centre.

The size of the area will depend in fact on the nature of the products concerned.

2.1.2. Conclusion of the contract (special conditions)

A distributor's agreement is a concensual contract which consists of an exchange of will of the parties, provided this has been freely expressed.

This rule is a pure and simple application of Article 1134 of the Civil Code . . . "freely formulated agreements have the effect of law on those who made them".

A distributor's agreement does not have to be in any particular legal form, it may be verbal but in practice it is nearly always drawn up as a privately executed instrument (document) designed to provide proof of the agreements concluded between the supplier and the distributor, although a document is the most common form for this type of contract, it is no less true that for the supplier and distributor alike, an exclusive distributorship is a business document which can be proved by any means.

In spite of whatever legal definition the parties may give to the contract, the Judges have sole jurisdiction to interpret the will of the contracting parties and decide on the legal definition given to the contract and to the legal position of the parties.

The Judges for example analyse the various clauses of a contract to make a distinction between a distributor and an agent.

2.1.3. The supplier's duties and rights

Exclusive sale to the distributor

The territory clause in an exclusive distributor's agreement allows the distributor to enjoy a monopoly on selling the supplier's products, the supplier undertaking to sell his products only to the distributor within that territory.

He cannot sell the product to a customer of the distributor either directly or through a distributor in another sales territory.

In this respect, all persons domiciled in the territory are deemed to be customers of the distributor.

However, if an order is sent direct to the supplier by a customer, he may fill the order but on behalf of the distributor. He becomes in some way the distributor's agent and must pay him the full value of the sale.

The products included in the exclusive distributorship must be strictly defined.

Furthermore, any supplier who refuses to give the distributor a list of the customers in his area so as not to reveal sales made through other traders, will be guilty of complicity in the act of unfair competition thus committed against the latter.

He becomes jointly and severally liable for the loss resulting from his deeds. The supplier is not liable on the other hand if deliveries were made after the expiry of the distributor's agreement.

Guarantee of supply

The supplier undertakes to regularly supply the granted products which the distributor orders from him on specific terms and at a specific price.

Any supplier who refuses to fill orders placed by the distributor within the quotas or only partly fills them or fills them late, without good reason, shall be contractually liable to the latter.

This would not be the case if such refusal to supply were justified by the distributor's failings. Such guarantee of supply extends to spare parts.

Supply of advertising material

The majority of distributor's agreements stipulate that the supplier shall supply substantial advertising material: signs, posters, signboards, literature, special offers etc. . .

Sometimes parts of the decorations of the distributor's premises are paid for by the supplier (shop front, painting, window etc. . .).

Warranty in respect of manufactuirng defects

As the distributor is a legally independent trader, the owner of the products which he previously bought from his supplier, his customers cannot take action for recision of contract directly against the supplier.

Only the distributor can make a direct claim on his supplier for damages to repair any loss suffered as a result of a redhibitory defect and cancellation of the sale.

However, the supplier may give a personal and direct warranty to the distributor's customers against manufacturing defects.

Nevertheless, the distributor cannot extend the warranty offered by the supplier of his own accord.

Guarantee against loss of value
The supplier's guarantee obligation extends to the partial loss of value of the items held in stock by the distributor as a result of a sudden and unilateral drop in price decided unilaterally by the supplier.

Guarantee of profit margin
In the majority of cases, an exclusive distributor's agreement provides for a selling price for the products as shown in the supplier's catalogue, this is the target price.

In return, the supplier undertakes to guarantee the distributor's profit margin, by a percentage of the catalogue price, which due to its fixed nature is called "commission", although this name is legally inaccurate.

While the supplier can therefore impose a maximum profit margin on his distributor, he cannot on the other hand impose a minimum margin or resale price.

Such a stipulation would in fact come up against legal provisions prohibiting imposed minimum prices.

2.1.4. The distributor's duties and rights

Exclusive purchase from the supplier
In exchange for his monopoly to sell the supplier's products in a given territory, the distributor undertakes not to buy and consequently not to sell similar of competitive products to those manufactured by his supplier.

This is the same as giving him exclusive rights to all the distributor's purchases in respect of a given range of products.

The Court of Cassation in fact overturned an order which upheld an action for unfair competition against a distributor by a supplier, the latter complaining that he had sold competing products while forbidden to do so under the contract.

Court in fact held that: "while the agreements which bound the parties were null and void, there was however a contractual situation of fact between them in the light of which they had arranged their commercial relations".

Basing its decision on the respondent's ignorance of the prohibitions which had been placed on him by a void contract, the Appeal Court did not draw any legal inference from its own findings.

However, the agreement may stipulate that the distributor is allowed to operate a competing distributorship.

The clause is legal but dangerous as it reduces the exclusive nature of the distributorship, the justification of the refusal to sell.

It does not however have this nature if the various distributorships together relate to products manufactured by groups of companies (parent company—subsidiaries) or financially affiliated companies.

Furthermore, the same trader may accumulate distributorships regarding totally different products without any problems.

Compliance with the territory granted

The distributor may not sell the products outside the area which has been allocated to him.

If he did, he would be contractually liable to the supplier and virtually criminally liable vis-a-vis other distributors as his behaviour would constitute unfair competition.

However, it may be stipulated that sales are possible outside the area either to customers from an unassigned area or the customers of another distributor provided that such sale is assigned to such other distributor. In which case, the distributor who sold outside his area must be considered as an agent of the distributor for the other area.

He is paid with a proportion of the profit margin set aside for the other distributor.

Quotas

The distributor must comply with the quota clause in the agreement which represents a quantity of products he undertakes to buy from the supplier and consequently sell to his customers over a given period.

Such quotas are given in an estimated statement prepared by the supplier in order to fix his production levels and prices.

They are also fixed in accordance with the investments already made and those to be undertaken, in the light of known and potential demand.

Quotas are most commonly fixed for one year, but may be fixed on an overall basis for several years.

They constitute one of the distributor's essential obligations, the non-performance of which will involve termination of the contract, even if such quotas are unusually high, the clauses of the agreement, even though they may be hard on the distributor, are considered as law between the parties.

Stock

The distributor must keep in his shop a predetermined stock of products, samples, spare parts and standard accessories in proportion to the needs of the customers in his area.

Furthermore, in carrying out repairs, he may only use parts sold to him by his supplier.

After-sales service

In most cases, the distributor is obliged to maintain, repair and even replace the equipment sold.

This obligation usually extends to passing customers, in other words customers of distributors other than those they approached for this service.

In such case, the distributor is considered to be carrying out an ancilliary duty to his agency.

Advertising the supplier's products

The interest in a distributor's agreement for the distributor lies in his sales monopoly on known and sought after products. It is therefore normal that he should contribute to distributing his supplier's advertising material.

But frequently the distributor has to organise advertising campaigns at his own expense or share in the expenses of campaigns conducted by the supplier.

Clauses which lay down such obligations must be faithfully executed.

Prices in the eyes of customs

Article 2 of the Decree of 27th February 1961 stipulates that in certain cases, which include distributors with exclusive import rights, the Administration calculates the normal price by seeking to combine the value, services and expenditure assumed by the said distributor in the same way as they would be assumed by a vendor in respect of a sale made to an independent purchaser in the country of import.

This Article lists precisely those services and expenses which exclusive import agreements usually make payable by distributor importers (market research and canvassing, advertising, exhibitions and fairs, warranties).

The Customs Administration tends to consider that the relationship between a supplier and a distributor is similar to that between two integrated companies, and jurisprudence holds that there is no presumption of reality of the price given to the distributor by the supplier and that it is up to the Administration to prove that such price is not the normal price.

While it is established that advertising expenses are fully borne by the exclusive importer distributor, such expenses must wholly or partly be included in the customs value of the imported goods. On the other hand, when it is established that the supplier directly bears part of such advertising costs and that the expenses finally borne by a distributor company do not exceed those which such company must normally pay, advertising expenses do not have to be included in the value to be declared to customs.

Fair Behaviour

The distributor must undertake not to act in any way which might cause the supplier a commercial loss.

Thus he must not abuse his position as distributor to represent himself as an agent acting in the name of the supplier, similarly if storage or agency agreements arise out of the distributor's agreement, the distributor who appropriates any sums or objects coming to the depositor would be committing an act of embezzlement.

Finally, a distributor who denigrates a supplier's methods or products or gives manufacturing secrets to competitors is committing an act of unfair competition.

Protecting the distributor against unfair competition

A trader obtaining products covered by an exclusive agency by indirect methods and selling them is an act of unfair competition.

A former distributor who sells stock which the supplier did not take back at the end of the contract and authorises him so to do is not unfair competition.

The distributor is only protected insofar as the exclusive nature of the contract is still valid.

It is the distributor's duty to prove by any means that the trader accused of unfair competition knew of the exclusive nature of the contract.

Distributor's failure to deliver

A customer of the distributor who has paid all or part of the price has no claim against the supplier if the distributor does not deliver the goods purchased.

He must therefore serve final notice on the distributor to deliver.

Miscellaneous obligations

An exclusive distributor's agreement may contain widely varying obligations incumbent on the distributor. There are usually many. Among the most common, the following may be quoted:

Attendance at exhibitions, obligation to engage qualified staff, keep certain books, carry out improvements, make specific investments, make exclusive use of a given credit institution in respect of credit sales, take back old equipment, apply sales methods laid down by the supplier.

The distributor is also bound to give the supplier certain commercial, economic and accounting information on a regular basis and allow him the right to inspect his business.

The supplier exercises technical control over the facilities and services through inspectors responsible for ensuring that all these directives are adhered to.

The distributor may not use certain practices to increase his volume of sales, in particular selling below the price fixed by the supplier.

If the supplier undertakes to indemnify the distributor in return for the various obligations placed on him, such indemnification is due as soon as the said distributor has complied with the main point of his obligations.

2.1.5. Liabilities of supplier and distributor during the term of the distributorship agreement

2.1.5.1. The supplier as against the distributor

The supplier's violation of any of his obligations towards his distributor makes him contractually liable to the latter who may claim damages.

In the event of serious breach of the contract, the distributor may apply for legal termination of the contractual bonds at the supplier's fault.

By way of example, a breach of contract is the supplier making direct contact with the distributor's customers inside the distributor's area.

The same holds true if the supplier publishes an advertisement in the press with a veiw to replacing him without the distributor's knowledge.

The supplier may be held liable not only for commercial loss (loss of earnings, adverse publicity suffered by the distributor) but he may also be ordered to compensate the latter for any expenses he may have incurred in complying with his obligations (improvements for example).

If the non-performance of supply obligations constitute a serious threat to the distributor, performance in kind may be demanded and the Judge may take all appropriate measures for this to be carried out, in particular by the appointment of an inspector.

Conversely, the supplier is no longer bound to fulfill his obligations if the distributor does not fulfill his own. In which case the contract is suspended and not improperly terminated.

Amendment of the agreement by the supplier

Where an agreement is amended at the supplier's initiative, producing inequality between the parties, and the distributor forced to accept such amendment or be in breach of contract, suffers a loss, the jurisdiction referred to can decide that the latter can claim reparation if the supplier has taken unfair advantage of his economic strength, attacking the special nature of their economic co-operation relationship.

Changes to the supplier's legal position

An exclusive distributorship is not concluded solely in respect of one person.

It therefore survives any transactions which affect the position or legal structure of the parties, the same holds true of a merger.

2.1.5.2. The supplier as against third parties

Although the supplier is not a party to a contract concluded between the distributor and the customer, the supplier may however be liable in certain cases (see guarantee against manufacturing faults).

Thus a car manufacturer who has known of his distributor's insolvency for a long time, is financially liable towards a loan company for the fraudulent acts committed by the distributor, providing such supplier had prerogatives and powers from the contract enabling him to put pressure on his distributor.

However, a supplier who, knowing the distributor's insolvency, withdraws his distributorship, is not bound to advise the latter's customers of the reason for such withdrawal.

The supplier cannot be held liable towards the customer if the contract concluded between the supplier and the distributor does not allow the customer to hold the supplier liable.

2.1.5.3. The distributor as against the supplier

The distributor's liabilities follow the same general principles as the supplier's.

Consequently, the sanctions for non-performance of the distributor's obligations are identical to those for non-performance of the supplier's obligations.

If the distributor's agreement has an avoidance clause, the Judges must apply it as soon as they note the non-performance of the distributor's obligations.

Similarly, irrespective of the reason, the distributor's failure to pay for the goods he has ordered makes him contractually liable and is justification for termination of contract.

Finally, the distributor's repayment or liquidation by Court Order are also reasons for termination usually provided in contracts. Furthermore, as the distributor is a firm buyer and becomes the owner of the goods on delivery by the supplier, the latter cannot make any claim on him in the event of bankruptcy.

This would not be so if a reservation of ownership clause were inserted in the sales agreement.

2.1.5.4. The distributor as against third parties

This liability is no different for distributors not only as regards the supplier's liability towards third parties but also that of any trader dealing with consumers.

2.1.6. Term and termination

A distinction must be made between an exclusive distributor's agreement for a specific term which terminates by reaching the expiry date of the contractual relationship and an exclusive distributors agreement of indeterminate term which, breach of contract aside, can be terminated at any time, even if continued co-operation is envisaged between the distributor and the supplier on the merger of the latter's company with another.

Termination is justified if the period of notice provided in the contract or failing that by the usages of the trade is complied with.

Thus there is no misuse of law provided it is noticed by the Judges pronouncing on the substance that the distributor had known for about ten months that he would cease to be authorised to sell the imported products in France by his supplier or when the supplier/distributor relationship had changed into a manufacture/wholesaler relationship and the distributor had been allowed an adequate period of time to reorganise his business.

Termination is also justified if the supplier breaks the contract due to his distributor's heavily encumbered financial position, the latter no longer offering adequate financial guarantees.

The same holds true in the event of collective action instituted against the distributor after submitting a statement of his affairs or on action by a creditor.

Non compliance with its undertakings by either party also justifies termination.

But failings in the provisions of the contract must be serious and of adequate gravity.

It was thus held that termination is justified in the event of serious and repeated violation of the basic clauses of an exclusive distributorship by either party making the continuance of the contractual bond impossible.

This is the case if the distributor sells competitive equipment or products outside the agreed territory or does not comply with the quota clauses.

The supplier can rightly terminate an exclusive distributor's agreement if the management of the distributor company changes providing a clause in the contract stipulated that it would terminate ipso jure in such circumstances.

Only judicial termination of a current contract can enable the supplier to conclude another contract with another distributor for example, the

Montereau Commercial Court rightly terminated the agreement and found against a distributor who, in exchange for payment of a sum of money in his favour, was to promote the sale of products manufactured by the supplier, the donor of the said sum, and who not only did no work but sold his business to a competitor of his supplier.

It is the duty of the Judge pronouncing on the substance to decide on the nature of the contract between the parties.

Thus the Court of Cassation quashed a judgment which, to dismiss a distributor's action for damages for improper termination of a contract of indeterminate term by the manufacturer, called the latter not a mutual agency but a commercial distributorship, thus permitting the supplier to revoke the contract at any time.

According to the Court of Cassation, in the case in point the Judges did not justify the designation of distributor's agreement and did not explain the distributor's pleadings which maintained that he could not be considered as a commercial agent or authorised agent tied to the supplier by a mutual commission.

In the event of termination of an exclusive distributor's agreement attributable to the supplier and distributor, the judges must ascertain the amount of liability incumbent on each party in the light of the blame attributed and the amount of the loss suffered by each of them.

Notice of termination

Unilateral termination of a contract of indeterminate term must be covered by a notice of termination, the duration of which is not bound to be fixed but a period of six months is in any eventuality adequate.

The notice need not be in any particular form provided the facts leave no room for ambiguity.

However, it would seem desirable that it should take the form of a registered letter with proof of delivery.

If the period of notice is too short, the notice is not null and void but its effects are extended to the expiry date of a normal period of notice counting from the day on which it was issued.

It is the duty of the Judge pronouncing on the substance to ascertain whether the supplier has given adequate notice to terminate a verbal distributor's agreement of indeterminate term.

Termination of contracts of determinate period

When an exclusive distributor's agreement has been concluded for a determinate period, it terminates on the expiry of that period.

If either party, usually the supplier, unilaterally terminates the contract in the absence of any blame attributable to the distributor before the specified expiry date, such termination shall be considered as improper and he must pay compensation for premature termination to the distributor.

The compensation may correspond to the distributor's loss of earnings during the period from the date of the termination to the contract's normal expiry date.

Thus the Court of Paris held that the supplier is at fault by terminating a contract when he has the option of waiting for the specified closing date, in the absence of a serious or repeated infringement of an essential contract clause.

The Court subsequently felt that the blame levelled at the distributor must be all the more serious as the contract approaches term.

The Court of Cassation reversed a decision which, deciding on the termination of an exclusive distributor's agreement to sell beauty products for a determinate period, decided on the termination with the blame falling on the supplier whereas it should have fallen on the distributor.

The Judges pronouncing on the substance raised the falsehood of the instructions given by the supplier to set up a distribution network and his concealment of the status of the beauty consultants from Social Security.

The Court of Colmar for its part held that the supplier may terminate a determinate period contract at his own initiative if the distributor fails so seriously and repeatedly in his essential undertakings that, under penalty of suffering an irreparable loss due to its nature and extent, he cannot limit his response to an objection to execution.

In fact, the instigator of a termination will rarely be held liable because, as exclusive distributor's agreements are usually concluded for a fairly short term, one or two years, the parties often wait for the end of the term to terminate them.

Recourse to law has in fact little chance of coming to a conclusion before the term stipulated in the contract.

Improper termination of contracts of indeterminate term

A supplier or distributor who terminates the contract while the other party is fulfilling his obligations normally, is in breach of contract.

However a simple mistake on the part of either party is not sufficient to justify termination; thus, non-compliance with or lack of notice provided in the contract constitutes improper termination.

In the event of improper termination, most frequently at the supplier's initiative, the distributor shall be entitled to reparation of the loss suffered due to the supplier's fault, such compensation shall be calculated according to the amount of the loss and will primarily be concerned with the distributor's loss of customers as a result of the improper termination, provided however he offers evidence thereof.

Jurisprudence held that there was improper termination on the part of the supplier:

- by falsely invoking reasons for termination provided in the contract.
- if the supplier wrongly invokes his distributor's failings in his obligations in order to oust him and thereby take advantage of the network of agents he has set up.
- if the termination was coupled with action designed to discredit the distributor in the eyes of his customers.
- if the termination was effected under unusual circumstances and in particular without reason or period of notice.
- if the supplier does not allow the distributor time to reconvert his com-

pany after being closely integrated into that of the supplier at the latter's wishes pursuant to a medium term co-operation plan.
- if the termination coincided with the setting up of another distributor in the granted territory.

On the other hand, the distributor's misconduct subsequent to the improper termination cannot justify it retrospectively.

Similarly, improper termination does not exist if the reason drawn from the distributor's reduced turnover proves accurate, neither does improper termination exist from the mere fact that the supplier has set up an agency or branch designed to replace the distributor after the expiry of the contract.

The Court of Cassation held that by not ascertaining whether the distributor's respective failings had caused each of them an equal loss, totally off-setting the damages they could each claim, the Judges pronouncing on the substance gave no legal foundation to their decision.

Renewal of an exclusive distributorship

In the absence of an express clause in the contract, the Courts held that on the expiry of the term, the parties would again be free, the supplier no more than the distributor being bound to renew the contract, even if a contract tactily renewed several times had become a contract of indeterminate term.

Thus there is no misuse of law if a clause authorising the parties to terminate the contract on a quarterly basis after three months notice has been complied with.

In the case of a verbal distributor's agreement of determinate term, a supplier who notifies his distributor within a period coming within the provisions of previous agreements between the parties and in accordance with normal practice, that the contract will not be renewed on expiry, is not at fault.

Fixing the starting point of the period of notice is the result of both the terms of the agreement and the circumstances of its performance.

Non renewal of the contract, most frequently by the supplier on expiry of the term, does not therefore constitute misconduct and does not entitle the distributor to any compensatory payment for the loss, even if he incurs a loss as a result, which will nearly always be the case.

This principle is based on contractual freedom on the expiry of the agreement; the supplier and distributor must be able to regain their freedom.

When commercial relations between a supplier and a distributor are continued after the expiry of a contract of determinate term, a further exclusive distributor's agreement of indeterminate term is created between the parties.

Application of the principle
In order to claim a right to review the contract, the distributor cannot invoke:

- the length of his commercial relations with his supplier, even lasting 40 years.
- lack of blame on his part.

- diversion of customers which in fact gives rise to the withdrawal of the distributorship.
- a verbal, public promise of indefinite renewal.
- the severity of the obligations which he only accepted with the prospects of a longer period to write off his costs.
- a conditional offer made by the supplier which was not approved by the distributor.

Exception to the principle

The Court of Cassation held that a supplier who, having made an offer to renew the contract which is accepted by the distributor, makes substantial amendments to the contract, is guilty of misconduct and owes reparation.

2.1.7. Indemnity

Reimbursement of expenses incurred by the distributor.

In principle, when the supplier terminates the contract, he is not bound to reimburse any expenses which the distributor has incurred because of the distributorship.

Exceptionally, he may be ordered to do so if he is guilty of misconduct in exercising his right of termination.

Reimbursement of wages paid by the distributor.

The Paris Court held that the partial non renewal of an exclusive distributor's agreement does not authorise the distributor to claim from his successor reimbursement of salaries and social security paid to his staff, invoking Article L 122.12 of the Labour Code in respect of changes to the employer's legal position.

Penalty clause

Exclusive distributor's agreements frequently include a penalty clause laying down a fixed overall sum for damages to be paid by the party taking the initiative in the termination.

A Judge may reduce or increase the agreed fixed compensation if it is manifestly too high or derisory in view of the actual size of the loss incurred, even if the parties made the penalty clause final and binding.

Such reduction may take account of the interest which the party applying for termination of the sale has drawn from its partial performance.

Damages payable by the distributor

If the liability for the termination falls on the distributor's non performance of his undertakings, he may be made to pay damages to the supplier in application of the common law principles of contractual liability and providing nothing of the kind is provided in the contract.

Furthermore, exercise of the avoidance clause does not prohibit the supplier from taking action for judicial termination for blameworthy non performance and obtaining damages to repair the loss suffered.

2.1.8. Specific application of EEC law

Although Article 85, paragraph 1, does not expressly mention an exclusive distributor's agreement as a prohibited practice, the EEC Commission decided that it constituted an understanding in the same way as horizontal agreements.

The exclusive distributor's agreement, a restictive practice, is therefore subject to the provisions of Article 85, paragraph 1, of the Treaty of Rome when it is likely to affect the trade of an EEC Member State and its object or effect is to prevent, restrain or alter competition within the Common Market.

The European Court of Justice held that the fact that a motor car manufacturer prohibits his distributors from selling cars abroad is likely to affect trade between Member States and is intended to noticeably restrict and alter competition within the Common Market.

Contracts covered

The application of Article 85 to exclusive distributorships covers only this type of contract concluded in respect of dealings between EEC member countries.

Contracts concluded between companies from one Member State concerning only that country's domestic market are subject to internal legislation alone and not Community legislation.

However, it has been recognised that general practice in such contracts could involve the compartmentalisation of the European Market if the number of distributors still available in a given national territory and the acuteness of the competition between manufacturers of that country, were to fall off too much.

The question thus put is to know whether certain contracts concluded between French companies would indirectly fall within the scope of Article 85.

The Commission on the other hand felt that the prohibition of Article 85 did not apply to an exclusive distributor's agreement concluded between a French manufacturer and a Swiss distributor, where the exclusive territory was restricted to the latter country, whereas it appeared from the facts of the case that the contract in question did not interfere with competition from the various manufacturers of similar products from the various Common Market countries in the territory of that country.

Thus in the case of a distributor's agreement with a supplier from another EEC country, protection will only be provided if the exclusive nature in question is not declared null and void by virtue of the provisions of Article 85.

In this case, the Judge to whom the action for unfair competition brought by the distributor was referred, had to postpone Judgement until the competent Commission to which an action to declare the said clause null and void was referred, had given its decision on the validity of the exclusive nature of the contract invoked in support of the action for unfair competition.

However, in order to avoid delaying action, Judges who postpone judgment must also issue a provisional judgment prohibiting acts of alleged unfair competition and make such prohibition subject to a daily fine.

Exemption from application of Article 85, paragraph 1

Rule 67/67 of 22nd March 1967 laying down the system of exemptions by category of exclusive sales or purchasing agreements in application of the provisions of Article 85, paragraph 3, of the Treaty of Rome, expired on 30th June 1983 and was replaced by the two Commission Rules of June 1983, the aim of which is to further open the Common Market to the producer, consumer, distributor.

1. The first Rule 1983/83 of 22nd June 1983, concerns exclusive distributor's agreements and repeats to a large extent the previous regulations to be able to enjoy exemption, exclusive distributor's agreements must comply with the following three conditions:

- the agreement must be concluded between 2 companies only.

In addition to the exclusive delivery undertaking, no other obligation must be imposed on the supplier other than the instruction not to deliver the products mentioned in the agreement to users in the granted territory.

No restriction of competition can be imposed on an exclusive distributor other than:

- the obligation not to manufacture or distribute competitive products to those covered by the contract throughout the term of the contract.
- the obligation to buy the products covered by the contract for resale only from the other party.
- the obligation to buy full ranges of products or minimum quantities.
- the obligation to carry out no advertising in respect of the products covered by the contract, to set up no branch and keep no warehouse for their distribution outside the granted territory. . .

Furthermore, exemption by category could not be obtained in respect of exclusive reciprocal distribution agreements concluded between manufacturers of identical products considered as similar by users.

Such agreements must therefore be covered by an individual decision of the Commission.

2. The second Rule No. 84/83 of 2nd June 1983 which concerns exclusive purchase categories, limits the maximum term of the exclusive purchase obligation to 5 years and does not allow this undertaking to be extended in respect of products which are not linked by their nature or commercial usage (see EEC study).

- As regard French jurisdiction:
- when an action whose result is linked to the validity of a territorial exclusivity clause is referred to French jurisdiction and furthermore, an action is instituted after which the competent EEC bodies must give judgment on the nullity of the said clause, French Judges must postpone judgment awaiting such decision.

On the other hand, if no European jurisdictional body has been referred to, there is no obligation on him to postpone judgement or refer the dispute to the Court of Justice provided that the interpreted EEC Rule of Law is perfectly clear.

The same holds true if the trader intends evading the exclusive nature of the distribution to which he is subject by stating that it is contrary to Article

85 of the Treaty of Rome, without providing grounds for such argument.

The European Court of Justice held that the EEC Commission's decision not to intervene under Article 85, paragraph 1, of the Treaty in exclusive distributor's agreements concluded between perfumers and retailers did not prevent the application and national provision prohibiting the refusal to sell.

2.1.9. Bibliography

Guyenot, "Exclusive sales agreements" *Quarterly Commercial Law Review* 1963.513.

Economic and legal study of exclusive sales agreements.

Social law revies, January, February 1965.

Buisson, de Lacger, Tandeau de Marsac, study on the exclusive distributor's agreements (Sirey, 1968).

Guyenot, *Commercial distribution contracts* (Sirey, 1968).

Plaisant, "Exclusive contracts" *Quarterly Commercial Law Review* 64.1.

Cosenard, *Exclusive concession of refusal to sell* (Dalloz, 1962), chronical p. 237, standing dictionary of company law:

Distributor.

Trehard, "The distributor, sale, credit, consumer", *Gazette du Palais,* 1978 1, doctrine 248.

"Distributor's agreements exclusive or otherwise," *Gazette du Palais* 279 2, doctrine 647.

"Termination of an exclusive distributor's agreement" *Commercial Agent,* N 36, p. 12.

"A new trader, the integrated distributor," *Gazette du Palais* 81.1, doctrine 227.

Proposal for a Euroean ruling on automobile distributors, sales and after sales agreements *Gazette du Palais* 13, 15 October 1985, p. 2.

Pigassou: "Integrated distribution," *Quarterly Commercial Law Review* 1980 473.

Bachet: Exclusivity clauses, doctoral thesis, Paris II, 277. . .

2.1.10. Legislation

See 2.1.1. *In fine.*

2.1.11. Case Law

(refer to notes in the bibliography).

2.2. Selective Distribution

2.2.1. Definition

The Supreme Court has defined the notion of selective distribution contract to mean a contract "in which the supplier agrees to furnish, in a specific area, one or more merchants selected by the supplier according to objective criteria based on quality, without discrimination or unjustified quantitative limits, and in which the distributor is authorized to sell other competing products."

2.2.2. Conclusion of the contract (special conditions)

The Commission on Free Trade requires this type of contract to be formulated in writing so that it may verify that the conditions imposed on distributors are applied in a uniform manner (see "Produits de Parfumerie", 1 December 1983, BOSP 28 December 1984, Rec. Lamy, no. 223).

2.2.3. The Supplier's Duties and Rights

2.2.3.1. The supplier's duties

In practice, there is one main obligation: that of supplying the selected distributor. There can be no justification for refusing to sell to this distributor.

Scope

- In the case of a selective distribution contract having a limited period of validity, if the selection criteria are not modified when the contract expires, then the contract must be renewed if the distributor continues to fulfill these conditions (cf. Trib. Commerce Paris, 15 May 1987, G.P. 30 June 1987, p. 15).
- Failure to renew despite the absence of modifications in the criteria which the distributor fulfills will be deemed a refusal to sell (CA—Paris, 11 February 1987, D. 1987, I.R. 64).

2.2.3.2. The supplier's rights

In any case, the producer has the sole right to determine the conditions under which his products are to be commercialized.

- Distributors may be selected according to qualitative criteria (Trib. Co. Paris, 14 May 1986, "Lettre de la Distribution", 1986, no. 6).
- Quantitative selection has been accepted by the Criminal Chamber of the Supreme Court (3 Nov. 1982) as part of its condemnation of unjustified quantitative limits. Quantitative limits must therefore be justified: for example, if their only purpose is to make sales outlets economically viable.
- The supplier has the sole right to decide what quantitative or qualitative criteria are to be required of future distributors.

Articles 7 and 8 of the 1 December 1986 decree do not apply to selective distribution agreements unless:

(1) The goal, or one of the goals pursued by such an agreement is to restrict the capacity of certain businesses to participate in free trade;
(2) The execution of such an agreement would have the effect of restricting free trade, either through the direct result of certain clauses, or through the accumulated constraints resulting from its combined stipulations.

2.2.4. The distributor's duties and rights

2.2.4.1. The distributor's duties

Selected distributors must respect the selectivity which the supplier seeks to achieve.

- The selected distributor may not sell the products concerned by the distribution network to an unauthorized distributor (Trib. Co. Paris, 14 May 1986, "Lettre de la Distribution", 1986 no. 6).
- The selected distributor may not sell the products concerned by the distribution network in a store which has not been authorized by the supplier according to the contractual stipulations defining selection criteria (Aix-en-Provence, 5e Ch., 20 May 1985, GP 1985.2.760 note J. P. Marchi).
- The selected distributor must respect the sales goals in the selective distribution contract if such goals have been established. Under European Community law, such an obligation is prohibited by article 85 of the Treaty, but seems to qualify for the exemption regulations (cf. BMW decision, 13 December 1974, JOCE, 3 February 1975, no. L 291).

2.2.4.2. The distributor's rights

- The selected distributor has the right to be supplied by the supplier who is party to the selective distribution agreement.
- The selected distributor maintains the right to procure merchandise from other suppliers.

2.2.5. Liabilities of supplier and distributor during the term of the distributorship agreement

2.2.5.1. The supplier as against the distributor

The supplier has valid reason to refuse to sell to a selected distributor who apparently sells the products covered by the selective distribution agreement to an unauthorized distributor (C Cass., 6 January 1987, unpublished, no. 85.12.441).

The burden of proof that the selective distribution contract has been violated lies with the supplier.

2.2.5.2. The supplier as against third parties

A supplier discovering that his products are being retailed by an unauthorized distributor may submit the matter for an emergency interim ruling in order to:

(1) have the products in the third party retailer's possession impounded (Paris, 18 March 1987, D. 1987 I.R. 94);
(2) have the products in the distributor's possession confiscated (Tribunal Co. Paris, 14 May 1986, "Lettre de la Distribution" 1986, no. 6).

Unauthorized distributors who sell products covered by a selective distribution contract are civilly liable.

In the same way, an unauthorized distributor who possesses brand-name merchandise covered by a selective distribution contract may be criminally responsible in virtue of article 422.2 of the Penal Code, which sanctions the use of a trademark without the holder's authorization (Cass. Crim., 24 February 1987, unpublished).

Unauthorized distributors may be convicted of misleading advertising for having created the impression that they were selected (Paris, 24 March 1987, D. 1987 I.R. 102).

2.2.5.3. *The distributor as against the supplier*

An authorized distributor may obtain damages from a supplier who refuses to renew their selective distribution contract, even though the distributor continues to fulfil the selection criteria.

Unauthorized distributor's recourse against the supplier—refusal to sell

2.2.5.4. *The distributor as against third parties*

The distributor has the same possibilities for recourse as the supplier. In most cases, it is the supplier, because of his right to choose his distribution network, who takes action against third party retailers.

2.2.6. Term and Termination

2.2.6.1. *Term*

The selective distribution contract may have a fixed or indefinite validity period.

2.2.6.2. *Termination*

The distribution contract may be terminated:

(1) by the will of both parties, having decided in the initial contract, or in a later agreement to put an end to their collaboration;
(2) by legal decision at the request of either one of the parties, for failure to respect the terms of the contract.

2.2.7. Indemnity

2.2.8. Specific applications of EEC law

The refusal to sell (along with the refusal to grant authorization) is not in itself called into question by Community law.

Under the terms of article 85 (prohibition of cartels), a distinction must be made between a refusal to grant authorization, which is due to concerted practices, and a refusal to grant authorization as an unilateral action.

In any case, the Court of Justice of the European Communities considers that in certain cases, such unilateral actions are the manifestation of a tacit commitment made by the producer to the authorized distributors.

Selection is allowed:

(1) for high quality, or highly technical products;
(2) for the recruitment of distributors offering the professional qualities and sales environment necessary for satisfactory product distribution.

Selection is prohibited, if it leads to unjustified quantitative limits.
The distributor must respect the conditions of selection.
The supplier cannot prevent a selected distributor from selling to other distributors (horizontal sales), as such a prohibition would have the effect of compartmentalizing the market.

If the distribution contract covers various phases of distribution (from wholesale to retail), the supplier may not prohibit "direct sales" or "jump sales", if such a prohibition could lead to free trade restriction. Only the absence of a wholesaling set-up, or, infrastructure may justify the prohibition to sell directly to consumers.

If the selected distributor violates his obligations, he may provoke the cancellation of the distribution contract, and, possibly that of the current supply contract as well (SABA decision, 15 December 1975, JOCE 1976 no. L 28, p. 19).

Selective distribution contracts receive negative clearance, when the selection conditions are necessary in order to ensure a regular distribution which does not affect free trade.

They may receive an exemption if, the restriction of free trade can be justified.

2.2.9. Bibliography

"Refus d'agréer ou de vendre en droit communautaire des ententes" (Refusal to grant authorization or to sell in Community cartel law), R. Kovar, *Cahier droit de l'entreprise* 5-1984.

2.2.10. Legislation

Articles 7, 8, and 36 of the 1 December 1986 Decree.

2.2.11. Case-Law

Criminal Supreme Court decision, 3 November 1982, GP 1982/2-658 note J. P. Marchi.

3. Franchise Agreements

3.1. Definition

Franchise is not governed by specific rules. There is no legal definition but principles may be drawn from the rules of the French Federation of Franchise, the AFNOR specification, case law and commentaries.

(a) The rules of the French Federation of Franchise (F.F.F.):
These rules give the following definition of franchise: "a means of cooper-

ation between two undertakings, franchisor on the one part, and one or several franchisees on the other part. It implies on franchisor's part:

- propriety of a company's name, of a trade name, of distinctive signs and symbols, of a trademark or of a service mark as well as of know-how which are provided to franchisees.
- an assortment of goods and/or services:
- offered for sale in an original and specific way;
- necessarily and entirely traded according to commercial techniques, which are uniform and have been previously tested and constantly improved and controlled.

The purpose of the said cooperation is to increase rapidly the number of contracting parties, through common action resulting from the association of individuals and capitals, but simultaneously preserving their respective independence within exclusive agreements".

(Definition of 1971 as amended and completed in 1966.)

(b) The AFNOR specification:

This largely resumes the characteristics of the said definition in its 2nd paragraph "Definitions" but emphasizes know-how and parties' independence.

(c) Caselaw:

The Paris Court of Appeal, 1978 (5th Chamber). Morvan Intercontinent (Bull Transp 1978 277) has provided a definition of the franchise agreement which outlines its characters in comparison with the licence agreement:

- assistance;
- know how.

The E.C.J. has decided for the first time upon the validity of franchise agreements when requested to give a preliminary ruling thereupon by the supreme Court of the EEC Member State, West Germany.

In a case dated January 1986, it laid out fundamental principles concerning distribution franchise agreements.

The court has declared that the contract submitted to it was valid in respect of most of its provisions, after having defined distribution franchise not as a method of distribution but rather as "a way for an undertaking to derive financial benefit from its expertise without investing its own capital".

("Pronuptia case".)

The said principles have been confirmed by the Court in respect of a manufacturing and exclusive distribution franchise agreement "Yves Rocher" and more recently in the "Computerland" case of 13 July 1987 which raises the question of the validity of a distribution agreement with goods manufactured by third parties and bearing their trademark.

See also the *Charles Jourdan* case concerning a problem of interference between several modes of sale of similar goods.

Several substantial elements of the franchise agreement may be outlined:

- exclusivity;
- license of trademark;

- a right to use franchisor's shop sign;
- assistance;
- know how;
- an assortment of goods and/or services.

When examined under its economic and commercial aspect franchise constitutes an original system of distribution of goods or provision of services. Four large categories of franchise agreements may be distinguished with six types deriving therefrom.

(a) The "four" large categories of franchise:

Manufacturing franchise
The main characteristic of this is that the franchisor himself manufactures the goods sold by his franchisees. Its development strategy is to concentrate on the manufacturing of notorious goods of good quality and to have them sold by franchisees who take advantage of the qualities and notoriety of the concerned goods, e.g.: Pingouin Stemm, Phildar, Rodier.

Distribution franchise
In this case the franchisor does not manufacture the franchised goods himself. He has them manufactured or purchases goods from various independent suppliers. He manages the sale of said goods through a franchisee's network that he creates, e.g.: Daniel Hechter, Pronuptia, Promoder, Lancel.

The three following characteristics may be drawn from industrial and distribution franchise agreements:

- all units shall have the same shop sign and conform to a standard in their appearance (lay-out of unit, shopwindow);
- the sale concerns a similar assortment of goods to which an identical commercial policy is applied;
- the said units are in fact a reliable image of "franchisor's pilots". Therefore, the franchisor tests the typical unit in order to ensure that his franchisees shall be commercially successful and shall make their investments profitable.

Service franchise
In a case dated 28 January 1986, the Court of Justice defined this type of contract as an agreement "under which franchisee offers a service under the business name or symbol and sometimes the trademark of franchisor, in accordance with franchisor's instructions".

This type of franchise is developing. The franchisor creates a service formula which is granted to his franchisees who shall be in charge of repeating the said formula in conformity with franchisor's methods, e.g.: Novotel, Holiday Inn, Europcar, Copy 2000.

Industrial franchise
Generally, only three categories of franchises are distinguished but it may be considered that industrial franchise is a category *sui generis* for the two following reasons:

- the franchisor and franchisee are businessmen;

- the contract concerned is complex since the franchisor not only communicates to franchisee his know-how, but also grants him the right to manufacture and sell the goods concerned, e.g.: Yoplait, Coca cola.

(b) The six types of franchise agreements arising from franchise:

Combined franchise
Some franchise agreements may be simultaneously manufacturing, distribution and service franchise agreements, e.g.: Simone Mahler.

Corner franchise
This consists of creating a privileged franchise area within a traditional trade, in which the franchisor's goods or services are offered for sale along with the franchisor's methods.

Associated franchise
This concerns franchises in which the franchisor has shares in the franchisee's capital and the franchisee owns shares in the franchisor's company.

Financial franchise
Some franchises require from franchisees substantial investments. Such a franchise may then be founded upon a separation between the investing franchisee and the administrator.

Multi franchise
In certain networks, franchisees manage several franchises belonging to the same system.

Pluri franchise
Franchisee may select several distinct franchises which, however, offer complementary services.

The franchise is a sector in full expansion. The concept is getting more accurate and complete over the years, even though there is a juridical paradox along with the evolution: indeed, at present, franchise which is not governed by specific rules corresponds to about 9% of the total turnover of retail trade, more than 80,000 local units in France.

3.2. Conclusion of the Contract (special conditions)

No special formal condition is imposed as regards the conclusion of the franchise contract. It is governed by the general rules of the law of contract. Nevertheless, it is noteworthy that according to the rules of the F.F.F., the agreement should be in clear written terms specifying the reciprocal obligations of both parties.

A franchise agreement preliminary may be provided for and followed by the franchise agreement itself.

The preliminary contract; the franchise preliminary agreement;

The basis of said agreement:
The franchise agreement is founded upon the transmission of know how,

the notoriety of a licensed trademark and franchisor's assistance. At the date of conclusion of the agreement the franchised candidate may not be aware of the value of said know how as well as of said trademark. Therefore, in order for the franchised candidate to get familiarized with the network of which he may become a member, it has been decided, in practice, to set up franchise preliminary agreements which shall enable the franchised candidate to try the advantages of such a system in a pilot centre.

Certain rules must preserve the confidentiality of the know how and of other methods which shall be provided to him. The said preliminary contract provides, *inter alia*, for reciprocal obligations:

- an obligation to negotiate: either party agrees to try to find out within an association the bases of the future agreements. Parties, however, do not undertake to sign a contract;
- an obligation of information and a non competition obligation;
- the franchised candidate shall be able to obtain certain information, commercial methods or secrets.

Although he remains free not to contract with the other party, he shall, however, not draw advantage therefrom by competing on an unfair basis. Consequently, non competition shall be provided for by certain clauses, during the term of the agreement and after termination.

Considering the failure of any legal rules at present, the contents of the franchise agreement is freely determined by the parties' contract.

As is witnessed by the contractual practice, it, in fact, varies a lot. There is not yet a standardized type of franchise agreement with proper formal and fundamental rules of several types of franchise agreements. The franchise agreement appears like a complex contract composed of several elements which could, if severed, constitute specific agreements but which, by reason of their composition, lose their autonomy and contribute to the creation of a new agreement.

The franchise contract being a contract with reciprocal obligations, obligations arise therefrom for both parties. Consequently, we shall analyze in turn the obligations imposed on franchisor and on franchisee.

3.3. The supplier's duties and rights

3.3.1. The supplier's duties

As regards obligations concerning signs attracting end-users:

As regards obligations to license the trademark:

"The trademark is a material sign serving to identify and distinguish products or services of any undertaking" according to the legal definition of the trademark pursuant to the law of 31 December 1964. As regards franchise, everything concerning the trademark is of importance, since same is an incorporal item with a value. The franchisor is necessarily the owner of a trademark that he shall assign to franchisee, in return for the payment of royalties.

The trademark shall have to be regularly filed and registered with the I.N.P.I., or with the competent authority within the contract territory. The said filing is aimed at protecting the trademark and taking legal action in case of trademark infringement, illicit imitation.

In fact, the codified rules of the French Federation of Franchise (F.F.F.) expressly provide that "Franchisor shall warrant the validity of his rights on the signs attracting end users, such as trademarks signs, emblems and grant to the franchisee a peaceful use of the same provided to hire.

Consequently, in the case of "trademark" infringement, the franchisee shall immediately inform franchisor, who, as the owner of an assigned trademark, shall do what is necessary in order to put an end to it.

Some agreements provide for a possible intervention of the franchisee, but being only the assignee of the trademark, it is much better for both parties' interests that franchisor, as owner of the trademark, mainly institutes the proceedings.

As regards the obligation concerning the right to use the sign

In the franchise agreement, the use of the sign by the franchisee is an indispensable element. The said obligation is necessarily imposed on the franchisor. In fact, the franchisor must be able to use all characteristic signs of the trademark, whether it be the sign, emblems or adverts.

The European Court of Justice (E.C.J.) has in its decision of 28 January 1986 ("the Pronuptia case") assimilated the assignment of trademark with the license of the sign considering that both elements are inseparable in this matter. The franchisor must be able to take the measures necessary for maintaining the identity and reputation of the network bearing his business name or symbol. It arises therefrom that, should the franchisor deprive the franchisee from the right to use the sign, the contract should be immediately terminated, since one of its substantial grounds would be failing.

As regards the obligations concerning the communication of know-how

According to Professor Mousseron: "know-how is a package of technical information not immediately assignable which is easily accessible and not patented". In respect of franchise, know-how is, in fact, a package of information concerning methods of manufacturing, trading, managing, financing goods and services. It is an experience which is secret, may not be used by someone who is a non patented experience and is not assignable by contract.

The communication of know-how enables the franchisee to reiterate his succeeding formula, by using the methods previously achieved by franchisor. "The AFNOR specification and the codified rules of the F.F.F. outline the characteristics of know-how: "it must be original and specific, not immediately accessible, approved and assignable."

As regards originality: The colmar Court of appeal, in a decision of 9 June 1982, *Felicitas* v. *Bernard Georges*, has outlined the idea of "relative originality" of know-how; it held that "it is noteworthy that the co-contractor, the future franchisee, does not know anything about the know-how, which once disclosed enables him in a few weeks to carry out an activity which he was unaware of". Thus, the originality may be measured in consideration of the franchisee, and the franchisor may establish proof of the communication once it has been "useful, necessary and efficient" for the franchisee.

In addition to the definition of the components of know-how, the contract shall provide for the conditions of the communication thereof.

It is possible to provide for three periods during which said know-how shall be communicated:

(a) Before opening unit

It is necessary to provide for the organization of an initial training for the franchisee and his staff.

(b) When opening unit

The franchisor shall constantly advise the franchisee (the cost of the said services shall be assumed by either party, in conformity with the provisions of the agreement).

(c) After opening unit

A permanent training shall be organized by the franchisor in conformity with the provisions of the agreement.

The information shall be given to the franchisee by circulars, notes, information reports, etc., in particular, for the introduction of new products, or improvement of the know-how.

Thus, the communication of know-how is very closely linked to the assistance given by the franchisor to the franchise.

As regards the obligations linked to assistance

The commercial, technical, financial, etc., assistance of franchisor to franchisee is fundamental, since it is an extension of the said know how and shall facilitate its regular adaptation to franchisee's requirements.

Assistance under normal circumstances

This may occur at three stages (cf.: the Pronuptia agreement notified to the E.E.C. Commission for exemption provides for three periods).

Before opening unit:

The franchisor shall furnish franchisee with advice as to location, search of unit. He shall communicate to the franchisee the manual procedures concerning the franchisee's unit; he shall advise the franchisee as to advertizing, the introduction of products, and shall provide all documents of management and all equipment for adverts.

When opening unit:

Technical assistance provided to franchisee shall be total for the first days in order to familiarize him with the know how.

After opening unit:

The franchisor is in charge of advertising on a national and international level, displays the assortment of goods and/or services.

The following information shall be given both by franchisor and franchisee: concerning the life of the network, the improvement of goods or the performance of services.

The franchisor makes sure that the know-how is well applied by franchisee but avoids interfering with franchisees' management (cf.: business management).

As regards assistance under exceptional circumstances:

Upon the franchisee's request, the franchisor shall provide him with an exceptional assistance justified by particular circumstances. In particular, should the franchisee be seriously ill, the franchisor may appoint a member of his staff to survey the franchisee's shop or engage a salaried employee on behalf of the franchisee:

Serious account assistance upon franchisee's request. . . But said services should remain exceptional because the franchisee and the franchisor are independent from one another. Otherwise both undertakings could be confused in the eyes of the public.

As regards obligations linked to territorial exclusivity

In the franchise agreement, the franchisor may agree not to conclude franchise agreement with third parties within the exclusive territory (but he may himself continue to sell within the territory. In return the franchisee agrees to purchase supplies exclusively or mainly from franchisor.

In certain cases exclusivity is total, the franchisee may purchase supplies only from the franchisor or suppliers determined by him (e.g.: Yves Rocher, Coryse Salome. . .) In other cases, exclusivity is partial, the franchisee must purchase supplies of only one category of certain specified products from the franchisor and may purchase supplies of other products as he wishes.

In this respect the position of the EEC Commission is interesting: in particular in its "draft regulation relating to exemption of certain categories of agreements of distribution and service franchise agreements" on the application of Article 85(3) of the Treaty. The exemption regulation applies if the franchisee sells products bearing exclusively the franchisor's trademark.

In the opposite case, namely if franchisee sells products bearing third parties' trademark, no exemption may be granted. The franchisor may not forbid franchisee to purchase supplies from any third party supplier but he may submit the said purchase of supplies to his consent which shall be impartial.

The franchisee in turn shall fulfil certain obligations, in return for services rendered to him.

3.4. The distributor's duties and rights

There are three fundamental principles in respect of the validity of clauses governing franchisee's obligations towards franchisor:

- The franchisor must be able to communicate his know-how to franchisee and provide him with the required assistance without running the risk of competition. The franchisee's obligation not to compete arises therefrom.

- It must be possible for the franchisor to take all measures necessary to preserve the identity and the reputation of the network symbolized by the shop sign. The franchisee's obligations to respect the identity of the franchised network arise therefrom.
- Finally, the franchisor must, in exchange for services rendered to the franchisee, be able to request from him payment of royalties. The franchisee's financial obligations arise therefrom.

As regards the non competition obligations:

According to ruling No. 16 of the Pronuptia case, "franchisor must be able to communicate his know-how to franchisees and provide them with the necessary assistance in order to enable them to apply his methods without running the risk that said know-how and assistance might benefit competitors even indirectly".

The said will to preserve the secret justifies the obligation of confidentiality and the clause of non competition imposed upon franchisee.

Confidentiality obligation:

This implies on the franchisee's part an obligation of confidentiality in respect of principles that are transmitted to him. He may not reveal the same to third parties, suppliers or competitors. On this point, Professor Le Tourneau has written that: "franchisee must jealously keep the secret as to know-how and methods which have been communicated to him by franchisor. Even though a contractual clause generally cautiously provides for said confidentiality obligation, it is not indispensable: said obligation arises from the contract." cf. *Le Franchisage* (J.C.P. editions N.I.), p. 13, 1985.

This obligation exists during the term of the contract and even survives after its termination.

If the franchisee infringes this principle, the balance of the contract would be threatened and he would expose himself to damages due to the franchisor under contractual liability.

Non competition clause:

This results from the obligation of confidentiality which pertains to the communication of know-how.

Thus, the E.C.J. held that the following clauses do not constitute restraints of competition:

- The clause prohibiting the franchisee, during the term of the contract and for a reasonable period after its termination, from opening a shop of the same or a similar purpose in an area where he may compete with a member of the network.
- The clause prohibiting the franchisee from transferring his shop without the franchisor's agreement, provided the said provision is intended to prevent competitors from indirectly benefiting from the know how and assistance provided.
- The said clause must be limited in time. In this respect, community law tends to limit its applicability to a year after termination of contract.
- Said clause must be limited as to the area: generally, it corresponds to the area previously granted.

- Said clause must be limited to a determined field of activity.

Indeed, even failing the existence of a non competition clause or should it be declared invalid, franchisee shall, in no case, once the contract is breached, act unfairly towards franchisor. In fact, franchisee shall not infringe franchisor's rights by willingly causing a confusion between both undertakings, which would result in an attraction of consumers. Such would be the case of: identical advertising slogans, sales of similar products, becoming a member of a competitive network or any methods establishing the use of previously communicated know-how.

Therefore, the European Court of Justice has declared valid the non-competition clause during the term of the contract and after its expiry, under certain conditions. Consequently, franchisee must be aware of the existing risk of loss of "his" customers when there is such a clause, if the contract is terminated upon expiration.

3.5. Obligations concerning the identity and reputation of the network

The European Court of Justice declares valid all clauses to the extent that it is indispensable "for maintaining the common identity and reputation of the franchised network" (article 3 of draft regulation).

Thus, franchisee has various obligations towards franchisor.

3.5.1. Obligation to comply with the commercial methods and to use the communicated know-how under franchisor's supervision

Franchisee has created a uniform network whose identity must be maintained. The reputation of the network also relies upon the use of finalized know-how; thus, franchisee must reiterate the built up system.

Thus the E.C.J. has held valid clauses imposing upon franchisee the obligation to sell the goods covered by the agreement exclusively in premises laid out and decorated in accordance with franchisor's instructions.

Similarly, the E.C.J. has held valid a clause prescribing the location of premises wherefrom it results that the franchisee may not transfer his shop to another location without franchisor's agreement (see: ruling No. 19 of the Pronuptia case). The franchisee shall consequently manage his shop with the specifications of commercial management, perform the planned investments, comply with the suggestions concerning stocks and with any instructions suggested by franchisor. However, the franchisor shall in no case impose minimum prices, which are prohibited by national legislation and principles of community law.

The AFNOR specification provides in paragraph 3.2.2.3.1. that: provided it is necessary for reiterating success and provided the said obligations shall not lead to the franchisor's characterized interference with the franchisee's management, the contract must provide for . . . the terms and conditions of supervision that franchisor reserves himself the right to perform (information which should be spontaneously furnished by franchisee, visits which may be made by franchisor, documents and literature which he may require)".

The only restraint upon said supervision is that it must not be an abuse, which would lead to interfering with the franchisee's activities and to a risk of confusion between both managements.

If, when supervising, the franchisor found irregularities, he should immediately point them out to the franchisee, requesting him to regularize them. Should the latter not comply with this instruction within a given time, the obligation would lie upon the franchisor to draw all necessary consequence, failing which he may be contractually liable towards other members of the network.

Indeed, like consumers they could seek the liability of a faulty franchisor who would no longer supervise the common identity and reputation of his network.

Obligation to point out any modification of his structure:

The franchisee shall operate his unit, himself, considering his qualities, since he has been selected and has been trained for managing in accordance with franchisor's specification.

It results therefrom that the Franchisee is prohibited from assigning the rights and obligations under the franchise agreement without the franchisor's approval. The franchisor being able to choose his franchisees freely (the franchise contract is *intuitu personae*) (cf.: E.C.J. *Pronuptia* case, ruling 20).

The contract may be terminated upon sale, "location gérance", suspension by the franchisee of its activities, upon increase or reduction of capital of a franchised company, or upon death.

However, the said clauses must be expressly mentioned in the franchise agreement, to the benefit of the franchisee thus warned.

Obligation to perform adequate advertizing

In most franchise agreements: national and international advertizing is determined by the franchisor who defines its contents in accordance with the standard prescribed by him; the cost thereof is divided between the franchisor and the franchisees.

Local advertizing is assumed by the franchisee, even though in exceptional cases, such as on the opening of franchisee's unit, it frequently occurs that the franchisor grants local advertizing aid.

Thus, local advertizing, for the benefit of the network, of the trademark, shall be carried out by the franchisee but shall first be submitted to franchisor's approval.

Similarly, the E.C.J. has expressly validated this clause in the following terms:

"Since advertizing helps to define the image of the network's name or symbol in the eyes of the public, a provision requiring the franchisee to obtain the franchisor's approval for all advertizing is also essential for the maintenance of the network's identity, so long as that provision concerns only the nature of the advertizing."

The obligation of supply:

The franchise agreement usually provides especially in the case of a distribution franchise an obligation of supply by the franchisee from the franchisor or suppliers designated or selected by same.

In this respect, the AFNOR specification at paragraph 3.2.2.3.3.: "Supply" expressly provides for the following measures:

> "To the extent that the agreement includes supply from franchisor or selected third parties, totally or partially and provided said clauses comply with the rules concerning restraints of competition, the agreement must include:
> (1) Elements of determination or the sufficient determinability of quantum and prices of supplies to franchisees.
> (2) The franchisor's agreement to comply up to said obligation of supply with franchisee's requests."

The said conditions comply with equity, in particular when providing that: to the extent that the franchisee may not get supplies of similar goods somewhere else, in counterpart it rests upon franchisor to comply with the franchisee's request at any time.

Concerning restrictive practices of trade, the E.C.J., in its ruling 21 of the *Pronuptia* case, enforced the said type of obligation holding that:

> "By means of the control exerted by franchisor on the selection of goods offered by franchisee, the public is able to obtain goods of the same quality from each franchise. It may in certain cases (e.g. the distribution of fashion articles) be impractical to lay down objective quality specifications. Because of the large number of franchisees, it may also be too expensive to ensure that such specifications are complied with".

Consequently the Court enforces said clauses in respect of distribution franchisee.

However, the franchisee must be able to obtain the goods from other franchisees. Concerning service franchise, the question is unanswered.

3.6. Financial obligations:

Pursuant to the European codified rules of franchise, "any franchise agreement implies a payment of any mode either by the franchisee or the franchisor in acknowledgment of services rendered by franchisor who provides his name, his method, his technology and his know how".

The price to be paid is usually divided in two parts:

The "redevance initiale forfaitaire (RIF) "also called franchise fee ("droit d'entrée") paid on signing the agreement.

The "Redevance d'exploitation Proportionnelle" (REP) or Royalties payable during the term of the agreement.

The "redevance initiale forfaitaire" or franchise fee:

It is paid for services provided generally to franchisee, before the very opening of his shop. In fact, it is paid in return for transfer of technical assistance, training, transfer of know how, use of franchisor's trademark and right to trade within a franchise system.

• Consequently, it corresponds to a franchise fee the amount of which shall vary from one franchisor to the other according to the notoriety of the exclusive territory, the number of franchisees and franchisor's expenses.

- It shall, however, be franchisee's interest to require that the contact mentions which services are thus paid.
- According to paragraph 3.2.2.3.2. "financial obligation" of the AFNOR specification "in any case, the agreement must precisely mention the financial counterpart of the obligation and the modes of payment."
- Some authors have proposed that the said franchise fee be paid not only on signing of the agreement but also on its renewal. However, the said argument seems excessive, since the franchisee also pays the proportional fee for services rendered in the future by franchisor.
- Finally some agreements do not provide for a franchise fee, services being compensated by the only proportional fee to be paid during the term of the agreement.

The "redevance exploitation proportionnelle (REP)" or royalties:

- This is regularly paid by the franchisee during the term of the agreement, generally per month.
- It shall be proportional to the achieved turnover.
- The percentage shall vary according to the importance of rendered services and shall vary from 2–10% of the tax free turnover. Some franchisors provide for a fixed minimum.
- The payment of said proportional fee is usually for use of trademark and shopsign services rendered to franchisee during the term of the contract, such as information, national advertizing, regular training, of supervision the brand image in respect of the whole network, and assortment if need be.
- The said fee is subject to VAT as regards the taxfree amount of fees; on paying, franchisee shall be able to deduct such amount.
- On a fiscal basis, on filing the franchise agreement with the tax administration, a set duty is payable.
- Thus, even though the REP is the usual payment for services provided by the franchisor, the franchisee is obliged to such payment in exchange of all advantages received. Therefrom, the agreement must list and specify the nature of services rendered, the modes of payment of the said fee and its amount.

In this respect, pursuant to the AFNOR specification, the agreement must carefully provide that the proportional fees shall be established objectively, on a verifiable basis and must specify, if need be, the minimum to be paid, in all cases."

3.7. Liability

The franchise agreement is not governed by specific legal rules. Thus, common law rules apply in respect of contractual and tortious liability.

Franchisor's liability:

As to franchisee

As a party to the contract, the franchisee may bring a legal action against franchisor, under contractual liability, every time he shall prove that franchisor has not carried out his contractual obligations. The franchisor shall then be compelled to remedy the damage resulting from the non performance of the franchise contract. Such will be the case if franchisor refuses to supply the franchisee within the time specified in the contract, or does not supply him with the agreed asssistance.

The franchisee may also bring a legal action against franchisor under tortious liability pursuant to Article 1382 of the Civil Code, whether the franchisor has caused harm to the franchisee which he is compelled to remedy or whether said harm is the result of carelessness or negligence (cf. Article 1383 of the civil Code).

As to the other members of the franchise network:

The other franchisees may bring legal action under contractual liability against the franchisor when for instance, the franchisor, when controlling finds irregularities at a franchisee's, he must immediately point them out to him and require him to remedy them immediately. If said the franchisee does not comply with the franchisor's request within a prescribed time, the franchisor shall draw all necessary consequences therefrom; otherwise, he may be sued under contractual liability towards the other members of the franchise network (to whom he is liable for protecting the brand image and maintaining the reputation of the franchise network).

Towards consumers:

(1) If the franchisor manufactures goods: his warranty as manufacturer of the goods may be operated, if the goods are defective or inadequate for their intended use: theory of hidden defects (Article 1641 et seq. of the Civil Code).

(2) The consumer may also bring an action against the franchisor, if he declares that he has been mistaken by a *semblance*, namely he believed that he was addressing a powerful undertaking with several branches in France and not an independent franchisee, member of a franchise network: the theory of appearance.

Until now, this action has not been successful but it is advisable for franchisor to provide in his commercial documents for shop signs, shop windows and any elements capable of identifying franchisee.

Franchisee's liability:

Towards franchisor:

Franchisee's contractual liability, namely that resulting from the non performance of his contractual obligations may also be sought.

Such will be the case, for instance, in respect of his obligation of confidentiality: if the franchisee publishes elements of know-how, commercial methods, etc., which should be kept confidential: his contractual liability may be sought and he shall be liable for damages.

Towards consumers:

If a consumer feels harmed by the action of the franchisee, he may seek the franchisee's liability. The same is a trader, artisan or independent manufacturer who is liable for his actions, even though he is submitted to many obligations which bind him to franchisor. Many questions of liability and of risks may be dealt with by insurance.

The franchisor may have finalized a standard agreement with his insurance company, but in any case it is franchisor's interest to request a serious insurance from his franchisees.

3.8. Term and termination:

3.8.1. Term

Frequently, the term of franchise agreements is limited. Such is the case for 90% of such agreements. The remaining are concluded for an indefinite term.

Agreements with an indefinite term

Such agreements are very rare because they are precarious and this is detrimental to the very idea of franchise which requires a definite term in order to be efficient. Agreements with an indefinite term may be terminated at any time by either party provided however that sufficient notice is given.

Agreements with a fixed term

The term of most franchise agreements is usually about five years. The said term may be extended in consideration of heavy investments or reduced to 3 years. However, this occurs rarely since in such a case, agreements with a fixed term would be similar to agreements with an indefinite term, as regards precariousness. The agreement with a fixed term may be tacitly renewed provided there is an explicit contractual clause.

If there is no renewal, each party shall resume their freedom upon expiry.

Termination of the franchise agreement:

Termination of the agreement may be sought either by franchisor or by franchisee. Either party shall invoke failures of the other. Failures must be sufficiently serious for termination to be well founded. It is for the court to examine said termination.

Cases of termination

The franchisor may terminate the agreement upon the franchisee's failure to make any payment of fees or goods, upon failure to comply with exclusivity, upon failure to respect the brand image, upon breach of the non-competition clause.

The franchisee may terminate the agreement if he considers that franchisor does no longer comply with his obligations of supply or if franchisor does no longer communicate his know how or if said know how was not regularly improved or disappeared.

Procedure:

Before instituting proceedings, it is necessary to have given the other, notice by registered letter, receipt requested or by a non judicial proceeding, to put an end to his failures, leaving him some time to remedy same.

Any inconsiderate breach shall be deemed to be an abuse by the courts (a reasonable notice of about 3 months shall be complied with).

Consequence of the breach: immediate effects

The franchisee has had the right to use the trademark and other distinctive signs such as shop signs, emblems, advertising methods on termination of this agreement and upon expiration of the notice period, the said distinctive signs shall disappear.

Franchisee shall remove the shop sign and all other signs bearing franchisor's trademark, which could possibly create confusion with his former network, failing which he may be sued for unfair competition.

If the franchise agreement provides for supplies or manufacturing of goods, it is necessary to provide that the franchisor shall purchase franchisee's inventory at a price to be fixed either by the parties or by an appointed expert. Failing such a clause, franchisee shall continue selling the remaining goods even though he may no longer use franchisor's distinctive signs.

The equipment whatever it be: commercial documents, advertising equipment, shall be returned to franchisor upon expiration of the agreement.

Differred consequences

This relates to the covenant not to compete, if it is provided for in the agreement.

The covenant not to compete forbids the franchisee, during the term of the agreement and for a certain period after termination, to engage either directly or indirectly in a similar business within the same territory.

The E.C.J. case of 28 January 1986 has expressly enforced the principle of the said clauses in the franchise agreements: "franchisor must be able to communicate his know how and provide them with the necessary assistance in order to enable them to apply his methods, without running the risk that said know how and assistance might benefit competitors, even indirectly".

The cases of 17 December 1986 and 13 July 1987 resume these arguments and rely expressly upon "the confidential and new aspect of the communication of know how, of the methods communicated to franchisees during the term of the contract which must not benefit competitors."

In order for the covenant not to compete to be valid, it must be restricted to a fixed period and to an area of business.

3.9. Damages

Generally the franchisee is not entitled to damages:

- Upon termination of the expiring agreement, in respect of an agreement with a sufficient notice, in respect of an agreement with a fixed term.
- Upon termination with a sufficient notice, in respect of an agreement with an indefinite term.

Damage shall only be awarded by the franchisor to the franchisee or by the franchisee to the franchisor upon abuse of breach (it is for the court to decide upon the existence of abuse of breach).

In order for the courts to award damage, it shall be necessary to prove:

(1) The other party's breach;
(2) Causation between breach and damage;
(3) Each item of the damage, carefully valuated, the mode of valuation thereof being justified.

e.g.: Damages equal to the amount of fees paid during the last twelve months if franchisee has committed a serious breach.

Upon breach of the *covenant not to compete* by the franchisee, the same may be held liable to pay damages to the franchisor.

According to some authors, the covenant not to compete must give rise, as under labour law, to "consumers' damages" paid by franchisor to franchisee. However, it is noteworthy that franchisee is an independent trader registered with the registry of Trade and Companies, who has benefited from consumers, in consideration of the licence of a well-known trademark and of the communication of know-how.

The know-how and the trademark belonging to franchisor, franchisee shall not be entitled to damages.

It is noteworthy that proceedings may be instituted against franchisee if he engages into business competing with franchisor's upon expiration of the agreement (confusion, disparagement, disorganization of the undertaking, cf. classification by Paul Roubier).

No contractual clause is required.

If successful, the said proceedings shall lead to an award of damages.

3.10. Assignment and transfer of the agreement

The franchise agreement is strongly characterized by the *intuitu personae* relationship. A certain number of consequences result therefrom. Article 5 of the rules of the F.F.F. provides for a selection of franchisees by franchisor. It provides that:

"The franchisor, after having selected his franchisees, only accepts applicants for new franchises who, after a careful examination, appear to him to have the personal qualities and necessary means to have reasonable chances to succeed".

Various consequences arise therefrom: In fact, if franchisee dies, sells his business or assigns shares of the company to a non approved third party, namely without franchisor's approval, or if there is an important charge in his management, franchisor shall be entitled to terminate the agreement which is founded upon reciprocal cooperation and trust.

This has been approved by the E.C.J. in ruling No. 20 of the Pronuptia case:

> "The prohibition of the assignment by franchisee of his rights and obligations under the contract without franchisor's approval protects the latter's right freely to choose franchisees, on whose business qualifications the establishment and maintenance of the network's reputation depend."

Therefore, many franchise agreements provide for an assignment clause following which "franchisee may not assign his interest in the franchise agreement to whatever party without the franchisor's approval, which shall be given or not within some specific period". Said assignment clause may be accompanied by a pre-emption clause according to which "upon assignment of the goodwill, franchisor shall exercise his right of preemption within a certain period and under the conditions provided for by the offer to purchase" (example of written clause). For, it is in the interest of both parties that the said clauses be expressly written in the franchise agreement.

CHAPTER 8
Ireland

R. John McBratney

1. Commercial Agency

1.1. Definition of various types of agencies and intermediaries

1.1.1. Independent

1.1.2. Employed

1.1.3. Others

In Irish law there is no statutory definition of an agent. The relationship of principal and agent is governed by the ordinary principles of the common law save in relation to retail petroleum sales agreements in respect of which S.I.70/1980 Restrictive Practices (Motor Spirit and Motor Vehicle Lubricating Oil) Order 1981 makes specific provisions. Consequently none of the above distinctions are relevant.

1.2. Conclusion of the Contract (Special Conditions)

Again the contract of principal and agent is no different from any other contract and can be made verbally or in writing. There are no special conditions.

1.3. The Principal's Duties and Rights

1.3.1. The principal's duties

"Legal systems which categorise types of agent and seek to lay down the incidents of the various legal relationships may well prescribe duties of principals towards their agents just as they prescribe duties of agents towards their principals. English law however has traditionally viewed the principal as the person requiring protection, against the wrongful use of the agent's powers, and have paid little attention to the position of the agent. Thus it was long ago held that the principal was under no duty to account on a fiduciary basis to the agent; and in general the view that the principal has fiduciary duties towards the agent is not one that is often put forward. Equally, the limited body of law relating to the common law duties owed by agents towards their principals has no obvious counterpart concerning duties owed towards agents by their principals."

Bowstead on Agency 15th edn., p. 208. Exactly the same statement applies to Irish law.

1.3.1.1. Commission

Any right of the agent to commission will depend on the proper interpretation of the contract whether the event has happened in relation to which the commission is to be paid.

1.3.1.2. Protection of agent, information

Again this will depend on the terms of the contract. If it is intended that certain information supplied by the agent to the principal is to be confidential, the terms of the contract should specifically so provide.

1.3.1.3. Supply of written statement

Not a concept known to Irish law.

1.4. The Commercial Agent's Duties and Rights

1.4.1. The commercial agent's duties

1.4.1.1. Trustworthiness, duty to inform

The agent bears fiduciary duties to the principal which require the agent in general terms not to allow himself to be placed in a position in which his own personal interests and his duties to his principal are in conflict unless he has made full and complete disclosure to the principal.

1.4.1.2. Del Credere

The agent is liable to indemnify his principal for the failure of the other contracting party.

1.4.1.3. Non-competition

This comes within the general duty set forth in 1.4.1.1.

1.4.1.4. Secrecy

It will depend on the nature of the information supplied. See 1.3.1.2.

1.4.2. The commercial agent's rights

1.4.2.1. Commission

See 1.3.1.1.

1.5. Liabilities of Principal and Agent during the Term of the Agency

1.5.1. The principal as against the agent

The agent is liable to the principal:

(a) to keep the money and property of his principal separate from his own;
(b) to account;
(c) to disgorge any secret profit received by agent.

1.5.2. The principal as against third parties

The third party is liable to the principal as if he had entered into the contract with the principal.

1.5.3. The agent as against the principal

The principal is liable to the agent for commission if it has been earned. See 1.3.

1.5.4. The agent as against third parties

The third party is liable to the agent only so far as the contract requires the third party to do something for or on behalf of the agent. Strictly, in such circumstances the agent is not acting as an agent but as a principal.

Where the agent is acting for an undisclosed principal, he, the agent, sues the third party in his own name. If the identity of the principal is disclosed, the third party has the right to use against the principal all defences that were available as against the agent prior to notice of the existence of the principal.

1.6. Term and Termination

1.6.1. Term

Whatever the contract provides. If no term is specified, it can normally be terminated by reasonable notice. What is reasonable will depend on the length of time the arrangement has continued and the terms of the agency. Damages will be awarded in the event of inadequate notice. The measure of damages will be the foreseeable damages the agent may suffer by reason of lack of reasonable notice, subject to the obligation of the agent to mitigate his loss.

1.6.2. Termination

See 1.6.1.

1.7. Indemnity

1.7.1. Indemnity for goodwill and/or clientèle

Save for S.I.70/1980 there is no protection of the agent in relation to goodwill or clientele.

1.7.2. Compensation for damages

See 1.6.1. and 1.7.1.

1.8. Specific Application of EEC Law

Apart from any provision of EEC law which is automatically binding on a Member State, there has been no implementation in Ireland of any community law in this field.

1.9. Bibliography

Bowstead on Agency; Chitty on Contract, vol. 2.

1.10. Legislation

S.I.70/1980.

1.11. Case law

Aluminium Design Ltd. v *Alcan Windows Ltd.* 1980, vol. 4, p. 622, unreported cases.
Irish Welding Co. Ltd. v *Philips Electrical (Ireland) Ltd.* 1976, vol. 6, p. 86.

2. Distributorship Agreements

2.1. Distribution

2.1.1. Definition

2.1.1.1. Exclusive/non-exclusive/exclusive purchasing

In Irish law there is no statutory definition relation to distributorship agreements nor is there a statutory definition of what is a distribution agreement. A distributorship agreement is recognized as being a contract where a manufacturer or supplier agrees with another that the other will purchase from the manufacturer or supplier goods and then the other sells the goods for his own account either to retailers or the ultimate consumer, usually within a defined geographic area.

The relationship between the supplier and the distributor is governed by the ordinary principles of contract applicable to all contracts. Consequently the terms of the contract determine whether it is for instance exclusive or non-exclusive and the words used in the contract will be the determining factor. While expressions such as exclusive or non-exclusive are as a matter of convenience frequently used to describe the type of agreement, they are not terms of art.

However, as a distribution agreement is primarily a contract for the sale and purchase of goods and may be the provision of services, the Sale of Goods Act 1893, as amended by the Sale of Goods and Supply of Services Act 1980, which are applicable to all contracts for the sale of goods and/or supply of services, also apply to distributorship agreements.

2.1.2. Conclusion of the contract (special conditions)

A distributorship agreement is no different from any other contract and can be made verbally or in writing. There are no special conditions as to the manner in which it is to be concluded.

2.1.3. The supplier's duties and rights

2.1.3.1. The supplier's duties

These are governed by the terms of the contract in accordance with the general principles of contract law. In relation to the sale of goods and then supply of any attendant services, the law has to a certain extent been codified by the Sale of Goods Act 1893, as amended by the Sale of Goods and Supply of Services Act 1980.

It imposes the following obligations on the supplier which subject to the terms of the contract are implied:

(a) a condition that the supplier has the right to the goods at the time the property is to pass (section 12(1)(a));
(b) a warranty that the goods are and will remain free, until the time when the property is to pass, from any encumbrance (section 12(1)(b));
(c) a condition that where the goods are sold by description that the goods will comply with the description (section 13);
(d) a condition that the goods supplied under the contract are of merchantable quality (section 14(2));
(e) if the distributor makes known to the seller the particular purpose for which the goods are being bought there is an implied condition that the goods supplied under the contract are reasonably fit for that purpose (section 14(4));
(f) if the contract is for a sale by sample there is an implied condition that:

(i) the bulk shall correspond with the sample in quality;
(ii) the buyer shall have a reasonable opportunity of comparing the bulk with the sample;
(iii) the goods shall be free from any defect, rendering them un-merchantable, which would not be apparent on reasonable examination of the sample (section 15(1)).

However under section 55 of the Act any such implied condition or warranty as between supplier and distributor may be negatived or varied by:

(a) express agreement;
(b) by the course of dealing between the parties; or
(c) by usage if the usage is such as to bind both parties to the contract

save that the condition referred to in section 12(1)(a) and the warranty referred to in section 12(1)(b) cannot be negatived.

In addition, under section 61(6) of the Act, which is highly relevant to suppliers who are not resident in Ireland, it is provided in relation to "a contract for the international sale of goods" that nothing in the Act shall prevent the parties to a contract from negativing or varying any right, duty or liability which is imposed by sections 12 to 15 referred to above.

"A contract for the international sale of goods" means a contract of sale of goods made by parties whose places of business (or, if they have none, habitual residences) are in the territories of different states and in the case of which one of the following conditions is satisfied:

(a) the contract involves the sale of goods which are at the time of the conclusion of contract in the course of carriage or will be carried from the territory of one state to the territory of another;
(b) the acts constituting offer and acceptance have been effected in the territories of different states;
(c) delivery of the goods is to be made in the territory of a state other than that within whose territory the acts constituting the offer and the acceptance have been effected.

Consequently, in relation to distributorship agreements between an Irish distributor and a foreign supplier/manufacturer there is the right to vary substantially the implied conditions and warranties in relation to the quality of the goods supplied.

If the supplier agrees to supply any service to the distributor, section 39 of the Sale of Goods and Supply of Services Act 1980 provides as follows:

"in every contract for the supply of a service where the supplier is acting in the course of a business, the following terms are implied—

(a) that the supplier has the necessary skill to render the service,
(b) that he will supply the service with due skill, care and diligence,
(c) that, where materials are used, they will be sound and reasonably fit for the purpose for which they are required, and
(d) that, where goods are supplied under the contact, they will be of merchantable quality within the meaning of section 14(3) of the Act of 1893".

However section 40 of the 1980 Act provides any term of a contract implied by virtue of section 39 may be negatived or varied by an express term of the contract or by the course of dealing between the parties or by usage, if the usage be such as to bind parties to the contract, except that where the recipient of the service deals as consumer it must be shown that the express term is *fair and reasonable* (see 2.1.5.2. below) and has been specifically brought to his attention.

There is an anti-avoidance provision in section 42 which provides as follows. Where the proper law of a contract for the supply of a service in the course of a business would, apart from a term that it should be the law of some other country or a term to the like effect, be the law of Ireland or where any such contract contains a term which purports to substitute, or has the effect of substituting, provisions of the law of some other country for all or any of the provisions of sections 39 and 40, those sections shall, notwithstanding that term, apply to the contract.

There is a similar anti-avoidance provision in relation to the sale of goods in section 55A of 1893 Act as amended by the 1980 Act.

2.1.3.2. The supplier's rights

These are governed by the terms of the contract in accordance with the general principles of contract law.

2.1.4. The distributor's duties and rights

2.1.4.1. The distributor's duties

These are similarly governed by the terms of the contract in accordance with the general principles of contract law.

2.1.4.2. The distributor's rights

These are similarly governed by the terms of the contract in accordance with the general principles of contract law.

2.1.5. Liabilities of supplier and distributor during the term of the distributorship agreement

2.1.5.1. The supplier as against the distributor

The supplier has the right to sue the distributor for any breach of the terms of the contract in accordance with the general principles of contract law. There is no legislation imposing statutory obligations on the distributor.

2.1.5.2. The supplier as against third parties

The supplier will be liable to third parties in accordance with the general law of contract and the provisions of the Sale of Goods Act 1893 as amended by the Sale of Goods and Supply of Services Act 1980.

In addition, where the third party *deals* with the distributor *as a consumer*, any variation to the implied conditions and warranties under sections 12 to 15 of the Act are void and in any other case the variation must be *fair and reasonable* in order to be enforceable.

A party to a contract "deals as a consumer" if:

(a) he neither makes the contract in the course of a business nor holds himself out as doing so; and
(b) the other party does make the contract in the course of a business; and
(c) the goods or services supplied under or in pursuance of the contract are of a type ordinarily supplied for private or consumption.

In relation to what is fair and reasonable, the Schedule to the 1980 Act provides that regard shall be had to the circumstances which were, or ought reasonably to have been, known to or in the contemplation of the parties when the contract was made. In particular regard is to be had to the following:

(a) the strength of the bargaining positions of the parties relative to each other;
(b) whether the customer received an inducement to agree to the term, or in accepting it had an opportunity of entering into a similar contract with other persons, but without having to accept a similar term.
(c) whether the customer knew or ought reasonably to have known of the existence of the term;
(d) where the term excludes or restricts any relevant liability if some condition is not complied with, whether it was reasonable at the time of the contract to expect that compliance with that condition would be practicable;
(e) whether any goods involved were manufactured, processed or adapted to the special order of the customer.

2.1.5.3. The distributor as against the supplier

The distributor has the right to sue the supplier for any breach of the terms of the contract in accordance with the general principles of contract law. There is no legislation imposing statutory obligations on the supplier other than the Sale of Goods Act 1893 as amended by the Sale of Goods and Supply of Services Act 1980.

2.1.5.4. The distributor as against third parties

The distributor is liable as the manufacturer of the goods in accordance with the general law of negligence to the user of the goods.

2.1.6. Term and termination

2.1.6.1. Term

2.1.6.2. Termination

See 1.6.

2.1.7. Indemnity

Again, the form and extent of indemnity (if any) will depend on the contract. As a general principle of contract law, an indemnity will be construed strictly so that the party seeking to rely on it will have to satisfy the Court that the damage which he has suffered comes within the terms of the indemnity.

2.1.8. Specific application of EEC law

See 1.8.

2.1.9. Bibliography

McMahon and Binchy, *Irish Law of Torts*, Professional Books, 1981

2.1.10. Legislation

Sale of Goods Act 1893
Sale of Goods and Supply of Services Act 1980

2.2. Selective Distribution

2.2.1. Definition

This type of distribution allows the supplier to ensure that the very high quality products and methods are used correctly so as to maximise their advantages.

For this purpose, the supplier designates a limited number of selected exclusive distributors. Each depot is allotted a main sales territory in which it must try to ensure the best possible distribution of the supplier's products.

Within the allotted territory only the distributor depot may set up further distribution points.

A distributor may do business outside its main territory but may not establish any branch in the territory of another distributor.

The supplier employs specially trained staff to give training courses at distribution depots and to carry out regular inspections of depots and to generally look after them.

2.2.3.1. The supplier's duties

- to guarantee the integrity of its selective distribution system and to maintain an up-to-date list of all authorised supplier's dealers.
- in the event of a large network, the supplier may undertake to organise a trustee responsible for answering enquiries as to whether particular dealers are members of the network.
- to supply the distributor with products of high quality.

2.2.4.1. The distributor's duties

- to sell supplier's products only to qualified persons, to certain classes of customers.
- to use its best endeavours to secure the widest possible distribution of supplier's products.
- to organise lectures and demonstrations for potential purchase groups and to carry out sales promotions by visiting customers and sending out circulars and advertising material.
- to have adequately qualified and trained staff capable of instructing, advising and generally looking after the purchasers of supplier's products.
- to maintain complete stocks of supplier's products, large enough to enable all orders to be filled promptly.
- to be able to display a representative cross-section of supplier's products

and to provide rooms and facilities for any demonstrations the supplier wishes.
- to check goods before selling them to the public.
- to promote the trade-mark via publicity, advertising and other customary means.
- to set up an after-sales service (replacement of articles and provision of advice to customers wishing to supplement a service).
- not to sell the products by mail order because of the objection to provide customers with advice.

However, a dealer is not prohibited from mailing equipment to a customer at the customer's own request.

Duration and Termination

Pursuant to EEC decisions, 10 years is the term for that kind of agreement.
Consequences of termination—see "exclusive distribution".

2.2.11. Case law

Judgment of the Court of Justice (EEC)
Case 107/82, 'AEG—Telefunken' (1983) ECR, 3151
'SABA II' OJ No. L376, 31 December 1983
'Grundig' of 10 July 1985, OJ No. L233/1
'Villeroy & Boch' of 16 December 1985 OJ No. L376/15.
'Ivoclar AG of Leichtenstein' of 27 November, 1985 OJ No. L369.

3. Franchise Agreements

3.1. Definition

"Franchising is a form of commercial co-operation, laid down in writing between independent undertakings, whereby one party, the franchisor, grants one or more other parties, the franchisees, the use of his trademark or tradename and any other symbols, to be used in the process of offering and rendering services, or selling of goods on the basis of a marketing system, developed by the franchisor, in exchange for which the franchisor receives a payment from the franchisee in such a way that the franchisor controls the use of the granted rights in order to guarantee a uniform presentation, quality and service to the consumers".

3.3.1. The supplier's duties

- to grant to the franchisee, in a determined territory, the exclusive right to use insignia know-how
- to undertake an obligation to train the franchisee and other persons nominated by him at a course to act in the business and to continue such training in respect of other personnel joining the business

- to give to the franchisee technical and commercial assistance in the search, the locating and the fitting out of the sales outlet
- to agree and to improve and develop the method and to provide such further training to the franchisee and other persons engaged in the conduct of the business as may from time to time appear to be necessary
- to supply the franchisee with advertising materials
- to give to the franchisee the benefit of its knowledge and experience in connection with any problems relating to the method
- to assist the franchisee in procuring supplies, services and equipment as may be required by the franchisee to commence and operate the business.

3.4.1. The distributor's duties

- Not to commence the business until he or other persons responsible for the management of the business have undergone the course of training provided by the franchisor
- to conform in all respects and at all times with the method as modified from time to time and that he will not do or suffer to be done anything additional to nor in accordance with the method without the previous consent in writing of the franchisor
- not to divulge or suffer to be divulged to any person any information concerning the business
- to undertake to promote and make every effort steadily to increase the business by such advertisement, signs and other forms of publicity
- to co-operate with the franchisor and his other franchisees in any advertising campaign, sales promotion programme or other activity in which the franchisor may engage
- to promote and protect the goodwill associated with the method
- to keep the premises and furnishing in a good state of repair and decoration and replace and renew the equipment so as to enhance the reputation of the trademark, the method and the business
- not to cause or permit anything which may damage or endanger the tradename, trademark or other intellectual property right of the franchisor
- not to use the trademark except in conjunction with the business and not to use any name or mark similar to or capable of being confused with the tradename
- not to grant any sub-licence in respect of the method or any part thereof
- to maintain sufficient stocks and employ sufficient staff to permit the operation of the business at its maximum capacity and with maximum efficiency
- not to take part in a competing company where the franchissee directly contributes in the firm's running
- to only sell the franchisor's products
- not to sell to the distributors who do not belong to the network
- to pay to the franchisor franchise fee calculated at a certain rate upon the gross invoice price
- not to sell the business without prior written consent of the franchisor.

Duration and Termination

Pursuant to decisions of the EEC Commission of 17 December, 1986 namely, Yves Roches and Pronuptia—five years is the normal term of the franchise agreement.

Consequences of termination

- the franchisee must return to the franchisor all stationery and signs bearing the trademark of the franchisor
- the franchisee must cease to make any use of the trademark

3.9. Bibliography

"Recent Developments in Franchising," *Journal of Business Law* (May, 1986).
"Passing Off and Trade Libel the 'Big Mac' case," *Journal of Business Law* (May, 1986).
"Camera Care—v—Aktiebolag," *Financial Times* (2nd April 1986).
"Franchising in Europe: Consequences of Pronuptia," *International Business Lawyer* (July/Aug., 1986).
"The Franchising Phenomenon," *Business & Finance* (9 Oct. 1986).
"The E.C. Context Peter Sutherland," speech re franchising (28 January 1987).
"Competition—Pronuptia and Yves Rocher," *Trends* (January 1987).
"Pronuptia—its legal consequences for E.E.C. Competition Law," A.I.J.A.
"Franchising," C.L.E.
"Re: Article 85, Treaty—Pronuptia de Paris," 87/17/E.E.C. 17 December 1986.
"Re: Article 85, Treaty—Yves Rocher," 87/14/E.E.C. 17 December 1986.

CHAPTER 9
Italy

Nicoletta Contardi,
Anna Maria Fulgoni,
Alessandra Pandarese

1. Commercial Agency

1.1. Definition of Various Types of Agencies and Intermediaries

1.1.1. Independent

1.1.1.1. "Agente Commerciale"

The "Agente Commerciale" in Italian law is an agent who performs his activities at his own risk, undertaking to promote, for a commission, the conclusion of contracts on a regular basis in a specific territory, on behalf of one or more principals (Art. 1742 Italian Civil Code–"CC", see section 1.10).

The present-day figure of a commercial agent dervies from the "Commissionario", who concluded transactions on his own behalf. The needs of commerce, which expanded to territories other than the place of residence of the trader, led to the entrusting to third parties of the promotion of the sale of the principal/trader's goods in certain specific territories. Thus a commercial agent "would not preclude direct contacts with customers, would receive a profit sharing as and for his compensation and, accordingly, a price share which would be easier to control than the earnings of other middle-men, and would perform his activity on an autonomous basis".[1] We may further distinguish among agents who work only for one principal (monomandatari) and those working for more principals (plurimandatari). Finally, we must point out the distinction between agents having the power to represent their principals (that is to conclude contracts which are binding for the principal) and those whose power is limited to the promotion of contracts on behalf of the principal (who shall be free to accept or not the agent's proposal).

---

[1] E. Molitor, "Sul Concetto di Agente di Commercio", in *Studi di Diritto Commerciale in onore di Cesare Vivante* (Ed. Foro It. Rome, 1931).

Agents with representative power are called in Italy "Rappresentanti di Commercio" (trade representatives). This definition should, however, be considered cautiously, because it is also the word commonly used for defining agents as a whole.

Although a commercial agent remains an autonomous worker, the prevailing provisions of law on commercial agency relationships contain certain aspects, which are typical of the employment contract, such as the right to a termination indemnity and some procedural rules. However, some of the aforesaid provisions (in particular those concerning litigation) apply only when the agent is a physical person and derive from the public policy principle common in Italian law of protection of the weakest contracting party.

1.1.1.2. The "Commissionario" (commission agent)

The "Commissionario" is still to be found in Italy, although he has largely been supplanted by the commercial agent. He is defined by the civil code as the "Mandatario" (see below), who is entrusted with purchasing or selling goods on behalf of the principal and in his own name. The commission agent can also be found with similar characteristics in Belgian, Dutch, German, French and Danish law. He is a subspecies of the Mandatario, but whilst the Mandatario is deemed to work for consideration, the commission agent works essentially for consideration. He is a Mandatario with authority to represent his principal, since he acts in his own name.

1.1.1.3. The "Mandatario" (mandatary)

The "Mandatario" was defined in the old Italian Commercial Code of 1882 (Art. 349) as "dealing with commercial transactions in the name and on behalf of the principal. The commercial mandate is not to be presumed free of consideration." The present civil code (Art. 1703) provides that the mandate has as its objects, "the performance of one or more authorized actions". The mandate is the basis for both the commercial agent and the commission agent, which evolved from it to meet the needs of the changing commercial world.

1.1.1.4. The "Procacciatore d'Affari" (business finder) and "Mediatore" (broker)

The "Procacciatore d'Affari" is not regulated by law; he differs from the commerical agent in that his collaboration is carried out on an irregular and discontinuous basis with no rights of exclusivity and no specific territory.[2]

The "Mediatore" although a figure within commercial distribution does not have the usual characteristics to be found in the others. He is "a person who puts into contact two or more parties for the conclusion of a transaction without being bound to either of them by relationships of collaboration, employment or representation".

Thus his commission will be earned upon the transaction and will not arise from any continuous or stable relationship with any party.

[2] Court of Appeal Florence, 8 Nov. 1958, in *Orientamenti Giurispr. del Lavaro* (1959), 308. Cass. 31 Jan. 1954, no. 251, in *Foro Padano* (1954), ii. 25.

1.1.2. Employed agents

Under Italian law there are two types of employed agents, the "Viaggiatore" (commercial traveller) and the "Piazzista" (salesman). The "Viaggiatore" normally carries out his activity in a specific territory, and the "Piazzista" in a specific city. Both of them carry out similar activities to those of commercial agents, but they differ from the last-mentioned as they are employed by the entrepreneur, enjoy an extensive welfare and social security assistance, as well as a protection from unjustified lay-off and bear none of the risks relative to their activity. However, they can still be remunerated in part by way of a commission, which in this case is an incentive to create a greater volume of business for the entrepreneur.

1.2. Conclusion of the Contract (Special Conditions)

There are no specific requirements for the form of an agency contract under Italian law: it can be in writing, or according to custom, or verbal. However, Art. 2 of the Collective Bargaining Agreement of 20 June 1956 (see section 1.10) which is enforceable *erga omnes*, provides that, when appointing an agent or representative, the following details shall be set forth in writing: territory, products, commissions and compensations, and term, whenever this is not indefinite, besides the names of the parties. Further, Law No. 204 of 3 May 1985 (see section 1.10) which regulates the agent's profession, provides that agents must be registered in a specific "roll" at the Chamber of Commerce of their place of residence. This law further indicates the requirements for the registration in that roll (such as school diplomas, examinations etc.). Should the agent be a legal entity, it also has to be registered in the roll and the legal representative thereof must have the prescribed requisites. These rules do not apply for agents residing in Italy, but performing their activity exclusively abroad. The aforesaid law provides that contracts entered into with agents not registered in the roll are void and penalties are payable in case of breach of it's provisions. According to certain legal authors,[3] however, such contracts will not be voided but may be transformed into other types of contracts, provided that the essential elements of the other type of contract are present, so that, e.g. a void agency contract may be transformed into a valid contract of "Procacciatore d'Affari"; in such case the agent will remain entitled to his commissions, but will lose the ancillary benefits attached to the agency contract, such as termination indemnity, notice, etc.

1.3. The Principal's Duties and Rights

1.3.1. The principal's duties

1.3.1.3. Supply of written statement

The principal is usually required to supply the agent with a periodic written statement of account, indicating the volume of business transacted and the

---

[3] R. Baldi, *Il Contratto di Agenzia*, 3rd edn. (Giuffrè, Milan, 1987), 262.

amount of the commissions due. It will also indicate which commissions have become payable as a result of customers having settled their accounts.

Information and assistance

The principal must put at the agent's disposal all the information as well as the advertising and information material necessary for him to carry out his promotional activities, and give him all the required assistance, e.g. answer customers' queries.

Social security contributions

ENASARCO, the National Institution providing Assistance and Welfare to Trade Representatives and Agents and their families, was created in 1939 and is actually regulated by Law of 2 February 1973 N.12 (see section 1.10). Registration with ENASARCO is compulsory for all commercial agents who work in Italy on behalf of Italian principals, or on behalf of foreign principals having a permanent establishment in Italy, and for all agents performing their activity abroad on behalf of Italian principals. Within three months from the effective date of the agency contract, principals must register their agents with ENASARCO. Later they must pay quarterly the relevant contributions amounting to 4% of the commission due to be borne by agent plus 4% to be borne by the principal. The principal shall pay the total figure of the contribution due and later deduct from the agent's commission the amount corresponding to his share of contributions.

1.3.2. The principal's rights

1.3.2.1. Right to give instructions to agent

According to Art. 1746 CC Agents shall perform their activity according to the instructions received from the principal. However, the instructions of the principal shall not be such to cancel the autonomy of the agent, who always remains an autonomous worker. Therefore the principal shall have no right to impose a specific working schedule on the agent; he may instead establish which clients should be visited more frequently and the kinds of business establishment to be contacted by preference, and those to be avoided.

1.3.2.2. The del credere provision

The "*del credere*" provision is a guarantee of the purchaser's solvency issued by the agent to the principal for the transactions concluded by him. This guarantee consists in charging the agent with a part of the loss incurred by the principal by reason of the customer's default. In order to be enforceable, the "*del credere*" provision must be expressly agreed upon by the parties in writing. According to the Collective Bargaining Agreement of 1956, which is enforceable *erga omnes*, the agent's liability is limited to 20% of the loss suffered by the principal and in any case it may never exceed one half of the commission due to the agent for that year. According to more recent collective bargaining agreements, which apply, however, only for the parties enrolled in the relevant trade unions or associations, the "*del credere*" commission is limited to 15% of the loss suffered by principal. Further, the "*del credere*" provision applies only in case of losses caused by default of the customer and not following to contestations concerning the quality of the goods supplied or of any other kind. Whenever the principal shall recover even part of his loss, the agent shall be entitled to a proportional refund of the *"del credere"* commission withheld by the principal.

1.4. The Commercial Agent's Duties and Rights

According to Art. 1746 CC, "the agent shall perform his assignment according to the instructions received and shall supply the principal with all information concerning the market conditions in his territory, and any other useful information in order to judge the convenience of any single business transaction."

1.4.1. The commercial agent's duties

1.4.1.1. Trustworthiness, duty to inform

The main duty of a commercial agent is that of performing his activity (the promotion of business on behalf of the principal) with diligence, that is, he shall ensure with his activity a continuous contact with customers, visiting them frequently, etc., in order to ensure the maximum amount of orders for the principal. The parties may also agree a minimum volume of orders to be met annually by the agent, and failure to reach said minimum may result in termination of the contract for negligence on the agent's part. Another duty of the agent is that of supplying the principal with all available information concerning market conditions and trends, customers' wishes, fashion trends, terms and conditions of competitors, customers' solvency, etc. Particularly detailed—as is easy to understand—must be the information concerning the advisability of each transaction and the customers' solvency: some authors even suggest that an agreement can be terminated upon repeated supply by the agent of wrong information on the advisability of a transaction due to the agent's negligence or incapacity.[4]

According to prevailing case-law, instead, the termination of an agreement would take place only in the case of the supply of wrongful or incomplete information concerning transactions actually promoted (and which thereafter turned out to be prejudicial to the principal).[5]

1.4.2. The commercial agent's rights

1.4.2.1. Commission

The principal must pay the agreed commission to the agent as consideration for the performance of the agent's activity on his behalf. This commission is usually a percentage of the business concluded and paid for by the customer and can be in a fixed amount or on a sliding scale, according to the volume of business transacted.

There are some discussions whether the agent may be compensated with a fixed periodical sum; however, this form of compensation may be admitted

---

[4] Formiggini, "Il Contratto di Agenzia", *UTET* (1958).
[5] Cass. 13 Mar. 1976, n. 911, in *Mass. Giur. It.*, col. 236.

only as a contribution to cover expenses or as advances to be set off with the commission to be paid in the subsequent months, but it is not acceptable as a usual form of compensation because it is against the very principle of the agent's figure, who is an autonomous worker who works at his own risk and shall be compensated according to his performance. Should certain business transactions proposed by the agent only come to a successful conclusion after the termination of the agency relationship, the agent shall remain entitled to the commission on those transactions. Further, in the absence of a valid agreement to the contrary, the agent remains entitled to a commission for the business directly transaction by the principal in the agent's territory.

Territory and exclusive right

The Exclusive right may be the object of a clause of the agency contract consisting in the fact that one or both parties agree to deal exclusively with the other party within the territory of activity of one agent. Exclusivity can be unilateral or bilateral; in the most frequent case of a bilateral exclusive right, the principal may not appoint other agents for the same products in the territory entrusted to that particular agent, while the agent may not transact business competing with those of the principal. Of course it is possible to enter into different forms of exclusivity agreements, varying according to the contractual power of the parties and the prevailing customs in that particular market area.

Powers of representation

Unless a specific power of representation of the agent is agreed upon (see above), the agent has no power to conclude contracts which are binding for the principal.

There are some very limited representation powers granted by Italian law to agents, such as the following: Art. 1745 CC recognizes a passive representation in "all declarations concerning performance of contracts entered into through the agents" and in "complaints relating to non-performance of a contract". This means that third party purchasers can file their complaints with the agent in the place where he operates.

Pursuant of Art. 1745 second para. CC. the Agent may also ask the Judge for urgent precautionary measures or attachments in order to protect the principal's rights deriving from the performance of contracts entered into through the agent.

The agent is not empowered to collect claims on behalf of his principal and, if he is exceptionally so authorized, he cannot grant extensions or discounts without his principal's authorization (Art. 1744 CC).

1.5. Liabilities of principal and agent during the Term of the Agency

1.5.1. The principal as against the agent

In the case where the agent has promoted and introduced a transaction and the principal does not execute this transaction, the agent is entitled to the commission which would have been paid had the principal carried out his duty.

Unless otherwise agreed, an agent remains entitled to commissions for transactions directly entered into by the principal in the agent's territory.

1.5.2. The principal as against third parties

An agent who has authority to enter into agreements will bind his principal and render him liable towards third parties for the unlawful behaviour of the agent within the limits of the duties and authority granted to him.

1.5.3. The agent as against the principal

Besides the agent's responsibilities as against the principal mentioned in 1.3 and 1.4 hereof, we can only say that, according to Art. 1747 CC, agents are required to give immediate notice to their principal of any reason which may inhibit the continuance of their activity, and that they are responsible for the damages caused to the principal, in case they fail to do so.

1.5.4. The agent as against third parties

Besides the responsibility of the agent without power to represent the principal for his engagement towards his customers, we do not find in Italian law particular cases of liability of the agent against third parties.

1.6. Term and Termination

1.6.1. Term

Italian agency agreements may be for a definite or indefinite term. Failing any indication of term, they are deemed to be for an indefinite term.

1.6.2. Termination

In case of agency agreements for a definite term, termination of the agreement coincides with the expiration of the term, although agreements may be terminated in advance, by reason of breach. However, the Collective Bargaining Agreements of 19 December 1979 and of 18 January 1977 (which apply only to the interested categories) provide that agency agreements entered into for a term exceeding six months may be terminated only by giving at least 60 days' notice before the expiration of the term.

In case of agency agreements entered into for an indefinite term, each party has the right to terminate the agreement by giving advance notice to the other party, at least 4 months before the date where the termination shall be effective, as provided by the Collective Bargaining Agreement of 1956 (which is enforceable *erga omnes*). In a case where the principal wishes to dismiss the agent before the expiration of the notice period, he is required to pay him an indemnity in-lieu-of-notice, amounting to 4/12 of the commissions earned in the preceding year.

1.7. Indemnity

1.7.1. Indemnity for goodwill and/or clientèle

In any case of termination of the agency agreement for reasons not attributable to the agent, the agent is entitled to an indemnity for the loss of clientèle. Said indemnity was introduced by the Collective Bargaining Agreement of 1974 and is calculated on the amount of all commissions earned after 1 January 1975. Its amount varies from 3% to 4% of the mentioned commissions according to the criteria indicated in the prevailing Collective Bargaining Agreements.

1.7.2. Compensation for damages

According to Art. 1751 CC, in any case of termination of the agency agreement, an indemnity is due to the agent. Such indemnity shall be calculated on all sums paid by the principal to the agent during the course of their relationship, including the sums paid as refund for expenses. The amount of said indemnity varies according to the business sector of the principal (industry or commerce), the length of the relationship, the total amount of the commissions earned by the agent, and other parameters; it may be in the range of 1% to 4% of the commissions.

1.8. Special Application of EEC-Law

Besides the new rules on jurisdiction introduced by the Brussels Convention of 1968, we cannot say at present that there are specific applications of EEC law in Italy in the captioned field, and that the prevailing Italian law dispositions on agency agreements do not contrast with the EEC Directive of 18 December 1986 concerning the independent commercial agents.

1.8.1. Applicable law and jurisdiction

Agency agreements concerning agents performing their activity in Italy may be governed by a different law than Italy's, provided that at least one party is not an Italian national and that the relevant clause has been entered into in writing simultaneously with the execution of the agreement. Whenever the agency relationship is governed by a foreign law, all indemnities due to the agent under Italian law are not applicable, and the registration with ENASARCO is not mandatory.

In case of controversies between the parties of an agency agreement governed by Italian law and whenever the agent is a physical person, performing his activity personally, the rules on the so-called "Labour Proceedings" apply (see section 1.10).

Such proceedings are held in front of the "Pretore" (Magistrate of the lower court, which has one judge), and with a much simpler procedure than that applicable for normal lawsuits.

In case one party is not an Italian national, and save for the dispositions of the applicable international conventions (e.g. the Brussels Conventions of 1968 between the member States of EEC), Italian law (see section 1.10) establishes that a foreigner can be summoned in front of an Italian Court in the following cases:

(a) When the foreigner has an office, or a branch in Italy;
(b) if he has appointed a representative with the authority to represent him in court;
(c) if the proceedings concern a contractual obligation arisen or to be performed in Italy;
(d) if the claim is connected with another claim on which the Italian judge has jurudiction;
(e) if the claim concerns provisionary measures to be enforced in Italy;
(f) if, in case of reciprocity, the foreign judge would have jurisdiction over an Italian.

Whenever an Italian judge shall decide a claim according to a foreign law, the parties will have the burden to provide him with the knowledge of the foreign law; whenever the parties fail to provide the judge with the necessary knowledge and the judge shall not be able to get this knowledge elsewhere, he shall decide according to Italian law.

1.10. Legislation

Considering the prevailing legislation in the field of commercial agency, we must distinguish between mandatory regulations (applicable *erga omnes*) and contractual regulations (applicable only with regards to the interested categories). Finally, we must consider that most of the regulations apply only with regards to "Agenti" in the strict meaning of said term, with the exclusion of any other similar figure.

The main mandatory rules on this subject are the following:
Arts. 1742–1752 CC;
Law 3 May 1985 No. 204 (Discipline of the Activity of Commercial Agents and Representatives);
Law 2 February 1973 (Nature and Duties of the National Institution of Welfare and Assistance for Trade Representatives and Agents—ENASARCO).

The contractural regulations consist in Collective Bargaining Agreements (Accordo Economico Collettivo—AEC), which are only binding for those parties adhering to the interested trade unions or associations. An exception to this principle is provided by AEC of 20 June 1956 for agents of industrial enterprises, which has been declared *erga omnes* by means of:
D.P.R. (Presidential Decree) of 16 January 1961 No. 145 and AEC of 30 June 1938 as modified by AEC of 13 October 1958 for agents of commercial enterprises, declared enforceable *erga omnes*, by means of D.P.R. of 26 December 1960 No. 1842.

Said AECs have been later amended by the AECs hereinafter mentioned; we must note, however, that the more recent AECs do not substitute completely the older ones, so that in some cases the rules of the preceding AEC, which have not been amended by the more recent one, continue to be applicable.

(a) AECs applicable to industrial enterprises: of 2 August 1965, 30 June 1969 and 12 December 1979;
(b) AECs applicable to commercial enterprises: 19 March 1964, 5 October 1968, 8 July 1971, 1 January 1977 and 24 January 1981.

There are further AECs for handicraft enterprises.
Following are the rules applicable in case of dispute:

Law of 11 August 1973, N.533, modifying the rules of Title IV of Book II of the code of civil procedure.
Art. 4 of the code of civil procedure.

2. Distributorship Agreements

2.1. Distribution

2.1.1. Definition

The distributor is a trader who buys goods from the supplier and resells them on his own behalf and on his own account. The distributor sets up a regular relationship with the supplier which can be either of limited or unlimited duration.

Frequently, in view of the regular relationship the distributor enters into special arrangements with the supplier such as holding stocks of the products, advertising in order to promote sales in a specific territory, fixing minimum sales and sales policy, providing reciprocal or unilateral exclusivity.

The special arrangements mentioned above may not differ from those provided in agency agreements and therefore confusion may arise. However, the distributor differs from the agent because he sells on his own behalf and not on behalf of his principal. Consequently, the distributor is not normally entitled to commission on contracts duly performed as the agent is, but he makes a profit on the difference between the purchase price and the resale price. Particularly in international contracts the parties frequently enter into both agency and distributorship agreements in order to be able to cope with the requirements of local customers, who sometimes may prefer buying from a local entity and on other occasions from a foreign supplier. There are no statutory provisions dealing with distributorships. Therefore distribution agreements are among those called "atipici" (not typical); this means that they are not expressly regulated in the Civil Code.

Courts and Authors give different interpretations concerning its nature. According to some precedents it is either a mere sale of goods or a mixed contract (mandate, sales and supply agreements).[6]

The prevailing precedents consider distributorship a "somministrazione" (supply contract) which is defined by Art. 1559 Italian Civil Code as "the

---

[6] Cass. 21 Apr. 1975, n. 1538, in *Mass. Giur. It.* (1975), pp. 424–25; Cass. 26 Sept. 1979, in *Giur. It.* (1980), 1, 1st edn. 1545 *et seq.*; trib. Napoli 15 Jan. 1979, in *Dir. e Giur.* (1979), p. 602 (n. Parfetti, *Ancora sul contratto di concessione e vendita*) 29 Nov. 1974, in *Dir. e Giur.* (1975), p. 584 et seq.

contract whereby a party undertakes, in return for a consideration, to supply goods regularly or periodically to the other one".[7]

Recently, courts have considered the distribution agreement as a different contract from those regulated in the Civil Code; and therefore they will decide on a case-by-case basis having regard to the characteristics of each particular contract.[8]

2.1.1.1. Exclusive/non-exclusive/exclusive purchasing

The distributor and the supplied may provide reciprocal or unilateral exclusivity. Consequently, the distributor may not sell in the same sector and in the same territory for several competing suppliers, nor may he manufacture and sell the same products on his own behalf.

On the other hand, the supplier may not appoint other distributors or traders directly in the distributor's territory.

One writer[9] believes that exclusivity clauses may be considered unlawful when they are not justified and have a monopolistic aim. However, if the distribution agreement is interpreted as a supply contract, exclusivity is regulated by Art. 1567 and 1568 Italian Civil Code,[10] and therefore are perfectly legal. Moreover, Arts. 1567 and 1568 do not limit the duration exclusivity.

However, if Art. 2596 Italian Civil Code (providing that the arrangements limiting competition are valid when they do not exceed five years would apply, problems could arise. But it is generally asserted that Art. 2596 applies *only* to single arrangements limiting competition which are not inserted contracts.

It has been held that Art. 2596 does not apply to exclusive-dealing provisions, since its nature is not the one of a competition provision in its strict sense. In fact, the activities of the contracting parties are not in direct competition, as they are at different levels.[11]

It must be noted that an exclusivity clause is valid only between parties and may not affect third parties who are allowed to sell in the exclusive territory.[12]

Art. 2596 is, instead, applicable to clauses limiting competition having their effect after the expiration of the agreement, which therefore may not

---

[7] Cass. 8 June 1976, n. 2094, in *Mass. Giur. It.*, col. 555; Cass. 13 May 1969, in *Mass. Giur. It.* (1976), col. 448; Cass 22 Dec 1969 n 4041, in *Mass. Giur. It.* (1969), col. 1600–1; Cass. 12 July 1965, n. 1473, in *Foro It.* (1966), i, col. 725.

[8] Oreste Cagnasso, *La concessione di vendita* (Giuffré).

[9] Ascarelli, *Patti di esclusiva, Patti di boicottaggio e concorrenza sleale*, in *Riv. Dir. Ind.* (1959), i. 5 *et seq.*

[10] Relevant Sections of the Italian Civil Code are given in translation on pp. 353–361 and unless otherwise indicated, all references are to this Code.

[11] The Courts of Cassation have held that Art. 2598 of the Italian Civil Code is not applicable to exclusive-dealing agreements, either with regard to time-limits or the duration of the agreements (see Corte di Cass. 18 July 1960, n. 2002, in *Giustizia Civile* (1960), i. 1747; Corte di Cass. 24 Oct. 1967, n. 2619, in *Giustizia Civile* (1967), i. 1940), nor with regard to the written form "ad probationem" (Corte di Cass., 20 Dec. 1973, p. 224), since "those agreements are not considered to restrict competition directly, but as a side-effect of the exclusion of third-party competitors from the collaboration which is established between the contracting parties".

[12] Court of Milan 18 July 1985, in *Giur. Ann. Dir. industriale* and all other judgments cited herein.

exceed five years and must concern a delimited territory and a determined activity. The validity of exclusivity clauses is due to the fact that Italy doesn't yet have domestic antitrust laws. However, as a member of the EEC, Italy is of course subject to the full impact or the competition rules of the Treaty of Rome.

2.1.2. Conclusion of the contract (special conditions)

There are no statutory provisions requiring particular formalities. The parties can freely choose how to enter into the agreement. However, Art. 1341 of the Italian Civil Code is highly relevant for certain clauses (clausole vessatorie) which might be included in distribution agreements, such as limitation liability, earlier termination clauses, limitation clauses, limitation of the right to raise opposition, limitation of freedom to deal with third parties, automatic extension of the contract, arbitration agreements and derogation to court jurisdiction.

According to Art. 1341 the clauses which establish in favour of the offerer who has drafted them in advance are invalid unless specifically accepted in writing. The purpose of Art. 1341 Italian Civil Code is the protection of the weaker party in the negotiation. The acceptance of these clauses is shown by a second signature after the reference of each single clause at the bottom of the signed agreement. According to Art. 1341 the exclusive clause must be specifically accepted in writing.

2.1.3. The supplier's duties and rights

Since no statutory provisions are expressly provided, the parties are free to determine their contractural obligation.[13] Some of the recurring clauses are required to above (see section 2.1.1. above).

The parties must not forget Art. 1341 (see section 2.1.2. above) and Art. 2596 (see section 2.1.1.1. above). The general rules on contracts (Art. 1321 *et seq.* of the Civil Code) apply whether or not the parties have agreed differently. Some rules, which are compulsory, may not be derogated by the parties. Provisions upon supply contracts may also apply to distribution contracts (see Arts. 1559–1570). In particular, according to Art. 1570 "to the extent that they are compatible with the provisions of the preceding articles, the provisions governing different types of contract may apply."

Art. 1566 may apply and parties must not forget that where they want to provide in their agreement a clause concerning "the right of first refusal in the stipulation of a future contract for the same purpose", this clause must not exceed 5 years. (Where the agreement provides longer duration, the latter is automatically reduced up to 5 years.)

2.1.3.1. The supplier's duties

See section 2.1.3. above.

---

[13] Fabio Bartolotti, "Guida alla stipulazione di contratti con agenti e concessione all'estero", ed. Sole 24 ore. (He refers to the most commonly recurring clauses in the distribution agreements.)

2.1.3.2. The supplier's rights

See section 2.1.3. above.

2.1.4. The distributor's duties and rights

See section 2.1.3. above.

2.1.4.1. The distributor's duties

See section 2.1.3. above.

2.1.4.2. The distributor's rights

See section 2.1.3. above.

2.1.5. Liabilities of supplier and distributor during the term of distributorship agreement

2.1.5.1. The supplier as against the distributor

The distributor is liable under contract and has to perform the contractual obligations charged to him.

2.1.5.2. The supplier as against third parties

Before the Italian Law on product liability D.P.R. n. 224 of 24 May 1988,[14] which implemented EEC Directive n. 85/374, the general principles of civil extracontractual liabilities of Art. 2043 of the Civil Code regulated the liability of the supplier/manufacturer as against third parties such as the consumers. According to Art. 2043 c.c., the consumers have to prove the fault of the supplier whenever they suffer damage. Today's industrialization makes this proof very difficult to obtain. For this reason European Law (Directive n. (85/374) based the supplier/manufacturer liability on object liability. Italian legislation, in application of this directive, now provides that the consumer doesn't have to prove the manufacturer's or intermediary's fault. He only has to prove the damage, the defects and the connection between them both.

On the other hand, it is the supplier/manufacturer who has to bring evidence which excludes his liability (Art. 6 D.P.R. 224/88 reproducing Art. 7 of EEC Directive 85/374).

It is also interesting to note that courts in some cases had to intervene in order to make up for the lack of legislation before Law D.P.R. N. 224/88 was introduced.

In fact a court stated as follows: "When the supplier supplies products which are dangerous by their own nature, consumers only have to prove the relation between the damage and the defective product supplier and not the supplier's fault in manufacturing."[15] Moreover, the court believed that it is impossible for consumers to prove defective manufacturing, especially where the production is standardized. Therefore, because of the particular

---

[14] D.P.R. No. 224 of 24 May 1988. For translation see pp. 000–000 below.
[15] Cass. 13 Mar. 1980, n. 1696, in *Mass. Giur. Civ.* (1980), 739; Cass. 2 Mar. 1973, n. 577, *Giust. Civ.*, in *Mass.* (1973), 296.

nature of the product, the supplier is held liable under Art. 2050 of the Civil Code.[16]

Furthermore, in a leading case[17] the Supreme Court stated that when the product had caused damage through its use and it had been destroyed, and because of this destruction the consumer was not able to prove the relationship between the damage and the defect, this relation must be presumed.[18]

2.1.5.3. The distributor as against the supplier

The distributor may be held liable under the contract and has duly to perform the contractual obligations.

2.1.5.4. The distributor as against third parties

The distributor is liable under contract as against the direct buyers and has to perform the contractual obligation charged on him.

It is generally asserted that Art. 1494 applies to distribution agreements. According to this provision the seller is liable for damages due to the defects of the goods sold unless he proves that he had no knowledge of the defect.

In general, as against all third parties, according to D.P.R. n. 244 of 24 May 1988, a wider protection is provided to the consumer against risks of defective goods; the distributor may be held liable for damages of defective goods, when the principal/manufacturer is unknown, unless the distributor indicates the principal on request (Art. 4 of D.P.R. 224/88). In any case, under the terms of that law, the distributor might be liable together with the principal.

2.1.6. Term and termination

2.1.6.1. Term

Distribution agreements can have a limited or unlimited duration. No limit of duration is provided for the clauses limiting competition during the life of agreement (see section 2.1.1.1. above).

2.1.6.2. Termination

While there is no legislation in Italy specifically addressed to the problem of termination, cancellation, or non-renewal of a distribution agreement, the general principles on contract apply.

Where parties provide a date of termination, they have to perform this obligation and terminate the agreement on the date thereof. The parties may provide an advance notice to communicate to the other parties when one of them wants the renewal of the agreement.

Where the agreement is of unlimited duration, the party who wants to terminate has to give an advanced notice to the other party. In particular, one writer[19] suggests that also Art. 1569, which requires advance notice by

---

[16] Ibid. and see below, pp. 000.
[17] Cass. 9 May 1969, n. 1595, in resp. *Civ. e Prev.* (1970).
[18] App. Roma 26 November 1976 in *Giur. merito* (1977). i. 1979, *Trib. Forli*, 7 May 1976, in *Giur. It.* (1978), i. 2.
[19] Baldi.

either party to terminate an agreement of unlimited duration, applies to distribution agreements ("Such notice must be given within the time agreed upon, or established by usage, or in the absence thereof, within a reasonable time with respect to the nature of the supply."). Furthermore, all general rules on the cancellation of a contract apply such as: Arts. 1418–1424 (nullità del contratto); Arts. 1425–1446 (annullamento del contratto); Arts. 1447–1452 (rescissione del contratto); Arts. 1453–1469 (risoluzione del contratto).

In particular, the Civil Code provides the general principal that in contracts requiring performances by both parties, if one of the parties fails to perform, the other party may demand either performance or termination of the contract, and may seek the payment of damages (Art. 1454). Moreover, Art. 1455 of the Civil Code, states that a contract may be terminated if breach by one of the parties has little importance in relation to the interests of the other party.

Finally, Art. 1341, which expressly refers to "the right to terminate from contract", could apply. These clauses must be accepted in writing (see section 2.1.2 above). Furthermore, a specific provision on termination is provided by the supply contract in Art. 1564 c.c. According to the courts, the last-mentioned applies to distribution agreements.[20]

2.1.7. Indemnity

In case of termination, the distributor does not have the right to an indemnity from the supplier.[21]

While the distributor has the right for indemnity for an earlier unlawful termination on agreement from the supplier, the parties may provide that in case one of them fails or is late in the performance, the party may indemnify the other one with a fixed amount (Art. 1382—clausola penale). In this case, the other party doesn't have to prove the damage.

There is no specific application in Italy of EEC-law on distribution agreements. However, with D.P.R. 224/88, Italy has given application to the Directive on product liability.

EEC Competition rules have a direct impact in the Member State, therefore when infringement of Arts. 85 (1) and 86 (1) arises, courts routinely refer to them, in addition to Art. 2598 (unfair competition of Civil Code).

2.2. Selective Distribution

2.2.1. Definition

With selective-distribution agreements, the supplier agrees to supply products only to a special number of distributors having particular characteristics for the purpose of reselling his products.

The Court stated the validity of arrangements selecting distribution and protected the selective-distribution system.[22]

[20] Cass. 24 Jan. 1959 n., in *Mass. Giur. It.* (1959), col. 46–47.
[21] Cass. 21 June 1974, n. 1888, in *Giur. It.* (1975), i, col. 1290.
[22] Cass. 21 Apr. 1975, n. 1538, in *Mass. Giur. It.* (1975), pp. 424–25; Cass. 26 Sept. 1979, in *Giur. It.* (1980), 1, 1st edn. 1545 *et seq.*; trib. Napoli 15 Jan. 1979, in *Dir. e Giur.* (1979), p. 602 (n. Parfetti, *Ancora sul contratto di concessione e vendita*) Nov. 29 1974, in *Dir. e Giur.* (1975), p. 584 et seq.

In one case the court followed the interpretation of The Court of Justice and stated that the way in which the distributors were selected was discriminatory and therefore was an act of unfair competition.[23]

For 2.2.2.–2.2.7. see above from sections 2.1.2. to 2.1.7.

There are no specific provisions for selective distribution.

2.2.8. Specific application of EEC-law

See the decision of the Supreme Court in Case-law, 2 below.

2.2.11. Case-law

1. Pretura di Vigevano ordinanza 17 November 1986, in *Riv. dir. Ind.* (1987), ii. 215. Pretura di Vigevano orded interim measures with the purposes of protecting the selective-distribution system of an important company distributing software and computers.

According to clause n. 7 of the distribution agreement the distributor was forbidden from using reproducing or licence copies of software. The judge considered that the behaviour of the distributors selling the computers and reproducing copies of the supplier's software was infringing the contract and being an act of unfair competition.

The judge stated that the two conditions for preliminary urgent measure *fumus boni juris* (at *prima facie* evidence of infringement of law) and *periculum in mora* (likelihood of serious and irreparable harm to the applicant unless measures are ordered) were met. In this way the court protects the selective-distribution system of the applicant.

2. Cass. 15 March 1985, n. 2018, in *Foro It.* (1985), p. 1663 with note of Pardolesi (see also the precedent mentioned herein). This case concerned the distribution of magazines and newspapers. The national collective agreement of 5 March 1969, presently not operative, provided a system in which the distributor of newspapers had to obtain, beside an administration leave, an authorization ("tesserino di prelevamento") released from a Commission composed by the association of supplier and the association of distributors.

The distributors excluded from this system of double barriers to entry in the market claimed before the special Commission for boycott, unfair competition, and invalidity of the arrangements.

As there is no antitrust legislation, the arrangements selecting distribution cannot be declared void according to Italian law. Therefore the court asked the Court of Justice for interpretation of Art. 85 EEC Treaty in relation to these arrangements.

The Court of Justice declared that selective distribution does not infringe Art. 85 no. 1 and Art. 86 no. 1 where the leave is granted following objective criteria and is not discriminatory.

---

[23] Cass. 8 June 1976, n. 2094, in *Mass. Giour. It.*, col. 555; Cass. 13 May 1969, in *Mass. Giur. It.* (1976), col. 448; Cass. 22 Dec. 1969, n. 4041, in *Mass. Giur. It.* (1969), col. 1600–1; Cass. 12 July 1965, n. 1473, in *Foro It.* (1966), i, col. 725.

Thereafter the Supreme Court followed the principle of the Court of Justice and stated that the criteria applied by the Commission were discriminatory.

Apart from this specific case which was held to be discriminatory and as being an act of unfair competition, generally, selective-distribution practices are legal and not void according to Italian legislation.

3. Franchise Agreements

3.1. Definition

In Italy the Italian Franchising Organization (Associazione Italiana del Franchising) has given the following definition of Franchising:

Franchising—Affiliazione commerciale—is a form of continuous collaboration for the distribution of goods or services between an Entrepreneur (Affiliante) and one or more Entrepreneurs (Affiliati) juridically and financially independent one from the other who enter into an agreement through which:

(a) the Affiliator grants to the Affiliate the utilization of its commercial formulae including the right to exploit its know-how (all techniques and knowledge necessary) and its distinctive signs together with other services and forms of assistance which permit the Affiliate to manage his business in the same image as that of the Affiliate.

(b) The Affiliate undertakes to adopt the Affiliator's commercial policy and image in the reciprocal interests of the parties themselves and the final consumer as well as to respect contractual conditions which have been fully agreed.

The term "Affiliazione" has been used in Italy to evidence the relationship between the franchisor and the franchisee.

3.1.1. Characteristics

The Italian contract of franchising is a mixed contract and one which is not governed in a specific way by any provisions of law either in the Civil Code or by Statute.

It is a contract both of supply, sale and a trade-mark licence and the courts will in any disputes arising out of a franchising contract in Italy look at which element or which elements of the contract prevails and will apply the provisions of Statute and Civil Code to the different kinds of contracts.

The contract of franchising in Italy is often identified with the distributorship contract and Italian doctrine has sometimes identified the main aspects of franchising as the giving of a series of services which are much closer than a mere trading relationship providing for secondary activities and supplementary services.

In Italy franchising agreements do not usually provide for front money to be paid by the franchisee and therefore the Italian franchisee must have available a certain initial capital and as well as a licence for the resale of the products on his premises.

In Italy we find exclusive franchising in which the franchisee may only sell the products of the franchisor and non-exclusive franchising in which the franchisee as well as selling the products of the franchisor, with the exclusion of competing products, is free to sell other products.

3.2–3.8. No special comment is called for.

3.9. Bibliography

Frignani, *Factoring Franchising Concorrenza* (Giapichelli, Turin, 1979).

Frignani, "Contributo ad una ricerca sui problemi dogmatici del Franchising (con particolare riferimento all'Italia)", in "nuovi tipi contrattuali, tecniche di redazione nella pratica commerciale—Quaderni di giurisprudenza commerciale" (Guiffrè, Milan, 1978).
Zanelli, "Il Franchising nella tipologia delle concessioni tra imprese in nuovi tipi contrattuali e techniche di redazione nella pratica commerciale, quaderni di giurisprudenza commerciale" (Giuffrè, Milan, 1978).
Baldi, *Il Contratto di Agenzia* (Giuffrè, 3rd ed., Milan, 1987).

3.10 Legislation

There is no specific legislation either in the Italian Civil Code or by Statute upon Franchising contracts in Italy.

1341. Standard conditions of contract. Standard conditions prepared by one of the parties are effective (1370) as to the other, if at the time of formation of the contract the latter knew of them or should have known of them by using ordinary diligence (1176).

In any case conditions are ineffective, unless specifically approved in writing, which establish, in favor of him who has prepared them in advance, limitations on liability (1229), the power of withdrawing from the contract or of suspending its performance, or which impose time limits involving forfeitures on the other party (2965), limitations on the power to raise defenses (1462), restrictions on contractual freedom in relations with third parties, tacit extension or renewal of the contract, arbitration clauses, or derogations from the competence of courts.

*   *   *

SECTION II

Penal Clause and Earnest

1382. Effects of penal clause. A clause by which it is agreed that in case of non-performance or delay of performance (1218) one of the contracting parties is liable for a specified penalty, has the effect of limiting the compensation to the promised penalty, unless compensation was agreed on for additional damages (1223).

The penalty is due regardless of proof of damage.

*   *   *

CHAPTER XI

NULLITY OF CONTRACT

1418. Causes of nullity of contract. A contract that is contrary to mandatory rules is void, unless the law provides otherwise.

A contract is rendered void by the lack of one of the requisites indicated in article 1325, unlawfulness (1343) of *causa*, unlawfulness of the motives in the case indicated in article 1345, and lack in the object of the requisites set forth in article 1346.

A contract is also void in the other cases established by law.

1419. Partial nullity. Partial nullity of the contract or the nullity of single clauses imports the nullity of the entire contract, if it appears that the contracting parties would not have entered into it without that part of its content which is affected by nullity.

The nullity of single clauses does not import the nullity of the contract when, by operation of law, mandatory rules are substituted for the void clauses (1339, 1354, 1679, 1815, 1932, 2066, 2077, 2115).

1420. Nullity in multilateral contracts. When there are more than two parties to a contract, and the performances of each of them are directed to the accomplishment of a common objective, nullity affecting the obligation of only one of the parties does not import the nullity of the contract unless, under the circumstances, the participation of that party must be considered essential (1446, 1459, 1466).

1421. Eligibility for action of nullity. Unless the law provides otherwise, nullity can be claimed by anyone who has an interest in it and can also be found, *ex officio*, by the judge.

1422. Imprescribability of action of nullity. The action for a declaration of nullity is not subject to prescription (2934 *ff.*), except for the effects of usucaption (1158 *ff.*) and of prescription of actions for restitution.

1423. Inadmissibility of validation. A contract that is void cannot be validated, unless the law provides otherwise (799).

1424. Conversion of void contract. A void contract can produce the effects of a different contract, of which it has the requisites of substance and of form, whenever, considering the objective sought by the parties, it must be deemed that they would have wished it if they had known of the nullity.

VOIDABLE CONTRACTS

SECTION I

Incapacity

1425. Incapacity of parties. The contract is voidable if one of the parties was legally incapable of contracting.

A contract made by a person incapable of understanding or intending is likewise voidable, when the conditions established by article 428 occur.

1426. Subterfuge used by minor. The contract is not voidable if a minor, by subterfuge, has concealed his minority (2), but a simple declaration by him that he has reached majority does not prevent an attack on the contract.

SECTION II

Defects in Consent

1427. Mistake, duress and fraud. A contracting party whose consent was given by mistake (1428 *ff.*), extorted by duress (1434 *ff.*) or obtained by fraud (1439 *ff.*), can demand annulment of the contract (1441) according to the following provisions.

1428. Relevance of mistake. Mistake is cause for annulment of a contract when it is essential (1429) and recognizable (1431) by the other contracting party.

1429. Essential mistake. Mistake is essential:

(1) when it concerns the nature or the object (1346 *ff.*) of the contract;

(2) when it concerns the identity of the object of the performance or a quality of said object which, according to common understanding or under the circumstances, should be considered determinative of consent;

(3) when it concerns the identity or personal qualities of the other contracting party, so long as the one or the others were determinative of consent;

(4) when the mistake was one of law and was the only or the principal reason for entering into the contract.

1430. Mistake in calculation. A mistake in calculation does not lead to annulment, but only to correction, of the contract, unless, producing a mistake as to quantity, it was determinative of consent.

1431. Recognizable mistake. A mistake is considered recognizable (1428) when, with respect to the content, the circumstances of the contract, or the quality of the contracting parties, it would have been detected by a person of normal diligence.

1432. Preservation of corrected contract. The mistaken party cannot demand annulment of the contract if, before he can derive injury from it, the other party offers to perform it in a manner which conforms to the substance and characteristics of the contract that the mistaken party intended to conclude.

1433. Mistake in declaration or transmission. The provisions of the preceeding article also apply when the mistake occurs in the declaration or when such declaration was inexactly transmitted by the person or office charged with it (2706).

1434. Duress. Duress is cause for annulment of a contract even if exerted by a third person.

1435. Characteristics of duress. Duress must be of such a nature as to impress a reasonable person and to cause him to fear that he or his property will be exposed to an unjust and considerable injury. In this respect, the age, sex and condition of the persons shall be considered.

1436. Duress directed against third persons. Duress is also cause for annulment of the contract when the threatened injury is directed toward the person or property of the spouse or of an ascendant or descendant of the contracting party.

If the threatened injury is directed toward other persons, annulment of the contract is left to the prudent appraisal of the circumstances by the judge.

1437. Reverential fear. Mere reverential fear is not cause for annulment of a contract.

1438. Threat to enforce right. A threat to enforce a right can be cause for annulment of a contract only when it is aimed at obtaining unjust benefits.

1439. Fraud. Fraud is cause for the annulment of the contract when the deception employed by one of the contracting parties was such that, without it, the other contracting party would not have entered into the contract.

When the deception was employed by a third person, the contract is voidable if it was known to the party who derived benefit from it.

1440. Incidental fraud. If the deception was not such as to compel consent, the contract is valid, even though without the deception it would have included different terms; however, the contracting party in bad faith is liable for damages.

SECTION III

Action for Annulment

1441. Eligibility. The annulment of a contract can be demanded only by those persons in whose interest it is established by law.

The incapacity of a convicted person in a state of legal interdiction can be pleaded by any interested person.

1442. Prescription. The action for annulment is prescribed (2934 *ff.*) in five years.

When voidability depends on a defect in consent (1427 *ff.*) or legal incapacity (1425), the time runs from the day on which the duress (1434) ceased, the mistake (1428) or fraud (1439) was discovered, the interdiction or disability ceased (429), or the minor attained majority (2, 1425).

In other cases the time runs from the day the contract was made (428, 775).

Voidability can be pleaded by the defendant in an action for performance of the contract, even if the action for annulment is prescribed (2934 *ff.*).

1443. Restitution against incapacitated contracting party. If a contract is annulled for incapacity of one of the parties (1425), such party is not bound to restore what he has received as performance to the other except to the extent to which it has benefited him.

1444. Validation. The contracting party entitled to sue for annulment can validate the voidable contract by a declaration containing a reference to the contract and to the cause for voidability thereof, and a declaration of intention to validate it (1423, 1451).

A contract is likewise validated if the contracting party entitled to sue for annulment, knowing of the voidability, has voluntarily performed it.

The validation has no effect if the person who does it is not in a condition to validly conclude the contract.

1445. Effects of annulment on third persons. Annulment that is not based on legal incapacity (1425) does not prejudice rights acquired by third persons in good faith by a non-gratuitous transaction, except for the effects of transcription (2652 no. 6) of the petition for annulment.

1446. Voidability of multilateral contract. In the contracts indicated in article 1420 the voidability of the obligation of only one of the parties does not permit the annulment of the contract, unless the participation of such party in the contract must, under the circumstances, be considered essential.

CHAPTER XIII

RESCISSION OF THE CONTRACT

1447. Contract concluded in state of danger. A contract by which one party assumes obligations under unfair conditions because of the necessity, known to the other party, of saving himself or others from a present danger of serious personal injury, can be rescinded on demand of the party who assumes such obligations.

In awarding rescission the judge can according to the circumstances award fair compensation to the other party for work performed.

1448. General action of rescission for lesion. If there is a disproportion between the performance of one party and that of the other, and such disproportion was the result of a state of need of one party, of which the other has availed himself for his advantage, the injured party can demand rescission of the contract.

The action is not admissible if the lesion does not exceed one-half of the value that the performance made or promised by the injured party had at the time of the contract.

The lesion must continue until the time when the action is instituted.

Aleatory contrcts (1872 *ff.*, 1934 *ff.*, 1970) cannot be rescinded for lesion.

The provisions concerning rescission of partition (761 *ff.*) are unaffected.

1449. Prescription. The action for rescission is prescribed (2934 *ff.*) in one year from the formation (1326) of the contract; but if the fact upon which the action is based constitutes a criminal offense, the last paragraph of article 2947 applies.

Rescindability of the contract cannot be claimed as a defence when the action is prescribed.

1450. Offer to modify contract. The contracting party against whom the rescission is demanded can avoid it by offering a modification of the contract sufficient to restore it to an equitable basis.

1451. Inadmissibility of validation. A rescindable contract can not be validated (1423, 1444).

1452. Effects of rescission on third persons. Rescission of the contract does not prejudice rights acquired by third persons, except for the effects of transcription (2652, 2690) of the petition for rescission.

CHAPTER XIV

DISSOLUTION OF CONTRACT

SECTION I

Dissolution for Non-Performance

1453. Dissolution of contract for non-performance. In contracts providing for mutual counterperformance, when one of the parties fails to perform his obligations, the other party can choose to demand either performance or dissolution of the contract, saving, in any case, compensation for damages (1223).

Dissolution can be demanded even when an action has been brought to demand performance; but performance can no longer be demanded after an action for dissolution has been brought.

The defaulting party can no longer perform his obligation after the date of the action for dissolution.

1454. Notice to perform. The other party can serve a written notice on the defaulting party to perform within an appropriate time, declaring that, unless performance takes place within such time, the contract shall be deemed dissolved.

The time can not be less than fifteen days, unless the parties have agreed otherwise or unless a shorter period appears justified by the nature of the contract or by usage.

If the time elapses without performance having been made, the contract is dissolved by operation of law.

1455. Importance of non-performance. A contract cannot be dissolved if the non-performance of one of the parties has slight importance with respect to the interest of the other.

1456. Express resolutive clause. The contracting parties can expressly agree that the contract will be dissolved if a specified obligation is not performed in the designated manner.

In this case, the dissolution takes place by operation of law when the interested party declares to the other that he intends to avail himself of the dissolution clause.

1457. Time essential to one party. If the time fixed for performance by one of the parties must be considered essential in the interest of the other, the latter, if he intends to demand performance of the obligation notwithstanding the expiration of the time, must so notify the former within three days, unless there is an agreement or usage to the contrary.

In the absence of such notice, the contract is deemed dissolved by operation of law, even if dissolution was not expressly agreed upon.

1458. Effects of dissolution. Dissolution of a contract for non-performance has retroactive effect as between the parties, except in the case of contracts for continuous or periodic performance, with respect to which the effect of dissolution does not extend to performance already made (1467).

Dissolution, even if expressly agreed upon (1456), does not prejudice rights acquired by third persons, except for the effects of transcription (2652 no. 1) of the action for dissolution.

1459. Dissolution in multilaterial contracts. Non-performance by one of the parties in the contracts indicated in article 1420 does not cause dissolution of the contract with respect to the others, unless the non-performance must, under the circumstances, be considered essential (1446, 1466).

1460. Defence based upon non-performance. In contracts providing for mutual counterperformance, each party can refuse to perform his obligation if the other party does not perform or offer to perform his own at the same time, unless different times for performance have been established by the parties or appear from the nature of the contract.

However, performance cannot be rejected if, considering the circumstances, such rejection is contrary to good faith (1371).

1461. Change in patrimonial conditions of contracting parties. Each party can withhold the performance due by him, if the patrimonial conditions of the other party have become such as obviously to endanger fulfilment of the counterperformance, unless adequate security is given.

1462. Clauses limiting pleading of defences. A clause providing that one of the parties cannot set up defences for the purpose of avoiding or delaying performance due by him has no effect on defences based on nullity (1418), voidability (1425) and rescission (1447) of the contract.

In cases in which the clause is effective the judge, if he finds that important reasons exist, can withhold sentence, requiring security if circumstances warrant it.

SECTION II

Supervening Impossibility

1463. Total impossibility. In contracts providing for mutual counter-performance, the party released for supervening impossibility of the performance due (1256) cannot demand performance by the other party, and he is bound to restore that which he has already received, in accordance with the rules concerning restitution of payments not due (2033 *f.*).

1464. Partial impossibility. When the performance of one party has become impossible only in part (1258), the other party has a right to a corresponding reduction of the performance due by him, and he can also withdraw from the contract if he lacks an appreciable interest in partial performance (1181).

1465. Contracts with translative or constitutive effects. In contracts which transfer ownership of a specified thing or constitute or transfer real rights (1376), destruction of the thing by a cause not imputable to the transfer does not release the transferee from the obligation of performance, even though the thing was not delivered to him.

The same provision applies if the translative or constitutive effect is deferred until the expiration of a time limit.

Whenever the object of the transfer is a thing specified only as to kind (1178), and the transferor has made delivery or the thing has been identified (1378), the transferee is not released from the obligation of counterperformance.

In all cases the transferee is released from his obligation if the transfer was subject to a suspensive condition (1353 *ff.*) and impossibility intervened before fulfilment of the condition.

1466. Impossibility in multilateral contracts. In the contracts indicated in article 1420, impossibility of performance by one of the parties does not cause dissolution of the contract with regard to the others, unless the performance not made must, under the circumstances, be considered essential (1446, 1459).

SECTION III

Excessive Onerousness

1467. Contract for mutual counterperformances. In contracts for continuous or periodic performance or for deferred performance, if extraordinary and unforeseeable events make the performance of one of the parties excessively onerous, the party who owes such performance can demand dissolution of the contract, with the effects set forth in article 1458.

Dissolution cannot be demanded if the supervening onerousness is part of the normal risk of the contract.

A party against whom dissolution is demanded can avoid it by offering to modify equitably the conditions of the contract.

1468. Contracts with obligations of one party only. In the case contemplated in the preceding article, if the contract is one in which only one of the parties has assumed obligations, he can demand a reduction in his performance or a modification of the manner of performance, sufficient to restore it to an equitable basis.

1469. Aleatory contracts. The provisions of the preceding articles (1467 *f.*) do not apply to contracts which are aleatory by their nature or by the intention of the parties.

*   *   *

1494. Compensation for damage. In all cases, the seller is bound to compensate the buyer for damage (1223 *ff.*) unless he proves that, without his fault, he had no knowledge of the defects.

The seller shall also compensate the buyer for the damage caused by defects in the thing.

*   *   *

1559. Notion. A supply contract is one by which a party binds himself to supply another with things continuously or periodically, in return for a price.

1560. Amount to be supplied. If the amount to be supplied is not established, it is deemed to correspond to the normal requirements of the customer as of the time of making the contract.

If the parties have established only a maximum and a minimum limit for the entire supply contract or for each instalment, the right to establish the quantity due, within those limits, vests in the customer.

If the quantity to be supplied is to be determined in relation to requirements and a minimum quantity was agreed upon, the customer is bound for the quantity corresponding to his requirements if this exceeds the agreed minimum.

1561. Determination of price. If the price in a periodic supply contract is to be determined according to the provisions of article 1474, the expiration date of each instalment and the place where these are to be delivered shall be taken into account.

1562. Payment of price. In periodic supply contracts, payment is made at the time of and in proportion to each instalment of performance.

In continuous supply contracts, the price is paid according to the customary terms.

1563. Maturity date of each instalment of performance. The time established for each instalment is presumed to have been agreed upon in the interest of both parties.

If the customer has the power to fix the maturity date of each instalment of performance, he shall give the supplier reasonable advance notice of the date.

1564. Resolution of contract. In case of non-performance of a single instalment by one of the parties, the other can request resolution (1453 *ff.*) of the contract if the default is significant and is such as to reduce confidence in the punctuality of subsequent performances.

1565. Suspension of supply. If the customer has failed to perform and the default is of slight importance, the supplier cannot suspend his performance of the contract without giving reasonable advance notice.

1566. Right of first refusal. An agreement is valid by which the customer binds himself to give a right of first refusal to the supplier in the stipulation of a future contract for the same purpose, provided that the duration of the obligation does not exceed five years. If a longer period is agreed upon, it is reduced to five years.

The customer shall notify the supplier of conditions proposed to him by third persons and the supplier, under penalty of forfeiting his right, shall declare within the established time limit or, in the absence thereof, within the period required by circumstances or usage, whether he intends to avail himself of his right of first refusal.

1567. Exclusive dealing clause in favour of supplier. If a contract contains an exclusive dealing clause in favour of the supplier, the other party cannot receive performances of the same kind from third persons nor, unless otherwise agreed, can he provide with his own means for the production of the things which form the subject matter of the contract.

1568. Exclusive dealing clause in favour of customer. If an exclusive dealing clause is stipulated in favour of the customer, the supplier cannot directly or indirectly make any performance of the same kind as that contemplated in the contract, within the territory for which the exclusive right was granted and for the duration of the contract.

A customer who assumes the obligation to promote the sale of the things for which he has exclusive rights within the territory assigned to him is liable for damages in case of non-performance of the obligation, even if he has performed the minimum requirements agreed upon in the contract.

1569. Indefinite time contract. If the duration of the supply is not established, each of the parties can withdraw from the contract by giving notice within the time agreed upon or established by usage or, in the absence thereof, within a reasonable time with regard to the nature of the supply.

1570. Reference. To the extent that they are compatible with the provisions of the preceding articles, the provisions governing the type of contract to which the single instalments of performance correspond apply to a supply contract.

*   *   *

Title IX

Unlawful Acts

2043. Compensation of unlawful acts. Any fraudulent, malicious, or negligent act that causes an unjustified injury to another obliges the person who has committed the act to pay damages.

*   *   *

2050. Liability arising from exercise of dangerous activities. Whoever causes injury to another in the performance of an activity dangerous by its nature or by reason of the instrumentalities employed, is liable for damages, unless he proves that he has taken all suitable measures to avoid the injury.

*   *   *

TITLE X

REGULATION OF COMPETITION AND SYNDICATES

CHAPTER I

REGULATION OF COMPETITION

SECTION I

General Provisions

*   *   *

2596. Contractual limits on competition. An agreement that limits competition shall be evidenced in writing (2725). It is valid if confined to a specified territory or a specified activity, and cannot exceed five years in duration.

If the duration of the agreement is not specified or is established for a period greater than five years, the agreement is valid for a period of five years.

*   *   *

ORDINARY SUPPLEMENT TO THE OFFICIAL GAZETTE, NO. 146, DATED 23RD JUNE 1988

PRESIDENTIAL DECREE

No. 224, dated 24th May 1988

Enactment of EC Directive no. 85/374 concerning the harmonisation of legislative, regulatory and administrative provisions by member states on liability for damage caused by defective products, under Art. 15 of Decree no. 183 dated 16th April 1987.

Based on Articles 76 and 87 of the Constitution;

Based on Decree no. 183 dated 16th April 1987 concerning the co-ordination of Community policy relating to Italy's membership of the European Community and the harmonisation of internal laws with Community regulations;

Based on EC Directive no. 85/374 covering the harmonisation of legislative, regulatory and administrative provisions by member states on liability for damage caused by defective products, indicated in Appendix C to Decree no. 183 dated 16th April 1987;

Whereas on 2nd May 1988, under Article 15 of the said decree of 16th April 1987, which delegates the government with the task of creating regulations to enact the directives in the said Appendix C, the draft of this Decree was duly submitted to the Presidents of the Chamber of Deputies and the Senate;

Whereas approval has been granted by the appropriate Committees of the Chamber of Deputies and the Senate;

Whereas the deliberations of the Council of Ministers were adopted at a meeting held on 20th May 1988;

Based on the proposals of the Minister for the Co-ordination of Community Policy, in agreement with the Ministers of Foreign Affairs, Justice, Finance, Agriculture and Forests, Industry, Commerce and Trades, Health and the Environment;

THE PRESIDENT HEREBY DECREES THE FOLLOWING:

Art. 1

Product liability

1. The producer shall be liable for damage occasioned by defects in its product.

Art. 2

Product

1. A product, for the purposes of these regulations, shall be any movable item, even if it forms part of another movable or immovable item.
2. Electricity shall also be regarded as a product.
3. Agricultural products of the soil and of animal husbandry, fishing and hunting, which have not undergone immediate processing, shall be excluded. Processing shall be defined as the subjection of the product to a treatment which changes its characteristics or adds other substances to it. Processing shall also include processes of an industrial nature, packaging and any other treatment, if they render it difficult for the consumer to check the product or create confidence in its safety.

Art. 3

Producer

1. The producer shall be the manufacturer of the finished product or a component thereof or the producer of a raw material.
2. In the case of agricultural products of the soil, and those of animal husbandry, fishing and hunting, the producer shall be the party subjecting them to processing.
3. Any party presenting itself as the producer by placing its name, brand name or other distinctive sign on the product or its packaging shall be regarded as a producer.
4. Any party importing a product into the European Community during the course of its business activities for the purposes of selling, leasing or any other form of distribution, and any party presenting itself as the importer into the European Community by adding its own name, brand name or other distinctive sign to the product or its packaging, shall bear the same liability as the producer.

Art. 4

Supplier's liability

1. Where the producer has not been identified, any supplier which has distributed the product during the course of its trading activities and failed to notify the injured party within three months of being requested to supply the identity and the domicile of the producer or the party which supplied the product, shall be subject to the same liability.
2. This request shall be made in writing and shall indicate the product which ocasioned the damage, the place and a reasonable approximation of the time it was purchased; it shall also include an offer of inspection of the product if it still exists.
3. If notification of the instigation of proceedings is not preceded by the request described in section 2 above, the defendant may provide the information required within three months.
4. In any event, if the supplier so requests at the first hearing of the first court hearing the case, the Judge may, if circumstances so justify, specify a later date not more than three months afterwards for the information specified in paragraph 1 to be provided.
5. The third party indicated as the producer or previous supplier may be called to the hearing under Article 106 of the Code of Civil Procedure and the agreed supplier may be excluded if the party indicated appears and does not contest the indication. In the case described in paragraph 3, the defendant may request reimbursement from the plaintiff of the expenses it has incurred in being brought to court.
6. The provisions of this article apply to products imported into the European Community, when the importer has not been identified, even if the identity of the producer is known.

Art. 5

Defective product

1. A product is defective when it does not provide the safety which could legitimately be expected of it in the circumstances, including:

(a) The manner in which the product has been placed on the market, its description, its obvious characteristics, the instructions and warnings supplied;
(b) The use to which the product can reasonably be put, and the behaviour towards it which one could reasonably expect;
(c) The time at which the product was placed on the market.

2. A product shall not be regarded as defective solely because a more highly perfected product has been on sale at any time.

3. A product shall be defective if it does not provide the safety normally provided by other examples of the same range of products.

Art. 6

Exclusion of liability

Liability shall be excluded:

(a) if the producer did not place the product on the market;
(b) if the defect which caused the damage did not exist when the producer placed the product on the market;
(c) if the producer did not manufacture the product for sale or any other form of distribution for gain, nor did it manufacture or distribute it during the course of its commercial activity;
(d) if the defect is due to the conformity of the product with a binding legal regulation or other binding provision;
(e) that the state of scientific and technical knowledge at the time the producer placed the product on the market did not yet make it possible to consider the product as defective;
(f) in the case of a producer or supplier of a component part or raw material, if the defect is due entirely to the design of the product in which the part or raw material is incorporated or to its conformity with instructions given by the producer which used it.

Art. 7

Placing of the product on the market

1. The product is placed on the market when it has been delivered to the producer, the user or an auxiliary of either, even if on approval or for testing.

2. The product has also been placed on the market when it has been delivered to the carrier or haulier to be sent to the purchaser or user.

3. Liability shall not be excluded if the product has been placed on the market by enforced sale, unless the debtor has specifically pointed out the defect to the judicial official presiding over the distraint of goods or by a document notifying the creditor taking the proceedings and deposited with the Registry where execution is taking place within fifteen days of the said distraint.

Art. 8

Proof

1. The injured party shall prove the existence of the injury, the defect and the causal connection between the defect and the injury.

2. The producer shall prove the facts which may exclude liability under the provisions of Art. 6. For the purposes of exclusion of liability under Art. 6, letter (b), it is sufficient to demonstrate that, given the circumstances, it is likely that the defect did not yet exist at the time when the product was placed on the market.

3. If it appears likely that the damage was caused by a defect in the product, the Judge may order that the costs of expert witnesses be paid in advance by the producer.

Art. 9

Plurality of liability

1. If more than one person is liable for the same injury, they shall all be jointly and severally liable for compensation.
2. The person paying compensation for the injury shall have recourse against the others in proportion to the amount of risk attributable to each of them, to the seriousness of any negligence involved, and the extent of the consequences arising therefrom. If there is any doubt, the compensation shall be equally divided.

Art. 10

Negligence by injured party

1. In the event of contributory negligence by the injured party, compensation shall be assessed under Art. 1227 of the Civil Code.
2. Compensation shall not be payable if the injured party was aware of the defect in the product and its potential dangers and nevertheless exposed himself to these dangers.
3. In the case of damage to property, negligence by the possessor shall be rated equally with negligence by the injured party.

Art. 11

Damage subject to compensation

1. The following shall be subject to compensation under this decree:

(a) damage resulting from death or personal injury;
(b) the destruction or deterioration of an item different to the defective product, provided it is of a type normally used for private use or consumption and thus used mainly by the injured party.

2. Damage to property shall be subject to compensation only inasmuch as it exceeds the sum of seven hundred and fifty thousand lire.

Art. 12

Exclusion of liability clauses

1. Any agreement which excludes or limits liability to the injured party under this decree shall be null and void.

Art. 13

Prescription

1. The right to compensation shall be prescribed after three years from the date when the injured party was or should have been aware of the damage, the defect and the identity of the party responsible.
2. In the event of aggravated damage, the prescription period shall not begin before the date on which the claimant was or should have been aware of damage serious enough to justify taking legal action.

Art. 14

Forfeiture of rights

1. The right to compensation shall be forfeited after a period of ten years from the date on which the producer or importer into the European Community placed the products which caused the damage on the market.
2. This forfeiture period shall be prevented only by application to a court unless the proceedings are extinguished, or by a request for admission of credit in bankruptcy proceedings, or if the party liable acknowledges the right.
3. Any document preventing the forfeiture of rights against one of the responsible parties shall not affect any of the others.

Art. 15

Liability under other legal provisions

1. The provisions of this decree do not exclude or limit any rights conferred upon the injured party by other laws.
2. The provisions of this decree shall not apply to nuclear accidents covered by decree no. 1860 dated 31st December 1962 and subsequent amendments thereto.

Art. 16

Temporary provision

1. The provisions of this decree shall not apply to products placed on the market before the date upon which the decree takes effect, namely before the 30th day of July 1988.

This Decree shall be affixed with the seal of State and inserted in the Official Digest of Legal Provisions of the Republic of Italy. It obliges any person concerned to observe it and ensure that it is observed.

Given in Rome, this 24th day of May 1988

COSSIGA

DE MITA, President of the Council of Ministers
LA PERGOLA, Minister for the Co-ordination of Community Policy
ANDREOTTI, Minister of Foreign Affairs
VASSALLI, Minister of Justice
AMATO, Treasury Minister
MANNINO, Minister of Agriculture and Forests
BATTAGLA, Minister of Industry, Commerce and Trade
DONAT CATTIN, Minister of Health
RUFFOLO, Minister of the Environment

Seen by Keeper of the Seals: VASSALLI

Registered at the Audit Office, this 4th day of June 1988
Acts of Government, register no. 74, page no. 24

Note:

The text of the notes published here has been drafted under Art. 10 paras. 2 and 3 of the text approved by Presidential Decree no. 1092 dated 28th December 1985, for the sole purpose of facilitating the reading of those provisions which have been modified or revoked. They are without prejudice to the validity and effect of the legislative acts reproduced here.

Note to Art. 4:

The wording of Art. 106 of the Code of Civil Procedure is as follows:

"Art. 106 (*Intervention at the instance of one party*) Either party may summon a third party to the hearing if it claims to have common cause with, or be guaranteed by, that party."

Note to Art. 10:

The wording of Art. 1227 of the Civil Code is as follows:

"Art. 1227 (*Contributory negligence by a creditor*). If negligence by a creditor contributed to causing the damage, compensation is reduced depending on the seriousness of the negligence and the nature of the consequence which resulted.
Compensation shall not be payable for negligence which the creditor could have avoided using normal common sense".

CHAPTER 10

Luxemburg

Guy Harles, Patrick Kinsch

1. Commercial Agency

1.1. Definition of Various Types of Agencies and Intermediaries

Luxemburg law does not provide for a statutory definition of the various types of agencies and intermediaries with the single exception of the employed commercial representative.

1.1.1. Independent

Legal writers define a commercial agent as being a merchant professionally acting on behalf of a businessman or an industrialist towards his clients.[1]

The Luxemburg courts have sometimes been called on to determine whether a given contractual relationship, purporting to be a contract of independent commercial agency, or other form of independent distribution, was not in fact a contract of employment (on which *see* 1.1.2.).

The question is of great practical importance, since contracts of independent agency are not regulated by specific statutory rules in Luxemburg, which provides the parties with considerable latitude as to the terms of their contract, while employment contracts must conform to far more stringent mandatory rules.

With agency contracts as with other similar agreements, the distinction between the "independent" provision of services and salaried employment is a source of considerable difficulty. While a carefully drafted contractual document might help, it will not in itself be considered as conclusive by the courts. However, the agent seeking to establish his salaried status will have to prove that despite the explicit terms of such a contract, the independence provided for therein is a sham; he will, in sum, have to prove subordination.

---

[1] A. Elvinger, 'Luxembourg' in Union Internationale des Avocats, *La représentation commerciale internationale*, Brussels, Etablissements Emile Bruylant, 1971.

Evidence will be sought by the courts in all aspects of the parties' contractual relationship.[2]

Finally, Luxemburg law, unlike other legal systems, does not have an *a priori* presumption either in favour of independence or of subordination. See also 1.1.2.

1.1.2. Employed

All labour contracts between employers and employees (whether employed agents or other) are regulated by a plethora of statutory enactments, rules and regulations, the most fundamental of which is the Act of Employees' Labour Contracts 1971[3] which provides in article 3:

> "par application de la définition générale qui précède, sont à considérer notamment comme employés privés au sens de la loi: toutes les personnes de l'un ou de l'autre sexe qui exercent sous quelque dénomination que ce soit, une occupation de la nature de celles déterminées ci-après:
>
> . . .
>
> f) activité de voyageur, représentant et agent, qu'ils travaillent pour le compte d'une ou de plusieurs firmes et quel que soit le mode de leur rémunération, pourvu qu'ils ne mettent en oeuvre un agencement industriel ou commercial personnel complet . . .".

It follows from this that commercial agents may be considered as employees whatever method of calculating their salaries is used (a commission or profit-sharing system is not in itself evidence of the absence of a contract of salaried employment). The statutory criterion is the existence of an "agencement industriel ou commerecial personnel complet", which again alludes to, rather than defines "complete personal industrial or commercial" independence, as opposed to subordination.

Cases have variously applied the criteria of the extent of the control that the principal has on the activities of the agent, the agent's authority to organize his own business, the possibility given to the agent to work for several principals,[4] and the fact that the agent has offices of his own or himself employs third persons.

Again, the Court may place a different interpretation on the relationship between the parties from the parties' own description in their agreement.[5]

Regulation of commercial agency
(i) No specific statute provides for the status of independent commercial agency. General principles of law thus apply and more specifically the provisions relating to agency (mandat) as they appear in articles 1984 to 2010 of the Civil Code.

---

[2] See Trib. arr. Luxembourg, 19 May 1983, *Kraus* v *Parries*, unreported (no. 28874); Cour Supérieure de Justice, 4 February 1988, *Wenzel and Majerus* v *Texaco Luxembourg*, unreported no. 9876) and on appeal to the Supreme Court: Cour de Cassation, 2 February 1989, (no. 799).

[3] Act on Employees' Labour Contracts 1971 loi du 12 novembre 1971 portrant réforme du règlement légal du louage de services des employés privés, Art. 3).

[4] Cour Supérieure de Justice, 19 April 1929, Pasicrisie luxembourgeoise, vol. 12, p. 139.

[5] Trib. arr. Luxembourg, 3 November 1966, Vol. 20, p. 295; 17 April 1953, R.D.T. 13.

The BENELUX Commission for the unification of law has elaborated a draft model law concerning commercial agency. Its draft was submitted to the interparliamentary advisory council of BENELUX on 24 May, 1965. This has not been ratified, transformed into national legislation or otherwise implemented in Luxemburg. No ratification or other implementation proceedings are currently in progress.

(ii) As the above impoies, the status of employed agents is identical to that of other employees and numerous mandatory provisions of law apply.

1.2. Conclusion of the Contract (Special Conditions)

A commercial agency agreement does not need to be in writing. The agreement is valid and binding once it has been agreed on by the parties. The agreement by one or the other of the parties may be implicit.

In accordance with article 109 of the Commercial Code, evidence of the existence and the content of the agreement—being a commercial contract—can be provided by any means. To avoid discussions, however, it is recommended that an agreement should be put in writing or its content established by an exchange of correspondence.

Registration of the commercial agency agreement is not a condition of its validity.

A commercial agent exercising his business in Luxemburg needs to have a licence to do business in the Grand Duchy of Luxemburg. A licence is granted by the Ministère des Classes Moyennes, the conditions being defined in detail by an Act of 1988 (which is mostly a re-enactment of existing statutory provisions).[6] There is some judicial authority for stating that the absence of a valid licence (for which criminal sanctions are provided) does not affect the validity of contracts entered into by the agent.

1.3. The Principal's Duties and Rights

1.3.1. The principal's duties

1.3.1.1. Commission

The agent is normally entitled by the terms of the agreement to receive a commission on the conclusion of a contract with the client. The parties may, however, agree that the commission will only become payable after actual payment is received from the client by the principal. The parties are free to determine the commission, both as to when it is paid and in its amount. The principal must also reimburse the agent all expenses incurred by him in fulfilling his contractual obligations.

1.3.1.2. Protection of agent, information

The principal normally undertakes, by contract, to provide to the agent with all available information concerning potential clients, market con-

---

[6] Loi du 28 décembre 1988 réglementant l'accès aux professions d'artisan, de commerçant, d'industriel ainsi qu'à certaines professions libérales (Mémorial A, no. 72, p. 1494). And see generally the Civil Code Art. 1993 and the Penal Code Art. 309.

ditions and the products or services to be offered. The parties are, however, absolutely free to agree on whatever conditions they believe suitable. The principal has no specific obligation.

1.3.1.3. Supply of written statement

This will normally be provided for by contract. Even in the absence of any contractual stipulations, a legal obligation to render accounts will be implied.

1.3.2. The principal's rights

The principal may expect from the agent the fulfilment in good faith and with due diligence of all express contractual stipulations and of all implied terms.

1.4. The Commercial Agent's Duties and Rights

1.4.1. The commercial agent's duties

1.4.1.1. Trustworthiness, duty to inform

It is a general principle of law that the agent has to inform the principal on a regular basis of the efforts he is making to fulfil his obligations and the outcome of his work. It is up to the parties to determine by agreement the frequency, extent and method of imparting such information.

1.4.1.2. Del credere

The agent may guarantee to the principal the performance, by the third party, of its obligations. Such a clause, however, is not general practice in Luxemburg. It cannot be implied from the contract; an express stipulation has to provide for it.

1.4.1.3. Non-competition

The commercial agent is an independent businessman and free to organize his activities. His obligations are defined in the commercial agency agreement. Commercial agency agreements frequently provide for the possibility for the agent to work at the same time for different principals.

In the absence of any specific agreement, the agent's freedom of activity is restricted only by general principles of good faith towards his principal. Disloyal conduct, if of sufficient gravity, will be considered illicit. Depending on the circumstances of the case, such conduct will be looked on as a mere breach of contract or as unfair competition. Remedies will in any event be given to the principal.

The parties are, however, free to insert into their agreement a clause of non-competition and to determine its content and its conditions.

The principal may undertake not to appoint another agent for the territory in question. The agent may undertake not to advertise outside his territory. Such provisions, if agreed, are valid. A modification of the territory has, unless otherwise provided for, to be agreed on by both parties.

In the absence of any stipulations, the agent is free to represent at the same time various principals which may compete with one another.

The parties to the agreement are free to stipulate that on the termination of their agreement, the agent shall not enter into competition with his former principal. For such a clause to be valid, however, it must be limited in time and space. If drafted in general terms, such limitation is void as being contrary to the constitutionally guaranteed freedom of trade.

1.4.1.4. Secrecy

The agent has a general obligation of confidentiality with regard to the information he receives from the principal and the work he is performing on his behalf.

While not required by statute, this obligation can easily be implied into the parties' contract as an aspect of the general obligation to perform contracts in good faith. Criminal sanctions will not normally apply, however, except under the most exceptional circumstances.[6]

1.4.2. The commercial agent's rights

1.4.2.1. Commission

The agent is entitled to the commission which has been agreed on in the commercial agency agreement (see 1.3.1.).

1.5. Liabilities of Principal and Agent during the Term of the Agency

1.5.1. The principal as against the agent

The relationship between the principal and the agent is governed by the agreement which has been entered into by the parties. The principal must fulfil all his duties under this agreement. If he does not comply with them, the agent may take action against him. The competent court is the Tribunal de Commerce.

1.5.2. The principal as against third parties

The principal may act against the third parties with whom the agent entered into an agreement on his behalf and in his name. A direct contractual relationship exists between these third parties and the principal, provided that the agent has disclosed to the third party the fact that he is acting on behalf of his principal.

1.5.3. The agent as against the principal

See 1.5.1.

1.5.4. The agent as against third parties

The agent when dealing with third parties acts in the name and on behalf of the principal. He thus has no direct contractual relationship with such third parties and only has a remedy in tort against them if, independently of any breach of contract, their fault causes him some personal loss.

1.6. Terms and Termination

1.6.1. Term

The commercial agency agreement may be entered into for a limited or unlimited period of time. If it has been entered into for a limited period of time, the parties are obliged to respect such a stipulation of the agreement and have to fulfil their obligations up to the contractual termination date. Such date may, however, be changed by mutual agreement.

If the agreement has been entered into for an unlimited period of time, it may be terminated by any party at any moment. Case law has, however, decided that such unilateral termination may only be made by with reasonable advance notice. This advanced notice depends on such criteria as the duration of the previous relationship and the importance of the agreement for the parties.[7]

1.7. Indemnity

1.7.1. Indemnity for goodwill and/or clientèle

The agent is not entitled to any indemnity for goodwill and/or clientèle as such. Goodwill and/or clientèle are deemed to belong exclusively to the principal.

1.7.2. Compensation for damages

General principles of law apply. Damages may only be awarded for an abusive termination of the agreement. The plaintiff has to prove the loss which was caused to him.

1.8. Specific Application of EEC Law

No cases are reported in which Luxemburg courts would have decided any specific point of EEC law.

2. Distributorship Agreements

2.1. Distribution

2.1.1. Definition

A distributorship agreement is an agreement between a supplier and an independent distributor, providing for the distribution by the distributor of the supplier's goods.

---

[7] Cour Supérieure de Justice, 6 March 1934, Pasicrisie luxembourgeoise Vol. 13, p. 213.

The distributor is a merchant buying the goods and selling them in his own name.

2.1.1.1. Exclusive/non-exclusive/exclusive purchasing

The agreement may be an exclusive or non-exclusive one and may or may not be limited to a given territory.

One Luxemburg case has defined an exclusive distributorship agreement as having the following three characteristics:[8]

(i)   the distributor, acting in his own name, sells to his own clientèle, this being the primary distinction between an exclusive distributor and a commercial agent;
(ii) the distributor's business is "integrated into the supplier's business": this is the criterion of economic subordination, as opposed to legal subordination, which characterizes salaried employment;
(iii) an exclusivity clause is inserted into the contract; this clause is often justified by the need to protect a trademark.

2.1.2. Conclusion of the contract (special conditions)

2.1.2.1. General

No legal provisions define any specific conditions to be fulfilled upon entry into a distributorship agreement. Both parties to such an agreement are businessmen. Thus business law applies to their relationship. The agreement may be an oral or a written one. The agreement and its content may be proven by whatever means available.

The agreement need not be registered with any authority. However, both parties to the agreement, if established in the Grand Duchy of Luxemburg, need a business licence.

See also under 1.2 above, the applicable principles being similar.

2.1.2.2. Defining the parties' respective obligations

One specific difficulty with the drafting of a distributorship agreement is that courts have sometimes considered such agreements as void on account of the fact that neither the price nor the quantity of goods supplied to the distributor by the supplier had been defined with precision in the initial contract.

Courts have tended to analyse distributorship agreements as agreements for the sale of goods between supplier and distributor; accordingly all conditions of validity of a sales contract apply.[9]

One reported case held that a distributorship agreement, drafted in 1966, could be declared void in 1983 as no contractual stipulation defined precisely the quantity of goods to be provided to the distributor over the years.[10]

---

[8] Trib. arr. Luxembourg, 8 October 1987, *Comptoir des Tabacs Fixmer* v *Interland S.A.*, unreported (no. 36366); see also Trib. arr. Luxembourg, 2 June 1986, *Wagener* v *Breuval & Cie S.A.*, unreported (no. 36,587).
[9] See especially the Civil Code Arts 1583 and 1591.
[10] Cour Supérieure de Justice, 12 January 1983, P, 25,429.

These cases are inspired in a well-established body of French case law almost systematically rendering void most forms of long-term distributorship agreements. The underlying rationale of that case law has been identified by French writers as the courts' desire to protect the economically dependent contracting party (the distributor).

The courts considered illegal the supplier's power arbitrarily to determine the fundamental characteristics of the contract, especially by unilaterally fixing the price by reference to the supplier's price list. Luxemburg courts sometimes have cited these legal writings with approval.[11]

It needs to be stressed, however, that the courts have, on the whole, hestitated to declare distribution contracts void on the sole ground of insufficient determination, in the original contract itself, of price and quantity. Various grounds have been given by the courts for upholding the validity of agreements while purporting to follow the principles laid down by French case law; generally, the courts have been able to discover an implied parties' intent as to the mode of determining price and quantity.[12]

It is perhaps not devoid of interest to note that in these Luxemburg cases the invalidity of the contracts was used as a defence by suppliers trying to fight a suit for wrongful termination of a distributorship contract, not by the (economically dependent) distributors.[12] The leading French cases had to deal with an altogether different situation.

2.1.3. The supplier's duties and rights

2.1.3.1. The supplier's duties

The supplier has to perform his contractual obligations in good faith and in accordance with their terms and conditions. His main duties are to keep the distributor informed of all market information and the modifications and improvement of the goods and services offered and sold.

2.1.3.2. The supplier's rights

The supplier may expect from the distributor the fulfilment of all his contractual obligations. He may in particular expect from the distributor the punctual payment of all goods and services sold and the feedback of market information.

2.1.4. The distributor's duties and rights

2.1.4.1. The distributor's duties

The distributor is obliged to respect the supplier's trade mark if any and the organization of his distribution network.

2.1.4.2. The distributor's rights

The distributor is entitled to receive punctual delivery of all goods and

[11] See e.g., Trib. arr. Luxembourg, 2 June 1986, *Wagener* v *Breuval* & Cie S.A., see footnote 8, at p. 13.
[12] See especially, Trib. arr. Luxembourg 23 January 1986, *Accinauto* v *Accinauto (Belgium) and Auto-Industrie*, unreported (no. 35,157) at pp. 7–8; 2 June 1986, *Wagener* v *Breuval* & *Cie S.A.*, (see footnote 8) at p. 13.

services ordered and may expect the supplier to refrain from selling directly to clients within the distributor's territory.

2.1.5. Liabilities of supplier and distributor during the term of the distributorship agreement:

2.1.5.1. The supplier as against the distributor

The relationship between the supplier and the distributor is a relationship of seller to purchaser within the framework of the distributorship agreement. Any litigious aspects would be solved on the basis of this contractual relationship. The competent court is the Tribunal d'Arrondissement siégeant en matière commerciale.

2.1.5.2. The supplier as against third parties

The supplier has no contractual relationship with third parties. They thus have no direct action against him. The European Directive concerning product liability is under discussion before Parliament.

2.1.5.3. The distributor as against the supplier

See 2.1.5.1 above.

2.1.5.4. The distributor as against the third parties

The distributor will enter into an agreement with the third parties. The terms and conditions of such an agreement have to be respected by both parties.

2.1.6. Term and termination

2.1.6.1. Term

The distributorship agreement may be entered into for a limited or unlimited period of time.

2.1.6.2. Termination

Agreements entered into for a limited period of time
Such agreements automatically come to an end at the expiration of the predetermined period of time, unless renewed. They may not be terminated before, unless both parties consent.

Agreements entered into for an unlimited period of time
These may in principle be denounced unilaterally, at any time, by one of the parties. The commercial consequences of unilateral termination by the supplier can be of the utmost gravity for the distributor. Courts have therefore—given the absence of any precise statutory framework such as that existing in Belgium—applied general principles of contract law (especially the principles relating to good faith and to abuse of rights) and defined the conditions of valid termination of a contract by the distributor.

According to the leading Luxemburg case,[13] a unilateral termination of an exclusive distributorship agreement will be deemed abusive (and the supplier will be liable for damages towards the distributor) unless it is

(i) *either* justified by very serious reasons (a concept most restrictively understood by the courts; it has for instance been held that the mere desire to replace an elderly distributor by someone more dynamic was an insufficient reason[14]);

(ii) *or* given with "sufficient" advance notice. Sufficient advance notice has been defined as sufficient for the distributor to be able, under the circumstances, to reorganize his business (or enter into an exclusive distributorship agreeement with another supplier) so as to enjoy a situation "equivalent" to that which the terminated agreement afforded him.[13]

2.1.7. Indemnity

2.1.7.1. Valid termination

No indemnity whatsoever is due to the distributor. In particular the Belgian concept of an *indemnité de clientèle*, based on principles of unjust enrichment, and independence of any fault on the supplier's side, is unknown under Luxemburg law.

It follows from this, in practice, that it is often of fundamental importance, if a case is being litigated, to determine the law applicable to a contract between a Belgian supplier and a Luxemburg distributor. In these cases the courts tend, in the absence of any express choice of law clause in the agreement itself, to apply Luxemburg law *qua lex loci solutionis*, the exclusive distributorship agreement being performed in Luxemburg. Accordingly claims for an *indemnité de clientèle*, based on Belgian law, will generally be denied.[15]

2.1.7.2. Invalid termination

On the criteria of validity, see 2.1.6.2.

Invalid termination will inevitably be considered as a breach of contract. The supplier will be liable for any direct or consequential loss suffered by the distributor.

While an *indemnité de clientèle* as such is not provided for by any statutory provision, it has been held that one of the elements of the damages the distributor is entitled to specifically includes the loss of his clientèle.[16] It might be useful to stress, again, that this indemnity is due to him only in case of invalid termination of the agreement (i.e. an abuse). It is in this respect that

---

[13] Cour Supérieure de Justice, 11 July 1972, *Flammant* v *Alfa-Laval*, P. 22, 194; see also Trib. arr. Luxembourg, 22 March 1984, *Burodatic* v *Triumph Adler AG*, unreported; 23 January 1986, *Accinauto* v *Accinauto (Belgium)*, unreported, (no. 35,057); 2 June 1986, *Wagener* v *Breuval & Cie S.A.*, (see footnote 8); 8 October 1987, *Fixmer* v *Interland*, unreported (no. 36,366).

[14] Cour Supérieure de Justice, 11 July 1972 (see footnote 13).

[15] See e.g., Trib. arr. Luxembourg, 14 July 1983, *Hartmann* v *International Motor Company*, unreported (no. 28,889).

[16] Trib. arr. Luxembourg, 2 June 1986, *Wagener* v *Breuval & Cie. S.A.*, (see footnote 8) at pp. 14–15.

the Luxemburg law of exclusive distributorship agreements differs most fundamentally from Belgian law.

2.2 Selective Distribution

Selective and non-selective distribution are treated on a similar basis, with the exception of competition law. In this respect, it has been held (in the context of the distribution of luxury products) that selective distribution agreements are normally valid under Luxemburg and EEC law and that they are opposable to third parties. Accordingly, a vendor who is not a member of the supplier's network of distributors is liable under unfair competition law towards the supplier and selective distributors.[17]

3. Franchise Agreements

Franchise agreements are frequently entered into by franchisors (who tend to be foreign) and Luxemburg franchisees.

No legislation, no reported cases and no bibliography exist on the specific subject of franchise agreements. The reader may rely on Belgian and French case law and legal writers.

Not surprisingly, a rather similar approach is taken by foreign franchisors in drafting the contracts with their Luxemburg franchisees, in so far as these contracts will generally not be anything other than adaptations of foreign model agreements. Some measure of caution is, however, called for. It is certainly true that no mandatory provisions of Luxemburg law specifically directed at franchise agreements will invalidate a contract, and it is true that the parties enjoy considerable freedom in adopting any set of contractual provisions (whether inspired by foreign model agreements or not). But some provisions of any agreement may conflict with the general rules of Luxemburg contract law; also, various public law rules—whether statutory or regulatory—will inevitably apply to certain aspects of the business conducted in Luxemburg.

[17] See Cour Supérieure de Justice, 1 October 1986, unreported, (no. 8782).

CHAPTER 11
THE NETHERLANDS

Robert Bosman,
Eric Keyzer,
Richard Norbruis,
J.M.C. Montijn-Swinkels
Gerard Van der Wal,
Corinna Wissels

1. Commercial Agency

1.1. Definition of Various Types of Agencies and Intermediaries

1.1.1. Independent

In 1966, the three Benelux countries signed the so-called Model-Act on Commercial Agency which has been ratified by the Netherlands on 12 July 1978. The Netherlands incorporated the Model-Act by introducing the new Art. 74 to 74s of the Dutch Commercial Code (Wetboek van Koophandel), which articles (hereafter also the "Articles") entered into force on 1 July 1977. Art. 74, para. 1 defines a commercial agency agreement as follows:

> "The agency agreement is an agreement pursuant to which one party, the principal, commits to the other party, the commercial agent, and the latter undertakes for a definite or an indefinite period and for remuneration, to act as an intermediary in concluding agreements and as the case may be, to conclude such agreements in the name and for the account of the principal without being subordinated to him."

The Articles apply irrespective of whether the principal or the commercial agent is a natural or legal person or whether the agency is the commercial agent's main or only an additional occupation. The Articles do not only apply to the sale of goods, but also the rendering of services, except that para. 2 of Art. 74 provides that the Articles "do not apply to agency agreements covered by the Act on Insurance Agency (Wet Assurantiebemiddeling)", which Act contains specific rules with respect to insurance agents. The Dutch statutory provisions on agency resemble in many instances the provisions on Dutch labor law. Both have as their main objective protection of the party who in economic respect is generally the weaker one: the employee and the commercial agent.

1.1.2. Employed

Apart from the Articles, the Dutch Commercial Code contains some provisions regarding the employed agent (Arts. 75 to 75c). Art. 75 defines the employed agent or salesman ("handelsreiziger") as follows:

> "The salesman agreement is the agreement pursuant to which one party, the salesman obligates himself to the other party, the principal, to visit persons as an employee of such principal, in order either to act as an intermediary in concluding agreements for the benefit of the principal, or to conclude such agreements in the name of the principal."

Arts. 75 to 75c aim to offer some additional protection to the salesman on top of the protection offered to him by Dutch Labour Law, by providing that certain of the provisions regarding commercial agency apply accordingly to salesmen.

1.1.3. Others

There are some other intermediaries, such as the Broker ("Makelaar") and the Stock Broker ("Commissionair") for which there are specific statutory provisions. Hereafter, however, we will not deal with the provisions regarding the salesman or other intermediaries, but instead focus on the provisions relating to commercial agency.

1.2. Conclusion of the Contract (Special Conditions)

There are no formal requirements. Any relationship that satisfies the definition referred to in 1.1.1. may be considered commercial agency irrespective of whether the agreement is in writing or concluded orally. Building contracts, for example, providing for all kinds of obligations which in itself may seem to have nothing to do with agency, may contain elements of agency, and therefore, trigger the statutory provisions on agency.

1.3. The Principal's Duties and Rights

1.3.1. The principal's duties

1.3.1.1. Commission

The principal's most important duty, of course, is to pay commission (see section 1.4.2.1. below).

1.3.1.2. Protection of agent, information

Art. 74c provides that: (first para) "The principal must do everything that is necessary on his part in the given circumstances to enable the commercial agent to do his work" and: (second para.) "He is obligated to warn the commercial agent forthwith, if he foresees that considerably fewer agreements will or will be permitted to be concluded than the commercial agent could expect".

The first paragraph is of a general nature and would include duties like putting the commercial agent in the position to actually act as the principal's agent, and to inform the agent of all particularities of the products or the services the agent is supposed to sell or to render. The wording "will be permitted to be" in the second paragraph or Art. 74c covers the commercial agent who is entitled to conclude agreements on behalf of his principal.

1.3.1.3. Supply of a written statement

Art. 74f provides that after each month the principal must supply a written statement of the commission due in respect of such month. The statement must be supplied prior to the end of the next succeeding month. Parties may agree in writing that this statement be supplied every two or three months. The principal must show the agent justificatory documents evidencing the principal's calculation of the commission due.

1.3.2. The principal's rights

The principal may exercise all the rights agreed to under the agreement concluded with a customer through or with the support of the commercial agent. Furthermore, the principal may, of course, keep the commercial agent to all the latter's duties.

1.4. The Commercial Agent's Duties and Rights

1.4.1. The commercial agent's duties

1.4.1.1. Trustworthiness, duty to inform

Agency is a relationship of trust. The commercial agent, therefore, must look after the principal's interest with due care (Art. 74a, first para.). He must supply the principal with all necessary information, particularly about all agreements in respect of which he acted as an intermediary or which he concluded for and on behalf of the principal (Art. 74a, second para.). Of course, the parties are free to agree that the commercial agent shall have all kinds of other duties such as: to inform the principal of any other agencies the commercial agent may accept, to inform the principal about the customer's solvency, to prohibit the agent to provide other kinds of services (repair, assembly), to trade second hand products, to promote the product, to warn the principal of any infringements of industrial property rights, etc.

1.4.1.2. Del credere

Article 74b addresses specifically the so called *del credere* stipulation, which generally takes the form of some sort of liability of the commercial agent to the principal for the obligations of the customer. Unless agreed otherwise in writing, a *del credere* stipulation may only render the commercial agent responsible for the customer's solvency. Furthermore, the commercial agent's liability may not exceed the agreed commission, unless the *del credere* stipulation was agreed in connection with a specific agreement or in respect of agreements which the commercial agent concluded in the principal's name. After having taken all specific circumstances of a case into consideration, the court may mitigate the agent's liability in as far as it exceeds the agent's commission, if there is an obvious disproportion between the risks of the agent on the one hand and his commission on the other. The commercial agent can only accept liability vis-à-vis the customer for obligations of such customer under any agreement, if such liability is accepted in writing. The rules of Article 74b have a mandatory character.

1.4.1.3. Non-competition

Although this is not specifically provided for in the Articles, it is pretty obvious that during the term of the agency the commercial agent is not supposed to compete with the principal, neither by accepting competing agencies, nor by competitively trading for his own account, since this would be contrary to the very purpose of the agency itself. To avoid any doubt, it may be advisable to include a specific provision for this in the agency agreement. Non-competition for a certain period after termination of the agency can only be validly agreed if agreed upon in writing. Art. 74p provides that the principal cannot successfully invoke such a non-competition clause if the agency has been terminated (i) by the principal without giving due notice, unless there was an urgent cause, (ii) by the agent for an urgent cause for which the principal was to blame, and (iii) by a court for reasons for which the principal is to blame. This Article has also a mandatory character.

The Court can be asked to annul all or part of any agreed upon non-competition clause if the agent is treated unreasonably, weighing the principal's interest in the clause against the possible disadvantages of it to the agent. The Court may on request mitigate a possible penalty on any infringement of any non-competition clause.

As has been stated before, a main feature of the Dutch provisions relating to agency is the protection of the commercial agent. Many agency provisions, therefore, are derived from Dutch Labour Law which offers quite some protection to the employee. The provisions relating to non-competition in Dutch Labour Law, for example, are very similar to the ones in Art. 74p and case law in respect of those labour law provisions plays an important role in the implementation of this Article.

1.4.1.4. Secrecy

The commercial agent is obligated to keep confidential the contents of the documents justifying the calculation of the commission that are showed to him pursuant to Art. 74f (see section 1.3.1.3. above).

1.4.2. The commercial agent's rights

1.4.2.1. Commission

Art. 74d provides that the commercial agent is entitled to the agreed commission (failing which he is entitled to a commission that is customary for the activities of the agent in the place where he carries out such activities) for the agreements concluded during the term of the agency, provided that either of the three following circumstances occur: (i) the agreement has been concluded through the agent's intermediary, (ii) the agreement has been concluded with a third party whom the commercial agent had already introduced earlier, or (iii) the agreement has been concluded with a third party belonging to a group of customers or established in a territory that was allocated to the commercial agent, unless it had been explicitly agreed that the commercial agent had no such exclusivity. This clarifies that the Articles presuppose an exclusive right of the agent. It is, therefore, for the sake of clarity, advisable to include some specific provisions on exclusivity in the agency agreement. The commercial agent has a mandatory right to a fair reward for agreements which had been prepared by him but which had been concluded only after termination of the agency. A fair reward would ordinarily be considered to be an amount equal to the agreed or customary commission. It could be less if, for example, the agent can be blamed for the termination of the agency or if the commission would also cover remuneration for services that should have been rendered by the agent in connection with the concluded agreement. Article 74e provides that the right to commission exists from the moment that the agreement with the third party has been concluded. If the agent's role in the transaction is only limited to acting as an intermediary, the order passed on to the principal will be considered accepted for purposes of calculating the right to commission, unless the principal within a certain period provided for in the agency agreement notifies the commercial agent that he refuses the order or to make a reservation in respect thereof. If no such specific period has been agreed upon, the relevant period will be one month. By virtue of this provision, the burden of proof in connection with the right on commission is shifted from the agent to the principal.

The commercial agent has no right on commission if it has been explicitly agreed that commission is subject to performance of the agreement and if the principal proves that non-performance of said agreement should not be for his account.

Force majeure on the part of the principal or the customer, insolvency of the customer which occurred after conclusion of the agreement, or the principal's decision for whatever reason not to carry out the agreement will, in principle, not impede the agent's right on commission.

Under certain circumstances, the commercial agent may be entitled to a remuneration if the principal did not use the agent's services or to a lesser extent than the agent could have expected.

1.5. Liabilities of Principal and Agent During the Term of the Agency

1.5.1. The principal as against the agent

The principal is liable to the agent for any commission payable. Commission is payable as from the fifth day of the month next succeeding the one during which the written statement must be supplied to the agent pursuant to Art. 74f (see section 1.3.1.3.). Further liabilities of the principal to the agent during the term of the agency agreement will depend on the contents of such agreement.

1.5.2. The principal as against third parties

If the agent's role was limited to acting as an intermediary, the principal will have to confirm the order to the customer in order to create an agreement of the principal with the customer. If, however, the agent was authorized to act for and on behalf of the principal, no such confirmation is necessary. The agent may also have unduly created the impression that he was authorized to represent the principal. Whether in such circumstances the principal is bound to the customer is a matter to be decided under the law of obligations that is applicable to such representation. The principal is liable to the third party for the proper performance of the agreement with the third party, in accordance with the terms of such agreement.

1.5.3. The agent as against the principal

The agent may be liable vis-à-vis the principal under a del credere provision, see above section 1.4.1.2. The agent is, of course, liable for the proper performance of all the obligations of the agent under the agency agreement insofar as these obligations do not infringe the Articles to the extent that they are of a mandatory nature.

1.5.4. The agent as against third parties

The commercial agent is, in principle, not liable to the customer, unless (i) the customer was rightly under the impression that the agent contracted in his own name and for his own account, or (ii) the agent explicitly accepted in writing liability for (certain of) the obligations under the agreement between the customer and the principal.

1.6. Term and Termination

1.6.1. Term

Art. 74 provides that an agency agreement may be for a definite or indefinite term.

1.6.2. Termination

The agency terminates:

(a) by mutual consent as to termination;
(b) if agreed for a definite period and not tacitly continued after this period, upon expiration of the definite period;
(c) if agreed for a definite period and tacitly continued after expiration of this period, in which case the agency agreement is considered concluded once again for the same term but not longer than for one year, ˙ after such term if not continued tacitly. This provision applies to any further tacit continuation (Art. 74i).
(d) if agreed for an indefinite period or for a definite period with the right to give intermediate notice, and if notice of termination is given by either party with due observance of the notice period, after such notice period;

the notice period will be four months, increased by one month after three years currency of the agency and by two months after six years currency of the agency. The notice period may not be shorter than one month and notice should be given by the end of a calendar month (Art. 74j);

(e) upon the death of the commercial agent (Art. 74k);

(f) upon the death of the principal if the heirs or the agent give notice of termination within nine months from the decease with a notice period of four months (Art. 74k);

(g) upon notice of termination for an urgent cause by either party (Art. 74l); and

(h) upon resignation of the agency agreement by the Court on request of either party, (i) for an urgent cause, or (ii) for change of circumstances of such a nature that reasonableness demands immediate termination within a short period of time (Art. 74m).

Specific performance cannot be claimed, because this would be contrary to the element of trust which is considered a basic feature of commercial agency. Non-observance of the notice period gives right to compensation only.

1.7. Indemnity

1.7.1. Indemnity for goodwill and/or clientèle

Apart from and in addition to the compensation of damages, the Articles provide the following in case of termination of the agency agreement (Art. 74o):

> "1. the commercial agent who through his activities has created or developed a group of customers and who has thus considerably increased the value of the principal's business, is entitled to a suitable compensation, unless this would not be within reason".
>
> 2. the amount of the compensation will not be more than that of the commission of one year calculated on the basis of the average of the five preceding years or, if the agreement has lasted a shorter period, on basis of the average of the entire period the agreement existed."

This goodwill compensation is due irrespective of whether the commercial agent can be blamed for the termination. The reasoning is that the nature of the termination does not diminish the increased value of the principal's business, possibly achieved by the commercial agent. Moreover, the Court is always entitled to reduce the goodwill compensation if it feels this to be fair.

Taking into consideration the explanatory observations of the Memory to the Bill introducing the Articles, the following conditions must be satisfied before a compensation for goodwill may be awarded: (i) the number of transactions or customers must be increased during the agency, thus increasing the value of the principal's business, (ii) such increase must have been the result of the agent's own efforts, and (iii) such increase must be considerable and, most importantly, permanent. The District Court of

Amsterdam decided that there is no right on goodwill compensation where the principal closed down his manufacturing plant and neither made any use of the group of customers that was created by the agent, nor transferred such group to any third party.[1] The District Court of 's-Hertogenbosch decided that an increase of turnover resulting from a longstanding customer of the principal will not lead to goodwill compensation for the agent.[2]

The goodwill compensation is a proprietary right which passes to the agent's heirs upon his decease.

1.7.2. Compensation for damages

In principle, either party who terminates the agency without due observance of the notice period owes the other party an amount equal to the commission for the time that the agency would have continued if proper notice had been given. In establishing this amount, the commission previously earned and all other circumstances are to be taken into account. In establishing the "commission previously earned", one should take into consideration the commission earned during the twelve months preceding the termination.[3] The Court may reduce this amount if it feels this to be appropriate. The damaged party is free to claim full compensation in lieu of the aforementioned fixed indemnity, but he must then prove the damages incurred (Art. 74n).

Compensation is not due by any party who terminates for a valid urgent cause, which is being defined as circumstances of such a nature that the party terminating cannot reasonably be expected to uphold the agency, even temporarily (Art. 74l). It is clear that this definition may lead to several court cases. In this respect, there is again a strong similarity with Dutch Labour Law which also allows for dismissal for an urgent cause. In agency conflicts, claimants, therefore, often refer to labour cases. The party terminating for a valid urgent cause may claim compensation from the other party if the latter can be blamed for the termination. The same applies if the Court resigns the agency agreement for a valid urgent cause. The amount of compensation is determined in accordance with Art. 74n, referred to above. The Court can also award compensation to either party if it resiliates the agency for a change of circumstances. In such a case, the Court is entitled to determine the amount of compensation according to its own views.

1.8. Specific Application of EEC Law

So far, there is no Dutch case law in which there has been specific application of EEC law to commercial agency. There is presently a Bill pending in Dutch Parliament aiming to implement the EEC Directive of 18 December 1986 relating to Commercial Agency. It is not expected that this implementation will bring about major changes in the Dutch provisions relating to commercial agency.

[1] 6 February 1980, Dutch Court Reports 1980, 459.
[2] 20 September 1985, Dutch Court Reports 1987, 112.
[3] District Court of Amsterdam, 6 February 1980, Dutch Court Reports 1980, 459; Court of Appeal Amsterdam, 6 December 1984, Dutch Court Reports 1986, 14.

1.8.1. Applicable law and jurisdiction

The Courts have held that an agency agreement made between an agent in the Netherlands and a principal having its place of business outside the Netherlands, relating to activities to take place in the Netherlands, will be governed by Dutch law. It is uncertain whether a clause in the agency agreement providing for a different foreign law would, in all circumstances, be enforceable in the Courts of the Netherlands. It might, however, be expected that such Courts will give prevalence to mandatory provisions of Dutch law if the agent, his place of business or his activities are closely connected with the Netherlands. The appropriate jurisdiction in the case of an agency agreement among parties that are subject to the EEC Judgement Convention of 1968 will be determined in accordance with this Convention.

1.9. Bibliography

Commerce Clearing House, *"Doing Business in Europe"*, para. 64-745.
Mees, Gouda Quint, *Nederlands Handels-en Faillissementrect*, Dorhout 9th ed. (1984), para. 2.81 ff.
Slagter, *Handelsagent, alleen-vertegenwoordiger en alleen importeur*, (TVVS, 1981), pp 1-9.
Geerlling, *Wijziging Wetboek van Koophandel, etc.*, (NJB, 1971), pp 377-91.

1.10. Legislation

Act of 23 March 1977, entered into force on 1 July 1977, introducing new Art. 74-74s in the Dutch Commercial Code.

2. Distributorship Agreements

2.1. Distribution

There is very little information available on distribution agreements in the Netherlands. For the more general provisions under Dutch law in respect of the conclusion of the contract, the supplier's and distributor's mutual rights and duties, their mutual liabilities, the term and termination of the contract, reference will be made to what is said hereafter in respect of franchise agreements in the Netherlands. In such a way unnecessary repetition of rules can be avoided.

2.1.1. Definition

Dutch law contains no specific provisions in respect of distribution agreements. General civil law is applicable.

All natural or legal persons not being agents and reselling goods may be called "distributors".

In general "distributor" refers to an independent contractor who purchases his goods from the manufacturer or another distributor (supplier) under an purchase agreement, and acts as a wholesaler or retailer.

2.1.2. Conclusion of the contract (special conditions)

There are no specific provisions under Dutch law in respect of the conclusion of a distribution agreement. General Dutch law is applicable.
See paragraph 3.2. of the section on franchise agreements.

2.1.3. The supplier's duties and rights

Again, there are no special provisions. A supplier may be obliged or entitled to all sorts of activities.

2.1.4. The distributor's duties and rights

For lack or special provisions, a distributor may be obliged or entitled to all sorts of activities: minimum purchase-requirements, use of specific trade marks and trade names, provision of specific services etc. Each time a distributor orders goods from the supplier, there will be a specific sales agreement for these goods, either orally or in writing.

The Dutch Competition Law (Wet Economische Mededinging) might be applicable to competition restrictions in the contract, (vertical price restraints, exclusivities, etc.) Legally binding agreements which will be in force for a term longer than one month have to be notified. The Minister for economic Affairs can declare an agreement partly or entirely non-binding; he can also issue a general non-binding decision for agreements of a specific feature, after consultation of the Commission Economische Mededinging (Fair Trade Commission). A ministerial decision has affect ex nunc. Horizontal price agreements are under discussion. Vertical price-fixing systems between one supplier and his distributors and sub-distributors on lower levels are not allowed for a number of durable consumer goods. So-called "collective" vertical price-fixing systems, which are agreements among suppliers to maintain certain prices in their distribution networks, are prohibited.

2.1.5. Liabilities of supplier and distributor during the term of the distributorship agreement

See paragraph 3.5. of the section on franchise agreements.

2.1.6. Term and termination

See paragraph 3.6. of the section on agreements. What is said there does *mutatis mutandis* equally apply to distribution agreements. (See also para. 2.1.7.).

2.1.7. Indemnity

The distributor has no legal right to compensation for goodwill. However, if there is a violation of good faith, compensation of damages could be possible.
Some examples:

- the length of the relationship as opposed to termination period; expec-

tations created, e.g. statements made explicitly or implicitly as to duration of the relationship, if the manufacturer/principal regularly discusses long-term market strategies and stimulates the distributor to make considerable expenditures in that respect (advertising, extra personnel, etc.) this would certainly be taken into account;
- timing aspects of the termination, e.g. just before or after a fair;
- was the distributorship the sole or the major source of income for the distributor;
- consequences of termination (will it cause considerable losses, will it be necessary to dismiss employees, is it or is it not difficult to find an adequate substitute, how long will it take to find such a substitute;
- motives of termination;
- customs in the distributor's branche.

The observation of a notice period of three to six months, depending on the circumstances referred to above, is advisable. It is advisable to provide for a notice period in the contract which should be a reasonable one from the distributor's point of view.

2.1.8. Specific applications of EEC law

There are no specific applications of EEC law.

2.1.8.1. Applicable law and jurisdiction

See paragraph 3.9.1. of the section on franchise agreements.

2.1.9. Bibliography

The legal features of distribution agreements are dealt with in the commentaries written on general civil law or in relation to the application of EEC-competition law.

2.1.10. Legislation

There is no specific legislation on distribution agreements.

2.1.11. Case law

There is no specific case law on distribution agreements (see section 2.2.12.).

2.2. Selective Distribution

2.2.1. Definition

Again, under Dutch law there is no definition of selective distribution. In practice the EEC-definition is used.

2.2.2. - 2.2.7.

See paragraphs 2.1.2.-2.1.7. above.

2.2.8. Specific applications of EEC law

There are no specific applications or EEC law.

2.2.8.1. Applicable law and jurisdiction

The maintenance of a selective distribution network in the Netherlands, will primarily depend on its compatability with EEC competition law, as far as this is applicable.

Often, selective distribution networks are jeopardized by outsiders who offer the products concerned to non-admitted dealers for resale to the public. The maintenance of the network will in that case depend on the legal possibilities to obtain an injunction against the outsider prohibiting him to continue his activities.

Dutch civil law determines the possibilities for obtaining such a decision. In the past the case law on selective distribution was primarily concerned with questions like vertical price-maintenance (infringements by non-admitted dealers). Recently, however, the debate in the case law has shifted to the prohibition of an outsider to deal.

Breach of contract

The following elements are decisive to obtain a positive judgment for the manufacturer:

- the outsider should have obtained products for resale by making use of a violation of the selective distribution contract by his supplier or a previous supplier.

  Tribunals often request proof that the selective distribution network is both legally and in fact closed. Dutch law does not demand an absolute closeness (com. the German "Lückenlosigkeit"). According to Dutch law, it will be sufficient to show that a manufacturer or distributor has undertaken - and continues to undertake - everything that is necessary to keep the system a closed shop.

- In case it can be proved that the network of a selective distribution system is functioning properly, it is for the outsider to prove that he is only selling products that leaked out of the system without any contractual violation by his supplier or previous supplier.
- There should be a relationship between the breach of contract by the admitted dealer, - e.g. violated provision -, and the interest the plaintiff tries to safeguard. Therefore, it is very important for internationally working networks to include the manufacturer as one of the parties in the distribution contract apart from a national representative or reseller.

2.2.9. Bibliography

The legal features of selective distribution are dealt with in the commentaries written on general civil law or in relation to the application of EEC-competition law.

2.2.10. Legislation

There are no specific provisions in Dutch law for selective distribution agreements.

2.2.11. Case law

Judgments of the Hoge Raad (HR) (Supreme Court), published in Nederlandse Jurisprudentie (NJ) (Dutch Court Reports).

HR 26.6.1964, NJ 1965, 170 and HR 18.12.1964, NJ 1965, 171, on the condition that the system is a closed shop.

HR 13.1.1961, NJ 1962, 245 and HR 12.1.1962 NJ 1962, 256, on the condition that there must be a relation between the violated provision and the interest the plaintiff wants to safeguard.

HR 18.5.1979, NJ 1975, 480, on the violation of the distribution network.

HR 27.1.1989, Rechtspraak van de Week (RvdW) 1989, 53, using a third party's violation of the contract, which is only contrary to good faith under certain conditions.

There are a large number of decisions of lower courts on selective distribution of parfumes and cosmetics, which have not been published. (See: notes with the article of E.H. Pijnacker Hordijk "De Nederlandse rechters en het Europese kartelrecht; een inventarisatie", SEW (1987, biz. 484).

3. Franchise Agreements

The franchising concept, developed in the United States and nowadays widely accepted in Europe, has become a well-known method of doing business in the Netherlands. Both the number of franchisors as well as the number of franchisees grew steadily. In the period from 1980-1987 the number of franchisors increased by 50% and the number of franchisees by 150%.

3.1. Definition

There are no Dutch laws which focus directly upon franchising. Until now, the special features of franchising have only been considered in the margin by legislation and courts: in June 1986 the Senate rejected a bill concerning competition law because of the fact that the bill did not create a special position for all franchising agreements;[4] the courts have decided some specific cases on social security and on commercial lease.

Most franchising organisations in the Netherlands (80%) are members of the Dutch Franchising Association. The members of the organisations subscribe to the European Code of Ethics of the European Franchising Federation.

For a definition of franchising the Dutch Franchising Association refers

---

[4] M.R. Mok, "Kartelrecht I, Nederland", *Tjeenk Willink* (Zwolle, 1987), p. 103. M.J.C. Deriks, "Focus op franchising", TVVS Nr. 87/3, p. 62 e.v.

to the definition in the EEC block exemption regulation for franchise agreements.[5]

In Dutch literature one of the definitions of franchising is the following:[6]

"Franchising is a contractually governed form of commercial operation between independent undertakers, whereby one party, the franchisor, gives one or more other parties, the franchisee(s), the right to use his trade name or trade mark or other distinguishing features, in the sale of products or services. This sale takes place on the basis of an exclusive marketing concept (system or formula) developed by the franchisor: in return, the franchisor receives royalties. The use of those rights by the franchisee is supervised by the franchisor in order to ensure uniform presentation to the public and uniform quality of the goods or services".

3.1.1. Characteristics

The essential characteristics of the franchise agreement in the Netherlands are the following:[7]

Collaboration

Franchising is a method of contractual collaboration between the franchisor and several franchisees according to agreed rules. Franchising is a method of commercialisation and distribution of products (and/or services) for producers, wholesalers and retailers as well as a method of commercialisation and distribution of services. Both the franchisor and the franchisee(s) benefit from the franchise agreement through the combination of their human and financial resources.

The intensity of the collaboration is the degree of tightness of the contract rules. If the collaboration does not go beyond the fixing of some premises which the franchisee can elaborate, the franchise formula is referred to as soft. The collaboration in that case only concerns the delivery of good, the elaboration of a marketing strategy and uniform sales system and the putting at franchisee's disposal of know how. On the other hand a tight and detailed scenario for the franchise formula may result in the qualification hard.

Independence

The franchisee is an independent entrepreneur, undertaking for his own account and at his own risk.

It may be important to establish the relationship between franchisor and franchisee as clear as possible in the franchise contract; otherwise a franchisee could be considered to be an employee of the franchisor and thus the franchisor would be under the obligation to pay social security premium and even income tax. This could occur, if the franchisee is for example sub-

---

[5] Regulation (EEC) No. 4087/88 of the European Commission of 30 November 1988. Art. 1(3)(a).

[6] E.M. Kneppers-Heynert, "Een economische en juridische analyse van franchising tegen de achtergrond van een property rights- en transactie kostenbenadering", *Drukkerij van Denderen B.V.* (1988), p. 264.

[7] E.M. Kneppers-Heynert, op. cit. F.W.J. Schalen, "Franchising, een nieuw perspectief" (Kluwer, Deventer, 1983), 20-24 and 94.

ordinated to a very large extent to the franchisor and the franchise fee is not established to be payment for a total franchise system but for example only a payment to obtain the lease of a building.[8] It is not sufficient to label a contract as "franchise contract": it has to be clear from the substance of the contract that there is no relationship of mere subordination.

The independence of the parties to a franchise contract requires that each must comply with the general rules of tax laws relative to independent enterprises as well as with the rules of bookkeeping and annual accounts.

Moreover, the franchisee needs an authorisation to start business and therefore must comply with the rules of the law concerning the establishment of new business (Vestigingswet Detailhandel en Vestigingswet Bedrijven).

Distinguishing capacity - uniformity

Only a product, service or commercial formula that is distinguishable from similar products, services and commercial formula can be eligible for franchising. The formula needs a specific reputation, originality and recognition. An essential characteristic of a franchising system is the uniform presentation. This uniformity has important advantages for the purchase, promotion and client tying.

Licence

The franchisor commits himself to place his formula at the disposal of franchisees. Consequently he licenses the right to use his trade name and/or trade mark(s) and possibly other distinguishable features as well as the commercial know how. In general the franchisor also provides for a theoretical and practical training of the franchisee, as well as for a continuing support in the form of advice and supervision.

Selection

The franchisor takes care of a careful preliminary selection of the franchisee(s). The identity and personality of the franchisee are of the utmost importance to the franchisor. Usually a franchisee may not grant a subfranchise without the consent of the franchisor.

Supervision

In order to protect the image of its trade name and/or trade mark(s), the franchisor controls the franchisee.

Payments

Implicit in any franchise agreement is that there shall be a payment made in one form or another by the franchisee to the franchisor in return for the services supplied by franchisor in licensing his trade name, trade mark(s) and know how. Often the franchisee pays an entrance fee for the initial expenses incurred by the franchisor with respect to the installation of the franchise formula, the research work, the recruitment costs, trainings etc.

The franchisee further pays royalties for the use of the trade name/ mark(s), for the business management, for the assistance, consultation and

---

[8] *Centrale Raad van Beroep*, d.d. 15 November 1985, Rechtspraak Sociale Verzekering 1986, 174.

supervision. Usually the franchisee also pays a monthly percentage of the turnover to the advertisement fund of the franchisor.

3.2. Conclusion of the Contract (Special Conditions)

As there is no Dutch franchise legislation and the franchise contract is not regulated under Dutch law as a specific contract, the general rules of Dutch contract law apply.

The Civil Code (Burgerlijk Wetboek), the Commercial Code and a number of other statutes codify the contract law in the Netherlands.[9] There is no distinction between civil contracts and commercial contracts. Accordingly, both codes apply to all persons and transactions, whether or not these transactions serve commercial purposes, and whether or not the parties are Dutch.

The codes contain a great number of rules that apply only when parties have not agreed otherwise.

Agreements generally do not need to be in written form.[10] Obviously, written agreements are preferable if only for evidentiary purposes. Moreover, the European Code of Ethics stipulates that "it is necessary and inherent to franchising that the basic agreement between franchisor and franchised firm(s) should be subject of a written contract".

Under Dutch law, a contract does not have to be written in Dutch. Whatever language the parties choose for purposes of interpretation, one controling language should clearly be selected by the parties for all purposes of the contractual relationship. If a contract provides for exclusive jurisdiction by the Dutch courts, a language that is commonly used in the Netherlands such as English, French or German, should preferably be chosen.

For a contract to be valid under Dutch law, the following basic requirements must be met:

(a) the parties must have agreed on the substance of their respective rights and obligations under the contract;
(b) the parties must be competent to contract;
(c) there must be an identifiable performance under the contract;
(d) the contract must have a permissable cause. The technical legal term "cause" is extremely difficult to explain. For all practical purposes, it may suffice to say that a contract does not have a permissable cause if it violates mandatory law or contravenes bonos mores or public order.[11]

If the requirement of a permissable cause is not met, the contract is null and void by operation of law. For example, contracts or provisions thereof *that violate European competition law are null and void by operation of law*. If any of the other requirements are not met, the contract is voidable. Thus, a contract can be nullified if one of the parties did not enter into it out of his

---

[9] E.P.A. Keyzer in S.R. Schuit, J.M. van der Beek, G.H. Zevenboom, B.E. Schifman, legal accounting and tax aspects of Doing Business in the Netherlands", *Dutch Business Law*, 3rd edn. (Kluwer, Deventer/Bosten, 1988) pp. 5–3 – 5–6.
[10] Burgerlijk Wetboek (BW) (Civil Code) Art. 1374(1).
[11] BW Art. 1356 et seq.

own free will, for example, if an agreement was reached between the parties on the basis of error, coercion or fraud.

A legal concept which may have significant implication for franchise contracts is the concept of good faith. Good faith is the guiding force behind Dutch contract law. All contracts must be construed and performed in good faith.[12] It is only in rare cases, however, that good faith can set aside a clearly stipulated contractual provision. This could occur, for example, if the provision concerned is manifestly not in accordance with the character of the contract, if one of the parties has a substantially stronger position, or if one of the parties could not be aware of the breach of the provision concerned. It has been established by case law that in certain circumstances it may be contrary to good faith to invoke an exclusion of liability-clause.[13]

3.3. The Supplier's Duties and Rights

3.3.1. The supplier's duties

- The franchisor commits himself to place his franchise formula, which has been tried and found to work, at the disposal of the franchisee. The trade name and trade mark(s), the products, the apparatus, the inventory, the house style, the publicity etc. . . . form an integral part of the formula.
- The franchisor bears the responsibility of a range of services and assistance with respect to: the installation and maintenance of the franchisee's administration, the training of the franchisee and its staff, advertising by or under supervision of the franchisor, business management, assistance in obtaining and implementing the technology of the franchise and guidance as to operating costs and margins that the franchisee should be achieving at any given time in his business.[14]
- The franchisor must provide for further development of the franchise formula through judiciously executed regional and national advertising, sales promotion and public relations, and through continuing research as to the management and marketing techniques.
- The franchisor must ensure that the franchisee receives a regular supply of goods and services of sound, genuine and saleable quality.

3.3.2. The supplier's rights

- The franchisor has a right to control the franchisee with respect to its performance of the contract, the quality of its execution of the franchising formula, the design of its business premises and its respect of the identity and uniformity of the formula. The franchisor is entitled to receive all relevant information.
- The franchisor can perform all his rights under the laws relating to intel-

---

[12] BW Art. 1374(3).

[13] Judgment of 19 May 1967 Hoge Raad (HR) (Supreme Court), 1967 Nederlandse Jurisprudentie (NJ) (Dutch Court Reports) No. 261; Judgment of 20 February 1976, HR, 1976 NJ No. 261; Judgment of 18 December 1981, HR, 1982 NJ No. 71; Judgment of 7 May 1982, HR, 1983 NJ No. 509.

[14] F.W.J. Schalen, op. cit. pp. 92-94.

lectual property rights. The important laws are the Benelux Merkenwet as to trade marks,[15] the Handelsnaamwet as to trade names,[16] the Benelux Tekeningen- en Modellenwet as to designs and modells,[17] the Auteurswet as to copyrights,[18] the Rijksoctrooiwet as to patents,[19] and the General Civil Law as to other rights, the performances of which would require and deserve the same protection as intellectual property rights the prior mentioned.

- The franchisor has a right to incorporate in the contract a non-competition and secrecy clause in order to prevent competitors from using the know how of the franchisor. Franchise contracts may contain non-competition clauses applicable during the contract as well as after breach or termination of the contract. The contracts in general contain detailed provisions as regarding duration and territorial extent of the non-competition obligations. *In view of the block exemption regulation for franchise contracts, the non-competition clause may apply in the territory where the franchisee exploited the franchise, during a reasonable period, with a maximum of one year after termination of the contract.*[20]
- Regarding the uniformity of the commercial franchise policy, the franchisor may wish to impose prices for the franchisee. Under present domestic Dutch law, the prices may be fixed, subject to any applicable pricing regulation. *On EEC-level, however, price fixing is considered contrary to article 85(1) of the Treaty of Rome. The franchisor can nevertheless communicate price guidelines which are not binding for the franchisee.*[21]

3.4. The Distributor's Duties and Rights

3.4.1. The distributor's duties

- The franchisee commits himself to exercise his entrepreneurial capacity among which his labour.[22]
- The franchisee has the obligation to pay a form or renumeration, which in general relates to an entrance fee and to the royalties in return for his right to use franchisor's trade name, trade mark(s) and know how.
- The franchisee is an independent entrepreneur, undertaking for his own account and at his own risk, but he is not free to decide how to use his labour and other assets. The franchisee must comply with the franchisor's standards and rules of business conduct; he is not free to decorate the business premises according to his own plans and designs and he is not free in composing the product/service assortment; he can only perform his own ideas if they fit in the formula of the franchise network, which he subscribed to.

---

[15] Benelux Merkenwet, 1962.
[16] Handelsnaamwet, 1921.
[17] Eenvormige Beneluxwet inzake Tekeningen of Modellen 1966.
[18] Auteurswet, 1912.
[19] Rijksoctrooiwet, 1910.
[20] Regulation No. 4087/88, Art. 3(i)(c).
[21] Regulation No. 4087/88, Art. 5(e).
[22] E.M. Kneppers-Heynert, op. cit., p. 265.

- The franchisee must supply the franchisor with operating data and financial ratios to facilitate the quality and management control.
- Unless otherwise agreed, the franchisee may not grant sublicensees or subfranchise contracts.
- The franchisee may be required to sell only products supplied for the franchisor or by the suppliers selected by him. *According to the franchise regulation such an obligation is acceptable only if, in view of the character of the franchise products, it is not possible through objective criteria to control the quality of the products sold by the franchisee.*[23] *Such an exclusive purchase obligation may, however, not prevent the franchisee from buying from other franchisees, belonging to the same network.*[24]

3.4.2. The distributor's rights

The franchisee has the right to operate under franchisor's trade name and trade mark(s). He furthermore has the right to make good use of the services provided by the franchisor.

3.5. Liabilities of Supplier and Distributor During the Term of the Distributorship Agreement

As mentioned before, general rules of Dutch contract law apply and good faith is the guiding principle of Dutch contract laws. All contracts must be construed and performed in good faith. As a general rule of contract, a contracting party, who committed a breach of contract, is liable for the damages which was the foreseeable result of the breach of contract, unless he can invoke force majeure.

Force majeure applies if the defaulting party can prove that its non-performance (or inadequate performance) is caused by facts or circumstances beyond its control. These facts or circumstances must not be the fault of, or the result of negligence on the part of, the defaulting party.

It is not necessary for force majeure to be provided for in the contract. The law grants this defence to any party, subject to the determination by the courts that the alleged facts and circumstances constitute force majeure. The parties to a contract can expand the scope of force majeure by enumerating facts and circumstances that exclude or limit liability. If the contract provides for a clearly defined peformance, and it is understood by the contracting parties that this performance is guaranteed, a non-performing party is stopped from pleading force majeure. Parties to a contract are always entitled to performance and can insist upon it as long as performance is physically possible.[25] Dutch law recognizes four types of excuses for non-performance: force majeure, the right to delay performance (exceptio non adimpleti contractus), change of circumstances (rebus sic stantibus clause) and unbearable hardship.

If a party fails to perform its obligations, the aggrieved party may seek the

[23] Regulation Nr 4087/88, Art. 3(i)(b).
[24] Regulation No. 4089/88, Art. 5(b)(c).
[25] BW Art. 1303.

following legal remedies: specific performance, damages, payable to the aggreived party and rescission of contract.

In principle default involves only the parties to the contract. However, in Dutch case law, it is often held that a third person who causes a party to default under a contract to the benefit of the third party, commits a tort against the non-defaulting party.

This leads to the distinction in Dutch law between contractual liability and tortuous liability.[26] The main rule of tort liability is contained in article 1401 of the Civil Code, which states that "every unlawful act which inflicts damage upon another obliges the person by whose fault the damages was caused to repair the same". While contractual liability can only be relied upon by one of the contracting parties, tortuous liability may be invoked by anyone.

3.5.1. The supplier as against the distributor

For a contract to be valid under Dutch law, the parties must have agreed on the substance of their respective rights and obligations under the contract. If the franchisor gives misleading information on the franchise formula or if he does not make full disclosure, the franchisee can start proceedings for nullity of the franchise agreement, based on the principle of imperfect consent. The relevant principles in such proceedings are error, coercion or fraud.

Where the franchisor sells a product to the franchisee, it is important to provide for warranty against hidden defects. The Civil Code contains a number of provisions concerning latent defects.[27] When goods sold have a latent defect, which makes them unsuitable for the intended use, the buyer is entitled to claim a reduction of the purchase price or to return the goods and claim a refund of the price. In spite of the wide wording of the provisions, they have been interpreted in a restricted way and as a result they are rarely applied. In the first place, the latent defects warranty is limited to the sale of specific goods (as opposed to generic goods). If the purchaser is entitled to the warranty against latent defects, he must exercise this right within a short period after discovery of the latent defect. The length of this period is not specified in the Civil Code; it depends on the characteristics of the goods and of the defect concerned and on other relevant circumstances. For practical purposes a good rule of thumb, based on case law, is that claims should be made within six weeks.[28]

3.5.2. The supplier as against third parties

If a third party suffers damage because of defective franchise goods sold to that third party, he has a direct course of action based on tort law against the franchisor/manufacturer.

The defectiveness of the product must be the result of fault in the production and control of the product on the part of manufacturer. In theory,

[26] BW Art. 1401 et seq.
[27] BW Art. 1504-1547.
[28] S.R. Schuit c.s., op. cit., pages 5-11.

the plaintiff must prove fault, although there is a tendency to alleviate the burden of proof.[29]

3.5.3. The distributor as against the supplier

If the franchisor discovers that the motives of the franchisee for entering into agreement were fraudulent, he can start proceedings for nullity on the basis of imperfect consent.

3.5.4. The distributor as against third parties

If a third party suffers damage because of a product sold by the franchise, there is first of all a contractual product liability. When the product has been supplied under a contract which contains an express warranty relating to the qualities or characteristics of the products sold, the damage caused may amount to a breach of contractual warranty and consequently result in contractual liability. The Supreme Court has held that there may be a breach of contract not only when the goods do not comply with the express stipulations of the contracts, but also if they do not comply with the reasonable expectations of the buyer.[30] The fact that a product causes damage presumes that the product did not meet the contract standards. The burden of proof that the defectiveness of the product was a result of force majeur lies with the seller.

In the absence of contractual liability the product liability may also be liability in tort. A distributor can be held liable for damages on the ground of negligence. His duty of care to prevent the marketing of products that embody a foreseeable risk of harm is not, however, as extensive as the duty imposed on the manufacturers.

Mention should be made of the EEC-Council Directive of 25th July 1985 on Product Liability, which must be incorporated in Dutch law before 1 August 1988. Pursuant to the regulation, future Dutch legislation (already finally approved by Parliament) will impose strict liability on producers.[31] According to article 3 of the regulation anyone putting his name, trade mark or other distinguishing feature on a product holds himself out as its producer.

3.6. Term and Termination

3.6.1. Term

Franchise agreement may be for an indefinite or a definite period of time.

3.6.2. Termination

It is important that franchise contracts contain provisions on termination,

---

[29] G.H.A. Schut, *Produktenaansprakelijkheid* (Zwolle 1979), p.81.

[30] HR, NJ 1972, 221.

[31] Council Directive of 25 July, 1985 on product liability, No L210/29, notified to the Member States on 30 July 1985; Draft Dutch Product Liability Act of September 1986 BW art. 1407a et seq.

including unilateral termination for cause. If a franchise agreement does not provide for the possibility of intermediate unilateral termination for cause, such termination is possible only on the basis of a judgment of the competent court.

In principle, the notice period for termination may be freely determined by contract, but should be reasonable from the franchisee's point of view.

Death or bankruptcy of one of the parties may usually result in intermediate termination of the agreement, since in franchising the personalities of the parties to the agreement are of major importance.

Failure to perform the obligations equally may be a cause for termination. If not established in the agreement, the court must establish the non-performance and consider whether it is serious enough to justify a rescission, in which even the contract is, if possible, rescinded with retroactive effect.[32]

Termination and lease

The provision of the Civil Code regarding the lease of commercial properties may be of importance in case of termination of the franchising agreement. The franchisor should be aware of his rights and duties with respect to its business premises upon termination of the franchise agreement.

In the Netherlands as in many other European countries, legislation exists which deals with commercial leases aimed at protecting the rights of the lessee who has developed a business in the leased premises and therefore must be protected against loss of his investment and his efforts through loss or termination of his lease.[33]

A problem for franchisors is to reconcile the franchising contract with the rights attaching to a commercial lease in order to ensure their right to remain on the premises when the contract expires or is terminated. Three situations may occur:

- The franchisor is owner of the premises. If he wishes to ensure the right of use of the premises, he shall have to match the duration of the franchise agreement with the duration of the commercial lease.[34] For that matter the consent of the cantonal courts is required in most cases. The same applies for the franchisor-lessee (franchisee is sublessee), although extra complications are likely in the event of termination of the lease between franchisor and proprietor.
- The franchisee is proprietor of the business premises. If the franchisor wishes to continue the use of the premises after termination of the franchise agreement, it is advisable that the parties enter into a preliminary agreement with respect to the transfer or lease of the premises by franchisee and franchisor.
- A third proprietor leases to the franchisee. The voluntary co-operation of this third party is necessary for the transfer, renewal or intermediate termination of the lease. A substitution procedure before the cantonal court

32 S.R. Schuit c.s., op. cit., p. 5-7.
33 BW Art. 1629 et seq.
34 BW Art. 1629.

may be possible if the lessee (franchisee) transfers its business to the franchisor or to a third party, appointed by the franchisor.[35]

3.7. Indemnity

Because the contract must be performed on the basis of good faith, it is possible that, in the light of the circumstances, damages will be due upon termination. For this reason, the mutual rights and obligations of the parties upon termination should be carefully stipulated in the franchise agreement itself.

There is no automatic right to goodwill compensation. The mutual rights and obligations of the parties upon termination may concern amongst others:

- the obligation for the franchisee to return franchise equipment and materials;
- the obligation for the franchisee to cease the use of trade name and trade mark(s);
- the obligation to respect the confidentiality clause, in order to prevent dissemination of know how during the post-contractual period;
- the right for the franchisor of repurchase of franchisee's stock and back-orders;
- or the right for the franchisee of continued sale without reference to the trade mark.

3.8. Specific Application of EEC Law

In the Netherlands, there is *no specific* application of EEC law. In November 1988 the EC-Commission issued a regulation exempting distribution and service franchise agreement from the prohibitions laid down by the competition rules. The regulation is directly applicable in all Member-States as of 1 February 1989.[36]

Applicable laws (B9)

A well known 1966 judgment of the Dutch Supreme Court (Hoge Raad) held that,[37] as a general rule, parties to an international contract are free to choose the legal system which will govern their contractual relationship. The freedom of choice implies that parties can have their contract governed by a legal system of a country with which the contract has no factual connection whatsoever.

A possible restriction of the freedom of choice is based on an interest analysis. The Dutch Supreme Court, stated that a state of the otherwise applicable law may have such a great interest in the application of certain provisions of its law, even outside its territory that Dutch courts should take this into account and should consequently apply those provisions in preference to the law chosen by the parties.[38]

---

[35] BW Art. 1653.
[36] Regulation (EEC) No. 4087/88 of the European Commission of 30 November 1988, Art. 1(3)(a).
[37] *The Alnati* case, HR, NJ 1967, 3.
[38] *American Express Company Inc.* v. *MacKay*, HR, NJ 1971, 1129.

It is unclear whether, subsequent to the making of a contract, the parties may change their choice of law or may elect for an applicable law in the absence of such a choice in the original contract. There are, in this respect, no clear rules established by the decisions of the various Dutch courts. However, even if this subsequent choice of law is considered valid, the rights of third parties may not be impaired.

In the event that a choice of law has not been made, the courts will try to determine with what country the contract has the closest connection, taking into account all the special circumstances of the case at hand. A natural consequence of this case by case approach is that the results are uncertain. A more predictable result is obtained when the courts employ, as they do with increasing frequency, the method whereby the domicile of the debtor of the obligation characterizing the contract determines the applicable law. The Dutch Supreme Court combines elements of both schools of thought.[39]

Jurisdiction

Parties to a contract may agree that all disputes arising out of their contract will be submitted only to a certain court or to certain arbitrators. Under Dutch law such agreements are valid.

Although choice of forum clauses are generally given effect, Dutch courts tend not to honour a forum clause if there would have been no competent court for such agreement. It should be noted, however, that one of the competent courts (enumerated in the Civil Procedure Code), is the forum actoris, i.e. the court under the jurisdiction of which the plaintiff is domiciled.[40]

Dutch courts that would have been competent but for that choice are inclined to honour a choice of forum clause that declares a foreign court exclusively competent. When, however, it seems likely that the foreign court will not honour Dutch mandatory provisions, Dutch courts will declare themselves competent in spite of the choice of forum clause.[41]

The problem of jurisdiction is also governed by the provisions of bilateral and unilateral treaties, which have priority to the national rules. The EEC-Convention on Jurisdiciton and the enforcement of civil and commercial judgments states that for a person domiciled in one of the original EEC-countries the forum actoris has no jurisdiction. The convention permits parties from the Treaty countries to agree upon choice of forum clause as long as they declare one or more courts in one or more Treaty countries competent. Other choice of forum clauses are not governed by the Convention: their validity is determined by the law of the countries concerned. The Treaty does not apply to: the status and capacity of natural persons, matrimonial law, wills and inheritances, bankruptcies, social security, and arbitration.[42]

Note that the European Code of Ethics advises to attribute competence to the courts of the place in which the head office of the franchisee is located.

---

[39] *Neska van de Beijer*, HR, NJ 1973, 121 and Topsoe Del Prado, HR, NJ 1973, 371.
[40] Wetboek van Burgerlijke Rechtavordering (Code on Civil Procedure) RV Art. 126, para. 1.
[41] For instance in the Salbandera-case, HR, NJ 1948, 609.
[42] Art. 1 and 17 of the EEC-Convention on Jurisdiction and the enforcement of civil and commercial judgments, Brussels, 27 September 1968.

CHAPTER 12

Portugal

Carlos de Oliveira Coelho,
Clementina Paiva,
Nuno Ruiz,
Ana Reis Santos

1. Commercial Agency

1.1. Definition of Various Types of Agencies and Intermediaries

1. Agency contracts have been existent for some time under Portuguese doctrine and legislation. It was only recently, however, that the contract ceased to be fully governed by the discretion of the parties concerned.

In fact, the agent's status was only recently accorded its legal sanction. This ruling was published by decree no. 178/86 on 3 July, where Article 1 defines the agency as follows:

" . . . the contract by means of which one of the parties undertakes to promote on behalf of another the conclusion of contracts in a defined area or a precise circle of clients in an autonomous, consistent manner, in exchange for payment."

2. Even if the law remains tacit on this point, doctrine maintains that the agent is a "merchant". Moreover, in accordance with Article 10 of the Commercial Registry Code, the agency contract " . . . when contracted in writing, its amendments and cancellations" are subject to registration. In our opinion, this means that (the agent) according to Portuguese law is a merchant.

3. The above-noted legal definition excludes the idea of a subordinate agent in the notion of the agent. The use of the expression " . . . in an autonomous manner. . . " means just that. Subsequent distinctions can only be based on supporting criteria. Thus, we may speak of an agent without representation rights—a standard position provided under Article 1—and the agent who has representation rights, a hypothesis covered by Article 2.

This latter solution, which is unusual under Portuguese law, can only be laid down in writing and would therefore become a true *ad substantiam* formality. In this case the written document would allocate representative powers to the agent.

Decree no. 178/86 only singles out within the general context of an agency contract the contract for a sub-agency, in which the agent becomes the principal for another agent.

The decree in fact only appraises the status of the agent. It does not deal with other social realities, where the position of intermediary is only established through the agency but where, in all events, the legislator prefers to regulate specific statuses (cf. insurance, forwarding agents).

1.2. Conclusion of the Contract (Special Conditions)

Under Portuguese law there are no legal provisions for legally concluding such a contract. In fact, when a particular aspect of the agency contract gives rise to certain questions, these will be decided by the law which will impose a peremptory legal decision and submit the contract to general provisions governing the conclusion of contracts.

The matter refers to the status of the agent and explains why Portuguese law opts for the subject of the rights and obligations of the agent to decide the question.

An example of this legal technique is provided in the *del credere* clause (one of many options chosen), where settlement is found under the section governing the agent's obligations.

Apart from the above cases, the order, drafting and conclusion of the contract is the same as for any other contract. Its order can be found under the general section of the Civil Code.

1.4. The Commercial Agent's Duties and Rights

1.4.1. The commercial agent's duties

1. In decree no. 178/86 of July 3, the agency contract is drafted from the viewpoint of the agent. Chapter II of the decree, the longest section, is entitled "Rights and Obligations of the parties". But Section I, enumerates the obligations (of the agent) and section II lists his rights. It would follow that the status of the "other party" has no autonomy, being only the opposing position to the agent.

2. A reading of this decree illustrates that the law consistently opposes the "agent" with the "other party", who is only referred to as a principal in Articles 19 and 23. All these legal provisions appear in the decree and occur when the status of the agent has been almost completely outlined.

3. Whatever the case, as this is the theory of the decree, we have to abide by it, and in this way we must justify the system we shall be adopting.

We have already pointed out that the agent's obligations are ordered before his rights. Bearing in mind that the decree is weighted on the protective side of the agent's status, this legislative slant may point to an attempt to mitigate this option.

1.4.1.1. Trustworthiness, duty to inform

Portuguese law does not mention this duty with the same distinctness accorded to the other duties. Whereas in the case of the others, it makes use of an individual provision, it acts quite differently for this obligation. In fact, the law states under paragraph 6 of Article 7 that the agent is bound to possess ". . . information that has been requested of him or which is required for proper management, particularly that concerning the solvency of his clients."

Subordination of this obligation is not solely dependent on the lack of formal autonomy for other obligations.

This clause has been drafted in such a way that one may conclude that it is only a simple kind of "good faith" general clause made more concrete by the obligation to be mindful of the interests of the other party. Since under Portuguese civil law the drafting of criteria which may be used for legal knowledge in the construction of a legal notion of "good faith" or for any other kind of "general clause" is quite recent, it is no simple task to explain the practical substantiation of this obligation, which has become a real legal obligation.

1.4.1.2. Del credere

According to Article 10, the agent can guarantee the execution of the obligations of a third party, if they relate to the contract that he has negotiated or concluded. This is what is meant by the *del credere* agreement.

This condition is only valid where there is a written document containing the acceptance by the agent.

1.4.1.3. Non-competition

The obligation of "non-competition" is sanctioned under Article 9. In this case, too, the clause is only valid when the condition appears in writing. In any case, its validity will extend only for a period of two years.

1.4.1.4. Secrecy

"The obligation for secrecy", the expression used in Article 8, means the prohibition of using or revealing to a third party a secret of the principal which has become the knowledge of the agent, either because it has been revealed to him, or because it was presumed for the exercise of his function as an agent.

1.4.2. The commercial agent's rights

1.4.2.1. Commission

The importance given to this obligation is self-evident, given that of the nine articles governing the rights of the agent, four are concerned with his commission.

The general principle is given in Article 16 where the right to commission for the agent is recognized for contracts that he has promoted or concluded with clients obtained by him. But this right is only valid following execution by the third party of his obligations (unless the *del credere* clause has been requested).

This general ruling is waived in the case of exclusive rights where the agent has the right to receive commission on contracts concluded by his principal.

The right to recover commission only after execution by the third party of the contract promoted by the agent is waived if stipulated in writing, because in this case the *del credere* clause becomes effective.

Finally, under Article 19, the agent may receive commission even in the event of non-execution by the third party, if this contractual failing is the fault of the principal.

Protection of the agent

The legal facilities created to protect the agent are covered by Article 13. The legal technicalities employed are the same as for those of obligations. That is to say, Article 13 appears as a sort of substantiation of good faith which Article 12—the equivalent, in the rights section of Article 6 in the obligations section—sanctions.

Among these various rights (enumerated in paragraphs (a) to (g)) the first four concern the right to be informed. Here it is still a question of rights which pertain to corresponding obligations of the principal.

The right to a written statement

According to Article 14 "the agent has the right to be told immediately if the other party is only able to conclude a number of contracts substantially lower than whatever was agreed, or that which circumstances had led one to expect."

1.5. Liabilities of Principal and Agent during the Term of the Agency—Questions of Civil Liability

There are no special provisions under Portuguese law governing agency contracts to cover the civil responsibility of the agent with respect to the principal and vice-versa. In our opinion, there are two reasons for this.

First, since the subject of civil liability covering all eventualities come under the umbrella of the civil code, there has been no reason to allocate an autonomous provision to a particular contract. So, the civil code will cover the problem of contractual responsibility and therefore of this contract.

Also, as neither the legal nature of either the principal or especially of the agent is passive in other legal respects, it is possible to admit that the legislator has opted not to enter into a controversy which has not yet arisen under Portuguese law.

Legal silence does not, however, imply ignorance of the ease with which the question may arise. Given the legal framework, we may be allowed to think that whatever the case in point, the situation will always be one of contractual civil liability.

In fact, if we concentrate on the agency contract it is obvious that the contractual perspective stands uppermost. But if we favour the "status" of the agent created by the contract, there will still be a contractual picture in sight. Effectively this "status" is characterised by the promotional character of contracts. Contractual non execution on the part of the agent or principal, one in relation to the other, will be tantamount to violation of the contract that they have signed. But if the situation shifts to the level of client relationships, it will still be within the scheme of the contract to record that a possible non execution should be declared.

This being the position of civil liability, there will be an obligation on the debtor to pay an indemnity. The amount of the indemnity to be paid will depend on the proof of damages incurred. The creditor will have the responsibility of proving non execution of the obligation. The debtor will be responsible for proving that the non execution is not incorrect.

1.6. Term and Termination

1. According to Article 24 of Decree 178/86 the agency contract may be terminated by:

(a) agreement of the parties;
(b) its expiry;
(c) non approval;
(d) cancellation.

2. The contract may be terminated if the parties have made a written agreement to this effect. Article 25 covers this method of termination.

3. Article 26 concerns termination of the contract through its *expiry*. In this case, the contract expires automatically on the basis of one of the following three conditions:

(a) after expiry of the agreed period of validity;
(b) if the condition arises to which the parties have subordinated the validity of the contract or when it appears certain that the condition cannot be fulfilled (depending on whether the condition is suspensive or resolutive respectively);
(c) death of the agent, or in the case of a collective body, its liquidation.

4. Article 23 governs *non-approval*. This kind of termination of the contract consists of the possibility of one party—for those contracts of an indeterminate length—to terminate the contract by communicating his decision in writing to the other contracting party with the following minimum warning:

(a) 30 days if the contract has been in existence for more than six months;
(b) 60 days if the contract is less than a year old;
(c) 3–12 months if the contract is more than a year old, in accordance with the importance, expectations of the parties and other circumstances of the case.

5. Finally, article 30 allows for the *cancellation* of the contract either in the event of its non execution or if circumstances arise which make the achievement of the contractual aims impossible or at least extremely difficult.

1.7. Indemnity

The two latter forms of termination of the agency contract (non-approval and cancellation) may give rise to an indemnity payment.

Non-approval

The right to an indemnity arises from the possible violation of time-scales determined in Article 28. This right is controlled under Article 29.

The law creates an alternative. It allows the wronged party by means of an illegal non-approval to choose between an indemnity which may compensate for damages suffered where the amount corresponds to the average monthly payment received over the preceding year, multiplied by the time still remaining for the conclusion of the rejected contract.

Cancellation

In this case the party cancelling the contract may still request an indemenity which may be determined according to the criteria of the Civil Code along the lines of the damages incurred.

In both cases

The agent retains the right, whatever the reason for terminating the contract, to a "Client Indemnity". This "Client indemnity" has been defined as " . . . compensation of the additional amount that the agent has obtained. It is a sort of additional compensation that the agent obtains for him thanks to the effort that he has made, to the extent that the principal always profits from the fruits of this activity, after termination of the agency contract".[1]

These reasons would lead us to believe, in line with legal doctrine, that this indemnity has no sanction value. In any case, Portuguese law has not definitively resolved the question, which thus remains open and subject to doctrinal and legal evolution.

Conflict of Laws

Portuguese law on agencies contains a clause on conflict of laws—Article 38—according to which:

> "Foreign legislation shall not apply to contracts governed by this law which develop exclusively or in a dominating fashion on national territory, regarding the method of terminating the contract, unless that legislation is more favourable."

This is an immediately applicable clause, for which the international legitimacy may be found under Article 7 of the Treaty of Rome on contractual obligations.

In any case this clause has already been the subject of criticism, as it is not fully compatible with the general principles of Portuguese international private law.

---

[1] Antonio Pinto Monteiro, *Agency Contact*, (Coimbra, 1987), p. 59.

1.8. Specific Application of EEC-Law

Decree no. 178/86 of July 3 1986, published prior to Directive no. 86/653/ CEE of the 18 December, embodied the agency contract and welcomed the solutions adopted by the Community order. The directive is generally valid for a number of aspects, where one needs to underline the obligations of agents and commercial travellers, the exclusivity, non competition and legal methods for terminating the contract. For certain aspects, the national system diverges from that arising from the directive. This is the case for provisions relating to the demand for commission (cf. Art. 18) and indemnity of clients (cf. Art. 33).

Up until now we have seen no sign of the Portuguese Council for Competition diverging from those aims prescribed by the Commission's Communication regarding exclusive representation contracts drawn up with commercial representatives.

There should not therefore be any conflict between the application of Decree no. 422/83 of December 3 1983 on restrictive commercial practices and the provisions of Directive 86/653/CEE relating to exclusivity and non competition.

1.9. Bibliography

Monteiro, Antonio Pinto, *Agency contract: Annotation of Decree no. 178/86 of July 3rd*, (Coimbra, 1987);
Nuno Ruiz, *International Agency Contract*, (ICEP, Lisbon, 1988).

1.10. Legislation

Decree no. 178/86 of July 3 1986.
Decree no. 422/83 of December 3 1983.

1.11. Case Law

Decision of the Council for Competition relating to Administrative Sanctions procedure no. 3/87, "Wasteels", not yet published.

2. Distributorship Agreements

2.1. Distribution

The matter discussed in this chapter has not so far been the subject of specific legislation, coming under the principle of contractual liberty expressed in no. 1 of Article 405 of the Civil Code: "Within the limits of the law, the parties have the power to fix freely the contents of the contracts, to sign contracts different from those anticipated in this . . ."

Thus, beyond the principal effects which characterise the structure of the contracts to be analysed, the parties may fix a multiplicity of other legal effects, the limits of which are circumscribed, on the one hand, by the principle of good faith, and on the other by the demands derived from the protection of the proper operation of the market, above all, the defence of competition.

With regard to the latter aspect, which we can consider has only been expressed in any significant manner as from the middle of 1984 (when the so-called Defencé of Competition Law—DL no. 422/83 of 3rd December, came into effect), it is necessary to underline right away, the resort, on the part of the national institutions responsible for the implementation of the rules of competition, to the criteria established in the community legal system, in order to check the legality of the agreements in force.

2.1.1. Definition

2.1.1.1. Exclusive/non-exclusive/exclusive purchasing

The *non-exclusive distributorship* contract, may be defined as an agreement whereby one of the parties buys from the other goods, for resale to third parties, acting in its own name and for its own account.

The only obligations which, in most cases, fall upon the non-exclusive distributor are:

- to buy a full range, or minimum quantities, of products
- to sell the products under the brand or presentation indicated by the other party.

But under *exclusive distribution*, one of the parties undertakes to supply the other with certain products, for resale, within a specific and limited geographical area.

Consequently, the supplier may not supply directly users within the territory granted. For his part, the distributor may be subject to the following obligations:

- not to manufacture or distribute competing products
- to buy exclusively from the other party, for resale purposes
- not to establish branches, agencies, warehouses or other installations outside the territory granted.

These are the aspects which until now, and notwithstanding their being considered practices restricting competition—Article 13 no. 1 (c) and (e) of DL no. 422/83—, have been judged to be justified by virtue of their contribution to the improvement of distribution, reserving to the users of the goods in question an equitable part of the benefits resulting therefrom (Article 15 no. 1 of the said legal document).

As already stated in the introduction, whenever the assumptions mentioned in the community regulations are present, the principles contained therein are applied direct, and we will not mention them, as they are the subject of a specific report.

The decisions of the Council for Competition regarding the application of Article 13 of Decree no. 422/83 of December 3 1983 to exclusive distribution contracts do not diverge substantially from those adopted by the European Commission in accordance with Article 85 of the E.C. Treaty, nor from principles arising from several rulings on category exemptions.

Nevertheless, in some cases, given the special nature of the national market and the characteristics of distributing certain products, Portuguese decisions have assumed certain special aspects. Such was the case of anti-competitive practices in the distribution of beers and "soft drinks", in relation to which the Council prohibited the concession of assistance to transportation, the practice of discounts on retail prices and the demand imposed on exclusive distributors not to sell competitive products. The fact of wanting to safeguard requirements peculiar to distribution competition in the national market has been considered as a proof of possible deviations from community discipline, in as much as its effectiveness or primacy has not been damaged (cf. The Activity Report of 1986 from the Council for Competition and Notice issued on the proposal for governing distribution contracts in the automobile sector.)

Where distribution contracts for beer and "soft drinks" are concerned, the Council for Competition has diverged from the application of Article 85 of the E.C. Treaty, because it felt that this concerned a marketing system which was not likely to have any significant effect on trade between member States. In any case, it emphasised that decisions from the Commission, judicial precedents from the European Community Court of Justice and Regulations on category exemptions express "Competition policy directions to which the application of national legislation may not be indifferent", even in the case where the application of community law aside, a uniform solution is not needed.

2.1.9. Bibliography

Nuno Ruiz, "Implicacões sectoriais da Aplicacão da lei da Concorrência" ("sectoral implications of the Application of the law of Competition), *Competition in Portugal for the 80's*, (Lisbon, 1985).

Martins, Maria Belmira and others, "O Direito da Concorrência em Portugal," *Concerning the Right of Competition in Portugal*, (Lisbon, 1986).

2.1.10. Legislation

Decree no. 422/83 of 3 December 1983.

2.1.11. Case law

Decision of the Council for Competition in administrative sanction procedures no. 5/86 "Centralcer", Journal of the Republic, II Series, 2nd Supplement dated 24 July 1987, p. 29.

Decision of the Competition Council of 16.12.85, relating to proceeding no. 1/85 (at present subject to judicial appeal) and Declaration of inapplicability no. 1/85.

2.2. Selective Distribution

Through *selective distribution* the supplier sells his products only to a certain number of authorised distributors. The selection of the points of sale can be made in several ways, and it is true that, in order to be compatible with the rules of competition, it must be made as a function of objective and qualitative criteria. Indeed, under the terms of article 13 no. 1 (e) of DL no. 422/83, any agreement between companies is considered to be a restrictive practice . . . if it implies:

"Refusing, directly or indirectly, without justification, to the purchase or sale of goods and the rendering of services, in particular by virtue of discrimination due to the identity of the buyer or seller".

However, "the lack of capacity of the purchaser, given the characteristics of the product or service, to ensure its resale under satisfactory technical conditions or to maintain an adequate after sale service", may be considered as a reason to justify the refusal to sell (Article 12–d) of DL no. 422/83).

The principles in force within the community legal system are also applicable in Portugal to contracts of this type.

2.2.8. Specific Applications of EEC-law

Up until now there has been no specific application of community law on the subject of selective distribution. In any case, that in no way means that efforts have not been made to adapt distribution circuits to the requirements contained in Article 85 of the E.E.C. Treaty, efforts which are closely linked to the editing of Article 13 of Decree no. 422/83, on the whole identical to the provision of the Treaty.

The question of selective distribution has been considered in depth by the Council of Competition with respect to a set of anti-competitive practices in the market of dermopharmaceutical products. In this respect, expressly invoking the experience of applying Community and French law, the Council has decided that the economic balance sheet of selective distribution systems must be the result of an individual appreciation because of their specific merit. For this reason, acceptance of the selection based on objective criteria of a qualitative kind is not unconditional: the criteria must also be adequate or proportional to the socio-economic interests that the distribution system aims at reaching. It is still indispensable that this concerns frank demands, that is to say the applicant for retailing may freely accede, if his financial interest is to do so.

Generally, on the subject of exclusive distribution as well as in relation to selective distribution, decisions of the Council for Competition attempt not to diverge from solutions which are a result of the application of community law by the Commission and the Court of Justice of the European Communities. Only in the case where the size of the companies concerned confronted with the small size of the national market make the effects of clauses admissible under other circumstances especially negative, can national law be applied more stringently with regard to justification conditions.

2.2.9. Bibliography

(See 2.1.9.)

2.2.10. Legislation

(See 2.1.10)

2.2.11. Case law

Decision by the Council of Competition in administrative sanction procedures no. 3/85, 4/85 and 5/85, "Phar", "Vichy", 'Ferraz Lynce" (cf. Journal of the Republic, "Diário da República," dated 24 July 1987, p. 15).

3. Franchise Agreements

3.1. Definition

It is customary to distinguish various types of franchising: that of *distribution*, in which the franchisee sells products manufactured by the franchisor, under the latter's brand or name, and benefitting from technical and commercial assistance; that of *services*, in which the franchisee offers a service under the franchisor's brand or trading name, following the latter's instructions; and *industrial*, in which the franchisee himself manufactures, following the franchisor's indications, totally or in part, the products he sells under the franchisor's trade mark.

3.3. The supplier's duties and rights

The franchisor is obliged to supply to the franchisee the means of marketing the products or services, which means may include the following aspects:

* engineering;
* marketing;
* assistance to the accounting organisation and professional training of the franchisee;
* the use of a sign which distinguishes the distribution network in which he participates. Should this distinctive sign be a trade mark, the franchising contract will include a licence for the use of the trade mark, subject to the rules of article 119 of the industrial Property Code (text given by DL no. 27/84 of 18th January and no. 40/87 of 27th January): the holder of the trade mark registration may, *by means of a written contract*, grant to someone else a licence to use, free of charge or for consideration, in a certain area or in the whole of the Portuguese territory, for all or some of the products or services, provided that this cannot lead the public into any error as to their origin or to the essential features for its appreciation. The use of the trade mark made by the licensee will be considered as made by the holder of the registration.

No. 1. The licensee, unless otherwise stated in the licensing contract, will enjoy all the faculties granted to the holder of the registration for all legal effects, and, in particular, to prove the right to the trade mark before any official body.

No. 2. If the licence is exclusive, no other may be granted while it remains in force.

No. 3. ....

No.4. The right obtained by means of the operating licence may not be disposed of without the express, written consent of the holder of the registration, unless otherwise stated the licensing contract.

For his part, it is for the franchisee to finance the investment, ensure the commercial function, as the sole person responsible for sales, and to remunerate the franchisor's services (normally, this compensation consists in the payment of a down payment, at the time of signing the contract, and of a regular amount to be paid as a function of the turnover).

3.8. Specific Application of EEC Law

Portuguese legal experience on the subject of franchise contracts is relatively recent. First of all, this form of commercial relationship constitutes, *grosso modo*, a novelty in Portugal, a country where, naturally franchisees are more numerous than the franchisors.

On the other hand, decisions made by the Community Commission and the Court of Justice are too recent for their effects to be visible for treating problems in the light of provisions governing contracts, industrial and commercial property rights and protection of competition.

Existing contracts have been modified in detail and commercial operators are keeping a close eye on the work of the European Commission in its adoption of the block exemption for franchises. The aim would appear above all to be to safeguard as much as possible the interests and financial freedom of the franchisees, whilst maintaining the basic characteristics of this kind of marketing system.

To conclude, it should also be mentioned that, in relation to some aspects not mentioned in this report—indemnity and dissolution—in the event of omission, it is suggested the rules relating to the agency contract, should be applied, with the necessary adaptations.

CHAPTER 13
United Kingdom

Leonard Hawkes, Fergus Randolph

1. Commercial Agency

1.1. Definition of Various Types of Agencies and Intermediaries

- An agency agreement exists when one party ("the principal") authorises another party ("the agent") to act on his behalf and the other agrees so to do.
- The agency agreement is often in contractual form, but the absence of a contract does not preclude an agency agreement.
- An agent must intend to act on behalf of his principal.[1]
- As is stated in the Notice on Exclusive Dealing Contracts with commercial agents:[2] " . . . he [the commercial agent] acts on the instructions and in the interest of the enterprise on whose behalf he is operating. Unlike the independent trader, he himself is neither a purchaser or a vendor, but seeks purchasers and vendors in the interest of the other party to the contract, who is the person doing the buying or selling".

1.2. Conclusion of the Contract (Special Conditions)

An Agency may arise in four situations:

(a) express agreement;
(b) implied agreement;
(c) without agreement under the doctrine of usual and apparent authority; and where a person has the authority of necessity;
(d) agency by ratification.

---

[1] *Vandyke v Fender* [1970] 2 QB 292.
[2] J.O. 1962 139/2921 (24 December 1962).

1.2.1. Express agreement

- No formality is generally required.[3]
- The extent of the agent's authority depends on the true construction of the words of appointment.[4]

1.2.2. Implied agreement

- The agreement can be implied from conduct in a particular occasion or from a relationship.
- An agent may also be authorized, impliedly, to do acts incidental to that which he has been authorized to do.[5]
- Note that an agent employed to sell something has no incidental authority to receive payment for it.[6]
- An agent acting in a particular market will be impliedly authorised to act in accordance with the custom of the market.[7] Note that the custom must not be unreasonable.

1.2.3. Agency without agreement

(a) *Apparent authority*: Where a principal represents to a third party that he, the principal, has authorized an agent to act on his behalf vis-a-vis his dealings with the third party, the principal will not be able to deny the truth of the representation and will be held by it even if he did not authorize it.[8]

(b) *Usual authority*: "The principal is liable for all acts of the agent, with or without the authority usually confided to an agent of that character, notwithstanding limitations as between the principal and the agent, put on that authority."[9]

(c) *Authority of necessity*: This doctrine covers those situations where due to necessity, the agent is entitled to create a contract between the principal and a third party,[10] to dispose of the principal's property,[11] or entitle the agent to claim compensation for efforts made, or expenditure incurred in such a way as to safeguard the interests of the principal.[12]

1.2.4. Agency by ratification

(a) The agent must purport to act on behalf of the principal.[13]
(b) The principal must have the capacity to do the act.[14]

---

[3] N.B. agents appointed under seal.
[4] *Weigall v Runciman* [1916] 85 LJ KB 187.
[5] *Waugh v H.B. Clifford & Sons* [1982] Ch 374.
[6] *Mynn v Jolliffe* [1834] IMI Rb. 326.
[7] *Graves v Legg* (1857) H & V 219.
[8] *The Shamah* [1981] Lloyds Law Reports 40.
[9] *Watteau v Fenwick* [1893] 1 QB 346.
[10] *The Winson* [1982] AC 939.
[11] *Sims & Co. v Midland Railway* (1913) IKB 103 at 112.
[12] *ibid* No. 10.
[13] *Keighley Maxsted & Co. v Durant* [1901] AC 240.
[14] *Rolled Steel Products (Holdings) Ltd v B.S.C.* [1982] All ER 1057.

(c) The principal must have been in existence at the time of the act.[15]
(d) The principal must ratify in time.[16]
(e) A nullity cannot be ratified.[17]

1.3. The Principal's Duties and Rights

1.3.1. The principal's duties

Whether disclosed or undisclosed, the principal generally is liable for the acts of his agents to the third party.

The principal may not set off against the third party any money owed to him by his agent.[18]

1.3.2. The principal's rights

The distinction must be made between a disclosed and an undisclosed principal.

Disclosed principal: the general rule is that such a principal may sue the third party.[19] The third party may not set off against the principal any debt which is owed to him by the agent.

Undisclosed principal: such a principal may only sue a third party in the following circumstances:

(a) when such action would not be inconsistent with the terms of the implied contract;
(b) when the third party cannot or does not wish to show that he only wanted to deal with the agent and no one else;[20]
(c) any action taken by the principal is subject to any defences which the third party has against the agent.[21]

1.4. The Commercial Agent's Duties and Rights

1.4.1. The commercial agent's duties

The general rule is that an agent is neither liable under nor entitled to enforce a contract he makes on behalf of his principal.[22]

However, the following exceptions exist:

(a) if the agent in fact intended to undertake personal liability;
(b) if the agent's liability is the usual course of business between particular parties or in relation to a particular class of agents;
(c) when the principal is undisclosed;[23]

---

[15] *Keher* v *Baxter* (1866) LR 2 CP 174.
[16] *Dibbins* v *Dibbins* (1896) 2 Ch 348.
[17] *Danish Mercantile Co.* v *Beaumont* (1951) Ch 680.
[18] *Werring* v *Farenck* (1807) 2 Comp 85.
[19] *Langton* v *Waite* (1868) LR 6 Eq 165.
[20] *Collins* v *A.G.R. Ltd* [1930] 1 Ch 1.
[21] *Browning* v *Provisional Insurance Co. of Canada* (1873) CR 5PC 263.
[22] *N & J Yassopulos* v *Ney Shipping Ltd* [1977] 2 Lloyd's Rep 478.
[23] *Sims.* v Bond (1833) 5 BP Ad 389.

(d) when the agent is in fact the principal;[24]
(e) when the principal does not exist.[25] [26]

When both the principal and agent are liable under the contract, the third party may lose his right to sue one of them if he has elected to sue the other.[27] [28]

Where a separate, collateral contract exists between the agent and the third party, as well as the main contract between the principal and the third party, rights and obligations will rest with the agent and third party as per the terms of that contract.[29]

When an agent purports to act for a principal when he has no authority to so do, then he will be liable to the third party.

When an agent is in such a situation, he will be liable even when he believes he has such authority to so act.[30]

However, the agent in this situation of an implied warranty of authority will not be liable to the third party when:

(a) the third party knows or should have known that the agent had no authority;[31]
(b) a representation is one of law;[32]
(c) the principal is liable to the third party on the grounds of apparent or usual authority.[33]
(d) where the agent is a Crown agent.[34]

An agent must carry out his instructions and must act with due care and skill. He is under a fiduciary duty in that he must not put himself in a position when his interest and his duty conflict and he must not, for example, accept commission from a third party without the principal's consent. Also, the general rule is that without specific authority, an agent cannot delegate the task to a sub-agent.

1.4.2. The commercial agent's rights

Commission: Although the agent has no legal right to commission, where there is a commercial agency, the courts are loathe to send away an agent empty-handed.[35] Commission is fixed by the contractual terms, but it is only payable in respect of work dealt with under the contract due to the efforts of the agent himself.[36]

Indemnity: A principal must indemnify his agent against all liabilities

[24] *Said v Butt* [1920] 3 K.B. 497.
[25] *Phonogram v Lane* [1982] QB 938.
[26] See section 9(2) of the European Communities Act 1972.
[27] *Debenham v Perkins* (1925) 113 LT 252.
[28] Note the Civil Liability (Contribution) Act 1978.
[29] *Chelmsford Auctions Ltd. v Poole* [1973] QB 542.
[30] *Younge v Toynbee* (1910) 1 KB 215.
[31] *Jones v Hope* (1880) 3 TLR.
[32] *Saffron Walden B.S. v Rayner* (1880) 14 Ch. D. 406.
[33] *Rainbow v Howkins* [1904] 2 KB 322.
[34] *Dunn v Macdonald* [1897] 1 QB 555.
[35] *Kofi Sunkersette Olev v A. Strauss & Co. Ltd.* (1951) AC 243.
[36] *Toulmin v Millar* (1887) 12 App. Case 746.

reasonably incurred by him in the execution of his authority.[37] The indemnity is due not only for contractual liability, but also for tortious liability. The agent is not entitled to an indemnity where the liability arose due to his such breach of duty.[38]

Lien: An agent, unless otherwise agreed, is entitled to a lien on all the property of the principal, which has come into his possession in the course of the agency.

1.5. Liabilities of the Principal and Agent during the Term of the Agency

See 1.3.1. and 1.4.1.

1.6. Term and Termination

The following circumstances can give rise to termination of an agency agreement:

(a) notice; where no time or period of notice is specified, the contract is determined on reasonable notice;
(b) conduct inconsistent with the continuance of the agency;
(c) insanity;
(d) death;
(e) bankruptcy.

The effects of the termination of an agency agreement are as follows:

- accrued rights are not affected by termination;
- when dealing with non-consensual agency, the methods of termination are slightly changed, i.e. notice must be given to the third party when terminating an apparent or usual authority.

1.7. Indemnity

See 1.4.2.

1.8. Specific Application of EEC Law

Unlike the German "Handelsvertreter", there is no particular social group identifiable in the UK as "commercial agents". The basic principles of agency law are an integral part of the common law and, until now, legislation has played a very minor role in the development of the law of agency in the United Kingdom.

There is the possibility that an agency agreement which would be exempt from the registration requirements of section 6(1) of the Restrictive Practices Act would nevertheless fall foul of the EEC competition rules because the latter will have regard to the economic reality of the agreement between the parties rather than its form. Nevertheless, UK law and the EEC rules treat agency agreements in a very similar fashion.

---

[37] *Thacker v Hardy* (1878) 4 Q.B.O. 685.
[38] *Lister v Romford Ice* [1957] AC 555.

In the future the UK position will change markedly following adoption of the EEC Directive on self-employed commercial agents (Directive 86/653/EEC of 18 December 1986). In current UK law the rights and duties of the principal and commercial agent depend on the express terms of the agency agreement made between them, supplemented by, or, in certain cases, overridden by, the common law rules which exist. Among other things, implementation of the Directive will provide in statutory form for:

(a) an express duty on the part of the agent to act "dutifully and in good faith";
(b) an express right to remuneration according to customary practice of reasonable remuneration;
(c) an express obligation on the principal to provide a statement of commission due and of supporting excerpts from the principals' records;
(d) an express provision ensuring that the agent is entitled in certain circumstances, on termination of the agency to receive either a lump-sum "indemnity" *or* compensation for damage. Such a provision will be new in UK law.

Recognizing that these and other provisions will effect fundamental changes, in order to adapt its legal system to accommodate the Directive, the United Kingdom has been granted an additional four years in which to implement the Directive, i.e. until 1 January 1994.

2. Distributorship Agreements

There are two main types of distribution agreement used in the UK, exclusive distribution and selective distribution agreements. These will be studied in turn below.

2.1 Distribution

2.1.1. Definition

2.1.1.1. Exclusive/non-exclusive/exclusive purchasing

There are two main types of exclusive distribution agreements, exclusive dealing agreements and exclusive purchasing agreements. The distinction between them is that, in an exclusive dealing agreement, a supplier agrees to appoint a dealer as the sole distributor of his goods within a defined area; in an exclusive purchasing agreement, the dealer agrees to take supplies exclusively from one single supplier—there are no territorial restrictions with the latter. The two relevant statutes are the Restrictive Trade Practices Act 1976 (RTPA) and the Competition Act 1980.

Exclusive dealing

Exclusive dealing under the R.T.P.A. 1976
The relevant statutory provisions on exclusive dealing are schedule 3(2) of

the Restrictive Trade Practices Act for goods and schedule 3(7) for services. Schedule 3(2) states:

"This Act does not apply to an agreement for the supply of goods between two persons neither of whom is a trade association, being an agreement to which no other person is a party and under which no restrictions as are described in S.6(1) above are accepted or no such information provisions as are described in S.7(1) are made other than restrictions accepted or provisions made for the furnishing of information:

(a) by the party supplying the goods, in respect of the supply of goods of the same description to other persons; or
(b) by the party acquiring the goods in respect of the sale, or acquisition for sale, of the goods of the same description".

This schedule *allows* two types of restriction to exist:

(a) those on the supply of goods imposed by the supplier on the dealer; and
(b) those on the holding of additional goods which compete with the suppliers goods.

However, although such restrictions are exempt under the RTPA 1976, they would be subject to the Competition Act 1980.

An agreement not subject to the exemption under schedule 3(2) of the RTPA must be submitted to the Office of Fair Trading for registration on the Register of Restrictive Trade Practices. Failure to register means that the restrictions are void and unenforceable. Whether registration is granted for such agreements will depend on the Office of Fair Trading's assessment of the market and in particular:

(a) the strength or weakness of inter-brand competition;
(b) the presence of dealer-to-dealer agreements;
(c) the presence of price fixing.

Exclusive dealing under the Competition Act 1980

Agreements exempt from the RTPA 1976 may be reviewed under the Competition Act 1980. The Office of Trading will consider the effects of restrictive clauses that would otherwise have been exempt under the RTPA. Points deemed by the Office to have beneficial consequences are:[39]

(a) control of the quality and type of goods or services provided, particularly where the corporate identity associated with the goods is important;
(b) increased operational efficiency and improved resource allocations arising from, for example, predictability of supply and/or demand or benefits of sale.

The Office of Fair Trading will view an exclusive dealing agreement favourably when there is strong inter-brand competition.

An agreement may be anti-competitive but not be referred to the Monopolies and Mergers Commission because the effect on the market is shown to be *de minimis.*[40]

[39] British Airport Authority: 22.2.84.
[40] British Railways Board: 18.5.83.

Exclusive purchasing

Exclusive purchasing agreements are subject to the provisions in both the RTPA 1976 and the Competition Act 1980. However, the provisions are materially exclusive; if an agreement falls under the RTPA 1976, then it cannot be reviewed under the Competition Act 1980. If it is exempt under schedule 3(2) of the RTPA 1976, it may be reviewed under the Competition Act 1980.

Exclusive purchasing under the RTPA 1976

Most exclusive purchasing agreements are exempt from the provisions by virtue of schedule 3(2)b. Section 9(5) of the Act is also important, dealing with restrictions regarding exclusivity. It states:

> "In determining whether an agreement for the supply of goods or for the application of any process of manufacture to goods is an agreement to which the Act applies by virtue of this Part, no account shall be taken of any term which relates exclusively to the goods supplied, or to which the process is applied, in pursuance of the agreement".

The exclusion from the Act applies only where the dealer re-sells the goods.

Exclusive purchasing agreements have been given dispensations from referral under section 21(2) of the RTPA,[41] which reads:

> "If it appears to the Secretary of State, upon the Director's representation, that the restrictions accepted or information provisions made under an agreement of which particulars are so entered or filed are not of such significance as to call for investigation by the Court, the Secretary of State may give directions discharging the Director from taking proceedings in the Court in respect of that agreement during the continuance in force of the directions."

Schedule 3(2) of the Act will only operate to exempt the agreement when the exclusive purchasing restrictions are the only restrictions in the agreement.

Exclusive purchasing under the Competition Act 1980

The Office of Fair Trading and the Monopolies and Mergers Commission will have regard to the following areas with regard to exclusive purchasing:

(a) foreclosure:[42] the closing of the relevant market to those supplies and dealing not involved in restrictive agreements;
(b) restraints on price competition: where prices of exclusive purchase dealing are higher than they would be if there was more competition;
(c) the specialist nature of the goods needing specialist dealers;
(d) the duration of the agreement.[43]

2.1.2. Conclusion of the Contract (special conditions)

The relevant law is based on UK contract law. Reference should be made to one of the standard works on the subject.

---

[41] Croda–Manox No. 5044 Register of Restrictive Trade Agreements.
[42] Car Parts H.C. 318 (February 1982).
[43] *A Report on the Supply of Petrol To Retailers in the U.K.* (1965) Cmmd. 264.

2.1.3.–2.1.7.—No special comment is called for.

2.1.8. Specific application of EEC law

On exclusive distribution agreeements, the Restrictive Trade Practices Act (RTPA) 1976 defines the classes of agreements to which it applies and catches agreements which are of a specified form (the "form based approach"). Agreements to which the RTPA 1976 applies must be registered. While the RTPA 1976 looks to the precise form of an agreement to determine whether or not it is registrable, EEC law looks to the economic effect of an agreement to determine whether it falls within the prohibition of Article 85(1). Nevertheless, both UK and EEC law adopt a benign attitude to exclusive distribution agreements. The combined effect of section 9(3) and schedule 3, paragraph 2 of the RTPA is that most exclusive distribution agreements, made between two parties, will fall outside the Act and will not be registrable. (Such agreements may however be subject to review under the Competition Act 1980.)

The permitted restrictions on competition set out in Regulation 1983/83/EEC would all be covered by the exemptions provided for in Article 9(3) and schedule 3, paragraph 2 of the RTPA 1976.

Exclusive purchasing agreements

Equally both UK and EEC law adopt a benign attitude to exclusive purchasing agreements for goods. The permitted restrictions on competition set out in Regulation 1984/83/EEC would all be covered by the exemptions provided for in Article 9(3) and schedule 3, paragraph 2 of the RTPA 1976.

Arguably, UK law may be less restrictive in some instances than EEC competition law (e.g. schedule 3, paragraph 2 of the RTPA 1976 may exempt from registration, agreements providing for mutual exclusive dealing which are not covered by exemption under EEC law). However, the better approach will be for parties to draft their agreements to conform to the block exemptions provided for in Regulations 1983/83/EEC and 1984/83/EEC, it being accepted law that an agreement "may affect trade between Member States" even though it is made between two parties who are themselves both in the same Member State.

In the light of the recent Department of Trade and Industry White Paper "DTI—the Department of Enterprise" (CM 278) and of the subsequent Green Paper "Review of Restrictive Trade Practices Policy" (CM 331, March 1988), it is clear that UK and EEC law will shortly become more closely aligned. It is proposed to introduce new law in the UK which will be based on a general effects based prohibition similar to that found in Article 85(1) of the EEC Treaty, together with a system of block exemptions. It is felt that this will avoid the fundamental weakness of the present law, namely that its coverage is too rigidly defined in terms of the form of agreements so that even some highly anti-competitive agreements may escape the law.

In addition the enforcement powers and sanctions will be strengthened and will include powers of entry and search of business premises similar to those available to the EEC Commission under Regulation 17/62. Provision will be made for substantial fines for serious breaches of the prohibition.

At paragraphs 1.4 and 1.5 of the Green Paper "Review of Restrictive Trade Practices Policy", the DTI has summarized what it sees as the future interplay between EEC and UK law as follows:

> "1.4. It will not be sufficient to leave Regulation in this area to the Competition law of the European Community (EC) since this catches UK agreements only when they affect trade between Member States. There is therefore still great scope for domestic restrictive agreements to be made which fall outside the scope of EC law. Moreover, the EC system is already overloaded.
> 1.5. The Government have concluded that the coverage of UK law should be defined in terms of the effects of agreements and concerted practices on competition, rather than in terms of their legal form, thus bringing the scope of the law into line with its purpose. This will have the added benefit of aligning our new national cartel law to EC cartel law as far as possible for the sake of consistency and simplicity."

2.2. Selective Distribution

2.2.1. Definition

Competition law will only intervene in these agreements when the criteria used to select the distributor become restrictive, i.e. when manufacturers exclude qualified dealers to maintain high prices or to attack those who allegedly engage in price-cutting.

Selective distribution does not involve the RTPA 1976, and thus the Competition 1980 is the relevant statute.

The first case studied by the Office of Fair Trading and Monopolies and Mergers Commission was *Raleigh*.[44] This showed that brand leaders should distribute to dealers with adequate back-up services and the case is important for its study of qualitative criteria.

Quantitative criteria were examined in *Sandersons*.[45] Here the Office of Fair Trading took a subjective view: quantitative criteria are not *per se* anti-competitive.

The Office of Fair Trading accepted two situations where quantitative criteria might be allowable:

(i)   to protect the supplier's brand name; and
(ii) to ensure that the cost of maintaining an outlet remains economic.

A third situation shown to be allowable[46] is where the restrictions allow the dealer to continue with a particular service.

2.2.2. Conclusion of the contract (special conditions)

The relevant law is based on UK contract law. Reference should be made to one of the standard works on the subject.

2.2.3.–2.2.7.—No special comment is called for.

---

[44] 27.2.81. (OFT Report).
[45] 27.8.81. (OFT Report).
[46] Distribution of Newspapers & Periodicals (May 1986).

2.2.8. Specific application of EEC law

Selective distribution agreements may be reviewed under the Competition Act 1980 which seeks to control vertical restraints of competition by firms with market power. Section 2 sets out the intention to control "anti-competitive practices". It was anticipated that there might have been a larger number of investigations under this Act than have in fact taken place. Accordingly, the EEC law concerning selective distribution agreements is more extensively articulated in the decisions of the Commission and judgments of the European Court of Justice than the UK law is in the findings of the Office of Fair Trading and of the Monopolies and Mergers Commission under the 1980 Act. However, both recognize objectively justified qualitative criteria for the selection of distributors and both recognize that, in certain circumstances, quantitative criteria for selection may be justified.

So far as quantitative criteria are concerned, there seems to be a slightly different approach. In EEC law quantitative criteria are treated as falling within the prohibition of Article 85(1) but may obtain exemption under Article 85(3) of the EEC Treaty. By contrast, the Office of Fair Trading did not declare quantitative criteria inherently anti-competitive in Sandersons.[47]

3. Franchise Agreements

3.1. Definition

Franchise agreements under the RTPA 1976

Four sets of provisions typically seen in franchise agreements are exempt under the RTPA:

(a) terms relating exclusively to the goods or services supplied, section 9(3) regarding goods and section 18(2) on services;
(b) Staffing restrictions: section 9(6) regarding goods and section 18(6) regarding services;
(c) territory and purchasing restrictions: schedule 3(1) regarding goods and schedule 3(7) regarding services;
(d) Restrictions regarding intellectual property: schedule 3.

S.9(3) and S.18(2)

The following clauses would appear to be exempt under sections 9(3) and 18(2):

(a) recommended retail prices (note that these are legal under the Resale Price Act 1976);
(b) restrictions on the price that the franchiser supplies goods to the franchisee;
(c) stocking requirements;
(d) ban on hiring out goods;
(e) best endeavours clauses imposed on the franchisee to sell franchisor's goods at the recommended resale price;

---

[47] 27.8.81. (OFT Report); see Green, *Commercial Agreements and Competition Law* (1986) at p. 528).

(f) the obligation on the franchisee to insure the relevant goods;
(g) restrictions on services (such as marketing advice) provided by the franchisor to the franchisee.

S.9(6) and S.18(6)

Sections 9(6) and 18(6) allow a restriction:

> "which effects or otherwise relates to the workers to be employed or not employed by any person, or as to remuneration conditions of employment, hours of work or working conditions of such workers".

In the case of *Association of British Travel Agents*[48]—the Court held that although the staff restrictions by themselves fell within the relevant sections and could be exempted when they were viewed together with other restrictions, it was felt that the staffing restrictions were against the public interest.

Schedule 3(1) and 3(7)

In order to be exempt under schedule 3(1) and 3(7), there must only exist those restrictions exempted under the schedule. However, when territorial restrictions are linked to restrictions relating exclusively to goods or services supplied, then such restrictions will be exempt under section 9(3) and 18(2) of the RTPA 1976.

Schedule 3

The Office of Fair Trading do not view the clauses of schedule 3 as being restrictive within the RTPA 1976.

Dispensation under S.21(2) RTPA 1976

Generally, the Office of Fair Trading view restrictions in franchise agreements sympathetically and are apt to grant dispensations under section 21(2) of the RTPA. Thus it is to a large degree safe to register a franchise agreement. However, before dispensation is given, the Office may require changes to some clauses in the agreement. In *Boosey & Hawkes plc Franchise Agreements,*[49] the Office asked for a restriction preventing the franchisee from buying foreign similar goods to be excluded from the franchise agreement.

Franchise agreements and the Competition Act 1980

Agreements exempt under the RTPA 1976 are subject to the Competition Act 1980.

The Monopolies and Mergers Commission will again tend to view franchise agreement restrictions sympathetically, but this will not be the case with exclusive purchase and supply obligations.[50]

When a group of franchisees begin working together for a common purpose in a "club", the latter could become a registerable agreement if there was a general standardization of prices, for example.

---

[48] (1984) ICR 12.
[49] D.G.F.T. *Annual Report* (1983).
[50] MMC, *Report on the supply of Ice Cream and Water Ices.*

3.2. Conclusion of the Contract (special conditions)

The relevant law is based on UK contract law. Reference should be made to one of the standard works on the subject.

3.3.-3.7.—No special comment is called for.

3.8. Specific application of EEC law

On the basis of the judgment in the *Pronuptia* case and the decisions which it has already taken in *Yves Rocher* and *ComputerLand*, the Commission has been able to establish clear principles regarding the compatibility of franchise agreements with Article 85. Accordingly, the Commission proposes to introduce a block exemption Regulation which will provide that franchise agreements for the supply of goods and services which fulfil certain defined criteria will not be notifiable to the Commission.

How does this affect the United Kingdom? In practical terms, it has little or no effect. Franchise agreements which are registerable under the Restrictive Trade Practices Act will still need to be registered with the Office of Fair Trading. The Director General of Fair Trading will still have to consider the agreements under the terms of the Act, but section 21(1)(a) gives the Director the discretion to refrain from taking proceedings before the court in respect of an agreement and for so long as he thinks it appropriate so to do, having regard to the operation of any directly applicable Community provision. It is the normal practice of the Director General of Fair Trading not to refer agreements to the court if they were exempt under Article 85(3).

However in the light of the recent Department of Trade and Industry White Paper "DTI—the Department of Enterprise" (CM 278) and of the subsequent Green Paper "Review of Restrictive Trade Practices Policy" (CM 331), it is clear that there will shortly be a thorough reform of the Restrictive Trade Practices Act 1976. The new law will be based on an effects based prohibition similar to that found in Article 85(1), together with a system of block exemptions. It is proposed that there would be a block exemption for franchising agreements. This would remove the registration requirements for qualifying franchise agreements.

APPLICATION OF EEC LAW ON COMMERCIAL AGENCY IN THE UNITED KINGDOM

SECTION 1: DIRECTIVE 86/653/EEC

[1] The EEC Directive on self-employed commercial agents was adopted on 18 December 1986 after some ten years of discussion. The purpose of Directive 86/653/EEC is to harmonize the laws of the Member States on the relationship between commercial agents and their principals and to strengthen the position of the commercial agent. There is little UK statute law on this area. In general the rights and duties of the principal and commercial agent depend on the express or implied terms of the agency agreement made between them. The terms of the agency agreement may be supplemented by or, in certain cases overridden by the common rules which exist.

[2] Article 22 lays down the transitional periods for implementing the Directive. Recognizing that the United Kingdom and Ireland will have to effect fundamental changes in order to adapt their legal systems to accommodate the Directive they have been granted an additional four years, compared with the other Member States, in which to implement the Directive. For Member States other than the United Kingdom and Ireland the Directive is to be implemented before 1 January 1990. The United Kingdom and Ireland must implement the Directive in relation to both future and existing contracts by 1994.

[3] The Directive requires Member States to select one of two specific alternatives in respect of two provisions, Article 7(2) and Article 17. Member States may take different positions on certain other points (Articles 2(2), 4(3), 13(2), 15(3) and 17(2)(a) second indent. The remainder of this paper discusses A) the effect of particular provisions on UK law and B) the likely attitude of the UK to those provisions (set out above) where a discretion is left as to implementation.

PART A

EFFECT OF PARTICULAR PROVISIONS ON EXISTING UK LAW

[4] *Scope:*

Article 2 of the Directive lists categories of commercial agents which are specifically excluded from the scope of the Directive. They include commercial agents when they operate on commodity exchanges or in the commodity market. In view of the importance of the London commodity exchanges this provision will need to be carefully defined in the UK's implementing legislation.

[5] *Rights and Obligations:*

At common law an agent has certain fiduciary duties which require that he should act in good faith. *Article 3* of the Directive introduces an express duty to act "dutifully and in good faith".

[6] *Remuneration:*

There are no compulsory provisions in United Kingdom law covering the level of remuneration for commercial agents although in general a term may be implied which requires "reasonable" remuneration to be paid. *Article 6* sets out, in the absence of an express agreement between the parties, the commercial agent's rights to remuneration according to customary practice in the place where he carries on his activities or, where their is no such customary practice, to such remuneration as is reasonable.

[7] There is no right in UK law to inspect the principal's books except in the case of litigation between the parties. *Article 12* provides that the principal shall be under an obligation to provide the agent with a statement of commission due and with all necessary information, including extracts from the principal's books, to check commissions due.

[8] *Conclusion and Termination of the Agency Contract*:

Article 16 provides that the Directive will not affect the laws of Member States relating to the immediate termination of the agency contract where (a) one party fails to carry out his obligations and (b) exceptional circumstances arise. "Exceptional circumstances" means circumstances which under the law of the Member State give grounds for immediate termination of the contractual relationship, such as force majeure or unforseeable, uncontrollable events. As to a) under UK law, where a party is in breach of contract the other party has the right to sue for damages and may also have the right to treat the agency contract as repudiated (and so cancel it).

Article 17 requires the Member States to include in their legislation a provision ensuring that the agent is entitled, in certain circumstances, on termination of the agency to receive either a lump-sum "indemnity" in accordance with the provisions of Article 17(2) *or* compensation for damage in accordance with the provisions of Article 17(3). Such a provision will be new in UK law.

[9] *Restraint of Trade*:

The general common law rule on agreements in restraint of trade is that they must be "reasonable" in ambit. There is detailed case law on what is and is not reasonable for this purpose. *Article 20* deals with agreements in restraint of trade and Article 20(4) provides that Article 20 will not affect the national laws that impose other restrictions on the validity or enforceability of restraint of trade agreements or which enable the courts to reduce the obligations on the parties resulting from such agreements. This provision appears to leave in place the commonlaw rule and the case law developed under it.

PART B

ATTITUDE OF THE UK TO DISCRETIONARY PROVISIONS

B.1. *Alternatives under Article 7(2) and Article 17*:

[10] Under Article 7(2) Member States must decide whether to extend the agents automatic entitlement to commission on transactions falling within a specific area or group of customers (Article 7(1)) to circumstances where the agents field of responsibility has not been given to him to the exclusion of other agents or the principal. It is likely that the UK will provide that this entitlement should only exist where the agent is granted exclusive rights to a geographical area or group of customers.

[11] *Article 17* poses a more difficult problem of implementation. It introduces a new concept into UK law. It is not yet clear which option will be adopted in the UK.

B.2. *Options under Articles 2(2), 4(3), 13(2), 15(3) and 17(2)(a)*:

[12] *Article 2(2)* allows Member States to exclude from the scope of the Directive persons whose activities as commercial agents are deemed by national law to be secondary. The UK government's intention is to exclude all persons whose activity as a commercial agent is not their primary business and all persons for whom the selling of goods from mail order catalogues is a "secondary activity".

[13] *Article 4(3)* requires the principal to inform the agent within a reasonable time of his acceptance, refusal or any non-execution of a commerical transaction secured by the agent. Bearing in mind that:

(a) commission becomes due when, under the agreement negotiated by the agent, the principal ought to have carried out the transaction, even if he has not actually done so (Article 10(b)) and;
(b) that when the transaction fails for reasons for which the principal is not to blame, the principal is obliged to inform the agent that the contract has not been performed (Article 4(3))

it is understood that the UK implementing legislation will not stipulate in addition that the principal must inform the agent of the execution of the transaction secured by the agent.

[14] *Article 13(2)* allows the Member States to provide that the agency contract will not be valid unless evidenced in writing. Current UK law does not require commercial contracts to be in writing and it is thought that the implementing legislation will retain this flexibility.

[15] It is felt that the three months period of notice provided for in Article 15(2) is sufficient and that it will be unnecessary to provide expressly for longer minimum periods of notice to be applicable in the fourth and subsequent years of agency agreements made for an indefinite period.

[16] Member States have the option of legislating to the effect that the inclusion of a clause in restraint of trade shall be taken into account when assessing the amount of an indemnity that is equitable under Article 17(1). [Whether this option is taken up is dependant in the first place on which alternative the UK will select in the application of Article 17(1).]